5th Edition

THE BLAIR HANDBOOK

Toby Fulwiler
University of Vermont

Alan R. Hayakawa
The Patriot-News
Harrisburg, Pennsylvania

Upper Saddle River, New Jersey 07458

Library of Congress Cataloging-in-Publication Data
Fulwiler, Toby
    The Blair handbook / Toby Fulwiler, Alan R. Hayakawa.— 5th ed.
    p. cm.
    Includes index.
    ISBN 0-13-193415-5
    1. English language—Rhetoric—Handbooks, manuals, etc. 2. English
language—Grammar—Handbooks, manuals, etc.   3. Report writing—Handbooks,
manuals, etc.   I. Hayakawa, Alan R.   II. Title.
    PE1408.F78 2006
    808'.042—dc22   2005034132

Editorial Director: Leah Jewell
Executive Editor: Paul Crockett
Editorial Assitant: Tara Culliney
**VP/Director, Production and
    Manufacturing:** Barbara Kittle
Production Assistant: Marlene Gassler
Copyeditor: Laura Patchkofsky
Text Permissions Specialist: Jane Scelta
Manufacturing Manager: Nick Sklitsis
Assistant Manufacturing Manager:
    Mary Ann Gloriande
VP/Director, Marketing: Brandy Dawson
Senior Marketing Manager: Windley Morley
Marketing Assistant: Kara Pottle
Media Project Manager: Alison Lorber
Senior Media Editor: Christian Lee
Director, Image Resource Center:
    Melinda Reo

Manager, Rights and Permissions:
    Zina Arabia
Manager, Visual Research: Beth Brenzel
Image Permissions Coordinator:
    Richard Rodrigues
Photo Researcher: Teri Stratford
Cover Visual Research: Karen Sanatar
Creative Design Director: Leslie Osher
Senior Art Director: Anne Bonanno Nieglos
Interior and Cover Designer:
    Wanda España/Wee Design Group
Full-Service Project Management: Karen
    Berry/Pine Tree Composition, Inc.
Composition: Pine Tree Composition, Inc.
Printer/Binder: Quebecor World Color Printing
Cover Printer: The Lehigh Press, Inc.
Text Type Face: 9/11 New Century Schoolbook

Credits and acknowledgments borrowed from other sources and reproduced, with permission, in this
textbook appear on pages 899–900.

Pearson Education LTD.
Pearson Education Singapore, Pte. Ltd
Pearson Education, Canada, Ltd
Pearson Education–Japan
Pearson Education Australia PTY, Limited

Pearson Education North Asia Ltd
Pearson Educación de Mexico, S.A.de C.V.
Pearson Education Malaysia, Pte. Ltd
Pearson Education, Upper Saddle River, NJ

10 9 8 7 6 5 4 3 2 1
ISBN 0-13-193536-4 (paper)
ISBN 0-13-193415-5 (case)

CONTENTS

*The  symbol indicates sections that have **WAC** boxes.
The **ESL symbol indicates sections that have **ESL** boxes.

xiv   Contents

BOXES

Checklist

Critical Thinking

ESL *ESL*

WRITING ACROSS THE CURRICULUM

HOW TO USE

The Blair Handbook

The following list of features in *The Blair Handbook* will help you find the information you need quickly and easily, making *The Blair Handbook* one of the most valuable references for college and beyond.

- **A Brief Contents** on the front inside cover lists all of the parts and chapters in *The Blair Handbook*. Locate the general topic you need to reference, and then turn to the page indicated.

- **An access code** provided on a card near the beginning of the book gives you access to **a valuable Web site**, which includes an electronic version of the book and many more online resources. Turn to the back of this card for a detailed list of what is available to you on *The Blair Handbook* Web site.

- **A more detailed Contents** following the title page lists every part, chapter, and section in the book. Use this Contents when you need to dig down to the section level.

- *The Blair Handbook* boxes, ✎ **WRITING ACROSS THE CURRICULUM (WAC)**, 🗋 *Checklist*, 🖋 *Critical Thinking*, and 🄴🅂🄻 *ESL*, found throughout the book, highlight common and important issues that will come up as you write. A **List of All Boxes** following the full Contents is provided to help you quickly find specific boxes by topic. Additionally, a special list of **WAC Boxes** can be found after the Index at the end of the book.

- **A list of supplementary material available with this book**, including information about the book's Web site, can be found in the Preface.

- **Documentation source maps** are designed to illustrate clearly the process for citing various types of sources. Annotated replications of original sources are presented along with step-by-step guidelines. Color is used carefully to help students

see where information is culled from a source and then where it is placed in a citation. Visual tools are provided throughout the research and documentation sections to simplify the research writing process.

- **A list of Editing Symbols** is on the rear inside cover for handy reference. Consult this list if your instructor uses revision and proofreading symbols when commenting on your writing.

- **The Glossary of Terms (Chapter 63)** in Part 9 is a convenient place to find the definitions for common terms. Significant words and phrases called out throughout the book can be found in this Glossary.

- **The Glossary of Usage (Chapter 64)**, also in Part 9, includes information on properly using words and phrases as you write. If you have questions about words not included here, try the Index, Glossary of Terms, or a dictionary for more information.

- **Two indexes** are provided at the end of the book. The **ESL Index** puts a list of topics for multilingual students in one convenient place. The easy-to-reference and comprehensive subject **Index,** which follows the ESL Index, covers virtually everything found in the book and is the best way to navigate the text if you know the specific topic or term you need to reference.

The following **sample page** illustrates how to navigate the book from page-to-page. ▶

The page number can always be found on the top outside corner of the page.

The running head on each page clearly calls out the chapter number, section letter, and a shortened title for easy naviagation.

Section headings include the chapter number, section letter, and section title for the material that follows.

Examples, including many with handwritten changes, illustrate concepts or show problems with their solutions at a glance. Examples can help students determine what to emulate or avoid as they write.

Activities provide opportunities to "explore", "apply," and/or "practice," a concept, strategy, or convention individually or collaboratively.

Boldface word or phrase indicates important terms that can be found in the Glossary of Terms.

Cross references provide a chapter number or a page number to locate information related to a topic being discussed.

Boxes (WAC, Checklist, Critical Thinking, and ESL) summarize key info for quick reference and review.

---

3 a   The elements of composition

To compose either an effective essay or a strong picture, the "composer" works with a number of compositional elements, which turn out to be remarkably similar from one medium to the other. Both pictures and stories contain **information** presented by a composer who has a particular **point of view** and **arranges** them in two-dimensional space.

In a study of
~~Studying~~ the effects of cigarette smoking, monkeys smoked the equivalent of dozens of cigarettes a day.

The monkeys were not conducting the study. This first part of the sentence is a dangling modifier.

1 Information

Both words and pictures convey information, but each does so in importantly different ways. In English, words are written sequentially, left to right, and so readers' attention is directed toward meaning according to where the text begins, where it goes next, and how it ends (see Chapter 2).

WRITING 3: APPLICATION ....

Select any unfamiliar book about which you are curious and preview it, using the two kinds of questions outlined here. Stop after ten minutes and write what you know about the text.

....

WRITING ACROSS THE CURRICULUM

Study Groups to Improve Reading Comprehension
Instructors across the curriculum assume you can understand and critically read whatever handouts, chapters, or whole texts they assign in their courses. This will most likely be true about material with which you have some personal experience or have encountered before. However, it may not be true about new material, especially in disciplines you may be encountering for the first time.

(COMPOSITE PAGE)

PREFACE

The fifth edition of *The Blair Handbook* is the clearest and most accessible edition we've ever put together. It continues to explain and illustrate the qualities of good writing as well as the logic behind conventions of grammar, spelling, punctuation, and usage. And it continues to insist that good writing results from imaginative composing, careful revising, and rigorous editing rather than a slavish following of mechanical prescriptions. At the same time, the new edition features careful attention to visual rhetoric, public forms of discourse, writing across the curriculum, and writing for the world of work.

We wrote the book to give students a comprehensive yet common-sense guide to improving their writing abilities. All editions of *The Blair Handbook* focus on the needs of undergraduate and working writers through a process approach, examining the overlapping stages of planning, drafting, researching, revising, and editing. The book addresses rhetorical issues of audience, purpose, situation, and voice as well as the more technical issues of style, grammar, and mechanics appropriate to contexts within and beyond the classroom.

A Balanced Author Perspective

A composition teacher with more than 35 years' experience teaching writing, Toby Fulwiler highlights the need for writers to gain confidence in their voices and ideas as well as to practice in a variety of formats and conventions. A practicing journalist with more than 25 years of experience writing and editing for newpapers, Alan Hayakawa understands the importance of conventional correctness and appreciates the way different writing situations and new technologies demand different approaches. For this reason, *The Blair Handbook* devotes time to both the whys and the hows of good writing. Students who know how to analyze and address individual rhetorical situations are more likely to succeed both across the curriculum and in the world beyond college.

Pedagogical Features and New Innovations

As a progressive alternative to traditional handbooks, this revised, fifth edition of *The Blair Handbook* has several important features that make this book an especially useful rhetoric and reference in writing classes, in classes across the curriculum, and in writing situations beyond the classroom.

HELP WHERE YOU EXPECT IT

The Blair Handbook offers compehensive coverage of all handbook concerns, organized according to the logic of the writing process: the opening section focuses on planning and drafting; later sections examine research, revising, and editing. Style, grammar, punctuation, and mechanics are presented as "editing" choices that writers make in the final stages of the writing process.

TEACHABLE TREATMENT OF THE PROCESS OF WRITING

The opening chapters of *The Blair Handbook* examine the creative but frustrating messiness of the writing process, offering ideas and strategies to help writers shape, organize, and give voice to their work. Detailed chapters cover many common purposes for college writing—reflecting on experience, explaining things, arguing positions, and writing about literature, as well as composing creative nonfiction, keeping journals, and constructing essay examinations.

ATTENTION TO VISUAL RHETORIC

This edition emphasizes the importance of visual rhetoric and design in the writing of even conventional college papers. The new Chapter 3 introduces students to critical terminology for understanding and talking about visual images while the handbook itself includes visual images throughout to illustrate the effective use of visual design.

ATTENTION TO PUBLIC DISCOURSE

New to this edition of *The Blair Handbook* is an increased emphasis on public discourse, including new chapters on "Reading Images Critically" and "Writing for the World." In addition, this edition includes expanded coverage of document design, creating Web pages, and making oral presentations.

EMPHASIS ON *WRITING ACROSS THE CURRICULUM* ✎

All editions of *Blair* have been written with both students and faculty across the curriculum in mind, taking great care to discuss rhetorical strategies and writing conventions of specific disciplinary areas to nonspecialist audiences. To the fifth edition we have also added *WAC Boxes* ✎ offering suggestions for assigning and responding to writing in disciplines across the curriculum and the world of work. Supplementary material for instructors and students are also available to support teaching and learning writing in disciplines across the curriculum and the world of work.

HELP FOR THOSE WHO SPEAK ENGLISH AS A SECOND LANGUAGE ESL

The Blair Handbook pays careful attention to the needs of second-language students. Graphically distinct boxes ESL throughout the text provide information on topics from grammar, idioms, and usage, to the how and why of rhetorical conventions. All these boxes have been critically re-examined and revised for the fifth edition.

EASY ACCESS TO CRITICAL INFORMATION ▯

Checklist boxes ▯ are provided throughout to call out key information in the preceeding section. These lists range from composing strategies, to figures of speech, to logical fallacies.

CRITICAL COVERAGE OF CRITICAL THINKING ✦

Students are given tips and encouragement for thinking critically about their writing throughout the text. Critical Thinking boxes ✦ prompt students to reassess their writing for clear and logical interpretations and explanations.

FULL COVERAGE OF ELECTRONIC RESEARCH METHODS

This latest edition of *The Blair Handbook* includes up-to-date strategies for planning, organizing, and writing research papers from sources found in the library, in the field, and on the Internet. Particular attention is paid to evaluating, using, and documenting the ever more complicated strands of electronic sources.

SPECIAL ATTENTION TO PLAGIARISM

Because of the ever-increasing ease of copying material from electronic souces, *The Blair Handbook* has greatly expanded the discussion of *plagiarism* in both intentional and unintentional forms. Clear explanations and illustrations of the do's and don't's of quoting and documenting will help students avoid breaches of academic ethics.

EDITING AS A MATTER OF CONVENTIONS, NOT RULES

The editing chapters focus on editing as a process focusing on effectiveness, usage, grammar, punctuation, and mechanics. Hand-edited examples illustrate how writers revise and edit, showing proven strategies for focusing loose paragraphs, strengthening weak sentences, and finding precise and suitable words. *The Blair Handbook* emphasizes grammatical and mechanical processes in everyday language and helps readers identify, analyze, and resolve confusing language problems.

UNIQUE DESIGN THAT FACILITATES QUICK REFERENCE

The four-color, carefully constructed design of the book helps students locate information quickly, as they can identify the parts of the book with their corresponding color bands. Thus, navigating the text becomes a visual as well as mental activity.

Supplements

The following supplements accompany the *Fifth Edition* to aid in teaching and learning:

FOR THE INSTRUCTOR

- **Instructor's Manual.** *Strategies and Resources for Teaching Writing with The Blair Handbook* offers guidance to new and experienced instructors for teaching composition. ISBN 0-13-195239-0

- **The Prentice Hall Resources for Writing** is a specially-designed set of supplements for the instructor that support timely classroom and composition topics. These supplements are free upon adoption of *The Blair Handbook, Fifth Edition.*

  - *Teaching Writing Across the Curriculum* by Art Young is written for college teachers in all disciplines and provides useful advice on teaching writing across the curriculum. ISBN 0-13-193664-6

  - *Teaching Civic Literacy* by Cheryl Duffy offers advice on how to integrate civic literacy into the composition classroom. ISBN 0-13-168060-9

- *Teaching Visual Rhetoric* by Susan Loudermilk provides an illustrated look at visual rhetoric and offers guidance on how to incorporate this topic into the classroom. ISBN 0-13-168058-7
- *Teaching Writing for ESL Students* by Ruth Spack addresses various strategies that can be employed to teach writing to nonnative speakers. ISBN 0-13-168059-5

FOR THE INSTRUCTOR AND STUDENT

- **NEW!** *Web Site with Interactive eBook (www.prenhall .com/fulwiler).* Every copy of *The Blair Handbook, Fifth Edition,* is packaged with a FREE access card that allows you to register for instant access to OneKey. This easy-to-use and valuable Web site offers the following resources and tools in one place:
  - *eBook with Personal Study Plan.* Whenever you write or do research, the eBook is just a click away. The eBook can be searched by table of contents, index, and heading number. Upon completion of a diagnostic test, the table of contents is customized and aligned to a series of quizzes that challenge students until they master each topic. The result is an "intelligent" study plan specific to each student's needs. Students can also annotate and highlight their eBook, just as they would a print book.
  - *OneKey Course Management.* All the resources available on our Web site are also available in CourseCompass, BlackBoard, and WebCT. Contact your sales rep for more information.
  - *English Tutor Center.* Actual composition instructors will review student papers for structure, style, organization, and grammar, providing feedback for the revision process. Tutors will also help students use the handbook and OneKey resources when writing and researching.
  - *Exchange.* This resource provides online portfolio building, instructor commenting, and peer review.
  - *Research Navigator.* This tool is the easiest way for students to start a research assignment or research paper. Students get extensive help on the research process and access to exclusive databases of credible and reliable source material, including the EBSCO Academic Journal and Abstract Database, *New York Times* Archive, "Best of the Web" Link Library, and the *Financial Times* Article Archive and Company Financials.
  - *Research and Documentation Website.* This site provides a quick guide to writing a research paper and documenting sources.
  - *Interactive, Self-Graded Exercises.* This resource provides additional exercises tied to every topic of every chapter in the handbook.

- **Writing and Grammar Practice for ESL Students.** This additional set of exercises has over 700 interactive activities on topics that ESL students find most difficult.
- *Blue Pencil Exercises.* This popular editing software provides contextual grammar and punctuation editing exercises at the paragraph level.
- *Diagnostic Tests and Personal Study Plan.* There are pre- and post-tests available for student self-assessment. These comprehensive tests are automatically graded and the results are broken down by the student's particular strengths and weaknesses. In areas where the student needs more practice, the software will automatically generate a personal set of quizzes and interactive tutorials until a level of mastery is reached.
- *Optional Plagiarism Detection Software.* MyDropBox allows instructors to submit papers for plagiarism detection or set up class accounts so that students can submit their papers themselves. MyDropBox provides its users with comprehensive plagiarism reports on all submitted documents, alerting the user to identified plagiarism. MyDropBox can be used not only to catch plagiarism, but to help students learn to avoid it altogether.
- *Understanding Plagiarism.* This section of the OneKey site helps students understand what plagiarism is and how to avoid committing plagiarism.
- **NEW!! Writing Matters *Videos.*** This video series includes anecdotes from instructors and students with tips on teaching and writing from the handbook, as well as interviews with professionals who discuss the importance of writing in their jobs.

- **NEW!! Student Workbook and Answer Key.** *The Blair Handbook Workbook for Writers* contains hundreds of additional exercises and activities with answers to help improve writing skills.

- **NEW!! *The Prentice Hall WAC PAC.*** A compilation of resources, designed to facilitate teaching and learning, Writing Across the Curriculum (WAC) includes *Papers Across the Curriculum* (edited by Judith Ferster), a series of sample student papers, and *A Prentice Hall Pocket Reader: Writing Across the Curriculum* (by Stephen Brown, University of Nevada–Las Vegas). If you would like to put additional emphasis on WAC in your composition course(s), please contact your Prentice Hall sales rep for more information.

- **Dictionary, Thesaurus, Writer's Guides, and Pocket Readers.** The following resources can be packaged with *The Blair Handbook, Fifth Edition.* These valuable student resources provide additional depth on specialized topics that may only be touched upon in the text and allow you to customize the handbook to your specific needs.

Contact your local Prentice Hall representative for discount pricing information.

- *The New American Webster Handy College Dictionary*
- *The New American Roget's College Thesaurus*
- *Writer's Guide to Research and Documentation*
- *Writer's Guide to Oral Presentations and Writing in the Disciplines*
- *Writer's Guide to Document and Web Design*
- *Writer's Guide to Writing About Literature*
- *A Prentice Hall Pocket Reader: Argument*
- *A Prentice Hall Pocket Reader: Literature*
- *A Prentice Hall Pocket Reader: Patterns*
- *A Prentice Hall Pocket Reader: Themes*
- *A Prentice Hall Pocket Reader: Writing Across the Curriculum*
- *Papers Across the Curriculum*

Acknowledgments

To our colleagues nationwide who agreed to share their collective wisdom on the teaching of writing in the Blair resource pamphlets: Pat Belanoff, State University of New York at Stony Brook; Wendy Bishop, Florida State University; Chris Burnham, University of New Mexico at Las Cruces; Deborah H. Holdstein, Governors State University; Harvey Kail, University of Maine; Ruth Spack, Tufts University; Dees Stallings, University of Maryland; John Trimbur, Worchester Polytechnic Institute; and Art Young, Clemson University.

To Jan Frodesen of the University of California, Santa Barbara, and Barbara Matthias, Iowa State University, who prepared and revised the ESL boxes, incorporating the newest understandings of how students learn English as a second language; and Sean McDowell and Dave Carlson of Indiana University, who prepared many of the activities in the text.

To the many students at the University of Vermont who asked and answered questions about learning to write and especially to those who allowed us to reprint samples of their essays, freewrites, and journal entries.

To Leah Jewell, editorial director, whose vision of contemporary writing instruction guided *The Blair Handbook, Fifth Edition,* to completion.

We would like to acknowledge the strong creative and supportive counsel of our Prentice Hall editor, Paul Crockett, whose vision guided the complicated revisions in this fifth edition. And a special thanks to editorial assistant Tara Culliney who helped all of us keep track of our manuscript in all its diverse stages. Also, thank you to Emily Cleary and Windley Morley, marketing managers, who shaped and implemented the marketing strategy.

We'd also like to thank Brandy Dawson, director of marketing, and Yolanda de Rooy, president of humanities and social sciences, for their enduring support of this project.

To our expert Prentice Hall production team, who took our handbook from manuscript to bound book: Karen Berry, Pine Tree Composition, production editor; Anne Nieglos, senior art director; Gail Cocker-Bogusz, art production manager; and Mary Ann Gloriande, assistant manufacturing manager.

To John Harvey of *The Oregonian,* who instilled respect for the language and for a writer's style; to John A. Kirkpatrick of *The Patriot-News* of Harrisburg, for his dedication to excellence in newspapering; to Ichiro Hayakawa and Frederick Romer Peters, who never met but shared a love of the English language that they passed on to their children; and to Barbara, for her boundless patience, support, and love.

And thanks finally and always to Laura for her continued patience and with this important, yet never-ending project.

REVIEWERS

Thank you to each and every reviewer who took time from their busy schedules to help us reach our goals for this fifth edition. A special thanks goes out to our reviewers from Reading Area Community College and the University of New Hampshire. Your willingness to share your impressions with the publisher and authors truly influenced the direction of this edition. It is a better book for your contributions and constructive feedback.

Joanne E. Gabel
Reading Area Community College

Michelle Cox
University of New Hampshire

Judith A. Schum
Reading Area Community College

Jacqueline A. Blackwell
Thomas Nelson Community College

Donna Singleton
Reading Area Community College

Michelle P. Ossa
Columbus State University

Katherine Ellen Tirabassi
University of New Hampshire

Belinda Westfall
Carl Albert State College

Paul Kei Matsuda
University of New Hampshire

James Allen
College of DuPage

Beth Howells
Armstrong Atlantic State
   University

Charles H. Cole
Carl Albert State University

Carol Eades
University of Kentucky

Cynthia H. Mayfield
York Technical College

Emily Dotson Biggs
University of Kentucky

Alexandra Duckworth
Richard Bland College

Cindy A. Renfro
Houston Community College

Sallie Wolf
Arapahoe Community College

Chere L. Peguesse
Valdosta State University

Lisa Gordon
Columbus State Community College

Donna Binns
Eastern Illinois University

James Boswell
Harrisburg Area Community
   College

Hope Burwell
Kirkwood Community College

Jonikka Charlton
Purdue University

Sandra Clark
Anderson University

Kathleen Furlong
Glendale Community College

Diana Roberts Gruendler
The Pennsylvania State
   University

Vasantha Harinath
North Central State College

David G. Hulm
Kirkwood Community College

Anita Knudson
Los Rios Community College

Mariann Kosub
Bowie State University

Deanna Mascle
Morehead State University

Homer Mitchell
SUNY–Cortland

Kathy Neal
York Technical College

Lisa Wilde
Howard Community College

Suzanne M. Swiderski
University of Iowa

Ray Watkins
Eastern Illinois University

Toby Fulwiler
Alan R. Hayakawa

THE BLAIR HANDBOOK

PART one

Reading and Writing in College

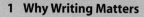

www.prenhall.com/fulwiler

chapter 1

Why Writing Matters

You can count on one thing—attending college will mean writing papers. Whether you are enrolled in a writing course or any other course, you'll be asked to write critical essays, research reports, position papers, book reviews, essay exams, and laboratory reports and sometimes to keep a journal. You may have tackled similar writing assignments in high school, so you've had some practice. Now that practice will be put to a test.

Recently we asked a class of first-year college students to talk about themselves as writers. Several began by describing where they wrote. Amy, for example, said she did most of her writing "listening to classical music and, if it is a nice day, under trees," while Jennifer felt "most comfortable writing on [her] bed and being alone." Others described their attitudes. John, for example, said he wrote best "under pressure." Becky, however, preferred writing when she "felt strongly or was angry about something," while Kevin "hated deadlines." In fact, there proved to be as many different perspectives on being a writer as there were students in the class. To continue our conversation, we asked more specific questions.

1 a   What is difficult about writing?

Everything about writing can seem difficult, from getting started to organizing, revising, and editing. Our own experience tells us this is so—and every published writer we know says the same thing. How, we wondered, would first-year college writers characterize their difficulties? Here is what they told us:

Jennifer: "I don't like being told what to write about."

Amy: "I never could fulfill the page requirements. My essays were always several pages shorter than they were supposed to be."

Jill: "I always have trouble starting off a paper . . . and I hate it when I think I've written a great paper and I get a bad grade. It's so discouraging, and I don't understand what I wrote wrong."

Omar: "Teachers are always nitpicking about little things, but I think writing is for communication, not nitpicking. I mean, if you can read it and it makes sense, what else do you want?"

Ken: "Putting thoughts down on paper as they are in your mind is the hardest thing to do. It's like music—anyone can play a song in his head, but translating it to an instrument is the hard part."

We weren't surprised by these answers since we too remember wondering: What did teachers want? How long was enough? How do you get thoughts into words? Why all the nitpicking?

WRITING 1: EXPLORATION

What do you find difficult about writing? Do you have a problem finding subjects to write about? Or do you have trouble getting motivated? Or does something about the act of writing itself cause problems for you? Explain in your own words by writing quickly for five minutes without stopping.

▣ Are any of your writing difficulties related to writing in a second language? For example, do you need to translate some ideas from your native language to English? Do problems with grammar or vocabulary make it difficult for you to communicate?

1   b   What do you enjoy about writing?

Though any writer will tell you writing isn't easy, most writers will also describe it as interesting and exciting. So we asked our first-year students what it was about writing that gave them pleasure:

Jolene: "If I have a strong opinion on a topic, it makes it so much easier to write a paper."

Rebecca: "On occasion I'm inspired by a wonderful idea. Once I get going, I actually enjoy writing a lot."

Casey: "I enjoy most to write about my experiences, both good and bad. I like to write about things when I'm upset—it makes me feel better."

Darren: "I guess my favorite kind of writing is letters. I get to be myself and just talk in them."

Like our students, we prefer to write about topics that inspire or interest us, and we find personal writing such as letters especially easy, interesting, and enjoyable.

WRITING 2: EXPLORATION

What kind of writing do you most enjoy doing? What do you like about it: communicating? exploring a subject? playing with words? something else?

1 c   What surprises are in store?

After talking with first-year students, we asked some advanced students about their writing experiences: "What has surprised you the most about writing in college?"

Carmen: "Papers aren't as hellish as I was told they'd be. In fact, I've actually enjoyed writing a lot of them—especially after they were done."

Aaron: "My style has changed a lot. Rather than becoming more complex, it's become simpler."

Kerry: "The most surprising and frustrating thing has been the different reactions I've received from different professors."

Rob: "I'm always being told that my writing is superficial—that I come up with good ideas but don't develop them."

John: "The tutor at our writing lab took out a pair of scissors and said I would have to work on organization. Then she cut up my paper and taped it back together a different way. This really made a difference, and I've been using this method ever since."

Chrissie: "Sharing papers with other students is very awkward for me. But it's extremely beneficial when I trust and like my group, when we all relax enough to talk honestly about one another's papers."

As you can see, most advanced students found ways to cope with and enjoy college writing. Several of them reported satisfying experiences when they shared their writings with each other. We are sorry that some students, even in their last year, could not figure out what their instructors wanted; we think there are ways to do that.

WRITING 3: EXPLORATION ....

Think about your experience with writing in the last school you attended. What surprised you—pleasantly or not—about the experience? What did you learn or not learn?

....

1 d Why is writing important?

We also asked these advanced students why, in their last year, they had enrolled in an elective writing class: "What made the subject so important to you?"

Kim: "I have an easier time expressing myself through writing. When I'm speaking, my words get jumbled—writing gives me more time, and my voice doesn't quiver and I don't blush."

Rick: "Writing allows me to hold up a mirror to my life and see what clear or distorted images stare back at me."

Glenn: "The more I write, the better I become. In terms of finding a job after I graduate, strong writing skills will give me an edge over those who are just mediocre writers."

Amy: "I'm still searching for meaning. When I write I feel I can do anything, go anywhere, search and explore."

Angel: "I feel I have something to say."

We agree with virtually all of these reasons. At times writing is therapeutic, at other times it helps us clarify our ideas, and at still other times it helps us get and keep jobs.

Look over the various answers given by the college seniors and select one.
Do you agree or disagree with the student? Explain.

1 e What can you learn from the experience of others?

Since our advanced students had a lot to say about writing, we asked
them to be consultants: "What is your advice to first-year college writers?"
Here are their suggestions:

Aaron: "Get something down!! The hardest part of writing is starting. Forget the introduction, skip the outline, don't worry about a thesis—just blast
your ideas down, see what you've got, then go back and work on them."

Christa: "Plan ahead. It sounds dry, but planning makes writing easier
than doing laundry."

Victor: "Follow the requirements of the assignment to a T. Hand in a
draft for the instructor to mark up; then rewrite it."

Allyson: "Don't think every piece you write has to be a masterpiece. And
sometimes the worst assignment turns into the best writing. Don't worry
about what the instructor wants—write what you believe."

Carmen: "Imagine and create; never be content with just retelling a story."

Rick: "When other people trash your writing, thank them and listen to
their criticism. It stings, but it helps you become a better writer."

Jason: "Say what you are going to say as clearly and as straightforwardly
as possible. Don't try to pad it with big words and fancy phrasing."

Angel: "Read for pleasure from time to time. The more you read, the better you write—it just happens."

Kim: "When choosing topics, choose something that has a place in your
heart."

These are good suggestions to any writers: start fast, think ahead, plan
to revise and edit, listen to critical advice, consider your audience, be clear,
read a lot. We hope, however, that instructors respond to your writing in critically helpful ways and don't "trash" it. Whether or not you take some of the

advice will depend on what you want from your writing: good grades? self-knowledge? personal satisfaction? clear communication? a response by your audience? When we shared these suggestions with first-year students, they nodded their heads, took some notes, and laughed—often with relief.

WRITING 5: EXPLORATION ....

What else would you like to ask advanced college students about writing? Find one and ask; report back.

::

1 f   What else do you want to know about writing?

Realizing that our first-year college writers had already received twelve years' worth of "good advice" about learning to write, we asked them one more question: "What do you want to learn about writing that you don't already know?" In parentheses, we have provided references to chapters of this handbook that answer these questions.

Emma: "Should I write to please the instructor or to please myself?" (See Chapter 5, "Analyzing a Rhetorical Situation.")

José: "I'm always being told to state my thesis clearly. What exactly is a thesis, and why is it so important?" (See 5a; also Chapters 9, "Writing to Explain"; 10, "Arguing and Persuading"; and 11, "Writing about Literature.")

Jolene: "How do I develop a faster way of writing?" (See Chapter 7, "Strategies for Invention and Discovery.")

Amy: "Is there a trick to making a paper longer without adding useless information?" (See especially Chapter 15, "Focused Revising.")

Sam: "How do I learn to express my ideas so they make sense to common, intelligent readers and not just to myself?" (See Chapter 5 and Part Eight, "Editing.")

Scott: "How can I make my writing flow better and make smooth transitions from one idea to the next?" (See Chapters 36, "Shaping Paragraphs," and 38, "Strengthening Sentences.")

Terry: "I want to learn to like to write. Then I won't put off assignments until the last minute." (See Chapter 4, "The Writing Process," and Part Two.)

Jennifer: "I have problems making sentences sound good. How can I learn to do that?" (See Chapters 36–45.)

John P.: "I would like to develop some sort of personal style so when I write, people know it's me." (See 5d.)

John K.: "I want to become more confident about what I write down on paper. I don't want to have to worry about whether my documentation is correct or my words are spelled right." (See Chapters 27, "Using Research Sources," and 58, "Spelling.")

Woody: "Now that I'm in college, I would like to be challenged when I read and write, to think and ask good questions and find good answers." (See Chapters 2, "Reading Texts Critically" and 3, "Reading Images Critically.")

Pat: "I don't want to learn nose-to-the-grindstone, straight-from-the-textbook rules. I want to learn to get my mind into motion and pencil in gear." (See Chapters 4, "The Writing Process," and 7, "Strategies for Invention and Discovery.")

Heidi: "I would love to increase my vocabulary. If I had a wider range of vocabulary, I would be able to express my thoughts more clearly." (See Chapter 43, "Choosing the Right Word.")

Jess: "I'm always afraid that people will laugh at my writing. Can I ever learn to get over that and get more confident about my writing?" (Reread this chapter "Why Writing Matters," and see Chapter 4, "The Writing Process.")

We can't, of course, guarantee that if you read and use *The Blair Handbook* your writing will get easier, faster, longer, clearer, or more correct. Or, for that matter, that your style will become more personal and varied, or that you will become a more confident and comfortable writer—no handbook can do that for you. Becoming a better writer depends on your own interest and hard work. It will also depend on your college experience, the classes you take, and the teachers with whom you study. However, whether in class or on your own, if you read *The Blair Handbook* carefully and practice its suggestions, you should find possible answers to all these questions and many more.

We admit that there was at least one concern for which we really had no good response. Jessica wrote, "My biggest fear is that I'll end up one semester with four or five courses that all involve writing and I'll die." Or maybe we do have a response: If you become comfortable and competent as a writer, you'll be able to handle all the writing assignments thrown your way. Even if you can't, Jessica, you won't die. It's just college.

SUGGESTIONS FOR WRITING AND RESEARCH

INDIVIDUAL

1.   Interview a classmate about his or her writing experiences, habits, beliefs, and practices. Include questions such as those asked in this chapter as well as others you think may be important. Write a brief essay profiling your classmate as a writer. Share your profile with a classmate.

2.   Over a two-week period, keep a record of every use you make of written language. Record your entries daily in a journal or class notebook. At the end of two weeks, enumerate all the specific uses as well as how often you did each. What activities dominate your list? Write an essay based on this personal research in which you argue for or against the centrality of writing in everyday life.

COLLABORATIVE

As a class or in small groups, design a questionnaire to elicit information about people's writing habits and attitudes. Distribute the questionnaire to both students and faculty in introductory and advanced writing classes. Compile the results. Compare and contrast the ideas of students at different levels and disciplines and write a report to share with the class. Consider writing a feature article for your student newspaper or faculty newsletter reporting what you found.

WRITING ACROSS THE CURRICULUM

Why Writing Matters

To find out how instructors across the various disciplines value writing, students in the class might conduct a collaborative survey of instructors from various disciplines across campus. An easy way to do this would be for each student in class to query one instructor in another course in which he or she is currently enrolled, asking questions that might include the following:

• Why does writing matter to you, personally?

• When and where did writing first become important to you?

• What kinds of writing do you most often do?

- How would you describe your writing habits: Where do you like to write—office, home, library? When? What conditions do you prefer? Do you listen to music or write in silence?

- What is the hardest part of writing for you? (And how do you overcome it?)

- What specific kinds of writing are most valued in your discipline and why?

- What are the most common problems you witness in student writing?

- What advice would you have for students who want to improve their writing?

Elect classmate editors and collate responses within the group and present your findings as a written report to your student paper or as a class book to be shared with interested college faculty, administrators, or committees.

chapter 2

Reading Texts Critically

College-level assignments ask you to expand your reading, thinking, and writing skills. That means being able to analyze the distinctions, interpretations, biases, and conclusions of others and make sense of their writing. **Critical reading** for research assignments involves evaluating the relative importance or credibility of each of your sources and placing them in a context of related opinions or findings. It includes gathering information, synthesizing it, and reaching new conclusions or findings of your own. College instructors expect you to make distinctions, develop interpretations, and render conclusions in your own writing that stand up to the critical reading of others. Although most of *The Blair Handbook* is about writing, this chapter is about critical reading and its relationship to, and influence on, critical writing.

2 a Reading to understand

Before you can read any text critically, you need to understand what you're reading. To do so, you need some context for the new ideas you encounter, some knowledge of the text's terms and ideas, and some awareness of the rules that govern the kind of writing you are reading.

Imagine, for example, reading Mark Twain's *The Adventures of Huckleberry Finn* with no knowledge of American geography, the Mississippi River, or the institution of slavery. Imagine reading about the national debt without understanding basic mathematics, principles of taxation, or the meaning of deficit spending. The more you know about any subject, the more you are capable of learning. The more you learn, the more you know—and the more careful and critical will be your reading, writing, and thinking about that subject.

Many college instructors will ask you to read about subjects that are new to you, so you won't be spending much time reading about what you already know. As you read one unfamiliar text after another, how can you manage to read successfully? How can you create a context, learn the background, and find the rules to help you read unfamiliar texts in unfamiliar subject areas? Let's look at how this might be done.

As an experiment, read the following short opening paragraph from an eight-paragraph *New York Times* story titled "Nagasaki, August 9, 1945." When you have finished, pause for a few moments and think about what you learned, how you learned it, and what you think the rest of the story will be about.

> In August 1945, I was a freshman at Nagasaki Medical College. The ninth of August was a clear, hot, beautiful, summer day. I left my lodging house, which was one and one half miles from the hypocenter, at eight in the morning, as usual, to catch a tram car. When I got to the tram stop, I found that it had been derailed in an accident. I decided to return home. I was lucky. I never made it to school that day.
>
> MICHAITO ICHIMARU

How did you do? Below, we've slowed down our own reading process to show what it was like:

1. We read the first sentence carefully, noticing the year 1945 and the name of the medical college, "Nagasaki." Through our prior historical knowledge, we *identified* Nagasaki, Japan, as one of the two cities on which the United States dropped atomic bombs at the end of World War II—though we did not remember the precise date.

2. We noticed the city and the date (August 9) and wondered if that was when the bomb was dropped. We *asked* (silently), "Is this a story about the bomb?"

3. Still looking at the first sentence, a reference to the writer's younger self ("I was a freshman"), we guessed that the author was present at the dropping of this bomb. We *predicted* that this would be a survivor's account of the bombing of Nagasaki.

4. The word *hypocenter* in the third sentence made us pause again. We *questioned* what the word meant. The language seemed oddly out of place next to the "beautiful, summer day" described in the second sentence. It sounded technical enough to refer to the place where the bomb went off. Evidence was mounting that the narrator may have lived one and a half miles from the exact place where the atomic bomb detonated.

5. In the next to last sentence of the paragraph, the author says that he was "lucky" to miss school. Why, unless something unfortunate happened at school, would he consider missing it "lucky"? We *predicted* that had the author gone to school "as usual," he would have been closer to the hypocenter, which we now surmised was at Nagasaki Medical College.

6. We then *tested* our several predictions by reading the rest of the essay— something that you, of course, can't do here. They proved correct: Michaito Ichimaru's story is a firsthand account of witnessing and surviving the dropping of the bomb, which in fact killed all who attended the medical college, a quarter of a mile from the hypocenter.

7. Finally, out of curiosity, we *consulted* an encyclopedia for "Nagasaki" and *confirmed* that 75,000 people were killed by this second dropping of an atomic bomb on August 9, 1945.

It is possible that your reasoning went something like ours, which we have reconstructed here as best we could. Of course, these thoughts didn't occur in a seven-step sequence at all, but rather in split-second flashes, simultaneously. Even as we read a sentence for the first time, we found ourselves reading backward as much as forward to check our understanding.

You'll notice that in our example, some parts of the pattern of identifying/questioning/predicting/testing/confirming occur more than once, perhaps simultaneously, and not in any predictable order. No two readers would—or could—read this passage in exactly the same way. However, our reading process may be similar enough to yours to show that reading is a messy trial-and-error process for everyone and that it depends as much on prior knowledge as on new information.

Whenever you read a new text or watch an unfamiliar event, you give it meaning by following a procedure similar to the one we did in the above example, trying to identify what you see, question what you don't understand, make and test predictions about meaning, and consult authorities for confirmation or information. Once you know how to read successfully for basic comprehension, you are ready to read critically.

WRITING 1: APPLICATION

Select a book you have been assigned to read for one of your courses and find a chapter that has not yet been covered in class. Read the first page of the chapter and then stop. Write out any predictions you have about where the rest of the chapter is going. (Ask yourself, for example: What is its main theme or argument? How will it conclude?) Finish reading the chapter and check its conclusion against your predictions. If your predictions were close, you are reading well for understanding.

ESL Reading Strategies Across Languages

If you learned to read in your native language before learning English, you can use some of the same strategies to read English. For example, some features of stories, explanations, or arguments may be the same in English as in your native language. Whenever you feel that you do not have a good understanding of the purpose or important features of something you are reading in English, take a moment to reflect on how you would have approached a similar text in your native language, and see whether you can use some of those same strategies.

You can also take advantage of information you gained through reading in your native language when you read in English. All readers relate new information in a text to what they already know; this helps them understand the text better and allows them to make predictions about what it will contain. As you read, try to be aware of any relevant information you know about the subject, whether you gained this information in English or in your native language.

Reading to Understand

1. **Identify.** Read first for what you recognize, know, and understand. Identify what you are reading about. Read carefully—slowly at first—and let meaning take hold where it can.

2. **Question.** Pause, and look hard at words and phrases you don't know or understand. See whether they make sense when you reread them. Compare them to what you do know, or place them in a context you understand.

3. **Predict.** Make predictions about what you will learn next: How will the essay, story, or report advance? What will happen? What theme or thesis will emerge? What might be the point of it all?

4. **Test.** Follow up on your predictions by reading further to see if they are correct or nearly correct. If they are, read on with more confidence; if they are not, read further, make more predictions, and test them. Trial and error are good teachers.

5. **Confirm.** Check your reading of the text with others who have also read it and see if your interpretations are similar or different. If you have questions, ask them. Share answers.

2   b   Reading critically

People read in different ways at different times. When they read a novel for pleasure or a newspaper to learn about current events, they read to find out "what happens." Doing this is reading for understanding. However, when they read a novel to write a paper on it or a newspaper to find evidence for an argument, they must read beyond the basic facts. They must analyze what they've read and assess the validity of the author's assumptions, ideas, and conclusions. Doing this is reading critically.

The rest of this chapter describes three strategies that lead readers from simply understanding texts to evaluating and interpreting them: previewing, responding, and reviewing. Although we will discuss this process of critical reading as three separate activities, it will become clear that they seldom occur in a simple one-two-three order.

One of our students, Richard, kept a detailed journal when he read a book titled *Iron John*. Richard shared with us both his thoughts and journal entries, some of which are reproduced here as an example of critical reading.

WRITING 2: EXPLORATION

Describe how you read a text when you need to understand it especially well, say, before an examination on it or when you plan to use its ideas in a paper.

1 Previewing

To preview a text, either look it over briefly before reading it or read it rapidly through once to get a general sense of what it says.

First questions

You should begin asking questions of a text from the moment you pick it up. Your first questions should be aimed at finding general, quickly gleaned information, such as that provided by the title, subtitle, and table of contents.

- What does the title suggest?

- What does the table of contents promise?

- What can I learn from the chapter titles or subheads?

- Who is the author? (Have I heard of him or her?)

- How current is the information?

You may not ask these questions methodically, in this order, and you don't have to write down your answers, but you should ask them before you read the whole text. If your answers to these questions suggest that a text is worthy of further study, continue with the previewing process.

Here are the notes Richard took in response to his first questions:

> The title itself, *Iron John*, is intriguing, suggests something strong and unbreakable. I already know and admire the author, Robert Bly, for his insightful poetry but have never read his prose.
>
> The table of contents looks like fun:
>
> 1. The Pillow and the Key
>
> 2. When One Hair Turns Gold
>
> 3. The Road of Ashes, Descent, and Grief
>
> 4. The Hunter for the King in Time with No Father
>
> 5. The Meeting with the God-Woman in the Garden

Second questions

Once you've determined that a book or article warrants further critical attention, it's helpful to read selected parts of it rapidly to see what they promise. Skimming leads to more questions. Capture your answers on note cards or in a journal.

- Read the prefatory material: What can I learn from the book jacket, foreword, preface?

- Read the introduction, abstract, or first page: What theme or thesis is promised?

- Read a sample chapter or subsection: Is the material about what I expected?

- Scan the index or notes: What sources have informed this text? What names do I recognize?

- Note words or ideas that you do not understand: Do I have the background to understand this text?

- Consider: Will I have to consult other sources to obtain a critical understanding of this one?

In skimming a text, you make predictions about coverage, scope, and treatment and about whether the information seems pertinent or useful for your purpose.

Here are the notes Richard took in response to his second group of questions:

> According to the blurb on the jacket: "*Iron John* is Robert Bly's long-awaited book on male initiation and the role of the mentor, the result of ten years' work with men to discover truths about masculinity that get beyond the stereotypes of our popular culture."

> There is no introduction or index, but the chapter notes in the back of the book (260–67) contain the names of people Bly used as sources. I recognize novelist D. H. Lawrence, anthropologist Mircea Eliade, poet William Blake, historian Joseph Campbell, and a whole bunch of psychologists—but many others I've never heard of.

These preview notes confirmed that *Iron John* is a book about men and male myths in modern American culture by a well-known poet writing a scholarly prose book in an informal style. Richard learned that Bly will not only examine current male mythology but also make some recommendations about which myths are destructive and which constructive.

Previewing is only a first step in a process that now slows down and becomes more time-consuming and critical. As readers begin to preview a text seriously, they often make notes in the text's margin or in a journal or notebook to mark places for later review. In other words, before the preview stage of critical reading has ended, the responding stage has probably begun.

WRITING 3: APPLICATION ....

Select any unfamiliar book about which you are curious and preview it, using the two kinds of questions outlined here. Stop after ten minutes and write what you know about the text.

....

2 Responding

Once you understand what a text promises, you need to examine it more slowly. You need to begin the work of evaluating its ideas, assumptions, arguments, evidence, logic, and coherence. You need to start developing your own interpretation of what the text is all about. The best way to do this is to **respond,** or "talk back," to the text in writing.

Respond to passages that cause you to pause for a moment to reflect, to question, to read again, or to say "Aha!" If the text is informational, try to capture the statements that summarize ideas or are repeated. If the text poses an argument (and many of the texts you'll be reading in college will do so), you need to examine the claims the text makes about the topic and to consider each piece of supporting evidence. (See Chapter 10 for more on arguments.) If the text is literary (a novel, play, poem, or essay), pay extra attention to language features such as images, metaphors, and dialogue. In any text, notice boldfaced or italicized words—they have been marked for special attention.

Ask about the effect of the text on you: How am I reacting? What am I thinking and feeling? What do I like? What do I distrust? Do I know why? But don't worry too much about answering all your questions at this point. (That's where reviewing comes in.)

Responding can take many forms, from **annotating** in the text margins to extensive **freewriting** in a **journal** or notebook (see Chapter 6), but it should involve writing. The more you write about something, the more you will understand it.

Annotating

To read any text critically, begin with pen or pencil in hand. If you own the book, mark places to be examined further, but be aware that mere underlining, checking, or highlighting does not yet involve you in a conversation with the text. If you don't own the text, write on sticky paper pasted in the margins or keep a running conversation in a notebook. To annotate look for:

- Points of agreement and disagreement with claims or assertions

- Convincing examples that support claims or assertions

- Implications or consequences of believing the author

- Personal associations with text material

- Connections to other texts you've read

- Recurring images, symbols, phrases, or ideas.

(For an example of an annotated page from *Iron John,* see page 19.)

The Fifties male had a clear vision of what a man was, and what male responsibilities were, but the isolation and one-sidedness of his vision were dangerous.

Examples in film? Books?

During the 1960s, another sort of man appeared. The waste and violence of the Vietnam war made men question whether they knew what an adult male really was. If manhood meant Vietnam, did they want any part of it? Meanwhile, [the feminist movement encouraged men to actually look at women,] forcing them to become conscious of concerns and sufferings that the Fifties male labored to avoid. As men began to examine women's history and women's sensibility, some men began to notice what was called (their *feminine* side) and pay attention to it. This process continues to this day, and I would say that most (contemporary men) are involved in it in some way.

How did they see it?

Examples? Easy Rider? Platoon?

There's something (wonderful) about this development—I mean the practice of men welcoming their own "feminine" consciousness and (nurturing) it—this is important—and yet I have the sense that there is something wrong. The male in the past twenty years has become more thoughtful, more gentle. But by this process he has not become more free. He's a nice boy who pleases not only his mother but also the young woman he is living with.

female-associated word—loaded

Why is pleasing people wrong? contradiction?

In the seventies I began to see all over the country a phenomenon that we might call the ("soft male.") Sometimes even today when I look out at an audience, perhaps half the young males are what I'd call soft. They're lovely, valuable people—I like them—they're not interested in harming the earth or starting wars.

How would Bly define free?

Should they be?

An annotated text page from *Iron John*

Freewriting

A second powerful way of responding to texts is to write freely about your reactions to the reading. All you do is write fast about an idea and see where your thoughts go. This **freewriting** often helps you clarify your own thoughts about the ideas in the text. When you freewrite, write to yourself in your own natural style, not worrying about sentence structure, spelling, or punctuation. Nobody else need ever read this; its purpose is to help you tie together ideas from your reading with the thoughts and experiences in your own mind. (For more details on freewriting, see 7b.)

In thinking about a main theme in *Iron John,* Richard did the following freewrite in his journal:

> 9/30   Bly praises the "Wild Man" in us, clearly separating "wildness" from barbarism and savagery—hurting others. Also suggests that modern men are wounded in some way—literally?—but only those who examine their wounds gain higher knowledge. In an interview I once heard him talk about warriors—men who seek action (mountain climbing? skiing? Habitat for Humanity?) to feel whole and fulfilled. So men (why not women too?) test themselves—not necessarily against other men—against nature or even themselves. Harvey says sailing is his warrior activity. Is backpacking mine?

Richard's freewriting shows the writer reacting to one idea in the text (*wildness*), moving to another (*being wounded*), digressing by remembering a TV interview, raising a question (*why not women too?*), and concluding by raising a question about himself (*Is backpacking mine?*). Freewriting generates questions at random, catches them, and leaves the answering for later.

Cross-referencing

To move beyond annotating (commenting on single passages) and freewriting, try **cross-referencing** (finding relationships among passages) in which you use a coding system to show that one annotation, passage, or idea is related to another. Some students write comments on different features of the text in different colors, such as reserving green for nature images, blue for key terms, red for interesting episodes, and so on. Other students write their notes first and then go back and number them, perhaps 1 for plot, 2 for key terms, and so on.

WRITING 4: APPLICATION ··

Keep a reading journal for an assigned reading from one of your courses. Write something in the journal after every reading session, including probing questions and freewriting. Annotate the text and create a cross-referencing system as you go along to see what patterns you can discover. Write about the results of these response methods in your journal: Did they help? Which ones worked best?

3 Reviewing

To review, you need both to reread and to *re-see* a text, reconsidering its meaning and the ideas you have about it. You need to be sure that you grasp the important points within the text, but you also need to move beyond that level to a critical understanding of the text as a whole. In responding, you started a conversation with the text so you could put yourself into the book's framework and context; in reviewing, you should consider how the book can fit into your own framework and context. As you review, keep responding, talking back to the text, but this time do so with more purpose and focus.

Reviewing will take different forms depending on how you intend to use the text—whether or not you are using it to write a paper, for example. In general, there are two ways to review a text you have read critically: you can interpret what it means, or you can evaluate its soundness or significance.

When you review a text, you examine its meaning and weigh its merits: What does it say? Is it credible? Why or why not? What's debatable? Texts with different purposes need to be examined accordingly. For example, an argument text tries to do one thing, an informational text something else, and a literary text something else again.

Argumentative texts

Argument texts make certain claims in advance and then support those claims with evidence. When you review an argumentative text, you examine and evaluate each part of the argument to see whether it is sound. If a critic argues that *Huckleberry Finn* is a racist book, look closely at the evidence, the claims, and the whole argument.

Review the **evidence.**

- Is it a *fact*—something that can be verified and that most readers will accept without further argument?

- Is it an *inference*—a conclusion drawn from an accumulation of facts?

- Is it an *opinion*—an idea that reflects an author's personal beliefs and may be based on faith, emotion, or myth?

While all three types of evidence have their place, the strongest arguments are based on accurate facts and reasonable inferences.

Review the **claims.** A claim is a statement that something is true or should be done.

- What is the claim and where is it stated? (Can you restate it in your own words?)
- Is every claim supported by sufficient *evidence?*
- Are you aware of *counterclaims* or contradictory evidence?

(See Chapter 10 for more on writing arguments.)

Informational texts

Reviewing informational texts such as reports and textbooks requires making sure the facts are true, the inferences are based on facts, and the opinions are based on knowledge. Informational texts don't make arguments, but they often draw conclusions from the facts they present. For example, a geology text explaining the theory of continental glaciation should explain the evidence that supports the theory. Ask these kinds of questions of informational texts:

- Do the facts justify the conclusions?
- Is any information that you expect to be there missing?
- Is the author's tone fair and reasonable?
- What is the basis for the author's expertise?

(See Chapter 9 for more on informational writing.)

Literary texts

Essays, short stories, poems, and plays may contain arguments and information, but their primary goal is more elusive—to make you feel, imagine, empathize, or understand. Interpreting and evaluating literature is often very personal, relying on individual associations and responses, but the strongest critical evaluations are based on textual evidence. Ask these kinds of questions about literary texts:

- How would you summarize the *plot?*

- Why are the *characters* believable or not?

- Of what importance is the *setting?*

- From what *point of view* is the text written and what difference does it make?

- What *images, words, or ideas* are repeated?

- What is the main *theme* or *themes* running through the text?

(See Chapter 11 for more information on analyzing and interpreting literary texts.)

Reading Critically

1. **Preview** a text first by questioning the title, table of contents, author's reputation, and date: do they seem relevant to you? If you are still interested in the source, ask similar questions of the preface or foreword, the introduction, sample pages, and index: does this text provide useful information?

2. **Respond** to a text by writing back to some of its assertions: ask further questions, freewrite possible answers, and write margin notes next to interesting or puzzling passages.

3. **Review an argumentative text** by examining the logic of the argument, the claims it makes, and the evidence that is presented to support these claims. Review an **informational text** by checking whether the facts justify the conclusion. Review a **literary text** by explaining in your own words its plot, character, setting, point of view, and theme.

SUGGESTIONS FOR WRITING AND RESEARCH

INDIVIDUAL

Select a short text. First read it briefly for *understanding,* to be sure it makes sense to you. Second, read it *critically* according to the methods described in this chapter. Finally, write a short (two-page) *review* of the text in which you explain its meaning and recommend or don't recommend it to other readers.

COLLABORATIVE

As a class or small group, agree on a short text to read and write about, following the suggestions in the individual exercise above. Share your written reviews in small groups, paying particular attention to the claims and evidence each writer uses. Rewrite your review, using the response you received from your group. (For more information about responding to other writers' texts, see Chapter 16.)

WRITING ACROSS THE CURRICULUM

Study Groups to Improve Reading Comprehension

Instructors across the curriculum assume you can understand and critically read whatever handouts, chapters, or whole texts they assign in their courses. This will most likely be true about material with which you have some personal experience or have encountered before. However, it may not be true about new material, especially in disciplines you may be encountering for the first time. According to Harvard researchers, one of the best ways to help you and other students in similar difficulties will be to create informal study groups in those classes. These groups will meet periodically, say over coffee, and share both questions and answers about the material.* While none of you may be experts about all the assigned reading, it's unlikely that all of you will find the same material confusing, so pooling your collective understanding by talking and reasoning it out almost always leads to improved understanding and better writing.

*The Harvard Assessment Seminars: Explorations with Students and Faculty about Teaching, Learning, and Student Life (1990).

chapter 3

Reading Images Critically

Of all five senses, the one most people trust first is their eyes. They believe what they see first hand, and they believe the photographs, films, or videos of others. Well-known examples of the power of visual images to shape public opinion and national policy include the photographs of Depression-era poverty, Vietnam war casualties, and Iraqi prisoner-of-war abuse; films of the Nazi Holocaust victims and JFK assassination; and videos of the Rodney King beatings, space shuttle disasters, and the 9/11 terrorist attacks.

Many Americans spend a substantial portion of their time watching visual images via television and computers as well as photographs, illustrations, charts, and advertisements in every possible media, including books, newspapers, magazines, pamphlets, posters, and billboards. Even the college curriculum is as much visual as verbal, including Internet research, computer graphics, and PowerPoint presentations. In other words, it is as important to read both visual and verbal texts with a critical eye in order to understand, discuss, and assess their worth.

This chapter examines those elements of visual literacy most likely to complement the verbal literacy emphasized in most first-year writing classes. We believe a critical understanding of visual texts helps students as both consumers of the frequent images they encounter in reading and viewing as well as producers who now so easily incorporate images into their own writing (see Chapters 17 and 18 and sample student essays in Chapters 9 and 10).

To illustrate the critical reading of visual images, the first part of this chapter draws on the collection of 77,000 black and white photographs compiled by the Farm Security Administration (FSA) under the Department of Agriculture from 1937 to 1945, now housed in the Library of Congress. As part of the New Deal programs to put Americans back to work during the Great Depression, the FSA commissioned out-of-work artists, historians, writers, folklorists, musicologists, and photographers to capture in text, tape, and celluloid as many elements as possible of American culture. The latter half of the chapter draws on contemporary visual images culled primarily from the colorful world of commercial advertising.

3   a   The elements of composition

To compose either an effective essay or a strong picture, the "composer" works with a number of compositional elements, which turn out to be remarkably similar from one medium to the other. Both pictures and stories contain **information** presented by a composer who has a particular **point of view** and **arranges** them in two-dimensional space. Likewise, stories are ordered in sequential time so that they illustrate certain **themes** or meanings, some emphasized more than others. In addition, images can serve focused rhetorical purposes in a manner similar to verbal texts, such as **describing, narrating, explaining,** and **persuading.**

1 Information

Both words and pictures convey information, but each does so in importantly different ways. In English, words are written sequentially, left to right, and so readers' attention is directed toward meaning according to where the text begins, where it goes next, and how it ends. A look at a daily newspaper or Web page reveals textual information further augmented by headlines, titles, subtitles, boldface, italics, and white space. By the time readers get to college, they have internalized many predictive strategies to help them critically understand a great variety of written texts (see Chapter 2).

Visual images present a different set of problems for critical readers. For example, in looking at a photograph or drawing, information is presented simultaneously so viewers can start or stop anywhere they like—at least theoretically. Since visual information is presented simultaneously, its general meaning may be apparent at a glance, while more nuanced or complicated

How many words are needed to convey this information?

meaning may take a long time to figure out and, even then, odds are it will vary from one viewer to another.

Look at the accompanying photograph, "Roadside Stand," taken by Walker Evans in 1936 near Birmingham, Alabama. It presents a lot of information at a glance, but what does the photograph say or mean? Why did Evans shoot it? What did he find of special interest there? What did he intend for viewers to take away?

What, among all those vegetables and words, do we focus on? Are you struck by the informality of the roadside market in contrast with today's modern supermarkets? Do you notice the careful order in what is otherwise a low-rent store? Or are you left wondering why the two boys are holding the watermelons? In this image, the visual information is augmented by the addition of verbal signs, but does that make the meaning any more clear? For instance, what is the relationship between the "*house-mover*" sign and the fish and farm market? What do we think of a merchant who advertises "*Honest Weights and Square Dealings*"? Is the sign reassuring or suspicious? While this photo supports the cliché "*a picture is worth a thousand words*," as it would take at least that many words to capture the details portrayed here, what, exactly, does that "*worth*" mean? Would a writer who used a thousand words to describe this scene point readers more specifically to one meaning rather than another?

In contrast to the multiple meanings possible in the Evans photograph would be an advertisement in a magazine or on television created to point you

What story is promised here?

toward a very specific meaning. For example, what kind of a movie experience do you anticipate when you look at the poster for the classic B&W film, *Touch of Evil*? Who is the villain? Who is the victim? And if the images alone don't tell you, how about the accompanying words, "murder, mystery, and suspense"?

In contrast to the roadside photograph and the suggestive film poster would be our more simple day-to-day reliance on visual images to convey practical information quickly and accurately, such as the weather forecast from a daily newspaper shown below.

To think critically about visual *information,* first identify what objects, facts, processes, or symbols are portrayed in the image. Taking all the information together, ask if there is a main or unifying idea: Is the meaning open to multiple interpretations, such as the Evans photograph? Is it suggested but not stated, as in the film poster? Or is it clear and unambiguous, as in the weather forecast? As a viewer, pausing to answer such questions will likely sharpen your critical faculties and increase your understanding of the visual information you encounter and help you use images more wisely in texts that you create.

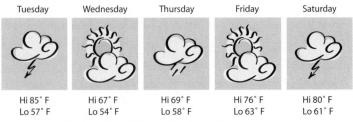

How long does it take to "read" this weather forecast?

2 Point of view

In written texts, *point of view* refers to the "person" from whose vantage point the information is delivered. Writing from the first person (I), the writer tells the story so you expect his personal perspective. Writing from the second person (you), the writer addresses readers directly and presumes to know something about them. Writing from the third person (he, she), the writer focuses on an external subject, without personal reference, so that her viewpoint is never directly stated. In photographs, drawings, or paintings, *point of view* refers to the place from which the image-maker looks at the subject—where the photographer places his camera, the artist her easel. For illustrative purposes, we'll continue to use photographic images to examine critical decisions that affect perspective.

Photographs that haven't been manipulated in a dark room or digitally by a computer don't lie. Nor do they tell the whole truth, either. Yes, they reproduce the subject in front of the camera, as it exists the moment the shutter is clicked, but they don't show anything to the left or right, above or below, or what went on before or after. A camera aimed east omits information north, west, and south, and so on. In other words, any photograph is the result of placing a camera in a certain place, at a certain height and distance, at a specific time of day, using a particular lens, film, and, possibly, filter. And all these decisions, about where, when, and how to place the camera, create the visual point of view. A good example of the limited truth revealed by photographs can be found in the real-estate advertisements, where the photograph of a house that's for sale doesn't reveal the landfill next door or the factory across the street—though you might infer such limitations from a low selling price or confirm them by driving past the house itself.

Look at the photograph of the Filipino lettuce pickers by Dorthea

Split-Level Ranch House

Split-level ranch with 4 bedrooms, 1.5 baths located close to town offers beautiful mountain & valley views on .43+/- acres. A lovely & spacious home with oak floors, fireplace in living room and woodstove in family room. Deck is ideal for dining & entertaining. **$195,000**
1 car garage.

What is the photographer's point of view?

Lange (above). What information does it convey? What first catches your attention—the dirt gullies, the big cabbages, the open sky, or the working pickers? If you are drawn first to the people, as most of us are, what is noteworthy about the people in this picture—size? posture? clothing? arrangement? Where has Lange placed her camera? How can you tell? And how does her camera placement affect the meaning you attach to the photo?

By way of contrast, look at Walker Evans's photograph (below) of the tenant-farmer family of Bud Fields set in rural Alabama. What do you no-

How does the camera judge these people?

tice first—the setting? the group? a specific face? What is your impression of either the whole group or of a specific individual? What words would you use to describe these people? Does the place from where the photo was taken influence how you judge these people? If so, in what way? If Evans placed the camera at eye level deliberately—which we suspect he did— what do you think he wanted viewers to think when looking at the photo?

To think critically about *point of view,* identify the place or stance from which the image maker viewed the subject. Ask about the effect this particular point of view has on how viewers think or feel about the subject. What would happen if the vantage point were somewhere else—above or below, left or right of what it is now? In other words, what would change in the image if the *point of view* were changed?

3 Arrangement

The term *arrangement* in visual texts might be compared to terms such as *order, organization,* or *structure* in verbal texts, though the differences are substantial. While writers arrange or put together a story, essay, or poem to take place over time—that is, the time it takes a reader to follow the text, line by line, through a number of pages—visual image makers arrange pictures in the two-dimensional space of their viewfinder, paper, or canvas so as to invite viewers to read in space rather than time. In visual texts, then, *arrangement* refers to the ways the various parts of a picture come together to present a single coherent experience to the viewer. As far as this handbook is concerned, all texts, whether verbal or visual, fact or fiction, are open to critical analysis by viewers who know what to look for.

One thing to look for is **pattern**—predictable, repeated elements within the visual field that the eye notices and seems attracted to. Just as sonnets, sestinas, and

What is the effect of pattern on meaning?

haiku follow patterns of line, so too do visual compositions, only lines here are created by light rather than words. Both documentary and commercial photographers often use visual patterns to lead viewers to an intended meaning. Look, for example, at Dorthea Lange's photo on the previous page, and ask about pattern: What does the curving pattern of the furrowed field lines have to do with the meaning of this photograph? What do the patterns of light and dark also contribute to meaning? And what is the role of the single human dwelling in this carefully plowed plain? What do all the elements taken together make us think or feel?

Lange took this photograph in 1938, so if we add historical hindsight to photographic pattern, our interpretation grows: we know that such power plowing of thousands of acres of the Great Plains was a precursor to the Depression-era dust bowl. If the visual imagery alone suggested loneliness, poverty, and abandonment, the historical knowledge only confirms it.

Another visual element at work in the Lange photograph is **balance**— the proportional weight of each visual component and how it does or does not hold the eye's attention. In Lange's photo, the larger dark shading of the left side is balanced by the smaller but lighter field on the right as the larger and darker land mass balances the smaller but lighter sky—balance is achieved because the light, which attracts more attention, is offset by a darker but larger mass. In addition to balancing light and dark as Lange does or as Jack Delano does in the photograph of school dancers below, what

How do size, number, and light make meaning?

Everything You Need to Earn a Better Grade, All in One Place!

www.prenhall.com/fulwiler

With the purchase of this new handbook, you get free access to a comprehensive, easy-to-use Web site.
This Web site will help you with your writing in college and beyond.
Follow the instructions below for instant access.

REGISTER for access to the Web site

1. Go to www.prenhall.com/fulwiler

2. Select the title/edition or book cover of your textbook.

3. Click on **Register**.

4. Depending on whether or not you have registered for another Pearson Education Web site, select **No, I Am a New User** or **Yes, Look Me Up**.

5. Enter the code below, and follow the on-screen instructions to complete the one-time registration.

PSFBK-TRAIL-CLUNG-FUMED-ELVIS-NINES

NOTE: This student access code is redeemable one time only! If you purchased a used book, go to the URL in Step 1, select your textbook, and follow the on-screen instructions for purchasing access to the Web site.

6. **LOG IN** - After you register, you can access the site any time by logging in at www.prenhall.com/fulwiler and clicking on the appropriate title/edition. Enter your log in name and password, click on **Log In**, and enjoy the wealth of resources available to you.

Fill in the boxes below so your user name and password will always be at your fingertips.

Name:	....
Email:	....
User name:	....
Password:	....

Turn the page to see a list of resources and tools available to you from this Web site. →

Everything You Need to Earn a Better Grade, All in One Place!

My Writing Center
- Build your own virtual *Study Plan* and custom version of the eBook
- Visit the *Prentice Hall English Tutor Center*, which offers personal tutoring by actual English instructors
- Use *Exchange* to build a writing portfolio and receive feedback from your peers

My eBook
- Search topics by table of contents or index
- Highlight, annotate, and take notes within the eBook

Practice and Assessment
- Take a diagnostic test to assess your writing skills
- Develop your writing skills using self-grading exercises
- Practice editing using *Blue Pencil*™ exercises

Research Navigator™
- Follow a series of clear research guidelines as you write your paper
- Access 25,000+ journal articles and the *New York Times* Archive
- Use the *AutoCite* Works Cited generation tool

And More
- View videos from professionals who write in their jobs
- See sample documents that model effective writing

Product and Technical Support are available 24/7 at: http://247.support.pearsoned.com

other visual elements might work in the same way? In the Delano photograph, try dividing the image vertically in two with an imaginary line separating the right from the left half of the photo. On the left side you see a dozen or so small figures, while on the right you see only part of one. What's the visual effect? Where does your eye travel? And what is the net effect? What's interesting to us is that each side seems to hold its own, allowing the eye to comfortably take in the activity in the whole gymnasium (we noticed the basketball hoop at building's end and remembered such rehearsals ourselves). The many smaller and darker dancers on the left seem offset by the larger and lighter dancer on the right. What difference, you might ask, does it make that the halves of the picture balance each other? How does this balance by numbers, size, and light contribute to a photo's meaning? As we see it, the visual balance adds a strong dimension of order and stability to the image, suggesting, perhaps, a world that is comfortable, safe, and secure. While the photograph portrays action on a small scale, it hints at peacefulness at large.

To think critically about *arrangement,* identify repeated elements within the visual image. Can you locate the center of gravity or weight in a given picture? Do you think the center was found or fabricated? Where do patterns of light/dark, large/small, and number lead the eye? How do pattern and balance contribute to meaning in a two-dimensional frame? What does the arrangement suggest about the meaning of the image?

4 Theme

Both verbal and visual texts may be said to have themes—statements that identify the larger meaning of the text being read or viewed. In verbal texts, this theme, thesis, or controlling idea (it's called lots of things) may be stated early (informational reports), late (feature stories), or accumulate by inference over the length of the whole text (personal essays and creative nonfiction). Though a visual text is usually perceived all at once in a single viewing, its theme may or may not be either strongly stated or quickly apparent. The themes of some of the photos we've looked at seem more obvious than others: for instance, Lange's photo of the Filipino lettuce pickers is a strong statement about the difficulty and dignity of work, while the more information-packed roadside vegetable stand by Walker Evans seems more difficult to pin down.

What determines whether a theme is obvious or even present in a photograph? Sometimes theme seems to be more in the eye of the beholder than the mind of the photographer—or so such a case could be made for Jack

What does the fine print tell you?

Delano's dancers; the viewers' associations with school gymnasiums and after-school dance classes may be responsible for our particular interpretation.

However, would you say the same thing of Marian Post Wolcott's photo of the movie theatre? What visual elements catch your attention? The man ascending the angled staircase? The graphic and stark light and dark patterns? And what do the verbal elements such as the large advertisement for Dr. Pepper or the cowboy movie poster help? In this photo, you may have to look at the fine print to decide this is not a nostalgic picture of times past in small-town America, but a chilling reminder of the dark side of the American past. Looking more closely, the eye is drawn to the center of the photo where the small print below the staircase, *"COLORED ADM. 10 CENTS,"* combines with the silhouetted figure ascending the staircase, to remind us that discrimination was once public policy.

Documentary photographers incorporate a number of strategies to shape the themes of material found in both the natural and developed world. That is, such photographers work within the same limits as nonfiction writers who are not supposed to invent material that doesn't exist. In fact, all the elements we've looked at so far—subject, point of view, arrangement—all contribute to the thematic content of a photograph. By shooting from far away rather than close up or cropping images in the darkroom, photographers focus viewer attention on the point they want to make.

Look, for instance, at two versions of Dorthea Lange photographs of a rural family that appears down and out on their luck. The close-up is well known and goes by the name of "Migrant Mother". The longer view reveals more of the whole family, the tent, and the setting. It is neither titled nor well known. In fact, we were surprised to find it when looking through the Dorthea Lange collection in the Library of Congress. What, we might ask, makes the close-up famous and the long shot run-of-the-mill? Is it only the fact that the camera is closer in one than the other? Is there something about the figures or facial expressions? Or is it a question of information, the one having more, the other less?

What is this woman's story?

To think critically about *theme*, notice your first reactions to an image: What caught your attention first? Second? What emotions did you feel and why? What ideas came to mind and where do you think they came from? How do the elements of *information, point of view,* and *arrangement* combine to make a thematic statement?

What caption would you give this photograph?

3 b   Words

Adding words to images brings us full circle, back to the specificity of verbal texts. In magazine ads, words point to or add details about an automobile, toothpaste, or food product. In television commercials, oral voiceovers tell us what meaning to attach to the image we are watching. And in political campaign posters, words enhance and embellish the image of a man or woman who seeks our vote. Text is often added to images to make sure the image is interpreted in a particular way. For example, in the photograph below, can you identify the man addressing a

Does this poster need a title?

crowd near the Washington monument? In case at first glance you didn't, the title of the poster tells you it is Martin Luther King giving his famous speech, "I Have a Dream" (1963). Without words, the King poster is still very powerful since the image pattern and balance keep your eyes fixed on King; and it is likely that many viewers would recognize King from television documentaries or history lessons. Here is a case where the words are only necessary to viewers unfamiliar with the man.

However, words may be added to images to create specific messages neither alone would convey. Look at the "Abusing" poster (below) and notice the interplay of words and image: What surprises you about this poster? Who do you think it is aimed at? What audience attitude or values did the creaters of the poster count on? Where would you imagine it being displayed? Where would you not display it? Regardless of your answers to these questions, it seems apparent that neither words nor image alone convey the same message as the two together.

Which is more important, word or image?

Can you compose a caption for this cartoon?

Each week, *The New Yorker* magazine runs a CARTOON CAPTION CONTEST on its back page, showing a cartoon drawing without words. Readers are invited to make up captions that would turn the drawing into a cartoon that makes a particular point. We found the drawing by Mike Twohy (above) in the April 25, 2005, issue of the magazine and began making up captions, which we found far more difficult than we imagined. Where do you begin? First we asked, what was possibly funny or surprising about this drawing? Of course, it's the researcher who's wearing a mouse costume instead of a lab coat. OK, but while the costume is out of the ordinary, especially in a laboratory setting, a man in a mouse costume, in and of itself, doesn't mean anything in particular and is not all that funny. So, how do you find words that, together with the drawing, create not only meaning, but humor? We now invite you to do the same, add words to this drawing so that it makes a point and is funny. After you've given it a good college try, check page 39 to see what captions *The New Yorker* judges most interesting.

Reproduced on the next page are the most interesting three captions to the "researcher in the mouse costume" cartoon selected by *The New*

Yorker and published in the May 9 issue. We noticed right away that each begins with the mouse costume, as we tried to, but then directs our attention to a different part of the cartoon to make what turn out to be very different points. Larson focuses on the mice ("their trust"), Futterman on the researcher ("myself"), and Baerkircher on the costume itself ("a thousand tiny lab coats").

THE FINALISTS

"First, you must gain their trust."
Russell Larson, Wallingford, Conn.

"More important, however, is what I learned about myself."
Roy Futterman, New York City.

"Well, it was just easier than making a thousand tiny lab coats."
Fred Baerkircher, Kent, Ohio.

Which caption do you prefer?

This image-first exercise is a simple illustration of the malleability of images, suggesting that images without words seldom have definitive meanings. While a single image may be worth many words, it takes only a few words to change what that meaning might be—a principle of reader/viewer manipulation exploited by commercial advertisers, political campaigners, and advocacy groups alike.

To think critically about the mixing of words with images, look at any poster, campaign ad, or commercial. What would be lost if either words or images were subtracted? Imagine how other words or images might change the meaning. *(If you have good ideas here, have you considered a career in advertising?)*

3 c Color

The images we've looked at so far have been in black and white since the visual elements actually stand out more clearly without the distraction of color. We also believe that black and white images have their own substantial place in the world of images, as the lack of color allows greater weight to be placed on compositional elements. We don't think, for instance, that any of the black and white photos looked at so far would be improved in any way by the addition of color—colored versions of "Filipino lettuce workers" or "Migrant Mother" would simply be different, not better, photographs.

That said, we realize that most of the commercial and aesthetic images you'll encounter today in magazines and films as well as on television and computer monitors will be in color, so we need to look critically at what color adds or subtracts. In verbal texts, the word "color" is metaphoric and commonly refers to rich details that flesh out a description; it's used the

What difference does color make?

Thinking Critically About Visual Images

Information: Identify what you are seeing, and ask why it is being presented.

Point of view: Identify where the image-maker stands, what is selected or omitted, and ask what the effect is.

Arrangement: Look where the eye most naturally falls, and ask where the center of gravity in the image is.

Theme: Notice your first reactions to the image, and ask what ideas or emotions come to mind.

Words: Ask what changes would occur in a text accompanied by an image if either words or images are removed. Do the words try to tell you what the image means?

Color: Notice whether it enhances or distorts the reality of the image, and ask if the color works with or against the other compositional elements in the image.

Persuasion: Identify the information in the image, and ask how its purpose, point of view, arrangement, and theme persuade you to think in one direction rather than another.

same way in sports broadcasts where the "color" commentator provides inside or detailed information about the game or players, to enrich the broadcast. In visual texts, color adds powerful dimensions in detail and enrichment that the more abstract black and white cannot. Most obviously, it shows us the world in the full range of colors that we see with our eyes. Look, for instance, at the photo (on page 40) of New York City firefighters raising an American flag at Ground Zero. The original is in color, but we added a black and white version for comparison. What is your reaction to seeing the two versions side by side? Which seems to you the more powerful? How does color figure into your answer?

Particular colors suggest specific moods. Think about your own personal reactions to different colors—what color would you select to paint a room? What is your favorite color for, say, clothing or cars? While these may differ greatly according to personal preferences, aren't there actually traditional symbolic values attached to different colors in literature and art? Why, for instance, does red often symbolize anger or war? Or black suggest danger or death? Or white stand for innocence or purity? Do you think the reasons for these associations arbitrary or logical?

Look at the two posters that seem to be inspired by the Iraq conflict. Describe your reaction to each one. What creates that reaction? Both posters use bird images to augment their message; which one do you find more effective? Does your preference have anything to do with your personal attitude toward the war? If you subtract your bias in favor of one message or the other, which poster is the more persuasive? Why? Finally, is the role played by color to augment each message predictable or surprising?

What color is peace?

What color is patriotism?

To think critically about color, notice whether it enhances or distorts the reality of the image. Imagine the image in shades of black, white, and gray: ask what would be lost, what gained if color were subtracted? Does the color work with or against the other compositional elements we've been looking at?

3   d   Images of persuasion

With the notable exception of radio, nearly every spoken or written message Americans encounter is accompanied by a visual component to strengthen the appeal. Institutions of every kind, profit and nonprofit alike, advertise their goods and services in carefully designed booklets, brochures, posters, billboards, bumper stickers, lawn signs, refrigerator magnets, commercials, and advertisements. Advertisements for commercial products use every trick in the persuasive book to sell you something. How many times have you seen on television Ford, Chevy, and Dodge trucks slogging through mud and conquering mountainous terrain to haul huge loads to difficult destinations and had the emotional response: *Wow! Gotta get me one of them tough trucks!*? Or how many times have large, colorful, and juicy images of

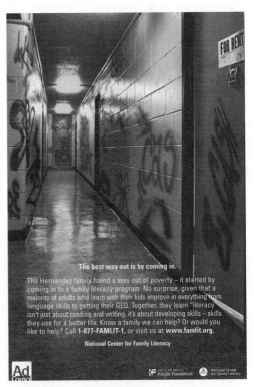

The best way out is by coming in.

The Hernandez family found a way out of poverty – it started by coming in to a family literacy program. No surprise, given that a majority of adults who learn with their kids improve in everything from language skills to getting their GED. Together, they learn "literacy" isn't just about reading and writing, it's about developing skills – skills they use for a better life. Know a family we can help? Or would you like to help? Call **1-877-FAMLIT-1**, or visit us at **www.famlit.org**.

National Center for Family Literacy

Ad

Knight Foundation   National Center for Family Literacy

What's the exit strategy?

Burger King cheeseburgers, Taco Bell tacos, and Subway submarine sandwiches made you hungry? Or Gap, Apple, and Nike made you want to be "with it"? Note that the truck ads are just as effective in black and white, the food ads stick exclusively to color, but hip ads can get away with anything.

Visual images sell ideas as well as products, and the emotional appeal of images can be just as strong in black and white as color. The accompanying photographic image shows the graffiti-covered walls of a narrow and shadowy hallway, a "FOR RENT" sign signifying a low-rent apartment building. Analyze this image: Why does the hallway so dominate the space on this poster in contrast to the small printed message at the bottom? What is the emotional effect created by the glaring and reflected light? While bright, is this a hallway in which you'd feel comfortable, a building in which you'd want to live? If the hallway image catches your attention, maybe you'll look closer look at the white print on the hallway floor that serves to title the image: *"The best way out is by coming in."* Now what does that mean—a hallway to exit rather than enter? (A definite yes here!) If so, what does it mean to "come in"? Where do your eyes go next in search of an exit strategy? To the next largest print on the poster, at the bottom, where the sponsoring agency is identified as the *National Center for Family Literacy*? If so, we reason, the way out has something to do with reading, writing, and communication skills. But who is the audience this poster is aimed at? In which magazines or on what bulletin boards would you exect to see it? Any that you regularly read?

In contrast to the realistic, gritty image of an apartment hallway, we found an equally interesting but simpler and more abstract public service advertisement sponsored by Project Safe (shown below). What are the persuasive elements in this message? The image or the print? Why so much blank space in the center? Why the white vertical lines? To lead our eyes to the bold horizontal print at the top of the bars? To be addressed directly as an ex-con, "you"? But is the ex (or existing) con the only or really intended audience? Who else might Project Safe have in mind? And what is the reason we're being warned? The answer seems found in the last and lowest lines in the ad, with the title, *"Gun Crimes Hit Home."* Gun crimes lead to jail time and a lot more hardship—avoid guns! And where would this ad be posted—A school? Community center bulletin board? Pool hall window? Telephone pole?

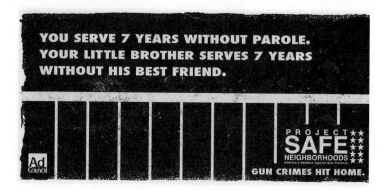

No one looks back fondly
on the time they spent in a parking garage.

In contrast to the persuasively serious is what might be called the persuasively comic, where the viewer is sold a product or idea through humor rather than dire warning. You've only to think about the television commercials that make you laugh aloud—and many are very, very funny. Still, commercials quickly become dated, so we won't refer to specific ones here. However, consider the advertisement to the right: Our eyes are drawn first to the dominant photograph that takes up most of the space on the page, showing what appears to be a teacher and her class of elementary school students sitting for a school photo. OK. But something seems out of order, not quite right. What on earth are they sitting in front of? A parking garage! Not at all the classic school building we've come to expect with such class photos. What gives? We laugh, of course it's sort of a joke—this would never happen—would it? And that, of course, is what the sponsor, the National Trust for Historic Preservation, wants to ensure. We laugh. We get the message. Preserve good buildings.

What's for sale here?

We'll end this chapter with one final favorite persuasive image, Brooke Shields dressed in white with cigarettes sticking out of her ears. We laugh, but again we ask, what gives?

- How is our attention caught?

- Who is the intended audience? Why do we think so?

- What dominant visual elements are at work here?

- What to do you believe about the ad?

- What do you question about the ad?

- What are the ad's unspoken assumptions?

- How necessary is the verbal text in the background?

As you know well, both words and pictures in the hands of skilled writers, artists, and photographers can be powerfully persuasive. Consequently, we believe both verbal language and visual images need to be viewed critically so that readers and viewers understand, first, the meaning of the message and, second, the intent behind the meaning. And we believe that, as writers and creators of images, the same critical understanding will advance your own writing and art. The balance of attention in the chapters to come focuses on your persuasive abilities, with and without images to support you.

SUGGESTIONS FOR WRITING AND RESEARCH

INDIVIDUAL

Choose any image from the Depression series of photographs in this chapter, and then make up a story to go along with the situation depicted. What clues in the picture did you choose to focus on? Why? Did these clues appeal to your emotional or rational sense? Write a paragraph each on this same picture as evidence for a historical interpretation, as an editorial making a cultural criticism, as a piece of forensic evidence in a court case, as a work of art, and as an advertisement. What visual elements within the photograph have greater or lesser importance depending on what kind of object you assume the photo to be?

COLLABORATIVE

As a class, complete the individual exercise above. Then, compare your answers to these questions to those of other students, and discuss the similarities and differences.

WRITING ACROSS THE CURRICULUM

Photographs as Disciplinary Documents

Choose any single image from the series of black and white Depression-era photographs in the first part of this chapter, and write a page or two, reimagining it through the eyes of a specific academic discipline:

- Imagine it as a document from which to infer **historical** change, by comparing it to a similar photo you might take today. Where would you go to take a contemporary photo with similar subject matter?

- Imagine it as an **economic or sociological** document from which you gather clues about these people's place in society. What details would you highlight? With what specific socioeconomic social group would you compare them today?

- Imagine the **poem** or **short story** you might write based on what you perceive to be the theme in the photograph. What verbal image would begin your poem? What character name would begin your story?

- Imagine the photo used in a **political** or **religious campaign:** who would use it and what purpose would the photo serve in the campaign?

- Imagine the photo as a **work of art.** What about the image is aesthetically strong and not dated? What contemporary photographer or aesthetic movement might this work have influenced?

- Imagine the photo as part of a poster for a current **advocacy group:** which group would it be and what would the poster say?
- Imagine the photo as an **advertisement** appropriated by a contemporary product to increase sales: what would the product be and how would you write the pitch?

chapter 4

The Writing Process

While there is no one best way to write, some ways do seem to work for more people in more situations than do others. Learning what these ways are may save you some time, grief, or energy—perhaps all three. This chapter describes the messy business we call the **writing process.** It takes a close look at how writers write from the time they select something to write about through their efforts at drafting, revising, and editing, until they send this writing out into the world. If you're interested in improving your writing, examine closely your own writing process: describe how you do it, identify what works and what doesn't, then study the ideas and strategies that work for others. Some of these are bound to help you.

4 a Describing writing as a process

It's time to examine your own writing habits: What do you do, for example, when you are assigned to write a paper due in one week? Do you sit down that day and start writing the introduction? Or do you sit down but do something else instead? If you don't work on the assignment right away, do you begin two days before deadline, or is your favorite time the night before the paper is due? Do you write a few pages a day, every day, and let your paper emerge gradually? Or do you prefer to draft it one day, revise the next, and proofread it just before handing it in?

What writing conditions do you seek? Do you prefer your own room? Do you like to listen to certain kinds of music? Do you deliberately go somewhere quiet, such as the library? Or do you prefer a coffee shop, a cafe, or a booth at McDonald's? And with what—a computer or a pen or pencil?

Which of the habits or methods described here is the right one? Which technique yields the best results? These are trick questions, since different ones work best for different individuals. There is no single best way to write. People manage to write well under wildly different conditions.

The rest of this chapter identifies five discrete but overlapping and often nonsequential phases of the process of writing—planning, composing, revising, researching, and editing—and explains how this handbook reflects this process.

ESL *Using Your Native Language When Composing in English*

You may want to compose in both your native language and English when working on a writing assignment. For example, you might brainstorm, make notes, or create outlines in your native language, or you could use native-language words or phrases when you're not sure of the English equivalents. Using your native language this way may help you avoid writer's block and develop fluency in English. However, because you want as much practice writing in English as possible, don't compose a whole essay first in your native language and then try to translate it into English. Periodically you should evaluate the effectiveness of your composing strategies. For instance, if you find that using a native language–English dictionary often results in unidiomatic constructions, you may want to become more familiar with a good English dictionary.

WRITING 1: EXPLORATION ....

Answer the questions posed on the opening pages of this chapter. Where, when, and how do you usually write? What are the usual results? With what do you need some extra help?

ESL If you sometimes write in your native language, compare the process you use when writing in it with the process you use when writing in English. Are any parts different? Why do you think this is so?

....

4 b   Planning

Planning consists of creating, discovering, locating, developing, organizing, and trying out ideas. Writers are doing deliberate planning when they make notes, turn casual lists into organized outlines, write journal entries, compose rough drafts, and consult with others. They also are doing less deliberate planning while they walk, jog, eat, read, browse in libraries, converse with friends, or wake up in the middle of the night thinking. Planning involves both expanding and limiting options, locating the best strategy for the occasion at hand, and focusing energy productively.

Planning comes first. It also comes second and third. No matter how careful your first plans, the act of writing usually necessitates that you keep planning all the way through the writing process, that you continue to think about why you are writing, what you are writing, and for whom. Part Two of this handbook focuses on the concerns that most writers face at the initial stages of a writing project: using a journal to help you create and discover ideas (Chapter 6), using invention and discovery techniques (Chapter 7), and focusing on your purpose, audience, and voice to guide your writing style (Chapter 5).

WRITING 2: APPLICATION ···

Describe the strategies you commonly use when you plan papers. How much does your planning vary from time to time or assignment to assignment? Now use your favorite planning strategy for twenty minutes to plan one currently assigned paper.

··

4 c Composing

At some point all writers need to move beyond thinking, talking, and planning and actually start writing. Many writers like to schedule a block of time—an hour or more—to compose their ideas, give them shape, see what they look like. One of the real secrets to good writing is learning simply to sit down and write. Remember that first drafts are concerned with ideas, with getting the direction and concept of the piece of writing clear. Subsequent writing, which includes revising and editing, is concerned with making the initial ideas ever sharper, more precise, and clearer.

While most writers hope their first draft will be their final draft, it seldom is. Still, try to make your early drafts as complete as possible—give each draft your best shot: compose in complete sentences, break into paragraphs where necessary, and aim at a satisfying form. At the same time, allow time for second and third drafts and maybe more. Sometimes it's hard to separate composing from the other stages of the writing process, so don't worry too much if they refuse to stay separate. In most serious writing, every phase of the process can be considered *recursive*—that is, moving back and forth almost simultaneously and maybe even haphazardly, from planning to revising to editing to drafting, back to planning, and so on.

WRITING 3: APPLICATION ....

Describe the process you most commonly use to draft a paper. Is your way of starting consistent from paper to paper? Now write the first draft for the paper you planned in Writing 2: Sit down, and for half an hour compose as much of the paper as you can, noting in brackets as you go along where you need to return with more information or ideas.

....

4 d   Revising

Somewhere in the midst of their writing, most writers revise the drafts they have planned and composed, and, of course, if research is required, that too is going on now. **Revising** involves rewriting to make the purpose clearer, the argument stronger, the details sharper, the evidence more convincing, the organization more logical, the opening more inviting, the conclusion more satisfying. We consider revising to be separate from editing, yet the two tasks may not always be separable. Essentially, revising occurs at the level of ideas, whereas editing occurs at the level of language. Revising means re-seeing the drafted paper and thinking again about its direction, focus, arguments, and evidence.

While it is tempting to edit individual words and sentences as you revise, revising before you edit saves time and energy. Revising to refocus or redirect often requires that you delete paragraphs, pages, and whole sections of your draft, actions that can be painful if you have already carefully edited them.

WRITING 4: APPLICATION ....

Does your usual process for revising a paper include any of the ideas discussed in this section? Describe how your process is similar or different.

Now revise the paper that you wrote in Writing 3, using any revision techniques with which you are comfortable.

4 e Researching

You may actually be researching all the way through the writing process, as you plan, compose, revise, and even edit. The importance of research cannot be overstated: serious writers need something to write about, and unless they are writing completely from memory, they need to locate ideas, authorities, specific information, and verifiable facts and figures. Even personal essays and experiential papers can benefit from researched information that substantiates and intensifies what the writer remembers.

As a college student, you do a form of **research** every time you write an analysis or an interpretation of a text: reading and rereading the text is the research. You do research when you compare one text to another. You do research to track down the dates of historical events. You do research when you conduct laboratory experiments, visit museums, interview people, or surf the Web.

Whenever you write about unfamiliar subjects, you have two choices: to research and find things out, or to bluff with unsupported generalizations. Which kind of paper would you prefer to read? Which kind of writing will you profit by doing?

WRITING 5: APPLICATION

Describe the kind of research assignments you have done in the past. Now locate additional research information to add to the paper you began drafting in Writing 3, using any research process with which you are familiar.

4 f Editing

Whether writers have written three or thirteen drafts, they want the last one to be perfect—or as near perfect as time and skill allow. When **editing,** writers pay careful attention to the language they have used, striving for the most clarity and punch possible. Many writers edit partly to please themselves, so their writing sounds right to their own ears. At the same time, they edit hoping to please, satisfy, or persuade their intended readers.

You edit to communicate as clearly as possible. After you've spent time drafting and revising your ideas, it would be a shame for readers to dismiss those ideas because they were poorly expressed. Check the clarity of your ideas, the logic and flow of paragraphs, the precision and power of your words, and the correctness and accuracy of everything from facts and references to spelling and punctuation.

Because there are so many different things to look for when you edit your writing, most of the last half of *The Blair Handbook* is devoted to editing issues, including matters of sentence and paragraph structure, grammar, spelling, and punctuation.

Reviewing the Writing Process

1. **Plan** to write by practicing invention strategies to help you find and clarify ideas. (See especially Chapters 6 and 7.)
2. **Compose a first draft** of your paper to see where your ideas are taking you. Plan to write later drafts to clarify, substantiate, or change those ideas. (See Chapters 8–13.)
3. **Revise** each paper by returning to its central idea and questioning its accuracy, evidence, and conclusions. (See Chapters 14–16.)
4. **Add current research** to your papers by locating authoritative, accurate, and detailed information in the library, on the Internet, or through interviews and observations. (See specific suggestions in Chapters 22–28.)
5. **Edit** your paper for clarity, grammar, punctuation, and mechanics. (See Part Eight.)

4 g English as a second language

All students in a writing class can grow as writers, those with extensive writing experience as well as those who have never written much. However, the ones faced with the greatest challenge may be students whose first language is not English. In addition to learning new strategies for composing and new forms for expressing what they know, non-native speakers must attend to the conventions of language that native speakers take for granted.

Besides possible grammar and vocabulary difficulties, students who grew up speaking another language may have to adjust to the expectations and traditions of the American classroom. For example, American academic prose is often less formal than that in many other countries. Students who have learned to write in more formal systems may find instructors suggesting that they make their writing more lively or personal. Also, while U.S. schools increasingly treat writing as a multiple-draft process, instructors in many other countries may expect a piece of writing to be finished correctly the first time through.

Throughout *The Blair Handbook* blue boxes provide information about the English language of particular interest to non-native speakers. The blue letters "ESL" in the contents identify each section that includes one of these specially marked boxes. This symbol in blue also appears before the special ESL writing suggestions found in many chapters in Parts One, Two, and Three. Finally, an ESL index is provided at the back of the book to help you locate topics that you may find helpful.

If English *is* your native language, you may still benefit from skimming the ESL boxes. They may give you a broader appreciation of foreign languages as well as English.

SUGGESTIONS FOR WRITING AND RESEARCH

INDIVIDUAL

Study your own writing process as you work on one whole paper from beginning to end, taking notes in your journal to document your habits and practices. Write an analytic sketch describing the way you write and speculating about the origins of your current habits.

COLLABORATIVE

With your classmates, form interview pairs and identify local professional writers or professors who publish. Make an appointment with one of these practicing writers, interview him or her about the writing process he or she practices, and report back to the class. Write a collaborative report about writers in your community; make it available to other writing classes or interested faculty.

WRITING ACROSS THE CURRICULUM

Planning to Revise

The writing process described in Chapter 4 represents an approximate way in which most published writers, both inside and outside the academy, write. Most of your professors, in other words, when they write books, articles, reports, and proposals plan, compose, revise, research, and edit to make sure their papers represent them well. At the same time, it is likely that in the busyness of academic life, some of these very same publishing instructors across the curriculum who assign papers make it sound as if one draft will do. That is, they assign a paper due at a particular date, but do not actually tell you that you ought to take this paper through the rigorous multidraft process they do in their own writing before you hand the paper in.

It's also clear that the busyness of your own academic schedule makes it difficult to do anything except last-minute, deadline writing: it's not unheard of to begin on Thursday evening a paper due Friday morning. (We know as undergraduates we've done it ourselves!) So here's what we propose: The next time you are assigned a substantial paper in any of your college classes, take it through the stages of the writing process described in this chapter, whether asked to or not. To make this happen, get out your paper or electronic date book, and write in process draft deadlines that guarantee, come the night before the paper is due, that the only remaining work is proofreading and printing your paper.

And the best way to guarantee this happens is to write out some kind of plan the very day you receive the assignment. Then write subsequent deadlines in at specific dates in your daily planner—a first draft due, a revised draft due, a certain amount of research done, and soon, until you've given that paper the time and energy it deserves. In other words, make your own quite specific deadlines to ensure a writing process that works. For example, here's a possible plan for a paper due in two weeks:

- First day, write planning notes in course notebook or journal.
- Second day, reserve one hour to begin serious first draft.
- Third night, if research is required, promise two hours at library.
- Fifth day, another hour for another serious draft sometime before evening.

- Weekend, find several hours each day to compose, research, and revise.
- Eighth day, ask for response from trusted reader (offer same back).
- Tenth day, revise and edit according to feedback received.
- Twelfth night, revise and edit.
- Night before paper is due: once over lightly—proofread and print final copy.

How will this extra short-term time pay off in the long run? You'll develop consistent, well-practiced writing skills. You'll get the better grades that good writers in all subjects get. And, since there are very few good jobs out there that don't require writing skills, you'll almost guarantee yourself the more serious attention on the job market that good writers get.

PART two

www.prenhall.com/fulwiler

chapter 5

Analyzing the Rhetorical Situation

The focus, structure, and style of every paper you write is determined by why you are writing (**purpose**), to whom (**audience**), and under what circumstances (**situation**). Taken together, purpose, audience, and situation largely determine the **voice** in which you write. While this chapter asks you to consider each of these elements analytically and in isolation, in truth, writers usually think about these elements intuitively and simultaneously. In any case, we believe the following discussion of the elements of rhetoric may be useful in writing an academic paper.

5 a Knowing the purpose

People write to discover what's on their minds, figure things out, vent frustrations, keep records, remember things, communicate information, shape ideas, express feelings, recount experiences, raise questions, imagine the future, create new forms, and simply for pleasure. They also write when they're required to in school, to demonstrate knowledge and solve problems. But no matter what the task, writers write better when they know what they want to accomplish. Following is a discussion of three broad and overlapping reasons for writing: **discovering, communicating,** and **creating.**

1 Writing to discover

Writing helps people discover ideas, relationships, connections, and patterns in their lives and in the world. In college, students write to discover paper topics, develop those topics, expand and explain ideas, and connect seemingly unrelated material in coherent patterns. In this sense, writing is one of the most powerful learning tools available.

Writing is especially powerful because it makes your language—and therefore your thought—stand still, allowing you to elaborate, critique, rearrange, and correct them. Playwright Christopher Fry once said, "My trouble is that I'm the sort of writer who only finds out what he is getting at by the time he's got to the end of it." In other words, his purpose and plan become clear only *after* he's written a whole draft—he's learned that the act of writing will help him find his way. But rather than considering this inventive power of writing "trouble"—to use Fry's word—you can consider it a solution to many other problems. Once you know that writing can generate ideas, advance concepts, and forge connections, then you can use it deliberately and strategically to help you write college papers.

2 Writing to communicate

The most common reason for writing in college is to say something to an audience. College students write essays, exams, and reports to instructors, as well as letters, applications, and resumés to potential employers. To communicate to instructors and employers alike, writing needs to be *purposeful* so both writer and reader know where it's going; it needs to be *clear* in order to be understood; and it needs to be *correct* in order to be believable.

Many academic assignments require a **thesis,** a statement of the writer's purpose, which the paper is expected to assert, explain, support, or defend. A thesis, broadly speaking, summarizes the main idea of a paper and makes that idea explicit to readers. Some papers, like this chapter, present the *thesis first,* in the first paragraph to summarize for the readers, in advance, what the paper will be about. Other papers present the thesis later in what might be called a *delayed-thesis* arrangement to show readers different sides of an idea before presenting the writer's conclusion. And still other papers, creative nonfiction, for example, *imply* a thesis but never state one directly.

Whether a thesis is obvious or required or not, serious college papers always answer that critical reader question, so what? Why does this paper exist? What's it about? Common college assignments include papers that reflect on personal experience (Chapter 8); explain concepts, procedures, and processes (Chapter 9); argue and persuade about issues (Chapter 10); and explore and interpret literary ideas (Chapter 11). In addition, some college assignments ask for creative dimensions (Chapter 12) while other ones test what you've learned (Chapter 13). These and so many other academic and nonacademic writing tasks have the common mission to communicate effectively to an audience other than the writer's self.

3 Writing to create

When you write to create, you pay special attention to the way your language looks and sounds—its form, shape, rhythm, images, and texture. Though the term *creative writing* is usually associated with poetry, fiction, and drama, it's important to see all writing, from personal narratives to research essays, as having creative potential. When you write to create, you pay less immediate attention to your audience and subject and more to the act of expression itself. Your goal is not so much to change the world or to transmit information about it, but to transform an experience or idea into something that will make your readers pause, see the world from a different angle, and perhaps reflect upon what it means. You want your language itself, not just the information it contains, to affect your readers emotionally or esthetically.

While most college assignments ask for communicative writing, nearly every assignment has room for creative dimensions. When writing for emotional or esthetic effect in an otherwise informative or argumentative paper, be especially careful that your creativity serves your communicative purpose. In other words, you want your creative language to enhance, not camouflage, the clarity of your ideas. For example, when Amanda recounted her experience picking potatoes on board a mechanical potato harvester on her father's farm, she made her readers feel the experience as she did by crafting her language to duplicate the sense of hard, monotonous work:

> Potatoes, mud, potatoes, mud, potatoes, that was all I saw in front of me. They moved from my right side to my left, at hip level. A conveyor belt never stopping. On and on and on. The potatoes passed fast, a constant stream. My hands worked deftly, pulling out clods of dirt, rotten potatoes, old shaws, and anything else I found that wasn't a potato. It was October, the ground was nearly frozen, the mud was hard and solid. Cold. Dirt had gotten into my yellow and yet brown rubber gloves, had wedged under my nails, increasing my discomfort.

This is a creative approach to nonfiction essay writing because Amanda uses a graphic, descriptive style to put readers at the scene of her experience rather than summarizing it or explaining explicitly what working on a farm meant to her. For more information on experimenting with form, style, or language, see Chapter 12, "Writing Creative Nonfiction."

WRITING 1: EXPLORATION ....

Describe a time when you used writing for each of the purposes described in the chapter: to discover, to communicate, to create. Each time, did you set out to use writing this way, or did the purpose emerge as you wrote? Which purpose do you address most often? Which do you most enjoy?

....

5 b   Addressing audiences

The better you know your **audience,** the better you're likely to write. Whether your writing is judged "good" or not depends largely on how well it's received by the readers for whom it's intended. Just as you change the way you speak depending on whom you're addressing—your boss, mother, professor, or between friend and younger brother—so you change the way you write depending on to whom you're writing. You don't want to over-explain and perhaps bore the audience, or underexplain and leave it wanting.

We believe all college papers need to be written to at least two audiences, maybe more: first, to the writer's self, so the author understands it; second, to the instructor who assigned the paper in the first place. In addition, in many classes, you may also be writing to other students or for publication to more public audiences. This section examines how expectations differ from one audience to the next.

1 Understanding college audiences

It might help to think of the different audiences you will address in college as existing along a continuum, with those closest and best known to you (yourself, friends) at one end and those farthest from and least known to you (the general public) at the other end:

Self———Family———Friends———Instructor———Public

While your audience concerns will always differ in particulars from somebody else's, every writer works along essentially the same continuum. For our purposes in the college handbook, the audience of most concern is the instructor who will read and respond to your writing.

2 Shaping writing for different audiences

The context you need to provide; the structure, tone, and style you use; and your purpose for writing can all be affected by your audience.

Context. Different audiences need different amounts of background information in order to understand your ideas. A smart writer will find out what and how much his or her readers already know about a topic before writing. For example, other students in a writing group (peers) might know who you mean when referring to a favorite singer, but the instructor might not have a clue.

Structure. Every piece of writing is held together in a certain way, beginning one place, moving to another, and finally ending. How a writer structures a paper depends in large part on what ideas or elements will work best with a particular audience. For example, if you were writing an argument for someone who disagrees with your position, you might begin with the evidence with which you both agree and then later introduce more controversial evidence.

Tone. The tone of a piece of writing conveys the writer's attitude toward both subject matter and audience. How do you want to sound to your readers? You may want different audiences to hear in different ways. For example, when writing to yourself, you won't mind sounding confused. When writing for instructors, though, you will want to sound confident and authoritative.

Style. The term "style" refers to the formality and complexity of a writer's language. What style is appropriate to what audience? You need to determine what style will be most effective in a given paper. Fellow students might be offended if you write in anything other than a friendly style, while some instructors might interpret the same style as disrespectful.

Purpose. The explicit purpose of a college writing assignment is often determined by an instructor rather than by the writer. However, there are unstated purposes embedded in any piece of writing, and these will vary depending on the audience being addressed. For example, is it important that your readers like you? or that they respect you? or that they give you good grades? Always ask yourself what you want a piece of writing to do for—or to—your audience and what you want your audience to do in response to your writing.

Let's follow the way writing generally needs to change as you move along the scale away from the audience you know best, yourself.

Writing to oneself

Every paper you write is addressed in part to yourself, and some writing, such as in journals, is addressed primarily to yourself. However, most reports, essays, papers, and exams are addressed primarily to other people—instructors, peers, parents, or employers. So, journal writing is one opportunity to write to yourself alone and not worry about context, structure, tone, or style. When you write to yourself, only purpose—your reason for writing—matters. (For more information on journal writing, see Chapter 6.)

Writing to peers

Your peers are your equals—friends and classmates, people of similar age, background, or situation. The primary difference between writing to yourself and writing to peers is the amount of context and structure you need to provide to make sure your readers understand you. If your paper is about a personal experience, you need to provide the explanations and details that will allow readers who did not have your experience to understand fully the events and ideas you describe. If your paper is about a subject that requires research, be sure to provide background information to make the topic comprehensible and interesting in a structure (e.g., chronological, logical, cause–effect) that makes sense. Be direct, honest, and friendly since peers will see right through any pretentious or stuffy language.

Writing to instructors

Instructors are among the most difficult audiences for whom to write because they usually make the assignments. They know what they want, and it's your job to figure out what that is. In addition, instructors often know more about your subject than you do. To complicate matters further, different instructors have quite different criteria for what constitutes good writing.

It is often difficult to know how much context to provide in a paper written for an instructor, unless the assignment specifically tells you. For example, in writing about a Shakespearean play to an English professor, should you provide a summary of the play when you know that he or she already knows it? Or should you skip the summary information and write only about ideas original with you? The safest approach is to provide full background, explain all ideas, support all assertions, and cite authorities in the field. Write as if your instructor needed all this information and it were your job to educate him or her.

One of your instructor's roles is to help you learn to write effective papers. But another role is to evaluate whether you have done so and, from a broader perspective, whether you are becoming a literate member of the college community. Therefore your implicit purpose when you write to instructors is to demonstrate, simultaneously, your understanding of literacy conventions, course knowledge, reasoning ability, and originality. Whew!

Writing to public audiences

Writing to an unknown public audience is difficult for all writers because the audience can be so diverse. The public audience can include both people who know more and those who know less than the writer; it can contain experts who will correct the slightest mistake and novices who need even simple terms explained; it can contain opponents looking for reasons to argue with the writer and supporters looking for reasons to continue support.

When you don't know your audience, provide context for everything you say: explain even well-known acronyms such as NCAA, NCTE, or ACLU; explain difficult ideas such as "postmodern"; provide brief background for all issues and ideas you refer to. Make your purpose and structure clear, with your opening paragraph letting this audience know something about what's to come. Adopt a tone that suits your purpose—fair or serious? angry or annoyed? comic or sarcastic?

At the same time, you usually have some idea of who these anonymous readers are or you wouldn't be writing to them in the first place. You need to be asking: What is their educational level? What are their political, philosophical, or religious beliefs? What are their interests? How can I best get them to listen to me?

WRITING 2: EXPLORATION

How accurate do you find the preceding discussion about different college audiences? Describe circumstances that confirm or contradict the description here. If instructors are not your most difficult audience, explain who is.

5 c   Understanding the situation

When you write college papers, you need to remember that you are situated within an academic community that may differ in important ways from home, high school, or work community. This larger academic community has clear expectations for what literate papers should accomplish and look like. While you cannot learn all the particular methods and conventions of every discipline (history, chemistry, sociology, and so on) within the larger community, you can be aware of the central values to which all members of the academic community subscribe.

- **Truth.** Regardless of department or discipline, college instructors are committed, at least nominally, to the pursuit of truth. (Never mind that "absolute truth" is elusive and may change from decade to decade—academics are committed to the pursuit!) Each academic discipline pursues new insights in a particular way—the sciences by close observation, testing, and replication; the social sciences by collecting and analyzing quantitative and statistical data; the humanities by studying individual expressions, and so on. A successful college paper will demonstrate that its writer can use the knowledge and methods of the discipline in which it has been assigned to reveal something that is true.

- **Evidence.** Scholars in all disciplines use credible evidence to support the assertions they make. Biologists make claims about the natural world and cite evidence to support those claims while art professors make claims about creative expression, and so on. As a college writer, you need to make claims, assertions, or arguments that you believe to be true; then support those with the best facts, examples, and illustrations available.

- **Balance.** It is difficult, even impossible, to prove that something is absolutely true. New information constantly calls old conclusions into question. Consequently, academic writers make even claims they believe to be true, cautiously, with balanced, judicious language. Balance in academic writing suggests that you present your own inferences, assertions, and arguments in neutral, serious, nonemotional language and be fair to opposing points of view.

5 d   Adopting a voice

Each individual speaks with a distinctive voice. Some people speak loudly, some softly, others with quiet authority. Some sound assertive or aggressive, while others sound cautious, tentative, or insecure. Some voices are clear and easy to follow, while others are garbled, convoluted, and meandering. Some create belief and inspire trust, while others do not.

An individual's voice can also be recognized in the writing he or she produces. A writer's voice, like a person's personality, is determined by many factors, such as ethnic identity, social class, family, or religion. In addition, some elements of voice evolve as a writer matures, such as how one thinks (logically or intuitively) and what one thinks (a political or philosophical stance). Writers also can exert a great deal of control over their language. They create the style (simple or complex), tone (serious or sarcastic), and many other elements. Writers try to be in control of as many elements of their writing voice as they can.

1 Defining voice

The word *voice* means at least two distinctly different things. First, it is the audible sound of a person speaking, as in a *high-pitched voice*, which distinguishes itself by auditory qualities such as pitch (high, low, nasal), pace (fast, slow), tone (angry, assertive, tentative), rhythm (regular, smooth, erratic), register (soft, loud), and accent (southern, British, Boston). However, since readers don't literally hear the writer's voice (except in readings) this meaning cannot be taken literally. However, the language on the page can recreate the sound of the writer talking. Careful writers control, as much as they can, the sound of their words in their readers' heads.

Second, *voice,* is a metaphoric term used to suggest who a person is and what he or she stands for. Written voices convey something of the writers behind the words, often including personal, political, philosophical, and social beliefs and biases.

WRITING 3: EXPLORATION ···

In your own words, describe the concept of voice. Do you think writers have one voice or many? How many do you have? Explain.

···

2 Analyzing the elements of voice

While readers experience a writer's voice as a whole expression, not a set of component parts, it may be helpful to look closely at the elements that comprise the whole and see which ones a writer can control.

Tone

Tone can be angry, anxious, joyous, sarcastic, puzzled, contemptuous, respectful, friendly, and so on. Writers control their tone by adopting a particular perspective or point of view, selecting words carefully, emphasizing some words and ideas over others, choosing certain patterns of inflection, and controlling the pace with pauses and other punctuation. For example, note how your tone might change as you speak or write the following sentences:

- The English Department was unable to offer enough writing courses to satisfy the demand this semester.

- Why doesn't English offer more writing courses?

- It's outrageous that so many students were closed out of first-year writing courses!

To gain control of the tone of your writing, read drafts of your paper aloud and listen carefully to the attitudes you express. (See Chapter 43 for specific examples of adjusting tone.)

Style

Style is found in the formality or informality, simplicity or complexity, clarity or muddiness of a writer's language. It's easy to see how the style in each of the following examples is adjusted to a different audience:

- Can't make the party tonight. Spent the day cutting wood and am totally bushed.

- I am sorry, but my critical essay will be late. Over the weekend, I overextended myself cutting, splitting, and stacking two cords of wood for my father and ended up with a sprained back. Would you be willing to extend the paper deadline for one more day?

To gain control of your style, think about how you wish to present yourself and shape your words, sentences, and paragraphs to suit the occasion. (For more on style, see any of the chapters in Part Eight.)

Structure

The structure of a text is how it's put together: where it starts, where it goes next, where the thesis occurs, what evidence fits where, how it concludes. Structure is the pattern or logic that holds together thoughtful writing, revealing something of the thought process that created it. For example, a linear, logical structure may characterize the writer one way while a circular, digressive structure another way. Skillful writers, of course, can present themselves one way or the other depending on whom they're addressing and why.

To gain control of an essay's structure, make an outline that reveals visually and briefly the organization and direction you intend. Some writers outline before they start writing and stick to the outline all the way through the writing. Others outline only after writing a draft or two to help control their final draft. And still others start with a rough outline, which they continue to modify as the writing modifies thought and direction.

Values and beliefs

Your values include your political, social, religious, and philosophical beliefs. Your background, opinions, and beliefs will be part of everything you write, but you must learn when to express them directly and when not to. For example, including your values would enhance a personal essay or other autobiographical writing, but it may detract attention from the subject of research essay.

To gain control of the values in your writing, consider whether the purpose of the assignment calls for an implicit or explicit statement of your values. Examine your drafts for words that reveal your personal biases, beliefs, and values; keep them or take them out as appropriate for the assignment. (For more on values, see Chapter 44.)

Authority

Your authority comes from confidence in your knowledge and is projected through the way you handle the material about which you are writing. An authoritative voice is often clear, direct, factual, and specific, leaving the impression that the writer is confident about what he or she is saying. You can exert and project real authority only over material you know well, whether it's the facts of your personal life or carefully researched information. The more you know about your subject, the more clearly you will explain it, and the more confident you will sound.

To gain control over the authority in your writing, do your homework, conduct thorough research, and read your sources of information carefully and critically. (See Chapter 2.)

WRITING 4: APPLICATION

Describe your own writing voice in terms of each of the elements outlined in this section (tone, style, structure, values, authority). Then compare your description with a recent paper you have written. In what ways does the paper substantiate your description? In what ways does it differ from your description? How do you account for any differences?

ESL Is your writing voice in English different from your writing voice in your native language? If you are aware of any differences, try to describe them in terms of the elements discussed in this chapter. Are there qualities of your voice in one language that you would like to transfer to your voice in the other language?

SUGGESTIONS FOR WRITING AND RESEARCH

INDIVIDUAL

1. Select a topic that interests you and write about it in each of the three modes described in this chapter. First, begin with discovery writing to yourself, perhaps in a journal. Second, write a letter to communicate with somebody about this interest. Third, write creatively about it in a short poem, story, or play. Finally, describe your experience writing in these different modes.

2. Select a paper written recently for an instructor audience and rewrite it for a publication, choosing either a student newspaper or a local magazine. Before you start, make notes about what elements need to be changed: context, structure, tone, style, or purpose. When you finish recasting the paper to this larger, more public audience, complete collaborative assignment 3. Make final revisions, taking into account your partner's observations, and send your paper to the publication.

3. Collect and examine as many samples of your past writing as you have saved. Also look closely at the writing you have done during this term. Write a paper in which you describe and explain this history and evolution of your voice and the features that most characterize your current writing voice.

COLLABORATIVE

1. Select a topic that your whole writing group is interested in writing about. Divide your labors so that some of you do discovery writing, some do communicative writing, and some write creatively. With scissors and tape, combine your efforts into a single coherent, creative piece of college writing, making sure that some of every member's writing is included in the finished product. Perform a reading of this collage for the other groups; listen to theirs in return.

2.   In a group of five students, select a topic of common interest. Write about the topic (either as homework or for fifteen minutes in class) to one of the following audiences: yourself, a friend who is not attending your school, your instructor, an appropriate magazine or newspaper. Share your writing with one another, and together list the choices you needed to make for each audience.

3.   Exchange recently written papers with a partner. Examine your partner's paper for the elements of voice. In a letter, each of you describe what you find. How does your partner's perception of your voice match or differ from your own? Now do individual assignment 2, including your partner's assessment as part of your analysis.

WRITING ACROSS THE CURRICULUM

Suggestions for Adjusting Your Voice

The concept of voice as applied to writing may not be well understood by instructors outside of English. Even in the discipline of English, voice is a slippery notion. It is not, in other words, a common a term applied to writing as, say, style, the meaning of which is universally accepted across the curriculum. At the same time, we think voice is a more inclusive term that includes style along with other dimensions of how you present yourself in a written document. Next time you are almost finished writing an important paper—when your thesis is solid, your evidence convincing, your organization clear—test the paper for voice by reading it out loud to yourself and asking the following questions:

- **Tone.** Listen to the *attitude* you hear: are you thoughtful? assertive? cautious? committed? or something else? Which do you intend? (Adjust words or phrases that don't communicate what you mean and change them.)

- **Style.** What image of yourself do you create through your language? Is it formal or informal? complex or casual? academic or popular? If not what you expect, make changes until it's right. (For example, to make more academic, take out the contractions and first-person pronouns; to sound more casual, put the contractions and first-person pronouns back in, etc.)

- **Structure.** What does your structure say about your manner of thinking? Is it careful and tight? loose? flexible? logical? intuitive? (For example, identify places where you choose to digress or speculate vs. Transition directly to a related thought—which best conveys your voice on this occasion?)

- **Values.** Do your beliefs show through when you speak on paper? Do you want them to? (Look for words that convey opinions or judgment vs. words that are more neutral or descriptive.)

- **Authority.** Where does your writing voice sound especially knowledgeable and confident? Where does it sound tentative and unsure? Where does it sound cautiously skeptical? Which do you want it to sound like, where? (Again, adjusting a few modifiers can change the tenor of your voice.)

chapter 6

Keeping Journals

ournals allow people to talk to themselves without feeling silly. They help students figure out and reflect on what is happening in their personal and academic lives. Sometimes students focus their journal writing narrowly, on the subject matter of a single discipline; other times they speculate broadly, on the whole range of academic experience; and still other times they write personally, exploring their private thoughts and feelings. College instructors often require that students keep journals to monitor what and how the students are learning. Just as often, however, students require journals of themselves, understanding that journals are more useful for the writer than for the reader.

6 a Understanding journals

Journals are daily records of people's lives (*jour* is French for "day"). Of course, journals don't need to be written in every day, and sometimes they go by other names: daybooks, logs, learning logs, commonplace books, or simply writer's notebooks. No matter what you call them, their function is similar—to capture and record ideas and events that are on your mind. The following discussion explores the character and quality of journals.

Sequence. Journals capture thoughts sequentially, from one day or time period to the next. Dating each entry allows you to compare ideas to both later and earlier ones and provides an ongoing record of your constancy, change, or growth. You thus end up documenting your learning over the course of a semester or a project.

Audience. Journals are written for oneself. A personal journal is a place to explore what's important to *you,* not to communicate information or ideas to someone else. An assigned journal, however, may initiate an informal conversation between you and your instructor. In this role, it has much in common with letters, e-mail, and other informal means of communication.

Language. The language of journals is whatever writers want it to be. Since your audience is yourself, use whatever language is comfortable. Your focus will be on ideas rather than on style, grammar, spelling, or punctuation.

Ownership. A personal journal is whatever the writer wishes it to be. A journal assigned by an instructor, however, may include an instructor's agenda more than the writer's own. If you're keeping a journal in college, you'll know which is which.

Writers keep "personal journals" because, of their own volition, they find them important. Instructors assign what might be called "academic journals" for several specific reasons: First, they want you to use writing to learn and think with in the hope you'll become a better learner and thinker. Second, instructors want to eavesdrop on your thinking to help them assess both your progress and the effectiveness of the course. As such, academic journals focus more consistently on ideas related to the course of study rather than students' personal lives. Ideally, an academic journal is a cross between private diaries, written solely for the writer, and class notebooks, which record only an instructor's words. Like diaries, journals are written in the first person about ideas important to the writer; like class notebooks, they focus on a subject under study in a college course.

Diary ———▶ *Academic journal* ◀——— *Class notebook*

Your journal includes your thoughts, reactions, reflections, and questions about your classes and ideas, written in your own language. Think of your academic journal as a personal record of your educational experience.

Describe your experiences with journals. Have you ever kept one for school before? In which class? With what result? Have you ever kept one on your own? With what result? Do you still keep one? What is it like? If you are unfamiliar with journals, what do you think of the idea of journal writing?

ESL Have you ever kept a journal in your native language? What was it like?

···

6 b   Keeping journals in college

Both personal and academic journals are useful to college writers because they provide places to record and play with thought and experience. In our classes, actually, we recommend that students keep both, one about their private lives and one about academic matters; sometimes they do this with separate notebooks, other times by dividing a loose-leaf notebook into two sections.

1 Journals in the writing class

Use your writing-class journal to find topics to write about, to try out introductions and arguments, to record relevant research and observations, to assess how the paper is turning out, and to make plans for what to do next. For example, in the following journal entry, John tells himself what to do in the next draft of a paper describing his coaching of an eighth-grade girls' soccer team:

> 9/16   I'm going to try to use more dialogue in my paper. That is what I really think I was missing. The second draft is very dull. As I read it, it has no life. I should have used more detail. I'll try more dialogue, lots more, in draft 3. I'll have it take place at one of my practices, giving a vivid description of what kids were like. I have SO MUCH MATERIAL. But I have a hard time deciding what seems most interesting.

Use your journal to record what you've learned about writing through class discussions, reading of other student papers, and reviewing your own writing. Near the end of the semester, John reflected in his journal about what he had learned so far:

> 11/29   I've learned to be very critical of my own work, to look at it again and again, looking for big and little problems. I've also learned from my writing group that other people's comments can be extremely helpful—so now I make sure I show my early drafts to Kelly or Karen before I write the final draft. I guess I've always known this, but now I actually do it.

WRITING 2: APPLICATION

Keep a journal for the duration of a writing project, recording in it all of your starts, stops, insights, and ideas related to the project. At the end, consider whether the journal presents a fair portrait of your own writing process.

2 Journals across the curriculum

Writing in a journal can help you learn virtually anything better. In science or mathematics, when you switch from numbers to words, you often see problems differently and keep track of your reasoning as it emerges. In addition, putting someone else's problem or question into your own language makes it yours and may lead you closer to a solution. In humanities and literature classes, journals allow you to speculate about the possible meanings of literary, historical, and philosophical problems without putting yourself on the line as you do in papers and exams.

One of the best uses for journals is making connections between college knowledge and personal knowledge. For example, when you record personal reflections in an academic journal, you may identify with and perhaps make sense of the otherwise distant and confusing past. When you write out trial hypotheses based on personal observations, you may eventually discover good ideas for research topics, designs, or experiments. In addition, writing a journal for one course may lead you to see connections to another, therefore helping integrate the many separate pieces of knowledge you are acquiring.

WRITING 3: APPLICATION

Keep a personal journal on your own for two weeks, writing faithfully for, say, fifteen minutes each day. Write about whatever is on your mind. Follow the "Guidelines for Keeping a Journal" at the end of this chapter. After two weeks, reread your entries and assess the worth of such writing to you.

6 c   Suggestions for using journals

Journals are useful even when you're not in an academic environment, since good ideas, questions, and answers don't always wait for convenient times. We suggest that you write often, in your most comfortable voice, and not worry about someone's evaluating you. The following selection of journal entries illustrates some of the ways journals can be used.

1 Planning

Journals can help you plan any project by providing a place to talk it over with yourself. Whether it's a research paper, a personal essay, or a take-home examination, you can make journal notes about how to approach it, where to start, or who else to consult before actually beginning a draft. Here is an entry from Peter's journal kept for his first-year writing class:

> 10/12   Well, I switched my research topic to something I'm actually interested in, a handicapped children's rehabilitation program right here on campus. My younger brother was born deaf and our whole family has pitched in to help him—but I've never really studied what a college program could do to help. The basis of my research will be interviews with people who run the program—I have my first appointment tomorrow with Professor Stanford.

Journal writing is ultimately unpredictable: it doesn't come out neat and orderly, and sometimes it doesn't solve your problem, but it does provide a place where you can keep trying to solve it.

2 Monitoring your writing process

Part of the content of a writing course is the business of learning to write. You can use a journal to document how your writing is going and what you need to do next to improve it. In the following example, Bruce reflects on his experience of writing a report:

> 10/3   I'm making this report a lot harder than it should be. I think my problem is I try to edit as I write. I think what I need to do is just write whatever I want. After I'm through, I then edit and organize. It's hard for me though.

Journals are good places to monitor your own version of the writing process and to document what helps you the most.

3 Writing to learn

The act of regular writing clarifies ideas and causes new ones to develop. In that sense, journal writing is an invention technique very much like freewriting. (See Chapter 7.) Julie, who kept a journal about all the authors she studied in her American literature course, noticed a disturbing pattern and wrote in her journal to make some sense of it:

> 2/4   So far, the first two authors we have to read have led tragic, unhappy lives. I wonder if this is just a coincidence or if it has something to do with the personality of successful writers. Actually, of all people, writers need a lot of time alone, by themselves, thinking and writing, away from other people, including, probably, close family members. The more I think about it, writers would be very difficult people to live with, that's it—writers spend so much time alone and become hard to live with.

To *write to learn* means trusting that as you write, ideas will come—some right, some wrong, some good, some bad—but you'll never know unless you try them out.

ESL *Journals for Second Language Writing*

Journals are useful when you are writing in a language other than your native language. Since you don't have to be concerned with correctness, you can work on developing fluency, experimenting with language, and trying out new vocabulary or sentence structures.

In an academic journal, your instructor will probably expect you to do more than summarize assigned reading.

To help you develop your English vocabulary, keep an ongoing list of new words as described in 43c. Include both vocabulary you learn in your classes and words or idioms that you hear outside class.

4 Examining values and beliefs

Writing in a journal is a good way to examine your beliefs in light of the social and political climate in which you grew up and which perhaps you took for granted. In the following example, Jennifer uses her journal to reflect on sexist language:

3/8   Sexist language is everywhere. So much so that people don't even realize what they are saying is sexist. My teacher last year told all the
"mothers-to-be" to be sure to read to their children. What about the fathers? Sexist language is dangerous because it so easily undermines women's morale and
self-image. I try my hardest not to use sexist language, but even I find myself
falling into old stereotypes.

Note that Jennifer recorded both her awareness of sexist language in society and her own difficulty in avoiding it.

5 Evaluating classes

Journals are good places in which to assess your classes, including both
what you're learning and what you're not learning. In the following entry,
Brian seemed surprised that writing can be fun:

10/28   English is now more fun. When I write, the words come out more easily
and it's not like homework. All my drafts help me put together my thoughts and retrieve memories that were hidden somewhere in the dungeons of my mind. Usually I
wouldn't like English, like in high school, but I pretty much enjoy it here. I like how you
get to hear people's reactions to your papers and discuss them with each other.

6 Letting off steam

Journals are good places to vent frustration when things aren't going
well, personally or academically. College instructors don't assign journals
to improve students' mental health, but they know that journals can help.
Kenyon writes about the value of keeping his journal for one semester:

12/1   This journal has saved my sanity. It got me started at writing. . . . I
can't keep all my problems locked up inside me, but I hate telling others, burden-
ing them with my problems—like what I'm going to do with the rest of my life.

In many ways, writing in a journal is like talking to a sympathetic audience; the difference, as Kenyon noted, is that the journal is always there,
no matter what's on your mind.

7 Reporting progress

Sometimes it's hard to see how much you've learned until you reread
your journal at the end of a term and notice where you began and where you
ended. Your writing may have been casual and fast, your thinking tentative,

your assessments or conclusions uncertain, but the journal gives you a record of who you were, what you thought, and how you've changed. Rereading a term's worth of entries may be a pleasant surprise, as Jeff found out:

> 11/21 The journal to me has been like a one-man debate, where I could write thoughts down and then later read them. This seemed to help clarify many of my ideas. To be honest there is probably fifty percent of the journal that is nothing but B.S. and ramblings to fulfill assignments, but that still leaves fifty percent that I think is of importance. The journal is also a time capsule. I want to put it away and not look at it for ten or twenty years and let it recall for me this period of my life.

Guidelines for Keeping a Journal

- Choose a notebook with which you are comfortable and with paper that you might enjoy writing upon.
- Try writing a journal on a laptop computer. One advantage of computer journals is that they make it easy for you to copy interesting or useful entries directly onto the paper you are working on.
- Date each entry. Also include the day of the week and the time if you like having more complete records. A journal allows you to watch your thoughts change over time.
- Write long entries. Plan to write for at least ten minutes at a crack, preferably longer, to allow your thoughts to develop as fully as possible. The more you write, the more you find to say.
- Include both "academic" and "personal" entries. If an academic journal, try a divider between academic and more personal entries.

WRITING 4: EXPLORATION

Look over the examples in this section and see if you can think up additional uses for journals. Can you provide any concrete examples from your own journal?

SUGGESTIONS FOR WRITNG AND RESEARCH

INDIVIDUAL

1. Select a well-known writer in your intended major who kept a journal (for example, Mary Shelley, Ralph Waldo Emerson, or Virginia Woolf in literature; Leonardo da Vinci, Georgia O'Keeffe, or Edward Weston in the arts; B. F. Skinner or Margaret Mead in the social sciences; Charles Darwin or Marie Curie in the natural sciences). Study the writer's journals to identify important characteristics and the purpose they probably served. Write a report on what you find, and share it with your class.

2. Review your journal entries for the past two weeks, select one entry that seems especially interesting, and write a reflective essay of several pages on it. How are the entry and the essay different? Which is better? Is that a fair question?

COLLABORATIVE

Bring duplicated copies of one journal entry written during the term. Exchange entries and discuss interesting features of the entries.

WRITING ACROSS THE CURRICULUM

Characteristics of Darwin's Journal

Many scientists, philosophers, and writers have kept journals both to find ideas and create a record of those ideas to return to at a later date. The following excerpt is typed from the handwritten journal Charles Darwin kept aboard the *Beagle* in 1836 as he sailed around the Galapagos Islands off the coast of Ecuador, speculating about the workings of nature and generating ideas for what would later become the theory of evolution in *The Origin of Species* (1857). Describe the characteristics of Darwin's journal entry that identify it as writing aimed solely at himself and not a wider public audience. Can you see the value in such speculations written down and dated?

> In the endless cycle of revolutions. by actions of rivers currents. & sea beaches. All mineral masses must have a tendency. to mingle; The sea would separate quartzose sand from the finer matter resulting from degradation of Felspar & other minerals containing Alumen.—This matter accumulating in deep seas forms slates: How is the Lime separated; is it washed from the solid rock by the actions of Springs or more probably by some unknown Volcanic process? How does it come that all Lime is not accumulated in the Tropical oceans detained by Organic powers. We

know the waters of the ocean all are mingled. These reflections might be introduced either in note in Coral Paper or hypothetical origin of some sandstones, as in Australia.—Have Limestones all been dissolved. if so sea would separate them from indissoluble rocks? Has Chalk ever been dissolved?

[*The Red Notebooks of Charles Darwin.* Ed. S. Herbert.
Cornel U. Press, 1980, pp. 37–38.]

7 *Strategies for Invention and Discovery*

Good writing depends on good ideas. When ideas don't come easily or naturally, writers need techniques for finding or creating them. Writers need to invent new ideas or discover old ones at all phases of the writing process, from finding and developing a topic to narrowing an argument and searching for good evidence. And knowing how to invent and discover ideas when none seems apparent is also the best antidote for writer's block, helping you get going even when you think you have nothing to say.

The main premise behind the techniques discussed in this chapter is "The more you write, the more you think." Language begets language, and more language begets more ideas. Virtually all writers have had the experience of starting to write in one direction and ending up in another; as they wrote, their writing moved their thinking in new directions—a powerful, messy, but ultimately positive experience and a good demonstration that the act of writing itself generates and modifies ideas. This occurs because writing lets people see their own ideas, on paper or on a computer monitor, and doing that, in turn, allows them to change those ideas. This chapter suggests ways to harness the creative power of language and make it work for you.

WRITING 1: EXPLORATION

Describe the procedures you usually use to start writing a paper. Where do you get the ideas—from speaking? listening? reading? writing? Do you do anything special to help them come? What do you do when ideas don't come?

7 a   Brainstorming

Brainstorming is rapid list making. You ask yourself a question and then list as many answers as you can think of. The point is to get out lots of possible ideas for later examination and review. Do not try to evaluate your ideas. Just record them as they occur to you, even those you think you will eventually reject. Sometimes you can generate ideas best by setting goals for yourself: what are five possible topics for a paper on campus issues?

1. overcrowding in campus dormitories

2. prohibiting cars for first-year students

3. date rape

4. multiculturalism and the curriculum

5. attitudes toward alcohol on campus

Sometimes you can brainstorm best by leaving the question open-ended: in thinking about the fourth topic, what do you already know about multiculturalism and the curriculum that interests you?

- racial diversity high among campus students

- racial diversity low among faculty

- old curriculum dominated by white male agenda

- new curriculum dominated by young feminist agenda

- how to avoid simplistic stereotypes such as those I've just written

In making such lists, jotting down one item often triggers the next, as is seen above. Each item becomes a possible direction for your paper. By challenging yourself to generate a long list, you force yourself to find and record even vague ideas in concrete language, where you can examine them and decide whether or not they're worth further development. You can also record the ideas you generate in your personal brainstorming sessions by drawing clustering diagrams.

7 b   Freewriting

Freewriting is fast writing. You write rapidly, depending on one word to trigger the next, one idea to lead to another, without worrying about conventions or correctness. Freewriting helps you find a focus by writing nonstop and not censoring the words and ideas before you have a chance to look at them. Try the following suggestions for freewriting:

- Write as fast as you can about an idea for a fixed period of time, say five or ten minutes.

- Do not allow your pen to stop moving until the time is up.

- Don't worry about what your writing looks like or how it's organized; the only audience for this writing is yourself.

If you digress in your freewriting, fine. If you misspell a word or write something silly, fine. If you catch a fleeting thought that's especially interesting, good. If you think of something you've never thought of before, wonderful. And if nothing interesting comes out—well, maybe next time. The following five-minute freewrite shows John's attempt to find a topic for a local research project:

> I can't think of anything special just now, nothing really comes to mind, well maybe something about the downtown mall would be good because I wouldn't mind spending time down there. Something about the mall . . . maybe the street vendors, the hot dog guy or the pretzel guy or that woman selling T and sweatshirts, they're always there, even in lousy weather—do they like it that much? Actually, all winter. Do they need the money that bad? Why do people become street vendors—like maybe they graduated from college and couldn't get jobs? Or were these the guys who never wanted anything to do with college?

John's freewrite is typical: he starts with no ideas, but his writing soon leads to some. This kind of writing needs to be free, unstructured, and digressive to allow the writer to find thoughts wherever they occur. For John, this exercise turned out to be a useful one, since he ultimately wrote a paper about "the hot dog guy," a street vendor.

ESL Freewriting to Develop Fluency

Writing in a second language can be frustrating when you are trying to pay attention to your ideas, sentence structures, word choices, spelling, grammar, and so on. Many ESL writers have discovered that freewriting helps tremendously with this problem. If you haven't tried freewriting before, you might find it hard at first not to stop and carefully check each sentence, but with continued practice this activity should help you to postpone editing and improve your fluency in English. If you have access to a computer, try invisible writing.

A computer can help you freewrite more freely by making your words invisible. This guarantees that you won't try to revise and edit at this early stage. Simply turn off your monitor or turn down the brightness until it is dark, and type away, focusing only on your current thoughts. After ten minutes, turn the brightness up and see what you have written.

7 c Looping

Looping is a sequenced set of freewrites. Each freewrite focuses on one idea from the previous freewrite and expands it. To loop, follow this procedure:

1. Freewrite for ten minutes to discover a topic or to advance the one you are working on.

2. Review your freewrite and select one sentence closest to what you want to continue developing. Copy this sentence, and take off from it, freewriting for another ten minutes. (John might have selected "Why do people become street vendors?" for further freewriting.)

3. Repeat step 2 for each successive freewrite to keep inventing and discovering.

7 d Asking reporters' questions

Writers who train themselves to ask questions are training themselves to find information. Reporters ask six basic questions about every news story they write: who? what? where? when? why? and how? Following this set of questions leads reporters to new information and more complete stories:

- *Who* or what is involved? (a person, character, or thesis)

- *What* happened? (an event, action, or assertion)

- *Where* did this happen? (a place, text, or context)

- *When* did it happen? (a date or relationship)

- *Why* did it happen? (reason, cause, or explanation)

- *How* did it happen? (a method, procedure, or action)

While these questions seem especially appropriate for reporting an event, the questions can be modified to investigate any topic:

Who or *what* is my central focus?

What happens as the paper progresses?

Where or *when* do I make my main point? On what page?

Are my *reasons* (my answers to the *why* question) ample and documented?

How well does my strategy work?

7 e Outlining

Outlines are, essentially, organized lists. In fact, outlines grow out of lists, as writers determine which ideas go first, which later, which are main, which subordinate. Formal outlines use a system of Roman numerals, capital letters, Arabic numerals, and lowercase letters to create a hierarchy of ideas. Some writers prefer informal outlines, using indentations to indicate relationships between ideas.

When Carol set out to write a research essay on the effect of acid rain on the environment in New England, she first brainstormed a random list of areas that such an essay might cover:

- What is acid rain?

- What are its effects on the environment?

- What causes it?

- How can it be stopped?

After preliminary research, Carol produced this outline:

   I. Definition of acid rain

  II. The causes of acid rain

     A. Coal-burning power plants

     B. Automobile pollution

 III. The effects of acid rain

     A. Deforestation in New England

        1. The White Mountain study

        2. Maple trees dying in Vermont

     B. Dead lakes

Note how Carol rearranged the second and third items in her original list to talk about causes before effects. The very act of making the outline encouraged her to invent a structure for her ideas. Moving entries around is especially easy if you are using a computer, because you can see many combinations before committing yourself to any one of them. The rules of formal outlining also cause you to search for ideas: if you have a Roman numeral I, you need a II; if you have an A, you need a B. Carol thought first of coal-burning power plants as a cause, then brainstormed to come up with an idea to pair with it.

Writing outlines is *generative:* In addition to recording your original thoughts, outlines actually generate new thoughts. Outlines most useful if you modify them as you write in accordance with new thoughts or information.

After an outline has been revised and is in its final form, it can be shared with the reader in the form of headings. In long papers—or textbooks such as this one—headings help readers follow the structure of the writer's presentation.

7 f Clustering

Clustering is a method of organizing ideas visually to reveal their relationships. Clustering is useful both for inventing and discovering a topic

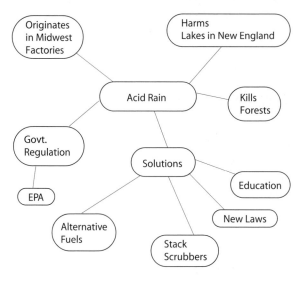

A clustering diagram

and for exploring a topic once you have done all your preliminary research. To use clustering, observe the following procedure:

1. Write a word or phrase that seems to be the focus of what you want to write about. (Carol wrote down "acid rain.")

2. Write ideas related to your focus in a circle around the central phrase and connect them to the focus phrase. If one of the ideas suggests others related to it, write those in a circle around *it* (Carol did this with her idea "solutions").

3. If one idea (such as "solutions") begins to accumulate related ideas, start a second cluster with the new term in the center of your paper.

7 g Talking

One of the most powerful invention techniques is simply talking with a partner or small group with the deliberate intention of helping each other find ideas. The directions are simple: sit across from each other for five or ten minutes and begin talking about possible topics or approaches or ways of finding sources. It doesn't matter who starts or finishes, since the principle at work here is that oral language, like written language, begets ideas. At some point it will be helpful to write down what you are talking about so that you have a record to return to.

Suggestions for Invention and Discovery

- **Brainstorm** a list of five possible topics to write about.
- **Freewrite** for ten minutes about the most interesting topic on your list.
- **Loop** back in your freewriting, selecting the most interesting or useful point, and freewrite again with that point as the focus.
- Ask the **reporters' questions** about the topic: who? what? when? where? why? and how?
- Make an **outline** of a possible structure for your paper.
- **Cluster** ideas about your topic and then on a related idea that occurs during the initial clustering.
- **Talk** with a partner or small group for ten minutes, helping each other find or advance one idea each.

SUGGESTIONS FOR WRITING AND RESEARCH

INDIVIDUAL

Explain your own most useful invention technique for finding ideas and support it with samples from your own earlier papers. Give clear directions to teach other writers how to use it.

COLLABORATIVE

Find a common writing topic by having each person in the group or class select one of the invention and discovery techniques described in this chapter and practice using it for ten minutes. Make a collective list of the topic ideas generated this way. Then ask each individual to select one topic and write for another five minutes. Again make a list of topics and the important ideas generated about them. Discuss the ideas together and try to arrive at a consensus on a common writing topic for the whole class to pursue. The most interesting part of this assignment will be comparing the variety of approaches chosen by different students on the same topic. This exercise is an excellent way to generate a *class book* (see 20d).

WRITING ACROSS THE CURRICULUM

Writing to Find Answers

The term "discovery" applies to the finding of ideas—either new ones out there somewhere in the world or old ones that you once knew but have since forgotten that you knew. The following example of writing to solve a problem was shared with us by a chemistry professor, teaching "Introduction to Chemistry."

The professor asked students to share with him their questions about the day's class by putting them in a box at the end of class. This anonymous student is puzzled by the instructor's explanation of the interaction between Transfer RNA (TRNA) and Messenger RNA (MRNA). In writing to the professor for clarification, however, the student answers her own question, but hands in the note anyway, perhaps to say thanks for the opportunity to solve the problem by writing about it.

Try the simple problem-solving technique of writing out where you're stuck or puzzled about any ideas in any classes and see if clarification comes through writing—letting your own eyes see the dilemma from a distance and providing you with helpful objectivity. No guarantees, of course, but your chances of answering questions or solving problems greatly increase simply by writing.

PART three

Composing

www.prenhall.com/fulwiler

93

chapter 8

Writing from Experience

Good stories can be told about virtually anything. Not only can good stories be about any subject, they can be quite simple and can take place in your own backyard—and you can tell them. Potential stories happen all the time—daily, in fact. What makes them actually become stories is recounting them, orally or in writing. Good stories are entertaining, informative, lively, and believable; they will mean something to you who write them and to your audience, who will read them.

All stories, whether they're true (nonfiction) or imagined (fiction), are accounts of something that happened—an event or series of events, after which something or somebody is changed. Whether the story is about "The Three Little Pigs" or *Huckleberry Finn* (both fiction), or about Darwin's *Voyage of the Beagle* or your own trip last winter to Mexico (nonfiction), it includes the following elements: a character (who?) to whom something happens (what?) by some method (how?), in some place (where?), at some time (when?), for some reason (why?). In other words, any time you render a full account of a personal experience, you answer questions about who, what, how, where, when, and why. Whether your story is engaging or not depends on the subject, your interest in telling it, and the skill with which you weave together these story elements.

WRITING 1: EXPLORATION ....

Think about the best stories you have read or listened to. What makes them memorable? What makes them believable?

ESL You might want to reflect on stories you have read or heard in your native language; do they translate well into English? Why or why not?

....

8 a Character

In personal experience writing, your main character is yourself, so try to give your readers a sense of who you are through your voice, actions, level of awareness, and description. The characters in a good story are believable and interesting; they come alive.

1 Voice

Your language reveals who you are—playful, serious, rigid, loose, stuffy, honest, warm, or whatever. In the following excerpt, in which Beth relates her experience playing oboe during a two-hour Saturday morning orchestra rehearsal, we learn she's serious, fun-loving, impish, and just a little lazy:

> I love that section. It sounds so cool when Sarah and I play together like that. Now I can put my reed back in the water and sit back and listen. I probably should be counting the rests. Counting would mean I'd have to pay attention and that's no fun. I'd rather look around and watch everyone else sweat.

2 Actions

Readers learn something about the kind of person you are from your actions. For example, when Karen recalls her thoughts playing in a basketball tournament, we learn something of her insecurity, fears, and skills all at once:

> This time, don't be so stupid, Karen—if you don't take it up court, you'll never get the ball. Oh, God, here I go. Okay, they're in a twenty-one—just bring it up—Sarah's alone—fake up, bounce pass—yes, she hits it! I got the assist!

3 Insight

One of the best ways to reveal who you are is to show yourself becoming aware of something, gaining a new way of seeing the world, a new insight. While such awareness can occur for apparently unexplainable reasons, it most often happens when you encounter new ideas or have experiences that change you in some way. In writing a paper about why she goes to the library to write a paper, Judith clarifies first for herself—then for her readers—the relationship between feeling safe and being creative.

> Two weeks ago, a female student was assaulted not far
> from where I live—that's why I've taken to locking my door so
> carefully. I am beginning to understand the importance of
> feeling safe in order to be creative and productive. Here, in the
> library, I feel secure, protected from real violence and isolated
> from everyday distractions. There are just enough people for
> security's sake but not so many that I feel crowded. And
> besides, I'm surrounded by all these books, all these great
> minds who dwell in the hallowed space! I am comfortable, safe,
> and beginning to get an idea.

4 Telling details

Describe yourself and other participants in your story in such a way that the details and facts help tell your story. A telling detail or fact is one that advances your characterization of someone without your having to render an obvious opinion. For example, you could characterize your little sister by pointing out the field hockey stick in the corner of her room, the photograph of the seventh-grade field hockey team on the wall, and the teddy bear next to her pillow. You could characterize her coach by pointing to the logo on her sweatshirt: "Winning isn't everything. It's the only thing."

WRITING 2: APPLICATION

Start to characterize yourself. Write four paragraphs, and in each one, emphasize one of these individualizing elements: voice, actions, awareness, and any telling details of your life. Select any or all that seem worthy of further exploration and write a few more paragraphs.

8 b   Subject

People write about their personal experiences to get to know and understand themselves better, to inform and entertain others, and to leave permanent records of their lives. Sometimes people recount their experiences casually, in forms never intended for wide circulation, such as journals, diaries, and letters. Sometimes they write in forms meant to be shared with others, such as memoirs, autobiographies, or personal essays. In college, the most common narrative forms are personal experience essays.

Subjects for good stories know no limits. You already have a lifetime of experiences from which to choose, and each experience is a potential story to help explain who you are, what you believe, and how you act today. Here are some of the topics selected by a single first-year writing class:

- playing oboe in Saturday orchestra rehearsals

- counseling disturbed children at summer camp

- picking strawberries on a farm

- visiting the library

- playing in a championship basketball game

- solo camping in Outward Bound

- touring Graceland in Memphis

- painting houses during the summer

When you write a paper based on personal experience, ask yourself: Which experience do I *want* to write about? Will *anybody else* want to read about it? Here are some suggestions. (See Chapter 7 for strategies to help you get started.)

1 Winning and losing

Winning something—a race, a contest, an award—can be a good subject, since it features you in a unique position and allows you to explore or celebrate a special talent. At the same time, the exciting, exceptional, or highly dramatic subjects such as scoring the winning goal in a championship game or placing first in a creative writing contest may be difficult to write about because they've been used so often that readers have very high expectations.

The truth is that in most parts of life there are more losers than winners. While one team wins a championship, dozens do not. So there's a large, empathetic audience out there who will understand and identify with a narrative about losing. Although more common than winning, losing is less often explored in writing because it is more painful to recall. Therefore there are fresher, deeper, more original stories to tell about losing.

2 Milestones

Perhaps the most interesting but also the most difficult experience to write about is one that you already recognize as a turning point in your life, whether it's winning a sports championship, being a camp counselor, or reading a particular book. People who explore such topics in writing often come to a better understanding of them. Also, their very significance challenges writers to make them equally significant for an audience that did not experience them. When you write about milestones, pay special attention to the physical details that will both advance your story and make it come alive for readers.

Be cautious, however, in choosing topics about intimate personal relationships, such as a romantic attachment, the death of someone you care about, or a divorce within your family, especially if the experience is recent. Writing about these and other close or painful experiences in your journal or diary can be immensely cathartic, but sharing them with instructors and classmates in a paper may be inappropriate. Because these emotional milestones evoke such intense reactions, it is difficult to write about them in a way that goes beyond the expression of strong feelings. Before you begin a paper on one of these sensitive topics, ask yourself—and your instructor—these questions: Can I present a fair and accurate account? Will my paper bring useful insights to my audience? Will it betray the confidence or invade the privacy of the other people mentioned?

3 Daily life

Commonplace experiences make fertile subjects for personal narratives. You might describe practicing for, rather than winning, the big game, or cleaning up after, rather than attending, the prom. If you are accurate, honest, and observant in exploring a subject from which readers expect little, you are apt to surprise them pleasantly and draw them into your story. Work experiences are especially fruitful subjects, since you may know inside details and routines of restaurants and retail shops that the rest of us

can only guess: How long is it before McDonald's tosses its unsold ham-
burgers? How do florists know which flowers to order when?

WRITING 3: APPLICATION ....

Make a list of a dozen experiences about which you could tell stories. Think
of special insight you gained as well as commonplace events that were in-
structive or caused change. Share your list with classmates and find out
which they would most like to hear about.

ESL You might want to reflect on your experiences learning English or
adjusting to a new culture.

....

8 c Perspective

The term *perspective* refers to the vantage point or position from which
one is telling a story. Perspective addresses this question: How close—in
time, distance, or spirit—are you to the experience? Do you write as if it
happened long ago or yesterday? Do you summarize what happened or put
readers at the scene? Do you explain the experience or leave it mysterious?
In other words, you can control, or at least influence, how readers respond
to a story by controlling the perspective from which you tell it.

Authorial perspective is established largely by **point of view.** Using
the **first person** (*I*) puts the narrator right in the story as a participant.
This point of view is usually the one used in personal experience writing,
as Beth, Karen, and Judith do in earlier examples.

The **third person** (*he* or *she*) establishes a distinction between the
person narrating the events and the person experiencing them and thus
tends to depersonalize the story. This perspective is more common in fiction,
but it has some uses in personal essays as well. In the following example,
for instance, Karen opens her personal experience essay from the imagined perspective of the play-by-play announcer who broadcasts the championship game; the point of view is first person, but from the perspective
of a third person:

> 2:15   Well folks, it looks as if Belmont has given up, the
>
> coach is preparing to send in his subs. It has been a rough
>
> game for Belmont. They stayed in it during the first quarter,
>
> but Walpole has run away with it since then. Down by

twenty with only six minutes left, Belmont's first sub is now approaching the table.

1 Once upon a time: past tense

The most natural way to recount a personal experience is to write in the past tense; whatever you're narrating *did* happen sometime in the past. Lorraine uses the past tense to describe an automobile ride with her Native American grandfather to attend a tribal conference:

> I sat silently across from Grandfather and watched him slowly tear the thin white paper from the tip of the cigarette. He gathered the tobacco in one hand and drove the van with the other. I memorized his every move as he went through the motions of the prayer, which ended when he finally blew the tobacco out of the window and into the wind.

Even though the governing tense for your personal narrative may be the past tense, you may still want to use other tenses for special purposes.

2 Being there: present tense

The present tense provides the illusion that the experience is happening at the moment; it leaves no time for your reflection. This strategy invites readers to become involved with your story as it is happening and invites them to interpret it for themselves.

If you want to portray yourself thinking rather than talking—in what is called **interior monologue**—you may choose to use fragment sentences and made-up words since the flow of the mind doesn't obey conventional rules of language. For example, when Beth describes her thoughts during orchestra rehearsal, she writes an interior monologue; we hear her talking to herself while trying to blow her oboe (note how she provides clues so that we understand what is going on around her):

> No you don't really mean that, do you? You do. Rats. Here we go . . . Pfff . . . Pff . . . Why isn't this playing? Maybe if I blow harder . . . HONK!! Great. I've just made a total fool of myself in front of everyone. Wonderful.

3 Mixing tenses

Writers often need more than one tense to tell a complete story. A writer telling most of a story in the present tense may switch to the past tense to provide additional important information, as Judith does in the opening paragraph of an essay on page 107 about personal safety:

> It is already afternoon. I fiddle with the key to lock the
> apartment door after me. I am not accustomed to locking
> doors. Except for the six months I spent in Boston, I have
> never lived in a place where I did not trust my neighbors.
> When I was little, we couldn't lock our farmhouse door; the
> wood had swollen and the bolt no longer lined up properly
> with the hole, and nobody ever bothered to fix it. I still remem-
> ber the time our baby-sitter, Rosie, hammered the bolt closed
> and we had to take the door off the hinges to get it open.

WRITING 4: APPLICATION ....

Write one page of a possible story using the first person, past tense, and a second page using the first person, present tense. From which perspective do you prefer to tell the story? Why?

....

8 d Setting

Experiences happen in some place at some time, and good stories describe these settings. To describe a believable physical setting, you need to recreate on paper the sights, sounds, smells, and physical sensations that allow readers to experience it for themselves. In addition to telling details that support your plot or character development, try to include **evocative details,** colorful details of setting and character that will let your readers know you were really there.

In the following example, Heather portrays details of the farm where she spent the summer picking strawberries:

> The sun is just barely rising over the treetops and there
> is still dew covering the ground. In the strawberry patch, the

deep green leaves are filled with water droplets and the
strawberries are big and red and ready to be picked. The
patch is located in a field off the road near a small forest of
Christmas trees. The white house, the red barn, and a
checkerboard of fields can be seen in the distance. It is 5:30
A.M. and the day has begun.

The evocative details are those which appeal to your senses, such as
sight, touch, and smell: *"dew covering the ground," "deep green leaves,"
"strawberries . . . big and red," "white house," "red barn,"* and *"checkerboard
of fields."*

The telling details of a setting reveal something essential about your
story without your explaining them (see also 7a4). For example, in telling
a story about your sister, you might describe the physical objects in her
room, which in turn describe important elements of her character: *"hockey
stick," "soccer ball," "gym bag," "sweatpants," "baseball jersey," "life-size posters
of Michael Jordan and Tiger Woods."* In other words, skillful description
helps you "tell" the story without interpreting its meaning for the reader.

WRITING 5: APPLICATION ···

Describe in detail one of the settings in which your experience took place.
Appeal to at least three senses, and try to include details that "tell" some
of your story without needing further explanation or overt value judgments on your part.

···

8 e   Sequence of events

In every story, events are ordered in some way. While you cannot alter
the events that happened in your experience, as a writer you need to decide
which events to portray and in what order to present them.

1 Selecting events

You have dozens of places to start and end any story, and at each point
along the way, many possible details and events are worth relating. Your
final selection should support the theme of your story. To decide which

events to portray, figure out how much detail you intend to devote to each one. In writing about her basketball career, Karen could have told about her four years playing in high school, her senior year alone, one game, or even less. Because she wanted to focus on a climactic point in great detail, she selected "even less"—she writes her entire six-page paper about the final six minutes in her final game.

In selecting events, consider using one of two strategies that writers commonly use to maintain reader interest: showing cause and effect and building suspense. When writers recount an experience to show **cause and effect,** they relate one event as bringing about another or several others (having an accident causing one to undergo physical therapy, meeting a person resulting in making a friend, taking a trip leading to the learning of a new language and new customs).

In using **suspense,** writers raise questions or pose problems but delay answering or solving them. If the writer can make the question interesting enough, the problem pressing enough, readers will keep reading to learn the answers or solutions—in other words, to find out what happens. Karen's paper asks indirectly, "What is it like to play a championship game from the perspective of a substitute player?"

2 Ordering events

The most common way to order events is to use **chronological order,** presenting events in the sequence in which they happened. Chronological order can be straightforward, following a day from morning to night as Heather does in her narrative about picking strawberries. Chronology orders Karen's six minutes at the end of one basketball game, and it orders Judith's evening trek to the library to study in safety. Sometimes, however, the sequence of events might be broken up, so that readers are introduced to an event in the present, with the rest of the story being a narrated flashback—an especially common strategy in films. In an experiential essay, for example, Judith might have begun her essay already sitting in the library and reflecting back on how she got there and why. In telling a story, the order of events is always a writer's choice.

WRITING 6: APPLICATION

Outline the sequence of events of your story in the order that makes the most sense. Is the arrangement chronological? If not, what is it? How do you decide which event to begin with? Which one to end with?

We can talk about the "why" of a story on two levels: First, *why* did the events occur in the story? What motivated or caused them? Well-told stories will answer this question, directly or indirectly. But we can also ask the writer. Of all the many stories you could write, *why* did you write this one? Or as every reader asks, at least tacitly: So what? What's the meaning or significance of this story? What did I learn by reading it? Well-told stories will also answer this question; readers will see and understand both why you wrote it and why they read it.

However, first drafts of personal experience narratives often do not reveal clear answers to these questions, even to the writers themselves. The purpose of a first draft is to get the events down on paper for a writer to look at; the reason for writing may not yet be apparent, even to the writer. In subsequent drafts, the meaning of these events—the **theme**—should become clearer to the writer because a major reason for writing about personal subjects is to put them in some kind of perspective, to reflect on them and find out how they contribute to the writer's current self. If some meaning doesn't emerge in the course of exploring the topic, the writer is well advised to switch topics.

In experiential stories, the theme isn't usually explicitly stated in the first paragraph as is the thesis statement in expository or argumentative writing. Instead, writers reflecting on personal experience may create a meaning that is not directly stated anywhere and that becomes clear only at the end of the narrative. Although any and all themes are possible, we will describe three broad categories that make especially good stories: slices of life, insights, and turning points.

1 Slices of life

Some stories simply let readers see what life is like for someone else. Such stories exist primarily to record the writer's memories and to convey information in an interesting way. Their primary theme is "This is what my life is like."

Beth's story of the Saturday orchestra rehearsal is a slice of life, as she chooses to focus on a common "practice" rather than a more dramatic "performance." After using interior monologue for nine paragraphs, in the last paragraph she speaks to the readers directly, explaining what the meaning of music is in her everyday life:

> As hard as it is to get up every Saturday morning, and as
> hard as it is to put up with some people here, I always feel

good as I leave rehearsal. A guest conductor once said:
"Music sounds how feelings feel." It's really true. Music
evokes emotions that can't be described on paper. Every
human feeling can be expressed through music—sadness,
love, hatred. Music is an international language. Once you
learn it you can't forget it.

2 Insights

In contrast to the many but routine experiences that reveal slices of life is the single important experience that leads to a writer's new insight, change, or growth. Such an experience is deeply significant to the writer, and he or she makes sure that readers see the full value of the experience, usually by explicitly commenting on its meaning. In the following passage, near the end of her essay, Judith locates a place in the library where she will study for her philosophy exam, reflecting that she needs not only comfort but safety in order to concentrate fully:

I find my place, an empty chair near a window, and slouch
down into it, propping my legs on the low table in front. If
my mother could see me, she'd reprimand me for not sitting
up straight. I breathe deeply, close my eyes for a moment,
and become centered, forgetting both last night's pizza and
tomorrow's philosophy exam. I need a few minutes to acclimate
to this space, relax, and feel safe before starting my work.

3 Turning points

Turning points are those moments in one's life when something happens that causes the writer to change or grow in some large, or small way—more than routine, less than spectacular—perhaps somewhere in between slices of life and profound insights. In fact, many of the best personal experience stories have for themes a modest change or the beginning of growth. Although such themes may be implied throughout the story, they often become clear only in a single climactic moment or episode. Mary's camp counselor story shows her progress from insecurity to confidence in gaining the trust of a ten-year-old. The following excerpt takes place after she has rescued Josh from ridicule by other campers:

He ran in and threw himself on my bed, crying. I held him, rubbing his head for over an hour. "I love you, Mary. You're the best big sister in the whole world and you're so pretty! I love you and don't ever want you to leave."

Writing from Personal Experience

After writing a first draft, address the following questions and revise accordingly:

- **Who** are you? What distinguishes you from others? How much of you is revealed in this story?
- **What** actually happens in this story? Is it clear to somebody who wasn't there with you?
- **How** do you choose to tell the story: first or third person? present or past tense?
- **Where** does this story take place? Will readers be able to see or feel it?
- **When** does this story take place? Is there a logical order for revealing these events?
- **Why** are you telling this story? What makes it significant? What do you want your readers to take from reading it?

WRITING 7: APPLICATION

Freewrite for ten minutes about the meaning of your story as you have written it so far, addressing some of these questions: What have you discovered about yourself? Were there any surprises? Does your story interest you? Why or why not? What do you want readers to feel or know at the end?

8 g   Sample student essay

The finished draft of Judith's personal reflective essay, "Writing in Safety," opens and closes with a walk to and from the library. It has a loosely narrative pattern and is written in the present tense to convey a sense of the events unfolding as we read them. Her essay tells a very simple story, since it's mainly about walking and sitting down. The journey emerges as a mental, almost spiritual, quest for safety—safety in which to think and create without fear. At the same time, the physical dimensions of her journey and the attention to descriptive detail make her journey believable.

Writing in Safety

Judith Woods

It is already afternoon. I fiddle with the key to lock the apartment door after me. I am not accustomed to locking doors. Except for the six months I spent in Boston, I have never lived in a place where I did not trust my neighbors. When I was little, we couldn't lock our farmhouse door; the wood had swollen and the bolt no longer lined up properly with the hole, and nobody ever bothered to fix it. I still remember the time our baby-sitter, Rosie, hammered the bolt closed and we had to take the door off the hinges to get it open.

I heft the book bag onto my shoulder and walk up College Street toward the library. As I pass and am passed by other students, I scrutinize everything around me, hoping to be struck with a creative idea for a topic for my English paper. Instead, my mind fills with a jumble of disconnected images, like a bowl of alphabet soup: the letters are there, but they don't form any words. Campus sidewalks are not the best places for creativity to strike.

Approaching the library, I see skateboarders and bikers weaving through students who talk in clusters on the library steps. A friendly dog is tied to a bench, watching for its owner to return. Subjects to write about? Nothing strikes me as especially interesting, and besides, my heart is still pounding from the walk up the hill. I wipe my damp forehead and go inside.

Inside the smoke-colored doors, the loud and busy atmosphere vanishes, replaced by the soft, soothing hum of air-conditioning and the hushed sound of whispering voices. The repetitive sound of the copy machine has a calming effect as I look for a comfortable place in which to begin my work.

I want just the right chair, with a soft cushion, and a low sturdy table for a leg rest. The chairs are strategically positioned with comfortable personal space around each one, so you can stretch your arms fully without touching a neighbor. I notice that if there are three chairs in a row, the middle one is always empty. If seated at a table, people sit staggered so they are not directly across from one another. People seem to respect each other's need for personal space.

Like a dog who circles her bed three times before lying down, I circle the reading room looking for the right place to sit. I need to feel safe and comfortable so I can concentrate on mental activity. Some students, however, are too comfortable. One boy has moved two chairs together and covered himself with his coat, and he is asleep in a fetal position. A girl sits at a table, head down, dozing like we used to do in first grade.

I find my place, an empty chair near a window, and slouch down into it, propping my legs on the low table in front. If my mother could see me, she'd reprimand me for not sitting up straight. I breathe deeply, close my eyes for a moment, and become centered, forgetting both last night's pizza and tomorrow's philosophy exam. I need a few minutes to acclimate to this space, relax, and feel safe before starting my work.

Two weeks ago, a female student was assaulted not far from where I live—that's why I've taken to locking my door so carefully. I am beginning to understand the importance of feeling safe in order to be creative and productive.

Here, in the library, I feel secure, protected from real violence and isolated from everyday distractions. There are just enough people for security's sake but not so many that I feel crowded. And besides, I'm surrounded by all these books, all these great minds who dwell in this hallowed space! I am comfortable, safe, and beginning to get an idea.

Hours later—my paper started, my exam studied for, my eyes tired—I retrace the path to my apartment. It is dark now, and I listen closely when I hear footsteps behind, stepping to the sidewalk's edge to let a man walk briskly past. At my door, I again fumble for the now familiar key, insert it in the lock, open the door, turn on the hall light, and step inside. Here, too, I am safe, ready to eat, read a bit, and finish my reflective essay.

SUGGESTIONS FOR WRITING AND RESEARCH

INDIVIDUAL

Write a personal experience essay based on Writings 2–6 in this chapter. Find a subject that will let you show some change or learning on your part. Plan to write this narrative in several drafts, each one exploring a different aspect of your experience.

COLLABORATIVE

As a class, write the story of your writing class so far in the semester. Each class member contributes one chapter (one page) to this tale. Each member chooses any moment (funny, momentous, boring, routine) and describes it so that it stands on its own as a complete episode. Choose two class members to collect all the short narrative chapters and weave them into a larger narrative with a beginning, middle, and end.

WRITING ACROSS THE CURRICULUM

Personal Perspectives in Academic Writing

Including a personal perspective in academic writing by including either personal experiences or first-person pronouns is a matter of debate both across the curriculum and within specific disciplines. Following are four arguments for the validity of personal perspectives in papers written in disciplines other than English:

1) It is usually easier to read than formal academic writing because it sounds like a real person speaking: it uses first-person pronouns, contractions, and colloquial language while avoiding disciplinary jargon and complicated sentences.

2) When used in conjunction with more academic writing it adds color, liveliness, and change of pace for the reader.

3) It provides pertinent evidence as when the author conducted an interview, observed a situation, or recalled a relevant experience.

4) It acknowledges the difficulty of absolute objectivity. What passes for fact today may be called into question tomorrow; for instance, only a few decades ago the extinction of dinosaurs was blamed on glaciers whereas currently it's blamed on a meteor hitting the earth.

Following are four arguments against personal perspectives in academic writing:

1) If used without good reason: For example, if every other statement of fact is preceded by "I think that …" it becomes tedious and irrelevant.

2) If used in place of hard evidence. For example, if your personal experience alone attests to the validity of a political or religious idea and other perspectives are excluded.

3) Convention expects it. For example, the following advice is still typical of some disciplinary style guides: "Although it is becoming increasingly common to see the use first person pronouns in aca-

demic texts, the use of the impersonal pronoun *one* is still generally preferred."

4) Including personal perspective may inhibit the striving for objectivity. Although perfect objectivity is impossible, the sincere effort to achieve it is highly valued in meaningful, reasoned dialogue.

When in doubt, consult your instructor. For further information on the advantages of blending experiential and academic perspectives, see Candace Speigelman's, *Personally Speaking: Experience as Evidence in Academic Discourse,* Southern Illinois University Press, 2004.

chapter 9

Writing to Explain

To explain something is to make it clear to somebody else who wants to understand it. Explaining is fundamental to most acts of communication and to nearly every type of writing, from personal to argumentative and research writing. Explanatory writing is also a genre unto itself: a newspaper feature on baseball card collecting, a magazine article on why dinosaurs are extinct, a textbook on the French Revolution, a recipe for chili, or a laboratory report.

Explanatory writing (also called *expository* or *informational* writing) answers questions such as these:

- What is it?

- What does it mean?

- How does it work?

- How is it related to other things?

- How is it put together?

- Why did it happen?

- What will its consequences be?

To write a successful explanation, you need to find out first what your readers *want* to know, then what they *already know* and what they *don't know*. If you are able to determine—or at least make educated guesses about—these audience conditions, your writing task becomes clear. When you begin to write, keep in mind three general principles that typify much explanatory writing: (1) it focuses on the idea or object being explained rather than on the writer's beliefs and feelings: (2) it often—not always—states its objective early in what might be called an informational thesis; and (3) it presents information systematically, according to a clear logic.

In writing classes, explanation usually takes the form of research essays and reports that emphasize informing rather than arguing, interpreting, or reflecting. The assignment may be to "describe how something works" or to "explain the causes and effects" of a particular phenomenon. This chapter explains how to develop a topic, articulate your purpose, and use strategies appropriate for your audience.

WRITING 1: EXPLORATION ....

How good are you at explaining things to people? What things do you most commonly find yourself explaining? What is the last thing you explained in writing? How did your audience receive your explanation?

ESL How is explaining things in your native language different from or similar to explaining things in English?

....

9 a   Topic

Topics with a limited, or specific, scope are easier to explain carefully and in detail than topics that are vague, amorphous, or very broad. For example, general subjects such as mountains, automobiles, or stereo systems are so broad that it's hard to know where to begin. However, a specific aspect of sound systems, such as compact discs (CDs) is easier. Within the subject of CDs, of course, there are several topics as well (design, manufacturing process, cost, marketing, sound quality, comparison to tape and vinyl recordings, etc.). If your central question focuses on how CDs are manufactured, you might well address some of these other issues (cost, marketing, comparison) as well, but only in so far as they illuminate and advance your focus on manufacturing. Effective explanations are detailed and developed, include examples, and are focused around a central question ("How are CDs made?" or "How do CDs differ from LPs?"). Of course, there may be other questions to be answered along the way ("How do CDs work?" "Why do CDs cost so much?"), but these are secondary.

Once you have a focused topic on a central question, you need to assemble information. If you're not an expert yourself, you'll need to consult authorities on the topic. Even if you are already an expert, finding supporting information from other experts will help make your explanation clear and authoritative. Keep your audience in mind as you begin your research. You don't want to waste time researching and writing about things your audience already knows or issues that are beyond the scope of your focused topic.

WRITING 2: APPLICATION

What would you like to explain? for what purpose? to whom? If you're not sure, do some freewriting or journal writing to help you discover a question.

9   b   Thesis

The **thesis** statement in an explanatory paper is simply the writer's declaration of what the paper is about. Stating a thesis early in an explanatory work lets readers know what to expect and guides their understanding of the information to be presented. In explanatory writing, the thesis states the answer to the implied question your paper sets out to address: What is it? How does this work? Why is this so?

QUESTION   Why do compact discs cost so much?

THESIS   CDs cost more than cassette tapes because the laser technology required to manufacture them is more complicated.

The advantage of stating a thesis in a single sentence is that it sums up the purpose of your paper in a single idea that lets readers predict what's ahead. Another way to state a single-sentence thesis is to convey an image, analogy, or metaphor that provides an ongoing reference point throughout the paper and gives unity and coherence to your explanation—a good image keeps both you and your readers focused.

QUESTION   How are the offices of the city government connected?

THESIS   City government offices are like an octopus, with eight fairly independent bureaus as arms and a central brain in the mayor's office.

The thesis you start with may evolve as you work on your paper—and that's okay. For example, suppose the more you learn about city government, the less like an octopus and the more like a centipede it seems. So, your first thesis is really a **working thesis,** and it needs to be tentative, flexible, and subject to change; its primary function is to keep your paper focused to guide further research.

WRITING 3: APPLICATION ....

Write out a working thesis for the topic you are explaining. If you are addressing a *when* or *how* question, find a controlling image or analogy that will hold all of the elements together.

....

9 c   Strategies

Good strategies that can be used to explain things include defining, describing, classifying and dividing, analyzing causes and effects, and comparing and contrasting. Which strategy you select depends on the question you are answering as well as the audience to whom you are explaining. You could offer two very different explanations to the same question depending on who asked it. For example, if asked "Where is Westport Drive?" you would respond differently to a neighbor familiar with local reference points ("One block north of Burger King") than to a stranger who would not know where Burger King was either. With this caution in mind on considering who is the receiver of the explanation, here is a brief overview of possible strategies:

QUESTION	STRATEGY
What is it?	Define

Example: A fairy tale is a story about fairies, giants, dwarfs, and so on, that takes place in imaginary places.

What does it mean?	Define

Example: The story of "Three Little Pigs" is a children's story that celebrates the work ethic.

QUESTION	STRATEGY
What are its characteristics?	Describe

<u>Example:</u> Animated cartoons are hand drawings made to move.

| How is it related to other things? | Compare and contrast |

<u>Example:</u> Fairy tales and cartoons convey cultural values to children in the same way that novels and plays convey cultural values to adults.

| How is it put together? | Classify and divide |

<u>Example:</u> An animated cartoon is composed of many individual images combined to tell a story.

| To what group does it belong? | Classify and divide |

<u>Example:</u> Cartoons, fairy tales, and nursery rhymes comprise an important part of children's literature.

| Why did it happen? | Analyze cause and effect |

<u>Example:</u> The strong wind can blow down the straw house because straw is not a substantial building material.

| What will its consequences be? | Analyze cause and effect |

<u>Example:</u> If you build a house of brick, it will withstand strong winds and not fall down.

If your paper is on a tightly focused topic and answers a narrow, simple question, you may need to use only one strategy. More often, however, you will have one primary strategy that shapes the paper as a whole and several secondary strategies that can vary from paragraph to paragraph or even sentence to sentence. For example, to explain why the government has raised income taxes, your primary strategy would be to analyze cause and effect, but you might also need to define terms such as *income tax* to classify the various types of taxes, and to compare and contrast raising income taxes to other budgetary options. In fact, almost every explanatory strategy makes use of other strategies: How, for example, do you *describe* a process without first dividing it into steps? How can you *compare and contrast* without describing the things compared and contrasted?

ESL Vocabulary for Explaining Things

- Description

consists of	has
displays	characterized by

Example: The gardenia *has* a sweet fragrance.

- Division

consists of	separated into
divided into	composed of

Example: The curriculum is *divided into* the humanities, the social sciences, and the natural sciences.

- Classification

categorized according to	categorized as
classified according to	classified as
grouped according to	

Example: History can be *classified as* a humanities discipline.

- Comparison

also	resembles
both ... and ...	similar to
like	the same as

Example: *Like* English, Spanish uses articles before nouns.

- Contrast

but	on the other hand
however	unlike
in contrast	yet

Example: *Unlike* English, Spanish does not always state the subject of a sentence.

- Cause and effect

as a result	so
consequently	therefore
for this reason	thus

Example: Some marathon runners do not pace themselves well, and *as a result* they may be unable to finish a race.

1 Defining

To define something is to identify it, to set it apart so that it can be distinguished from similar things. Writers need to define any terms central for reader understanding in order to make points clearly, forcefully, and with authority.

Formal **definitions** are what you find in a dictionary. They usually combine a general term with specific characteristics:

A computer is a programmable electronic device [*general term*] that can store, retrieve, and process data [*specific characteristics*].

Usually, defining something is a brief preliminary step accomplished before you move on to a more important part of the explanation. When you need to define something complex or difficult or when your primary explanatory strategy is definition, you will need an extended definition consisting of a paragraph or more. This was the case with Mark's paper explaining computers, in which he defined each part of a typical computer system. After defining the central processor unit (CPU), he defined computer memory:

Computer storage space is measured in units
called "Kilobytes" (K). Each K equals 1,024 "bytes" or
approximately 1,000 single typewriter characters. So 1 K
equals about 180 English words, or a little less than half of a
single-spaced typed page, or maybe three minutes of fast
typing.

Personal computers generally have their memories
measured in "megabytes" (MB). That means 1 MB equals
1,048,567 bytes (or 1,000 K), which translates into
approximately 400 pages of single-spaced type. One gigabyte
(GB) equals 1,000 MB or 400,000 pages of single-spaced type.
A 100 GB hard drive holds a lot of typed pages!

2 Describing

To describe a person, place, or thing means to create a verbal image so that readers can see what you see; hear what you hear; or taste, smell, and feel what you taste, smell, and feel. In other words, effective descriptions appeal to the senses. Furthermore, good descriptions contain enough sensory detail for readers to understand the subject, but not so much as to distract or bore them. Your job, then, is to include just the right amount of detail so that you put readers in your shoes.

To describe how processes work is more complicated than describing what something looks like: in addition to showing objects at rest, you need to show them in sequence and motion. You need to divide the process into discrete steps and present the steps in a logical order that will be easy for readers to follow. This is easier to do with simple processes, such as making a peanut butter and jelly sandwich, than for complex processes, such as manufacturing an automobile.

To help orient your readers, you may also want to number the steps, using transition words such as *first, second,* and *third.* In the following example, taken from an early draft of his paper, Keith describes the process of manufacturing compact discs:

> CDs start out as a refrigerator-sized box full of little plastic beads that you could sift your hands through. They are fed into a giant tapered corkscrew—a blown-up version of an old-fashioned meat grinder. As the beads pass down the corkscrew, they are slowly melted by the heated walls.
>
> At the bottom of their descent is a "master recording plate" onto which the molten plastic is pressed. The plastic now resembles a vinyl record, except that the disc is transparent. The master now imprints "pits," rather than grooves, around the disc, the surface resembling a ball of Play-Doh after being thrown against a stucco wall—magnified five thousand times.

3 Comparing and contrasting

To compare two things is to find similarities between them: to contrast is to find differences. **Comparing and contrasting** at the same time helps people understand something two ways: first, by showing how it is related to similar things, and second, by showing how it differs. College assignments frequently ask you to compare and contrast two authors, books, ideas, and so on.

People usually compare and contrast things when they want to make a choice or judgment about them: books, food, bicycles, presidential candidates, political philosophies. For this reason, the two things compared and contrasted should be similar: you'll learn more to help you vote for president by comparing two presidential candidates than a presidential candidate with a Senate candidate; you'll learn more about which orange to buy by comparing it with other oranges (*navel, mandarin*) than with apples, plums, or pears. Likewise, it's easiest to see similarities and differences when you compare and contrast the same elements of each thing. If you describe one political candidate's stand on gun control, describe the other's as well; this way, voters will have a basis for choosing one over the other.

Comparison-and-contrast analysis can be organized in one of three ways: (1) a *point-to-point analysis* examines one feature at a time for both similarities and differences; (2) a *whole-to-whole analysis* first presents one object as a whole and then the other as a whole; (3) a *similarity-and-difference analysis* first presents the similarities, then the differences between the two things, or vice versa.

Use a point-to-point or similarity-and-difference analysis for long explanations of complex things, such as manufacturing an automobile, in which you need to cover everything from materials and labor to assembly and inspection processes. But use a whole-to-whole analysis for simple objects that readers can more easily comprehend. In the following whole-to-whole example, a student explains the difference between Democrats and Republicans:

> Like most Americans, both Democrats and Republicans believe in the twin values of equality and freedom. However, Democrats place a greater emphasis on equality, believing equal opportunity for all people to be more important than the freedom of any single individual. Consequently, they stand for government intervention to guarantee equal treatment in matters of environmental protection, minimum wages, racial policies, and educational opportunities.
>
> In contrast, Republicans place greater emphasis on freedom, believing the specific rights of the individual to be more important than the vague collective rights of the masses. Consequently, they stand for less government control in matters of property ownership, wages and the right to work based strictly on merit and hard work, and local control of schools.

Note how the writer devotes equal space to each political party, uses neutral language to lend academic authority to his explanation, and emphasizes the differences by using parallel examples as well as parallel sentence structure. The careful use of several comparison-and-contrast strategies makes it difficult for readers to miss his point.

An *analogy* is an extended comparison which shows the extent to which one thing is similar in structure and/or process to another. Analogies are effective ways of explaining something new to readers, because you can compare something they are unfamiliar with to something they already know about. For example, it might help you to understand how a heart functions by comparing it to a water pump. Be sure to use objects and images in analogies that will be familiar to your readers. (See the box on pp. 161–163 in Chapter 10 for a discussion of *false analogies,* arguments that inaccurately portray things that are different as being similar.)

4 Classifying and dividing

People generally understand short more easily than long, simple more easily than complex. One way to help readers understand a complicated topic is to **classify and divide** it into simpler pieces and to put the pieces in context.

To *classify* something, you put it in a category or class with other things that are like it:

Like whales and dolphins, sea lions are aquatic mammals.

To *divide* something, you break it into smaller parts or subcategories:

An insect's body is composed of a head, a thorax, and an abdomen.

Many complex systems need both classification and division to be clear. To explain a stereo system, for example, you might divide the whole into parts: headphones, record player, graphic equalizer, tape deck, CD player, preamplifier, amplifier, radio, and speakers. To better understand how these parts function, you might classify them into categories:

Inputs	Radio
	Record player
	Tape deck
	CD player
Processors	Preamplifiers
	Amplifiers
	Graphic equalizers

Outputs   Speakers
               Headphones

Most readers have a difficult time remembering more than six or seven items at a time, so explaining is easier when you organize a long list into fewer logical groups, as in the preceding example. Also be sure that the categories you use are meaningful to your readers, not simply convenient for you as a writer.

5 Analyzing causes and effects

Things don't change unless some force causes them to change. Usually, one thing happens because something else happened; then it, in turn, makes something else happen. You sleep because you're tired, and once you've slept, you wake up because you're rested, and so on. In other words, you already know about cause and effect because it's a regular part of your daily life. A **cause** is something that makes something else happen; an **effect** is the thing that happens.

Cause-and-effect analyses are most often assigned for college papers to answer *why* questions: Why are the fish dying in the lake? The most direct answer is a *because* statement:

Fish are dying *because* oxygen levels in the lake are too low.

The answer, in other words, is a thesis, which the rest of the paper must defend and support:

There are three reasons for low oxygen level . . .

Cause-and-effect analyses also try to describe possible future effects:

If nitrogen fertilizers were banned from farmland that drains into the lake, oxygen levels would rise, and fish populations would be restored.

Unless there is sound, widely accepted evidence to support the thesis, however, this sort of analysis may lead to more argumentative writing. In this example, for instance, farmers or fertilizer manufacturers might complicate the matter by pointing to other sources of lake pollution—outboard motors, paper mill effluents, urban sewage runoff—making comprehensive solutions harder to reach. Keep in mind that most complex situations have multiple causes. If you try to reduce a complex situation to an overly simple cause, you are making the logical mistake known as *oversimplification.*

. . . .

Decide which of the five strategies described in this section best suits the primary purpose of the explanatory paper you are drafting. Which additional or secondary strategies will you also use?

. . . .

9 d Organization

If you explain to your readers where you're taking them, they will follow more willingly; if you lead carefully, step by step, using a good road map, they will know where they are and will trust you.

Your method of organization should be simple, straightforward, and logical, and it should be appropriate for your subject and audience. For example, to explain how a stereo system works, you have a number of logical options: (1) you could start by putting a CD in a player and end with the music coming out of the speakers; (2) you could describe the system technically, starting with the power source to explain how sound is made in the speakers; (3) you could describe it historically, starting with components that were developed earliest and work toward the most recent inventions. All these options follow a clear logic that, once explained, will make sense to readers.

. . . .

Outline three possible means of organizing the explanatory paper you are writing. List the advantages and disadvantages of each. Select the one that best suits your purpose and the needs of your audience.

. . . .

9 e Neutral perspective

First, you need to understand that absolute neutrality or objectivity is impossible when you write about anything. All writers bring with them assumptions and biases that cause them to view the world—including this explanatory project—in a particular way. Nevertheless, your explanations will usually be clearer and more accessible to others when you present them as fairly as possible, showing as little bias as possible—even though doing this, too, will depend on who your readers are and whether they agree or disagree with your biases. In general, it's more effective to emphasize the thing explained (the object) rather than your personal beliefs and feelings. This perspective allows you to get information to readers as quickly and efficiently as possible without you, the writer, getting in the way.

To adopt a neutral perspective, write from the third-person point of view, using the pronouns *he, she,* and *it.* Keep yourself in the background unless you have a good reason not to, such as explaining your personal experience with the subject. In some instances, adopting the second-person *you* adds a friendly, familiar tone that keeps readers interested.

Be fair; present all the relevant information about the topic, both things you like about it and things you dislike. Avoid emotional or biased language. Remember that your goal is not to win an argument, but to convey information.

9 f   Sample student essay

In the following paper, Katie Moll discovered an unexpected and disturbing controversy surrounding the television cartoon show, *The Smurfs.* The essay records her step-by-step attempt to explain and understand the truth about her favorite childhood program. Here is an instance where information found on the Internet first created a problem to solve, then provided the solution. Katie's essay concludes with a personal postscript that poses interesting questions for all who rely on Web-based research. Note that illustrations serve the important function of showing the characters who are the subject of her essay.

The Smurfs as Political Propaganda

Katie Moll

Saturday morning cartoons were a large part of my childhood. They brought enjoyment and laughter, and they sometimes taught moral lessons. I grew up surrounded by shows like *Fraggle Rock, Rainbow Brite, The Jetsons,* and *Reading Rainbow.* My personal favorite, however, was *The Smurfs,* a cartoon focused on a village of small, blue, elf-like creatures that lived in mushrooms and were always content with their lives. Much to my despair, they were taken off

the air after the 1980s. It wasn't until about a year ago that the Smurfs were
brought to my attention again, when I chose to attend a theme party dressed as
one of the Smurf characters such as Brainy, Handy, or Smurfette. However, after
checking every party store around, I could find no costumes. When I checked the
Internet for Smurf costumes, I found more than I
bargained for, as Web sites popped up with titles
such as "Sociopolitical Themes in the Smurfs" and
"Papa Smurf Is a Communist." How could they make
such claims about my favorite cartoon? And then I
wondered, could this be true? Was *The Smurfs*
television show really political propaganda?

To check this story further, I searched the Web with the keyword "Smurfs,"
which took me to "The Smurfs Official Site" at www.smurf.com/homepage.html.
It had nothing about the communist theory, but then again, why would it? This
was the home page promoting the cartoon, so I doubted it would slander the
program. However, I did obtain useful background information on the origin of
The Smurfs. The creator of the Smurf characters was Peyo, the pen name of Pierre
Culliford, who lived and worked in Brussels, Belgium. The Smurfs first appeared
as a comic strip in 1958. It was not until 1981 that *The Smurfs* became an
animated television series designed by the team of William Hanna and
Joseph Barbera. Nothing on the Smurf home page suggested that either Peyo or
Hanna-Barbera had subversive intentions, so I began to think the theory was a
complete hoax. But I wanted to find out more.

Then, amidst a jumble of commercial topics, I found a Web site called "The Smurfs as a Paradigm for Communist Society" that suggested, "The Smurfs were actually a well-devised piece of communist propaganda to erode American society from within" (Gozer, para 2).

Five points of comparison between the Smurf cartoon show and a Russian communist society make the author's case: (1) Papa Smurf, the wise leader of the Smurf community, looks like Karl Marx and (2) wears red pants; (3) all Smurfs work according to their ability and receive according to their needs; (4) the villain, Gargamel, acts like a greedy capitalist; and (5) his cat, Azreal, represents "third-world despotisms that are clinging onto the coattails of first-world capitalism." He concludes, saying, "these five points provide very strong evidence pointing to the conclusion that the TV show 'The Smurfs' is indeed a paradigm for communist society" (para 8).

"Strong evidence"? It is hard to take this 500-word Web site very seriously. It is short; the supporting detail in each paragraph is sketchy; some of the arguments (Papa Smurf as Karl Marx!) are far-fetched; and the author is not accountable, providing no name and no credentials, though an e-mail address, n9620080@cc.wwu.edu, is included. However, a second Web site, Sociopolitical Themes in *The Smurfs* by J. Marc Schmidt, outlines in much more detail the basis for a Marxist interpretation: "Unlike many other cartoons, or indeed other television programmes, *The Smurfs* is about an entire society and its interactions with itself and with outsiders, rather than the adventures of a few characters. Hence, I believe it is, in short, a political fable, in much the same way that *The Lion, the Witch and the Wardrobe* was a fable about Christianity. Rather than Christianity, however, *The Smurfs* is about Marxism" (para 2).

Note that Schmidt does not label *The Smurfs* "propaganda," but describes the cartoon series in the same terms as other respected "political fables" such as those by C. S. Lewis, something to be studied or learned from rather than be brainwashed by. In Schmidt's words, "I am not accusing *The Smurfs* of being some kind of subversive kiddie propaganda" (para 3).

Schmidt believes Peyo to be a socialist rather than a card-carrying communist, calling the Smurf village "a Marxist utopia" rather than a police state like the old Soviet Union (para 5). The evidence Schmidt assembles is thoughtful and far more convincing than Gozer's hasty claims. For example, he points out that the Smurf village is "a perfect model of a socialist commune or collective" (para 5), that "the Smurfs are all completely equal" (para 6), that "everyone is equally a worker and an owner" (para 7), and that "they wear the same kind and colour of clothes" (para 9).

I found the Schmidt Web site to be quite convincing. For one thing, all that

he says about the Smurfs and Smurf village matches what I remember about the

show. Once he points out those similarities, I can see his point. For another thing,

the Schmidt article on the Web site is carefully written, with clear explanations

and concrete examples. In addition, Schmidt includes his whole name along with

an e-mail address, j_marc_s@hotmail.com—an indication that he is willing to be

responsible for his ideas. Because of the way Schmidt spells certain words

(programme and colour), a first reading of his site suggests that his English is

British rather than American, in which case he may have more objective distance

from the cartoon show than an American author would.

However, when I looked at a third Web site that addressed this

propaganda issue, "Papa Smurf Is a Communist," I became confused again. At

first glance, this site seemed to have been written from an angry capitalist

perspective, upset that communist connections are hidden in the children's

cartoon. Even the feel of this Web page was different, with a menacing black

background and dark red letters as opposed to the more neutral tones on the

other Web sites. At first, I was annoyed by its aggressive tone, but when I read

it a second time, I found myself laughing. This Web site is not serious at all!

Instead, it is making obvious fun of the communist propaganda theory, as the

following excerpt illustrates:

> Yes, that is correct, Papa Smurf and all of his little Smurf minions are not
>
> the happy little characters Hanna-Barbera would have us believe! The
>
> cartoon was really created by the Russian government in order to

indoctrinate the youngest members of Western society with communist

beliefs and ideals, thus destroying their resistance to the imminent

Russian invasion that was to occur when this generation (my

generation) grew up.

When I read "Imminent Russian invasion," I said wait a minute. While it is

true that during the Cold War many Americans feared a nuclear war with Russia,

I didn't think anyone actually feared an invasion. And when he claimed that the

word *Smurf* was an acronym standing for "Small Men Under Red Father" I found

myself laughing again. And in yet another passage, this anonymous author

argues that Papa Smurf resembles Stalin more than Marx:

I feel that Stalin is most likely the man that Papa Smurf was modeled

after. Marx believed more in the system of socialism, not communism.

What is the difference, you may ask? Well, under both systems

everything is supposedly shared equally among all members of the

society; however, under the socialist system there are free elections for

the leadership of the society, whereas under the communist system

there are no elections. I sure as hell don't remember Papa Smurf being

elected leader. . . . [but] Stalin's appearance also highly resembles that

of Papa Smurf. His beard may not be as perfect as that of Marx, but look

at that round face! (para 7)

The author does not reveal his or her identity but does provide an e-mail

address, commiesmurfs@hotmail.com, to which readers can respond, along with

twenty reader responses printed at the end of the site such as these two:

–"Your page was one of the funniest things I have read in a long time! Great job on it—I especially like the shot [an image on the Web page] of Papa Smurf with the hammer and sickle in his hat!"

–"The site made me open my eyes and realize that communism only exists not in society but in most of our pop culture as well. Being concerned, I am now proposing 'CASCO' (Canadians Against Smurf Communism) to rid the evils of the Smurfs on Sunday mornings; they are shown on a regular basis in Canada. Spread the news."

To make sense of three different Web sites, each pointing to similarities between *The Smurfs* and Marxism, I looked more carefully at the sequence in which the sites were created. Who, in other words, started this comparison? Fortunately, each site was dated. The brief Gozer site was created in September 1997. The anonymous and obvious parody, "Papa Smurf," was created in March of the same year—six months *earlier* than Gozer—so the parody was first. The only serious site, Schmidt's, was not created until sometime in 1998 (exact month not available). In other words, the most obvious parody of the cartoon show, the anonymous "Papa Smurf," seemed to start a small chain reaction, with the Gozer site second and Schmidt's last.

Curious to see whether there were any connections among the three Web sites, I sent e-mail queries to each site. I never heard from the anonymous creator of the earliest site, "Papa Smurf," but I received responses from the other two authors. J. Marc Schmidt responded promptly, identifying himself as a high school teacher living in Sydney, Australia (hence the British spellings), and explaining that he created his site after attending a museum exhibit on

cartoon animation in which he found hard-to-believe interpretations of many

animated shows. Schmidt writes, "I started thinking more and more about

socialism, and eventually the idea just clicked. Anyway, for good or bad, that

incomprehensible blurb was the seed, which led me to write an essay called

'Sociopolitical Themes in the Smurfs.' I turned it into a Web site and put it on

the Internet."

The author of the Gozer site also responded, providing his real name, Eric

Lott, but asking me not to give out his personal e-mail address. Lott writes:

"In honest truth, it was/is not intended as a parody. Personally, I am an

anarcho-socialist. I began thinking this up . . . and developed it into a monologue.

Most people I gave [it] to found it quite amusing."

After reading the comic, the amusing, and the serious interpretations of the

socialist Smurfs, I realized I had to take another look at the cartoon myself. I

obtained a copy of one Smurf episode by borrowing it from a friend's younger

sister (who else would collect such videotapes?) and tried to watch it with an open mind, as if I were young again.

This untitled episode portrayed Smurfette in danger of being captured by the cat, Azreal, but rescued just in time by Papa and the other Smurfs. After having read all the political ideas about *The Smurfs,* however, I found it difficult to watch an episode with an open mind. As soon as it was over, I began seeing possible socialist connections myself. For example, when Papa Smurf rounds up the rescue team, is he a communist dictator taking charge? When the villain, Gargamel, orders his cat to catch Smurfette, is he a capitalist dictator delegating his dirty jobs to the workers? Is the chase scene a reminder of the constant war between the free world and communism? Does the color red symbolize communism?

It was then I also realized that I could take virtually any children's story and make it mean something else. Do Santa Claus and Little Red Riding Hood wear red because they are communists? Do Santa's elves make toys because they are slaves? Is the Big Bad Wolf a greedy capitalist? While these interpretations are possible, I don't believe they were ever intended by the creators of these stories.

Postscript

Browsing the Internet after writing this paper, I found an interpretation of the popular children's television show *Teletubbies,* suggesting that one of the Teletubbies characters is a homosexual role model. According to "Parents Alert: Tinky Winky Comes Out of the Closet," an article published in the February 1999 edition of the *National Liberty Journal*—a newsletter edited and published by the

Rev. Jerry Falwell—"Tinky Winky has the voice of a boy yet carries a purse . . . is purple—the gay-pride color; and his antenna is shaped like a triangle—the gay-pride symbol" (qtd. in Reed). At this point, however, I stopped reading. Who really cares whether it's possible that Tinky

Winky is gay—or a Marxist, for that matter. Not me.

Thinking about my Smurf investigation now, I think the real topic was neither *The Smurfs* nor the Marxists, but what I found out about the Internet itself. First, for anybody with access to a computer, the Internet is the greatest medium ever devised for the unlimited practice of free speech. Second, the Internet is also the greatest repository of both fact and fiction ever devised—but there's nobody to tell you for sure which is which, sometimes not even the author! This idea clearly needs further investigation and elaboration, but to tell the truth, I don't have the time. I'll leave that topic, along with the Teletubbies, for my next paper.

* * *

Works Cited

Gozer. *The Smurfs* as a Paradigm for Communist Society. 27 Sep. 1997. 7 Oct.

  2001 http://www.ac.wwu.edu/~n9620080/smurf.html.

Lott, Eric. Personal e-mail. 4 Dec. 2001.

Papa Smurf Is a Communist. 16 Mar. 1997. 8 Oct. 2001 http://geocities.com/

CapitolHill/Lobby/1709.

Reed, David. "Falwell's Newspaper Attempts to Label Teletubbies Character as

Gay." 10 Feb. 1999. 9 Nov. 2001 http://www.sfgate.com/cgibin/article.cgi?

file=/news/archive/1999/02/10/national0333EST0476.DTL.

Schmidt, J. Marc. Sociopolitical Themes in the Smurfs. 7 Oct. 1998. 8 Oct. 2001

http://www.geocities.com/Hollywood/Cinema/3117/sociosmurf2.htm.

---. Personal e-mail. 3 Dec. 2001.

The Smurfs Official Site. 2005. 7 Oct. 2001 http://www.smurf.com/

homepage.html.

Teletubbies. PBS Kids. 2005. 8 Nov. 2001 http://pbskids.org/teletubbies.html.

SUGGESTIONS FOR WRITING AND RESEARCH

INDIVIDUAL

1. Write a paper explaining any thing, process, or concept. Use as a starting point an idea you discovered in Writing 2. When you have finished one draft of this essay, look back and see whether there are places where your explanation could be improved through use of one of the explanatory strategies explained in this chapter.

2. Select a writer of your choice, fiction or nonfiction, who explains things especially well. Read or reread a passage of explanatory writing in his or her work and write an essay in which you analyze and explain the effectiveness of the explanation you find there.

COLLABORATIVE

Form writing groups based on mutual interests; agree as a group to explain the same thing, process, or concept. Write your explanations separately and then share drafts, comparing and contrasting your different ways of explaining. For a final draft, either (1) rewrite your individual drafts, borrowing good ideas from others in your group, or (2) compose a collaborative single paper with contributions from each group member.

WRITING ACROSS THE CURRICULUM

Guidelines for Writing to Explain

The following guidelines for writing clear explanations should be helpful in principle for most writers writing to unknown audiences:

1. Organize in a pattern that's logical and easy to follow: cause should come before effect while inference should follow after facts, and so on.
2. Prefer simple sentences to complicated constructions, but selected compound and complex sentences, by varying the pattern, will add to readability and decrease boredom.
3. Write to the point, eliminate unnecessary words, and avoid digressions unless you have a good reason for doing so.
4. Prefer common language to technical jargon, short words to long ones.

However, each of these points may need modifying if the writer fully understands the needs of the audience. For example, an audience familiar with the technology you are describing will want you to use technical jargon to save time and be more efficient. Likewise, expert readers in academic disciplines such as history and philosophy may view longer sentences and complicated constructions as positive evidence of familiarity with disciplinary knowledge. In sum, writing to explain clearly depends on both your skills as a writer and your knowledge of the audience to whom you are writing.

As an exercise, list the names of three instructors for courses you are now taking in three different disciplines, and closely examine the syllabus for each course. What does the syllabus tell you about the type of language expected in each discipline? To be more specific, match the way each syllabus is written with the four points of clarity above. Does the syllabus match each point? Where does it depart? What do you think are the reasons for those departures? How easy or difficult for you are the lectures and readings in this course? In your opinion, is the syllabus language a fair predictor of the ease or difficulty of the course?

chapter 10

Arguing and Persuading

Argument is deeply rooted in the American political and social system, in which free and open debate is the essence of the democratic process. Argument is also at the heart of the academic process, in which scholars investigate scientific, social, and cultural issues, hoping through the give-and-take of debate to find reasonable answers to complex questions. Argument in the academic world, however, is less likely to be about winning or losing—as it is in political and legal systems—than about changing minds or altering perceptions about knowledge and ideas.

Argument as rational disagreement, rather than as quarrels and contests, most often occurs in areas of genuine uncertainty about what is right, best, or most reasonable. In disciplines such as English, history, and philosophy, written argument commonly takes the form of interpretation, in which the meaning of an idea or text is disputed. In disciplines such as political science, engineering, and business, arguments commonly appear as position papers in which a problem is examined and a solution proposed.

The purpose of writing argument papers is to persuade other people to agree with a particular point of view. Arguments focus on issues about which there is some debate; if there's no debate, there's no argument. College assignments commonly ask you to argue one side of an issue and defend your argument against attacks from skeptics.

10 a   Elements of argument

In a basic position paper assignment, you are asked to choose an issue, argue a position, and support it with evidence. Sometimes your investigation of the issue will lead you beyond polar positions toward compromise—a common result of real argument and debate in both the academic and political worlds. In other words, such a paper may reveal that the result of supporting one position (**thesis**) against another (**antithesis**) is to arrive at yet a third position (**synthesis**), which is possible now because both sides have been fully explored and a reasonable compromise presents itself.

This chapter explains the elements that constitute a basic position paper: an arguable issue, a claim and counterclaim, a thesis, and evidence.

1 Issues

An issue is a controversy, something that can be argued about. For instance, mountain bikes and cultural diversity are things or concepts, not in themselves issues. However, they become the foundation for issues when questions are raised about them and controversy ensues.

ISSUE   Do American colleges adequately represent the cultural diversity of the United States?

ISSUE   Should mountain bikes be allowed on wilderness hiking trails?

These questions are issues because reasonable people could answer them in different ways; they can be argued about because more than one answer is plausible, possible, or realistic.

Virtually all issues can be formulated, at least initially, as yes/no questions about which you will take one position or the other: pro (if the answer is yes) or con (if the answer is no).

ISSUE   Should mountain bikes be allowed on trails in Riverside Park?

PRO   Yes, they should be allowed to share pedestrian trails.

CON   No, they should not be allowed to share trails with pedestrians.

2 Claims and counterclaims

A **claim** is a statement or assertion that something is true or should be done. In arguing one side of an issue, you make one or more claims in the hope of convincing an audience to believe you. For example, you could make a claim that calls into question the educational experience at Northville College:

CLAIM   Northville College fails to provide good education because the faculty is not culturally diverse.

Counterclaims are statements that oppose or refute claims. You need to examine an opponent's counterclaim carefully in order to refute it or, if you agree with the counterclaim, to argue that your claim is more important to making a decision. For example, the following counterclaim might be offered against your claim about the quality of Northville College education:

COUNTERCLAIM   The Northville faculty are good scholars and teachers; therefore, their cultural backgrounds are irrelevant.

You might agree that "Northville faculty *are* good scholars and teachers" but still argue that the education is not as good as it would be with more diversity. In other words, the best arguments provide not only good reasons for accepting a position but also good reasons for doubting the opposition. They are made by writers who know both sides of an issue and are prepared for the arguments of the opposition.

3 Thesis

In an argument, the major claim your paper makes is your **thesis:**

THESIS   Northville College should enact a policy to make the faculty more culturally diverse by the year 2010.

In taking a position, you may make other claims as well, but they should all work to support this major claim or thesis:

CLAIM   The faculty is not culturally diverse now.

CLAIM   A culturally diverse faculty is necessary to provide a good education for today's students.

CLAIM   The goal of increased cultural diversity by the year 2010 is achievable and practical.

In arguing a position, you may state your thesis up front, with the remainder of the paper supporting it (*thesis first*), or you may state it later in the paper after weighing the pros and cons with your reader (*delayed thesis*). As a writer, you can decide which approach is the stronger rhetorical strategy after you fully examine each claim and the supporting evidence. Each strategy, thesis first or delayed, has its advantages and disadvantages (see 10f).

4 Evidence

Evidence makes a claim believable. **Evidence** consists of facts, examples, or testimony that supports a claim. For example, to support a claim that Northville College's faculty lacks cultural diversity, you might introduce the following evidence:

EVIDENCE   According to the names in the college catalog, 69 of 79 faculty members are male.

EVIDENCE   According to a recent faculty survey, 75 of 79 faculty members are Caucasian or white.

EVIDENCE   According to Carmen Lopez, an unsuccessful candidate for a position in the English department, 100 percent of the faculty hired in the last ten years have been white males.

Most arguments become more effective when they include documentable source material; however, shorter and more modest argument papers can be written without research and can profitably follow a process similar to that described here.

WRITING 1: EXPLORATION

An issue debated by college faculty is whether or not a first-year writing course should be required of all college students. Make three claims and three counterclaims about this issue. Then select the claim you most believe in and write an argument thesis that could form the basis for a whole essay.

ESL Consider similarities and differences in how arguments are developed in English and in your native language. Do arguments in your native language use claims and counterclaims?

10 b   Issue

You'll write better and have a more interesting time if you select an issue that interests you and about which you still have real questions. A good issue around which to write a position paper will meet the following criteria:

- It is a real issue about which there is controversy and uncertainty.

- It has at least two distinct and arguable positions.

- Resources are available to support both sides.

- It is manageable within the time and scope of the assignment.

In selecting an issue to research and write about, consider both national and local issues. You are likely to see national issues explained and argued in the media:

Are SAT scores a fair measure of academic potential?

Should handgun ownership be outlawed in the United States?

Does acid rain kill forests?

The advantages of national issues include their extensive coverage by television and radio, national newspapers such as the *New York Times* and *Washington Post,* and national newsmagazines. The broad coverage of national news is likely to provide evidence and supporting claims from many sources. In addition, you can count on your audience's having some familiarity with the subject. The disadvantage is that it may be difficult to find local experts or a site where some dimension of the issue can be witnessed.

Local issues derive from the community in which you live. You will find these issues argued about in local newspapers and on local news broadcasts:

Should a new mall be built on the beltway?

Should mountain bikes be allowed in Riverside Park?

Should Northville College require a one-semester course introducing students to diverse American cultures?

The advantage of local issues is that you can often visit a place where the controversy occurs, interview people who are affected by it, and find generous coverage in local news media. The disadvantage is that the subject won't be covered in the national news. Evidence and claims in support of your thesis may be more limited.

Perhaps the best issue is a national issue (hikers versus mountain bikers) with a strong local dimension (this controversy in a local park). Such an issue will enable you to find both national press coverage and local experts (see 10g).

....

Make a list of three national and three local issues about which you are concerned. Next, select the three issues that seem most important to you and write each as a question with a yes or no answer. Finally, note whether each issue meets the criteria for a good position paper topic.

....

10 c Analysis

The most demanding work in writing a position paper takes place *after* you have selected an issue but *before* you actually write the paper. To analyze an issue, you need to conduct enough research to explain it and identify the arguments of each side.

In this data-collecting stage, treat each side fairly, framing the opposition as positively as you frame the position. Research as if you are in an honest debate with yourself. Doing so may even cause you to switch sides—one of the best indications of open-minded research. Furthermore, empathy for the opposition leads to making qualified assertions and heads off overly simplistic right versus wrong arguments. Undecided readers who see merit in the opposing side respect writers who acknowledge an issue's complexity.

1 Context

Provide full context for the issue you are writing about, as if readers know virtually nothing about it. Providing **context** means answering these questions: What is this issue about? Where did the controversy begin? How long has it been debated? Who are the people involved? What is at stake? Use a neutral tone, as Issa does in the essay on pages 153–161 in discussing the mountain bike trail controversy:

> With all these new riders, there is a need for places to ride,
> and this is where the wilderness trail controversy begins. The
> mountain bike is designed to be ridden on dirt trails, logging
> roads, and fire trails in backwoods country. However, other trail
> users who have been around much longer than mountain
> bikers prefer to enjoy the woods at a slow, leisurely pace. They

find the rapid and sometimes noisy two-wheel intruders
unacceptable. . . .

2 Claims for (pro)

List the claims supporting the pro side of the issue. Make each claim
a distinctly strong and separate point, and make the best possible case for
this position, identifying by name the most important people or organizations that hold this view. Issa makes the following claims for opening up
wilderness trails to mountain bikes:

1. All people should have the right to explore the wilderness so long as they do
    not damage it.

2. Knobby mountain bike tires do no more damage to hiking trails than Vibram-
    soled hiking boots.

3. Most mountain bike riders are respectful of the wilderness and courteous to
    other trail users.

3 Claims against (con)

List the claims supporting the con side of the issue—the counterclaims.
It is not important to have an equal number of reasons for and against, but
you do want an approximate balance.

1. Mountain bike riders ride fast, are sometimes reckless, and pose a threat to
    slower moving hikers.

2. Mountain bike tires damage trails and cause erosion.

4 Annotated references

Make an alphabetical list on note cards or computer files of the references you consulted during research, briefly identifying each according to
the kind of information it contains. The same article may present claims
from both sides as well as provide context. Following are two of Issa's annotated references:

Buchanan, Rob. "Birth of the Gearhead Nation." *Rolling Stone* 9 July 1992: 80-85.

   Marin Co. CA movement advocates more trails open to mountain bike use.

   Includes history. (pro)

Schwartz, David M. "Over Hill, Over Dale on a Bicycle Built for . . . Goo."

    Smithsonian June 1992: 74-84. Discusses the hiker vs. biker issue,

    promotes peaceful coexistence; includes history. (pro/con)

Annotating your list of references allows you to check and rearrange your claims at any time during the writing process. In addition, if you write and organize your references now, your reference page will be ready to go when you've finished writing your paper.

WRITING 3: APPLICATION

Select one of the issues you are interested in, establish the necessary context, and make pro and con lists similar to those described in this section, including supporters of each position. Make the best possible case for each position.

10 d Position

Once you have examined the two positions fairly, weigh which side is the stronger. Select the position that you find more convincing and then write out the reasons that support this position, most compelling reasons last. This will be the position you will most likely defend; you need to state it as a thesis.

Start with a thesis

Formulate your initial position as working thesis early in your paper-writing process. Even though it is merely something to start with, not necessarily to stick with, it serves to focus your initial efforts in one direction and it helps you articulate claims and assemble evidence to support it.

WORKING THESIS   Hikers and mountain bikers should cooperate and support each other in using, preserving, and maintaining wilderness trails.

Writers often revise their initial positions as they reshape their paper or find new evidence. Your working thesis should meet the following criteria:

- It can be managed within your confines of time and space.

- It asserts something specific.

- It proposes a plan of action.

WRITING 4: APPLICATION

Take a position on the issue you have identified. Formulate a working thesis that you would like to support. Test your thesis against the criteria listed for good theses.

10 e Argument

Your argument is the case you will make for your position, the means by which you will try to persuade your readers that your position is correct. Good arguments need solid and credible evidence and clear and logical reasoning.

1 Assembling evidence

A claim is meaningless without evidence to support it. Facts, examples, inferences, informed opinion, and personal experience all provide believable evidence.

Facts and examples

Facts are verifiable and agreed upon by everyone involved regardless of personal beliefs or values. Facts are often statistical and recorded in some place where anybody can look them up:

Water boils at 212 degrees Fahrenheit.

Northville College employed 79 full-time faculty and enrolled 1143 full-time students in 1999.

Five hundred Japanese-made "Stumpjumper" mountain bikes were sold in the United States in 1981.

Examples can be used to illustrate a claim or clarify an issue. If you claim that many wilderness trails have been closed to mountain biking, you can mention examples you know about:

The New Jersey trails at South Mountain, Eagle Rock, and Mills Park have all been closed to mountain bikes.

Facts and examples can, of course, be misleading and even wrong. For hundreds of years malaria was believed to be caused by "bad air" rather than, as we know today, by a parasite transmitted through mosquito bites; however, for the people who believed the bad-air theory, it was fact.

Inferences

The accumulation of a certain number of facts and examples should lead to an interpretation of what those facts mean—an *inference* or a **generalization.** For example, if you attend five different classes at Northville College and in each class you find no minority students, you may infer that there are no minority students on campus. However, while your inference is reasonable, it is not a fact, since your experience does not allow for your meeting all the students at the college.

Facts are not necessarily better or more important than inferences; they serve different purposes. Facts provide information, and inferences give that information meaning.

Sometimes inference is all that's available. For example, statistics describing what "Americans" believe or do are only inferences about these groups based on information collected from a relatively small number of individuals. To be credible, however, inferences must be reasonable and based on factual evidence.

Expert opinion

Expert opinion makes powerful evidence. A forest ranger's testimony about trail damage caused by mountain bikes or lug-soled hiking boots reflects the training and experience of an expert. A casual hiker making the same observation is less believable. To use expert opinion in writing arguments, be sure to cite the credentials or training that makes this person's testimony "expert."

Personal testimony

A useful kind of evidence is testimony based on personal experience. When someone has experienced something firsthand, his or her knowledge cannot easily be discounted. If you have been present at the mistreatment of a minority student whether as the object or an observer of the incident, your eyewitness testimony will carry weight, even though you are not a certified expert of any kind. To use personal testimony effectively, provide details that confirm for readers that you were there and know what you are talking about.

2 Reasoning effectively

To build an effective argument, consider the audience you must persuade. If you were writing about the mountain bike controversy and taking a pro-biker position, for example, you would ask yourself these questions:

■ Who will read this paper?

Members of an environmentally conscious hiking club? members of a mountain bike club? your instructor?

■ Where do I think my readers stand on the issue?

Hikers are often opposed to mountain bikes, and mountain bikers are not, but you would need more information to predict your instructor's position.

■ How are their personal interests involved?

Hikers want the trails quiet and peaceful; bikers want to ride in the wilderness, and your instructor may or may not care.

■ What evidence would they consider convincing?

A hiker would need to see convincing examples of trails not being damaged by mountain bike use; bikers would accept anecdotal testimony of good intentions, and you're still not sure about your instructor.

The more you know about the audience you're trying to sway, the easier it will be to present your case. If your audience is your instructor, you'll need to make inferences about his or her beliefs based on syllabus language, class discussion, assigned readings, or personal habits. For example, if your instructor rides a mountain bike to work, you may begin to infer one thing; if he or she assigns Sierra Club readings in the course, you infer something else; and if the instructor rides a mountain bike *and* reads Sierra Club publications, well, you've got more homework ahead. Remember that inferences based on a single piece of evidence are often wrong; find out more before you make simple assumptions about your audience. And sometimes audience analysis doesn't work very well when an instructor, in an effort to help you learn to develop a persuasive position paper, assumes a deliberately skeptical role, no matter which side of an issue you support. It's best to assume you will have a critical reader and to use the best logic and evidence available. Following are some ways to marshal careful and substantial evidence.

First, establish your credibility. Demonstrate to your audience that you are fair and can be trusted. Do this by writing in neutral, not obviously biased, language—avoid name-calling. Also do this by citing current sources by respected experts—and don't quote them out of context. Do this also by identifying elements that serve as common ground between you and the audience—be up front and admit when the opposite side makes a good point.

CREDIBLE   Northville College offers excellent instruction in many areas; however, its offerings in multicultural education would be enhanced by a more diverse faculty.

LESS CREDIBLE   Education at Northville College sucks.

Second, use logic. Demonstrate that you understand the principles of reasoning that operate in the academic world: Make each claim clearly and carefully. Make sure you have substantial, credible evidence to support each claim. Make inferences from your evidence with care; don't exaggerate or argue positions that are not supported by the evidence. Use **logic** to infer reasonable relationships between pieces of evidence.

LOGICAL   Because 75 of 79 faculty members are white and 69 of 79 are male, hiring more blacks, Hispanics, Native Americans, and women, when they are available, would increase the cultural diversity of the faculty.

ILLOGICAL   Because most of the Northville faculty are white men, they must be racists and should be sent to another country.

Third, avoid false arguments. For more than two thousand years, since the time of the ancient Greeks and Romans, the principles of false logic have been recognized by careful debaters and audiences alike. Study these logical **fallacies** (see the WAC box "False Arguments (Fallacies)" at the end of the chapter). Avoid using them in making your arguments, and also recognize when others try to use them on you. Although false arguments do not necessarily lead to false conclusions, they weaken the writer's credibility with readers who recognize the faulty logic. The illogical argument above contains three fallacies. It "begs the question" (it has not been established that the whole faculty is racist); it "does not follow" that racists should be sent to another country; and it "oversimplifies" by proposing a simplistic solution to a complex problem.

Fourth, appeal to your audience's emotions. It's fair to use means of persuasion other than logic to win arguments. Write with vivid details, concrete language, and compelling examples to show your audience a situation that needs addressing. It is often helpful, as well, to adopt a personal tone and write in friendly language to reach readers' hearts as well as minds

EMOTIONAL
APPEAL

When Bridgett Jones, the only black student in Philosophy 1, sits down, the desks on either side of her remain empty. When her classmates choose partners for debate, Bridgett is always the last one chosen.

WRITING 5: APPLICATION

Develop an informal profile of the audience for your position paper by answering the questions posed in this section. Make a list of the kinds of evidence most likely to persuade this audience.

10 f   Organization

To organize your paper, you need to know your position on the issue: what is the main point of your argument? In other words, move from a *working thesis* to a *final thesis:* confirm the working thesis that's been guiding your research so far, or modify it, or scrap it altogether and assert a different one. You should be able to articulate this thesis in a single sentence as the answer to the yes/no question you've been investigating. (See 10d.)

THESIS

Wilderness trails should be open to both mountain bikers and hikers.

THESIS

Wilderness trails should be closed to mountain bikes.

Your next decision is where in this paper you should reveal your thesis to the reader—in your opening or strategically delayed until later?

1 Thesis-first organization

Leading with a thesis, the most common form of academic argument, tells readers from the beginning where you stand on the issue. One good way to organize a thesis-first argument is to make the remainder of the essay defend your claim against counterclaims, support your thesis with evidence, and close with a restatement of your position. In this organization, your thesis occupies both the first and last position in the essay, making it easy for your readers to remember.

1. **Introduce and explain the issue.** Make sure there are at least two debatable sides. Pose the question that you see arising from this issue; if you can frame it as a yes/no, for/against construction, both you and your reader will have the advantage throughout your answer of knowing where you stand.

   > Minority students, supported by many majority students at Northville College, have staged a week-long sit-in to urge the hiring of more minority faculty across the curriculum. Is this a reasonable position? Should Northville hire more minority faculty members?

Limiting Generalizations

When you make general claims, you should carefully limit your statements so that the generalizations are accurate and believable. Claims that are too broad may cause your readers to doubt the strength of your argument. Use these techniques to limit your general claims:

- Use adverbs such as *often, usually, seldom,* or *frequently* if something is not always true.

  > Due to the recent budget cuts, students *often* cannot enroll in the courses they need for graduation.

- Add *many, most,* or *a majority of* to limit the subject's range.

  > Because of the recent budget cuts, *many* students cannot enroll in the courses they need for graduation.

- Use *may, might,* or *could* if you are not certain of a claim about the future.

  > Raising tuition ~~will~~ *may* deprive some students of a college education.

- Add an expression of probability (*it is possible/probable/likely that* ...) before the general claim to show that you cannot be absolutely sure of the result.

  > *It is very likely that raising* ~~Raising~~ tuition will prevent some students from getting a college education.

2. **Assert your thesis.** Your thesis states the answer to the question you have posed and establishes the position from which you will argue. Think of your thesis as the major claim the paper will make.

> Northville College should enact a policy to make the faculty more culturally diverse as soon as reasonably possible.

Writers commonly state their thesis early in the paper, at the conclusion of the paragraph that introduces the issue.

3. **Summarize the counterclaims.** Before elaborating on your own claims, explain the opposition's counterclaims. Doing that gives your own argument something to focus on—and refute— throughout the rest of the paper. Squeezing the counterclaims between the thesis (2) and the evidence (5) reserves the strongest places—the opening and closing—for your position.

COUNTERCLAIM 1 Northville College is located in a white middle-class community, so its faculty should be white and middle-class also.

COUNTERCLAIM 2 The Northville faculty are good scholars and teachers; therefore, their race is irrelevant.

4. **Refute the counterclaims.** Look for weak spots in the opposition's argument, and point them out. Use your opponent's language to show you have read closely but still find problems with the claim. To refute counterclaim 1, you could make a statement like this:

> If the community in which the college is located is "white middle-class," all the more reason to offer that diversity in the college.

Your refutation is often stronger when you acknowledge the truth of some of the opposition's claims (demonstrating your fairness) but point out the limitations as well. To refute counterclaim 2, you could say this:

> It's true that Northville College offers excellent instruction in many areas; however, its instruction in multicultural education would be enhanced by a more diverse faculty.

5. **Support your claims with evidence.** Spell out your own claims clearly and precisely, enumerating them or being sure to give each its own full-paragraph explanation, and citing supporting evidence. This section will constitute the longest and most carefully documented part of your essay. The following evidence supports the thesis that Northville needs more cultural diversity:

> According to the names in the college catalog, 69 of 79 faculty members are male.

According to a recent faculty survey, 75 of 79 faculty members are white.

According to Carmen Lopez, an unsuccessful job candidate for a position in the English department, all faculty hired in the last ten years have been white males.

6. **Restate your position as a conclusion.** Near the end of your paper, synthesize your accumulated evidence into a broad general position, and restate your original thesis in slightly different language.

    While Northville College offers a strong liberal arts education, the addition of more culturally diverse faculty members would make it even stronger.

2 Delayed-thesis organization

Using the delayed-thesis type of organization, you introduce the issue and discuss the arguments for and against, but you do not obviously take a side until late in the essay. In this way, you draw readers into your struggle to weigh the evidence, and you arouse their curiosity about your position. Near the end of the paper, you explain that after carefully considering both pros and cons, you have now arrived at the most reasonable position. Concluding with your own position gives it more emphasis. The following delayed-thesis argument is derived from the sample student essay at the end of this chapter.

1. **Introduce the issue and pose a question.** Both thesis-first and delayed-thesis papers begin by establishing context and posing a question. Following is the question for the mountain bike position paper:

    Should mountain bikes be allowed on wilderness trails?

2. **Summarize the claims for one position.** Before stating which side you support, explain how the opposition views the issue:

    To traditional trail users, the new breed of bicycle [is] alien and dangerous, esthetically offensive, and physically menacing.

3. **Refute these claims.** Still not stating your own position, point out your difficulties with believing this side:

    Whether a bicycle—or a car or horse for that matter—is "alien and . . . esthetically offensive" depends on your personal taste, judgment, and familiarity. And whether it is "dangerous" depends on how you use it.

In addition, you can actually strengthen your position by admitting that in some cases the counterclaims might be true:

> While it's true that some mountain bikers—like some hikers—are too loud, mountain biking at its best respects the environment and promotes peace and conservation, not noise and destruction.

4. **Summarize the counterclaims.** You are supporting these claims and so they should occupy the most emphatic position in your essay, last:

> Most mountain bikers respect the wilderness and should be allowed to use wilderness trails.

5. **Support your counterclaims.** Now give your best evidence; this should be the longest and most carefully documented part of the paper:

> Studies show that bicycle tires cause no more erosion or trail damage than the boots of hikers and far less than horses' hooves.

6. **State your thesis as your conclusion.** Your rhetorical strategy is this: after giving each side a fair hearing, you have arrived at the most reasonable conclusion:

> It's clear that mountain bikers don't want to destroy trails any more than hikers do. The surest way to preserve America's wilderness areas is to establish strong cooperative bonds among the hikers and bikers, as well as those who fish, hunt, camp, canoe, and bird-watch, and encourage all to maintain the trails and respect the environment.

WRITING 6: APPLICATION

Make two outlines for organizing your position paper, one with the thesis first, the other with a delayed thesis. Share your outlines with your classmates and discuss which seems more appropriate for the issue you have chosen.

10 g Sample student essay

In the following paper, Issa explores whether or not mountain bikers should be allowed to share wilderness trails with hikers. In the first part of the paper he establishes the context and background of the conflict; then he introduces the question his paper will address: "Is any resolution in sight?" Note his substantial use of sources, including the Internet and interviews, cited in the MLA documentation style (see Chapter 30). Issa selects a delayed-thesis strategy, which allows him to air both sides of the argument fully before revealing his solution, a compromise position: so long as mountain bikers follow environmentally sound guidelines, they should be allowed to use the trails. Finally, note the use of selected photos to illustrate the essay. While photos are not essential to Issa's argument, the visual information adds depth, increases credibility, makes the paper more attractive to read, and suggests a serious commitment to the assignment on the part of the student.

On the Trail: Can the Hikers Share with the Bikers?

Issa Sawabini

The narrow, hard-packed dirt trail winding up the mountain under the spreading oaks and maples doesn't look like the source of a major environmental conflict, but it is. On the one side are hikers, environmentalists, and horseback riders who have traditionally used these wilderness trails. On the other side, looking back, are the mountain bike riders, who want to use them too. But the hikers don't want the bikers, so trouble is brewing.

The debate over mountain bike use has gained momentum recently because of the increased popularity of this form of bicycling. Technology has made it easier for everyone to ride these go-anywhere bikes. These high-tech wonders incorporate exotic components including quick gear-shifting derailleurs, good brakes, and a more comfortable upright seating position—and they can cost up to $2,000 each (Kelly 104). Mountain bikes have turned what were once grueling hill climbs into casual trips, and more people are taking notice.

Mountain bikes have taken over the bicycle industry, and with more bikes come more people wanting to ride in the mountains. The first mass-produced

mountain bikes date to 1981, when 500 Japanese "Stumpjumpers" were sold; by 1983 annual sales reached 200,000; today the figure is 8.5 million. In fact, mountain biking is second only to in-line skating as the fastest-growing sport in the nation: "For a sport to go from zero to warp speed so quickly is unprecedented," says Brian Stickel, director of competition for the National Off Road Bicycle Association (Schwartz 75).

With all these new riders, there is a need for places to ride, and this is where the wilderness trail controversy begins. The mountain bike is designed to be ridden on dirt trails, logging roads, and fire trails in backwoods country. However, other trail users who have been around much longer than mountain bikers prefer to enjoy the woods at a slow, leisurely pace. They find the rapid and sometimes noisy two-wheel intruders unacceptable: "To traditional trail users, the new breed of bicycle [is] alien and dangerous, esthetically offensive and physically menacing" (Schwartz 74).

"The problem arises when people want to use an area of public land for their own personal purpose," says Carl Newton, forestry professor at the University of Vermont. "Eventually, after everyone has taken their small bit of the area, the results can be devastating. People believe that because they pay taxes for the land, they can use it as they please. This makes sense to the individual, but not to the whole community." Newton is both a hiker and a mountain biker.

When mountain bikes first came on the scene, hikers and environmentalists convinced state and local officials to ban the bikes from wilderness trails (Buchanan 81; Kelly 104). The result was the closing of many trails to mountain bike use: "Many state park systems have banned bicycles from narrow trails. National Parks prohibit them, in most cases, from leaving the pavement" (Schwartz 81). These trail closings have separated the outdoor community into the hikers and the bikers. Each group is well organized, and each group believes it is right. Is any resolution in sight?

The hikers and other passive trail users have a number of organizations, from conservation groups to public park planning committees, who argue against allowing mountain bikes onto narrow trails traditionally traveled only by foot and horse in the past. They believe that the wide, deeply treaded tires of the mountain bikes cause erosion and that the high speeds of the bikers startle and upset both hikers and horses (Hanley; Schwartz 76).

The arrival of mountain bikes during the 1980s was resisted by established hiker groups, such as the Sierra Club, which won debate after debate in favor of closing wilderness trails to mountain bike activities. The younger and less well organized biking groups proposed compromise, offering to help repair and maintain trails in return for riding rights, but their offers were ignored. "Peace was not given a chance. Foes of the bicycle onslaught, older and better connected, won most of the battles, and signs picturing a bicycle crossed with a red slash began to appear on trailheads all over the country" (Schwartz 74).

In Millburn, New Jersey, trails at South Mountain, Eagle Rock, and Mills Park have all been closed. Anyone caught riding a bike on the trails can be arrested and fined up to $100. Local riders offered an amendment calling for trails to be open Thursday through Sunday, with the riders helping maintain the trails on the other days. The amendment was rejected. According to hiker Donald Meserlain, the bikes "ruin the tranquillity of the woodlands and drive out hikers, bird watchers, and strollers. It's like weeds taking over the grass. Pretty soon we'll have all weeds" (Hanley).

Many areas in western New York, such as Hunter's Creek, have also been closed to mountain bike use. Anti-biking signs posted on trails frequently used by bicyclists caused a loud public debate as bike riding was again blamed for trail erosion.

Until more public lands are opened to trail riding, mountain bikers must pay fees to ride on private land, a situation beneficial to ski resorts in the off season: "Ski areas are happy to open trails to cyclists for a little summer and fall income" (Sneyd). For example, in Vermont, bike trails can be found at the Catamount Family Center in Williston, Vermont, as well as at Mount Snow, Killington, Stratton, and Bolton Valley. At major resorts, such as Mount Snow and Killington, ski lifts have actually been modified to the top of the mountains, and each offers a full-service bike shop at its base.

However, the real solution to the conflict between hikers and bikers is education, not separation. In response to the bad publicity and many trail closings, mountain bikers have banded together at local and national levels to educate both their own member bike riders and the non-riding public about the potential alliance between these two groups (Buchanan 81).

The largest group, the International Mountain Bike Association (IMBA), sponsors supervised rides and trail conservation classes and stresses that mountain bikers are friends, not enemies, of the natural environment. "The IMBA wants to change the attitude of both the young gonzo rider bombing downhill on knobby tires and the mature outdoorsman bristling at the thought of tire tracks where boot soles alone did tread" (Schwartz 76). IMBA published guidelines it hopes all mountain bikers will learn to follow:

1. Ride on open trails only.

2. Leave no trace.

3. Control your bicycle.

4. Always yield trail.

5. Never spook animals.

6. Plan ahead. (JTYL)

The New England Mountain Bike Association (NEMBA), one of the largest East Coast organizations, publishes a home page on the Internet outlining goals: "NEMBA is a not-for-profit organization dedicated to promoting land access, maintaining trails that are open to mountain bicyclists, and educating riders to use those trails sensitively and responsibly. We are also devoted to having fun" (Koellner).

At the local level, the Western New York Mountain Bike Association (WNYMBA) educates members on proper trail maintenance and urges its members to cooperate with local environmentalists whenever possible. For instance, when angry cyclists continued to use the closed trail at Hunter's Creek, New York, WNYMBA used the Internet (see insert) to warn cyclists against continued trail use: "As WNYMBA wishes to cooperate with Erie County Parks Department to the greatest extent possible on the use of trails in open parks, WNYMBA cannot recommend ignoring posted signs. The first IMBA rule of trail is 'ride on open trails only'" (JTYL). As of the summer of 2005, Hunter's Creek remains closed to mountain bike use, and all serious mountain bikers in the western New York region respect this.

Trails Menu

Show trails for: [All counties ‡]
[Go]

```
open   Allegany State Park
open   Allegheny National Forest
open   Golden Hill
open   Hunters Creek
open   Letchworth
open   McCarty Hill/Rock City SF
```

Educated mountain biking, like hiking and horseback riding, respects the environment and promotes peace and conservation, not noise and destruction. Making this case has begun to pay off, and the battle over who walks and who rides the trails should now shift in favor of peaceful coexistence. "Buoyed by studies showing that bicycle tires cause no more erosion or trail damage than the boots of hikers, and far less than horses' hooves, mountain bike advocates are starting to find receptive ears among environmental organizations" (Schwartz 78).

Even in the Millburn, New Jersey, area, bikers have begun to win some battles, as new trails have recently been funded specifically for mountain bike use: "After all," according to an unnamed legislator, "the bikers or their parents are taxpayers" (Hanley).

The Wilderness Club now officially supports limited use of mountain bikes, while the Sierra Club also supports careful use of trails by riders so long as no damage to the land results and riders ride responsibly on the path. "In pursuit of happy trails, bicycling organizations around the country are bending backward

over their chain stays to dispel the hell-on-wheels view of them" (Schwartz 83).

Education and compromise are the sensible solutions to the hiker/biker

standoff. Increased public awareness as well as increasingly responsible riding will

open still more wilderness trails to bikers in the future. It's clear that mountain

bikers don't want to destroy trails any more than hikers do. The surest way to

preserve America's wilderness areas is to establish strong cooperative bonds

among the hikers and bikers, as well as those who fish, hunt, camp, canoe, and

bird-watch, and to encourage all to maintain the trails and respect the environment.

★ ★ ★

Works Cited

Buchanan, Rob. "Birth of the Gearhead Nation." *Rolling Stone* 9 July 1992: 80-85.

Hanley, Robert. "Essex County Mountain Bike Troubles." *New York Times* 30

May 1995: B4.

JTYL (ed.). Western New York Mountain Bike Association Home Page. Western

New York Mountain Bike Association. 4 Oct. 1995 http://128.205.166.43/

public/wnymba/wnymba.html.

Kelly, Charles. "Evolution of an Issue." *Bicycling* May 1990: 104-105.

Koellner, Ken (ed.). New England Mountain Bike Association Home Page. 19 Aug.

1995. New England Mountain Bike Association. 30 Sep. 1995

http://www.ultranet.com/~kvk/nemba.html.

Newton, Carlton. Personal interview. 13 Nov. 1995.

Schwartz, David M. "Over Hill, Over Dale on a Bicycle Built for . . . Goo."

Smithsonian June 1992: 74-84.

Sneyd, Ross. "Mount Snow Teaching Mountain Biking." *Burlington Free Press* 4

Oct. 1992: E1.

Western New York Mountain Bike Association (WNYMBA) Home Page. 1 May

2005. WNYMBA, 9 July 2005. www.wnymba.org

SUGGESTIONS FOR WRITING AND RESEARCH

INDIVIDUAL

1.   Write a position paper on the issue you have been working with in Writings 2–6. Follow the guidelines suggested in this chapter, using as much research as you deem appropriate.

2.   Write a position paper on an issue of interest to your class. Consider topics such as (1) student voice in writing topics, (2) the seating plan, (3) the value of writing groups versus instructor conferences, or (4) the number of writing assignments.

COLLABORATIVE

1.   In teams of two or three, select an issue. Divide up the work so that each group member contributes some work to (1) the context, (2) the pro argument, and (3) the con argument (to guarantee that you do not take sides prematurely). Share your analysis of the issue with another group and receive feedback. Finally, write your position papers individually.

2.   Follow the procedure for the first collaborative assignment, but write your final position paper collaboratively.

WRITING ACROSS THE CURRICULUM

False Arguments (Fallacies)

The following arguments are recognized as false across the college curriculum. People make such arguments when they do not have enough evidence to support their claims, often not knowing that they are fallacious. Learn to recognize faulty logic and avoid it.

Ad hominem (to the person). Attempts to refute a statement by attacking a supporter rather than the logic of the argument.

Professor Jones is a bigot, so of course he thinks current policies are not biased.

Calling Professor Jones a bigot is an attempt to dismiss his argument without addressing its merits.

False authority. Suggests that the opinion of a particular person, often a celebrity, is authoritative, regardless of his or her expertise.

My roommate has lived in this town for fifteen years, and she says the college has favored white men in its hiring for as long as she can remember.

The writer's roommate is not in a position to know why the majority of faculty members are white men. There may be reasons other than a biased hiring policy.

Bandwagon. Encourages people to accept a position simply because others already have.

More than three-fourths of American colleges have required courses on cultural diversity; so should Northville College.

For various reasons, Northville might approach the situation in other ways. Although evidence of others' decisions can be persuasive, it is not definitive.

Begging the question. Treats a questionable statement as if it had already been accepted.

Northville College must change its discriminatory hiring policies to attract a more culturally diverse faculty.

Are the policies discriminatory? Could there be other reasons for large numbers of white male faculty?

False analogy. Incorrectly claims that two things that are similar in one way are similar in other ways as well.

Just as polar bears don't hang around with black panthers, so white students shouldn't be part of a community that includes black students.

Is fur color the only reason polar bears don't hang around with black panthers?

False cause. Assumes that if one event happened after another, the earlier event must have caused the later one.

When Fay Wong transferred from culturally diverse Southfield College to predominantly white Northville College, her grades fell dra-

matically. Being a token minority student obviously distracted her from her studies.

There could be other explanations to explain the drop in grades.

False dilemma (either/or argument). Presents a situation as allowing only two options when there are actually more.

Northville College will have to fire some of its white male faculty and replace them with minority and female instructors or remain a biased institution.

The college could also hire minority and female instructors when replacing retirees, or it could add new positions to the faculty.

Non sequitur (does not follow). Presents a conclusion that does not logically follow from its premises.

Eddie Murphy is a great comedian, so he would be an excellent college teacher.

Murphy's talents as a comedian don't either prove or disprove that he would be a good college teacher.

Oversimplification. Reduces a complex system of causes and effects to an inaccurate generalization.

The teaching of traditional American values will be eroded if the Northville faculty becomes more culturally diverse.

Are not equality and tolerance for differences traditional American values?

Slippery slope. Assumes that if an action or event is allowed to occur, it will lead to more extreme actions or events.

If Northville College offers a course in cultural diversity, pretty soon the whole curriculum will be overrun with courses in ethnic studies.

Have all the colleges that offer a course in cultural diversity subsequently been compelled to add courses in ethnic studies to their curriculum?

Exercise: To learn how each of these ten classical fallacies works, construct your false example for each one. Then reconstruct the sentence so that it avoids making a false argument.

chapter 11

Writing About Literature

To write about literature in college usually means to write analytical essays about poetry, fiction, and drama. To analyze a poem, a story, or a play means reading it, hearing it, looking closely at its language, comparing it with similar things, noticing how it affects you, and all the time asking, how does it work and why does it have this effect?

11 a Interpretive essays

The best literary texts to write about are those that may, at first, seem most problematic—texts whose meaning seems to you somewhat slippery and elusive. Such texts give you, the interpreter, multiple meanings to look for and select from in order to make a case for one meaning rather than another. As a writer about literature, your job is to convince someone, another reader, that your interpretation is reasonable, valid, and deserves attention.

A typical literary assignment asks you to read a poem or story and write about what it means, which act of interpretation draws upon all of your reasoning and writing skills: you may have to *describe* people, settings, and situations; *retell* events and actions; *define and use* literary terminology; *analyze* selected passages; and *explain* how they work, perhaps by *comparing* or *contrasting* the text with others. Finally, you will *argue* for one meaning rather than another. In other words, develop a *thesis* and defend this *thesis* with sound *reasoning* and convincing *evidence*.

This chapter explores numerous ways of developing textual interpretations, using for illustrative purposes Gwendolyn Brooks's poem "We Real Cool." Brooks's poem is especially useful because it is short and quickly read, yet can be looked at in multiple ways. Our questions about this text, as well as the strategies for finding answers, are virtually the same ones we would use with any text—fiction, nonfiction, or poetry.

Read, now, this poem by Gwendolyn Brooks about pool players at the Golden Shovel pool hall, and follow along as we examine different ways of determining what it means.

We Real Cool

THE POOL PLAYERS.
SEVEN AT THE GOLDEN SHOVEL.

We real cool. We
Left school. We

Lurk late. We
Strike straight. We

Sing sin. We
Thin gin. We

Jazz June. We
Die soon.

WRITING 1: EXPLORATION ....

After reading "We Real Cool," freewrite for ten minutes to capture your initial reaction. Ask yourself these questions: What did it remind me of? Did I like it? Do I think I understand it? What emotions did I feel?

....

11 b Exploring texts

A good topic for an interpretive essay addresses a question that has several possible answers. If you think the meaning of a text is obvious, you will have no real need to interpret it for somebody else. In addition, it helps to choose a topic that interests or intrigues you, because if it doesn't, chances are it won't interest or intrigue your readers either.

No matter what text you are interpreting, however, you need to figure out what it means to you before you can explain it well to someone else.

Plan to read it more than once, first to get the gist, then to understand what it seems to mean on a literal level. When you read it a second time, more slowly, mark passages that interest or puzzle you, making notes in the margin, on stick pads, or in a journal. As you do this, catch possible answers and solutions (hypotheses) to your queries, rereading as many times as necessary to further your understanding.

In selecting a text to interpret, ask yourself these questions:

■ What are some of the different ways of reading this text?

■ With which perspective or possibility do I most agree?

■ Which passages in the text support this reading?

■ What evidence do I need to assemble to convince an audience of my interpretation?

WRITING 2: APPLICATION ....

Select a text that you are interested in interpreting, and write out the answers to the questions above. Do not at this time worry about developing any of these answers thoroughly.

11 c Interpretive communities

Let's pause for a minute to look at what mindsets we might bring to the reading of a text in the first place. How you read and interpret a text depends on who you are. Who you are depends on how you've been shaped by your upbringing, background, and the various communities to which you belong. All of us belong to many communities: families (immediate and extended), social groups (dormitories, reading groups, athletic teams), economic groups (low, middle, or high), organizations (Brownies, Boy Scouts, Democrats, Masons), geographic locales (rural, urban, suburban, North, South), and institutions (school, church). Your membership in one or more of these communities determines, in one way or another, how you see and respond to the world.

The communities that influence you most strongly are called **interpretive communities;** they influence the meaning you make of the world. People who belong to the same community as you do are likely to have similar assumptions and therefore likely to interpret things as you would. If you live in an urban black community, jazz and rap music may be a natural and constant presence in your life; if you live in a rural white community, country and western music may be the norm; at the same time, as a member of either group you might also belong to a larger community that surrounds itself with rock or classical music. All this means is that people who belong to different communities are likely to have different—not better or worse—perspectives from yours.

Before writing an interpretive essay, it is helpful to ask, "Who am I when I am writing this piece?" You ask this to examine the biases you bring to your work, for each of us sees the world—and consequently texts—from our own particular vantage point. Be aware of your age, gender, race, ethnic identity, socioeconomic class, geographic location, educational level, political or religious persuasion. Ask to what extent any of these identities emerges in your writing.

College is, of course, a large interpretive community. Various smaller communities exist within it called disciplines—English, history, business, art, and so on. Within any discipline there are established ways of interpreting texts. Often when you write an interpretive essay, you will do so from the perspective of a traditional academic interpretive community. Take care to follow the conventions of that community, whether you are asked to write a **personal interpretation,** in which you deliberately identify yourself and your biases, or an **analytical interpretation,** in which you remove your personal perspective as much as possible from your writing.

1 Personal Interpretation

In writing from a personal or subjective perspective, the interpreter and his or her beliefs and experiences are part of the story and need to be both expressed and examined. In examining "We Real Cool," for instance, explaining your background may help the reader understand why you view the poem as you do. You may compare or contrast your situation to that of the author or characters in the text. Or you might draw upon particular experiences that cause you to see the poem in a particular way. For example, Mitzi's response (reprinted in full chapter's end) begins with memories inspired by the poem:

"We Real Cool" is a sad poem. It reminds me of the gang in high school who used to skip classes and come back smelling of cigarette smoke and cheap liquor—not that I knew it was cheap back then.

It is increasingly common for good interpretive essays to include both analytical and personal discussions, allowing you to demonstrate your skill at closely reading texts while acknowledging your awareness of the subjective nature of virtually all interpretive acts. To move in a more analytic direction, Mitzi would need to quote and discuss more lines directly from the poem, as she does later in her essay:

These "cool" dropouts paid for their rebellion in drug overdoses, jail terms, police shootouts, and short lives. They "Die soon," so we never know where else their adventurous spirits might have taken them.

2 Analytical interpretation

In critically analyzing a text, writers focus as much as possible on its content and deliberately leave themselves, the interpreters, in the background, minimizing personal presence and bias. If you are asked to write this way—to avoid first-person pronouns or value judgments—keep your attention on actual passages in the text and avoid language that reveals your personal biases. In reality, of course, authors reveal their presence by all the choices they make: what they include, what they exclude, what they emphasize, and so on. But when you are aware that your own situation affects the inferences and judgments you make about others, you can take steps to keep your focus on the subject and off yourself.

In writing about "We Real Cool," for example, your first reaction may be more personal than analytical, focusing on your own emotions by calling it a *sad poem,* as Mitzi does, or by expressing value judgments about the poem's characters:

I think these guys are stupid, cutting their lives short drinking, stealing, and fighting.

However, a more analytical response would be to drop the first person (*I think*) and the judgment (*these guys are stupid*) and to focus more closely on the text itself, perhaps quoting parts of it to show you are paying close attention:

The speakers in the poem, "The Pool Players," cut their lives short by hanging out at "The Golden Shovel," fighting, drinking, stealing, and perhaps worse.

11 d Interpretations

There is no formula for arriving at or presenting an interpretation in essay form, but readers, especially English instructors, will expect you to address and explain various elements of the text that usually contribute substantially to what it means. Convincing interpretive essays often, but not always, include the following information, commonly in this order:

1. an overview of the text, identifying author, title, and genre and *briefly* summarizing the whole text

2. a description of form and structure

3. a description of the author's point of view

4. a summary of the social, historical, or cultural context in which the work was written

5. an assertion or thesis about what you believe the text means—your main business as an interpreter

Note that a **thesis,** whether explanatory (see 9c), argumentative (see 10a), or interpretive, is essentially a statement or passage that identifies the central point of the paper. To be persuasive and believable, any thesis needs to be supported with substantial and credible evidence. While some interpretive essays may include all of the elements listed above, others will emphasize some of the elements while downplaying others. For example, an interpretive essay that focuses on authorial point of view may not say much about form, structure, or historical context.

1 Identify and summarize the text

Essays about literature, like all essays, should begin by answering some basic questions: What genre is this—poem, play, novel, short story? What is its title? Who is the author? When was it published? In addition, especially if you are writing to readers unfamiliar with the text, it helps to provide a brief summary or background information. For example, in summarizing "We Real Cool" you might write:

> "We Real Cool," a poem by Gwendolyn Brooks, condenses the life story of pool-playing high school dropouts to eight short lines and foreshadows an early death on the city streets.

2 Explain the form and organization

To examine the organizational structure of a text, ask: How is it put together? Why start here and end there? What connects it from start to finish? For example, by repeating words, ideas, and images, writers call attention to them and indicate that they are important to the meaning of the text. No matter what the text, some principle or plan holds it together and gives it structure. Texts that tell stories are often organized as a sequence of events in chronological order. Other texts may alternate between explanations and examples or between first-person and third-person narrative. You will have to decide which aspects of the text's form and organization are most important for your interpretation. The following example pays close attention to Brooks's overall poetic structure:

> The poem consists of a series of eight three-word sentences, each beginning with the word "We." The opening lines "We real cool. We / left school" explain the characters' situation. The closing lines "We / Jazz June. We / Die soon" suggest their lives will be over soon.

3 Describe the author's perspective

From what point of view is the text written? In an article, essay, editorial, or textbook (all classified as nonfiction), you can expect the author to write about what is true as he or she sees it—just as we are doing in this textbook. However, in a work of poetry, fiction, or drama the author's point of view may be quite different from that of the character(s) who narrate or act in the story. If you can describe or explain the author's perspective in your interpretive essay, you provide readers with clues about the author's purpose. For example, Kelly's essay (reprinted in full at chapter's end) opens by making a distinction between Brooks the poet and her characters, "Seven at the Golden Shovel":

> Gwendolyn Brooks writes "We Real Cool" (1963) from the point of view of the members of a street gang who have dropped out of school to live their lives hanging around pool halls—in this case "The Golden Shovel." These guys are semiliterate and speak in slangy street lingo that reveals their need for mutual support in their mutually rebellious attitude toward life.

What he doesn't say, but clearly implies, is that Brooks herself is a mature and highly skilled user of formal English, and that in the poem she adopts the persona or mask of semiliterate teenagers in order to tell their story from what she imagines is their perspective.

4 Place the work in context

What circumstances (historical, social, political, biographical) produced this text? How does this text compare or contrast with another by the same author or a similar work by a different author? No text exists in isolation. Each was created by a particular author in a particular place at a particular time. Describing this context provides readers with important background information and indicates which conditions you think were most influential. "We Real Cool" could be contextualized this way:

> "We Real Cool" was published in 1963, a time when the civil rights movement was strong and about the time that African Americans coined the phrase "Black is beautiful." The poem may have been written to remind people that just because they were black did not mean they necessarily led beautiful lives.

5 Explain the theme of the text

In fiction, poetry, and drama, and reflective essays, the main point usually takes the form of an implicit **theme,** which is seldom stated outright in a creative text. A main reason for writing an interpretive essay is to point out this theme as you see it. To do so, you might ask: So what? What is this really about? What do I think the author meant by writing this? Your answer to this "so-what?" question, of course, will generate the thesis statement of your interpretive essay, as Kelly does here about "We Real Cool" at the end of his first paragraph:

> The speakers in the poem, "We," celebrate what adults would call adolescent hedonism—but they make a conscious choice for a short, intense life over a long, safe, and dull existence.

When you write from a subjective perspective, you make it clear that your interpretation is based on your own personal reactions as much as on the content of the text, and that other readers will necessarily read it differently. The controlling idea or theme of Mitzi's subjective interpretation of "We Real Cool"—often called a "reader-response" essay—is revealed in her opening paragraph, in which she compares the narrators of the poem to the gang members of her own high school.

6 Support your interpretation

Analytical interpretations are usually built around evidence from the text itself: summarize larger ideas in your own language to conserve space; paraphrase more specific ideas also in your own words; and quote directly to feature especially colorful or precise language. If you include outside information for support, comparison, or contrast reasons, document carefully where it came from. Most of the preceding examples referred to specific lines in the poem, as does this passage from Kelly's essay:

> Instead of attending school, planning for their future, or finding work, these seven "Lurk late," "Strike straight," "Sing sin," "Thin gin," and "Jazz June." Watch out for this bunch. If you see them coming, cross the street.

Subjective interpretations also include textual evidence, but often passages from the text are cited as prompts to introduce the writer's own memories, associations, or personal ideas, as in Mitzi's essay. The more specific and concrete your examples, the better.

> I think everybody who ever went to a public high school knows these guys— at least most of them were boys—who eventually "Left school" altogether and failed to graduate. They dressed a little differently from the rest of us—baggier pants, heavier boots, dirtier shirts, and too-long hair never washed—and if there were girls—too much makeup or none at all.

WRITING 3: APPLICATION ....

Look at the text you plan to interpret, and make brief notes about each of the elements described in this section.

....

11 e   Different literary genres

All the examples so far have come from a single short poem. If you are interpreting a work of fiction or nonfiction, or something else altogether

Glossary of Literary Terms

- **alliteration** The repetition of initial consonant sounds (*"On the bold street breaks the blank day."*)
- **antagonist** A character or force opposing the main character (the *protagonist*) in a story.
- **climax** A moment of emotional or intellectual intensity or a point in the plot where one opposing force overcomes another and the conflict is resolved.
- **epiphany** A flash of intuitive understanding by narrator or character in a story.
- **figurative language** Language that suggests special meanings or effects such as metaphors or similes; not literal language. (*"She stands like a tree, solid and rooted."*)
- **imagery** Language that appeals to one of the five senses, especially language that reproduces something the reader can see or imagine. (*"His heart was an open book, pages aflutter and crackling in the wind."*)
- **narrator** Someone who tells a story; a *character narrator* tells the story from a personal perspective (Huckleberry Finn) while an *omniscient narrator* tells a story about other people.
- **persona** A *mask,* not the author's real self, worn by the author to present a story or poem.
- **plot** The sequence of events in a story or play.
- **point of view** The vantage point from which a story or event is perceived and told.
- **protagonist** The main character or hero of a plot.
- **rhyme** The repetition of sounds, usually at the ends of lines in poems, but also occurring at other intervals in a line (*moon, June, noon*).
- **rhythm** The rise and fall of stress sounds within sentences, paragraphs, lines, and stanzas.
- **symbol** An object that represents itself and something else at the same time. A *black rose* is both the color of the rose and the suggestion of something evil or death-like.
- **theme** The meaning or thesis of a text.

such as an art exhibit, a concert, a play, or a film, the basic elements of interpretation still apply—with a few differences.

Poetry

Of all language genres and forms, poetry exhibits the most intensive and deliberate use of language. With certain exceptions, poetic texts are far shorter than even short stories or one-act plays. Consequently, when interpreting poems, pay special attention to specific words, phrases, and lines; quote exactly to support your points; and familiarize yourself with the basic poetic terms you learned in high school: line, stanza, rhyme, rhythm, meter, metaphor, and image.

2 Fiction

To write about a novel or short story, explain how the main elements function: the *narrator* (who tells the story), *plot* (what happens in the story), one or more *characters* (who are acting or being acted upon), *setting* (where things are happening), and *theme* (the meaning of the story). Be sure to keep in mind that the author who writes the story is different from the characters in the story and that what happens in the story is different from the meaning of the story.

3 Drama

Plays are a special kind of fiction that are meant to be acted out on a stage; consequently, all the elements of fiction apply, except that since the characters are acting out the story, a narrator is seldom present. In drama, the setting is limited to what is contained on the stage, what the characters are thinking is usually not available to the audience, and the actors who play the parts are crucial to the play's success. Remember, too, that plays are structured according to acts (usually from one to five), which are in turn divided into scenes.

4 Film

Fictional films are discussed in terms similar to those for fiction and drama (plot, character, setting, theme). However, additional elements also come into play: camera angles, special effects, and unlimited settings. Because of the complexity of orchestrating all of these elements, the film director rather than the screenwriter is often considered the "author" of a film.

Writing Interpretive Essays

When you have completed the first draft of your interpretive essay, address the following questions:

- Do you identify the author, the title, and the date this text was published, early in your text? If not, should you?
- Have you provided a brief summary of what happens (plot) on the literal level in the text?
- Where do you explain the meaning or importance of this text?
- Is your approach to this interpretive essay objective or subjective? Why do you choose the one approach over the other?
- Have you provided evidence from the text itself for all assertions? If not, should you?
- Have you correctly documented any assertions not your own or any passages of text that you quote or paraphrase? (See 27d.)

5 Nonfiction

The elements of a nonfiction story are similar to those of fiction, except that everything in the text is supposed to have really happened. For this reason, the author and the narrator of the story are one and the same.

Informational nonfiction—essays, reports, textbooks, photos, film, and video—is also meant to be believed; however, here you might say that "ideas," "arguments," and "images" are the main characters to be discussed and evaluated.

6 Other media

In interpreting other kinds of texts—paintings, sculptures, quilts, buildings, concerts, and so on—always explain to your reader the basic identifying features, be they verbal, visual, musical, or something else: What is it? What is its name or title? Who created it? What are its main features?

Where is it? When did it take place? As with your interpretation of literary works, your interpretation of works in other media can identify a theme and can respond to the theme in subjective, personal ways and more objective, analytical ways.

This chapter concludes with two brief interpretive papers from which some of the foregoing illustrations have been taken. The first one might be called an objective or *critical essay,* while the other might be called a subjective or *personal essay.*

Analytic response to "We Real Cool"

Kelly writes a short analytical interpretation of "We Real Cool," called "High Stakes, Short Life," keeping himself in the background, writing in the third-person point of view. He presents his thesis early and supports it afterward with frequent quotations from the text, amplifying and explaining it most fully in his last paragraph.

High Stakes, Short Life

Kelly Sachs

Gwendolyn Brooks writes "We Real Cool" (1963) from the point of view

of the members of a street gang who have dropped out of school to live their

lives hanging around pool halls—in this case "The Golden Shovel." These guys

are semiliterate and speak in slangy street lingo that reveals their need for

mutual support in their mutually rebellious attitude toward life. The speakers in

the poem, "We," celebrate what adults would call adolescent hedonism—but

they make a conscious choice for a short, intense life over a long, safe, and dull

existence.

For the "Seven at the Golden Shovel," companionship is everything. For many teenagers, fitting in or conforming to a group identity is more important than developing an individual identity. But for these kids, none of whom excelled at school or had happy home lives, their group *is* their life. They even speak as a group, from the plural point of view, "We," repeated at the end of each line; these seven are bonded and will stick together through boredom, excitement, and death.

From society's point of view, they are nothing but misfits—refusing to work, leading violent lives, breaking laws, and confronting polite society whenever they cross paths. Instead of attending school, planning for their future, or finding work, these seven "Lurk late," "Strike straight," "Sing sin," "Thin gin," and "Jazz June." Watch out for this bunch. If you see them coming, cross the street.

However, the most important element of their lives is being "cool." They live and love to be cool. Part of being cool is playing pool, singing, drinking, fighting, and messing around with women whenever they can. Being cool is the code of action that unites them, that they celebrate, for which they are willing to die.

The poet reveals their fate in the poem's last line. Brooks shows that the price of coolness and companionship is higher than most people are willing to pay. In this culture, the fate of rebels who violate social norms is an early death ("We / Die soon"), but to these seven, it is better to live life to the fullest than hold back and plan for a future that may never come. They choose, accept, and celebrate their lives and "Die soon."

Personal response to "We Real Cool"

In the following essay, "Staying Put," Mitzi writes about her personal reaction to Brooks' poem, describing how it reminds her of her own high school experience. Mitzi's theme, the sad lives of ghetto gangs versus the safer, happier life she leads, opens and closes the essay and provides the necessary coherence to hold it together. While she quotes the text several times, her primary supportive examples come from her own memories.

Staying Put

Mitzi Fowler

Gwendolyn Brooks' "We Real Cool" is a sad poem. It reminds me of the gang in high school who used to skip classes and come back smelling of cigarette smoke and cheap liquor—not that I knew it was cheap back then. I think everybody who ever went to a public high school knows these guys—at least most of them were boys—who eventually "Left school" altogether and failed to graduate. They dressed a little differently from the rest of us—baggier pants, heavier boots, dirtier shirts, and too long hair never washed—and if there were girls—too much makeup or none at all.

They had their fun, however, because they stayed in their group. They came late to assemblies, slouched in their seats, made wisecracks, and often ended up like the characters in <u>The Breakfast Club</u>, in detention after school or on Saturday morning.

And no matter how straitlaced and clean-cut the rest of us were, we always felt just a twinge of envy at these careless, jaunty rebels who refused to follow rules, who didn't care if they got detentions, who didn't do homework, and whose parents didn't care if they stayed out all night. I didn't admit it very often—at least not to my friends—but some part of me wanted to have their pool hall or whatever adventures, these adult freedoms they claimed for themselves. However, I was always afraid—chicken, they would have said—of the consequences, so I practiced piano, did my algebra, and stayed put.

Then I think of the poem's last line and know why I obeyed my parents (well, most of the time), listened to my teachers (at least some of them), and stayed put (if you don't count senior cut day). These "cool" dropouts paid for their rebellion in drug overdoses, jail terms, police shootouts, and short lives. They "Die soon," so we never know where else their adventurous spirits might have taken them. In the end, this poem just makes me sad.

SUGGESTIONS FOR WRITING AND RESEARCH

INDIVIDUAL

1.   Write an interpretive essay about a short text of your choice. Write the first draft from an analytic stance, withholding all personal judgments. Then write the second draft from a personal stance, including all relevant private judgments. Write your final draft by carefully blending elements of your first and second drafts.

2.   Locate at least two reviews of a text (book, recording, exhibit) with which you are familiar, and analyze each to determine the reviewer's critical perspective. Write your own review of the text, and agree or disagree with the approach of the reviewers you analyzed. If you have a campus newspaper, consider offering your review to the editor for publication.

COLLABORATIVE

As a class or small group, attend a local concert, play, or exhibition. Have each student take good notes and, when he or she returns home, write a review of this event that includes both an interpretation and a recommendation that readers attend it (or not). Share these variations on the same theme with others in your class or group and explore the different judgments that arise as a result of different perspectives.

WRITING ACROSS THE CURRICULUM

Insights from Literature Throughout the Disciplines

In disciplines other than English, there are occasions to introduce themes, characters, and insights derived from reading fiction, drama, and poetry in assigned papers. As with personal anecdotes, literary perspectives would supplement rather than replace more discipline-specific or objective information in science, social science, humanities, and fine arts courses. Below are some examples of how literature might be included in papers other than English classes.

History, political science, or American studies. In writing a paper about social, cultural, or political conditions during the Civil War, adding insights from well-known fiction about the same period, such as Mark Twain's *The Adventures of Huckelberry Finn* or Harriet Beecher Stowe's *Uncle Tom's Cabin,* would show both your breadth of knowledge and illustrate your larger understanding of the issues being discussed in your paper.

Psychology or sociology. In writing a paper on adolescent psychology or social norms, using fictive examples such as sixteen-year-old Holden Caufield from J. D. Salinger's *The Catcher in the Rye* or a character from the Harry Potter series (book or film) would provide an apt example to demonstrate an interdisciplinary understanding of your topic—you are not just writing from textbook or lecture material.

Religion or art history. A paper examining Medieval or Renaissance ideas about Christianity might introduce ideas from Dan Brown's *The Da Vinci Code* or Nicolas Kazinzakis's *The Last Temptation of Christ,* either to support or refute the argument of another critic could illustrate both your literary and ability to extract parallels from your private reading.

Biology or history of science. Referencing or including an example from Michael Crichton's *Jurassic Park* (book or one of the several films) in a paper on evolution might provide a lively and apt illustration of the contemporary view that dinosaurs were warm-blooded and therefore fast-moving creatures rather than cold-blooded and sluggish. Again, the fictive reference reinforces textbook understanding and adds a lively, interesting dimension to an otherwise fact-based paper.

Exercise: Make a short list of novels, films, plays, or poems that might include appropriate material in a paper written for one course other than English you are now enrolled in.

12 *Writing Creative Nonfiction*

The term *creative nonfiction* describes much of the good writing that appears in magazines such as *The New Yorker, Harper's,* and *GQ,* as well as many works on the nonfiction best-seller lists. Writers of creative nonfiction commonly borrow stylistic and formal techniques from the fast-paced visual narratives of film and television as well as from the innovative language of poetry, fiction, and drama. Many current nonfiction prose writers find the traditions of continuity, order, consistency, and unity associated with conventional prose insufficient to convey the chaotic truths of the contemporary life. This chapter examines some creative writing strategies and suggests appropriate venues within the academic curriculum where such prose strategies could be useful. (Many of the ideas presented here were first articulated by Winston Weathers in his groundbreaking book *An Alternate Style: Options in Composition* [Hayden, 1980].)

12 a Lists

Lists can break up and augment prose texts in useful, credible, and surprising ways. Lists of names, words, and numbers add variety, speed, depth, and humor to texts. And lists are everywhere we look, as Joan Didion illustrates in making the case that Las Vegas weddings are big business in this excerpt from "Marrying Absurd":

> There are nineteen such wedding chapels in Las Vegas, intensely competitive, each offering better, faster, and, by implication, more sincere

services than the next: Our Photos Best Anywhere, Your Wedding on a Phonograph Record, Candlelight with Your Ceremony, Honeymoon Accommodations, Free Transportation from Your Motel to Courthouse to Chapel and Return to Motel, Religious or Civil Ceremonies, Dressing Rooms, Flowers, Rings, Announcements, Witnesses Available, and Ample Parking.

Didion's list of competitive wedding services convinces us she has observed carefully, she's not making this stuff up; without her saying it, we see some level of absurdity in the way this town promotes marriage.

Lists need not be clever so much as purposeful. That is, you include a list of names, items, quotations, and so on to show readers you know your stuff: you've done your homework, read widely or observed carefully, taken good notes, and made sense of what you've found. Lists deepen a text by providing illustrations or examples.

When first-year student Craig examined sexist stereotypes in children's toys, he made the following list of dolls on a single shelf at a local discount store:

> To my left is a shelf of Barbie: Animal Lovin' Barbie, Wet 'n Wild Barbie, Barbie Feelin' Pretty Fashions, Barbie Special Expressions, Super Star Barbie Movietime Prop Shop, Step 'n Style Boutique, My First Barbie (Prettiest Princess Ever), Action Accents Barbie Sewing Machine, Barbie Cool Times Fashion, Barbie and the All-Stars, Style Magic Barbie, a Barbie Ferrari, and tucked away in a corner, slightly damaged and dusty, Super Star Ken.

This list simply documents by name the products on the toy shelf, actually adding a dimension of authenticity and believability to the writer's case that, yes, the Barbie image has a considerable influence on children.

However, lists that are quick to read may not be quick to write; an effective list that appears to be written by free association may, in fact, have been laboriously constructed as the writer ransacked his memory or her thesaurus for words, then arranged and rearranged them to create the right sound or sense effect.

12 b Snapshots

Writing prose snapshots is analogous to constructing and arranging a photo album composed of many separate visual images. Photo albums, when carefully assembled, tell stories with clear beginnings, middles, and endings, but with lots of white spaces between one picture and the next and no transitions explaining how the photographer got from one scene to the next. In other words, photo albums tell stories piecemeal, making the viewer fill in or imagine what happened between shots. Prose snapshots function the same way as visual snapshots, each connected to the next by white space and leaps of reader imagination. Sometimes individual snapshots are numbered to suggest deliberate connectedness; other times each is titled to suggest its ability to stand alone like chapters within books; sometimes they appear on a page as block paragraphs.

Margaret Atwood wrote snapshots to emphasize the dangers of men's bodies in the following passage from her essay "Alien Territory" (1983):

> The history of war is a history of killed bodies. That's what war is: bodies killing other bodies, bodies being killed.
>
> Some of the killed bodies are those of women and children, as a side effect you might say. Fallout, shrapnel, napalm, rape and skewering, anti-personnel devices. But most of the killed bodies are men. So are most of those doing the killing.
>
> Why do men want to kill the bodies of other men? Women don't want to kill the bodies of other women. By and large. As far as we know.
>
> Here are some traditional reasons: Loot. Territory. Lust for power. Hormones. Adrenaline high. Rage. God. Flag. Honor. Righteous anger. Revenge. Oppression. Slavery. Starvation. Defense of one's life. Love; or, a desire to protect the men and women. From what? From the bodies of other men.
>
> What men are most afraid of is not lions, not snakes, not the dark, not women. What men are most afraid of is the body of another man.
>
> Men's bodies are the most dangerous things on earth.

Note how the white space between one snapshot and another gives readers breathing space, time out, time to digest one thought before supping at the next. The white space between snapshots actually exercises readers' imagination as they participate in constructing some logic that makes the text make sense—the readers themselves supply the connectives, construct the best meaning, which, nevertheless, will be very close to what skillful authors intend.

Snapshot is fun, in part because each snapshot is short and therefore composing is quick and progress seems easy. At the same time, the real secret to a successful snapshot essay is putting them together in some right order, some thematic that's as strong and sure as if you had written straight narration or exposition. Writing snapshots on a computer is especially fun since you can order and reorder indefinitely until you arrive at a satisfying arrangement. Composing snapshot essays on easy-to-shuffle 3″ × 5″ cards also works. In either case, assemble and arrange as you would pictures in a photo album, playfully and seriously: begin at the beginning, weave in several themes, begin in the middle, alternate time, begin with flashbacks, try multiple voices in alternate fonts, and so on.

12 c Playful sentences

No matter what your form or style, sentences usually remain your main units of composition, explaining the world in terms of subjects, actions, and objects, suggesting that the world operates according to cause and effect—that something (a subject) does something (acts) that causes something else to happen (an object). English prose is built around complete and predictable sentences such as those in which this paragraph is written. Sometimes, however, writers use sentences in less predictable, more playful ways.

Fragment sentences suggest fragmented stories. Stories different from the stories told by conventional subject–verb–object sentences. Fragment sentences, of course, can be used judiciously in conventional writing so long as the purpose is crystal clear and the fragment is not mistaken for fragmentary grammatical knowledge. However, creative nonfiction writers use fragments in more surprising ways as well. A flash of movement. A bit of a story. A frozen scene. Fragments force quick reading. Ask for impressionistic understanding. Suggest parts rather than wholes.

Fragment sentences suggest, too, that things are moving fast. Very fast. Hold on. Remember the snapshot passage from Margaret Atwood's "Alien Territory"? Note how fragments emphasize the sharp dangers of men's bodies:

> Some of the killed bodies are those of women and children, as a side effect you might say. Fallout, shrapnel, napalm, rape and skewering, anti-personnel devices. But most of the killed bodies are men. So are most of those doing the killing.
>
> Why do men want to kill the bodies of other men? Women don't want to kill the bodies of other women. By and large. As far as we know.

Atwood's fragments make the reader notice sharply the brutal and jarring truths she is writing about men, violence, and war.

Write fragments so your reader knows they are not mistakes. Not ignorance. Not sloppiness or printer error or carelessness. Purposeful fragments can be powerful. Deliberate. Intentional. Careful. Functional. And brief.

A **labyrinthine sentence** is quite the opposite of the fragment sentence because it seems never to end; it won't quit, and goes on and on and on, using all sorts of punctuational and grammatical tricks to create compound sentences (two or more independent clauses joined by a comma and a conjunction such as *and* or *but*) and complex sentences (one independent clause with one or more dependent clauses) and is written to suggest, perhaps, that things are running together and are hard to separate—also to suggest the "stream of consciousness" of the human mind, in which thoughts and impressions and feelings and images are run together without the easy separation into full sentences or paragraphs complete with topic sentences—the power (and sometimes confusion) of which is illustrated in the passage below, by James Agee, as he imaginatively enters the thoughts of the people he is profiling in *Let Us Now Praise Famous Men* (1941), the poor Alabama tenant farmers:

> But I am young; and I am young and strong and in good health; and I am young and pretty to look at; and I am too young to worry; and so am I for my mother is kind to me; and we run in the bright air like animals, and our bare feet like plants in the wholesome earth: the natural world is around us like a lake and a wide smile and we are growing: one by one we are becoming stronger, and one by one in the terrible emptiness and the leisure we shall burn and tremble and shake with lust, and one by one we shall loosen ourselves from this place, and shall be married, and it will be different from what we see, for we will be happy and love each other, and keep the house clean, and a good garden, and buy a cultivator, and use a high grade of fertilizer, and we will know how to do things right; it will be very different:) (?:)

Agee's long connected sentence creates the run-together, wishful, worried, desperate internal dream of his subjects in a way a conventional paragraph could not. Notice, too, that punctuation and grammar are conventional and correct—up to the end, where punctuation marks are used in unexpected ways to suggest something of the confusion and uncertainty these people live with daily. You may also write run-on or fused sentences in which punctuation does not function in expected ways. Use both fragment and labyrinthine sentences to create special effects, but be wary of grammatically incorrect sentences, such as run-ons and comma splices, since they make even liberal teachers suspicious.

12 d Repetition/refrain

Writers repeat words, phrases, or sentences for emphasis. They repeat words and phrases to remind us to think hard about the word or phrase repeated. They repeat words and phrases to ask us to attend and not take for granted. They repeat words and phrases to suggest continuity of idea and theme. And, sometimes, they repeat words and phrases to create rhythms that are simply pleasing to the ear.

The following paragraph opens Ian Frazier's book-length study *The Great Plains:*

> Away to the Great Plains of America, to that immense Western short-grass prairie now mostly plowed under! Away to the still empty land beyond newsstands and malls and velvet restaurant ropes! Away to the headwaters of the Missouri, now quelled by many impoundment dams, and to the headwaters of the Platte, and to the almost invisible headwaters of the slurped up Arkansas! Away to the land where TV used to set its most popular dramas, but not anymore! Away to the land beyond the hundredth meridian of longitude, where sometimes it rains and sometimes it doesn't, where agriculture stops and does a double take! Away to the skies of the sparrow hawks sitting on telephone wires, thinking of mice and flaring their tail feathers suddenly, like a card trick! Away to the airshaft of the continent, where weather fronts from two hemispheres meet and the wind blows almost all the time! Away to the fields of wheat and milo and Sudan grass and flax and alfalfa and nothing! Away to parts of Montana and North Dakota and South Dakota and Wyoming and Nebraska and Kansas and Colorado and New Mexico and Oklahoma and Texas! Away to the high plains rolling in waves to the rising final chord of the Rocky Mountains!

Frazier's singing chant invites us, in one sweeping passage, to think about the Great Plains as geography, biology, history, and culture. Along the way he uses fragments and lists and exclamation marks to invite readers to consider this arid and often overlooked part of America.

Repetition and refrain, along with lists, snapshots, fragments, and labyrinthine sentences, are stylistic devices that add an emotional dimension to the otherwise factual material of nonfiction prose—without announcing, labeling, or dictating what those emotions need be. The word play of creative nonfiction allows nonfiction prose to convey themes more often conveyed through more obviously poetic forms.

12 e   Double voice

In any given essay, writers may try to say two things at the same time. Sometimes they question their own assertions; sometimes they say one thing out loud and think another silently to themselves; sometimes they say one thing that means two things; sometimes they express contradictions, paradoxes, or conundrums; and sometimes they establish that most of us have more than one voice with which to speak.

Double voices in a text may be indicated by parentheses—the equivalent of an actor speaking an "aside" on the stage (see what I mean?) or in films, the internal monologue of a character revealed as voiceover or through printed subtitles while another action is happening on screen. Or it may be shown by changes in the size or type of font, a switch to *italics,* **boldface,** or CAPITAL LETTERS signaling a switch in the writer's voice. Or the double voice may occur without distinguishing markers at all. Or it may be indicated by simple paragraph breaks, as in the following selection from D. H. Lawrence in his critical essay on Herman Melville's *Moby-Dick* from *Studies in Classic American Literature,* where he uses fragments, repetition, and double voice:

> Doom.
> Doom! Doom! Doom! Something seems to whisper it in the very dark trees of America.
> Doom of what?
> Doom of our white day. We are doomed, doomed. And the doom is in America. The doom of our white day.
> Ah, well, if my day is doomed, and I am doomed with my day, it is something greater than I which dooms me, so I accept my doom as a sign of the greatness which is more than I am.
> Melville knew. He knew his race was doomed. His white soul, doomed. His great white epoch, doomed. Himself doomed. The idealist, doomed. The spirit, doomed.

Here, Lawrence critiques Melville by carrying on a mock dialogue with himself, alternating his caricature of Melville's voice with his own whimsical acceptance of Melville's gloomy prophesy. Lawrence's essay seems written to provoke readers into reassessing their interpretations of literary classics, and so he provokes not only through the questions he raises but through his style as well—note his poetic use of repetition and sentence fragments that contribute to his double-voice effect.

Double voice may also be offset spatially, in double columns or alternating paragraphs. In trying to capture the experience of running a 26.2-mile marathon, student Paige alternated voices in separate snapshot-style paragraphs (one double stanza for each mile). In the following example from her third set of snapshots, her first voice is in the race (present tense, italics) while her second voice is remembering the training (past tense, non-italic, or roman, font):

> *Mile 3: Make sure you are going the right pace. Slow down a little, you're going too fast. Let people pass you. Don't worry; they will burn out and you'll glide by later. Don't make a mistake.*

My typical training week went like this:

   Monday: a two-mile warm-up at a slow pace; then three miles at a faster pace; finally, two miles slowing down, cooling off. After: a leg strength workout.

   Tuesday: a medium long run, ten miles at a medium pace.

A word of caution

Wise writers will master both conventional and unconventional styles and formats, using each as occasion and audience demand. Proficiency in one is a poor excuse for sloppiness or neglect of the other. Creative nonfiction techniques, used carefully and judiciously on selected writing tasks, are fun to write and enjoyable to read, and at the same time they are able to convey the emotional and aesthetic dimension of ideas so difficult to express in conventional prose. Yet such stylistic devices are easy to overuse and exaggerate, resulting in predictable, routine, or overly cute expressions that lose the very edge they are trying to achieve and that made them effective in the first place. Check with your instructor before handing in an unconventional paper in response to a conventional assignment.

SUGGESTIONS FOR WRITING AND RESEARCH

INDIVIDUAL

1. Select one or more of the following techniques to compose your next essay: lists, snapshots, playful sentences, repetition, or double voice.
2. Recast an essay previously written in one or more of the experimental techniques above. Compare and contrast the effects created by each version.

COLLABORATIVE

As a class, compose a snapshot profile of your class, using one snapshot from each writer to piece together one thematically consistent but stylistically varied profile.

WRITING ACROSS THE CURRICULUM

Creative Nonfiction Across the Disciplines

Creative nonfiction is an accepted genre in the field of English, a genre that includes exemplary writers from George Orwell, Virginia Woolf, and E. B. White through Tom Wolfe, Hunter S. Thompson, Joan Didion, Truman Capote, Norman Mailer, and Margaret Atwood. We asked professors from other disciplines to name significant *creative nonfiction* about their discipline. Following are some of their suggestions:

An **anthropologist** suggested Kent Nerburn's *Neither Wolf nor Dog: On Forgotten Roads with an Indian Elder,* a narrative of the toils and truths of a 78-year-old Lakota man that refuses to romanticize the life of contemporary native Americans along with Anne Fadiman's *The Spirit Catches You and You Fall Down: A Hmong Child, Her American Doctors, and the Collision of Two Culture,* mapping out the controversies raised by the collision between Western medicine and holistic healing traditions of Hmong immigrants. And any book written by Loren Eiseley.

A **botanist** suggested two books blending science with humor: George Gaylord Simpson's *Attending Marvels,* a tongue-in-cheek field journal of Argentine fossil hunting in the Patagonian wilderness in the early 1930s and John Steinbeck's *Log of the Sea of Cortez,* what he called "a hilarious account" of Steinbeck's travels with a marine biologist in the Baja region of California in 1940. And any book by Stephen Jay Gould.

An **economist** recommended a single anthology called *The Literary Book of Economics,* an anthology with dozens of essays ranging from Shakespeare, Milton, and Swift, to Emerson, Krakauer, and Vonnegut, each exploring some aspect of economics: Entrepreneurship, Markets, Supply and Demand, Government Regulations, Labor Markets, Free Trade, Unemployment, Cost–Benefit Analysis, and so on.

A **geologist** mentioned John McPhee's book-length study *Basin and Range,* along with many shorter essays exploring elements of place and geography such as "From Birnam Wood to Dunsinane," "Oranges," and "Searching for Marvin Gardens." And any works by John Muir, Edward Abbey, or Barry Lopez.

A **sociologist** named Kai Erikson's *A New Species of Trouble: The Human Experience of Modern Disasters,* a look at how various communities and victims have dealt with man-made disasters. He also recommended several books by Tracy Kidder: *The Soul of a New Machine,* stories portraying the evolution of the modern fast-paced work ethic and *House,* which takes readers to the heart of the American dream: the excitement and frustration of building a family's first house.

Exercise: As a class, spread out and ask professors in disciplines other than English to name the most exciting, unorthodox, or experimental writing about their discipline. Collate their suggestions and read the book that sounds most interesting to you. (We'll call this pleasure reading, so you don't need to do anything else but enjoy the book!)

13 Writing Essay Examinations

Essay examinations typically require students to sit and compose responses to instructors' questions at a single sitting for fifty minutes or more. As such, they seldom allow much room for revision, researching, or editing, thereby demanding pretty good off-the-cuff writing skills. Instructors assign essay exams instead of "objective" tests (multiple choice, matching, true/false) because they want students to go beyond identifying facts and to demonstrating mastery of course concepts in their own language.

Of course, the best preparation for taking an essay exam is to acquire a thorough knowledge of the subject matter, which means if you've attended class, read assigned texts, and completed other assignments, you should be in good shape. If you've taken good notes, kept journals, annotated readings, and discussed course material with other students, you should be in even better shape. So, while there is no substitute for a thorough knowledge of the course subject, certain writing strategies may enhance your presentation of information. This chapter outlines suggestions for writing under examination pressure.

13 a Understanding questions

1 Read the whole examination

You've heard this before, but we'll say it once more: before answering a single question, quickly read over the whole exam to assess its scope and focus. Figure out how much time you'll have for each question and stick to that estimate if you can. If you are given a choice among several questions, select questions that, taken together, demonstrate your knowledge of the whole course rather than answering two on pretty much the same topic. Finally, decide which questions you are best prepared to answer, and respond to those first. Answering questions you know relaxes you, warms you up intellectually, and gives you confidence to tackle the tougher ones.

2 Attend to direction words

Take a moment to analyze each question before you write: read it several times, then underline the direction word that identifies your task to keep you on track.

Define or *identify* asks for the distinguishing traits of a term, subject, or event, but does not require an interpretation or judgment. Use appropriate terminology learned in the course. For example, the question *Define John Locke's concept of tabula rasa* is best answered by using some of Locke's terminology along with your own.

Describe may ask for a physical description (*the setting of a play*) or it may request an explanation of a process, phenomenon, or event (*the culture and practices of the mound builders*). Answering description questions requires specific detail and apt examples.

Summarize asks for an overview or a synthesis of the main points. If asked to *summarize the impact of the Battle of Gettysburg,* hit the highlights, but don't get bogged down in details.

Compare and contrast asks that you point out both similarities and differences, between two or more subjects, so be sure to do both.

Analyze asks that you write about a subject in terms of its component parts. If asked to *analyze the typical seating plan of a symphony orchestra,* examine one part at a time.

Interpret asks you to explain the meaning of something. If asked to *interpret a Flannery O'Connor short story,* focus on the theme you think most important and provide relevant quotations from the text to back you up.

Explain asks what causes something (*List three causes of the Civil War*), how something works (*How are compact disks manufactured?*), or what something means (*Explain the function of color in the work of Picasso*). Note that while the first two examples call for value-neutral responses, the third really asks for interpretation. So, *explain,* like *discus,* is really a catchall term that requires careful attention on your part.

Evaluate, like *critique,* asks for a judgment based on clearly articulated analysis and reasoning (*Evaluate this questionnaire and eliminate weak* *questions).* Back up your evaluation with good reasons, which may include citing other's opinions that support your own.

Discuss, like *explain* or *comment,* is a general request, which allows you considerable latitude. If asked to *discuss the effects of monetarist economic theories on current Third World development,* you should be using terms and ideas found in the course readings and lectures, though it is implied that you will add your own insights as well.

13 b   Writing good answers

Instructors give essay exams to find out how much students know about course content and how expertly they can discuss it, which suggests that written answers should use course concepts in a clearly organized and appropriate way. If they were interested in testing only for specific facts and information, they could give true/false or multiple-choice tests. The following strategies will help you write more carefully composed answers.

1 Outline

Take one or two minutes per question to make an outline of your answer. If asked to compare and contrast three impressionist painters, decide in advance which three you will write about and in which order. A brief written outline in the margins of the test or your paper will help focus information and present it in a logical rather than haphazard order.

2 Lead with a thesis

The surest way to receive full credit on an essay question is to answer the question briefly and directly in your first sentence. In other words, if possible, state your answer as a **thesis** statement, which the rest of your essay explains, supports, and defends (here, again, outlining will help).

3 Remember how to organize a five-paragraph essay

A five-paragraph essay is often taught in high school as a way to write a satisfying, if formulaic, short essay. To write one, you open with a broad, general first paragraph that states your main idea or thesis. You follow with three paragraphs that support this main idea. You conclude. It turns out that learning to write the five-paragraph theme is actually excellent training for writing essay exams, as it gives you an easy template to follow while wrestling with ideas on the spot in a short period of time.

❹ Include details, examples, and illustrations

Good writing contains specific information that lets readers see for themselves the evidence for your position. Use as many supportive specifics as you can; memorize names, works, dates, and ideas as you prepare for the exam so you can recall them accurately if they are needed. Individual statistics alone are not worth much, but when used as evidence along with

Strategies for Writing Essay Examinations

1. **Skim the whole examination and block your time.** Read quickly through the whole exam so that you know what you're being asked to do, and allot blocks of time for tackling each section.

2. **Choose your essay questions carefully.** The essay questions you answer should allow you to write on what you know best. Choose a mix of answers to show your range of knowledge.

3. **Focus on direction words.** For each question you have chosen, it is important to recognize what your instructor is really asking, for this understanding enables you to answer the question successfully.

4. **Plan and outline each essay.** Prepare a rough outline of your answer by identifying the key points you need to make and organizing them well.

5. **Write thesis-first essays.** Doing this illustrates your confidence in knowing the answer and setting out to prove it. (For more information on thesis-first-organized essays, see 10f.)

6. **Include specifics—details, examples, illustrations.** Backing up statements with evidence shows your mastery of the subject matter. Include short, accurate, powerful quotations where relevant, citing each by author, title, and date, as necessary. To help you remember, focus on key words and jot them in the margins near your answer.

7. **Use the terms and methods used by the discipline.** Enter in the conversation of a particular discipline by using its accepted terms and methods.

8. **Provide context but stay focused.** Explain all your points as if your audience did not have the understanding your instructor does, but keep all your information focused on simply answering that one question. If you know more than time allows you to tell, end your answer with an outline of key points that you would discuss if you had more time.

9. **Proofread your answers** in the last five minutes before handing in the finished exam. Even this short step back from composing will allow you to spot errors and omissions.

strong reasoning, these specifics make the difference between mediocre and good answers.

5 Provide context

In answering a question posed by an instructor who is an expert in the field, it is tempting to assume no context is needed. However, since you are being asked to demonstrate how much *you* understand, treat each question as an opportunity to show how thoroughly you know the subject. Explain, if ever so briefly, concepts, terms, and background information that amplifies your answer.

6 Use disciplinary language

Use, define, explain, and correctly spell all technical terms used in the course. Essay exams implicitly test your facility with the language as well as explicitly test your knowledge of its concepts.

SUGGESTIONS FOR WRITING AND RESEARCH

INDIVIDUAL

In preparation for an essay examination in one of your courses, conduct an analytical reading of your course syllabus, asking questions such as:

- In reading the descriptive overview of the course, which words seem most important?
- What are the main subheadings into which the course is divided?
- How much time is allocated for each subdivision of course content?
- What is the title or stated agenda of each scheduled class?
- How would you describe the voice of the syllabus—stern, authoritarian, loose, relaxed, etc.?
- What specific tasks do course assignments ask you to do?

On the basis of this analysis, outline the most important issues, concepts, and information that you should study for the upcoming exam.

COLLABORATIVE

Form a small study group of students who are taking the same course. First, do an individual analysis of the syllabus as described above. Then, pool your answers and see if additional answers emerge about the relative importance of some topics compared to others. (A successful conclusion to either of these exercises, of course, will be the measure of how well you do taking the examination.)

WRITING ACROSS THE CURRICULUM

Evaluating Essay Examinations

Following are two examples of answers to an essay question from a music history examination that asks: Explain the origin and concept of neoclassicism, and identify a significant composer and works associated with the development of this music. Which do you think is the better answer and why?

> **Essay 1** Neoclassicism in music is a return to the ideas of the classical period of earlier centuries. It is dry and emphasizes awkward and screeching sounds and does not appeal to the listener's emotions. It does not tell a story but presents only a form. It is hard to listen to or understand compared to more romantic music such as Beethoven composed. Neoclassical music developed in the early part of the twentieth century. Stravinsky is the most famous composer who developed this difficult music.

> **Essay 2** Neoclassical music developed as a reaction against the romantic music of the nineteenth century. Stravinsky, the most famous neoclassical composer, took his style and themes from the eighteenth-century classical music of Bach, Handel, and Vivaldi rather than Beethoven or Brahms. Stravinsky emphasizes technique and form instead of story or image, with his atonal compositions appealing more to the intellect than the emotions. Rite of Spring (1913) and Symphony of Psalms (1940) are good examples.

Hint: Both answers are approximately the same length, and both are approximately correct. However, the better one will be more carefully organized, contain more information, use more disciplinary terms, and be more academically objective, won't it?

PART four

www.prenhall.com/fulwiler

199

chapter 14

The Revising Process

A first draft is a writer's first attempt to give shape to an idea, argument, or experience. Occasionally, this initial draft is just right and the writing is done. More often, however, the first draft shows a general direction that needs further thinking and redirecting. An unfocused first draft, in other words, is not a mistake but rather a start toward a next, more focused draft.

No matter how much prior thought writers give to a particular paper, once they begin composing, the draft begins to shift, change, and develop in unexpected ways. Each act of writing produces new questions and insights to be incorporated into the emerging piece of writing. While inexperienced writers view revising as an alien activity that doesn't come easily, experienced writers view revising as the primary way of developing thoughts to be shared with others.

14 a Understanding revising

The terms *revising, editing,* and *proofreading* may seem similar, but there is good reason to understand each as a separate process, each contributing to good finished writing.

Revising is re-seeing, rereading, and rethinking your thoughts on paper until they fully match your purpose. It's conceptual work focuses on units of meaning larger than the sentence.

Editing, in contrast, is changing language more than ideas. It's primarily stylistic work, where writers test each word or phrase to see that it is accurate, appropriate, necessary, generally sentence-level work.

Proofreading is checking a manuscript for accuracy and correctness. It is the last phase of the editing process, completed after conceptual and stylistic concerns have been addressed. Proofreaders review spelling, punctuation, capitalization, and usage to make sure no careless mistakes continue to the final draft.

Try to revise before you edit so you don't waste time on passages that later get cut from your manuscript. At the same time, it's especially easy to violate this guideline as writers are always circling back through the stages, editing when now they should be revising and vice versa. Nonetheless, you will save time if you revise before editing and edit before proofreading.

ESL *Revising Versus Editing*

Revising the content and organization of ideas is different from editing for word choice and grammatical correctness. It's especially difficult when writing in a second language, to postpone concerns about word choice and grammar. Consequently, ESL writers commonly edit prematurely. Although you may want to do some editing in early drafts, remember that taking time to revise content is very important and that you should work on revision before you do any extensive editing.

■

WRITING 1: EXPLORATION ....

Describe any experience you've had with revising papers: Was it for a school assignment or some writing on your own? Why did you revise? How many drafts did you do? Were you pleased with the result? Was your audience?

....

14 b Planning

To begin revising, return to the basic questions of purpose, audience, and voice: Why am I writing? to whom? in what voice?

1 Questions of purpose

It is often easier to see your purpose—or lack thereof—most clearly after you have written a draft or two. Ask: Why am I writing this paper? Do all parts of the paper advance this purpose? What is my rhetorical strategy: to narrate, explain, interpret, argue, reflect, or something else?

2 Questions of audience

Make sure your paper is aimed accurately at your readers by asking: What does my audience know about this subject? What does my audience need to know to understand the point of my paper? What questions or objections do I anticipate my audience raising? (Try to answer these questions as you revise.)

3 Questions of voice

Make sure your paper satisfies you. Revise so you say what you intend in the voice you intend by reading out loud and asking which passages sound like me speaking and which don't. (Enjoy those that do; fix those that don't.)

Creating Titles

Titles catch the attention of readers and provide a clue to the paper's content. If a title doesn't suggest itself in the writing of your paper, try one of these strategies:

- Use one strong, short phrase from your paper.
- Present a question that your paper answers.
- State the answer to the question or issue your paper will explore.
- Use a clear or catchy image from your paper.
- Use a famous quotation.
- Write a one-word title (or a two-word title, a three-word title, and so on).
- Begin your title with the word *On*.
- Begin your title with a gerund (*-ing* word).

14 c   Revising strategies

You cannot revise if you haven't first written, so write early and leave time to revise later. Good college papers are seldom written in one draft the night before they are due. When you plan in advance, you'll have the opportunity to take advantage of some of the dozen **revising strategies** other writers have found useful. While they won't all work for you all the time, some will be useful at one time or another.

1 Impose false due dates

Write the due date for a final draft on your calendar; then fool yourself
a little by adding in earlier, self-imposed due dates for first, second, or third
drafts. Your self-imposed intermediate due dates will guarantee you the
time you need to revise well.

2 Establish distance

Let your draft sit for a while, overnight if possible; then reread it to
see whether it still makes sense. A later reading allows you to see whether
there are places that need clarification, explanation, or development that
you did not see close up. You can gain distance also by reading your draft
aloud—hearing instead of seeing it—and by sharing it with others and listening to their reactions.

3 Reconsider everything

Reread the whole text from the beginning: every time you change something of substance, reread again to see the effect of these changes on other
parts of the text. If a classmate or instructor has made comments on some
parts of the paper and not on others, do not assume that only the places
where there are comments need revision.

4 Believe and doubt

Reread your draft twice, first as if you wanted to believe everything you
wrote (imagine a supportive friend), putting check marks in the margins
next to passages that create the most belief—the assertions, the discussion,
the details, the evidence. Next, reread your draft as if you were suspicious
and skeptical of all assertions, putting question marks next to questionable
passages. Be pleased with the check marks, and answer the question marks.

5 Test theme and evidence

When you make changes in theme or thesis, review the whole manuscript to make sure all parts remain consistent. When you find multiple
bits of evidence to support your major idea, keep in mind that facts make
the strongest evidence. Inferences based on accumulated facts are also powerful; however, opinion can be strong or weak depending on the source.

6 Make a paragraph outline

The most common unit of thought in a paper is the paragraph, a group of sentences set off from other groups because they focus on the same main idea. A paragraph outline creates a map of your whole paper that shows whether the organization is effective or needs changing. Number each paragraph and write a phrase describing its topic or focus. Check to make sure each subject of each paragraph leads logically to the next.

7 Make a new file for each revision

Each time you revise a draft, give that version a new number (e.g., draft 1, 2, etc.) so that you automatically save your earlier draft in a separate file. That way, if you become unhappy with your revisions, you can always return to the earlier copy.

8 Review hard copy

When revising with a computer, print out hard copies of your drafts on scrap paper and see how they read. Hard copy lets you scan several pages at a time and quickly flip pages in search of certain patterns or information.

9 Rewrite introductions and conclusions

Once started, papers grow and evolve in unpredictable ways: An opening that seemed appropriate in an earlier draft may no longer fit. The closing that once nicely ended the paper may now fail to do so. Examine both introduction and conclusion to be sure they actually introduce and conclude. (See also Chapter 37.)

10 Listen for your voice

In informal and semiformal papers—in fact, in most college papers—your language should sound like a real human being speaking. Read your paper aloud and see whether the human being speaking sounds like you. If a formal style is requested, the language should sound less like you in conversation and more like you giving a presentation—fewer opinions, more objectivity, no contractions.

11 Let go

View change as good, not bad. Many writers become overly attached to the first words they generate, proud to have found them, now reluctant to abandon them. Learn to let your words, sentences, and even paragraphs go. Trust that new and more appropriate ones will come.

12 Start over

Sometimes the best way to revise is to start fresh. Review your first draft, then turn it face down and start again. Starting over generates your best writing, as it doesn't lock you into old constructions, eliminates dead-end ideas, and opens up new possibilities. (Many writers have discovered this fact accidentally by losing a file on a computer and thus being forced to reconstruct; almost every one of them will tell you they wrote a better draft because they started over.)

WRITING 2: EXPLORATION

Look over the suggestions for revision in this section. Which of them have you used in the past? Which seem most useful to you now? Which seem most farfetched?

SUGGESTIONS FOR WRITING AND RESEARCH

INDIVIDUAL

Select any paper that you previously wrote in one draft but that you believe would profit from revision. Revise the paper by following some of the revision strategies and suggestions in this chapter.

COLLABORATIVE

As a class, brainstorm favorite revision strategies and write these on a board or overhead projector screen. Put check marks by those used by most students. Put asterisks next to any ideas not already mentioned in this chapter. Promise yourself to use at least one new strategy next time you revise a paper.

WRITING ACROSS THE CURRICULUM

I Write Every Paragraph Four Times

We found the following comment by nature writer Adolph Murie especially interesting because it so mirrors not only our own approach to rewriting, but that of many college faculty teaching in various subjects across the curriculum:

> I write every paragraph four times: once to get my meaning down, once to put in everything I left out, once to take out everything that seems unnecessary, and once to make the whole thing sound as if I had only just thought of it.
>
> *The Grizzlies of Mt. McKinley*

Murie's first rewrite of a paragraph is essentially writing-to-learn, as he lets the words on paper interact with his evolving thoughts to make his meaning clear—the writing leading the thinking! He knows this is a draft to get him started, a draft he knows he'll keep rewriting. His second rewrite is to add more depth by adding more details, facts, insights, whatever—which makes the paragraph rich, but overly long. His third rewrite is essentially editing for economy, as he tests each word to make sure it pulls its own weight and needs to be there. His final rewrite is especially intriguing, as he now revises for voice—to make sure it sounds like him speaking honestly and casually.

Exercise: In pairs or small groups, research the revision habits of a favorite or famous writer. If you cannot find such information, interview a professor, teacher, or person in your community who is known to write and publish. Find out about the revision strategies he or she most often uses. Summarize your findings according to the strategies described in this chapter and any others that your chosen writer uses. With your classmates, reorganize the research of individual members or teams by strategy. Each member or small group will assume responsibility for preparing a report on one strategy, discussing the information collected from all the chosen authors about that strategy. These reports can be assembled in a class book.

chapter 15

Focused Revising

Have you ever found yourself running out of ideas, energy, or creativity on what seemed to be a perfectly good topic for a paper? Have you ever been told to rewrite, revise, review, redo, or rethink a paper but not known exactly what those suggestions meant? Have you ever written a paper you thought was carefully focused and well researched but also was dull and lifeless?

Odds are you're not alone. When anyone writes a first draft—especially on an assigned topic to which he or she has given little prior thought—it's easy to summarize rather than analyze, to produce generalities and ignore specifics, to settle for clichés rather than invent fresh images, to cover too much territory in too little time. In fact, most first drafts contain more than their share of summary, generalization, superficiality, and cliché, since most first-draft writers are feeling their way and still discovering their topic.

The best way to shape a wandering piece of writing is to return to it, reread it, slow it down, take it apart, and build it back up again, this time attending more carefully to purpose, audience, and voice. Celebrate first-draft writing for what it is—a warm-up, a scouting trip—but plan next to get on with your journey in a more deliberate and organized fashion. Sometimes you already know—or your readers tell you—exactly where to go. Other times, you're not sure and need some strategies to get you moving again. This chapter offers four specific strategies for restarting, reconceiving, and refocusing a stuck paper.

15 a   Limiting

Broad topics lead to superficial writing. It's difficult to recount a four-week camping trip, to explain the meaning of *Hamlet,* or to solve the problems of poverty, crime, or violence in a few double-spaced pages. You'll almost always do better to cover less ground in more pages. Instead, can you *limit* your focus to one pivotal day on the trip? Can you explain and interpret one crucial scene? Can you research and portray one real social problem in your own backyard?

1 Limit time, place, and action

When a first draft attempts to describe and explain actions that took place over many days, weeks, or months, try limiting the second draft to actions that took place on one day, on one afternoon, or in one hour. Limiting the amount of time you write about automatically limits the action (what happened) and place (where it happened) as well. For example, in the first draft of a paper investigating the homeless in downtown Burlington, Dan began with a broad sweep:

> In this land of opportunity, freedom takes on different meaning for different people. Some people are born to wealth; others obtain it by the sweat of their brows, while average Americans always manage to get by. But others, not so fortunate or talented, never have enough food or shelter to make even the ends of their daily lives meet.

While there is nothing inherently wrong with this start, neither is there anything new, interesting, or exciting. The generalizations about wealth and poverty tell us only what we already know; there are no new facts, information, or images to catch our attention and hold it for the pages still to come.

Before writing his second draft, Dan visited the downtown area, met some homeless people, and observed firsthand the habits of a single homeless man named Brian; then he limited his next draft to what he witnessed one morning:

> Dressed in soiled blue jeans and a ragged red flannel shirt, Brian digs curiously through an evergreen bush beside a house on Loomis Street. His yellow mesh baseball cap bears no

emblem or logo to mark him a member of any team. He wears it low, concealing any expression his eyes might disclose. After a short struggle, he emerges from the bush, a Budweiser can in hand, a grin across his face. Pouring out the remaining liquid, he tosses the can into his shopping cart among other aluminum, glass, and plastic containers. He pauses, slides a Marlboro out of the crumpled pack in his breast pocket, lights it, and resumes his expedition.

While only one small act happens in this revised first paragraph—the re-trieving of a single beer can—that act anticipates Dan's forthcoming story of how unemployed, homeless people earn money. By describing instead of evaluating or interpreting this scene, he invites readers to make their own inferences about what it means. In other words, writing one specific, accu-rate, nonjudgmental scene asks readers to interpret and therefore engage more deeply in the text.

2 Limit scope

One technique for limiting the scope of any type of paper is to identify the topic of any one page, paragraph, or sentence in which something im-portant or interesting is introduced. Begin your next draft with that specific topic, focusing close now and limiting the whole draft to only that topic. For example, in a paper arguing against the clear-cutting of forests, focus on one page describing the cutting of Western red cedar; limit the next whole draft to that single subject. In a paper examining the exploitation of women in television advertising, focus on one paragraph describing a single beer ad; limit the next whole draft to that single subject. By limiting your scope in this fashion, you deepen your exploration.

WRITING 1: APPLICATION

Devote a portion of your journal or class notebook exclusively to exploring the revision possibilities of one paper. For your first entry, reread the paper you intend to revise, and limit either the time or scope that you intend to cover in the second draft.

15 b   Adding

A sure way to increase reader interest in a paper, and your own interest as well, is to *add* new and specific material to that overly general first draft. Whether you are arguing about the effects of mountain bikes on the wilderness, explaining the situation of the homeless people downtown, or interpreting the poems of Gwendolyn Brooks, it is your job to become the expert on this subject in your writing class. On first drafts, neither your instructor nor classmates expect you to be this authority; on subsequent drafts, their expectations increase.

1 Add expert voices

Locate new information to add to your later drafts by reading widely and listening carefully. Get to the library and locate sources that supplement and substantiate your own voice. Quote the experts, identifying who they are and why they should be listened to. Also get out into the field and talk to people who are the local experts on your subject. Quote these experts and include their voices in your next draft.

Although textual quotations are helpful and expected in academic papers, they are seldom so lively as interview quotations from local people. In many instances where little may have been published on local issues, the only way to get up-to-date local information is to talk to people. Quoting people directly not only adds new and credible information to your paper; it invariably adds a sense of life as well. For example, a team of first-year students collaborated to write a profile of the local Ronald McDonald House, a nonprofit organization providing free room and board for the families of hospital patients. In their first draft, they researched the local newspaper for introductory information on the origins of this institution. It was useful information, but without much life:

> The McDonald's corporation actually provided less than
> 5 percent of the total cost of starting the Ronald McDonald
> House. The other 95 percent of the money came from local
> businesses and special-interest groups.

For their second draft, the group interviewed the director of the Ronald McDonald House and used her as an additional and more current source of information. In fact, they devoted the entire second draft to material collected through interviews with the director and staff at the house. In the following sample, the director substantiates the information from the initial newspaper story but adds more specific, local, and lively details:

> "Our biggest problem is that people think we're
> supported by the McDonald's corporation. We have to get
> people to understand that anything we get from McDonald's is
> just from the particular franchise's generosity—and may be no
> more than is donated by other local merchants. Martin's, Hood,
> and Ben and Jerry's provide much of the food. McDonald's is
> not obligated to give us anything. The only reason we use their
> name is because of its child appeal."

Their final profile of the Ronald McDonald House included information ranging from newspaper and newsletter stories to site descriptions and interviews with staff, volunteers, and family.

2 Add details

If you quickly review this chapter's samples of revision by *limiting* and *adding,* you will notice the increase in specific detail. Focusing close, interviewing people, and researching texts all produce specific information that adds both energy and evidence to whatever paper you are writing. In the can collecting paper, the visual details make Brian come alive—"*the soiled blue jeans,*" "*red flannel shirt,*" "*yellow mesh cap,*" "*Budweiser can,*" "*Marlboro cigarette pack.*" In the Ronald McDonald revisions, newspaper statistics add authority ("*5 percent McDonald's corporation contribution*") while the interview information adds specificity ("*Martin's,*" "*Hood,*" "*Ben and Jerry's*").

WRITING 2: APPLICATION ·

Identify texts, places, or people that contain information relevant to your paper topic and go collect it. If you are writing a paper strictly from memory, close your eyes and visit this place in your imagination: Describe the details and re-create the dialogue you find there.

· ·

15 c   Switching

Another strategy for focusing a second or third draft is to deliberately alter your customary way of viewing and thinking about this topic. One sure way to change how you see a problem, experience, or idea is to *switch* the perspective from which you view it (the point of view) or the language in which you portray it (the verb tense).

1 Switch point of view

Switching point of view from which a story, essay, or report is written means changing the perspective from which it is told. For example, in re-counting personal experience, the most natural point of view is the first person (*I, we*) as we relate what happened to us. Here Karen writes in the first person in reporting her experience participating in the Massachusetts women's basketball tournament:

> We lost badly to Walpole in what turned out to be our final
>
> game. I sat on the bench most of the time.

However, Karen opened the final draft of her personal experience basket-ball narrative with a switch in point of view, writing as if she were the play-by-play announcer broadcasting the game at the moment, in this case moving to third person *and* adopting a new persona as well:

> Well folks, it looks as if Belmont has given up; the coach is
>
> preparing to send in his subs. It has been a rough game for
>
> Belmont. They stayed in it during the first quarter, but Walpole
>
> has run away with it since then. Down by twenty with only six
>
> minutes left, Belmont's first sub is now approaching the table.

In her final draft, Karen opened from the announcer's point of view for one page, then switched for the remainder of the paper to her own first-person perspective, separating the two by white space.

In research writing, as opposed to personal narrative, the customary point of view for reporting research results is third person (*he, she, it*) to em-phasize the information and deemphasize the writer. For example, the pro-file of the Ronald McDonald House begins, as you might expect, with no reference to the writers of the report:

> The Ronald McDonald House provides a home away from
> home for out-of-town families of hospital patients who need to
> visit patients for extended periods of time but cannot afford to
> stay in hotels or motels.

However, in one of their drafts, the writers switched to first person and explained their personal difficulties in reporting on this situation:

> In this documentary, we had a few problems with getting
> certain interviews and information. Since the house is a refuge
> for parents in distress, we limited the kinds of questions we
> asked. We didn't want to pry.

2 Switch tense

Switching verb tense means switching the time frame in which a story or experience occurs. While the present tense is a natural tense for explaining information (see the first Ronald McDonald example above), the most natural tense for recounting personal experience is the past tense, as we retell occurrences that happened sometime before the present moment—the same tense Karen adopted in draft one of her basketball essay. However, her final draft is written entirely in the present tense, beginning with the announcer and continuing through to the end of her own narrative.

The advantage of switching to the present tense is that it lets readers participate in the drama of the moment, waiting along with you to find out what will happen next. The disadvantage is that the present tense is associated with fiction—it's difficult to be writing while you're playing basketball. It's also difficult to reflect on your experiences if you're pretending they are occurring as you are writing.

3 Switch sides

Another way to gain a new revision perspective is to switch sides in arguing a position: write one draft supporting the "pro" side, then write a second draft supporting the "con" side. The real advantage of switching sides for a draft is that you come to understand your opponent's point of view better and so argue more effectively against it in your final draft.

Write in your journal about a past experience, using the present tense and/or third-person point of view. Then reread the passage and describe its effect on you as both writer and reader.

15 d Transforming

To *transform* a text is to change its form by casting it into a new form or genre. In early drafts, writers often attend closely to the content of their stories, arguments, or reports but pay little attention to the form in which these are presented, accepting the genre as a given. However, recasting ideas and information into different genres presents them in a different light. The possibilities for presenting information in different genres are endless, since anything can become anything else. Consequently, keep in mind that some transformations are useful primarily to help you achieve a fresh perspective during the revision process, while others are appropriate for presenting the information to readers.

In the world outside of college, it is common for research information to be reported in different genres to different audiences. For example, in a corporate setting, the same research information may be conveyed as a report to a manager, a letter to the president, a pamphlet for the stockholders, and a news release for public media—and show up later in a feature article in a trade publication or newspaper. As in the working world, so in college: information researched and collected for any paper can be presented in a variety of forms and formats.

1 Transform personal experience from essay to journal

The journal form encourages informal and conversational language, creates a sense of chronological suspense, is an ideal form for personal reflection, substitutes dates for more complex transitions, and proves especially useful for conveying experience over a long period of time. For example, Jeff used the journal format to tell the story of his month-long camping trip with the organization Outward Bound. Following is an excerpt, edited for brevity, in which he describes his reactions to camping alone for one week:

Day 4   I find myself thinking a lot about food. When I haven't eaten in the morning, I tend to lose my body heat faster than when I eat. . . . At this point, in solo, good firewood is surprisingly tough to come by. . . .

Day 5   Before I write about my fifth day of solo, I just want to say that it was damn cold last night. I have a −20 degree bag, and I froze. It was the coldest night so far, about −25. . . .

Day 7   I haven't seen a single person for an entire week. I have never done this before, and I really don't want to do it again—not having anyone to talk to. Instead of talking, I write to myself. . . . If I didn't have this journal, I think I would have gone crazy.

2 Transform to letters

An issue might be illuminated in a lively and interesting way by being cast as a series or exchange of letters. Each letter allows a different character or point of view to be expressed. For example, Issa's argument on mountain bike use in wilderness areas could be presented as a series of letters to the editor of a local paper arguing different sides of the controversy: from a hiker, a horseback rider, a mountain bike rider, a forest ranger, a landowner, and so on.

3 Transform to a documentary

Radio, film, and television documentaries are common vehicles for hearing news and information. Virtually any research paper could be made livelier by being cast as a documentary film or investigative feature story. Full research and documentation would be required, as for formal academic papers; however, writers would use the style of the popular press rather than the MLA or APA. In fact, the final form of the profile of the Ronald McDonald House was written as a script for *60 Minutes* and opened with a Mike Wallace–type reporter speaking into a microphone.

Smith: Hello, this is John Smith reporting for *Sixty Minutes*.

Our topic this week is the Ronald McDonald House. Here I am,

in front of the house in Burlington, Vermont, but before I go

inside, let me fill you in on the history of this and many other

houses like it.

The final paper included sections with the fictional Smith interviewing actual staff members as well as some sections presented neutrally from the camera's point of view:

> Toward the back of the house, three cars and one
>
> camper are parked in an oval-shaped gravel driveway. Up
>
> three steps onto a small porch are four black plastic chairs
>
> and a small coffee table containing a black ashtray filled with
>
> cigarette butts.

4 Transform to any medium of expression

The possibilities are endless: song, play, poem, editorial, science fiction story, laboratory report, bulletin, brochure, commercial, public address, political speech, telephone conversation, e-mail exchange, World Wide Web page, poster, "Talk of the Town" for *The New Yorker,* sound bite, environmental impact statement, conference paper, video game, philosophical debate.

WRITING 4: APPLICATION ....

Propose a transformation for a paper you are writing or have recently written. List the advantages and disadvantages of this transformation. Recast your paper (or a part of it) in the new genre and describe the effect.

....

15 e Experimenting

Standard academic conventions are accepted ways of doing certain things, such as using an objective voice in research reports and placing the thesis first in position papers. These conventions have evolved over time, for a reason. When carefully followed, they transmit ideas and information in a clear, predictable, and direct manner, avoiding confusion, complexity, and subjectivity. Although in many cases these conventions work well, successful writers sometimes invent unorthodox strategies and experiment with new forms to express their ideas. In order to decide whether a conventional or an unorthodox form is preferable in any part of your paper, try both to see which more appropriately presents your ideas in their best light. Sometimes an act as simple as changing time, tense, point of view, or genre can totally change the effect of a piece of writing.

When and under what circumstances should you limit, add, switch, or transform? While there are no rules, you might try using these strategies whenever you feel stuck or in need of new energy or insight. But be sure to weigh gains and losses whenever you use new focusing techniques.

Focused Revising

When you have finished the first draft of a paper, address one or more of the following questions:

1. How could this topic be **limited** so that it covers less in more detail?

2. What research information could I **add** to this paper to make it more convincing?

3. What would be the effect on this paper if I **switched** from past to present tense or from objective to subjective point of view?

4. In what **form** would the final draft of this paper be most effective?

Disregarding academic conventions in early drafts should seldom be a problem; however, disregarding them in final drafts is riskier, so check with your instructor. Be sure that in gaining reader attention in this way, you do not lose credibility or cause confusion.

SUGGESTIONS FOR WRITING AND RESEARCH

INDIVIDUAL

1. Write the first draft of a personal experience paper as a broad overview of the whole experience. Write the second draft by limiting the story to one day or less of this experience. Write the third draft using one of the other techniques described in this chapter: adding, switching, or transforming. Write the final draft any way that pleases you.

2. Write the first draft of a research-based paper as on overview of the whole issue you intend to deal with. In the second draft, limit the scope to something you now cover in one page, paragraph, or sentence. In the third draft, adopt one of the focused revision strategies described in this chapter: adding, switching or transforming. For your final draft, revise in any way that makes your presentation more effective.

COLLABORATIVE

For a class research project, interview college instructors in different departments concerning their thoughts about transforming academic papers into other genres. Write up the results in any form that seems useful.

WRITING ACROSS THE CURRICULUM

Imagining Revision

Review the examples below and invent your own imaginatively focused version of a paper you need to write somewhere across the curriculum. Compare the result with a more traditional draft. What are the strengths and weaknesses of each?

Art history: Review a local art exhibit in the form that might appear in both the local and campus newspapers.

Biology: Write a science fiction story after the fashion of your own favorite author, book, or movie; include carefully researched biological facts and principles, but take one imaginative leap (fiction, not fact) that creates a problem for your local community.

Business: Invent a product case study including perspectives from several corporate points of view (marketing manager, CEO, technical support) as well as several consumers with realistic but colorful complaints.

Communications: Recreate a fictional television talk show debate with perspectives similar to those of a Chris Matthews, Don Imus, or Rush Limbaugh interviewing an expert about a critical issue in contemporary communications.

Education: Write an editorial supporting a local school board decision with a major impact on local schools; then write half a dozen letters to the editor in response to the editorial.

Geology: Interview the survivor of a natural disaster such as a forest fire, flood, tornado, or drought; then research the same event on the Internet and in the library. Write an account of this event as it might appear in *Time* or *Newsweek* magazine.

History: Adopt the role of an important historical figure and compose a fictive letter exchange between this figure and his or her historical nemesis.

Literature: Invent the missing chapter or compose an alternate ending for a literary work you are studying in your English class; be sure to replicate the style and form of the work, and make your new content consistent with the content and theme of the original.

Political science: Write a public opinion column on a troublesome political issue in the style of a syndicated columnist representing a particular point of view such as conservative George Wills or liberal Ellen Goodman; conclude with letters to the editor sparked by the column.

Psychology: Contrast two major psychological theorists by sitting them down in a coffee shop (or bar or mall or talk show debate) for a conversation about a current issue of some psychological importance.

Sociology: Write an advice column as commonly published in newspapers in response to a question of some social concern after the fashion of Ask Abbey or Anne Landers; include both fictitious names and situations.

16 Responding to Writing and Peer Review

All writers can use a little help from their friends. Few great books or good stories were written by one author in one draft without some kind of help along the way. This is not to say that individual authors do not compose their own work, for of course they do. But even the most skillful writers benefit from suggestions by editors, reviewers, teachers, and friends. In like manner, your writing will improve if you share it with classmates, consider their reactions, and revise accordingly. This chapter explores ways to give and get writing help.

16 a Asking for help

Writers can profit from help at virtually every stage of the writing process—brainstorming ideas, seeking research leads, proofreading—but it's while they're revising that most writers seek the help of potential audiences to find out what in their writing is strong, what weak, because then they still have a chance to do something about it. Following are some suggestions for getting help as you seek to finish your writing.

1 Identify the kind of help you want

When you share a draft with a reader, specify what you want. If you want help with ideas, tell your reader not to worry about grammar, mechanics, or style. If you are firm about your ideas but want help with style or proofreading, specify that need. If you do want a general reaction, say so—but be prepared to hear about everything and anything.

2 Ask specific questions

If you wonder whether you've provided enough examples, ask about that. If you want to know whether your argument is airtight, ask about that. If you are concerned about your tone, ask about that. Also mark specific places in your paper about which you have questions, whether a word, a sentence, or even a paragraph.

3 Ask global questions

Ask whether the larger purpose is clear. Ask whether the reader can identify your theme, thesis, or main point. Ask whether the paper seems right for its intended audience. Ask for general reactions about readability, evidence, and completeness. Ask what objections or problems your reader would anticipate from other readers.

4 Listen, don't defend

Pay close attention to what you hear. You have asked for help, so now listen to what's offered. While listening to oral comments, stay quiet and take notes, interrupting only when you don't understand something. When reading written responses, read them twice before accepting or rejecting them.

5 Maintain ownership

Don't act on responses with which you disagree. If you don't understand or believe what someone tells you to do, don't do it. This is your paper, and you will live with the results.

WRITING 1: EXPLORATION ....

Describe the best written or oral response to a piece of your writing that you remember. What were the circumstances? Who was the respondent? Explain whether the response was deserved or not.

16 b   Giving responses

When you find yourself in a position to help other writers, keep the following basic ideas in mind:

- **Respond to the writer's requests.** If you are asked whether the thesis is clearly stated, for example, address that question before commenting on logic of the writer's reasoning, the accuracy or authority of the evidence, or other issues.

- **Follow the Golden Rule.** Give the kind of response that you would like to receive yourself. Remember how you feel being praised, criticized, or questioned. If you remember what helps, what hurts, and what makes you defensive, you'll give better help to others.

ESL *The Language of Making Suggestions*

Here are some tips on writing suggestions for your classmates:

- Use words or phrases that indicate a statement is your opinion only.

  | I think | in my opinion | from my perspective |
  | I feel | in my viewpoint | |

- Use *could* and *might* (suggestion) rather than *should* or *ought* (direction).

  You *could* clarify the cause–effect relationship in the last paragraph.

  Not: You should clarify.…

- Avoid negative phrases unless you need them to state your opinion clearly.

  I didn't understand how the second example was related to the first one.

  Not: Your second example wasn't related to the first.

- Use verbs like *seems* or *appears* to qualify your opinions.

  The conclusion *seems* to shift to another topic.

  The ideas at the end of your essay *appear* to be repeating ones that you stated earlier. Is that what you intended?

- Use questions if you are not sure that you interpreted the writer's ideas correctly.

  You seem to be disagreeing with the author in one place but agreeing with her in another. *Did I misunderstand your point?*

- **Attend to the text, not the person.** Focus on the text and not the writer's person. Writers, like all people, have egos easily bruised by careless or cruel comments.

- **Praise what deserves praise.** Most writers accept critical help when they also receive complimentary help, and in most papers there is something that is praiseworthy. But writers can sense hollow praise, so avoid praising what doesn't deserve it.

- **Ask questions rather than give advice.** It's your turn, now, to respect ownership. Asking questions gives writers room to solve their own problems. Of course, when asked, give answers or suggest alternatives if you have them.

- **Focus on major problems first.** Address conceptual problems first, mechanical ones later on. Early drafts that are marked for every possible misspelling, typo, and grammatical slip can overwhelm writers, making them reluctant to revise at all. At the same time, most writers want such proofreading help on near-final drafts, so it pays to check what the writer wants when.

16 c   Writing responses

Responding to writing in writing, as most instructors do, is both common and convenient. "Talking back" to a piece of writing by commenting directly on the manuscript takes less time and is therefore more efficient than discussing every idea orally. You can annotate a classmate's manuscript as you would a published work. It is easy to make written comments specific, identifying particular words, sentences, paragraphs, or examples that need attention. Also, written comments leave a record for writers to refer to later, when they actually get around to the rewriting.

The disadvantage to writing comments directly on papers is the possibility that misunderstandings will arise because you are not present to clarify. Try to ask questions rather than give answers and, again, follow the Golden Rule. The following suggestions may help:

Comment in pencil. Ink is permanent. Red ink looks bloody. Pencil, on the other hand, is soft, gentle and erasable. Many writers have already developed negative associations from teacher's red ink comments that correct what's wrong rather than praise what's right. Don't do that to your classmates.

Use clear symbols. Consider using professional editing symbols to comment on a classmate's paper. (They are printed on the last page of this book.) Or use obvious symbols that anyone can figure out—underlining or circling phrases that puzzle you or writing question marks in the margin. Put brackets where a missing word or phrase belongs.

Describe your most recent experience in receiving written comments from someone. Were the comments helpful? Did the respondent follow the suggestions given in this section? How did the comments influence your revisions?

....

16 d   Responding through conferences

One-to-one conferences provide the best and most immediate help writers can get. After reading a paper alone and quietly, sitting together, you can read passages aloud and make both general and specific comments about the writing. An oral conference helps as a follow-up to written comments, as conversations between writer and reader promote community, friendship, and understanding.

Conferences also make it easy to address both global and specific writing concerns at the same time. Finally, writer and reader can clarify misunderstandings as soon as they arise. However, it is harder to make tough, critical comments face to face, so readers are often less candid than when they make written comments. Also, conferring together in any depth about a piece of writing takes time.

The suggestions for making effective written responses also apply to oral conferences; however, there are additional things to keep in mind:

Converse in a comfortable setting. A place that's warm and casual can make a great difference in creating a friendly, satisfying discussion. When digressions occur, as they will if you're relaxed together, use them to learn new things about the subject and about each other; many such digressions circle back and help the writer. Even in the friendliest setting, however, if you don't discuss the writing itself, the writer will not be helped.

Ask follow-up questions. Ask clarifying questions to help writers advance their revision. When you have already written out responses, use the oral conference time to ask deeper or follow-up questions so together you can search for appropriate solutions.

....

Confer with a writer about his or her paper. Follow the suggestions given in this section. Describe in a journal entry how they worked.

....

16 e Responding in writing groups

Many serious writers belong to writing groups in which members both give and receive help with their writing. When a particular writer's work is featured, that writer receives a response from each member of the group; in other sessions, this person gives responses.

Writing groups allow a single writer to hear multiple perspectives on a draft, which provide either more consensus or more options for revision. They also allow an interpretation to develop through the interplay of different perspectives, often creating a cumulative response that existed in no single reader's mind before the session. Finally, writing groups can give writers more confidence by providing them with a varied and supportive audience.

At the same time, groups that meet outside of a classroom setting can be difficult to coordinate, since they involve people with varied schedules. Furthermore, the multiple audiences provided by groups may be intimidating and threatening to a writer. Since writing groups involve more people, require more coordination, take more time, and are less likely to be familiar than conferences with one other person, the following suggestions may help.

1 Form a group along common interests

Writing groups are useful in classes because the people are usually working on similar projects. You can take advantage of having everyone together at one time and place to give each other help. Writing groups can also be created outside of class by interested people who get together regularly to share their writing.

2 Focus on the writing

The goal of writing groups is to improve one another's writing and to encourage one another to write more. Pass out copies of the work in advance for silent reading prior to class, or read drafts aloud during the group meetings, with other group members following along on copies. After members have read or heard the paper, share your reactions, each in turn.

3 Keep groups small

In-class writing groups can have as few as three or as many as five members; time constraints make groups larger than five cumbersome groups. Smaller groups need less time, larger groups need more time. Groups that meet outside of the classroom have fewer size and time limits.

4 Allocate time fairly

Sometimes a meeting is organized so that each member reads a paper or a portion of a paper. At other times a meeting may focus on the work of one member, and members thus take turns receiving responses at different meetings. If papers are to be read, it generally takes two minutes to read a typed, double-spaced page out loud. Discussion and comment time should match or exceed the oral reading time on each paper. Groups that meet on their own should experiment to determine how much they can read and discuss at each session, perhaps varying the schedule from meeting to meeting.

SUGGESTIONS FOR WRITING AND RESEARCH

INDIVIDUAL

Investigate what has been written about peer writing groups. Check, in particular, for work by Kenneth Bruffee, Peter Elbow, Anne Ruggles Gere, Thom Hawkins, and Tori Haring-Smith. Write a report to inform your classmates about your discoveries.

COLLABORATIVE

Form interview pairs and interview local published writers about the way in which response by friends, family, editors, or critics affects their writing. Share results orally or in a collaboratively written report.

WRITING ACROSS THE CURRICULUM

Ten Questions to Ask Writers About Their Writing

Writing groups work across the curriculum, whether structured by instructor or students, because almost any writer profits from the response of other readers. To save time and energy, we'd suggest the groups be small, three to five members, and that each group create its own guidelines for when and where to meet and how to operate. At the same time, many writing groups have found the following questions useful in providing feedback to writers.

1. Where did this idea come from? (The origin of the idea may provide useful clues as an aid to further revision.)

2. What idea holds the whole piece together? (Where's the center? Can you point to a page or paragraph?)

3. When you were writing, who were your imagined readers? (Is there any place you think your readers might still be confused?)

4. Where else could you find information to support or expand this topic? (All papers profit from research knowledge.)

5. Whom could you interview to provide more information or another perspective on this topic? (Interview quotations add life to most papers.)

6. Can you provide some background or context for this idea?

7. Can you provide any examples or illustrations to show what you mean?

8. Can you think of two alternative ways to begin this paper?

9. Can you think of two alternative ways to end this paper?

10. Can you think of two alternative titles?

PART five

www.prenhall.com/fulwiler

229

chapter 17

Designing Documents

Design is the process of arranging and presenting your writing for others to read. Whether you present your writing as a college paper, a newsletter, or a Web page, you are creating a *document* of one kind or another. Your objective is to present your work in a neat, attractive form that makes its organization apparent and your purpose clear.

17 a Objectives of design

Good design is *transparent:* it calls attention to your work, not to itself. If a magazine cover catches your eye and you think, "That looks interesting, I want to read that," the design is doing its job.

Here are some objectives of good design and sample ways to achieve them.

1. **Attract attention.** Choose layout, title, type font, illustrations, and graphics to spark interest.

2. Create **flow.** Help readers move through your document. To remove obstacles, put background information or statistics in tables or boxes where they don't disrupt your narrative or argument.

3. Show **hierarchy.** Make items of similar importance resemble each other (this list is an example). In a college paper, set off major sections with subheadings, white space, or initial capitals.

4. Reinforce **contrast.** If your paper advances with one side of an argument, consider summarizing the opposing view in a box or "sidebar."

5. Use **graphics.** Charts make numbers easier to understand. Drawings or photos can convey information more efficiently than words.

6. Create **emphasis.** A pull-out quotation calls attention to an important concept. Boldface type highlights key terms.

7. Offer **choices.** If your writing is linear, readers tend to start at the beginning and slog through to the end. By removing selected elements from the main path, you allow readers to choose whether, for example, they want to read background information or stay with your main thread. This technique is important on the World Wide Web. (See 18a.)

8. **Hold attention.** Break up long, uninterrupted stretches with graphics or typographical devices such as subheadings or initial capitals. (See 17c.)

17 b Layout

Most college instructors ask you to use 8½ ×11″ paper. Use paper heavy enough to prevent type on the following pages from showing through. Use an inkjet or laser printer.

Set page **margins** at one inch at the top, bottom, and sides of body text. In Microsoft Word, go to File, Page Setup. Click on View, Print Layout to see the proportion of type to white space. **Double space** text unless instructed otherwise.

If the **title page** is also the first page of your paper, put your name, your instructor's name, the course title, and the paper's due date at the top left-hand corner, each on a separate, double-spaced line using your regular typeface. Don't indent.

On the next double-spaced line, center the title of the paper. Use a typeface slightly larger than your body type. Don't underline or italicize your title or put it in quotation marks. Double-space again, and begin the body of text. (For an example of this style, see 30k.)

If your instructor asks for a separate title page, follow his or her guidelines or those of your discipline. (See 30k and 31k for examples in MLA and APA formats.)

In the upper right-hand corner of each manuscript page, put your last name or an abbreviated title followed by the page number, separated by a single space. Do not use slashes, parentheses, periods, the abbreviation *p*, or the word *page*. (See 30k.) Your word processor can automatically insert your last name, title, and page number in a "header." The Word command is View, Header and Footer.

Rules for Indenting and Spacing

- Indent the first word of each paragraph five spaces.
- Space once after each word; space once after end punctuation if you write on a computer, otherwise check with your instructor.
- Space once after a comma, semicolon, or colon.
- Do not space between words and quotation marks, parentheses, or brackets. [See Chapters 56, 57.]
- Do not space between quotation marks and end punctuation or between double and single quotation marks. [See 56a, Chapter 56.]
- Do not space after a hyphen except in a suspended construction. *The rest of the staff are half- and quarter-time employees.* [See 60b–60d.]
- Do not space on either side of a dash, which consists of two hyphens. *Only two players remained—Jordan and Mario.* [See 57b.]
- Space before and after a slash only when it separates lines of poetry. [See 57e.]
- To display quotations of more than four typed lines, use block format. [See 56a.]
- Underlining spaces between underlined words is optional, but be consistent.

Columns

By tradition rooted in the use of the typewriter, college papers are usually produced in a single column of type, but your instructor may permit other formats. Newsletters and brochures are often set newspaper style with two, three, or more columns per page. Multiple columns provide shorter lines of text, which can be easier to read and offer greater design flexibility. In Word, click on Columns on the toolbar or use the commands under Format, Columns to specify the number of columns and the width of the gutter between them.

17 c   Typography

Today, the computer has all but completely replaced the typewriter. Word processing lets you choose what type face you use.

A **type font** consists of a typeface in various sizes with variations such as **bold** and *italic*. A **serif font**—like this one—has little strokes at the ends of each letterform. A **sans serif font** consists of type without serifs. For body text, serif type is easier to read. Use sans serif type in informal settings and in charts, captions, headings, and labels.

For the body text, use a font with proportional spacing (which varies with letter width) such as Times Roman, Marin, Bookman, Palatino, or New Century Schoolbook. If your instructor specifies a typeface that looks like a typewriter's, choose Courier, which has fixed spacing for each letter. Avoid unusual fonts. Choose a  **point size** that is easy to read, usually 12 points. The wider each line of type, the larger the point size needed for easy reading.

`12-point`
`Courier`
`(serif,`
`fixed`
`spacing)`
	12-point
	New Century
	Schoolbook
	(serif, propor-
	tional spacing)
		12-point
		News Gothic
		(sans serif,
		proportional)

1 Titles and headings

After selecting the body type, pick a typeface for your title and for headings.

Designing Documents

(Chapter title, 16-point News Gothic bold)

Tools for designing

(First-level heading, 12-point News Gothic bold)

Typography

(Second-level heading, 12-point News Gothic)

Title pages and headings

(Third-level heading, 12-point Times New Roman bold)

Justified or Ragged?

Your word processor can set type **ragged-right,** with an uneven right margin like this, or **justified,** with even margins on both sides, like the body text of this book. Word has icons in its format toolbar for ragged-right, centered, ragged-left, or justified type. Justified type is easier to read than ragged-right type, especially in a proportional font. Make sure, however, that the computer does not leave large spaces between words. Also check hyphenation. If your word processor makes many hyphenation errors, turn off hyphenation and hyphenate manually.

2 Pull-out quotations

One way to refresh readers' interest in a long passage of text is to use a pull-out quotation. You can set off your own words, highlight an important statistic, or select a compelling quotation. Pull-out quotations are easily created on a word processor.

Within a passage of text, create a box approximately the size you need. (In Word the command is Insert, Text

You can set off your own words . . . or select a compelling quotation.

box.) Copy the words you want from your text into the box. Use slightly larger type. If you use a quotation, include attribution. Then flow the text around the box (Format, Text box).

Another way to break up a passage or introduce a new section is to use a large **initial capital.** This is a capital letter several sizes larger than body type, with the text flowing around it. (The Word command is Format, Drop Cap.)

3 Lists and tables

A **list** of related items needs only a few simple typesetting techniques.

- Indent the list to set it off from the body type.

- Write all items in parallel grammatical form.

- Use letters, numbers, or typographical elements to introduce each item.

Most word processors can format lists automatically. Select the paragraphs in question and click on the toolbar icon for numbers or bullets.

DESIGNING YOUR DOCUMENT	DESIGN CHECKLIST
1. Set page layout	▪ Instructor's preferences
2. Set line spacing	▪ Title page elements
3. Select type fonts	▪ Page numbering
4. Plan tables, graphics	▪ Graphics, illustrations

An array or **table** can make numbers easier to understand. For a simple series, you can set up a table using tab stops.

Median Income by Age of Householder

15–24 YEARS	25–34	35–44	45–54	55–64	65+	ALL HOUSEHOLDS
$27,699	44,473	53,240	58,218	44,992	23,048	42,148

2000 Census

To compare more than one series of numbers, use tab stops or your word processor's table function. (In Word, use the toolbar's Insert Table button.) The following array of numbers is four columns wide by seven rows deep. Put the table near the text it illustrates.

Median Income by Age, 1993–2000

	1993	1999	2000
15–24	$22,740	26,017	27,689
25–34	36,793	43,591	44,473
35–44	48,063	52,582	53,240
45–54	54,350	58,829	58,218
55–64	39,373	46,095	44,992
65+	20,879	23,578	23,048

Bureau of the Census

17 d   Graphics

The term **graphics** refers to methods of presenting information in non-verbal forms, including charts, graphs, and illustrations.

A **line graph,** sometimes called a **fever graph,** can make data easy to see.

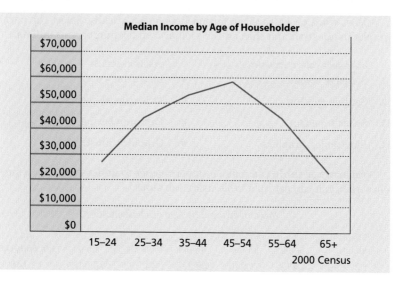

A **bar graph** can compare multiple sets of data.

A **pie chart** translates proportions into sections of a circle to compare parts to the whole.

Many computer programs can create graphics like these. Enter the data in a spreadsheet program and use its tools to create a graph. Pick the type of chart, give it a title, and copy it into a word-processor document. If you don't have the software, you can make simple graphs and charts by hand and include them in your paper. Keep them neat and easy to read, and identify the source of the data.

Use **color** for a specific reason, not just for its own sake. Color can convey information, as it does in a photograph. The colors in the bar graph and pie chart in this section distinguish elements and link them with their descriptions. If you can't print in color, many graphics programs can differentiate areas with shading.

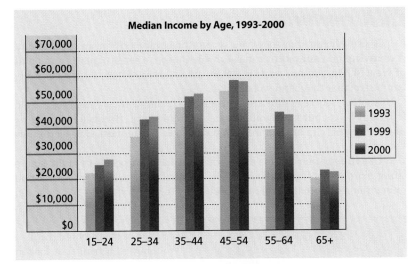

Median Income by Age, 1993-2000

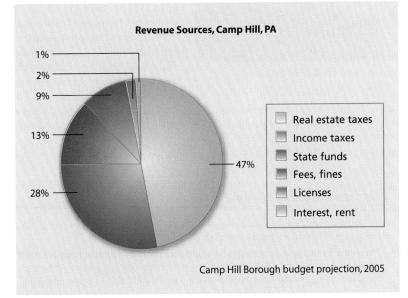

Revenue Sources, Camp Hill, PA

Camp Hill Borough budget projection, 2005

17 e   Illustrations

A **sketch** can show how you set up the equipment for an experiment. A **drawing** or a **snapshot** can establish a mood, a sense of place, or a point of view. When you are writing about art or architecture, a picture really can be worth a thousand words.

Another source of illustration is **clip art,** simple illustrations once sold in cutout books but now available in electronic form. Because it is generic and simplistic, clip art can make a paper look amateurish. Be careful how you use it.

Use illustration not for decoration but for a purpose—to make something more understandable or easier to visualize or to convey information or emotion. A photo that relates specifically to your writing— "We followed Queen's Garden Trail through Bryce Canyon"—is more effective than a stock photograph— "We followed a trail that looked something like this."

Queen's Garden Trail, Bryce Canyon

Your school's computer lab probably has a **scanner** you can use to put an image in electronic form. Once your image is in electronic form, the tools available in Word or photo-editing software such as Adobe Photoshop can help you adjust the image, and your word-processing program can place it on the page. Mounting a photographic print or drawing on a page is also acceptable. If you use an image you did not create, be sure to obtain permission.

Design Resources Online

Combining text, headlines, and images on your computer to create papers or publications is sometimes called **desktop publishing.**

■ Resources for designing paper and Web documents can be found at http://desktop publishing.com/open.html. The site contains technical tips, theoretical discussions, free type fonts and clip art, and electronic bulletin boards you can use to discuss design questions.

■ Another desktop publishing site is http://desktoppub.about.com/.

- Learn about the history and the uses of various type styles at Typographic. http://www.rsub.com/typographic/

- The online version of Patrick J. Lynch and Sarah Horton's Web Style *Guide: Basic Design Principles for Creating Web Sites* gives an overview, much of which applies to publishing on paper as well. http://www.med.yale.edu/caim/manual/index.html

- Terry Sullivan's site All Things Web explains how design for Web pages differs from that of print documents. http://www.pantos.org/atw/basics.html

- See the front page designs of more than 300 newspapers, updated every day at http://www.newseum.org/todaysfrontpages/

- The Yahoo! directory has links to collections of graphic elements and tips at http://dir.yahoo.com/Arts/Design_Arts/Graphic_Design/Web_Page_Design_and_Layout/Graphics/

Placing an Image in Text

In Word, select the approximate point in the text at which you want to insert the image. You can copy the image from another application and paste it into your document. Or select Insert, Picture, From File, Browse (to the file you want) and click Insert. To adjust the picture's size, position, and relation to the type, go to the picture toolbar. If the toolbar is not visible, select View, Toolbars, Picture. With the picture selected, click on the toolbar's Format Picture icon. Use the Size tab to adjust the horizontal or vertical measure until the image fits (as long as Lock Aspect Ratio is selected, the proportions of the image will remain the same). Use the Layout tab  to position the image left, right, or center and to determine how the type flows around the image.

WRITING 1: EXPLORATION

Look for examples of different kinds of design in newspapers and magazines. If your school library has a collection of student papers, look at some of them as well. What design techniques appeal to you, and which ones are unappealing? Which ones look dated or appear to be trying too hard? Pick a half-dozen examples, and for each one write down two or three things you think the designer or author is trying to achieve through design.

WRITING ACROSS THE CURRICULUM

Designing Documents for Specific Audiences

With the help of a librarian or a professor, find copies of newsletters or Web pages produced by students and professionals in at least two different academic disciplines. What design similarities appear across the disciplines? within each discipline? What differences across disciplines? Pick a Web page or newsletter you find visually appealing and effective. Describe the major elements and how they contribute to communicating the author's message.

chapter 18

Writing for the Internet

By helping you share ideas across the campus or across the globe, Internet writing raises special questions about your purpose and your audience. Why are you writing, and for whom, and in what electronic format? If you're a college student, you grew up in a world that is increasingly digitized and interconnected. If you haven't already done so, you will almost certainly soon begin corresponding by e-mail, sending *instant messages* to friends, or *chatting* with groups online. You might join a *newsgroup* or an *e-mail list* to find people who could help your research move further, publish research discoveries and analysis for others to critique, or post a photo-illustrated essay on the World Wide Web to seek feedback from classmates. You might display your writing and editing for prospective employers or create an online journal, called a *weblog* or a *blog,* to share personal observations, family news, or comments on current events. It's a wired world, and writing is a big part of it.

Your audience will differ in each situation. Each makes possible different kinds of interaction with other Internet users. You'll usually write with a primary audience in mind. For many Internet publications, there's a secondary audience to consider too—people who happen upon your writings for other reasons and might need more context or explanation.

18 a   Writing for the Web

On a Web page, you can present text, charts, photographs, video clips, and audio recordings. But readers can't take in all these things at once. In

Web Jargon

World Wide Web pages: text, graphics, and images presented simultaneously on a computer screen. When they hear "Internet," the Web is what many people think of first.

Web site: a group of related Web pages.

Navigation: creating or following paths within and among Web pages.

Hyperlink: the key navigation tool of the Web. Using hyperlinks, or links for short, any Web page can be "next to" any other page.

E-mail: electronic mail, sent to one person or to many simultaneously.

Instant messages: written messages exchanged online in real time. Quick, personal, and informal.

Chat: similar to instant messages, but open to more than two people at a time. An online "space" for chat is a *chat room*.

Newsgroup: a collection of written entries from numerous authors on an individual topic.

E-mail lists: lists of people interested in a list's particular topic. E-mail sent to the list address reaches members as individual messages or as a daily summary.

Blog (or weblog): an online journal devoted to personal reflection, commentary, or news about topics of interest to its author.

Blogosphere (or blogspace): the "universe" of blogs, a loose-knit online community in which blog authors—"bloggers"—share their thoughts, document facts, exchange opinions, and—sometimes—engage in seemingly endless debate.

print, you'd set the order in which readers would proceed. On the Web, readers pick their own paths among alternatives you construct.

1 Web audiences

Readers on the Web often don't read in the same ways as print readers. They scan rather than read deeply. They skip from section to section, page to page, or site to site, looking for items that spark their interest. Others are seeking for specific information. If they don't find it quickly, they move on. If they think they might find what they need, they stick around a little longer. If they do find useful information, they linger until the supply runs out or they find enough.

A 2000 study by Stanford University and the Poynter Institute (a newspaper-industry think tank) found that even though many Web sites offer photos and graphics, a surprising number of readers focus first on words—headlines, captions, or stories. Readers' patterns of scanning combined with insights about what causes readers to pause and "drill deeper" suggests some general strategies for Web writers. Some of the following ideas might sound like design issues rather than writing strategies. That's because the Web makes the connections between organization, design, and writing even more important.

The first Web page readers encounter should provide most of the following items or, at least, links to them:

The subject—what's the site about?

Authorship—whose work is this?

Purpose—why was it created?

Contents—beyond the home page, what other content is available?

Context—is there information for readers new to the topic?

Organization—are there links to major sections? How does the reader navigate the site?

Paths—where did the information come from? Where can readers learn more?

Date—when was the site created and last modified?

2 Manageable chunks

You can make some educated guesses about what your specific audience wants. Site visitors might be seeking specific information, or they might be interested in your perspective and opinions. Whatever you most want readers to see and whatever you believe they will need or find interesting, display that information prominently.

Break information into small, easily comprehensible *chunks*. Online readers prefer not to scroll through long screens, which shortens their effective attention spans. You can help by linking to separate pages of background information, answers to common questions, how or why you created the site, and other side issues.

Writing for Web Readers

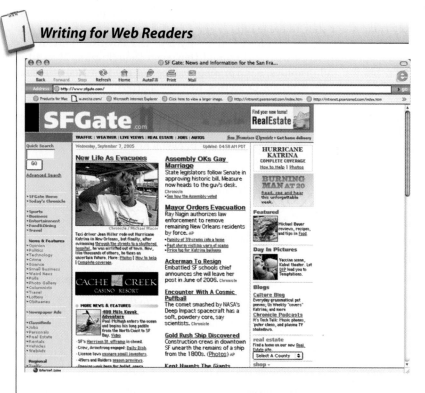

How readers view a Web site	How to design for Web readers
Often begin with written text	Make captions, titles, and openings engaging and informative. Don't let graphics hinder reading.
Look for navigation signs	Use organization strategies common to other sites (such as a column of links repeated on the side of each page).
Read "shallow but wide"	Categorize. Don't hide important data "deep" in any one category. Write brief, clear headings that tell what follows.
Scan rather than read	Create lists. Put keywords in boldface.
Read first sentences only	Make every word count.

Breaking Up Information

Lists make information accessible. Concise writing saves readers time. Compare these two examples:

Mission

The Chicago Opera Theater was founded in 1974. The mission of the Theater is to provide first-class productions, drawing from the operatic repertoire of some of the greatest works of the 17th, 18th, and 20th centuries. The Theater aims to produce intimate and innovative performances that are accessible to everyone and to discover and assist the development of the most talented young artists in the United States. The Theater further intends to make itself an integral part of the cultural landscape of Chicago.

Mission

Founded in 1974, the Chicago Opera Theater's mission is

- To provide first-class productions of operatic repertoire, including the greatest works of the 17th, 18th, and 20th centuries.

- To produce intimate and innovative performances that are accessible to everyone.

- To discover and develop the most talented young artists in the United States.

- To become an integral part of Chicago's cultural landscape.

Both examples contain the same information, but the second, which is what the opera company actually wrote, is easier to read and remember. This technique is effective in print as well.

3 Nonlinear writing

Breaking information into chunks gives readers a choice of routes through your material. They can read background information first or jump to your conclusions. They can examine your sources to judge the quality of your research. They can go first to illustrations. But you must *anticipate* these moves and create paths for them.

Suppose you're writing for a history class about the roots of the Civil War. The Whig Party and the Compromise of 1850 will be familiar to your professor and classmates, but other readers will need more background. To find an organization pattern, make a cluster diagram of main ideas.

What was in the compromise?

Consequences of the compromise of 1850

Who were the Whigs? Who compromised with whom?

How slavery's spread was affected

What the Fugitive Slave Act meant to slaves, to abolitionists

Did the comprise work?

What it meant for the Union

Grouping and expanding these elements begins to suggest how a Web presentation of your research could be structured, a page or more for each section. These groupings will become the major elements of your presentation. You can use an embellished cluster diagram, like the one below, or outline each major element on a page of its own and arranged into sequence to create what is called a "storyboard" presentation.

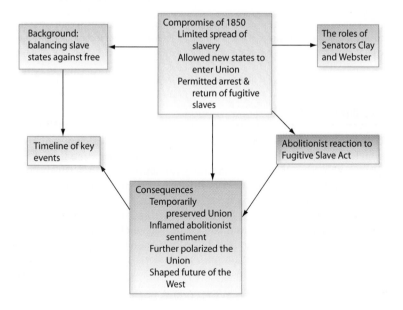

4 Links and navigation tools

Once you map the structure, you can begin to imagine what each section will contain and what paths readers will need between sections. For example, a main reference to the Fugitive Slave Act should link to its impact among abolitionists. If you have a preferred sequence in mind, use a *next* link to connect each chunk to the next.

A **navigation bar** is a consistent set of links providing access to all pages in a site. Every page should be available directly or indirectly from the home page. Each page should include a link to other pages in its section, to other sections, and to the home page, so readers can see where they are at all times. The anchors for navigation links can be images such as buttons or pictures, or just words. A simple set of navigation links for the Compromise of 1850 paper might look like this.

Home: Compromise of 1850   Elements of Compromise   Timeline
Fugitive Slave Act   Clay and Webster   Consequences

Put a navigation bar at the top and bottom of every page, or down one side. Make navigation tools visually consistent, and keep them in the same position on every page.

5 Photos on Web pages

If you include a photo that belongs to someone else, be sure you have permission, and give credit. File size is an important consideration when including photos on your pages. Digital photos are usually produced for print at a resolution of 300 dots per inch, or dpi, but that resolution results in file sizes that load very slowly over dial-up Internet connections. Use a photo-editing program to create 72 dpi versions of your photos. Readers will appreciate the faster loading.

6 Resources for Web site builders

If you want to learn HTML, tutorials on the Web can get you started. Check out "A Beginner's Guide to HTML," a primer from the National Center for Supercomputing Applications at the University of Illinois at Urbana–Champaign, birthplace of the graphical Web browser, at http://archive.ncsa.uiuc.edu/General/Internet/WWW/HTMLPrimer.html. For a

Navigation links repeated on all pages.

Front page describes purpose, displays main areas.

An overview of site structure is apparent from front page organization.

This is a University of Wisconsin–Madison site dedicated to finding high-quality academic information on the Web.

print reference, try *HTML 4 for the World Wide Web* by Elizabeth Castro (Peachpit, Berkeley, 2000). For others, search on the term "HTML tutorial."

18 b   E-mail, newsgroups, and instant messages

If you have access to a computer, you're probably familiar with electronic mail and instant messaging, two important forms of one-to-one communication online. E-mail lists, newsgroups, and chat enable one-to-many interactions. This section focuses on writing in these formats. For tips on how to find and use e-mail lists and newsgroups for research, see 24d.

1 E-mail do's and don't's

You can use e-mail to contact people who can provide information or help you find it, conduct interviews, or verify facts or quotations. Here are a few e-mail rules from the world of business, some learned by painful experience.

In academic or business e-mail, write more formally than you would when corresponding with friends. Capitalize appropriately and spell conventionally. Don't use slang or informal abbreviations (great, not gr8). Don't assume the recipient will understand IMHO (in my humble opinion) or ROFL (rolling on the floor laughing).

E-mail magnifies emotion. If you're angry or excited, draft, save, and wait a while before you send. If you have something negative to say—"Your answers seem to contradict one another. Why?"—avoid e-mail if you can. In person or on the telephone, you can modulate your voice and not sound hostile. In e-mail, a challenging question can appear hostile, attempts at humor can fall flat or be misunderstood, and any expression of anger or cynicism can be magnified.

E-mail is forever, so think before you send. Even if you delete your files and the recipient does the same, copies can survive on servers at various points of Internet transmission. You might regret something you wrote, but you might not be able to erase it.

Just as e-mail can live forever even though you'd prefer that it wouldn't, e-mail messages can vanish if you don't take care to save them. To document an e-mail conversation for research or business, save and print a copy that includes all headers and routing codes.

Keep it simple. Until you know your correspondent's style, be aware that many people will recognize and answer only one or two questions per e-mail.

2 Newsgroups and e-mail lists

E-mail lists and newsgroup lists allow one writer to reach many people with similar interests. Information submitted (or *posted)* to a newsgroup, sometimes called a discussion group, is collected on a computer "bulletin board." Readers interested in a group's topic electronically visit the board to read messages and submit their own. If you subscribe to an e-mail list, you receive and send messages by e-mail.

Some lists and groups require you to become a member before posting or reading messages. A request for membership for research purposes will usually be accepted, and almost all lists are free. Many have archives in which you can read prior discussions.

The e-mail do's and don't's discussed previously also should guide your posting to a list or newsgroup. In addition, before you post a query, do your homework. Most groups and lists publish frequently asked questions (FAQs, pronounced *fax*) and answers. Read them. The FAQs often will tell you whether you're in an appropriate group, list the key contacts, answer many preliminary questions, tell you how to post, and describe any special protocols. (For an example, see 24c.) If there's an archive, search it for your specific topic before posting. The sources you contact will appreciate not having to repeat information they have already published.

In your initial contact, identify yourself and your purpose. Provide context: If you have a question about a specific message, provide a link or a brief, attributed quotation. If you want a direct reply rather than post to the list or group, include your e-mail address.

3 Instant messages and chat

When you correspond by e-mail, each exchange can take minutes or days. By contrast, instant messaging (IM) and chat are "real-time" modes—people who are online at the same time can send messages that appear immediately on one another's screens.

Instant messaging usually links two people online, whereas chat can involve any number. Either can be an appropriate information-gathering method in certain circumstances, for example, if a person you wanted to interview consented to an IM conversation or a chat with you and a collaborator. Remember in an academic or business conversation to write in appropriately formal ways (see 18b1).

While conducting an interview by chat or instant messages, keep a word-processing file open and periodically copy and paste the entire conversation into it, saving as you go. When the conversation is finished, enter the time, the date, and the full names, screen names, and titles of the people involved. Save the file, and print a copy for your business or research records.

18 c   Weblogs

Weblogs, or blogs, are online, public journals. Blog postings frequently link to related material on other sites and permit readers to post comments. Thus blogs connect with one another and with their readers. Over the last few years, blogging has moved from an obscure form of Internet scribbling to a collectively powerful force in commerce, journalism, and politics. How are bloggers causing this earthquake? They are *writing*.

There are nearly as many reasons for writing in a weblog as there are bloggers—in March 2005 the search site Technorati (www.technorati.com) said it counted 7.8 million blogs and estimated that the number had doubled every five months for the past 20 months.

What are all these people writing about? Whatever interests them—whatever they're thinking about, reacting to, struggling to understand, or trying to explain.

Blog hosts and blog tools:

Many host sites offer free blog accounts. A blog is basically a simple Web page, with the most recent journal entries at the top, but hosting software makes it possible to publish without knowing HTML. Other sites offer tools for editing or data gathering. There's a useful directory at Weblogs Compendium (http://www.lights.com/weblogs/hosting.html), or search on "blog host."

Search tools now cover the world of weblogs. Visit www.technorati.com, www.icerocket.com, www.blogdigger.com, or search for "blog search."

RSS, or Really Simple Syndication, is an important Weblog tool that provides a way for readers to get summaries of their favorite blogs and for publishers to let readers know when sites are updated. Find tools and info at http://allrss.com/. There's an RSS search engine at www.feedster.com.

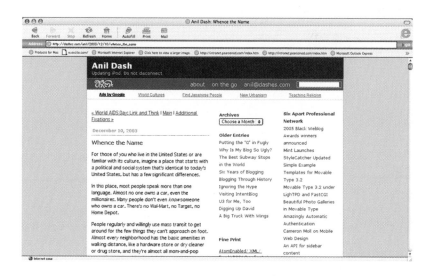

WRITING ACROSS THE CURRICULUM

Writing Across the Internet

Pick a Web site that you have found useful for research. How is it organized? What did you notice first, and how did you discover its organization? If you had difficulty finding anything, how did you resolve it? What would you do to improve the site's usefulness for visitors like you?

For a class other than your writing class, find a related e-mail list or newsgroup. Search the archives or current posts for information related to what you're studying. Compare the writing to the materials you've read in that class. What are the similarities and differences? How would you explain them?

Do you have a favorite blog? If not, browse until you find one that appeals to you. What do you like about it? What can you discern about the author's purpose? For what audience is the blog written? If comments are posted, what do they tell you about the site's readers?

If you were starting a weblog, what would you write about? Narrower question: What would you write about today? What three other blogs would you want to link to? What would your choice of links tell readers about you?

chapter 19

Writing for the World

Beyond the classroom, a world of writing situations awaits. If you record news of your community or advocate action or policy, you will be engaging in what is sometimes called *public writing* or *civic writing*. Public writing includes persuasion, in editorials, letters to the editor, position papers, and legal briefs. Writing reports is a key task in government and the social sciences. Journalism is a special form of report writing. And even if you are not a journalist, understanding how journalists write can help you attract news coverage of issues or events.

In business, you might write to apply for a job, to explain a proposed transaction, or to confirm an agreement. You might report on marketing prospects or the solution to a problem. You might create a brochure to describe a company's services or write advertising copy to persuade consumers to buy a product.

As you meet these situations in business and public affairs, you'll recognize familiar writing purposes: *inform, explain, persuade, advocate.* The techniques you are developing in college will serve you well in the world beyond.

19 a   Reports

When you are asked to report, you are usually being asked to describe a problem, conflict, or situation. Conventional news reporting often stops there. In business, reporting often goes further, to evaluating possible solutions and making recommendations.

Begin by understanding the purpose, the audience, and the scope of your task. Next, gather information. That step is called researching or *reporting.* Then write, organizing the information in ways that support your purpose.

Here are some common reporting purposes:

Describe an event, its consequences, and people's reactions. This is a common purpose for news stories. People's reactions help readers understand the event's importance and meaning.

Identify a problem, investigate its nature and extent, and propose a solution.

Document the process and results of a research process or experiment.

Document a person's actions or behavior. This could be anything from a police report to a physician's statement to a nomination for a heroism award.

Compare alternatives (an equipment purchase, how to start a nonprofit organization) and recommend a decision or course of action.

For whom are you writing? Journalists often imagine an individual or group whose characteristics are a composite of real readers they know. Within an organization, a *primary audience* is the people who will make decisions based on your report. A *secondary audience* comprises those who will be affected by that decision. An *immediate audience* consists of people—your editors or your immediate supervisors—who will read your report first.

As you gather information, ask the journalist's familiar questions— *who, what, when, where, why,* and *how.* Depending on the situation, some of these questions will be more important than others. *What* is the condition of city parks? *How much* will it cost to improve them? In a study of consumer behavior, *why* did a new product do poorly in the marketplace? *Who* bought it, and who didn't? Why not? In a public opinion poll, *how many* voters think health care should be a private responsibility, and how many think it should be guaranteed to everyone?

Here's a basic strategy for organizing a report:

State the problem and the purpose (inform, analyze, recommend): *City parks have a backlog of deferred maintenance. Equipment is worn or unusable. Buildings need repair. What can or should be done?*

Provide background information or context: *Spending has been cut over several years. Other budget areas had pressing needs.*

Convey facts: *Further deferral of maintenance will damage some buildings past the point of repair. Growth in youth sports participation requires more maintenance of athletic fields.*

List alternatives: *Close less-used parks; shift money from other budget areas; charge user fees; raise taxes.*

Recommend action: *Form a group of park users and managers to budget repairs over five years and recommend a mix of shifted resources and new revenue. Bring recommendations to city council by beginning of next budget cycle.* (Some reports, including progress reports and news reports, need not involve a recommendation or a conclusion.)

As you write, distinguish fact from opinion. Identify your own opinions clearly. (In news reporting, your opinion is less important than the opinions of people affected by the events you describe.) In most reports, a fact or a prediction carries more weight than an emotional characterization: *The park maintenance supervisor says the roof of the pavilion needs to be replaced. If it leaks, repairs will be much more expensive.* That is more useful than *The park maintenance supervisor says the pavilion roof is in a "disgraceful condition."*

19 b   Pamphlets and brochures

A *pamphlet* or *brochure* is one way to provide information about a product or service. Often no more than a single sheet of paper, a pamphlet is easy and inexpensive to produce. For businesses and organizations, pamphlets provide a quick, portable format to give out information, including schedules, contact information, and more.

The Mendocino Wine Country pamphlet on page 256 follows a common format: a single $11 \times 17''$ sheet (twice the size of a standard $8\frac{1}{2} \times 11''$ sheet) folded in sections and printed on both sides. This flyer was designed to tell visitors where to find wineries on California's redwood coast.

What? A map, description of grape-growing regions and a list of wineries.

Where? Mendocino County on the northern California coast.

When? Winery hours and visiting policies are listed.

Who? The Mendocino Growers Alliance.

With a word-processing computer, simple image-editing tools, and a printer, you can design and produce a basic flyer. (For more on designing documents, see Chapter 17.) Adapting the pamphlet format to the Web frees you from the restrictions of paper sizes (see page 257).

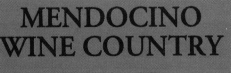

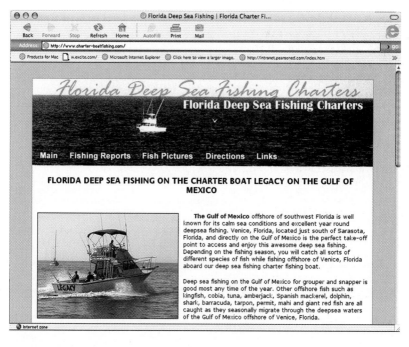

19 c Newsletters

If you belong to an academic organization, a nonprofit group, or a club of people with a shared interest, chances are you receive a *newsletter,* a periodic publication that keeps members of a group up-to-date on developments of interest. Since the advent of the personal computer, newsletters have led to a whole area of computing known as desktop publishing, meaning that layout, illustration, and typographical chores that once required professional assistance can now be performed at your own computer keyboard. A newsletter also makes an excellent marketing tool for a small business, especially when sent to customers by e-mail.

The editor of a special-interest newsletter has one key advantage: there's less need to guess about who is reading. The audience consists of people already familiar with the topic or newcomers curious enough to browse a while. The mix of devotees and newbies will determine how you balance articles between introductory and advanced material (see page 258).

DENISON UNIVERSITY

Library Links

Volume 5, Issue 3   *http://denison.edu/library/*   Spring 2005

National Library Week April 10 -16

It is National Library Week, a time to celebrate the contributions of libraries, librarians and library workers to their schools, campuses and communities.

As part of this annual event the William Howard Doane Library will be hosting the following events and displays.

National Library Workers' Day

Tuesday, April 14

Show your appreciation for your favorite library worker!

Spring Lemonade Stand

Thursday, April 14
10:30 a.m. - 12:00 p.m.
In front of the library. (Rain site - Library Atrium)

Senior Student Workers Display

New book area across from the Circulation Desk

Denison Faculty and Staff READ posters

Atrium Overlook Area

Granville Bicentennial Display

Located in the display case in the 3rd floor Gallery west of the office door

National Library Week 2005 marks the fifth year of The Campaign for America's Libraries, a multi-year public education campaign sponsored by the ALA and libraries across the country to speak loudly and clearly about the value of libraries and librarians in the 21st century.

Local Celebrities Grace Read Posters

In the fall of 2004 the Denison Library launched it's first in a series of local celebrity READ posters. The purpose of the READ poster campaign is to promote the Denison libraries, literacy and reading. Denison University's celebrites were excited about donating their time to this cause.

Nedda Ahmed, Fine Arts Liaison Librarian, designed the posters. She and Star Andrews, Reserves Specialist, photographed the celebrities in their own environments with their favorite books.

Introduced at the "Welcome Back" Lemonade Stand last fall, the posters are currently on display in the library's Atrium area. The display includes posters of Library Director Scottie Cochrane and her husband Louis Middleman, President Dale Knobel, Provost

David Anderson, Studio Art Professor Ran Abram, Communication Professor Laurel Kennedy, Black Studies professor John Jackson, History Professor Catherine Dollard and husband Economics Professor Ted Burczak and their children, Spanish Professor Eduardo Jaramillio, and History Professor Don Schilling.

In addition to articles and news reports of interest to subscribers, a newsletter should include the *who, what,* and *why* of its existence. It should list the key officers of the organization, such as the president, secretary, treasurer, and editors of the newsletter itself. It also should give subscription information and mailing addresses for the organization and its editorial offices. If the newsletter is published online or sent as e-mail, these elements can appear as links.

19 d Press releases

A basic way to attract newspaper or television coverage of an event is to send out a press release. There is no fixed format for a press release, but any press release must tell *who, what, when,* and *where.* Often a little background information will be needed to explain *why* or *how.*

You can find out how long before an event to send a release by calling a newspaper's *city, sports,* or *features desk* or the *assignment editor* of a television newsroom. Online publications have *content producers* who work for *content editors.* Give as much advance notice as you can, since reporters, like college students, manage their time by planning ahead whenever possible.

Press Release Guidelines

If your organization has letterhead stationery or a logo, use it.

Include basic contact information: officers' names, mailing address, phone number, e-mail addresses, Web address.

Check for *who, what, when, where, why,* and *how.*

Double-check your facts. Then check them again, especially times, dates, addresses, and phone numbers.

Always include your name and phone number or that of someone in your organization who can provide more information.

Ask each news organization whether to send releases by postal mail, fax, or e-mail.

Ask for the name of the person to contact for the type of information you're sending, and mark the release for that person's attention.

Follow up with a phone call to make sure the release was received and ask whether you can answer any questions.

Try to think like a reporter or an assigning editor, who upon reading your release will be thinking, "Why is this event newsworthy? What's happening? Who will be there? Someone of particular interest? Members of the general public? Who will want to read or hear about it? If I write a story, how can it be illustrated? What will make the most interesting photographs or video footage?" Television of course relies heavily on film, but photography is increasingly important to newspapers. Online publications can use either still photos or video. If a "photo opportunity" will happen at a specific time, be sure to say so in the release. And remember, you're trying to catch people's attention, so keep your writing interesting.

19 e   Advocacy

Want to change the world? Spread the word about what needs changing. Whether you're proposing to amend a local ordinance or calling for international action against AIDS, you need to reach people who are willing to listen and consider your call to action. You can publish your arguments on a personal Web page or develop them on a weblog, e-mail them to a list of friends, post them on a relevant newsgroup, write to a public official, or send a letter to the editor of a magazine or newspaper. Many newspaper editorial pages accept guest opinion pieces.

In college writing, you have learned to assemble relevant facts and to employ logic, expecting your audience to respond in a fair-minded and reasonable way if approached in a similar manner. This strategy is a good starting point for public advocacy.

1 Letter to the editor

Think of a letters column as a continuing conversation. Readers write in to discuss what they have read, and other readers respond in turn. Magazines usually restrict their letters columns to comments on their own articles. In many newspapers, pretty much any topic can be fair game, but it helps to refer to a recent, relevant article.

Get to the point. Brevity might be the soul of wit, but in a newspaper letters column, it also is essential to getting published. Identify the topic, state any new facts, and make as clear and as logical a point as you can. You can close with an appeal to morality, patriotism, or emotion. The stronger your logic, the greater the power of such an appeal.

> To the Editor:
>
> The article "More homes become call centers" (May 5) states, "Most of the home-based agents work part-time or as independent contractors, so employers don't pay for . . . benefits. Unions, which represent employers at some large call centers, will be hard-pressed to reach workers spread across thousands of homes, analysts say."
>
> When did it become an undisguised employer objective to eliminate jobs that entail health insurance and benefits? When did blatant anti-union strategy become part of the business plan?
>
> So much for the rhetoric of employers, who keep insisting that our state needs business tax cuts to create good jobs.
>
> *Terry Stark*
> Harrisburg

This writer fit the topic, an argument, and an emotional closing into just over 100 words.

Sign and date the letter, and include your return address and telephone number. Most newspapers will not publish a letter without being able to contact the writer for verification.

2 Writing to public officials

Asking a government agency or nonprofit organization for action is a little different from writing to a newspaper. Public agencies have clearly defined missions that they are duty-bound to fulfill, so the first step is picking the responsible agency and persuading its officials that the problem you see is their responsibility.

May 12, 2005

The Honorable Judd Gregg
The Honorable Kent Conrad
Senate Office Building
Washington, D.C. 20510

Dear Senators Gregg and Conrad,

Following the passage last month of H. Con. Res. 95 outlining the budget for fiscal 2006, the approval of oil exploration in the Alaska National Wildlife Refuge seems increasingly likely.

In the past, I have written to oppose oil drilling in the refuge, as even the highest predicted levels of production will only postpone the coming energy crisis. However, I could accept oil development more readily if I could be assured that the nation would use the time it generates to solve an underlying problem—overdependence on fossil fuels. We should

> immediately raise fuel economy standards for all cars and trucks.
>
> encourage alternative sources by requiring utilities to credit consumers for solar energy contributed to the grid.
>
> support research and development in solar, wind, hydrogen, and cogeneration with grants and regulatory assistance.

The policy you craft in the Budget Committee in the coming months will go a long way to determining what our energy landscape looks like when the oil from the wildlife refuge has been consumed.

Sincerely yours,

Roosevelt Symington

43 Big Bend Road
Cave City, KY 42127

The letter is addressed to the chairman and ranking Democrat of the Senate Budget Committee. The structure is familiar: State the situation; argue from facts; conclude by urging action.

Addresses and Salutations for Public Officials

Official	Written address	Salutation
The president	The President The White House Washington, D.C. 20500	Dear Mr. (Madam) President
U.S. senator	The Honorable Jane Smith Senate Office Building Washington, D.C. 20510	Dear Senator Smith
U.S. representative	The Honorable Jane Smith House Office Building Washington, D.C. 20515	Dear Mrs. (or Ms.) Smith
Governor	The Honorable John Doe The Capitol Harrisburg, PA 17120	Dear Governor Doe
State senator	The Honorable John Smith Senate Chambers, State Capitol Des Moines, IA 50319	Dear Senator Smith
State representative	The Honorable Jane Smith House Chambers, State Capitol Talahassee, FL 32399	Dear Mrs. (or Ms.) Smith
Mayor	The Honorable Jane Smith Office of the Mayor City Hall San Francisco, CA 94102	Dear Mayor Smith

WRITING ACROSS THE CURRICULUM

"6 RMS RIV VU"

This chapter is about writing situations you will encounter beyond the college campus. In an unfamiliar situation, look for models you can emulate. If you've never written a real-estate brochure, a help-wanted ad, or a product review, a few minutes of study will get you started in the right direction.

But don't simply copy the examples you find. As you study them, look for unique writing conventions—"6 RMS RIV VU"—and decide whether they'll work in your situation and how you can freshen them. And as you write, notice and evaluate your own conventions. Should some habits acquired in school be modified for business, professional, or social situations? For example, when writing academic papers you probably used conventional paragraph structure with five space indents; in business settings, the convention may favor block paragraphs separated by white space and no indentations. In other words, develop your "eye" and "ear" for writing in your new situation, and trust it.

20

Portfolios and Publishing Class Books

Revised and edited final drafts are written to be read. At the minimum, your audience is your instructor; at the maximum, it's the whole world—an audience for student writing now made possible by everyone's access to the Internet. In writing classes, the most common audience, in addition to the instructor, is the class itself. This chapter explores two common avenues of presenting your work in final published form via a writing portfolio and class books.

20 a Writing portfolios

In simplest terms, a **writing portfolio** is a collection of your writing contained within a single folder. This writing may have been done over a number of weeks, months, or even years. A writing portfolio may contain writing that you wish to keep for yourself; in this case you decide what's in it and what it looks like. Or a portfolio may contain work you intend to share with an audience to demonstrate your writing and reasoning abilities.

One kind of writing portfolio, accumulated during a college course, presents a record of your work over a semester

and will be used to assign a grade. Another type of portfolio presents a condensed, edited story of your semester's progress in a more narrative form. In addition, portfolios are often requested by prospective employers in journalism and other fields of professional writing; these samples of your best work over several years may determine whether or not you are offered a job as a writer or editor.

20 b   Course portfolios

The most common type of portfolio assigned in a writing course contains the cumulative work collected over the semester plus a cover letter in which you explain the nature and value of these papers. Sometimes you will be asked to assign yourself a grade based on your own assessment.

The following suggestions may help you in preparing a *course portfolio:*

Make your portfolio speak for you. If your course portfolio is clean, complete, and carefully organized, that's how you will be judged. If it's unique, colorful, creative, and imaginative, that, too, is how you'll be judged. So, too, will you be judged if your folder is messy, incomplete, and haphazardly put together. Before giving your portfolio to somebody else for evaluation, consider whether it reflects how you want to be presented.

Attend to the mechanics of the portfolio. Make sure the folder containing your writing is the kind specified and that it is clean and attractive. In the absence of such specification, use a pocket folder, which is an inexpensive means of keeping the contents organized and secure. Put your name and address on the outside cover. Organize the material inside as requested. And turn it in on time.

- **Include exactly what is asked for.** If an instructor wants three finished papers and a dozen sample journal entries, that's the minimum your course portfolio should contain. If an employer wants to see five samples of different kinds of writing, be sure to include five samples.

- **Add supplemental material judiciously.** If you believe that supplemental writing will present you in a better light, include that too, but only after the required material. If you include extra material, attach a note to explain why it is there. Supplemental writing might include journals, letters, sketches, or diagrams that suggest other useful dimensions of your thinking.

- **Include perfect final drafts.** Show that your own standard for finished work is high. Final drafts should be printed double-spaced on one side only of high-quality paper, be carefully proofread, and follow the language conventions appropriate to the task—unless another format is requested.

- **Demonstrate growth.** The signal value of portfolios in writing classes is that they allow you to demonstrate how a finished paper came into being. Consequently, instructors commonly ask for early drafts to be attached to final drafts, the most recent on top, so they can see how you followed revision suggestions, how much effort you invested, how many drafts you wrote, and how often you took risks. To build such a record of your work, date every draft of each paper.

- **Demonstrate work in progress.** Course portfolios allow writers to present partially finished work that suggests future directions and intentions. Both instructors and potential employers may find such preliminary drafts or outlines valuable. When you include such tentative drafts, be sure to attach a note explaining why it's not quite finished.

- **Attach a table of contents.** For portfolios containing more than three papers, attach a separate table of contents. For those containing only a few papers, embed your table of contents in the cover letter.

- **Include a cover letter.** The cover letter represents your own most recent assessment of the work you completed over the semester, serving two primary purposes: (1) as an introduction explaining the portfolio's contents and (2) as your own self-assessment of the quality of the work. Following is an excerpt from Kelly's letter describing the evolution of one paper:

> In writing the personal experience paper, I tried three
> different approaches, two different topics, and finally a
> combination of different approaches to my final topic. My first
> draft [about learning the value of money] was all summary
> and didn't show anything actually happening. My second
> draft wasn't focused because I was still trying to cover too
> much ground. At this point, I got frustrated and tried a new

topic [the hospital] but that didn't work either. Finally, for my last draft, I returned to my original topic, and this time it worked. I described one scene in great detail and included dialogue, and I liked it better and so did you. I am pleased with the way this paper came out when I limited my focus and zeroed in close.

The following excerpt describes Chris's assessment of her work over the whole semester:

As I look back through all the papers I've written this semester, I see how far my writing has come. At first I thought it was stupid to write so many different drafts of the same paper, as if I would beat the topic to death. But now I realize that all these different papers on the same topic went in different directions. This happened to some degree in the first paper, but I especially remember in my research project, when I interviewed the director of the Ronald McDonald House, I really got excited about the work they did there, and I really got involved in the other drafts of that paper.

I have learned to shorten my papers by editing and cutting out needless words. I use more descriptive adjectives now when I'm describing a setting and try to find action verbs instead of "to be" verbs in all of my papers. I am writing more consciously now—I think that's the most important thing I learned this semester.

20 c Story portfolios

A *story portfolio* is a shorter, more fully edited and finely crafted production than a cumulative course portfolio. Instead of including a cover letter and all papers and drafts written during the term as evidence for your self-assessment, a story portfolio presents the evolution of your work and thought over the course of the semester in narrative form. In a story portfolio, you include excerpts of your papers insofar as they illustrate points

Guidelines for Creating Course Portfolios

- **Date, collect, and save in a folder** all papers written for the course.

- **Arrange papers in chronological or qualitative order,** depending on the assignment, last drafts on top, earlier drafts in descending order behind.

- **In an appendix, attach supplemental writing** such as journal excerpts, letters, class exercises, quizzes, or other relevant writing.

- **Review your writing and compose a cover letter** explaining the worth or relevance of the writing in the portfolio. Consider the strengths and weaknesses of each individual paper as well as of the combined collection. Provide a summary statement of your current standing as a writer as your portfolio represents you.

- **Attend to the final presentation.** Include all writing in a clean, attractive folder; organize contents logically; attach a table of contents; write explanatory memos to explain unusual materials, and make sure the portfolio meets the minimum specifications of the assignment.

in your development as a writer. In addition, you include excerpts of supplemental written records accumulated at different times during the semester, including such items as (1) early and dead-end drafts of papers, (2) journal entries, (3) in-class writing and freewriting, (4) comments on papers from your instructor, and (5) comments from your instructor and classmates about your papers

In other words, to write a story portfolio, you conduct something like an archeological dig through the written remains of your work in a class. By assembling this evidence in chronological order and choosing the most telling snippets from these various documents, you write the story that explains, amplifies, or interprets the documents included or quoted. The best story portfolios commonly reveal a theme or set of issues that run from week to week or paper to paper throughout the semester. As you can see, a story portfolio is actually a small research paper, presenting a claim about your evolution as a writer with the evidence coming from your own written sources.

We encourage students to write their story portfolios using an informal voice as they might in a journal or letter. However, some students choose a more formal voice. Some prefer to write in the third person, analyzing the semester's work as if it were someone else's. We also encourage them to experiment with the form and structure of their story portfolios, so that some present their work as a series of dated journal entries or snapshots while others write a more fluid essay with written excerpts embedded as they illustrate this or that point. The following pages from Karen's portfolio exemplify the format and content of one type of story portfolio:

When I entered English 1, I was not a confident writer and only felt comfortable writing factual reports for school assignments. Those were pretty straightforward, and personal opinion was not involved. But over the course of the semester I've learned that I enjoy including my own voice in my writing. The first day of class I wrote this in my journal:

> 8/31   Writing has always been hard for me. I don't have a lot of experience writing papers except for straightforward things like science reports. I never did very well in English classes, usually getting B's and C's on my papers.

But I began to feel a little more comfortable when we read and discussed the first chapter of the book—a lot of other students besides me felt the same way, pretty scared to be taking English in college.

I decided to write about our basketball season last year, especially the game that we lost. Here is a paragraph from my first draft:

> We lost badly to Walpole in what turned out to be our final game. I sat on the bench most of the time.

As I see now, that draft was all telling and summary—I didn't show anything happening that was interesting or alive. But in a later draft I used dialogue and wrote from the announcer's point of view and the result was fun to write and my group said fun to read:

> Well folks, it looks like Belmont has given up, the coach is preparing to send in his subs. It has been a rough game for Belmont. They stayed in it during the first quarter, but Walpole has run away with it since then. Down by twenty with only six minutes left, Belmont's first sub is now approaching the table.

You were excited about this draft too, and your comment helped me know where to go next. You wrote:

Great draft, Karen! You really sound like a play-by-play announcer—you've either been one or listened closely to lots of basketball games. What would happen if in your next draft you alternated between your own voice and the announcer's voice? Want to try it?

This next excerpt comes from a story portfolio that included twelve pages of discussion and writing samples and concluded with this paragraph:

I liked writing this story portfolio at the end of the term because I can really see how my writing and my attitude have changed. I came into class not liking to write, but now I can say that I really do. The structure was free and we had plenty of time to experiment with different approaches to each assignment. I still have a long way to go, especially on my argument writing, since neither you nor I liked my final draft, but now I think I know how to get there: rewrite, rewrite, rewrite.

Suggestions for Preparing a Story Portfolio

■ **Assemble your collected writing in chronological order,** from beginning to end of each paper, from beginning to end of the semester.

■ **Reread all your informal work** (in journals, letters, instructor comments) and highlight passages that reflect the story of your growth as a writer.

■ **Reread all your formal work** (final papers, drafts) and highlight passages that illustrate your growth as a writer. Note especially if a particular passage had evolved over several drafts in the same paper—these would show you learning to revise.

■ **Arrange all highlighted passages in order** and write a story that shows (a) how one passage connects to another and (b) why each passage is significant.

■ Before writing your conclusion, reread your portfolio and **identify common themes or ideas or concerns** that have occurred over the semester; include these in your portfolio summary.

WRITING 1: APPLICATION

Using the guidelines in the box above, select the items to be included in a story portfolio. You may wish to use your computer's copy function to assemble a manuscript of selected extracts from papers, journal entries, freewriting, and other writing stored in your hard drive files or on disk.

Make notes on this new manuscript of where you want to insert writing that is available only on hard copy, such as handwritten notes from instructors and classmates. Also make notes of the reasons for your selections for use in writing the narrative of a story portfolio.

20 d Publishing class books

Publishing a class book is a natural end to any class in which interesting writing has taken place. A **class book** is an edited, bound collection of student writing, usually featuring some work from each student in the class. When the book is published before the last class of the semester, a class discussion can be organized to examine the themes, style, and structure of the finished book. Responsibility for compiling and editing such a book is commonly assigned to class volunteers, who are given significant authority for design and production of the book. Volunteers who edit class books may find the following guidelines helpful:

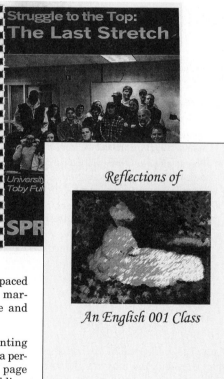

- **Establish manuscript guidelines.** Discuss with the class what each submitted paper should look like: single- or double-spaced typing, typeface, font size, margins, justification, and title and author names.

- **Set page limits.** Since printing charges are usually made on a per-page basis, discussion of page length is related to final publication cost.

- **Ask for camera-ready copy.** To simplify and speed the publishing process, have each student prepare his or her own manuscript to submit to the editors.

- **Set deadlines.** Arrange for manuscript deadlines (when papers are due from contributors to editors) as well as final publication deadlines (when published books are available to students).

- **Organize the essays.** Arrange collected essays according to some logic—theme, content, quality, or author's last name.

- **Establish a graphics policy.** Discuss with the class how much space to leave in each essay for clip art, downloaded Web pictures, or photos.

- **Write an introduction.** Write an introduction to explain to readers the nature of the reading experience to follow. Introductions vary in length from a paragraph to several pages.

- **Prepare a table of contents.** Include author's name, essay title, and first page number for each essay.

- **Ask the instructor to write an afterword.** Instructors may write about the assignment objectives, impressions of the essays, or reactions to the class or add any other observation that seems relevant to the book.

- **Collect student writer biographies.** Conclude with short (50–100 word) serious, semiserious, or comical biographies of the student writers.

- **Design a cover.** Design the cover or commission a classmate to do so. (Color cardboard covers cost extra but are usually worth it.)

- **Arrange for publication.** Explore with local print shops the production costs and a timetable to produce copies for all students in the class.

- **Divide editorial responsibilities.** Class books are best done by editorial teams consisting of two or more students who arrange among themselves the various duties described above.

WRITING ACROSS THE CURRICULUM

Discussing Class Books

Class books make excellent final projects for any small class or seminar in which writing is required. Try the suggestions in this chapter, and plan to have all class books distributed (or purchased) and read by the final class.

To prepare for a final class discussion, send out, in advance, a copy of the discussion questions below. Then invite the class book editors to lead a discussion in which students respond to these questions:

- Which are your favorite titles and why?
- What, besides your own, is your favorite essay and why?
- What ideas or techniques did you learn from classmates' essays?
- In your own essay, what are your favorite passages?
- In your own essay, what would you like to change?
- Which essay reveals the most substantial research?
- Which essay writer has the most interesting voice?
- In which essays are graphics used most effectively and why?

chapter 21

Making Oral Presentations

P ublic speaking is another way of "publishing" ideas that originate in written form. In speaking, as in writing, it's important to present ideas with confidence, clarity, accuracy, and grace: in the professions, in business, and in government, good writers and speakers get listened to, promoted, and rewarded; poor ones do not. While the art of public speaking can be addressed more comprehensively in speech class, we believe all writers should pay some attention to the oral publication of their ideas.

21 a   The assignment

The following suggestions have proved useful to successful public speakers:

Identify your purpose. What is your report supposed to accomplish? Is the purpose to present information, raise questions, argue a position, or lead the class in an activity? Regardless of your instructor's reason for making this assignment, to do a good job you'll need to believe in, understand, and know your subject. Choose a subject and a point of departure that you care about and believe in so you have the curiosity to do effective research and the passion to speak with conviction.

Know your audience. What you say and how you say it depends on to whom you are speaking. In most class settings, your audience is composed of your instructor and classmates; the best oral report will reach both effectively. To keep them interested, plan to teach them something they don't already know. Don't cover material already covered in class or in the textbook, nor material unrelated to the course. Instead, build deliberately on issues, ideas, or information that stems from familiar class material, and present new information in that context.

Collaborate. If collaboration is called for or allowed, the following guidelines might help: (1) Arrive at a consensus about what your task entails; (2) divide tasks according to ability; do your own part promptly, and hold others accountable for doing theirs; (3) meet often enough outside class so material is ready when the oral report is due; (4) plan in advance who will report what and for how long.

21 b   Speaking texts

Texts that are spoken need to be simple, clear, and direct. The following ideas follow such a process:

Invent. Allow time for thinking, planning, inventing, discovering—don't try to prepare your whole oral report the night before it is due.

Compose. Even if you don't intend to read your report out loud, write it out in full to see how it looks and where it's going. Once a talk is composed, even roughly, it's easy to make an outline from it from which to speak.

Research. Find current and detailed information to convey. Cite textual sources, quote local experts, report survey results, explain on-site visits. Google is an enormous help!

Outline. Effective oral reports are spoken rather than read, with the speaker making eye contact with the audience as much as possible. Consequently, the "final draft" of an oral report is a "speaking outline" or notes to be glanced at as needed.

Create listening signposts. The old advice for making speeches goes like this: *"Tell what you're gonna tell 'em. Tell 'em. Then tell 'em what you've told* *'em.*" It makes sense to be repetitious in this way with oral presentations because it's hard for audiences to remember and keep track of what they hear. *Listening signposts*—words that signal what's coming—help do this. For example, tell your audience you are going to make three points about gun control legislation, then enumerate each to help you remember.

Prepare note cards. In a short report, a one-page speaking outline is all you need. For longer or more complex reports that include quotations and statistics, use index cards to follow as you move from point to point in your talk.

Start strong. In oral delivery it's especially important to get everyone listening at the same time, so speakers commonly use questions, stories, or jokes to catch quick attention. If you tell a story or joke, make sure it pertains to your subject.

Finish strong. Many speakers map out their conclusion first, then work backward to make sure the text leads them there. With only five, ten, or fifteen minutes, be sure that when time is up, you've made the point you intended.

Write simply for oral delivery. Simple, jargon-free language is easiest to understand at a single hearing; repeating key words and phrases helps reinforce the listening memory.

Edit your reading text. If your material is complex and your time short, you may choose to read your report out loud. While it's less engaging, unless you're an excellent reader, it does guarantee that you say exactly what you meant precisely and economically. Triple-space your reading copy, use a large font, leave wide margins to pencil in extra notes, and start new paragraphs on new pages. For timing purposes, plan two and a half minutes for each page of double-spaced text ($8\frac{1}{2}'' \times 11''$).

WRITING 1: EXPLORATION

What do the professionals say in a speech? Evaluate the content of a speech delivered by a professional public speaker, such as a guest lecture at your college, a television or radio news anchor's report of a single story, or a speech broadcast on CNN, C-Span, or Court TV. Take notes on what the speaker did to identify the theme or thesis of the speech and to capture the audience's attention at the beginning. Jot down listening signposts. Consider whether the speech ended with a strong conclusion.

21 c Speaking in public

Presenting to a group means leaving your comfortable seat and moving front and center for attention. A recent poll identified public speaking as the greatest fear of most Americans. Even famous actors and speakers feel anxiety before performing before live audiences, and they learn to use their nervous energy to keep a sharp edge while performing. Nervousness is unavoidable; accept it, and try to harness this energy to help your performance. The following suggestions may help to alleviate this fear.

Rehearse. Run through your oral presentation in the privacy of your room to check your understanding and to set your pace to make sure you can deliver the talk in the time allotted. Rehearsing your talk out loud several times beforehand will help you understand your own material better as well as give you confidence when you walk to the front of the room. Rehearsing in front of a mirror and recording your rehearsals can help you to see your presentation from the perspective of a listener.

Make the room your own. Set up the room to suit the purpose of your presentation. If that means rearranging desks, tables, screens, or lecterns, don't hesitate to do so. If there is a lectern front and center but you don't plan to use it, move it to one side. If you use the lectern, stand still and rest your hands on it—that will help you control any shaking. If you prefer your audience in a semicircle or in groups instead of straight rows, ask them to sit that way. Taking control of your space makes you comfortable and gives you ownership of your time in front of the class.

Maintain eye contact with friendly audience members. While it's important to look around at the whole audience and make everyone feel as if you are addressing him or her, return periodically to the faces most receptive to your words—to smiles or nods or friends—for these will boost your confidence and keep you going smoothly.

Speak point by point. The reason for sticking to your outline or note cards is to present information in an economical and orderly fashion. If your report is supposed to last ten minutes, jot the starting time on your notes and stick to ten minutes. If you speak too fast, the audience can't follow you; if you speak too slowly, people get restless—so strive for balance.

Leave time for questions. When giving oral reports, it is customary to allow your audience time to ask questions. Plan for this time, show your willingness to discuss further what you know, and always answer succinctly and honestly; if you don't know an answer, say so.

21 d   Creative options

Depending on your task and time, you may want to enhance your presentation with some of the following materials or activities:

Use handouts. Many talks are augmented by handouts (outlines, poems, stories, ads, articles) illustrating points made in the talk or as a text to attend to at some time during the presentation. Prepare handouts carefully, make sure they are legible, document them if they are borrowed from another source, and make enough for everyone in your audience.

Use *prepared* visual aids. Many talks are made more powerful when accompanied by illustrations or examples of what is being talked about. Visual aids include videos, films, maps, charts, sketches, photographs, posters, computer graphics, or transparencies shown on overhead projectors. With computer programs such as PowerPoint (see the WAC box on page 280), it is easy to prepare professional-quality visual aids.

Use *process* visual aids. It often helps to illustrate something on the spot in front of your audience, something often called for during a question-and-answer session. Media that help you write or sketch things out include blackboards, flip charts, and overhead projectors. Arrange for these aids in advance and bring chalk or markers.

Use audio aids. Some talks are best advanced when accompanied by music or oral recordings. Audience attention picks up noticeably when you introduce sounds or voices other than your own into your presentation. A sound or visual recording may be the featured text in your presentation, or it may provide useful accompaniment.

***Be* a visual and audio aid.** For some topics, a live demonstration may be appropriate. Be sure to have all the props, supplies, and equipment you need for your demonstration, whether it involves how to play the trombone or how to dress for in-line skating. Even if you do not demonstrate a process, you can use *body language* to your advantage. Smiling at your audience, in addition to making eye contact, will help to establish a friendly connection. Natural gestures can help you maintain your audience's interest and can reinforce what you are saying. Body language also includes the sound of your voice; volume, speed of delivery, emphasis, tone, and pitch all add meaning to the words you say.

Ask your audience to write. If you want to engage your audience quickly and relax yourself at the same time, ask people to write briefly before you speak. For example, on the subject of "alcohol on campus," ask people to jot down their own experience with or knowledge of the subject on blank paper, telling them their notes will remain private. After a few minutes, ask them to talk about—not read—their ideas with a neighbor for several more minutes. Talking aloud to seatmates pulls them in deeper still, and the oral buzz in the room makes everyone—especially you—more comfortable. To resume control, ask for several volunteer opinions and use these as a bridge to your own presentation.

WRITING ACROSS THE CURRICULUM

Guidelines for PowerPoint Presentations

PowerPoint has become the standard visual aid program for making presentations across the curriculum. In classrooms equipped with computer projectors, it allows you to show text, slides, graphics, and photos, as well as moving images, to help you supplement oral presentations in any course of study. The following tips will help you create an effective presentation.

- **Check out** the space in advance. Make sure the room can be darkened and that the screen isn't facing the light. Check sight lines to be sure the whole audience can see.

- **Estimate the distance** from the farthest seat to the screen. Use the sign-painter's rule of thumb: one-inch letters can be read from ten feet, two-inch letters from twenty feet, etc. Adjust type accordingly. (On a monitor, 72-point type is about one inch high.)

- **Consider readability** when choosing colors for background and type. Complementary colors (red on green) may be hard to see while other combinations (black on yellow) may need to be toned down. Choose light colors for backgrounds.

- **Keep it simple.** Follow an outline of your presentation, using slides to highlight major points. Fill-in details orally.

- **Make organization visible.** If your outline has three main sections, consider beginning with a slide listing points I, II, and III. Then show the main points of Section I in one or more slides, followed by the main points of Section II, and so on.

- **Use art carefully.** If a photo or graphic is the best way to convey information, use it. Most clip art cartoon figures convey little information and look amateurish.

- **Avoid unnecessary animation.** Moving type, elements that fade into or out of view, and/or animated graphics tend to distract from what you're saying.

- **Consider a printed handout** for important information you want your audience to carry away from your presentation.

- **Rehearse** with a tape recorder and a computer so you can watch and listen to your presentation at the same time.

PART six

Writing with Research

www.prenhall.com/fulwiler

Before agonizing too long over your next research project, stop to consider that all research really means, in or out of college, is asking questions to which you do not already know the answer, then looking for the answers. In your nonacademic life you conduct practical research of one kind or another every time you search the classifieds for a used car, comparison shop for a laptop at Staples, Costco, and Best Buy, log onto Amazon.com in search of a book, browse the Internet for a spring-break vacation spot, or sample tunes on the Internet before purchasing one for your I-Pod. You may not make formal note cards, and you never report the results in writing, but whenever you ask questions and then systematically look for answers, you are researching.

In college, the research you conduct is academic rather than practical, designed to result in a convincing paper rather than a practical purchase or an action. Academic research is part of the writing process for many college papers requiring you to report, explain, argue, or interpret, as you seldom begin such papers knowing all you need to know: to fill in knowledge gaps, you conduct research. In fact, one type of assignment, often called a *research essay, paper,* or *report,* is often assigned in classes across the curriculum to familiarize you with the research process that informs knowledge in particular disciplines.

WRITING 1: EXPLORATION ....

What research in or outside if school settings have you conducted recently? What started it? How did it turn out?

....

22 a Understanding research

Research projects usually occupy several weeks or months and are often the most important papers you write during a semester, so study the assignment carefully, begin work immediately, and allow sufficient time for the many different activities involved.

Strategies for Managing the Research Process

- **Ask questions.** Write out as many questions as you can think of that might lead to interesting research. Often, preliminary general questions lead to more specific ones.
- **Read extensively.** Texts of all kinds, in libraries, bookstores, and on the Internet, provide the knowledge you don't already possess to begin, continue, and complete research projects.
- **Question knowledgeable people.** Start with people you know. If they can't help, ask who can. Then broaden that circle to include people with specialized knowledge.
- **Seek out firsthand information.** No matter how many answers texts and people offer, your own observation and experience also count.
- **Evaluate your sources and double-check the information you find.** Sources vary in their accuracy and objectivity. Confirm the information you gather by checking more than one reliable source.
- **Write at every stage.** Take reading notes, interview notes, and observation notes. Write out hunches and hypotheses. Construct arguments and propositions. Try introductions and conclusions. The more you write, the more you'll have to write about.

1 Examine the assignment

First, think about the aims of the course in which the research project is assigned. What themes has the instructor emphasized? What research questions contribute to the goals of this course? In other words, before selecting a topic, assess the instructor's probable reasons for making the assignment in the first place.

Examine both the subject words and the direction words. **Subject words** (*historical, geographical, social,* etc.) specify the area of the investigation. **Direction words** (*propose* or *explain*) specify your purpose for writing—whether you should argue or report or do something else.

2 Ask good questions

To begin with, make a list of all the ways your personal interests dovetail with the content of the course. What subjects have you enjoyed most? What discussions, lectures, or labs were most engaging? What recent news both interests you and relates to the course material? After each item, list the questions that might lead you to interesting research, then select the one that meets the following conditions:

- It's a question to which you don't already know the answer.

- It requires more than a yes or no answer.

- It's a question that you have a reasonable chance of answering.

In the following example, a general subject is turned into a specific question.

GENERAL SUBJECT   *What's the health of the environment in the state of Vermont?* [too broad, not sure where to begin]

GENERAL TOPIC   *How do governmental and corporate policies in the state of Vermont protect the environment?* [narrower, but this could be a book]

FOCUSED TOPIC   *Which corporations in Vermont have policies that protect the environment?* [more specific, but the "which" question would generate a list rather than a full-fledged examination of an issue]

FINAL TOPIC   *How does Ben and Jerry's Ice Cream Company make a profit and protect the environment at the same time?* [specific place to read about, visit, and find people to interview]

3 Write with authority

Whenever you undertake research, you join an ongoing conversation among a select community of people who are knowledgeable about the subject. As you collect information, you also begin to be knowledgeable and gain an authoritative voice. Your goal should be to become enough of an expert on your topic that you can teach your classmates and instructor something they didn't already know about your topic. One good way to write like an expert is to translate all the crucial information about your topic into your own words. Do this on note cards, in journal entries, and throughout paper drafts so your final draft will be written in your own strong voice.

4 Keep an open mind

Don't be surprised if, once you begin researching, questions and answers multiply and change. For example, suppose you start out researching local recycling efforts, but you stumble upon the problem of finding buyers for recycled material. One source raises the question of processing recycled materials, another on manufacturing difficulties with recycled material, while another source turns the whole question back to consumer education. All of these concerns are related, but if you attempt to study them all with equal intensity, your paper will be either very long or very superficial. Chances are one of these more limited topics may interest you more than the first question you started with—which is as it should be. Follow your strongest interests, and you'll go deeper with more satisfaction and write a better paper in the bargain.

ESL ▸ *Becoming an Authority*

If you have been educated outside the United States, you may feel it is inappropriate to act as an authority, especially on an unfamiliar topic. In U.S. colleges, however, students are expected to develop a sense of authority regarding their topics. This enables them to present interesting ideas of their own rather than repeating what others have said.

Becoming an authority means working hard to become an expert and thus master your writing project. The following guidelines should help:

- Learn enough about your topic to become the class expert.
- Read your sources critically, analyzing what they say and why they might be saying it. (See Chapter 2.)
- Think carefully about which sources to use and how to use them in your paper. (See 27a–27b.)
- Make sure your paper includes ideas of your own, not just summaries of what other people have said.

22 b   Working with a thesis

When an answer to your research question starts to take shape, form a *working thesis,* which will be a preliminary or tentative answer to your initial question. As you investigate further, you will look for information that either substantiates, refutes, or modifies this thesis. When additional research leads you in a different direction, be ready to redirect your investigation and revise your thesis.

Whether or not you already have a working thesis will determine what type of research you undertake. **Informational research** is conducted when you don't know the answer to the question or don't have a firm opinion about the topic. You enter this kind of investigation with an open mind, focusing on the question, not on a predetermined answer. As you become more knowledgeable, your information will begin to answer the question you started with—at which point you'll begin shaping the main point of your paper. Such research might be characterized as thesis-finding.

Persuasive research, however, is conducted to prove a point you already believe in. You enter such projects having already formulated a working thesis—the tentative answer to your question, the side of a debate or argument you want to support. For example, even as you began research on the environmental policies of Ben and Jerry's Ice Cream Company, local and national media publicity had led you to believe this company was environmentally friendly; in other words, you began with a belief to verify, so you'd be surprised if further research disproved your initial hunch. However, you might find out that publicity about a company was one thing, but getting the scoop from employees was something else, causing you to revise your first thesis. The best papers will be those that most honestly report what's closest to the truth, even a different truth than you started with. (For more detailed information on working with theses, see Chapters 9 and 10.)

WRITING 2: APPLICATION ....

Select a topic that interests you and that is compatible with the research assignment. List ten questions about this topic. Select the question that most interests you and freewrite a possible answer for ten or more minutes. Why does it interest you? Where would you start looking to pursue answers further?

....

22 c   Keeping a research log

A **research log** can help you keep track of the scope, purpose, and possibilities of any research project. Such a log is essentially a journal kept in a paper notebook or on a notebook computer in which you write to yourself about the process of doing research by asking questions and monitoring the results. Questions you might ask include the following:

- What subject do I want to research?

- What information have I found so far?

- What do I still need to find?

- Where am I most likely to find it?

- What evidence best supports my working thesis?

- What evidence challenges my working thesis?

- How is my thesis changing from where it started?

Writing out answers to these questions in your log clarifies your tasks as you go along, forcing you to articulate ideas and examine supporting evidence critically. Novice researchers often waste time tracking down sources that are not really useful. But posing and answering questions in writing as you investigate will make research more efficient. When you keep notes in log form, record them by date found and allow room to add cross-referencing notes to other entries. The following entries are from a first-year student's handwritten research log:

11/12   With over a hundred thousand hits on Google (!), I decided to limit my research by going to the library. In checking the subject headings, I couldn't seem to find any books specifically on ozone depletion. But the reference librarian suggested I check periodicals because it takes so long for books to come out on new science subjects. In the General Science Index I found a dozen articles that pointed me in the right direction—now all I need to do is actually start reading them.

11/17   Conference today with Lawrence about the ozone hole thesis—said I don't really have so much a thesis as a lot of information aiming in the same direction—whatever that means. Suggested I look at what I've found already and then back up to see what question it answers—that will probably point to my thesis.

....

Keep a research log for the duration of one research project. Write in it as often as you think or research about your subject. When your project is finished, review your log and assess how it helped you and determine whether you'll keep one for your next project.

....

22 d   Finding your way

Research writing benefits from the multistage process of planning, composing, revising, and editing. In research writing, however, managing information and incorporating sources present special problems.

1 Make a schedule

After developing some sense of the range and amount of information available, write out a schedule of when you will do what in either your research log or daily calendar. For example, block out specific time to begin an Internet search. Write in a day for a first library visit. Arrange interview appointments well in advance, with time to reschedule in case a meeting has to be postponed. And allow enough time not only for writing but also for revising and editing.

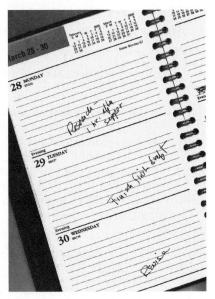

2 Include primary and secondary sources

To conduct any kind of research, you need to identify appropriate sources of information, consult and evaluate these sources, and take good notes recording the information you collect. You also need to understand how each source works as evidence.

Primary sources consist of original documents and accounts by participants or eyewitnesses, as opposed to descriptions or interpretations by other researchers. **Secondary sources** are articles, books, chapters, Web pages, and people whose information is obtained from other sources rather than firsthand experience who have their own opinions about your research subject.

For example, if you were exploring the development of a novelist's style, primary sources would include the novels themselves, as well as, for example, the novelist's manuscripts and correspondence or contemporary interviewer's account of the novelist's views on writing. Other people's reviews and critical interpretations of the novels would be secondary sources. If you were researching the Ben and Jerry's Ice Cream Company, plant visits, employee interviews, and published financial documents would be primary sources from which to shape your own opinions, while articles *about* the company by journalists would be secondary sources.

What constitutes a primary source will differ according to the field and your research question. For example, the novel *Moby Dick* is a primary source if you are studying it as literature. However, information in *Moby Dick* is a secondary source if you are investigating nineteenth-century whaling and referring to its descriptions of harpooning.

Most research essays use both primary and secondary sources. Primary sources ground the essay in firsthand knowledge and verifiable facts; secondary sources supply the authoritative context for your discussion and provide support for your own interpretation or argument. Most research essays are based on library and Internet sources. However, some of the most interesting research essays are also based on **field research** that derives from site visits and firsthand interviews with people who have expert knowledge of your subject. In other words, you conduct field research simply by going places, observing carefully, and reporting what you find.

WRITING 4: APPLICATION

On one page of your research log, design a research plan that includes library, Internet, and field investigations. In this plan, list sources you have already found as well as those you hope to find.

3 Choose your approach

Written research can be reported in one of two distinctly different ways: **thesis-first** as in conventional academic papers or **delayed-thesis** as in journalism and popular nonfiction. Academic research papers usually are written *thesis-first,* where the writer reports the answer to the research question early in the paper and substantiates the answer in the balance of the paper. Such papers written in the sciences and social sciences commonly begin with a paragraph-length abstract that summarizes the findings of the whole paper before the reader even reads the paper. The purpose of this form is to present information in the most rapid and economical way possible in order to be most useful to subsequent researchers.

A clear thesis-driven paper not only helps readers quickly understand what your research turned up, it also helps you, the writer, organize your thoughts and energies when writing. To write your thesis-first paper in academic style, you might address the following questions:

- Is it interesting? An informational thesis should answer a question that is worth asking: *Why is the cartoon show, The Smurfs, thought to be communist propaganda?* A persuasive thesis should take a position on a debatable issue and include a proposal for change: *Mountain bikes should be allowed on wilderness trails.*

- Is it precise and specific? Instead of arguing in favor of less pollution in the lake, explain how to stop the zebra mussel infestation.

- Is it manageable? Try to split the difference between having to much information and not enough.

- Does it adequately reflect my research and the expected shape of my paper? Your thesis should state the major point of your paper.

(To read a thesis-first academic paper, read Andrew Turner's "The Two Freedoms of Henry David Thoreau" at the end of Chapter 30.)

In contrast to academic papers, research writing in popular nonfiction such as you find in newspaper feature articles and *The New Yorker* magazine is usually presented with *delayed theses,* so that readers follow along with the writer on his or her search for an answer. (Sometimes, in fact, such a paper might end with more questions than a specific answer.) While it takes longer for readers to find the results of the research, the paper is usually more exciting to read as readers become progressively more curious to find the answer to the question that began the paper but won't be revealed until the paper's end.

To write your research in the style of popular nonfiction, consider asking the following questions in your paper:

- Where did I look first to answer my question? What did I find out? What did I not find out?

- When I checked the World Wide Web, how many sources did I find? How many useful sources did I find? What made a source useful? What did I not find?

- What places did I physically visit? What did each look like? What did I find out there? What was missing?

- What person or people did I talk to? Who granted me an interview? When, where? What did each person look like? What did the setting look like? What did I learn there? What other leads did I find?

- What further questions have occurred as I've tried to answer the first question?

- When did I turn to the library? Where did I look—books, periodicals, databases, other sources? How many of what kind did I find? How many did I read? What did I learn?

- Where and when did one source contradict another? How did I decide which to believe?

- How did I conclude my search? How satisfied am I now? Did I find one answer to my question? More than one answer? No answer?

- What related questions would I pursue, had I more time? Another life?

(For an academic paper with a delayed thesis approach, see Katie Moll's "The Smurfs as Communist Propaganda" at the end of Chapter 9.)

4 Revise, revise, revise

When drafting, you must follow your strongest research interests and try to answer the question you most care about. However, sometimes what began as informational research may become argument as the process of drafting the paper tips your original neutrality one way or another. Or a research investigation that starts out to prove a thesis may, as you draft, become a more neutral, informative paper of various perspectives, especially when multiple causes or complications surface in what had seemed a straightforward case.

Be ready to spend a great deal of time revising your draft, adding new research information, and incorporating sources smoothly into your prose.

Such work takes a great deal of thought, and you'll want to revise your paper several times. (Consult Part Four for helpful strategies on revising your draft.)

5 Edit and proofread

Editing a research paper requires extra time. Not only should you check your own writing, but you should also pay special attention to where and how you use sources (see Chapter 27) and use the correct documentation style (see Part Seven). The editing stage is also a good time to assess your use of quotations, paraphrases, and summary to make sure you have not misquoted or used a source without crediting it.

SUGGESTIONS FOR WRITING AND RESEARCH

INDIVIDUAL

1.   Select a research topic that interests you and write an exploratory draft about it. First, write out everything you already know about the topic. Second, write out everything you want to know about the topic. Third, identify experts you can contact. Finally, make a list of questions you need answered. Plan to put this paper through a process that includes not only planning, drafting, revising, and editing but also locating, evaluating, and using sources.

2.   Keeping in mind the research topic you developed in assignment 1 above, visit the library and conduct a search of available resources. What do you find? Where do you find it? Show your questions to a reference librarian and ask what additional electronic databases he or she would suggest. Finally, don't forget the Internet, an ever-expanding source of information on virtually any topic you can think of.

3.   After completing assignments 1 and 2 above, find a person who knows something about your topic and ask him or her for leads about doing further research: Whom else would this person recommend you speak with? What books or articles would he or she recommend? What's the first thing this expert would do to find out information? Finally, look for a "virtual" person, someone available through an e-mail listserv or on the Internet with whom you might chat to expand your knowledge.

WRITING ACROSS THE CURRICULUM

Collaborative Research Projects

Of all writing assignments, those involving research profit most from collaboration, no matter what the subject area. In the corporate, business, and scientific worlds, nearly all work is collaborative, including posing, processing, and solving problems; reaching decisions; evaluating production; and writing reports. For most complex problems, two heads are better than one, and three are better than two. If your assignment lends itself to collaboration, and if your instructor approves, find out with which classmates you could work. The following suggestions will aid collaboration:

- **Start with either group or topic.** Either form a group you want to work with and then choose a topic you all want to research, or choose a topic that interests you and see whether you can interest others in joining you.

- **Control size.** Small groups (two to three people) work better than large groups, because they make it easier to find time to meet outside of class and to synthesize the information found.

- **Organize.** Divide tasks early, specifying who will do what when. Divide tasks equitably. And divide tasks so that members best use their different skills, abilities, and interests.

- **Share.** Agree to duplicate the reading, interview, and observation notes so that each member has full sources of information.

- **Compose.** A group writing a single paper can write together by (1) blending voices, passing the drafts back and forth, each writer overwriting the others each time; (2) sequencing voices, each writer writing a different section (as in chapters in a book); or (3) weaving voices, so that the final product has different writers' voices emerging at different times throughout the paper.

- **Synthesize.** Ask each group member to write his or her own version of what the paper might be. Share early drafts and look for consensus in topic and thesis. If no consensus emerges, share research but write separate papers.

- **Revise and edit.** Near the end, rebalance the workload, with different members volunteering to type, prepare references, edit, proofread, and reproduce the final paper. To encourage group ownership of the project, conduct a round-robin reading, whereby each member takes a turn editing the final draft.

- **Assess responsibility.** Ask group members to privately rank individual contributions to assess equity. When all group members meet their responsibilities and deadlines, all should receive the same reward; when they don't, they shouldn't.

chapter **23** *Conducting Library
Research*

What is it like today, researching in a modern college library? When our first-year students finished a major research project, we asked them to describe their library research experience, and here are some of their comments:

Frances: "I could find all the library sources from just one computer search instead of looking one place for books, another for periodicals, and still another for films and CDs. It was awesome!"

David: "The quality of my research was much better when I went to the library . . . the sources were more informative and more trustworthy."

Elena: "Researching in the library puts you in a scholarly mood—you look harder and goof off less."

Tammy: "The library lady helped me when I was stuck. When you research at the library, you never feel alone."

Some topics might favor Internet research while other topics might favor local field research. But the most comprehensive collection of *reliable* information for college research assignments remains the library. Unlike information from the Internet and field, library sources are screened by experts and critics before being catalogued and shelved. Just because it's cataloged, of course, doesn't certify it's accurate, true, or the last word, but expert screening increases the odds that the information is trustworthy. In addition, the reference librarian is on your team and can usually guide you to the right places.

23 a   Planning library research

To learn about the library, go there, walk slowly through it, read the signs, poke your nose into nooks and crannies, and browse through a few books or magazines. If there is an introductory video, pause to see it. If there is a self-paced or guided tour, take it. Read informational handouts and pamphlets. By the time you leave, know how to find the following:

The **online catalog,** a computerize database that tells you which books and other sources your library owns and where they are located.

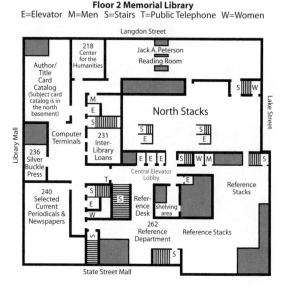

Floor 2 Memorial Library
E=Elevator M=Men S=Stairs T=Public Telephone W=Women

The **stacks,** where books and periodicals are stored.

The **circulation desk,** where you check out and reserve books and get information on procedures and resources.

The **periodical room,** which houses current issues of magazines, journals, and newspapers.

The **reference room,** which contains general reference works, such as dictionaries and encyclopedias, along with guides and indexes to more specific sources information.

To take full advantage for library resources, keep the following suggestions in mind:

Visit early and often. As soon as you receive a research assignment, visit the library to find out what resources are available for your project. Even if your initial research indicates a wealth of material, you may not be able to find everything the first time as a book may be checked out or your library may not subscribe to a certain periodical, or there are still resources you haven't learned about.

Take notes. Even in this computerized world it helps to bring index cards to the library—3″ × 5″ cards for bibliographical information and 4″ × 6″ cards for notes—from your first visit on. Good substitutes, of course, include your laptop computer or research log notebook.

Check general sources first. Look at dictionaries, encyclopedias, atlases, and yearbooks for background information about your topic. An hour spent with these general sources will give you a quick overview of the scope and range of your topic and will lead you to more specific information.

Ask for help. Talk to librarians. At first you might show them your assignment and describe your topic and your research plans; later you might ask them for help in finding a particular source or ask whether they know of any sources that you have not checked yet. Librarians are professional information experts, so use them.

23 b   Finding sources of information

Most of the information you need to find will be contained in reference books, in other books, and in periodicals (journals, magazines, and newspapers). To locate these sources, you'll need a variety of tools including the *online catalog* and *databases* as well as *periodical indexes*. To use these resources efficiently, use the following four-step process:

1. Consult *general reference works* to gain background information and basic facts.

2. Consult the *online catalog* to identify library books on your topic.

3. Consult paper and online *indexes to periodicals* to find relevant articles.

4. Consult *other sources* as needed.

1 Consult *general reference works*

Use **databases** (also called indexes) at your college or university library to locate general reference sources. Databases are guides to the

What You Need to Know About Keyword Searching

When you are looking for materials on a particular topic, a keyword search is often your best bet. A keyword search is a comprehensive way to search and tells the computer to look for your word or words anywhere in a record—in the title, the author name, the subject headings, the journal title, or the abstract. Keyword searching allows you to combine terms in different ways using Boolean connectors to either broaden or narrow your search results. Truncation is another powerful keyword searching tool that allows you to add greater flexibility to your searches by telling the computer to search for variant word endings. Both techniques are described below.

BOOLEAN CONNECTORS

▶ **BOOLEAN CONNECTORS**

Boolean Connector		Examples		Search Result
	and	▶ forests and vermont ▶ wetlands and ecology		Retrieves records containing *both* terms; *narrows* the search.
	or	▶ lakes or ponds ▶ color or colour		Retrieves records containing *either or both* terms; *broadens* a search.
	not	▶ vermont not new hampshire		*Excludes* records containing the second term; *narrows* the search.

TRUNCATION

Truncation	*Example*	*Search Result*
Use a truncation symbol at the end of a word or a root word, and the computer will search for all its different word endings.		*The use of "*" retrieves . . .*
Different databases use different symbols (?, *, |, or #), so check the online help to learn what symbol to use.	environment*	environment environmental environmentalist environmentalists environmentalism environmentally environments

material published within works, sometimes within books but more often within periodicals (magazines, journals, newspapers), which are published at set periods throughout the year. They focus on particular areas of interest, and their information is more current than that found in books. Because so many periodical issues are published each year and because every issue can contain dozens of articles on various topics, using a periodical index or database is essential to finding the article you need. Each index or database covers a particular group of periodicals. Make sure that the index you select contains the journals, magazines, and newspapers that you want to use as sources.

General reference works provide background information and basic facts about a topic. The summaries, overviews, and definitions in these sources can help you decide whether to pursue a topic further and where to turn next for information. The information in these sources is necessarily general and will not be sufficient by itself as the basis for most research projects—in fact, general reference works are not strong sources to cite in research papers.

Many indexes, called **full-text databases,** allow you to print out the full text of an article you find, thus simplifying your search process. But beware: some texts are abbreviated when they are stored on the computer, and others omit accompanying information such as sidebars or graphics. In some cases, you may have to pay to retrieve the full text of an article. If an article looks important but is not retrievable in full text form, be sure seek out the periodical (paper or electronic version) and read the article.

Whichever search tool you use, there is nothing magic about information transferred over a computer. You will need the same critical skills you use to evaluate printed materials, although the clues may be harder to understand when you find documents online. Is the author identified? Is that person a professional in the field or an interested amateur? What are his or her biases likely to be? Does the document you have located represent an individual's opinion or peer-reviewed research?

Following are some of the most useful general reference works to provide context and background information for research projects:

Almanacs and yearbooks. Almanacs and yearbooks provide up-to-date information, including many statistics, on politics, agriculture, economics, and population. See especially *Facts on File: News Digest* (1940–present), an index to current events reported in newspapers worldwide. (Also in CD-ROM form, 1980–present.) and *World Almanac and Book of Facts* (1868–present), which reviews important events of the past year as well as data on a wide variety of topics, including sports, government, science, business, and education.

Atlases. Atlases such as the *Hammond Atlas of the World,* the *National Geographic Atlas of the World,* and the *Times Atlas of the World* can help you identify places anywhere in the world and provide information on population, climate, and industry.

Biographical dictionaries. Biographical dictionaries contain information on people who have made some mark on history in many different fields. Consult the following: *Contemporary Authors* (1962–present), containing short biographies of authors who have published during the year; *Current Biography* (1940–present), containing articles and photographs of people in the news; and *Who's Who in America* (1899–present), the standard biographical reference for living Americans.

Dictionaries. Dictionaries contain definitions and histories of words along with information on their correct usage.

Encyclopedias. Encyclopedias provide elementary information, explanations, and definitions of virtually every topic, concept, country, institution, historical person or movement, and cultural artifact imaginable. One-volume works such as the *Random House Encyclopedia* and *The Columbia Encyclopedia* give brief overviews. Larger works such as *Collier's Encyclopedia* (24 volumes) and the *New Encyclopedia Britannica* (32 volumes, also online) contain more detailed information.

The best way to locate and search for general reference works is to use the **databases** available online at most university libraries. Access is usually restricted, so check to see which of the following databases your university subscribes to.

Academic Search Premier. Indexes over 3,400 scholarly publications including humanities, sciences, social sciences, education, engineering, languages, and literature in full-text access.

ArticleFirst. Indexes over 15,000 journals in business, humanities, medicine, science, and social science.

Expanded Academic ASAP. Indexes over 2,000 periodicals in the arts, humanities, sciences, and social sciences, as well as many newspapers.

Factiva. Full-text access to major newspapers, business journals, and stock market reports.

LexusNexus Academic. Indexes a wide range of magazines, newspapers, and government documents, all available full-text.

WRITING 1: APPLICATION ....

Look up background information on your research topic, using at least
three databases and three general reference works described in this section.

....

2 Consult specialized reference works

Also plan to use university online **databases** to search for s*pecialized
reference works* that contain detailed and technical information in a particular field or discipline. They often contain articles by well-known authorities and sometimes have bibliographies and cross-references that can
lead to other sources. Access is usually restricted, so check to see which
databases your university subscribes to.

A major online system commonly found in college libraries is *Dialog,*
which offers more than 400 specialized databases. Some of the most commonly used databases (content identified by title) within *Dialog* include
Arts and Humanities Search (1980–present), ERIC (Educational Resources
Information Center, 1966–present), MLA International Bibliography
(1963–present); PsycINFO (1967–present), Scisearch (1974–present), and
Social Scisearch (1972–present).

To use *Dialog,* you usually need the assistance of a reference librarian. The library is charged a fee for each search, calculated according to the
time spent and the number of entries retrieved. Some libraries have the
person requesting the search pay the fee; others limit the time allotted for
each search. Be sure to ask what your library's policy is.

3 Consult the online catalog

All catalogs provide the same basic information. They list items by
author, title, and subject; describe their physical format and content;
and tell where in the library to find them. Consult the online catalog to
find all books, journals, newspapers, and audiovisual material the
library owns. Most online catalogs can be accessed from locations outside
the library.

Plan to use the library catalog in several ways. If you already know
the title of a work, the catalog confirms your library owns it and tells where
it's located. You can also browse the catalog for works relevant to your topic.
And you can also search the online catalogs of other libraries via the World
Wide Web. Many libraries can obtain a work owned by another library

through an interlibrary loan, a process that may take anywhere from a few days to a few weeks.

Note: You will not find individual journal articles listed in the catalog; to find those you will need to consult the periodical indexes.

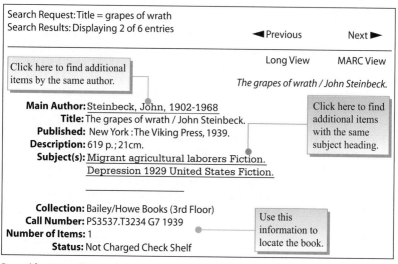

Search Request: Title = grapes of wrath
Search Results: Displaying 2 of 6 entries

◀ Previous   Next ▶

Long View   MARC View

Click here to find additional items by the same author.

The grapes of wrath / John Steinbeck.

Main Author: Steinbeck, John, 1902-1968
Title: The grapes of wrath / John Steinbeck.
Published: New York : The Viking Press, 1939.
Description: 619 p. ; 21 cm.
Subject(s): Migrant agricultural laborers Fiction.
Depression 1929 United States Fiction.

Click here to find additional items with the same subject heading.

Collection: Bailey/Howe Books (3rd Floor)
Call Number: PS3537.T3234 G7 1939
Number of Items: 1
Status: Not Charged Check Shelf

Use this information to locate the book.

Record from an online catalog

Online catalog systems vary slightly from library to library, though all systems follow the same general principles. Most online catalogs allow you to search with partial information. For example, if you know that the title of a novel begins with the words *Love Medicine* but you can't remember the rest of it, you can ask the catalog computer to search for the title *Love Medicine*. It will present you with a list of all works that begin with those words.

Most online catalogs also allow you to perform keyword searches, allowing the computer to search different parts of the record at once. To perform a keyword search, use the words you've identified as describing your topic, linked by *and* or *or* as appropriate. For example, if you're trying to research fictional accounts of Dakota Indians, you can search for *"Dakota Indians" AND "fiction."* The computer will present you with a list of works that fit that description.

```
Search Request: T=LOVE MEDICINE
Search Results: 4 Entries Found                              Title Index
--------------------------------------------------------------------T257
1   LOVE MEDICINE:   A NOVEL.   ERDRICH LOUISE <1984>  (BH)

    LOVE MEDICINE AND MIRACLES
2     SIEGEL BERNIE S <1986>       (BH)
3     SIEGEL BERNIE S <1988>       (DA)

    LOVE MEDICINE AND MIRACLES LESSONS LEARNED ABOUT SELFHEALING
    FROM A SURGEON'S EXPERIENCE WITH EXCEPTIONAL PATIENTS
4     SIEGEL BERNIE S <1986>       (BH)
-------------------------------------------------------------
COMMANDS:   Type line # to see individual record
            O   Other options
            H   Help

NEXT COMMAND:
```

Results of a title search in an online catalog

```
Search Request: T=LOVE MEDICINE
BOOK - Record 1 of 5 Entries Found                          Long View
------------------------------Screen 1 of 1------------------------------T259
Author:        Erdrich, Louise.
Title:         Love medicine : a novel
Edition:       1st ed.
Published:     New York : Holt, Rinehart, and Winston, c1984.
Description:   viii, 275 p. ; 22cm.
Subjects(LC):  Indians of North America--North Dakota--Fiction.
-------------------------------------------------------------
   LOCATION;           CALL NUMBER            STATUS
1 Halley Stacks        PS3555.R42 L6 1984     Not checked out

COMMANDS:   P Previous screen
            O Other options
            H Help

NEXT COMMAND:
```

Full information on a book in an online catalog

How to use call numbers

To find books your library owns, use the book's call number to locate it in the stacks. Most academic libraries use the Library of Congress system, whose call numbers begin with letters. Some libraries still use the older Dewey Decimal System, whose call numbers consist entirely of numbers. In either case, the first letters or numbers indicate the general subject area. Because libraries shelve all books for a general subject area together, this portion of the call number tells you where in the library to find the book you want. Be sure to copy a book's call number exactly as it appears in the catalog. When you have located your book in the stacks, look at other books in the area to see if any of those might also be useful.

4 Other sources of information

Government documents. The U.S. government publishes numerous reports, pamphlets, catalogs, and newsletters on most issues of national concern. Consult the *Monthly Catalogue of United States Government Publications* and the *United States Government Publications Index,* both available electronically.

Nonprint media. Records, CDs, audiocassettes, videotapes, slides, photographs, and other media may also be located through the library catalog.

Pamphlets. Pamphlets and brochures published by government agencies and private organizations are generally stored in a library's vertical file. The *Vertical File Index: A Subject and Title Index to Selected Pamphlet Material* (1932/35–present) lists many of the available titles. Many are also available via the World Wide Web.

Special collections. Rare books, manuscripts, and items of local interest are commonly found in a special room or section of the library.

Maps and geographic information systems (GIS). Maps and atlases depict much more than roads and state boundaries, including information on population density, language patterns, soil types, and much more.

WRITING 2: APPLICATION ....

Identify three distinct kinds of information in your library's holdings (book, periodical, other), locate these, and take notes on both their usefulness and the process you used to obtain each.

....

23 c   Taking notes

Taking good notes will make the whole research process easier, enabling you to locate and remember sources and helping you use them effectively in your writing. For short research projects requiring only a few sources, it is easy to take careful notes in a research log or class notebook and refer to them as needed when writing your paper. Or you can photocopy or print out whole articles or chapters and take them home for further study. However, for any research project requiring more than a few sources, use either a card-based system or laptop computer to record and sort sources and information.

1 Make bibliographic notes

A bibliographic note identifies the source, not what's in it. When you locate a useful source, write all the information necessary to find that source again on a 3″ × 5″ index card or computer equivalent, using a separate "card" for each work. Do this as you find each source, even before taking notes from the source. If you create *bibliographic notes* as you go along, then at the end you can easily arrange them in alphabetical order to prepare the reference list required at the end of formal academic papers. (For complete information on bibliographic information appropriate for each discipline, see MLA, APA, or other documentation conventions in Chapters 30–33.)

2 Make information notes

Make paper or electronic notes to record the relevant information found in your sources. To write a research essay, you'll work from these note cards,

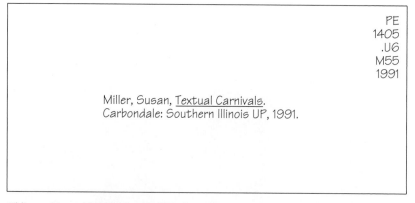

PE
1405
.U6
M55
1991

Miller, Susan, <u>Textual Carnivals</u>.
Carbondale: Southern Illinois UP, 1991.

Bibliographic card for a book using MLA documentation style

so be sure they contain all the information you need from every source you intend to use. Also try to focus them on your research question, so that their relevance is clear when you read them later. If using paper cards, use 4″ × 6″ index cards for information and 3″ × 5″ for bibliographic sources. These different sizes will also help keep the two sets separate. A typical note card should contain only one piece of information or one idea to allow you to arrange and rearrange the information in different ways as you write. At the top of each note card, identify the source through brief bibliographic identification (author and title), and note the page numbers on which the information appears. Personal notes, including ideas for possible use of the information or cross-references to other information, should be clearly distinguished from material that comes from the source; they might be put at the bottom in parentheses.

3 Quote, paraphrase, or summarize as needed

When recording information, you must take steps to avoid **plagiarism** (see Chapter 28). Do this by making distinctions among quoting directly, paraphrasing, and summarizing. A **direct quotation** is an exact duplication of the author's words in the original source. Put quotation marks around direct quotations on your note cards so that you will know later that these words are the author's, not yours. (See 27d, "Paraphrase.") A **paraphrase** is a restatement of the author's words in your own words. Paraphrase to simplify or clarify the original author's point. A paraphrase must restate the original facts or ideas fully and correctly. (See 27d, "Sum-

Information to Be Recorded on Bibliographic Cards

FOR BOOKS

1. Call number or other location information
2. Full name(s) of author(s)
3. Full title and subtitle
4. Edition or volume number
5. Editor or translator
6. Place of publication
7. Publisher and date of publication
8. Inclusive page numbers for relevant sections in longer works

FOR PERIODICALS

1. Full name(s) of author(s)
2. Full title and subtitle of articles
3. Periodical title
4. Periodical volume and number
5. Periodical date
6. Inclusive page numbers of article
7. Library call number or other location information

marize.") A **summary** is a brief condensation or distillation of the main point of the original source. Like a paraphrase, a summary should be in your own words, and all facts and ideas should be accurately represented. (See 27d3.)

The major advantage of quoting is that it allows you to decide later, while writing the paper, whether to include a quotation or to paraphrase or summarize. In general, copy direct quotations only when the author's words are particularly lively or persuasive. Photocopying machines and computer printers make it easy to collect direct quotations, but be sure to highlight the pertinent material or make notes to yourself on the copy so you can remember later what you wanted to quote and why. For ease of organizing notes, many researchers cut out the pertinent quotation and paste it to a note card.

A good paraphrase can help clarify a difficult passage by simplifying complex sentence structure and vocabulary into language with which you are more comfortable. Be careful not to distort the author's ideas. Use paraphrases when you need to record details but not exact words.

Lewis, <u>Green Delusions</u>, p. 230
Reasons for overpopulation in poor countries

Some experts believe that birth rates are linked to the "economic value" of children to their parents. Poor countries have higher birth rates because parents there rely on children to work for the family and to take care of them in old age. The more children, particularly sons, the better off the family is financially. In wealthier countries parents have fewer children because they cost more in terms of education and they contribute less.

(Based on Caldwell and Cain—check these further?)

Note card containing a paraphrase

Because a summary boils a source down to its essentials, it is particularly useful when specific details in the source are unimportant or irrelevant to your research question. You may often find that you can summarize several paragraphs or even an entire article or chapter in just a few sentences without losing any useful information. It is a good idea to note when a particular card contains a summary so you'll remember later that it leaves out detailed supporting information.

Quotation, Paraphrase, and Summary

As you take notes, use this box to help you choose which note-taking technique is best for your purposes.

- **Direct quotation** duplicates the exact words from a source. Keep direct quotations brief, and put prominent quotation marks around them on your note cards.

- **Paraphrase** restates the author's ideas in your own words simply, clearly, and accurately. This device captures content without exposing you to the risk of unacknowledged quotations, and thus your text may run as long as the original.

- **Summary** condenses the main point(s) of an original passage. Summarize in your own words, and use quotation marks around any of the author's language you include.

....

Describe the most important, useful, or surprising thing you have learned about the library since exploring it as part of your research project. Share your discovery with classmates, and listen to theirs. Are you comfortable in the library? Why or why not? How does technology help or hinder the research process? Explain in an online journal entry and share this with the class.

....

Thinking Critically About Library Sources

Ask the following questions of each source you read before deciding to use it.

- **Subject.** Is the subject *directly related* to my research question? Does it provide information that supports my view? Does it provide helpful context or background information? Does it contain quotations or facts that I will want to quote in my paper?

- **Author.** What do I really know about the author's reputation? Does the book or periodical provide any biographical information? Is this author cited by other sources? Am I aware of any biases that might limit the author's credibility?

- **Date.** When was this source published? Is it sufficiently up to date to suit my purpose? Does it represent common, widely accepted views or does it introduce a new perspective or discovery?

- **Publisher.** Who published this source? Is it a major publisher, a university press, or a scholarly organization that would subject material to a rigorous review procedure?

- **Counterauthority.** Does the source address or present counterarguments on issues I intend to discuss? Each point of view is essential for examining an issue completely.

WRITING ACROSS THE CURRICULUM

Suggestions for Talking with Librarians

The following suggestions apply to any research situation in any discipline where the writer wants to advance the research project and learn more about the way libraries work.

- Bring with you a copy of the research assignment and be prepared to describe the course/discipline for which you are conducting the research. Also bring along a copy of the course syllabus.

- Be ready to explain the assignment in your own words: purpose, format, length, number of sources, and due date.

- Identify any special requirements about sources: Should information come from government documents? rare books? films?

- Describe the particular topic you are researching and the tentative question you have framed to address the topic.

- Describe any work you have done so far: Web sites, books, or periodicals looked at, log entries written, people interviewed, and so on.

- Think about it this way: Reference librarians don't like to sit around with nothing to do. The more difficult the questions, the more interesting their work.

24

Conducting Internet Research

The Internet offers information of all kinds—entertainment, news, opinion, advertisement, vanity publishing, propaganda, reference, and academic writing. Because no one person or agency is "in charge," the Internet can be at once exciting and frustrating to use. Many students turn first to the World Wide Web to look up information of any kind. For academic research, using the Internet effectively requires good search skills and the ability to evaluate sources for their relevance and reliability. Supplementing Internet information with other sources can help you avoid many pitfalls. This chapter focuses on how to search for information. Evaluating Internet sources for their value to your research is covered further in Chapter 26.

24 a   Search engines

1 Search engine design

The commercial search sites Yahoo! and Google exemplify two different approaches to searching. Yahoo! is primarily a *directory,* an index organized in the manner of a library subject catalog. Directory listings usually are evaluated by human editors. In contrast, Google's principal search service uses *crawlers,* automated programs that evaluate sites in part by counting the number of times key terms appear in them and the other sites that link to them.

Directories are particularly useful at the beginning of research, providing an overview of a subject and the topics and issues within it. For example, if you enter the term *molecular biology* in a Yahoo! directory search, you'll be offered links to subcategories such as *molecular biology: imaging* or *molecular biology: computational*. The individual sites returned will contain many gateway (specialized index) and overview sites.

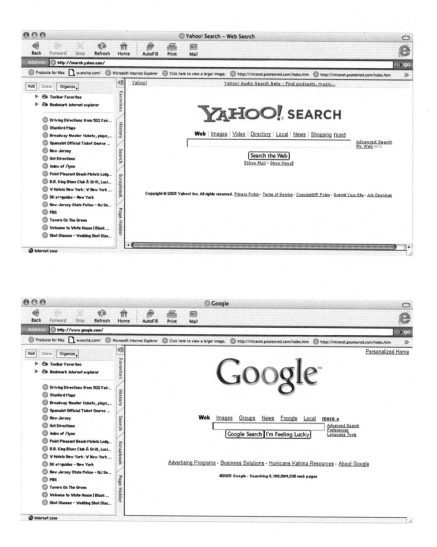

A Google search on a similarly general term yields an assortment of individual sites, including reference sites, gateways, course outlines, and journal archives. Some of these resources might be of great value, but it can be hard to know where to start.

On the other hand, when your search terms are more specific, such as *molecular biology evolution creationism,* a crawler search is often a more useful tool. To see the differences, try those two searches in a Google Web search and a Yahoo! directory search. To learn more about search engines and how they work, visit Search Engine Watch (www.search enginewatch.com). For a tutorial on Internet searching, visit the University of California at Berkeley site at http://www.lib.berkeley.edu/Teaching Lib/Guides/Internet/.

Academic Search Resources on the Internet

For academic research, you'll need search tools that focus on resources that are useful to students and other academic writers. Here are some places to start, each of which can lead to many others.

- The Internet Public Library, http://www.ipl.org/. The University of Michigan School of Information maintains this site.

- Invisible Web, www.invisible-web.com/. Chris Sherman and Gary Price compile a directory of academic and government search tools.

- University of Wisconsin Internet Scout, http://scout.wisc.edu/. This ongoing project finds and lists academic resources on the Internet.

- Infomine, http://infomine.ucr.edu. The University of California at Riverside operates this broad academic directory.

- RefDesk.com, http://www.refdesk.com/. This is a noncommercial site dedicated to research of all kinds.

- Reference.com, http://www.reference.com: dictionaries, thesauri, encyclopedias, and more.

- Library of Congress Online Catalog, http://catalog.loc.gov/.

- Metasearch. A *metasearch engine* such as Dogpile (www.dogpile.com), ez2www (http://ez2www.com), or Vivísimo (http://vivisimo.com) feeds search terms to several search engines at once, often mixing results from directories with results found by crawlers.

24 b   Limiting your search

When you enter a word or phrase in a search engine, the program re-trieves a list of pages containing your search terms. Sometimes that list is impossibly long. Searching for *music* on Google locates 108 million pages; limiting the search to *classical music* yields a mere 4.5 million. Even searching for *composer Edvard Grieg* retrieves 6,560 pages. Nar-rowing further to *composer Grieg biography* yields manageable and use-ful results.

Most search engines have an "advanced search" or help page that tells how it works and describes any special tools. For example, if you enter more than one word in Google, by default it returns only pages that con-tain *all* your search terms. That's why *classical music* yields fewer pages than *music* or *classical*. To search within those results, simply add an-other term: *American classical music.*

Some search engines use *stemming,* a way of searching for related words at the same time. Searching for *parent* would also produce refer-ences to *parents, parenting,* and *parental*. Others let you use an asterisk to include multiple forms: *parent**. On engines that do not use stemming, you must search separately: *parents' rights, parent's rights,* and *parental rights*. Consult the help page of each search engine for details.

Search engines allow you to combine terms in logical ways. Using what is called Boolean logic, you can search for *rights and parent or par-enting or parental* and accomplish the same thing as three separate searches (*parent's rights, parents' rights, parental rights*). You can also ex-clude terms: *rights and parent's or parents' or parental not grandparents.*

Search Engine Tips

Archived pages: Google stores "cached" versions of pages that you can call up when the live page is no longer available. If a search engine finds a page that turns out to be unavailable, try Google's "cached" link to see if an archived version exists.

Search within a Web site: If you find a likely site but can't find the specific item you're looking for, enter the site's home address plus specific search terms like this: *site:* http://www.pennlive.com/pennstate football (note the spaces separating the URL and the search terms). The search engine will list all the pages on that site that contain your terms. (Some engines use *host* rather than *site* for a site search.)

Most search engines ignore prepositions (*in, on, around*) and other small, common words. To guarantee that a word is included, put a space and plus sign in front of it: *breakfast +in bed* yields more specific results than *breakfast bed* but doesn't eliminate all the *bed and breakfast* results. To search for an exact phrase, put it in quotation marks: *"breakfast in bed."*

Try some of these searches on the Google advanced search page and note the different results each one yields. (Some sites code these functions in other ways; check the help files.) The point of this exercise is that when you're having trouble finding what you need, be ready to try lots of different approaches.

24 c Search strategies

1 Maximizing search effectiveness

When you find a Web site devoted to your topic, look for links to other sites, and follow them to see whether they lead to other useful information. If you find a dead link, check your typing and try again. Then shorten the Web address. For example, the Vietnam Veterans of America site has a massive page of links "About the War." If you can't bring up www.vva.org/about_ the_war.htm, try www.vva.org/, and look for links, or do a site search. (See "Search Engine Tips" box.)

Be sure to examine several different sites on the same subject. Similar sites may provide different information or have different degrees of reliability. Some provide reference information; some contain primary sources; others make sales pitches.

2 Documenting a search

Here are some tips for documenting Web searches:

■ In a research notebook, record search terms you use, the URLs of sites you visit, and the dates you visited.

■ When you locate a useful site, print a copy of the page and, if your printer doesn't automatically print the URL, record it and the date and time in your notebook or on the printout.

■ If you're using your own computer, save useful locations in your browser's bookmark or favorites file.

More Internet Resources

Here are some specialized, academic, and reference resources.

- Amazon.com, http://www.amazon.com/: Lists books in print and out-of-print titles, including publication data and readers' reviews, and suggests related titles. You don't have to buy the books; use the information to find them in a library.

- Bartleby.com, http://www.bartleby.com: Offers complete, searchable text of works of literature, poetry, and criticism.

- Biographical dictionary, http://www.s9.com/biography/

- CIA World Factbook, http://www.cia.gov/cia/publications/factbook/: Comprehensive information on every country.

- Information Please, http://www.infoplease.com: Online almanac with topics from architecture to biography to historical statistics to weather.

- Learn the Net Inc, http://www.learnthenet.com/english/index.html: Web tours and training.

- Social Science Research Network, http://www.ssm.com: Abstracts of current papers in accounting, economics, and legal scholarship.

- U.S. Census Bureau, http://www.census.gov: A primary source for government demographic and economic data. Also see Statistical Abstract of the United States, http://www.census.gov/stat abstract.

24 d   E-mail, lists, and newsgroups

Once you have an **e-mail address,** you can correspond with people around the world—if you know their addresses. To search for an e-mail address, try Search.com at http://www.search.com/search?channel=10 or an e-mail address metasearch at http://my.email.address.is/. People often post their e-mail addresses on their own Web sites, and institutions such as universities often have faculty e-mail directories on their Web pages. If you know someone works at an institution but can't find his or her e-mail address, try writing to a contact address provided on the Web site.

E-mail lists help you communicate with selected groups of people. If you write to an e-mail list, your message is delivered to all members of the list.

Information submitted (or *posted*) to a **newsgroup** is collected on a computer "bulletin board." Readers interested in a group's topic must electronically visit the board to retrieve messages.

1 Newsgroups

The oldest newsgroups began on a network called Usenet to create groups outside Usenet and provide search tools that cover Usenet groups. (At Google, www.google.com, click the Groups link, then follow the Usenet link).

Many of the tens of thousands of Usenet groups are open to the public. Some require membership, which is usually easy for researchers to obtain. (Note that unmoderated groups can contain irrelevant or objectionable material or heated debate.) Google, Yahoo, and other gateways now host groups that are not part of Usenet.

Usenet Categories

The name of a Usenet group describes its contents hierarchically: *sci.astro.hubble* is a science group devoted to astronomy, specifically data from the Hubble Space Telescope. Wikipedia, the online encyclopedia at http://en.wikipedia.org/, lists eight major Usenet categories.

- **comp.***: Computer-related discussions (*comp.software, comp.sys.amiga*)
- **misc.***: Miscellaneous topics (*misc.education, misc.forsale, misc.kids*)
- **news.***: Discussions and announcements about news (meaning Usenet, not current events) (*news.groups, news.admin*)
- **rec.***: Recreation and entertainment (*rec.music, rec.arts.movies*)
- **sci.***: Science-related discussions (*sci.psychology, sci.research*)
- **soc.***: Social discussions (*soc.college.org, soc.culture.african*)
- **talk.***: Talk about various controversial topics (*talk.religion, talk.politics*)
- **humanities** *Fine arts, literature,* and *philosophy* (*humanities.classics, humanities.design.misc*)
- Other broad categories include *rec.* for recreation and *alt.* for alternative, a huge miscellaneous category.

The archives of a scholarly newsgroup can be a gold mine for a patient researcher. They can also help you find people knowledgeable about your topic whom you can contact directly, usually by e-mail.

Before you post a query to a newsgroup or contact a member, do your homework. Most major groups list frequently asked questions (FAQs) and answers. The FAQs (pronounced fax) often will tell you whether you're in an appropriate group, list the key contacts, and answer many preliminary questions. The sources you contact will appreciate not having to repeat information they have already set out for you.

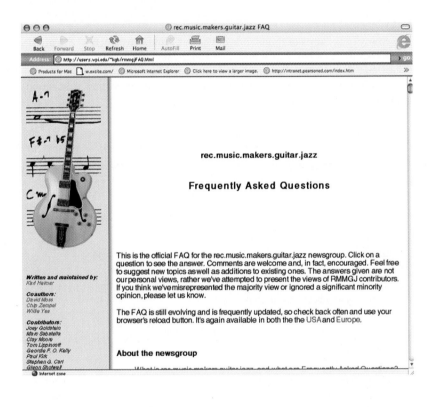

2 E-mail lists

Both newsgroups and e-mail lists allow one writer to reach many readers with similar interests. The difference is that while a newsgroup posting must wait for interested readers to find it, anything you post to a list will quickly be delivered to list members' inboxes. Many lists have Web pages with FAQs that include the name and address of the moderator and instructions for joining or leaving the list. Many also have searchable archives available to members of the list. A request for membership for research purposes will usually be accepted. And most members will welcome questions from newcomers, especially those who have familiarized themselves with the list's FAQs or archives before posting.

List Search and Writing Lists

You can search academic and professional e-mail lists and newsgroups by title or topic groups.yahoo.com or groups.google.com. CataList www.lsoft.com/lists/listref.html searches all the public lists created with the pioneering list program called Listserv.

Here are two lists of many devoted to writing and electronic research:

CARR-L Computer Assisted Reporting and Research, hosted by the University of Louisville, http://www.louisville.edu/it/listserv/archives/carr-l.html. Membership required.

Poynter Institute, http://talk.poynter.org. A collection of discussion lists for professional reporters and editors, including sections on writing online. Membership required.

WRITING ACROSS THE CURRICULUM

How to Read an Internet Address

Every site on the Internet has a unique electronic address called the *universal resource locator,* or URL. In addition to identifying a specific computer file, a URL also includes information about the owner of the site. Here are the parts of a URL:

<http://iana.netnod.se>

Internet	server	second-level	country code top-level
mode	name	domain name	domain name
			(Sweden)

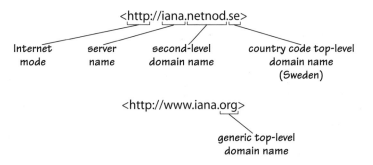

<http://www.iana.org>

generic top-level
domain name

The top-level domain name (.*se* or .*org* in these examples) tells in what country or type of organization the site originates. Here are the generic top-level domain names:

- **.aero** aviation groups or companies
- **.biz** businesses
- **.com** commercial/business
- **.coop** cooperative association
- **.edu** educational institution
- **.gov** government agency
- **.info** informational site, including commercial
- **.museum** accredited museums worldwide
- **.mil** military
- **.name** reserved for individuals
- **.net** news and other networks, including broadband service providers
- **.org** nonprofit agency
- **.pro** professionals and professional organizations

Looking at the top-level domain name can give you a clue about the purpose and viewpoint of a Web site: **.com** and **.biz** sites are commercial, oriented toward sales; **.coop, .pro,** and **.org** may have commercial or political purposes but also may promote general public welfare; **.mil** and **.gov** are official sites; **.edu** and **.museum** are primarily educational and cultural; **.info, .name,** and ~ can be almost anything.

Research is an active and unpredictable process requiring serious investigators to find answers wherever those happen to be. Depending on your research question, you may need to seek answers by visiting museums, attending concerts, interviewing politicians, observing classrooms, or following leads down some wooded trail. Investigations that take place outside the library are commonly called **field research**.

After our first-year students completed a writing project in which field research played a central part, we asked them what they thought of this kind of research. Here is what they told us:

John: "Without question, it was interviews that gave me the most current and interesting information for my forestry paper. I could ask my own questions and not have to dig through useless information to get the answer."

Angel: "When I quoted Congressman Sanders's personal views on gun control, his voice made my voice stronger and more believable."

Jose: "Field research was very frustrating to me. No one would ever return my phone calls or answer my questions directly."

Kate: "I enjoy field research because I'm more personally involved in it. It's harder than library or Web research—calling and making appointments and going places—but it is more entertaining."

Field research adds liveliness, immediacy, and credibility to a research paper, especially when used in conjunction with library and Internet research. In fact, it's always a good idea to learn as much as you can about the subject of your research via a library or Web search before conducting an interview; the people you talk to will see that you're informed and will give you more detailed information. At the same time, good field research often takes more time and preparation than browsing the Web or an online catalog, so it can also be frustrating.

Field researchers collect primary source information not yet recorded or assessed by somebody else, and so they have the chance to uncover new facts and develop original interpretations. To conduct such research, you first need to determine which people, places, things, or events can give you the information you need. Then you must go out in the field and either **observe** by watching carefully or **interview** by asking questions of a particular person.

25 a Planning

Unlike a library, which bundles millions of bits of every kind of information in a single location, "fields" are everywhere, including on-campus (academic departments, administrative offices, labs, libraries, dining and sports facilities, and dormitories) as well as the neighborhood beyond the campus (theaters, malls, parks, playgrounds, farms, factories, and so on). Field information is not cataloged, organized, indexed, or shelved for your convenience. Obtaining it requires diligence, energy, and careful planning.

- **Consider your research question as it now stands.** What field sources are available that would bolster your argument or add to your report?

- **Select your contacts and sites.** Find the person, place, thing, or event most helpful to you. Decide whether you will collect observations, conduct interviews, or do both.

- **Schedule field research in advance.** Interviews, trips, and events don't always work according to plan. Allow time for glitches, such as having to reschedule an interview or return for more information.

■ **Do homework before you go.** Visit the library or conduct a Google search before conducting extensive field research. No matter from whom, where, or what you intend to collect information, there's background information that can help you make more insightful observations or formulate better interview questions.

■ **Take extensive notes in your research log.** Record visits, questions, phone calls, and conversations in a research log: write from the very beginning about topics, questions, methods, and answers. Record even dead-end searches, to remind yourself that you tried them.

Thinking Critically About Field Sources

When using field sources on or off campus in writing classes or across the curriculum, analyze each source's underlying assumptions, determine the reliability and credibility of the source, and develop an interpretation of your source's information that helps you answer your research question. To assess the value of field resources, ask yourself the following questions:

■ **What is the most important point this source makes?** How does it address my research question? How might this point fit into my paper and how should I articulate it?

■ **What evidence did the source provide that supports this point?** Is it strong or weak? Can I use it and build on it? Should I question or refute it?

■ **Does the information support my working thesis?** If so, how? How can I express the support in writing?

■ **Does the information challenge my working thesis?** If so, how? Can I refute the information or contradiction? Or should I revise my thesis to take the new information into account?

■ **Does the information support or contradict information collected from other sources?** How so? How can I resolve any contradictions? Do I need to seek other sources for confirmation?

■ **Is the source reliable?** Does any of the information from this source seem illogical or not credible? Has any of the information been contradicted by a more authoritative source?

■ **Is the source biased?** Does the interview subject have a reason to be biased in any way? Would the selection of a different site have produced different information?

Begin a field research log by speculating on the feasibility of using field research information to help answer your research question. Identify two sites you might visit and three subjects you might interview.

....

25 b   Interviewing

If you are comfortable talking to strangers, then you have a head start on being a good interviewer. In many respects, a good interview is simply a good conversation. If you consider yourself shy, don't worry, for you can still learn how to ask good interview questions that will elicit useful answers. Your chances of obtaining good interview material increase radically when you've thought about what questions you want to pose ahead of time. The following guidelines should help you conduct good interviews:

Select the right person. People differ in both the amount and kind of knowledge they have. Not everyone who knows something about your research topic will be able to give you the information you need. Ask yourself (1) exactly what information you need, (2) why you need it, (3) who is likely to have it, and (4) how you might gain it.

Most research projects benefit from more than one perspective, so plan on more than one interview. For example, to research Lake Erie pollution, you could interview someone who lives on the shore, a chemist who knows about pesticide decomposition, a vice president of a nearby paper company, and people who frequent the waterfront.

Do your homework. Before you talk to an expert about your topic, make sure you know something about it yourself. Be able to define or describe your interest in it, know the general issues, and learn what your interview subject has already said about it in books, articles, or interviews. In this way, you will ask sharper questions, get to the point faster, and be more interesting for your subject to talk with. Plan appropriate questions.

Create a working script. A good interview doesn't follow a script, but it usually starts with one. Before you begin an interview, write out the questions you plan to ask and arrange them so that they build on each other—general questions first, specific ones later. If you or your subject digresses, your questions can reminder you to get back on track.

Ask both open and closed questions. Different kinds of questions elicit different kinds of information. Open questions place few limits on the answers given: Why did you decide to major in business? What are your plans for the future? Closed questions specify the information you want and usually elicit brief responses: When did you receive your degree? From what college? Open questions usually provide general information, while closed questions supply details.

Ask follow-up questions. Listen closely to the answers you receive. When the information is incomplete or confusing, ask follow-up questions requesting clarification. Such questions are seldom scripted, so plan on using your wits to direct your subject toward the information you consider most important.

Use silence. If you don't get an immediate response to a question, wait a bit before asking another one. In some cases, your question may not have been clear and you will need to rephrase it. But in many cases your interview subject is simply collecting his or her thoughts, not ignoring you. After a slight pause, you may hear thoughtful answers worth waiting for.

Read body language. Be aware of what your subject is doing while answering the questions. Does he or she look you in the eye? fidget and squirm? look distracted or bored? smile? From these visual cues you may be able to infer when your subject is speaking most frankly, doesn't want to give more information, or is tired of answering questions.

Take good content notes. Many interviewers take notes on a pad that is spiral-bound on top, which allows for quick page flipping. Don't try to write down everything, just major ideas and telling statements in the subject's own words that you might want to use as quotations in your paper. Omitting small words, focusing on the most distinctive and precise language, and using common abbreviations make note taking more efficient.

Take good descriptive notes. Note your subject's physical appearance, facial expressions, and clothing, as well as the interview setting itself. These details will be useful later when you reconstruct the interview, helping you represent it more vividly in your paper.

Tape-record with permission only. If you plan to use a tape recorder, ask for permission in advance. The advantage of tape recording is that you have a complete record of the conversation. Sometimes on hearing the person a second time, you notice important things you missed earlier. However, sometimes tape recorders make subjects nervous and be aware that transcribing a tape is time-consuming. It's a good idea to have pen in hand to catch highlights or jot down additional questions.

Confirm important assertions. When your subject says something especially important or controversial, read back your notes aloud to check for accuracy and to allow your subject to elaborate. Some interviewers do this during the interview, others at the end.

Review your notes. Notes taken during an interview are brief reminders of what your subject said, not complete quotations. You need to write out the complete information they represent as soon after the interview as you can, certainly within twenty-four hours. Supplement the notes with other remembered details while they're still fresh, recording them on note cards or directly into a computer file that you can refer to as you write your paper.

Interview electronically. It is possible and useful to contact individuals via telephone, electronic mail, or the Internet. Phone interviews are quick and obvious ways of finding out information on short notice. If your interviewee has an e-mail address, asking questions via this medium is even less intrusive than telephoning as your subject can answer when doing so is convenient—quickly, specifically, and in writing.

WRITING 2: EXPLORATION ....

Describe any experience you have had as either interviewer or interviewee. Drawing on your own experience, what additional advice would you give to researchers setting out to interview a subject?

....

ESL   *Conducting Interviews in English*

Interviewing someone, especially in a foreign language, can be challenging. Before you conduct an interview, consider whether you will feel comfortable taking notes and listening at the same time. If your interview subject doesn't object, you may want to use a tape recorder.

To take notes efficiently in an interview, develop a list of abbreviations beforehand to facilitate note taking. Don't hesitate to ask your interview subject to repeat or clarify information, but be polite. It is usually more polite to make a request than to use a command or statement.

POLITE REQUESTS

Could you please repeat that statistic?

Would you please explain that to me?

25 c   Surveying

Surveys are commonly used in the social sciences to collect data from more than one person. A survey is a structured interview in which respondents are all asked the same questions and their answers tabulated and interpreted. Researchers usually conduct surveys to discover attitudes, beliefs, or habits of the general public or segments of the population. They may try to predict how soccer moms will vote in an election, determine the popularity of a new movie with teenage audiences, compare the eating habits of students who live off campus to those of students who eat in college dining halls, and so on.

For research purposes, respondents to surveys can be treated like experts because they are being asked for opinions or information about their own behavior. However, to get useful answers, you must ask your questions skillfully. Wording that suggests a right or wrong answer reveals the researcher's biases and preconceived ideas more than the subject's candid responses. Furthermore, the questions should be easy to understand and answer, and they should be reviewed to make sure they are relevant to the research topic or hypothesis. The format for questioning and the way the research is conducted also have an influence on the responses. For example, to get complete and honest answers about a sensitive or highly personal issue, the researcher would probably use anonymous written surveys to ensure confidentiality. Other survey techniques involve oral interviews in which the researcher records each subject's responses on a written form.

Surveys are usually brief to gain the cooperation of a sufficiently large number of respondents. And to enable the researcher to compare answers, the questions are usually closed, although open-ended questions may be used to gain additional information or insights. Surveys are treated briefly here because, in truth, the designing of good survey questions, distributing of surveys, and assessment of the results is a highly complex and sophisticated business. To get some idea of the steps involved in formulating an effective survey, consult either of the following helpful Internet sources:

- *Questionnaires and Surveys: A Free Tutorial,* http://www.statpac.com/surveys/

- *Creative Systems Research, The Survey System,* http://www.surveysystem.com/sdesign.htm

A further complication arises if the survey you are considering requests sensitive information (such as personal experience with drugs, alcohol, or sex) from identifiable subjects. All colleges and universities have "human subject" boards or committees, which need to approve any research that could compromise the privacy of students, staff, or faculty. Consequently, consult your instructor before launching any survey on or off campus.

However, the simple, informal polling of people to request opinions takes place quite often in daily college life, such as every time a class takes a vote or a professor asks the class for opinions or interpretations about texts. In one case, a student who was writing a self-profile wanted to find out how she was perceived by others. First, Anna made a list of ten people who knew her in different ways—her mother, father, older sister, roommate, best friend, favorite teacher, and so on. Next, she invited each to make a list of five words that best characterized her. Finally, she asked each to call her answering machine on a day when she knew she would not be home and name these five words. In this way, she was able to collect an original outside opinion (field research) in a nonthreatening manner that she then wove into her profile paper, combining others' opinions with her own self-assessments. The external points of view added an interesting (and sometimes surprising) view of herself as well as other voices to her paper.

WRITING 3: APPLICATION

Invent a simple survey (no more than five questions) to generate external information about any paper topic you are working on. To implement the survey, plan to use a one-page paper handout, a brief e-mail message, or the telephone to collect responses. Perhaps the easiest way to do this is to try it out on your classmates first.

25 d Observing

Another kind of field research calls for closely observing people, places, things, or events and then describing them accurately to show readers what you saw and experienced. While the term *observation* literally denotes visual perception, it also applies to information collected on site through other senses. The following suggestions may help you conduct field observations:

Select a good site. Like interviewing, observing requires that you know where to go and what to look for. Have your research question in mind and identify places where observation might yield useful information. For example, historical research on a small town might be enhanced by visits to the county courthouse, the town clerk, or the local cemetery.

Do your homework. To observe well, you need to know what you are looking for and what you are looking at. If you are observing a political speech, know the issues and the players; if you visit an industrial complex, know what is manufactured there. Researching background information at the library or elsewhere will allow you to use your site time more efficiently.

Plan your visit. Learn not only where the place is located on a map but also how to gain access; call ahead to ask directions. Find out where you should go when you first arrive. If relevant, ask which places are open to you, which are off limits, and which you could visit with permission. Find out about visiting hours; if you want to visit at odd hours, you may need special permission. Depending on the place, after-hours visits can provide detailed information not available to the general public.

Take good notes. At any site there's a lot going on that casual observers take for granted. As a researcher you should take nothing for granted. Keep in mind that without notes, as soon as you leave a site you forget more than half of what was there. Review and rewrite your observation notes as soon after your site visit as possible. Make your notes as precise as possible, indicating the color, shape, size, texture, and arrangement of everything you can.

Taking field notes is a lot easier in a notebook with a stiff cover so you can write standing, sitting, or squatting; a table may not be available. Double-entry notebooks are useful for site visits because they allow you to record facts in one column and interpretations of those facts in the other. Unless you're a very skilled typist, a laptop computer may be more trouble than it's worth.

Visual images also provide excellent memory aids, so consider sketching, photographing, or videotaping the site you visit. If you speak your notes into a tape recorder, you will also pick up the characteristic sounds of the site.

WRITING ACROSS THE CURRICULUM

The Role of the Researcher in Field Research

The researcher is present, one way or another, in all research projects, but never more so than in field research. When using textual sources such as books, articles, Web sites, and pamphlets, the researcher is able to rely on language created by other people—to credit, discredit, or question. However, in field research, the researcher plays a larger role in creating the language of the source. In other words, the researcher participates directly in both the creation and the evaluation of interview and site-visit material used in writing research essays.

- The researcher directly shapes interview material through (1) the questions asked, (2) the site chosen, and (3) the language in which notes are taken.

- The researcher shapes on-site material selecting the site by placing a camera one place and not another and by selecting what to focus on and what to ignore. In like manner, the location and audio level of a tape recorder affect what is heard and what is not.

- The researcher assigns value to the field sources through the way they are collected (notes, tapes, photos) as well as how they are recorded, developed, transcribed, and saved.

Account for your preparation, participation, and perspective in any field research that you have undertaken sometime in the recent past, which may include a chemistry experiment, a geology laboratory, an author interview, a natural resources field trip, an art class drawing expedition, or a sociological survey.

26 *Evaluating Research Sources*

I n order for writers to use research sources to support claims made in research projects, they need to ask two critical questions of each source: (1) Is the source itself credible? (2) Does it help my paper? This chapter provides guidelines for evaluating the credibility and usefulness of sources found on the Internet, in the library, and in the field.

26 a Evaluating library sources

Many of the books, periodicals, and documents in special collections have been recommended for library acquisition by scholars and librarians with special expertise in each of the many subject areas the library catalogs. While the Internet now provides additional and more easily accessed sources on every imaginable topic, these sources are not subject to the same screening and cataloging process as library sources and need additional critical appraisal. (See 26b.)

Regardless of origin, all information sources need to be questioned by your critical intelligence for credibility and usefulness. Though the library remains the main repository of knowledge on a college campus, you cannot use even library sources without subjecting each source to careful scrutiny. Two of the main reasons for questioning a source found in the library have to do with *time* (when was it judged true?) and *perspective* (who said it was true and for what reason?).

1 Locate date

Most library documents, especially those created since the advent of copyright laws at the end of the nineteenth century, include their date of publication on or inside the cover of the document itself, in most cases a fact that you can rely on. In some cases, such as articles first published in one place, then reprinted in another, you may have to dig harder for the original date, but if you check the permissions page, you'll find it.

However, one of the main reasons library sources lose reliability, and hence credibility, is the simple passage of time. Sources become outdated and, therefore, unreliable. For example, compare any fifty-year-old atlas or encyclopedia entry about African, Asian, or European nations with the latest edition of the same work, and you'll find changes so striking as to make the older source completely outdated. Geographical, political, or statistical information valid in 1955 has inevitably changed by 2005—in many cases, radically so. Pay attention to the date a source was created, and reflect on what may have happened since then.

At the same time, dated information may still be highly useful—which is why old texts remain in the library. Once you know the source date, you can decide whether or not it will still help your paper. If you are studying change over time, for example, old statistical information would be useful baseline data to demonstrate what has changed since. But if you are studying current culture, the dated information may actually be misleading. In other words, when evaluating whether a dated source serves your purpose, know what that purpose is.

2 Identify perspective

The second critical question to ask of any source is what point of view or perspective it represents. *Who* created the source and for *what purpose?* This second critical question is more difficult to answer quickly because the author's point of view is seldom identifed or summarized on the source itself. And when it is, this information, being a creation of the author, cannot always be believed.

To trust a source, you need to learn to analyze its assumptions, evidence, biases, and reasoning—which together constitute the author's perspective. In essence, you need to ask:

■ What is this writer's purpose—scholarly analysis, political advocacy, entertainment, or something else?

■ Will a quick perusal of the Introduction or first chapter reveal what the writer assumes about the subject or audience?

■ Can you tell which statements are facts, which are inferences drawn from facts, and which are strictly matters of opinion?

■ Does a first reading of the evidence persuade you?

■ Is the logic of the position apparent and/or credible?

■ Are there relevant points the writer *doesn't* mention?

■ Do the answers to these questions make you more or less willing to accept the author's conclusions?

Although at first it may seem daunting or even futile to try to answer all these questions about every source, have patience and give the research process the time it needs. At the beginning of a research project, when you're still trying to gain context and overview and you've looked at only one source, it's difficult to recognize an author's purpose and viewpoint. However, as you read further and begin to compare one source to another, differences will emerge, especially if you read extensively and take notes. The more differences you note, the more critically aware you become and the more you know why, how, and where a source might help you. *Remember, the more you learn, the more you learn.* Will it be useful?

3 Critically review

To critically review a library source yourself, reread Chapter 2 and plan to ask both first and second questions of the text (see pp. 15–16). In short, the answers to first questions are generally factual, the result of probing the text (identifying the title, table of contents, chapter headings, index, and so on). The answers to second questions are more inferential, the result of analyzing the assertions, evidence, and language of the text (identifying the perspective of author and sources).

To gain a larger perspective on an especially interesting source, consult the opinion of experts about the published source by (1) looking at reviews of the work when it was published in places such as *Book Review Digest*, (2) doing a subject search for the author in the library's catalog or general periodical index, and (3) doing a Google search by author or title on the World Wide Web.

WRITING 1: APPLICATION

Find any text applicable to your current research that advocates a position or makes an argument. Look at the copyright date. Read the Introduction. Review the Table of Contents. Skim read the first chapter. What can you infer about the author's purpose, assumptions, and point of view? How persuasive is the argument? Finally, check your own analysis against a source review you find in *Book Review Digest* or on the Internet.

Thinking Critically About Library Sources

When you have selected your library sources and are prepared to read them more thoroughly and take notes, apply your critical thinking skills to the following issues:

- **Publication date.** What is the significance of the publication date for your purposes? Consult the *Book Review Index* to locate reviews of the book sources at the time of publication to help you evaluate their credibility. For articles in general-interest magazines and scholarly or professional journals, you can often find useful commentary in letters to the editor of subsequent issues.

- **Author perspective.** In each source, what are the author's point of view and purpose? Are the claims made in the text reasonable? Is the evidence based on fact, inference, or opinion? Is the language careful or careless, neutral or biased, calm or strident? Does the author take other perspectives into account?

- **Critical reviews.** Does the information in one source support or contradict that in other sources? Do a subject search of the author in the library catalog, in a general periodical index, or on the World Wide Web to find out how the author is viewed by other experts and how your source fits in with the author's other works.

26 b   Evaluating Internet sources

Although the Internet provides marvelous information sources, it can also be a trap for unwary researchers. Material published on the Internet does not have to meet the same standards of fairness, accuracy, or statistical validity as, say, a peer-reviewed journal or a daily newspaper. Anyone with a computer and a modem can publish personal opinion, commercial pitches, satire, bogus claims, even bomb-making instructions, on the World Wide Web. So how do you distinguish the credible from the questionable? And what do the differences mean for your research writing?

To identify an Internet source, look first at the electronic address or Uniform Resource Locator (URL). The extension at the end, such as .com or .gov, is called the *top-level domain name*. It indicates the type of organization sponsoring the site. (See box in 24d.)

The domain extensions are your first clue to the nature of the source. Those with .gov and .mil can be expected to present official information. Nonprofit organization sites—.org—usually reflect the viewpoint of the sponsoring organization. For examples of how a point of view can saturate

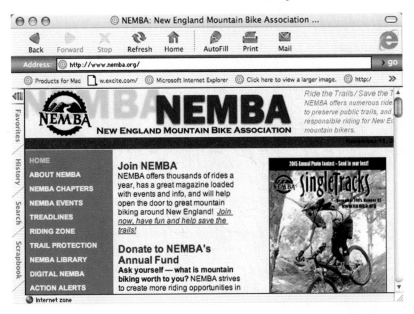

a site, visit the Sierra Club (www.sierraclub.org), the New England Mountain Bike Association (www.nemba.org), or any other special-interest site you are interested in. Pages designated .com and .biz can be promotional, sales-oriented, or informational. The top-level domain .info—for information—is not yet common, but it will be available to all Internet users wanting to publish information of almost any kind. Personal sites with a tilde (~) or .name in the URL usually represent one person's point of view, and in that case you have to make a judgment about that individual's credibility and relevance to your project.

An address extension isn't a certain indicator of a site's value. If you're writing about history, for example, you may find a .edu site covering your topic published by a history class at another school. For your purposes, that site is a secondary source that you may not want to use directly, but it might contain useful links to primary sources that are highly relevant. Similarly, a commercial site isn't usually a primary source for information about history, but it can be a primary source for what the sponsor says about itself or perhaps for trends in marketing.

Question every Internet source as thoroughly as you would a print source. If the source has a print counterpart, such as a peer-reviewed journal or a respected periodical, you may assign it roughly the same credibility as its print cousin. But most Internet sources are not so easy to classify. Try asking a reporter's questions—*who, what, when, where, why,* and *how.*

Who is the author?

- Look for an individual's name. Check the top and bottom of the page and in the URL.

- Look for a link that says "about us" or "about this site."

- Does the author have credentials as a scholar, scientist, physician? experience? college degrees?

- Does the author have a connections to a university? a publication? a government agency? an advocacy group?

- If no individual is named, is there a sponsoring organization? What can you tell about that organization's purpose, credibility, or politics?

- Look for links to the author's or agency's home page.

- Look for a way to contact the author or sponsoring organization by e-mail, phone, or letter to ask further questions.

- If you cannot tell who created the site or contact its sponsor, assign the site a low credibility, and don't rely on its information.

What ideas or information does the site present?

- Look for familiar concepts and terminology. Are they used in the ways you would expect?

- Summarize the site's claims or central ideas in your own words. How does the site fit your research needs?

- Examine how clearly the author distinguishes facts from opinions or speculation. Be wary of speculation. Be especially wary of any author who presents opinion or speculation as fact.

- When opinions are expressed, are they part of a balanced presentation or one that is biased toward one point of view? What tips you off? Which is more trustworthy? Why?

- Is any key information missing? Why do you think it's not there?

- If advertising is present, is it clearly labeled and separate from the factual material? Does the information in the site tend to support the aims of the advertisers?

How is the information presented?

- Examine how carefully the site is constructed, an indication of the educational level and sophistication of its creators. If the site contains spelling or grammatical errors or unexplained jargon, do you trust it? Will your readers?

- Do the graphics and multimedia features contribute to the content or detract from it?

- Are there links that help you put the information in context?

Where does the information come from?

- How carefully does the author identify the source of material not his or her own? Are links provided so you can check for yourself? Documenting sources increases a site's credibility, as it shows respect for standards of accuracy and verifiability.

- Are there related print sources for the information? How credible are they?

- Has the information been refereed or peer-reviewed?

When was the site created?

- A site more than a year old suggests information could be outdated. If there is no date, check the links to see whether the sites they point to are current. How important is the datedness or currency of the information to your purpose?

- If the site is not dated, how does that affect your assessment of its credibility?

Identifying the Ownership of Internet Resources

Every Internet domain name, such as *randomnumbers.com* or *google.com,* must be registered, and you can look up the name of each registered owner. Registries also usually contain e-mail addresses or postal addresses. The tool for finding this information is called *WHOIS.* Click on the WHOIS button at Network Solutions (www.netsol.com). Enter only the second-level and top-level domain name (*google.com,* not www.google.com), and WHOIS returns the owner's name and contact information. However, a site that makes you search for this information, rather than providing it, should not inspire confidence.

Critically Evaluating Two Web Sites

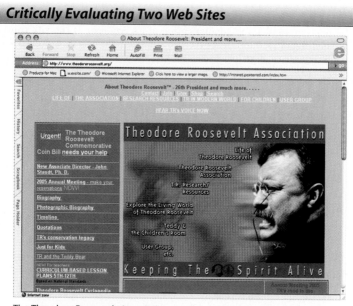

The Theodore Roosevelt Association site (http://www.theodoreroosevelt.org).
Reprinted by permission of Theodore Roosevelt Association.

The Almanac of Theodore Roosevelt site (http://www.theodore-roosevelt.com).

Here's the situation. You are looking for primary source material about Theodore Roosevelt, the 26th president of the United States, especially contemporary photographs and facsimiles of manuscripts. After ruling out several sites by actors who impersonate Roosevelt for special occasions and after reading a good biographical sketch at www .AmericanPresident.org, a University of Virginia site, you have narrowed your search to two very similar sites, the Theodore Roosevelt Association (www.theodoreroosevelt.org) and The Almanac of Theodore Roosevelt (www.theodore-roosevelt.com). Both appear to have primary documents, including many contemporary photographs. The two sites share a very positive view of Roosevelt—neither contains any material critical of him, but the sites' origins differ. Which would make the more reliable source? Here's how the "reporter's questions" help differentiate the two.

The Theodore Roosevelt Association site (www.theodoreroosevelt.org):

- **Who?** The site says it's the official publication of an association chartered by Congress in 1920. Officers of the association are named. The appointment of a new director is announced.
- **What?** A wealth of facts, a timeline, images of pages from Roosevelt's diaries, and photos. The diary pages and photos are representations of primary sources, and they are identified and dated.

- **Where?** A mailing address, e-mail link, and phone numbers are provided.
- **When?** Home page isn't dated, but the site includes information on an upcoming meeting and one that occurred very recently.
- **Why?** A mission statement says the organization exists "to instill in all who may be interested an appreciation …" of Roosevelt.
- **How?** Site mixes some primary materials with secondary accounts to present a positive view of Roosevelt.

The Almanac of Theodore Roosevelt site (www.theodore-roosevelt.com):

- **Who?** No author is identified on the home page. The site appears to be the work of one person with a great enthusiasm for all things related to "TR."
- **What?** The site has extensive texts of writings and speeches by Roosevelt. There are many photos, most of which do not have captions or dates. There are a number of facsimiles of documents, but many lack identification. Some photos appear on both the association and almanac sites.
- **Where?** There is no mailing address or phone number.
- **When?** The site says it was modified within the past week.

- **Why?** A mission statement says the site was created to "preserve and expand upon the memory and ideals of Theodore Roosevelt."
- **How?** The site mixes historical documents with advocacy, such as offering readers a chance to vote (for Roosevelt) in a History Channel poll on "Who is the greatest American?"

SOME CONCLUSIONS

Both sites show a heavy pro-Roosevelt bias, so their stories of Roosevelt's actions and triumphs (which for this purpose are secondary sources) need to be checked against other, more balanced accounts. The almanac site, the work of one person who presents no scholarly credentials, is an example of an excellent "fan site," a collection of materials gathered to express and spread the author's enthusiasm for the subject. The absence of key information about photographs and some other materials limit its usefulness for scholarly research. Many items here that appear to be primary documents would need to be supported by other sources.

While the association site apparently began with similar enthusiasms, the group's longevity and official recognition and the fact that it appears to have hired professional staff enhance its credibility. The association shows greater respect for research standards by providing more information about the primary documents it presents.

To judge for yourself, visit the sites online. Be aware that they may have changed substantially since this writing.

■

26 c   Evaluating field sources

Everything said about critically questioning library sources would hold true for field sources if people and places were as carefully documented, reviewed, and cataloged. Evaluating the credibility of an interview subject or usefulness of a Web site is just as important as a print or electronic source. It is often more difficult for readers to track down field sources than text sources.

1 Interviews

An interview is usually a one-time event. The subject may no longer be available for cross-checking or may change his or her mind. Be careful to find out whether an individual speaks for an organization or for him- or herself alone. Get permission in advance from the interviewee if you plan to tape-record. Then after the interview subject agrees to be recorded, start the recorder, and ask again for permission to record so you have confirming evidence of that agreement. Basically, what you will be doing is "freezing" the interview, but take copious notes anyway. Then transcribe the whole session to allow you to quote exactly what was said but also to pick and choose from a variety of accurate statements.

Once an interview is taped, you can apply to it all the critical and analytical questions you would to a written source, asking for other opinions to verify certain statements or, if your interviewee is a public figure, looking up his or her record in a newspaper index or biographical review. If you cannot tape-record, take notes as carefully as possible; review main points with your subject before the interview ends, and then, at your leisure, apply as many as possible of the same analytical procedures to your notes as you would to a cataloged text.

For example, in writing a paper about local lake pollution, you might interview a biology professor who teaches a college course on lake pollution. In her office, she tells you that the most severe pollution is caused not by paper mills but by farm fertilizer—which surprises you. After transcribing your tape (or reviewing your notes), you cross-check her assertion by talking to other experts in the state department of natural resources and by reviewing text sources found in the library or on the World Wide Web. Note how you've been critical in two ways: first, you sought out an expert whose credentials gave her advance credibility; second, you sought to verify her statements by confirming them with other reliable sources.

2 Site visits

Any research essay written about a topic with local dimensions gains credibility when it shows evidence the writer has investigated it firsthand, whether it's electric automobiles or local graveyards. For example, a recent first-year research paper focused on the practical introduction of electric automobiles into America's car culture. Adam visited the local organization promoting these cars, interviewed the manager, and test-drove one of the electric vehicles. While his paper also included conventional sources from periodicals, it gained extra credibility from his personal account, his interview quotations, statements from brochures, and photographs of the vehicle he took for a test ride.

When you visit a place to locate evidence to support the claims you make in a paper, make photographic or video records of what it looks like and what you find. Take copious notes about time, sensory details, location, size, shape, color, number, and so forth. Pictures and careful verbal descriptions essentially freeze your visit and will help you in writing the paper in several ways. First, in writing your paper, you may include photographs as well as specific details that would be difficult to invent had you not been present—both of which add credibility for original research. Second, even if you do not include photos or directly quote your notes, they will still jog your memory about what, exactly, you found and thus help you write more accurately. Finally, these recordings—assuming they are relatively objective in perspective and language—will help you maintain a neutral rather than a biased perspective.

On the one hand, evaluating the usefulness of an interview or site visit is simple: ask yourself whether the details gathered on your visit to the site support the assertions made by your paper. (See the WAC box below for further tips on evaluating field research.) In his electric car essay, for instance, Adam was able to testify positively to the automobile's quietness and ample acceleration as well as negatively, noting his fear the battery would run down before he returned to a charging station.

On the other hand, evaluating any field source becomes more complicated when you realize that you are both the creator and evaluator of the material at the same time. In site visits, the material is out there, and in and of itself, it has no meaning or value until you, the recorder, assign it. This material has not been filtered through the lens of another writer. *You* are the interpreter of what you witness, and when you introduce field evidence, it's your own bias that will show up in the way you use language; you will lead your reader one way or another depending on whether you describe the lake water as *cloudy, murky,* or *filthy* or label the electric car as *slow, hesitant,* or *a dog.* In other words, you assign a value to (evaluate) your field evidence by the way you present it in your paper.

WRITING 2: APPLICATION

List two field sources for a current research paper. Examine each for evidence of your role in creating it and for evidence of your bias. Which source did you find more trustworthy? Which one helped your paper more? Why? Looking back, what would you have done differently during your interview or site visit? How do you plan to make up for any limitations of your field research?

WRITING ACROSS THE CURRICULUM

Questions to Ask Any Source, Any Time, in Any Discipline

To evaluate the authenticity, accuracy, or reliability of any source found in the library, on the Internet, or in the field, apply the same prompt newspaper reporters use to make sure they've covered all the bases in writing news stories—*asking who, what, where, when,* and *why.* For evaluation purposes, however, you ask these questions about an information source to see whether or not you can trust it. If you do these source tests, you'll have extra and especially credible information to add to the body of your paper. Here's how it works:

- **Who?** What author or agency is speaking? If a printed or electronic document, run a name check on the World Wide Web or in the library catalogue to find the author's credentials or in one of the library's invaluable *Who's Who* reference books. If checking an interview subject, examine any evidence of expertise available, from job title to neighborhood opinion. When a document has no verifiable authorship, it is not a strong source. In your main text, if you have important information about author credibility, include it in a signal phrase introducing quoted material.

- **What?** Whatever information in a source interests you, check at least two other sources claiming to have the same information and look for similarities and/or differences. In your main text, include some acknowledgment that you've checked more than one source.

- **Where?** Notice the location of the source: an article in an academic journal will count more than one in a popular magazine, which will count more than an anonymous Web site. In your main text, mention strong academic sources in a signal phrase or parentheses.

- **When?** How recent is the information? This year's is better than last, which is better than last decade, etc. In your main text, if your source is recent, include that information in a signal phrase or parentheses.

- **Why?** Sometimes it's apparent that a source exists with a particular bias—a media commercial promoting a new product, a newspaper editorial supporting government policy, electoral campaign literature, etc. Information from such sources is best balanced by information from more neutral sources as well. In your main text, acknowledge your awareness of biased sources.

chapter 27

Using Research Sources

L ocating potential sources for a research project is one thing; deciding which ones to include, where to use them, and how to incorporate them is something else. Some writers begin making use of their sources in early exploratory drafts, perhaps by trying out a pithy quotation to see how it brings a paragraph into focus. Others prefer to sift and arrange their note cards in neat stacks before making any decisions about what to include in their essays. No matter how you begin writing with sources, there comes a time when you will need to incorporate them finally, smoothly, effectively, and correctly into your paper.

27 a Controlling sources

Once you've researched and begin composing your essay, you need to decide which sources to use, how, and where. You can't make this decision on the basis of how much time you spent finding each source, but rather on how useful it is in answering your research question.

Serious research is vital and dynamic, which means it's always changing. Just as you can't expect your first working thesis to be your final thesis, you can't expect to know in advance which sources are going to prove most fruitful. And don't think that you can't collect more information once you've begun drafting. At each step in the process you see your research question more clearly and know better what sources you need to answer it. Similarly, and perhaps especially when engaging in field research, writers of research essays often gain an increased sense of audience as their research progresses, which pays off in increasingly reader-oriented writing.

27 b Organizing sources

You need to control your sources rather than letting them control you, so somtime after you've begun collecting information, generate a **working outline** of your major ideas—"working" because it's imporant that outlines change as ideas evolve. It's more helpful to compose an outline separate from your research notes than to compose one from your notes. The former will have the logic of a coherent set of thoughts while the latter will only have logic formed by what sources you've found so far. Outline first and you won't be tempted to find a place for every note and to gloss over areas where you haven't done enough research.

Once you have outlined or begun drafting and have a good sense of the shape and direction of your paper, arrange the note cards so that they correspond to your outline, and put bibliographic cards in alphabetical order by the author's last name. Integrate field research notes as best you can, depending on their format. Finally, go back to your outline and annotate it according to which source goes where, and which points as yet have no sources to back them up. By doing this, you can see whether there are any ideas that need more research. In addition, look for connections between one source and subsequent sources.

Next, decide on some balance among your sources so you remain the director of the research production, your ideas on center stage, and your sources the supporting cast. Keep in mind that referring too often to a single source—unless it is itself the focus of your paper, as in frequent references to the text *Moby-Dick* because it's the text you are interpreting—suggests overreliance on a single point of view. If you find yourself referring largely to one source—and therefore one point of view—make sure that you have sufficient references to add other points of view to your paper.

WRITING 1: APPLICATION ....

Draft a tentative thesis and working outline for your research paper. Then arrange your note cards according to that outline. Look for too many references to a single source as well as places where you've no external sources to support you. This procedure is equally easy with card or computer notes. Plan on rearranging this initial plan as many times as needed as ideas evolve.

....

27 c   Integrating information

The notes you made during your research may be in many forms. For some sources, you will have copied down direct quotations; for others, you will have paraphrased or summarized important information. For some field sources, you may have made extensive notes on background information, such as your interview subject's appearance. Simply because you've quoted or paraphrased a particular source in your notes, however, doesn't mean you have to use a quotation or paraphrase from this source in your paper. Make decisions about how to use sources based on your goals, not on the format of your research notes.

MLA Handbook for Writers of Research Papers

SIXTH EDITION

Joseph Gibaldi

If you've taken source notes in your own words to help with paraphrasing and summarizing an expert's ideas, and carefully set off quotations with quotation marks, you're in good shape to integrate them smoothly into your own textual ideas. Different disciplines have different conventions for documentation. The examples in this chapter use the documentation style of the Modern Language Association (MLA), the style preferred in English and foreign language departments. (For documentation styles of specific disciplines, see Chapters 29–34.)

1 Integrating quotations into your paper

Direct quotations will be most effective when you integrate them smoothly into the flow of your paper. You can do this by introducing the source and reason for the quotation in a phrase or sentence. Readers should be able to follow your meaning easily and see the relevance of the quotation immediately.

Introduce quotations

Readers need to know who is speaking, so introduce quoted material with a **signal phrase** (sometimes called a **attributory phrase**) so the reader knows the source and purpose of quotation.

If the source is well known, name alone will be enough.

Henry David Thoreau asserts in *Walden,* "The mass of men lead lives of quiet desperation" (5).

If your paper focuses on the published work itself, introduce a quotation with the work's title rather than the author's name, as long as the reference is clear.

Walden sets forth one individual's antidote against the "lives of quiet desperation" led by the working class in mid-nineteenth-century America (Thoreau 5).

If either author or source is not well known, introduce the quotation with a brief explanation to give your readers enough context to understand the quotaton.

Mary Catherine Bateson, daughter of anthropologist Margaret Mead, has become, in her own right, a student of modern civilization. In *Composing a Life,* she writes, "The twentieth century has been called the century of the refugee because of the vast numbers of people uprooted by war and politics from their homes" (8).

A strong argument in favor of outlining sometime during the writing process is found in *The Handbook of Technical Writing:* "Outlining provides structure to your writing by assuring that it has a beginning (introduction), a middle (main body), and an end (conclusion)" (Brusaw, Alred, and Oliu, 426).

Quote smoothly and correctly

To use a *direct quotation* you must use an author's or speaker's exact words. Slight changes in wording are permitted, but these changes must be clearly marked. Although you can't change what a source says, you do have control over how much of it you use. Too much quotation can imply that you have little to say for yourself. Use only as long a quotation as you need to make your point. Remember that quotations should be used to support your points, not to say them for you.

To *shorten* a quotation, so that only the most important information is included, integrate it smoothly and correctly in the body of your paragraph to provide minimal disruption for your reader. Unless the source quoted is itself the topic of the paper (as in a literary interpretation), limit brief quotations to no more than two per page and long quotations to no more than

one every three pages. The following examples illustrate both correct and incorrect use of quoted material.

ORIGINAL PASSAGE

The dialogue throughout the movie is once again its weakest point: The characters talk in what sounds like Basic English, without color, wit or verbal delight, as if they were channeling Berlitz. The exceptions are Palpatine and of course Yoda, whose speech (voiced by Frank Oz) reminds me of Wolcott Gibbs' famous line about the early style of *Time* magazine: "Backward ran sentences until reeled the mind." (Roger Ebert review of *Star Wars Episode III: Revenge of the Sith, Roger Ebert.com*)

DISTORTED QUOTATION

According to film critic Roger Ebert, all the characters in *Star Wars Episode III: Revenge of the Sith* "talk in what sounds like Basic English, without color, wit or verbal delight, as if they were channeling Berlitz."

The exceptions noted by Ebert in the original passage are missing.

According to film critic Roger Ebert, all the characters, with
the exceptions of Yoda and Palpatine, "talk in what sounds
like Basic English, without color, wit or verbal delight, as if
they were channeling Berlitz."

Omit or substitute words judiciously

Cutting out words for the sake of brevity is often useful, but do not distort meaning. Indicate omitted words by using **ellipsis** points (three dots
within a sentence, four to indicate a second sentence). Indicate any changes
or additions with brackets. (See 57c–57d for more on ellipses and brackets.)

In reviewing the last episode of the *Star Wars* saga, film critic
Roger Ebert claims that, "The dialogue throughout the [*Revenge
of the Sith*] . . . sounds like Basic English, without color, wit or
verbal delight, as if they were channeling Berlitz."

*While use of the ellipsis and bracket are technically correct, the missing words
indicated by the ellipsis leave out Ebert's exceptions and again distort the meaning of the original passage.*

Use block format for long quotations

Brief quotations should be embedded in the main body of your paper
and enclosed in quotation marks. All of the previous examples are brief and
would be embedded within paragraphs as normal sentences. According to
MLA style guidelines, a brief quotation consists of four or fewer typed lines.

However, longer quotations (more than five lines) should be set off in
block format, indented, but spaced the same as the normal text.

■ Introduce the quotation in the last line of normal text with a sentence that
ends with a colon.

■ Indent ten spaces, then begin the quote. Do not use quotation marks as the
indentation signals a direct quotation.

■ Include the page number after end punctuation in parentheses.

In *The Magical Classroom,* Michael Strauss says:

> If they were candid, most magicians would say they are trying to
> entertain us by hiding the truth. They challenge us to discover
> what they have hidden. And we respond by trying to figure out the
> underlying causes of the magical effects and illusions we see. Like

scientists, we search for the truth, for what might be hidden from our senses. (2)

Verbs Used in Signal Phrases

The verb you choose for a signal phrase should accurately reflect the intention of the source. Notice that some of these verbs require an object.

acknowledge	concede	illustrate	report
admit	conclude	imply [this idea]	reveal
agree	declare	insist	say
argue	deny	maintain	show
assert	emphasize	note	state
believe	endorse [this idea]	observe	suggest
claim	find	point out	think
comment	grant	refute [this idea]	write

Explain and clarify quotations

Sometimes you will need to explain a quotation in order to clarify why it's relevant and what it means in the context of your discussion.

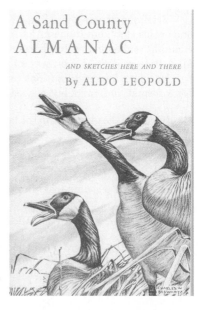

A Sand County
ALMANAC

AND SKETCHES HERE AND THERE

By ALDO LEOPOLD

In *A Sand County Almanac,* Aldo Leopold invites modern urban readers to confront what they lose by living in the city: "There are two spiritual dangers in not owning a farm. One is the danger of supposing that breakfast comes from the grocery, and the other that heat comes from the furnace" (6). Leopold sees city-dwellers as self-centered children, blissfully but dangerously unaware of how their basic needs are met.

You may also need to clarify what a word or reference means. Do this by using square brackets. (See 57d.)

Adjust grammar for clarity

A passage containing a quotation must follow all the rules of grammatical sentence structure: tenses should be consistent, verbs and subjects should agree, and so on. If the form of the quotation doesn't quite fit the grammar of your own sentences, you can either quote less of the original source, change your sentences, or make a slight alteration in the quotation. Use this last option sparingly, and always indicate any changes with brackets.

UNCLEAR
In *A Sand County Almanac,* Aldo Leopold follows various animals, including a skunk and a rabbit, through fresh snow. He wonders, "What got him out of bed?" (5).

It is not clear whether "him" refers to the skunk or the rabbit.

CLEAR
In *A Sand County Almanac,* Aldo Leopold follows various animals, including a skunk and a rabbit, through fresh snow. He wonders, "What got [the skunk] out of bed?" (5).

GRAMMATICALLY INCOMPATIBLE
In *A Sand County Almanac,* Aldo Leopold said that living in the city is a "spiritual danger" if people "supposing that breakfast comes from the grocery."

To be grammatically correct, the writer needs to change supposing from a gerund (-ing word) to the verb form suppose. *One way is to make the change inside the quotation marks with brackets.*

GRAMMATICALLY COMPATIBLE
In *A Sand County Almanac,* Aldo Leopold said that living in the city is a "spiritual danger" if people "[suppose] that breakfast comes from the grocery."

Another option is to start the quotation one word later.

GRAMMATICALLY COMPATIBLE
In *A Sand County Almanac,* Aldo Leopold said that living in the city is a "spiritual danger" if people assume "that breakfast comes from the grocery."

Still another option is to recast the sentence completely.

GRAMMATICALLY COMPATIBLE
According to Aldo Leopold, city dwellers who assume "that breakfast comes from the grocery" are out of tune with the world of nature (*A Sand County Almanac* 6).

When to Quote

Direct quotations should be reserved for cases in which you cannot express the ideas better yourself. Use quotations when the original words are especially precise, clear, powerful, or vivid.

- **Precise.** Use quotations when the words are important in themselves or when the author makes fine but important distinctions.

  Government, even in its best state, is but a necessary evil; in it worst state, an intolerable one.

  THOMAS PAINE

- **Clear.** Use quotations when the author's ideas are complex and difficult to paraphrase.

  Paragraphs tell readers how writers want to be read.

  WILLIAM BLAKE

- **Powerful.** Use quotations when the words are especially authoritative and memorable.

  You shall know the truth, and the truth shall make you free.

  THE KING JAMES BIBLE

- **Vivid.** Use quotations when the language is lively and colorful, when it reveals something of the author's or speaker's character.

  Writing, I'm more involved in it, but not as attached.

  KAREN, STUDENT

WRITING 2: APPLICATION ....

Read through your research materials, highlighting any quotations you might want to incorporate into your paper. Use your research log to explore why you think these words should be quoted directly. Also note where in your essay a quotation would add clarity, color, or life; then see if you can find one to serve that purpose.

....

27 d   Paraphrasing and summarizing

Taking notes is often a combination of quoting directly, paraphrasing, and summarizing. On the one hand, it's important to have direct quotes to incorporate judiciously your text; on the other hand, it helps to write as many research notes as possible in your own words to make sure you understand them—which is where the skill of paraphrasing and summarizing become important. Remember that another author's ideas, even restated in your own words, need to be documented and attributed (see Chapter 28).

1 Paraphrase

When you **paraphrase,** you restate a source's ideas in your own words. The point of paraphrasing is to make the ideas clearer by simplifying and explaining the author's original language to both your readers and to yourself, and to express the ideas in the way that best suits your purpose. In paraphrasing, attempt to preserve the intent of the original statement and to fit the paraphrased statement smoothly into the immediate context of your essay.

The best way to make an accurate paraphrase is to stay close to the order and structure of the original passage, to reproduce its emphasis and details. However, don't use the same sentence patterns or vocabulary or you risk inadvertently plagiarizing the source.

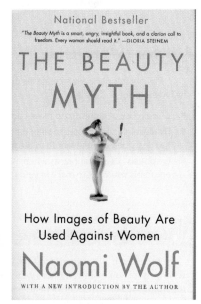

National Bestseller

"The Beauty Myth is a smart, angry, insightful book, and a clarion call to freedom. Every woman should read it." —GLORIA STEINEM

THE BEAUTY
MYTH

How Images of Beauty Are
Used Against Women

Naomi Wolf

WITH A NEW INTRODUCTION BY THE AUTHOR

If the original source has used a well-established or technical term for a concept, you do not need to find a synonym for it. If you believe that the original source's exact words are the best possible expressions of some points, you may use brief direct quotations within your paraphrase, as long as you indicate these with quotation marks.

Keep in mind why you are including this source; doing so will help you to decide how to phrase the ideas. Be careful, though, not to introduce your own comments or reflections in the middle of a paraphrase unless you make it very clear that these are your thoughts, not the original author's or speaker's.

ORIGINAL
PASSAGE

The affluent, educated, liberated women of the First World, who can enjoy freedom unavailable to any woman ever before, do not feel as free as they want to. And they can no longer restrict to the subconscious their sense that this lack of freedom has something to do with—with apparently frivolous issues, things that really should not matter. Many are ashamed to admit that such trivial concerns—to do with physical appearance, bodies, faces, hair, clothes—matter so much.

NAOMI WOLF, *THE BEAUTY MYTH* (9)

INACCURATE
PARAPHRASE

In *The Beauty Myth,* Naomi Wolf argues that First World women, who still have less freedom than they would like to have, restrict to their subconscious those matters having to do with physical appearance—things that are not really important to them (9).

ACCURATE
PARAPHRASE

In *The Beauty Myth,* Naomi Wolf asserts that First World women, despite their affluence, education, and liberation, still do not feel very free. Moreover, many of these women are aware that this lack of freedom is influenced by superficial things having primarily to do with their physical appearance—things that should not matter so much (9).

When to Paraphrase

Paraphrases generally recreate the original source's order, structure, and emphasis and include most of its details.

- **Clarity.** Use paraphrases to make complex ideas clear to your readers.
- **Details.** Use paraphrases to tailor the presentation of details that an author or speaker has described at great length to the goals of your paper.
- **Emphasis.** Use paraphrases when including an author's or speaker's point suits the emphasis you want to make in your paper.

ESL Strategies for Paraphrasing

Writers who are inexperienced at paraphrasing in English sometimes just substitute synonyms for some of the author's words, keeping the sentence structure and many of the words the same. This kind of paraphrasing is unacceptable in academic writing; it can be considered a form of plagiarism. (See 28a.) Here are some suggestions that may help you write effective paraphrases:

- Before you begin writing a paraphrase of a sentence or passage, make sure that you understand the author's meaning. Look up in a dictionary any words you don't know, and ask a native speaker of English about any idioms or slang with which you are unfamiliar.

■ Look away from the original source and put the ideas into your own words.

■ If you are paraphrasing a passage, don't paraphrase the information one sentence at a time. Instead, try to express the meaning of the entire passage.

■ Consider the context of the sentence or passage you are paraphrasing. Are there any references that are clear only from the surrounding sentences? Make sure you have given your readers enough information to understand your paraphrase.

■ Use a thesaurus to find synonyms if you need to, but use only words you are familiar with. Not every synonym for a word listed in a thesaurus will be appropriate in your sentences.

WRITING 3: APPLICATION ....

Read through your note cards for any passages you quoted directly from an original source. Find source quotes that now seem wordy, unclear, or longer than necessary. Paraphrase notes that you expect to use in your paper. Exchange your paraphrases and the originals with a classmate, and assess each other's work.

....

2 Summarize

To distill a source's words down to the main ideas and state these in your own words is to summarize. A **summary** includes only the essentials of the original source, not the supporting details, and is consequently shorter than the original.

Keep in mind that summaries are generalizations and that too many generalizations can make your writing vague and tedious. You should occasionally supplement summaries with brief direct quotations or evocative details collected through observation to keep readers in touch with the original source.

Summaries vary in length, and the length of the original source is not necessarily related to the length of the summary you write. Depending on the focus of your paper, you may need to summarize an entire novel in a sentence or two, or you may need to summarize a brief journal article in two or three paragraphs. Remember that the more material you attempt to summarize in a short space, the more you will necessarily generalize and abstract it. Reduce a text as far as you can while still providing all the information your readers need to know. Be careful, though, not to distort the original's meaning.

ORIGINAL
PASSAGE

For a long time I never liked to look a chimpanzee straight in
the eye—I assumed that, as is the case with most primates,
this would be interpreted as a threat or at least as a breach of
good manners. Not so. As long as one looks with gentleness,
without arrogance, a chimpanzee will understand and may
even return the look.

JANE GOODALL, *THROUGH A WINDOW* (12)

INACCURATE
SUMMARY

Goodall learned from her experiences with chimpanzees that
they react positively to direct looks from humans (12).

ACCURATE
SUMMARY

Goodall reports that when humans look directly but gently
into chimpanzees' eyes, the chimps are not threatened and
may even return the look (12).

When to Summarize

As you draft, summarize often so that your paper doesn't turn into a string of undigested quotations.

- **Main points.** Use summary when your readers need to know the main point the original source makes but not the supporting details.
- **Overviews.** Sometimes you may want to devise a few sentences that will effectively support your discussion without going on and on. Use summary to provide an overview or an interesting aside without digressing too far from your paper's focus.
- **Condensation.** You may have taken extensive notes on a particular article or observation only to discover in the course of drafting that you do not need all that detail. Use summary to condense lengthy or rambling notes into a few effective sentences.

WRITING 4: EXPLORATION ....

Review any sources on which you have taken particularly extensive notes.
Would it be possible to condense these notes into a briefer summary of the
entire work? Would it serve your purpose to do so? Why or why not?

....

3 Identify Internet sources in *signal phrases*

When you quote, paraphrase, or summarize *authoritative* sources from
the World Wide Web—and there are many such sources on the Web—you

need to be sure to emphasize the nature of that authority when you introduce the source. Although library and field sources also need to be introduced carefully, readers don't regard them with quite the skepticism and distrust they've learned while surfing the Net.

For example, in looking for information about the zebra mussell infestation in Lake Champlain, a team of students located the following sources on the Internet, noting the first two, a university site (.edu) and a nonprofit site (.org), were more likely to be impartial than the third commercial site (.com).

Zebra Mussels and Other Nonindigenous Species
. . . Zebra mussels also had colonized New York's Finger **Lakes, Lake Champlain,** Wisconsin's **Lake** Winnebago, Kentucky **Lake,** and nearly 100 smaller inland **lakes . . .**
www.seagrant.wisc.edu/communications/great**lake**s/GLnetwork/exotics
.html - 23k - Cached - Similar pages

Invasive Species Lake Champlain
. . . **Zebra Mussel** Monitoring Program - Excellent explanation of the **Lake Champlain** Basin Program's **Zebra Mussel** Monitoring program. . . .
www.lclt.org/invasive.htm - 47k - Cached - Similar pages]

Zebra Mussel filters by ZeeStop Filter designed to stop **Zebra Mussels**
. . . your **lake** water line from sand, silt and the ever present **Zebra Mussel . . . Lake Champlain,** Mississippi River, Erie Canal, Hudson River and most **lakes . . .**
www.zeestop.com/

However, the researchers were able to use both the educational and the commercial information by carefully specifying what was to be learned by each source in careful signal phrases introducing block quotations.

Information supplied by The University of Wisconsin, Sea Grant Institute details the destructive nature of the zebra mussel in fresh water lakes:

> The prolific mollusk tends to biofoul and restrict the flow of water through intake pipes, disrupting supplies of drinking, cooling, processing and irrigating water to the nation's domestic infrastructure. The mussel also attaches to boat hulls, docks, locks,

breakwaters and navigation aids, increasing maintenance costs and impeding waterborne transport.

The pesky zebra mussel had given rise to new commercial enterprises to help lakefront homeowners cope with the destructive mollusks. For example, Zeestop.com promises:

> The use of a Zeestop Filter should prolong the life of your entire plumbing system. Valve seats and washers should last longer without the grit that shortens their life expectance. Hot water tanks should not accumulate sediment brought in with the water, leading to longer element life. Other water filters such as carbon filters should not need to be replaced as often.

27 e   Incorporating visual images

It is easy to incorporate visual images into papers, portfolios, and Web pages to inform, entertain, and engage readers in ways text alone does not. Images are often included in verbal texts to break up dense textual space or signal a shift in content. While readers appreciate such images, they seldom pay close attention to them. Whenever possible, use images to expand understanding rather than merely decorate the paper you're writing. Here are some possibilities:

■ Use images that save you a thousand words. For example, many of the images that illustrate Chapter 3 in this handbook are especially rich in visual information.

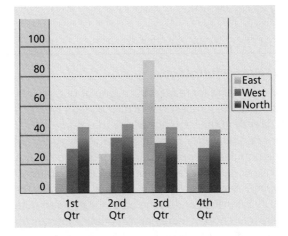

- Use images that convey useful information quickly in the shorthand way of charts and graphs, as does this *Regional Sales Distribution* chart above.

- Use images that make abstract ideas concrete. It would take a lot of words and a long time to describe a cartoon character such as a Smurf to somebody who has never seen the television show.

- Control the size and layout of images using a computer program such as *MS Paint* or *Adobe Photoshop* or by judicious cutting and pasting with scissors and tape.

- Position images where they belong—or as near as possible—in your text.

- Refer to in text to explain reason for being in text.

- Label each image appropriately, following conventions such as MLA style in formal papers (*Figure 1: Roadside Stand Near Birmingham, AL, by Walker Evans*) or more casually as we did with captions in Chapter 3.

- If publishing on a Web site, make sure the image is in public domain (as is the Walker Evans photograph on page 360) or secure permission from the copyright holder.

WRITING ACROSS THE CURRICULUM

Embedding Source Information

Whether you are writing for readers in college or out, you always need to credit your sources. The simplest way of giving credit is embedding source information directly in the sentence where the source is used and not attaching a separate reference page at the end. Embedded references are used in all the popular—as opposed to academic—periodicals, including *Time, Newsweek, Harpers, The New Yorker, The Atlantic Monthly, GQ, Sports Illustrated, Esquire, Elle,* etc., as well as in *The New York Times, The Los Angeles Times, The Washington Post,* and all the other local papers in the country.

Embedded references in more popular publications are not as detailed or precise as academic systems such as MLA or APA require (see Part Seven of this handbook); however, they always include enough information for a curious reader to track down the source if necessary. For example, in Chapter 3 of this textbook, we identified photographs by photographer, title, and date without referring to more specific source location:

> In the accompanying photograph, "Roadside Stand," taken by Walker Evans in 1936 near Birmingham, Alabama, different viewers may find different messages.

In choosing this embedded reference style, we knew that a curious reader could find more about a particular photo or photographer simply by conducting a search with that most wonderful research tool, Google!

In like manner, *The New Yorker* uses an embedded style, as illustrated in Jonathan Weiner's article, "The Tangle" (April 11, 2005):

> "In August 2003, Cox and Banack reported in *Neurology* their discovery of high concentrations of BMAA in the bat tissues and in the cycad seeds."

While Weiner doesn't give us the volume number or page, interested readers can locate the Cox and Banack article should they wish to.

Another kind of embedded documentation is used in book reviews, where reviewers cite precise identifying information at the beginning of the review (title, author, total pages, publisher, price) but do not include specific page references when they include a quotation. For example, in reviewing *A Land of Ghosts,* by David Campbell, *New York Times* book reviewer Elizabeth Royte writes:

"Darwin gushed upon entering the Brazillian rain forest; Campbell writes more coolly, though with precision. At a rubber estate, "six hammocks are pregnant with indolent men.""

So, our advice is this: when writing college papers, always use the appropriate academic documentation for the discipline in which you are writing. However, when you are writing to an audience outside the academy, try embedded documentation. The bottom line is, one way or another, always credit your sources.

chapter 28

Avoiding Plagiarism

The rule is simple: When you use other people's ideas or language in writing a paper, you need to give credit to those people whose ideas and words you have used. If you don't, you have stolen their ideas or words and are guilty of plagiarism. In Western culture, plagiarism is a serious offense, one that has cost writers, reporters, artists, musicians, and scientists their reputations, jobs, and enormous amounts of money. Plagiarism is especially serious within academic communities where the generation of original research, ideas, and words is the central mission of the institution.

The Internet has made the copying of research sources especially easy, which saves researchers an enormous amount of time. However, easy Internet copying has also made both intentional and unintentional plagiarism easy. To avoid plagiarizing, you need to know exactly *what it is* and *how to avoid committing it.*

28 a What plagiarism *is*

Plagiarism is putting one's name on a paper written by a friend and passing it in. Plagiarism is buying a term paper from an Internet term-paper factory and pretending to have written it. Plagiarism is downloading a report from the Internet and pretending to have written it. And plagiarism is pasting in a phrase, sentence, paragraph, passage, or portion of anybody else's work in any paper and not giving that author credit. In any of these flagrant examples, the intent to plagiarize is deliberate and obvious, something that serious and honorable students would never do.

However, plagiarism also occurs when well-meaning students get careless in taking notes from library or Internet sources or in copying those notes into paper drafts. Following are three examples of *unintentional* plagiarism: (1) A student copies a passage word-for-word from an Internet site and pastes it word-for-word into a paper, but forgets to include quotation marks or author attribution. (2) A student summarizes, but does not directly quote, a published author's idea and omits both author name and source title. (3) A student credits an author's idea in a signal phrase (According to John Smith . . .) but omits quotation marks around the author's exact phrases. None of these may be intentional, but each is an act of plagiarism, and each could be easily avoided by clearer knowledge and more careful research and writing practice.

28 b   What plagiarism is *not*

Writers don't need to attribute everything they write or say to specific sources. For example, what we call *common knowledge* does not need documentation. You do not need to credit common historical, cultural, or geographical information that an educated adult American person can be expected to know. Nor do you need to attribute to specific authorities the factual information that appears in multiple sources such as the dates of historical events (the sack of Rome in 410 AD, the Declaration of Independence in 1776), the names and locations of states and cities, the general laws of science (gravity, motion), or statements of well-known theories (feminism, liberalism, evolution).

You don't need to document phrases in widespread use in your own culture (global warming, cloning, urban sprawl). Nor do you need to document what is well known in the field in which you are writing that can be found in textbooks and lectures. For example, in a paper written about Sigmund Freud for a psychology professor, don't document the terms *libido* or *superego*. In a paper written for English, history, art, or philosophy, don't document *Victorian, the Roaring Twenties, modern,* or *postmodern.* In other words, within a given interpretative community, basic ideas and knowledge can be assumed to be the common property of all members of that community. However, specific positions or interpretations within a community do need to be specifically identified: how fellow psychotherapists Jung and Adler viewed Freud; how one specific critic viewed Victorian manners compared to another critic; and so on.

28 c   Recognizing and avoiding plagiarism

If the author of an article, book, or Web site offers unique opinions or interpretations about any type of common knowledge (see examples above), these should be credited using the proper documentation style. For example, in writing a paper for an English or film professor about comic book heroes portrayed in the movies, you decide to use this passage in Roger Ebert's review of *Spider-Man* for *Chicago Sun Times,* May 3, 2002:

> "Remember the first time you saw the characters defy gravity in *Crouching Tiger, Hidden Dragon?* They transcended gravity, but they didn't dismiss it: They seemed to possess weight, dimension and presence. Spider-Man as he leaps across the rooftops is landing too lightly, rebounding too much like a bouncing ball. He looks like a video game figure, not like a person having an amazing experience."

Now, Ebert's whole review is readily available on the Internet, easily accessed via the Internet Movie Database (http://www.imdb.com/), so that it's easy to block and copy parts of it to paste directly into the paper you are writing. *(In an academic paper, the citation would appear on a "Works Cited" (MLA) or "Reference" (APA, CMS) page; if academic style is not required, including author and title in a signal phrase would give proper credit.)* If the research writer does not follow proper citation guidelines, he or she might inadvertently plagiarize, as the following examples illustrate.

- It is plagiarism if the student cut and pasted the *Spider-Man* passage above directly into the paper without acknowledging that it was written by Roger Ebert.

    - To fix, credit in a signal phrase (*According to Roger Ebert . . .*), put the passage in quotation marks, and in an academic paper, identify where the passage came from and when it was published on a "Works Cited" page (MLA), "References" page (APA), or footnote (CMS) page as appropriate (see Chapters 30–33).

■ It is plagiarism if the student wrote: *The problem with* Spider-Man *is the video-game quality of the characters who bound from roof to roof and don't seem to be affected by gravity—unlike the more realistic figures in the movie* Crouching Tiger, Hidden Dragon. In this case the student lifts Ebert's idea in clearly identifiable ways, but does not quote Ebert directly.

  ■ To fix, credit in a signal phrase (***Roger Ebert claims*** *the problem with* Spider-Man *is the video-game quality* . . .) and, if an academic paper, identify where the passage came from and when it was published in the appropriate academic convention.

■ It is plagiarism if the student lifted key portions of Ebert's exact language from the passage without using quotation marks: *Roger Ebert claims that the characters in* Crouching Tiger, Hidden Dragon *transcended gravity, but they didn't dismiss it.* Though Ebert is credited with the idea, he is not credited with the language.

  ■ To fix, put quotation marks around the words borrowed: *Roger Ebert claims that the characters in* Crouching Tiger, Hidden Dragon *"transcended gravity, but they didn't dismiss it."* Again, if this is an academic paper, identify where the passage came from and when it was published on the appropriate reference page.

WRITING ACROSS THE CURRICULUM

Guidelines for Avoiding Plagiarism

Plagiarism is a serious offense in every field and department across the curriculum. In simplest terms, it's the act of copying somebody else's work and passing it off as your own. In addition to the many obvious cases described in this chapter, it's also plagiarism to copy the results of a neighbor's biology experiment in your lab report; it's plagiarism to copy a chart or graph from an economics textbook and not attribute it; and it's a form of plagiarism to hand in somebody else's field notes and claim them as yours. Below are simple guidelines for avoiding plagiarism:

● For all copied sources, note *who said what, where,* and *when.*

● When using quoted material, do not distort or intentionally modify an author's meaning.

- Print out and save at least the first page of all online material, making sure it contains the Internet address and date.

- Hand copy identifying information (name, title, date, place of publication) on all photocopied or printed source pages.

- In using direct quotations, place all exactly copied language in quotation marks.

- In writing a paraphrase or summary, credit the author *and* recast the original material into your own language.

- Identify all borrowed ideas and language with appropriate references using the appropriate documentation system (MLA, APA, CMS, etc.).

PART seven

Writing in the Disciplines

www.prenhall.com/fulwiler

chapter 29

Understanding the College Curriculum

ood writing satisfies the expectations of an audience in form, style, and content. But different audiences come to a piece of writing with different expectations, so writing that is judged "good" by one audience may be judged "less good" by another. Although all college instructors value good writing, each area of study has its own set of criteria by which writing is judged. For instance, the loose form, informal style, and speculative content of a reflective essay that please an English instructor might not please an anthropology instructor, who expects form, style, and assertions to follow the more formal structures established in that discipline. This chapter provides a broad outline of these different criteria and points to some important similarities for writing across the curriculum.

29 a Differences among disciplines

As a rule, knowledge in the humanities focuses on texts and on individual ideas, speculations, insights, and imaginative connections. Interpretation in the humanities is thus relatively subjective. Accordingly, good writing in the humanities is characterized by personal involvement, lively language, and speculative or open-ended conclusions.

In contrast, knowledge in the social and physical sciences is likely to focus on data and on ideas that can be verified through observing, measuring, and testing. Interpretation in these disciplines needs to be objective.

Accordingly, good writing in the social and physical sciences emphasizes inferences based on the careful study of data and downplays the personal opinion and speculation of the writer.

But boundaries between the disciplines are not absolute. For example, at some colleges history is considered one of the humanities, while at others it is classified as a social science. Geography is a social science when it looks at regions and how people live, but it is a physical science when it investigates the properties of rocks and glaciers. Colleges of business, engineering, health, education, and natural resources all draw on numerous disciplines as their sources of knowledge.

The field of English alone includes not only the study of literature but also literary theory and history, not only composition but also creative and technical writing. In addition, English departments often include linguistics, journalism, folklore, women's studies, African American studies, and sometimes

speech, film, and communications. In other words, within even one discipline, you might be asked to write several distinct types of papers: personal experience essays for a composition course, interpretations for a literature course, abstracts for a linguistics course, short stories for a creative writing course. Consequently, any observations about the different kinds of knowledge and the differing conventions for writing about them are only generalizations. The more carefully you study any one discipline, the more complex it becomes, and the harder it is to make a generalization that doesn't have numerous exceptions.

Formal differences exist among the styles of writing for different disciplines, especially in the conventions for documenting sources. Each discipline has its own authority or authorities, which provide rules about such issues as spelling of technical terms and preferred punctuation and editing mechanics, as well as documentation style. In addition, if you write for publication in a magazine, professional journal, or book, the publisher will have a *house style,* which may vary in some details from the conventions listed in the authoritative guidelines for the discipline in which you are writing. The following table lists the sources of style manuals for various disciplines:

DISCIPLINE	STYLE
Languages and literature	Modern Language Association (MLA) (See Chapter 30.)
Social sciences	American Psychological Association (APA) (See Chapter 31.)
Humanities	*Chicago Manual of Style* (CMS) (See Chapter 32.)
Sciences	
Life sciences	Council of Science Editors (CSE) (See Chapter 33.)
Chemistry	American Chemical Society
Physics	American Institute of Physics (AIP) (See Chapter 33.)
Business	Varies (See Chapter 34.)
Journalism	Associated Press (AP)
Medicine	American Medical Association (AMA)

29 b   Similarities among disciplines

Regardless of disciplinary differences, certain principles of good writing hold true *across* the curriculum.

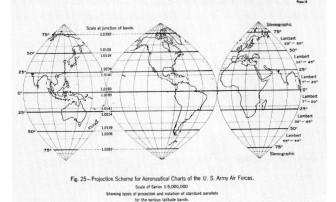

Fig. 25 – Projection Scheme for Aeronautical Charts of the U. S. Army Air Forces.
Scale of Series 1:5,000,000
Showing types of projection and notation of standard parallels
for the various latitude bands.

1 Knowledge

Each field of study attempts to develop knowledge about a particular aspect of the physical, social, or cultural world in which we live. For example, the physical sciences observe nature to learn how it works, while history and anthropology examine civilizations over time, sociology looks at human beings in groups, and psychology attempts to explain the operation and development of the individual human mind. In writing for a particular course, keep in mind the larger purpose of the field of study, especially when selecting, introducing, and concluding your investigation.

2 Method

Each field has accepted methods of investigation. Perhaps the best known is the scientific method, used in most of the physical and social sciences. One who uses the scientific method first asks a question, then poses a possible answer (a hypothesis), then carries out experiments in field or laboratory to test this answer, and finally, if it cannot be disproved, concludes that the hypothesis is correct. However, while research in the social sciences follows this scientific pattern, some disciplines, such as anthropology, rely instead on the more personal approach of ethnographic study. Literary research may be formal, historical, deconstructive, and so on. It is important to recognize that every discipline has its accepted—and its controversial—methods of study. Any conclusions you discuss in your writing should reflect that awareness.

3 Evidence

In every field, any claim you make about the subject of your study needs to be supported by evidence. If, in order to identify an unknown rock, you scrape it with a known rock in the geology laboratory, the scratch marks of the harder rock on the softer rock will be part of your evidence to support your claims about the unknown rock. If you analyze Holden Caulfield on the basis of his opening monologue in *The Catcher in the Rye,* his words will be evidence to support your interpretation. If you conduct a survey of students to examine college study habits, counting and collating your findings will be evidence to support your conclusions. In other words, although the *nature* of evidence varies greatly from one discipline to another, the *need* for evidence is constant. In some cases, when you need to support an assertion, you will consult certain sources for evidence and will need to have clear documentation for these sources. (Chapters 30–33 provide detailed guidelines for documenting sources in various disciplines.)

4 Accuracy

Each field values precision and correctness, and each has its own specialized vocabulary for talking about knowledge. Writers are expected to use terms precisely and to spell them correctly. In addition, each discipline has developed formats in which to report information. When you write within a discipline, you should know the correct form in which to communicate a literary analysis in English, a research report in sociology, or a laboratory report in biology. Each discipline also values conventional correctness in language. Your writing will be most respected when it reflects standard use of grammar, punctuation, and mechanics.

chapter 30

MLA: Writing in Languages and Literature

This chapter describes the aims, style, and forms required for most kinds of writing in English, comparative literature, and foreign languages where the primary focus is on the study of texts. Many specialized areas, such as film and cultural studies, also follow the conventions described here. Papers in language and literature use the documentation system of the Modern Language Association (MLA).

30 a Aims

Language and literature courses are concerned with reading and writing about texts such as poems, novels, plays, and essays written by published authors as well as by students. (The term *text* is defined here broadly to include films, visual arts, advertisements—anything that can be read and interpreted.) What sets literary studies apart from most other disciplines, including others in the humanities, is the attention devoted to all elements of written language. In these courses, writing is not only the means of study but often the object of study as well: Works are examined for their *form* and *style* as well as their *content*. Texts are read, listened to, discussed, and written about so students can discover what these texts are, how they work, what they mean, and what makes them exceptional or flawed. Moreover, literary studies often draw on ideas from other disciplines. For instance, reading a single novel such as Charles Dickens's *David Copperfield* can teach readers a little about sociology, psychology, history, geography, architecture, political science, and economics as well as the esthetics of novel writing.

When you write in language and literature, you can focus on a text's ideas, authors, formal qualities, or themes. For such essays, you usually refer mainly to **primary sources,** the text itself and perhaps other works to which you may compare it. You can also consider the culture that produced the text, the text's relationship to other texts, its place in history, and its politics. You may refer to **secondary sources,** writing by others about the text or about the context in which the primary text was written. Modern literary study may engage in any of five basic activities with texts:

- **Appreciating** texts. You write about the text's most moving or interesting features, the beauty or strangeness of the setting, the character with whom you most identify, the plot as it winds from beginning to end, or the turns and rhythms of the language.

- **Analyzing** texts. You ask questions such as *How is it put together?* or *How does it work?* Analysis involves looking at a text's component parts (chapters, for example) and the system that makes it work as a whole (such as the plot), defining what they are, describing what they are like, and explaining how they function.

- **Interpreting** texts. You ask, *What does it mean? How do I know what it means?* and *Why was it made?* Interpretations often vary widely from reader to reader and may provoke quite a bit of disagreement.

- **Evaluating** texts. *How good is it? What makes it worth reading?* and *How does it compare with other texts?* These are questions of judgment, based on criteria that might differ considerably from person to person. One reader might judge a poem good because its rhythm and imagery are pleasing (esthetic criteria), while another reader may praise the same poem because it subverts common assumptions about power relationships (political criteria), and a third may do so because it evokes fond childhood memories (personal criteria). However, a fourth reader might look for underlying assumptions or values (philosophical criteria), and a fifth might contrast it to another poet's work (comparative criteria).

- **Inferring cultural values.** You can also use literature to study culture by asking, *What are the values of the people depicted in the text?* and *How do the scenes, settings, and characters reveal the character of the broader culture?* To find answers to these and other questions, it is common to compare the text with other texts produced at the same or different times.

30 b   Style

Writing in languages and literature demands clarity, variety, and vitality to create a strong connection between the writer and reader. Direct, unpretentious language and an engaging tone are valued over obscure terminology and an artificially formal style. Observing the standard conventions of grammar, punctuation, and mechanics is expected, as are creative deviations.

Because literary studies center so closely on the multitude of ways readers approach texts, writing can range from the highly personal to the highly theoretical, from deeply impressionistic to sharply rational, from journalistic to experimental to political. Indeed, a single essay may knit together all these styles.

As a student, you may do much of your writing in language and literature in a relatively conventional academic style—asserting a thesis and supporting it with textual evidence and reasoned insight. But do not be surprised if you find yourself responding in different styles and voices for different kinds of assignments.

30 c   Writing about texts

The papers assigned in language and literature courses are likely to fall into two categories: those that focus on your own personal responses to one or more texts and those that require researching and synthesizing additional material before coming to your own conclusions. (See Chapter 11 for more on writing about texts.)

1 Writing essays without research

Some assignments ask for your own responses to a text, asking you to include personal experiences and background to write a paper. Other assignments ask you to base your response exclusively on the way a text is put together, its form, and its imagery. (See 11d.) Either way, be sure to quote from the work directly whenever doing so can help clarify a point you are making.

In either case, such papers are most interesting to both write and read when they move beyond summarizing either the text's plot or the instructor's notes. Your particular insights into the meaning and working of a text should constitute the body of any such paper. Your conclusions may be tentative and exploratory rather than assertive and conclusive, but they should always represent a careful, detailed reading.

2 Writing research essays

Research assignments require you to read, evaluate, and synthesize what other critics have said about a work or to compare the work with other works or with historical events. You will be expected to develop your own thesis based on your close reading of the work and to introduce secondary sources as a way of supporting, expanding, or contrasting your views with those of other critics. Such assignments commonly ask you to consult biographies, letters, journals, and interviews about the writer to provide historical or social context to the text. Such sources should help you develop and support a thesis or point of view that is ultimately your own and, at the same time, to acknowledge or document where other material and ideas came from.

30 d   MLA style: Documenting sources

The Modern Language Association (MLA) system is the preferred form for documenting research sources when you write about literature or language.

■ All sources are briefly documented in the text by an identifying name and page number (generally in parentheses).

■ A Works Cited section at the end of the paper lists full publication data for each source cited.

■ Additional explanatory information provided by the writer of the paper (but not from external sources) goes either in footnotes at the foot of the page or in a Notes section after the close of the paper.

The MLA system is explained in more detail in the *MLA Handbook for Writers of Research Papers,* sixth edition (New York: MLA, 2003) aimed specifically at undergraduate writers, as well as *The MLA Style Manual and Guide to Scholarly Publishing,* second edition (1998) aimed at graduate students and faculty.

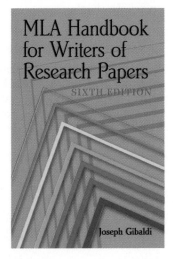

MLA Handbook
for Writers of
Research Papers
SIXTH EDITION

Joseph Gibaldi

The MLA system provides a simple, concise, and thorough way for writers to acknowledge their research sources. In the MLA system, authors use footnotes and/or endnotes to provide additional, explanatory information, but not to cite information provided by external sources. Whenever possible, the MLA system includes explanatory information in the text itself and limits the use of footnotes or endnotes. Pay careful attention to the practical mechanics of documentation so that readers can readily identify, understand, and locate your sources.

1 Conventions for in-text citations

In-text citations identify ideas and information borrowed from other writers and refer readers to the Works Cited list at the end of the paper, where they can find complete publication information about each source. The disciplines of languages and literature are less concerned with the date at which something was written than with the internal qualities of texts. Therefore, the brief MLA citations in the text feature *author names, text titles,* and *page numbers* while other disciplines in which currency is most important (the sciences and social sciences) feature dates instead of titles within the text. MLA style is economical, providing only as much in-text information as readers need in order to locate more complete information in the Works Cited list. Following are brief examples of how in-text citation works while the balance of the chapter includes sample entries formatted for the Works Cited page. A sample paper using MLA documentation concludes the chapter.

1. Single work by one or more authors

When you quote, paraphrase, or summarize a source, include the last name of the source's author, if known, and, in parentheses, the page or pages on which the original information appeared. Do not include the word *page* or the abbreviation *p.* or *pp.* You may mention the author's name in the sentence or put it in parentheses preceding the page number(s).

> Carol Lea Clark explains the basic necessities for the
> creation of a page on the World Wide Web (77).

> Provided one has certain "basic ingredients," the Web
> offers potential worldwide publication to individuals (Clark 77).

Note that a parenthetical reference at the end of a sentence comes before the period. No punctuation is used between the author's last name and the page number(s).

If you cite a work with two or three authors, your in-text parenthetical citation must include all authors' names: (*Rombauer and Becker 715*), (*Child, Bertholle, and Beck 215*). For works with more than three authors, you may list all the authors or, to avoid awkwardness, use the first author's name and add *et al.* (Latin for "and others") without a comma: (*Britton et al. 395*).

2. Two or more works by the same author

If your paper has references to two or more works by the same author, either mention the title of the specific work in the text or include a shortened version of the title (usually the first one or two important words) in the parenthetical citation.

> According to Lewis Thomas in <u>Lives of a Cell</u>, many bacteria become dangerous only if they manufacture exotoxins (76).

> According to Lewis Thomas, many bacteria become dangerous only if they manufacture exotoxins (<u>Lives</u> 76).

> Many bacteria become dangerous only if they manufacture exotoxins (Thomas, <u>Lives</u> 76).

If both the author's name and a shortened version of the title are in a parenthetical citation, a comma separates them, but there is no comma before the page number.

3. Unknown author

When the author of a work is unknown, use either the complete title in the text or a shortened version of it in the parenthetical citation, along with the page number.

> According to <u>Statistical Abstracts</u>, the literacy rate for Mexico stood at 75 percent in 1990, up 4 percent from census figures ten years earlier (374).

> The literacy rate for Mexico stood at 75 percent in 1990, up 4 percent from census figures ten years earlier (<u>Statistical</u> 374).

4. Corporate or organizational author

When no author is listed for a work published by a corporation, organization, or association, indicate the group's full name in any parenthetical reference: (*Florida League of Women Voters 3*). If the name is long, cite it in the sentence and put only the page number in parentheses.

5. Authors with the same last name

When you cite works by two or more authors with the same last name, include the first initial of each author's name in the parenthetical citation: (*C. Miller 63; S. Miller 101–04*).

6. Works in more than one volume

When your sources are in more than one volume of a multivolume work, indicate the volume number for each citation before the page number, and follow it with a colon and one space: (*Hill 2: 70*). If your source is in only one volume of a multivolume work, don't include the volume number in the text, but do on the Works Cited list.

7. One-page works

When you refer to a work that is one page long, do not include the page number in your citation.

8. Quotation from an indirect source

When a quotation or any information in your source is originally from another source, use the abbreviation *qtd. in.*

> Lester Brown of Worldwatch believes that international agricultural production has reached its limit and that "we're going to be in trouble on the food front before this decade is out" (qtd. in Mann 51).

9. Literary works

In citing literary prose works available in various editions, provide additional information (such as chapter number or scene number) for readers who may be consulting a different edition. Use a semicolon to separate the page number from this additional information: (*331; bk. 10, ch. 5*). In citing poems, provide only line numbers for reference; include the word *line* or *lines* in the first such reference. Providing this information will help your audience find the passages *in any source where those works are reprinted.*

> In "The Mother," Gwendolyn Brooks remembers "[. . .] the
>
> children you got that you did not get" (line 1); children that
>
> "never giggled or planned or cried" (30).

Cite verse plays using act, scene, and line numbers, separated by periods: (*Hamlet 4.4.31–39*).

10. More than one work in a citation

To cite more than one work in a parenthetical reference, separate them with semicolons: (*Aronson,* Golden Shore *177; Didion 49–50*).

11. Long quotation set off from text

Set off quotations of *four or more lines* by indentation. Indent the quotation one inch or ten spaces from the left margin of the text (not from the paper's edge), double-space, and omit quotation marks. The parenthetical citation follows end punctuation (unlike shorter, integrated quotes) and is not followed by a period.

> Fellow author W. Somerset Maugham, admiring Austen,
>
> but not blindly, had this to say about her dialogue:
>
>> No one has ever looked upon Jane Austen as a great
>>
>> stylist. Her spelling was peculiar and her grammar often
>>
>> shaky, but she had a good ear. Her dialogue is probably as
>>
>> natural as dialogue can ever be. To set down on paper
>>
>> speech as it is spoken would be very tedious, and some
>>
>> arrangement of it is necessary. (434)

2 Conventions for endnotes and footnotes

MLA notes are used primarily to offer comments, explanations, or additional information (especially source-related information) that cannot be smoothly or easily accommodated in the text of the paper. Use notes also to cite several sources within a single context if a series of *intext* references might detract from the readability of the text. In general, however, omit additional information, outside the "mainstream" of your text, unless it is necessary for clarification or justification.

If a note is necessary, insert a raised (superscript) numeral at the reference point in the text; introduce the note itself with a corresponding raised numeral, and indent it.

TEXT WITH SUPERSCRIPT

The standard ingredients for guacamole include

avocados, lemon juice, onion, tomatoes, coriander, salt, and

pepper.[1] Hurtado's poem, however, gives this traditional dish

a whole new twist (lines 10-17).

NOTE

[1]For variations, see Beard 314, Egerton 197, Eckhardt 92, and Kafka 26. Beard's version, which includes olives and green peppers, is the most unusual.

The references listed in the notes should appear in the Works Cited list.

Notes may be placed either at the bottom of the page on which the text reference appears (*footnotes*) or be included double-spaced on a separate page at the end of your paper (*endnotes*). Endnote pages should be placed between the text of the paper and the Works Cited section, with the title "Note" or "Notes."

30 e   Conventions for list of *Works Cited*

All sources mentioned in academic or professional writing should be identified on a concluding list of *works cited*. These entries are formatted in specific ways so that the reader can readily find information.

Format. After the final page, title a separate page "Works Cited," one inch from the top, centered, but not underlined or in quotation marks.

Exception: If you are required to list all the works you have read in researching the topic—not just those to which you have actually referred in your text or notes—you should title this list "Works Consulted" rather than "Works Cited."

Double-space between the Works Cited title and your first entry. Begin each entry at the left margin, indenting the second and all subsequent lines of each entry five spaces. Double-space both between and within entries. If the list runs to more than one page, continue numbering pages in sequence but do not repeat the title.

Order of entries. Alphabetize the entries according to authors' last names. If two or more authors have the same last name, alphabetize by first name or initial. For entries by an unknown author, alphabetize according to the first word of the title, excluding an initial *A, An,* or *The.*

1. Book by one author

Benjamin, Jessica. *The Bonds of Love: Psychoanalysis, Feminism, and the*
    Problem of Domination. New York: Prometheus, 1988.

2. Book by two or three authors

Zweigenhaft, Richard L., and G. William Domhoff. *Blacks in the White*
    Establishment. New Haven, CT: Yale UP, 1991.

Author names after the first are identified first name first, and the final author's name is preceded by *and.*

3. Book by more than three authors

Belenky, Mary Field, et al. *Women's Ways of Knowing: The Development of Self,*
    Voice, and Mind. New York: Basic, 1986.

If a work has more than three authors, you may use the Latin abbreviation *et al.* or list all the authors' names in full as they appear on the title page.

4. More than one book by the same author

Nelson, Mariah Burton. *Are We Winning Yet?: How Women Are Changing Sports*
    and Sports Are Changing Women. New York: Basic, 1991.

---. *The Stronger Women Get, The More Men Love Football: Sexism and the*
    American Culture of Sports. New York: Harcourt, 1993.

If your Works Cited list contains more than one source by the same author(s), in the second and all additional entries replace the author's name with three hyphens (no spaces) followed by a period. The hyphens represent the *exact* name of the author in the preceding entry. If a source's author is

GENERAL FORMAT FOR BOOK CITATIONS, MLA

one space   one space   one space   one space

Author(s). Book Title. Place of publication: Publisher, year of publication.

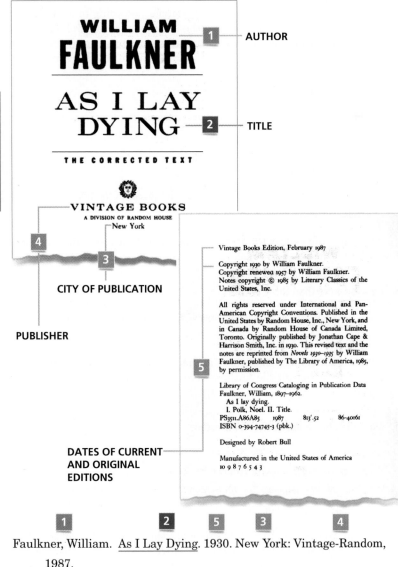

WILLIAM
FAULKNER — 1 — **AUTHOR**

AS I LAY
DYING — 2 — **TITLE**

THE CORRECTED TEXT

VINTAGE BOOKS
A DIVISION OF RANDOM HOUSE
New York

4

3

CITY OF PUBLICATION

PUBLISHER

Vintage Books Edition, February 1987

Copyright 1930 by William Faulkner.
Copyright renewed 1957 by William Faulkner.
Notes copyright © 1985 by Literary Classics of the
United States, Inc.

All rights reserved under International and Pan-
American Copyright Conventions. Published in the
United States by Random House, Inc., New York, and
in Canada by Random House of Canada Limited,
Toronto. Originally published by Jonathan Cape &
Harrison Smith, Inc. in 1930. This revised text and the
notes are reprinted from *Novels 1930–1935* by William
Faulkner, published by The Library of America, 1985,
by permission.

Library of Congress Cataloging in Publication Data
Faulkner, William, 1897–1962.
   As I lay dying.
   I. Polk, Noel. II. Title.
PS3511.A86A85   1987   813'.52   86-40161
ISBN 0-394-74745-3 (pbk.)

Designed by Robert Bull

Manufactured in the United States of America
10 9 8 7 6 5 4 3

5

**DATES OF CURRENT
AND ORIGINAL
EDITIONS**

1   2   5   3   4

Faulkner, William. As I Lay Dying. 1930. New York: Vintage-Random,
1987.

5

1 AUTHOR OR EDITOR NAME.

Last name first, comma, and rest of the name as it appears on the publication. Period. If a work has more than one author, second and later names are listed first name first, and separated by commas (for example, *Smith, Robert, Michael Jones, and Susan Morse*). Period. If more than one work by the same author, substitute three hyphens for the author's name after the first entry:

> Faulkner, William. As I Lay Dying. 1930. New York: Vintage-Random,
>
> 1987.
>
> ---. Light in August. New York: Modern Library, 1932.

2 BOOK TITLE.

List titles and subtitles fully, capitalizing them as in the original. Underline (or *italicize*) the titles of entire books and put quotation marks around the titles of essays, poems, and short works within larger works. Period. Do not underline the period that follows the title.

3 CITY OF PUBLICATION.

List first city of publication. If the name of a foreign city could be unfamiliar to readers, add abbreviation for the country. (See the section on abbreviations in Chapter 62.) Use a comma to separate city from country; use a colon to separate place from the publisher.

4 PUBLISHER.

Abbreviate publishers' names—for example, *Vintage* for *Vintage Books*. Omit words such as *press, publisher, inc.* Use *UP* for *University Press* (*Wisconsin UP*) or *P* (*U of Mississippi P*). If the title page indicates that a book is published under an imprint—for example, *Vintage Books* is an imprint of *Random House*—list both imprint and publisher, separated by a hyphen (*Vintage-Random*). Use a comma to separate the publisher from the publication date.

5 DATE OF PUBLICATION.

List year of publication as it appears on the copyright page. Period. If no publisher, place of publication, or date of publication is provided, use *n.p.* (for both publisher and place, to be clarified by its relation to the separating colon) or *n.d.* (for date).

not identical to that in the preceding entry, list author names in full. Two or more works with the same author are alphabetized according to title; a work by a single author precedes works by that author and one or more collaborators.

5. Book by a corporation, association, or organization

Society of Automotive Engineers. *Effects of Aging on Driver Performance.*

Warrendale, PA: Society of Automotive Engineers, 1988.

Alphabetize by the name of the organization.

6. Revised edition of a book

Peek, Stephen. *The Game Inventor's Handbook.* 2nd ed. Cincinnati, OH:

Betterway, 1993.

For second or any subsequent editions of a book, place the appropriate numerical designation (*2nd ed., 3rd ed.,* etc.) after the name of the editor, translator, or compiler, if there is one. If not, place it after the title.

7. Edited book

Schaefer, Charles E., and Steven E. Reid, eds. *Game Play: Therapeutic Use of*

Childhood Games. New York: Wiley, 1986.

For books with a listed editor or editors but no author, place the name of the editor(s) in the author position, followed by *ed.* or *eds.*

8. Book with an editor and an author

Hemingway, Ernest. *Conversations with Ernest Hemingway.* Ed. Matthew J.

Bruccoli. Jackson: UP of Mississippi, 1986.

Books with both an editor and an author should be listed with the editor following the title, first name first, preceded by the abbreviation *Ed.*

9. Book in more than one volume

Waldrep, Tom, ed. *Writers on Writing.* 2 vols. New York: Random, 1985-88.

The total number of volumes is listed after the title. When separate volumes were published in different years, provide inclusive dates.

10. One volume of a multivolume book

Waldrep, Tom, ed. *Writers on Writing.* Vol. 2. New York: Random, 1988.

When each volume of a multivolume set has an individual title, list the volume's full publication information first, followed by series information (number of volumes, dates).

Churchill, Winston S. *Triumph and Tragedy.* Boston: Houghton, 1953. Vol. 6 of

   The Second World War. 6 vols. 1948-53.

11. Translated book

Hammarskjold, Dag. *Markings.* Trans. Leif Sjoberg and W. H. Auden. New York:

   Knopf, 1964.

12. Book in a series

McLeod, Susan, ed. *Strengthening Programs for Writing Across the Curriculum.*

   New Directions for Teaching and Learning Ser. 36. San Francisco: Jossey-

   Bass, 1988.

Immediately after the title, and the series information: the series name, neither underlined nor in quotation marks, and the series number, both followed by periods. Book titles within an underlined title are not underlined.

13. Reprinted book

Evans, Elizabeth E. G. *The Abuse of Maternity.* 1875. New York: Arno, 1974.

Add the original publication date after the title; then cite the current edition information.

14. Introduction, preface, foreword, or afterword

Gavorse, Joseph. Introduction. *The Lives of the Twelve Caesars.* By Suetonius.

   New York: Book League of America, 1937. vii-xvi.

Jacobus, Lee A. Preface. *Literature: An Introduction to Critical Reading.* By

   Jacobus. Upper Saddle River, NJ: Prentice, 1996. xxvii-xxxiii.

Nabokov, Vladimir. Foreword. *A Hero of Our Time.* By Mihail Lermontov. Garden
   City, NY: Doubleday-Anchor, 1958. v-xix.

List the author of the introduction, preface, foreword, or afterword
first, followed by the title of the book. Next insert the word *By*, followed by
the full name of the author of the whole work if different from the author
of the piece or the last name only if the same as the author of the shorter
piece.

15. Work in an anthology or chapter in an edited collection

Charen, Mona. "Much More Nasty Than They Should Be." *Popular Writing in
   America: The Interaction of Style and Audience.* 5th ed. Eds. Donald
   McQuade and Robert Atwan. New York: Oxford UP, 1993. 207-08.

Gay, John. *The Beggar's Opera. British Dramatists from Dryden to Sheridan.* Eds.
   George H. Nettleton and Arthur E. Case. Carbondale: Southern Illinois UP,
   1975. 530-65.

Enclose the title of the work in quotation marks unless it was originally published as a book, in which case it should be underlined. The title
of the anthology follows the book title and is underlined. At the end of the
entry, provide inclusive page numbers for the selection. For previously published nonscholarly works, you may, as a courtesy to your reader, include the
year of original publication after the title of the anthologized work. Follow
this date with a period.

16. Two or more works from the same anthology or collection

Kingston, Maxine Hong. "No Name Woman." Kirszner and Mandell 46-56.

Kirszner, Laurie G., and Stephen R. Mandell, eds. *The Blair Reader.* 2nd ed.
   Eds. Laurie G. Kirszner and Stephen R. Mandell. Upper Saddle River, NJ:
   Prentice, 1996.

Tannen, Deborah. "Marked Women." Kirszner and Mandell 362-67.

When citing two or more selections from one anthology, list the anthology separately under the editor's name. Selection entries will then need
to include only a shortened cross-reference to the anthology entry, as illustrated above.

17. Periodical article reprinted in a collection

Atwell, Nancie. "Everyone Sits at a Big Desk: Discovering Topics for Writing."

English Journal 74 (1985): 35-39. Rpt. in *Rhetoric and Composition: A*

Sourcebook for Teachers and Writers. 3rd ed. Ed. Richard Graves.

Portsmouth, NH: Boynton/Cook, 1990. 76-83.

Include the full citation for the original periodical publication, followed by *Rpt. in* ("Reprinted in") and the book publication information. Provide inclusive page numbers for both sources.

18. Article in a reference book

"Behn, Aphra." *The Concise Columbia Encyclopedia.* 1983 ed.

"Langella, Frank." *International Television and Video Almanac.* 40th ed. New

York: Quigley, 1995.

For signed articles in references books, begin with the author's name. For commonly known reference works (*Concise Columbia*), you need not include full publication information or editor's names. Page and volume numbers are also unnecessary when the entries in the reference book are arranged alphabetically.

19. Anonymous book

The End of a Presidency. New York: Bantam, 1974.

Alphabetically arrange anonymous books (and most other sources lacking an author name) in the Works Cited list by title, excluding *A, An,* or *The.*

20. Government document

United States. Cong. House. Committee on Energy and Commerce. *Ensuring*

Access to Programming for the Backyard Satellite Dish Owner. Washington:

GPO, 1986.

If the author is identified, begin with that name. If not, begin with the government (country or state), followed by the agency or organization. Most U.S. government documents are printed and published by the Government Printing Office in Washington, DC. You may abbreviate this office *GPO.*

21. Dissertation

UNPUBLISHED

McGuire, Lisa C. "Adults' Recall and Retention of Medical Information." Diss.

Bowling Green State University, 1993.

Enclose the title of an unpublished dissertation in quotation marks, followed by the abbreviation *Diss.* and the name of the university and the year.

PUBLISHED

Boothby, Daniel W. *The Determinants of Earnings and Occupation for Young*

Women. Diss. U. of California, Berkeley, 1978. New York: Garland, 1984.

For a published dissertation, italicize or underline the title, list the university and year as for an unpublished dissertation, and then add publication information as for a book, including the order number if the publisher is University Microfilms International (UMI). The descriptive abbreviation *Diss.* still follows the title.

22. A pamphlet

McKay, Hughina, and Mary Brown Patton. *Food Consumption of College Men.*

Wooster: Ohio Agricultural Experiment Station, 1943.

Cite a pamphlet just as you cite a book. Remember the abbreviations *n.p., n.d.,* and *n.pag.,* where publication information is missing. Also see item 23.

23. A book with missing publication information

Palka, Eugene, and Dawn M. Lake. *A Bibliography of Military Geography.* [New

York?]: Kirby, [198-?].

The MLA practice is to provide missing publication information if possible. If the information you provide does not come from the source itself—that is, if you succeed in finding missing information through another source—you should enclose this information in brackets in the Works Cited entry [*198-?*]. If a date of publication can only be approximated, place a *c.* before it, the abbreviation for the Latin *circa,* or "around." You may also use the abbreviations *n.p.*—depending on placement in your entry, this abbreviation stands for either "no place" or "no publisher"— *n.d.* ("no date"), or *n.pag.* ("no pages").

24. Religious texts

Holy Bible, King James: Modern Phrased Version. New York: Oxford UP, 1980.

Use a period to separate chapter from verse in in-text citation (Luke 2. 12).

Quran: The Final Testament (Authorized English Version) with Arabic Text.
Trans. Rashad Khalifa. Fremont: University Unity, 2000.

25. Article, story, or poem in a monthly or bimonthly magazine

Hawn, Matthew. "Stay on the Web: Make Your Internet Site Pay Off." *Macworld*
Apr. 1996: 94-98.

Abbreviate all months except May, June, and July. Hyphenate months for bimonthlies, and do not list volume or issue numbers.

26. Article, story, or poem in a weekly magazine

Updike, John. "His Mother Inside Him." *New Yorker* 20 Apr. 1992: 34-36.

27. Article in a daily newspaper

Finn, Peter. "Death of a U-Va. Student Raises Scrutiny of Off-Campus Drinking."
Washington Post 27 Sept. 1995: D1.

If an article in a newspaper is unsigned, begin with its title. Give the name of the newspaper as it appears on the masthead, excluding *A, An,* or *The.* If the city is not in the newspaper's name, it should follow the name in brackets: *Blade [Toledo, OH].* Include with the page number the letter that designates any separately numbered sections; if section are numbered consecutively, list the section number (*sec. 2*) before the colon, preceded by a comma.

28. Article by an unknown author

"Conventionalwisdomwatch." *Newsweek* 13 June 2005: 5.

GENERAL FORMAT FOR JOURNAL ARTICLES, MLA

one space   one space   one space   one space   one space

Author(s). "Article Title." <u>Journal Title</u> volume number (year of publication):

    page numbers.

Indent second line five spaces.

TITLE OF PERIODICAL

TITLE OF ARTICLE   **AUTHOR**

VOLUME NUMBER   **DATE**

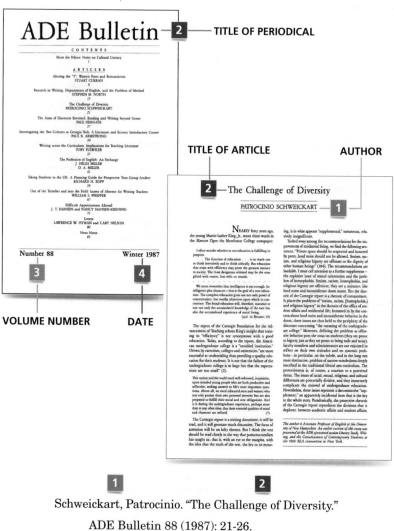

MLA MLA MLA

Schweickart, Patrocinio. "The Challenge of Diversity."

<u>ADE Bulletin</u> 88 (1987): 21-26.

1 **AUTHOR NAME.**

Last name first, comma, then rest of the name as it appears on the article. Period. If more than one author, second and later names are listed first name first, separated by commas, with *and* before last author (*Smith, Alan, Brian Jones, and Michelle Watts*). If four or more authors, you may list only first author followed by *et al.* (and others). If more than one work by the same author, substitute three hyphens for the author's name after the first entry:

> Schweickart, Patrocinio. "The Challenge of Diversity." *ADE Bulletin* 88
>
> (1987): 21-26.
>
> ---. "Reading Ourselves." *Speaking of Gender*. Ed. Elaine Showalter.
>
> New York: Routledge, 1989. 88-98.

2 **TITLES.**

List titles and subtitles fully, capitalizing as in the original and put quotation marks around the titles of articles, poems, and short works in the periodical. Period. Underline book titles within **article titles** ("A Reassessment of Faulkner's As I Lay Dying"). Use single quotation marks around the titles of short works within article titles ("T.S. Eliot's 'Ash Wednesday' Revisited"). *Italicize* or underline **periodical titles** (*ADE Bulletin*).

3 **VOLUME, ISSUE, AND PAGE NUMBERS.**

For journals paginated separately by issue (as in this example), list volume number, period, and issue number (12.2), followed by year of publication (in parentheses) and a colon: then page numbers. For journals paginated continuously, include the volume number before the year, but omit the issue number. Separate inclusive page numbers with a hyphen (*42-54*). Up to 99, use all the digits for the second page numbers, and above 99 list the last two digits only (*130-38*) unless the full sequence is needed for clarity (*198-210*). If page numbers are not consecutive, use the first page number, followed by a plus sign: 84+.

4 **DATE OF PUBLICATION.**

Place the year of publication for periodicals within parentheses, followed by a colon and a space to the page numbers. Never use season for a journal.

29. Article in a journal paginated by volume

Nelson, Jennie. "This Was an Easy Assignment: Examining How Students

Interpret Academic Writing Tasks." *Research in the Teaching of English* 34

(1990): 362-96.

If page numbers are continuous from one issue to the next throughout the year, include only the volume number and year, not the issue or month.

30. Article in a journal paginated by issue

Tiffin, Helen. "Post-Colonialism, Post-Modernism, and the Rehabilitation of Post-

Colonial History." *Journal of Commonwealth Literature* 23.1 (1988): 169-81.

If each issue begins with page 1, include the volume number followed by a period and the issue number. Do not include the month of publication.

31. Anonymous article

"Fraternities Sue Hamilton College over Housing Rule." *Chronicle of Higher

Education* 41.46 (1995): A39.

As with an anonymous book or magazine, if no author is listed for an article, begin your entry with the title and alphabetize by the first word, excluding *A, An,* and *The.*

32. Microform or microfiche article

Mayer, Caroline E. "Child-Resistant Caps to Be Made 'Adult-friendly.' " *Washington

Post* 16 June 1995: A3. CD-ROM. Newsbank. (1995) CON 16: B17.

If the listing is derived from a computer-based reference source such as *Newsbank,* you may treat it exactly as you would any other periodical. To help your audience locate the source as quickly as possible, however, you should include the descriptor *CD-ROM,* the name of the service (*Newsbank*), and the available section/grid information.

33. Editorial

"Sarajevo Reborn." Editorial. *New York Times* 21 Feb. 1996, natl. ed.: A18.

If the editorial is signed, list the author's name first.

34. Letter to the editor and reply

Kempthorne, Charles. Letter. *Kansas City Star* 26 July 2002: A16.

Massing, Michael. Reply to letter of Peter Dale Scott. *New York Review of Books* 4 Mar. 2005: 57.

35. Review

Ross, Alex. Rev. of "Kafka's Trial" by Poul Ruders. *New Yorker* 28 Mar. 2005: 80.

"Talk to Me Now" by Jack Dahl. *New West News* 15 Jan. 2002: 24.

Works Cited entries for reviews should begin with the reviewer's name, if known, followed by the title of the review, if there is one. *Rev.* of precedes the title of the work reviewed, followed by a comma, then the word *by* and the name of the work's author. If the work of an editor, translator, etc., is being reviewed instead of an author's, an abbreviation such as *ed.* or *trans.* replaces the word *by*. If a review is unsigned and untitled, list it as *Rev. of* [title] and alphabetize it by the name of the work reviewed. If the review is unsigned but titled, begin with the title. If the review is of a performance, add pertinent descriptive information such as director, composer, or major performers.

Electronic sources include both databases, available in portable forms such as CD-ROM, diskette, or magnetic tape, and online sources accessed with a computer connected to the Internet.

Databases

The Works Cited entries for electronic **databases** (newsletters, journals, and conferences) should be listed like entries for articles in printed periodicals: cite the author's name; the article or document title in quotation marks; the newsletter, journal, or conference title; the number of volume or issue; the year or date of publication (in parentheses); and the number of pages if available.

Portable databases are much like books and periodicals. Their entries in Works Cited lists are similar to those for printed material, except you must also include the following items:

- The medium of publication (*CD-ROM, diskette, magnetic tape*)

- The name of the vendor, if known (this may be different from the name of the organization that compiled the information, which must also be included)

- The date of electronic publication, in addition to the date the material originally may have been published (as for a reprinted book or article)

GENERAL FORMAT FOR MAGAZINE AND NEWSPAPER ARTICLES, MLA

one space   one space   one space   one space

Author(s). "Article Title." <u>Publication Title</u> Date of publication: page numbers.

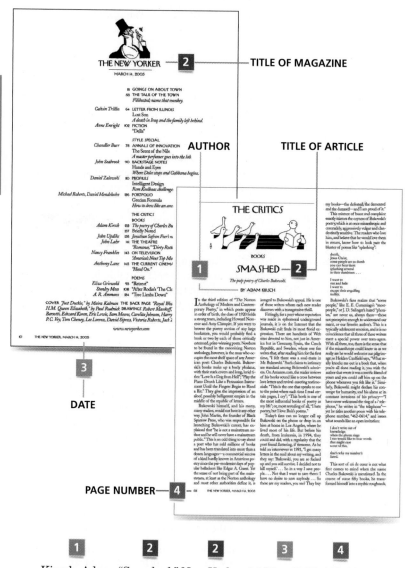

2 ⟶ TITLE OF MAGAZINE

AUTHOR   TITLE OF ARTICLE

3

DATE

PAGE NUMBER — **4**

1   **2**   **2**   **3**   **4**

Kirsch, Adam. "Smashed." <u>New Yorker</u> 14 Mar. 2005: 132-36.

1 AUTHOR NAME.

Last name first, comma, then rest of the name as it appears on the article. Period. If more than one author, second and later names are listed first name first, separated by commas, with *and* before last author (*Smith, Alan, Brian Jones, and Michelle Watts*). If more than one work by the same author, substitute three hyphens for the author's name after the first entry:

Kirsch, Adam. "Smashed." <u>New Yorker</u> 14 Mar. 2005: 132-36.

---. "The Lazy Gardener." <u>New York Sun</u> 28 Sept. 2005: A24.

2 TITLES.

List titles and subtitles fully, capitalizing as in the original. Put quotation marks around the titles of articles, poems, and short works in the periodical. Period. Underline book titles within **article titles** ("The Effect of Sunshine in Faulkner's <u>Light in August</u>"). Use single quotation marks around the titles of short works within article titles ("What's Cool in 'We Real Cool'?") *Italicize* or underline **periodical titles** and omit introductory articles (*New Yorker*, not <u>*The New Yorker*</u>).

3 DATE.

For daily, weekly, or biweekly magazines and newspapers, give day, month, and year of publication (*14 Mar. 2005*), but omit volume and issue numbers. Colon. Abbreviate all months except May, June, and July followed by a period (*Jan., Apr.*). If no date of publication, use *n.d.* in parentheses (*n.d.*).

4 PAGE NUMBERS.

Separate page numbers in a range with a hyphen (*42-54*). Up to 99, use all the digits for the second page numbers, and above 99 list the last two digits only (*130-38*) unless the full sequence is needed for clarity (*198-210*). If the page numbers are not consecutive (as in a newspaper), place a plus sign after the final consecutive page (39+, 52-55+). Period.

36. CD-ROM database, periodically updated

James, Caryn. "An Army as Strong as Its Weakest Link." *New York Times* 16

Sept. 1994: C8. *New York Times* Ondisc. CD-ROM. UMI-ProQuest. Oct. 1994.

If a database comes from a printed source such as a book, periodical, or collection of bibliographies or abstracts, cite this information first, followed by the title of the database (underlined), the medium of publication, the vendor name (if applicable), and the date of electronic publication. If no printed source is available, include the title of the material accessed (in quotation marks), the date of the material (if given), the underlined title of the database, the medium of publication, the vendor name, and the date of electronic publication.

37. CD-ROM nonperiodical

"Rhetoric" *The Oxford English Dictionary.* 2nd ed. CD-ROM. Oxford: Oxford UP,

1992.

List a nonperiodical CD-ROM as you would a book, adding the medium of publication and information about the source, if applicable. If citing only part of a work, underline the title of the selected portion or place it within quotation marks, as appropriate.

38. Diskette or magnetic tape

Doyle, Roddy. *The Woman Who Walked into Doors.* Magnetic tape. New York:

Penguin Audiobooks, 1996.

List on the Works Cited page as you would a book, adding the medium of publication (e.g., *Diskette, Magnetic tape*).

Online sources

Documenting information from the Internet follows the same basic guidelines as documenting other texts—who said what, where, and when. However, in citations of Internet sources, two dates are important—the date the text was created, published, or revised and the date you found the information (the access date). When both publication and access dates are available, provide them both. However, many www sources are often updated or changed, leaving no trace of the original version, so always provide the access date to show when this information was available. Thus, most electronic source entries will end with an access date immediately followed by the electronic address in angle brackets: *23 Dec. 1999* <http://www.cas.usf.edu/english>.

The following guidelines are derived from the MLA Web site at <http://www.mla.org/style_faq4>. To identify a World Wide Web source, include all the relevant items in the following order, each followed by a period except the date of access:

1. **Author** (or editor, compiler, or translator). Give the person's full name, if known, last name first; if the name is unknown, include any alias given.

2. **Title.** Enclose the title of a poem, short story, or article in quotation marks. Include the title of a posting to a discussion list or forum in quotation marks, followed by *Online posting*. Underline book titles.

3. **Editor, compiler, or translator.** Include the full name, if not cited earlier, followed by the appropriate abbreviation (*Ed., Comp.,* or *Trans.*). Also see items 7 and 8 on pages 785–786.

4. **Print source information.** Include the same information you would give for a printed citation.

5. **Title of scholarly project, database, personal, or professional site** (underlined). If there is no title, include a description such as *Home page*. Include the name of an editor if available.

6. **Identifying number.** For a journal, include the volume and issue numbers.

7. **Date of electronic publication.** Include latest date of site revision if available.

8. **Discussion list information.** Include the full name or title of the list or forum.

9. **Page, paragraph, or section numbers.** Include only if your source includes them; do not count paragraphs or sections yourself if your source lacks numbering.

10. **Sponsorship or affiliation.** Include the name of any organization or institution sponsoring this site.

11. **Date of access.** Include the date you visited this site.

12. **Address.** Enclose in angle brackets; if hyphenation is necessary, do so after angle brackets or period (see 40 below).

GENERAL FORMAT FOR ONLINE SOURCES, MLA

Author(s). "Article Title." <u>Title of Site</u>. Date of electronic publication. Page, paragraph,

or section number for specific reference. Sponsoring body. Date of access

<electronic address>.

Padgett, John B. "William Faulker." <u>Mississippi Writers Page</u>. 15 Apr. 2005.

3 University of Mississippi English Department. 8 June 2005 **4**

<http://www.olemiss.edu/mwp/dir/faulkner_william/index.

html>.

1 **AUTHOR OF MATERIAL ON WEB SITE.**
Last name first, comma, then rest of the name. Follow rules for citing books and periodicals (*Padgett, John B.*). Period. If no author is listed, begin with page title (*Mississippi Writers Page*).

2 **TITLE OF MATERIAL ON WEB SITE.**
Enclose title of poem, short story, or other short work in quotation marks ("William Faulkner"). Underline or *italicize* the site title and subtitle. Period. If no title is obvious, use home page name as title (found in URL).

3 **NAME OF SPONSORING ORGANIZATION.**
Usually found at bottom of site home page (*University of Mississippi English Department*). Period.

4 **PUBLICATION INFORMATION.**
List two dates for each Internet site: first, place the date the site was created or last revised, immediately after the title (*15 Apr. 2005*). Period. Second, give the date you accessed the site (*8 June 2005*) followed directly by the URL.

5 **ELECTRONIC ADDRESS (URL).**
Enclose the site address between angle brackets (*< >*) at end of the entry *<http://www.olemiss.edu/mwp/dir/faulkner_william/index.html>*. Period.

39. Work from an online database

Conniff, Richard. "Approaching Walden." Yankee. 57.5 (May 1993): 84. *Article*
   First. OCLC. Bailey Howe Library, U. Vermont 2 Jun. 2005 <http://
   firstsearch.oclc.org>.

Give the print publication information, name the database (underlined), name of vendor, name of library, date of access, and URL.

40. Professional site

Yellow Wall-Paper Site. U of Texas. 1995. 4 Mar. 1998 <http://www.cwrl.utexas
   .edu/~daniel/amlit/wallpaper/wallpaper.html>.

41. Government or institutional site

"Zebra Mussels in Vermont." Home page. State of Vermont Agency of Natural
   Resources. 3 May 1998 <http://www.anr.state.vt.us/dec/waterq/smcap.htm>.

42. Article in a journal

Erkkila, Betsy. "The Emily Dickinson Wars." *The Emily Dickinson Journal* 5.2
   (1996) 14 pars. 2 Feb. 1998 <http://www.colorado.edu/EDIS/Journal>.

43. Book

Twain, Mark. *The Adventures of Tom Sawyer.* Internet Wiretap Online Library.
   Camegie Mellon U. 4 Mar. 1998 <http://www.cs.cmu.edu/Web/People/rgs/
   sawyr-table.html.>.

44. Poem

Poe, Edgar Allan. "The Raven." *American Review,* 1845. The Poetry Archives.
   4 Mar. 1998 <http://tqd.advanced.org/3247/cgibin/dispgi?poet=poe
   .Edgar&poem>.

45. Article in a reference database

"Jupiter." Britannica Online. Vers. 97.1.1 Mar. 1997. *Encyclopaedia Britannica.* 29
    Mar. 1998 <http://www.eb.com:180>.

46. Posting to a discussion list

"New Virginia Woolf Discussion List." Online posting. 22 Feb. 1996. The Virginia
    Woolf Society, Ohio State U. 4 Mar. 1998 <gopher://dept.english.upenn
    .edu:70//OrO-1858-?Lists/20th/vwoolf>.

47. E-mail, listserv, or newsgroup (Usenet) message

Fulwiler, Toby. "A Question About Electronic Sources." E-mail to Alan
    Hayakawa. 23 Jan. 2004.

Superman. <superman@200.uvm.edu>. "Writing Committee Meeting."
    Distribution list. University of Vermont. 24 Jan. 2001.

Include the author's name or Internet alias (if known, alias first, period)
followed by the subject line (in quotation marks) and the date of the posting. Identify the type of communication (*Personal e-mail, Distribution list,
Office communication*) before the access date. The source's e-mail address
is optional, following the name in angle brackets; secure permission before
including an e-mail address.

48. File transfer protocol (FTP), telnet, or gopher site

King, Jr., Martin Luther. "I Have a Dream Speech." 28 Aug. 1963. 30 Jan. 1996
    <telnet://ukanaix.cc.ukans.edu>.

Substitute the abbreviation *ftp, telnet,* or *gopher* for *http* before the
site address.

49. Synchronous communications (MUD, MOO, IRC)

StoneHenger. The Glass Dragon MOO. 6 Feb. 2004. Personal interview. 6 Feb.
    2004 <telnet://surf.tstc.edu>.

Synchronous communications take place in real time; when they are
over, an archive copy may remain, or they may simply be erased. After the
posting date, include the type of discussion (e.g., *Personal interview, Group
discussion*) followed by a period.

50. Home page—personal

Fulwiler, Anna. Home page. 1 Feb. 1998 <http://www.uvm.edu/~afulwile>.

51. Home page—college course or academic department

Huges, Jeffrey. Fundamentals of Field Science. Course home page. Sep.-Dec.

2005. Botany department. University of Vermont, 6 May 2005

<http://www.uvm.edu/~plantbio/grad/fn>.

List instructor or department name, course or department title, the words *course* or *department home page,* for course offering add inclusive dates, department name, school, date of access, and URL.

52. Online newspaper

Sandomir, Richard. "Yankees Talk Trades in Broadcast Booth." *New York Times*

on the Web 4 Dec. 2001. 5 Dec. 2001 <http://www.nytimes.com/pages/

business/media/index.html>.

53. Online magazine

Epperson, Sharon. "A New Way to Shop for a College." *Time.com* 4 Dec. 2001.

5 Dec. 2001 <http://www.time.com/time/education/article/

0,8599,183955,00.html>.

54. Online encyclopedia

Stanford Encyclopedia of Philosophy. Ed. Edward N. Zalta. 1995. Stanford U.

5 Dec. 2001 <http://plato.stanford.edu/contents.html>.

55. Online work of art

Van Gogh, Vincent. *The Olive Trees.* 1889. Museum of Modern Art, New York.

5 Dec. 2001 <http://www.moma.org/docs/collection/paintsculpt/recent/

c463.htm>.

56. Online interview

Plaxco, Jim. Interview. Planetary Studies Foundation. Oct. 1992. 5 Dec. 2001

<http://www.planets.org/>.

57. Online film or film clip

Columbus, Chris, dir. *Harry Potter and the Sorcerer's Stone.* Trailer. Warner

Brothers, 2001. 5 Dec. 2001 <http://hollywood.com>.

58. Online cartoon

Bell, Darrin. "Rudy Park." Cartoon. *New York Times on the Web* 5 Dec. 2001.

5 Dec. 2001 <http://www2.uclick.com/client/nyt/rk/>.

59. Electronic television or radio program

Chayes, Sarah. "Concorde." All Things Considered. Natl. Public Radio. 26 July

2000. 7 Dec. 2001 <http://www.npr.com/programs/atc/archives>.

60. Weblog entry

Rickey, Anthony. "Three Years of Hell to Become the Devil" Weblog posting.

8 June 2005. 10 June 2005 <http://www.threeyearsofhell.com/>.

Author name or pseudonym, title of site (if any) followed by the words "Weblog posting," date of site, date of access, and URL.

4 Documenting other sources

The manner in which MLA format applies to other sources can be inferred with reasonable accuracy from the principles for documenting books, periodicals, and online sources, the entries beginning with *author, title, medium identification, publisher,* and *date.* Following are specific examples of how to document other types of media.

61. Cartoon

Davis, Jim. "Garfield." Cartoon. *Courier* [Findlay, OH] 17 Feb. 1996: E4.

62. Film or videocassette

Casablanca. Dir. Michael Curtiz. Perf. Humphrey Bogart and Ingrid Bergman.

Warner Bros., *1942.*

Fast Food: What's in It for You. Prod. The Center for Science in the Public

Interest and Churchill Films. Videocassette. Los Angeles: Churchill, 1988.

Lewis, Joseph H., dir. *Gun Crazy.* Screenplay by Dalton Trumbo. King Bros., 1950.

Begin with the title, followed by the director, the studio, and the year released. Optionally, you may include the names of lead actors, producer, and the like between the title and the distribution information. If your essay is concerned with a particular person's work on a film, begin with that person's name, arranging all other information accordingly.

63. Personal interview

Holden, James. Personal interview. 12 Jan. 2005.

Morser, John. Professor of Political Science, U of Wisconsin. Telephone interview.

    15 June. 2001.

Begin with the interviewee's name and specify the kind of interview and the date. Identify the interviewee's position if relevant to the purpose of the interview.

64. Published or broadcast interview

Sowell, Thomas. "Affirmative Action Programs." Interview. All Things

    Considered. NPR. WGTE, Toledo. 5 June 1990.

For published or broadcast interviews, begin with the interviewee's name. Include appropriate publication information for a periodical or book and appropriate broadcast information for a radio or television program.

65. Print advertisement

Cadillac DeVille. Advertisement. *New York Times* 21 Feb. 2004, natl. ed.: A20.

Begin with the name of the product, followed by the description *Advertisement* and normal publication information for the source.

66. Unpublished lecture, public address, or speech

Graves, Donald. "When Bad Things Happen to Good Ideas." National Council of

    Teachers of English Convention. St. Louis, 21 Nov. 1989.

Begin with the speaker, followed by the title (if any), the meeting (and sponsoring organization, if needed), the location, and the date. If it is untitled, use a descriptive label (such as *Speech*) with no quotation marks.

67. Personal or unpublished letter

Friedman, Paul. Letter to the author. 18 Mar. 1999.

Personal letters and e-mail messages are handled nearly identically in Works Cited entries. Begin with the name of the writer, identify the type of communication (e.g., *Letter*), and specify the audience. Include the date written if known, and the date received if not. To cite an unpublished letter from an archive or private collection, include information that locates the holding (for example, *Quinn-Adams Papers. Lexington Historical Society. Lexington, KY*).

68. Published letter

King, Jr., Martin Luther. "Letter from Birmingham Jail." 28 Aug. 1963. *Civil*

    Disobedience in Focus. Ed. Hugo Adam Bedau. New York: Routledge, 1991.

    68-84.

Cite published letters as you would a selection from an anthology. Specify the audience in the letter title (if known). Include the date of the letter immediately after its title. Place the page number(s) after the publisher information. If you cite more than one letter from a collection, cite the entire work in the Works Cited list, and indicate individual dates and page numbers in your text.

69. Map

Ohio River: Foster, KY, to New Martinsville, WV. Map. Huntington: U.S. Corps of

    Engineers, 1986.

Cite a map as you would a book by an unknown author. Underline the title, and identify the item as a map or chart.

70. Performance

Rumors. By Neil Simon. Dir. Gene Saks. Broadhurst Theater, New York. 17 Nov. 1988.

Bissex, Rachel. *Folk Songs*. Flynn Theater. Burlington, VT. 14 May 2000.

Identify the pertinent details, such as title, place, and date of performance. If you focus on a particular person in your essay, such as the director or conductor, lead with that person's name. For a recital or individual concert, lead with the performer's name.

71. Audio recording

Springsteen, Bruce. "Devils & Dust." *Devils & Dust.* New York: Sony BMG Music

Entertainment, CN 93900, 2005.

Depending on the focus of your essay, begin with the artist, composer, or conductor. Enclose song titles in quotation marks, followed by the recording title, underlined. Do not underline musical compositions identified only by form, number, and key. If you are *not* citing a compact disc, specify the recording format. End with the company label, the catalog number if known, and the date of issue.

72. Television or radio broadcast

"Emissary." *Star Trek: Deep Space Nine.* Teleplay by Michael Pillar. Story by Rick

Berman and Michael Pillar. Dir. David Carson. Fox. WFLX, West Palm

Beach, FL. 9 Jan. 1993.

If the broadcast is not an episode of a series or the episode is untitled, begin with the program title. Include the network, the station and city, and the date of broadcast. The inclusion of other information—such as narrator, writer, director, or performers—depends on the purpose of your citation.

73. Work of art (photograph, painting, sculpture, etc.)

Holbein, Hans. Portrait of Erasmus. Musée du Louvre, Paris. The Louvre

Museum. By Germain Bazin. New York: Abrams, n.d., 148.

Begin with the artist's name. Follow with the work's title, and conclude with the location. If your source is a book, also give pertinent publication information.

30 f   Sample MLA research paper

The following research essay was written by a first-year college student, Andrew Turner, in response to an assignment to write about a major American author using both primary and secondary sources in formal MLA style.

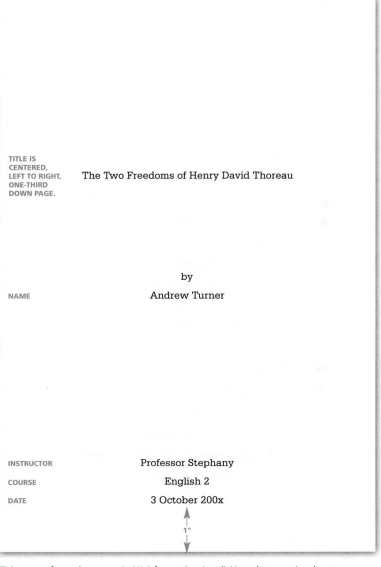

TITLE IS CENTERED, LEFT TO RIGHT, ONE-THIRD DOWN PAGE.

The Two Freedoms of Henry David Thoreau

by

NAME

Andrew Turner

INSTRUCTOR

Professor Stephany

COURSE

English 2

DATE

3 October 200x

1"

Title page of a student essay in MLA format (optional). Note that margins shown are adjusted to fit space limitations of this book. Follow actual dimensions shown and your instructor's directions.

Turner 1

Andrew Turner

Professor Stephany

English 2

3 October 200x

The Two Freedoms of Henry David Thoreau

Henry David Thoreau led millions of people throughout the world to think about individual freedom in a new way. During his lifetime, he attempted to live free of unjust governmental constraints as well as conventional social expectations. In his 1849 essay "On the Duty of Civil Disobedience," he makes his strongest case against governmental interference in the lives of citizens. In his 1854 book <u>Walden: Or, Life in the Woods</u>, he makes the case for living free from social conventions and expectations.

Thoreau opens "Civil Disobedience" with his statement that "that government is best which governs not at all" (222). He argues that a government should allow its people to be as free as possible, providing for the needs of the people without infringing on their daily lives. Thoreau explains: "The government does not concern me much, and I shall bestow the fewest possible

NAME · INSTRUCTOR · COURSE · DATE PAPER DUE · DOUBLED SPACED · WRITER OPENS WITH THESIS. · WRITER IDENTIFIES BY FULL TITLE THE TWO WORKS TO BE EXAMINED. · ABBREVIATED TITLE IS USED AFTER WORK HAS BEEN IDENTIFIED BY FULL TITLE. · WRITER'S LAST NAME AND PAGE NUMBER APPEAR ON EACH PAGE. · DO NOT JUSTIFY RIGHT-HAND MARGIN. · ONLY THE PAGE NUMBER IS NEEDED WHEN SOURCE IS INTRODUCED IN THE SENTENCE.

Turner 2

thoughts on it. It is not for many moments that I live under a government" ("Civil" 238).

In other words, in his daily life he attends to his business of eating, sleeping, and earning a living and not dealing in any noticeable way with an entity called "a government."

Because Thoreau did not want his freedom overshadowed by governmental regulations, he tried to ignore them. However, the American government in 1845 would not let him. He was arrested and put in the Concord jail for failing to pay his poll tax—a tax he believed unjust because it supported the government's war with Mexico as well as the immoral institution of slavery. Instead of protesting his arrest, he celebrated it and explained its meaning by writing "Civil Disobedience," one of the most famous English-language essays ever written. In it, he argues persuasively that "under a government which imprisons any unjustly, the true place for a just man is also a prison" (230). Thus the doctrine of passive resistance was formed, a doctrine that advocated protest against the government by nonviolent means:

MLA MLA MLA

Turner 3

How does it become a man to behave

INDENTED
10 SPACES
BECAUSE
QUOTATION
IS MORE
THAN
4 LINES

toward this American government today?

I answer that he cannot without disgrace

be associated with it. I cannot for an

instant recognize that political

organization as my government which is

the <u>slave's</u> government also. (224)

SIGNAL
PHRASE
INTRODUCES
AUTHOR

According to Charles R. Anderson, Thoreau's other writings, such as "Slavery in Massachusetts" and "A Plea for Captain John Brown," show his disdain of the "[N]ortherners for their cowardice on conniving with such an institution" (28). He wanted all free American citizens, North and South, to revolt and liberate the slaves.

In addition to inspiring his countrymen, Thoreau's view of the sanctity of individual freedom affected the lives of later generations who shared his beliefs (King). "Civil Disobedience" had the greatest impact because of its "worldwide

PARTIAL
QUOTATION
IS WORKED
INTO
SENTENCE IN
GRAMMATIC-
ALLY
SMOOTH
WAY.

influence on Mahatma Gandhi, the British Labour Party in its early years, the underground in Nazi-occupied Europe, and Negro leaders in the modern [S]outh" (Anderson 30). In other words, for nearly

Turner 4

150 years. Thoreau's formulation of passive
resistance has been a part of the human struggle
for freedom ("Gandhi").

Thoreau also wanted to be free from the
everyday pressure to conform to society's
expectations. He believed in doing and possessing
only the essential things in life. To demonstrate his
case, in 1845 he moved to the outskirts of Concord,
Massachusetts, and lived by himself for two years
on the shore of Walden Pond (Spiller et al. 396-97).

IDENTIFICATION OF WORK WITH MORE THAN THREE AUTHORS.

Thoreau wrote <u>Walden</u> to explain the value of living
simply, apart from the unnecessary complexity of
society: "Simplicity, simplicity, simplicity! I say, let
your affairs be as two or three, and not a hundred
or a thousand" (66). At Walden, he lived as much as
possible by this statement, building his own house
and furniture, growing his own food, bartering for
simple necessities, attending to his own business
rather than seeking employment from others
(<u>Walden</u> 16–17).

ABBREVIATED SHORT TITLE AFTER FIRST REFERENCE

SHORT TITLE IS INCLUDED BECAUSE MORE THAN ONE TITLE APPEARS ON WORKS CITED PAGE.

Living at Walden Pond gave Thoreau the
chance to formulate many of his ideas about living
the simple, economical life. At Walden, he lived

MLA MLA MLA

Turner 5

simply in order to "front only the essential facts of life" (66) and to center his thoughts on living instead of on unnecessary details of mere livelihood. He developed survival skills that freed him from the constraints of city dwellers whose lives depended on a web of material things and services provided by others. He preferred to "take rank hold on life and spend [his] day more as animals do" (117).

While living at Walden Pond, Thoreau was free to occupy his time in any way that pleased him, which for him meant writing, tending his bean patch, and chasing loons. He was not troubled by a boss hounding him with deadlines or a wife and children who needed support. In other words, "he wasn't expected to be anywhere at any time for anybody except himself" (Franklin). His neighbors accused him of being selfish and did not understand that he sought most of all "to live deliberately" (<u>Walden</u> 66), as he felt all people should learn to do.

Then as now, most people had more responsibilities than Thoreau had, and they could

PAGE NUMBERS SUFFICE WHEN CONTEXT MAKES SOURCE CLEAR.

BRACKETS INDICATE CHANGE IN WORDING SO PRONOUN CONFORMS TO SENTENCE GRAMMAR.

Turner 6

not just pack up their belongings and go live in the
woods—if they could find free woods to live in.
Today, people are intrigued to read about Thoreau's
experiences and are inspired by his thoughts, but
few people can actually live or do as he suggests in
<u>Walden</u>. In fact, most people, if faced with the
prospect of spending two years removed from
society—from modern plumbing, automobiles,
television, telephone, and e-mail—would think of it
as punishment or banishment rather than freedom
(Poger).

WRITER'S
CONCLUSION
REPEATS
THESIS.

    Practical or not, Thoreau's writings have
inspired countless people to reassess how they live
and what they live for. Though unable to live
exactly as he advocated, readers everywhere
remain inspired by his vision of independence,
equality, and, above all, freedom.

MLA MLA MLA

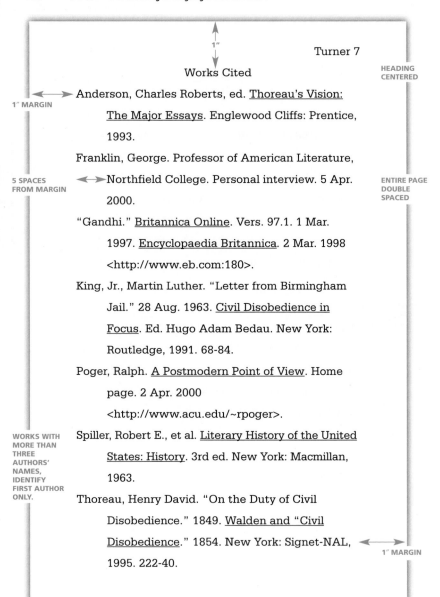

1″

Turner 7

Works Cited

Anderson, Charles Roberts, ed. <u>Thoreau's Vision:</u>
<u>The Major Essays</u>. Englewood Cliffs: Prentice,
1993.

Franklin, George. Professor of American Literature,
Northfield College. Personal interview. 5 Apr.
2000.

"Gandhi." <u>Britannica Online</u>. Vers. 97.1. 1 Mar.
1997. <u>Encyclopaedia Britannica</u>. 2 Mar. 1998
<http://www.eb.com:180>.

King, Jr., Martin Luther. "Letter from Birmingham
Jail." 28 Aug. 1963. <u>Civil Disobedience in</u>
<u>Focus</u>. Ed. Hugo Adam Bedau. New York:
Routledge, 1991. 68-84.

Poger, Ralph. <u>A Postmodern Point of View</u>. Home
page. 2 Apr. 2000
<http://www.acu.edu/~rpoger>.

Spiller, Robert E., et al. <u>Literary History of the United</u>
<u>States: History</u>. 3rd ed. New York: Macmillan,
1963.

Thoreau, Henry David. "On the Duty of Civil
Disobedience." 1849. <u>Walden and "Civil</u>
<u>Disobedience</u>." 1854. New York: Signet-NAL,
1995. 222-40.

Turner 8

AUTHOR'S
NAME IS NOT
REPEATED.
NAME IS
REPLACED
BY 3
HYPHENS
FOLLOWED
BY A PERIOD.

---. <u>Walden: Or, Life in the Woods</u>. New York:

Harcourt, 1987.

MLA MLA MLA

chapter 31

APA: Writing in the Social Sciences

This chapter describes the aims, style, forms, and documentation conventions associated with disciplines in the social sciences: psychology, sociology, anthropology, political science, economics, social work, and education. The system of documentation described here is based on guidelines published by the American Psychological Association (APA).

31 a Aims

The social sciences examine the fundamental structures and processes that make up the social world. Sociology examines social groups; political science examines the methods of governance and social organizations; anthropology examines social cultures; economics examines the allocation and distribution of resources among social groups; and psychology examines the mind as both a biological and social construction. The social sciences use methodical and systematic inquiry to examine and analyze human behavior, commonly asking questions such as the following:

- What is society? Can it be isolated and observed? How can it be described?

- How do social and psychological systems function? What forces hold them together or lead to their breakdown?

- Why do social organizations and individuals behave the way they do? Can governing laws be identified, explained, and understood?

Most writing in the social sciences explains findings based on factual research: either *empirical research*—based on firsthand observation and experimentation—or the wide reading that results in a *literature review*. Social scientists must also interpret their factual findings in a carefully reasoned manner and based on clear evidence that is objectively presented.

31 b   Style

Writing in the social sciences must be clear, with connections among ideas explicitly stated. Language should be precise and informal diction discouraged. However, social science writing need not be dull or dry. Readers of the social sciences look for clarity, smoothness, and economy of expression. Writers should therefore avoid unnecessary jargon, wordiness, and redundancy.

Stylistic Guidelines for Writing in the Social Sciences

As you write and revise, keep the following guidelines in mind:

- Write from a **third-person point of view.** (First-person experience is considered inappropriate for conveying empirical data because, in calling attention to the writer, it distracts from the information.)
- Use the **past tense** to describe methods and results ("Individuals responded by …"); use the **past** or **past perfect tense** for literature reviews ("The study resulted in …,""Jones has suggested …"); use the **present tense** to report established knowledge or to discuss conclusions ("The evidence indicates …"). Use tenses consistently.
- Use the **technical language** of the discipline correctly, but avoid excessive jargon. Use plain, direct language. Choose synonyms with care.
- Include **graphs, charts,** and **illustrations** when they convey information more readily than words. Label them clearly.
- Incorporate **numbers, statistics,** and **equations** clearly and accurately. Include explanations.

31 c   Writing about texts

Two common forms of social science writing are reports of original research and reviews of published research.

1 Research reports

Empirical studies, those based on surveys and experiments, are common in the social sciences. In political science, a study might be based on an opinion poll about an election; in psychology, on the effects of a particular stimulus on behavior. The conventional form for research reports varies somewhat from discipline to discipline. However, many social science reports use the following basic structure:

Title page. The title of your report summarizes the topic of the paper. Center the title on the page, and underneath it type your name, your instructor's name, the course title, and the date.

Abstract. Your abstract summarizes the study and its results in approximately 100 words. A good abstract will explain what you did and what you found in simple, direct language so readers can then decide whether to read the report for details. It is best to write it after you complete the text itself. The abstract page follows the title page.

Introduction. Begin the report by defining the problem the study examines and outline how you set out to solve that problem. Discuss the background of the problem and include a brief literature review of any previously reported studies of the problem or issue. End by discussing your own purpose and rationale for the study and stating your hypothesis. The introduction has no heading.

Method. Explain how you studied the problem your report addresses. This section is often divided into three subsections: subjects or participants (describing the type, number, and selection of people in the study); apparatus (including any materials or statistical programs and their function); and procedure (summarizing the steps involved in conducting the study).

Results. In this section (headed "Results"), report the findings and conclusions of your study, including any findings that do not support your hypothesis. Use tables to present your results when doing so is clearer or more concise than a description in words. In this section, remain descriptive, not interpretive or evaluative.

Discussion. In this final section (headed "Discussion"), interpret what the results mean. Begin with a statement of whether or not your study supported your hypothesis. Consider what your work contributes to an understanding of the problem you set out to study. You may speculate on any theoretical implications or implications for further experiments. (This is the only section of a formal report in which the *first person* may be appropriate, as you may want to identify an opinion or theory as your own.)

References. List all the references cited in the report at the end on a separate page (headed "References"; see 31d3.)

2 Literature reviews

In addition to being included as part of research reports, literature reviews (sometimes called surveys) are often written as independent documents. Preparing a literature review exposes you to knowledge generated by social science methodology and also acquaints you with the conventions of experimentation and documentation.

Reviews are generally written in the style of an essay, with one paragraph devoted to each article surveyed. While the precise form, length, and name of these papers may vary slightly in different disciplines, they will generally contain the following parts:

Title. Create a title that concisely describes the subject area that is surveyed in the paper.

Introduction. Begin the report with a brief introduction to the subject and a chronological listing of the articles to be reviewed.

Summary. Summarize the main conclusion of each article reviewed. Include brief quotations that succinctly state the researchers' findings, and make some suggestion of how you interpret their implications.

Conclusion. Conclude the report with a cumulative summary of the survey. Assess the most important articles in the review and suggest possible implications for further research.

References. List all the articles cited in the report on a separate page titled "References." (See 31d3.)

31 d APA style: Documentating sources

Disciplines in the social sciences—psychology, sociology, anthropology, political science, economics, social work, and education—use the name-and-date system of documentation put forth by the American Psychological Association (APA). This citation style highlights dates of publication because the currency of published material is of primary importance in these disciplines.

Also, listing *all* the authors (up to six) is more strongly emphasized in the APA than in the MLA system as collaborative authoring is common in the social sciences so all authors are entitled to credit. For more about the foundations and purposes of the APA system, see the *Publication Manual of the American Psychological Association,* 5th edition (Washington DC: APA, 2001). For "Frequently Asked Questions" about the *Publication Manual* and APA style, please consult http://www.apastyle.org/faqs.html.

1 Conventions for in-text citations

1. Single work by one or more authors

Whenever you paraphrase or summarize material in your text, you should give both the author's last name and the date of the source. For direct quotations, you should also provide specific page numbers. You may also provide page references, as a convenience to your readers, whenever you suspect they might want to consult a source you have cited. Page references in the APA system are always preceded, in text or in the reference list, by the abbreviation *p.,* in the case of a single page, or *pp.,* in the case of multiple pages.

According to the APA system, authors' names, publication dates, and page numbers (when listed) should be placed in parentheses following citable material. If any of these elements are identified in the text referred to in the parenthetical citation, they are not repeated in the citation.

> Exotoxins make some bacteria dangerous to humans
>
> (Thomas, 1974).
>
> According to Thomas (1974), "Some bacteria are only
>
> harmful to us if they make exotoxins" (p. 76).

We need fear some bacteria only "if they make exotoxins" (Thomas, 1974, p. 76).

For a work by *two authors,* cite both names each time the source is cited.

> Smith and Hawkins (1990) agree that all bacteria
>
> producing exotoxins are harmful to humans.

> All known exotoxin-producing bacteria are harmful to
>
> humans (Smith & Hawkins, 1990).

The authors' names are joined by *and* within your text, but APA convention requires an ampersand (&) to join authors' names in parentheses.

For a work by *three to five authors,* identify all the authors by last name the first time you cite a source. In subsequent references, identify only the first author followed by *et al.* ("and others").

> The most recent study supports the belief that
>
> alcohol abuse is on the rise (Dinkins, Dominic, Smith,
>
> Rogers, & White, 1989). . . . When homeless people were
>
> excluded from the study, the results were the same
>
> (Dinkins et al., 1989).

If you are citing a source by *six or more authors,* identify only the first author in all the references, followed by *et al.*

2. Two or more works by the same author published in the same year

To distinguish between two or more works published in the same year by the same author or team of authors, place a lowercase letter (*a, b, c,* etc.) immediately after the date. This letter should correspond to that in the reference list, where the entries will be alphabetized by title. If two appear in one citation, repeat the year (Smith, 1992a, 1992b).

3. Unknown author

To cite the work of an unknown author, use the first two or three words of the entry as it appears in the reference list (usually by the title). If the words *are* from the title, enclose them in quotation marks or underline them, whichever is appropriate.

> *Statistical Abstracts* (1991) reports the literacy rate for
>
> Mexico at 75% for 1990, up 4% from census figures 10
>
> years earlier.

> Many researchers now believe that treatment should not
>
> begin until other factors have been dealt with ("New Evidence
>
> Suggests," 1987).

4. Corporate or organizational author

If a citation refers to a work by a corporation, association, organization, or foundation, spell out the name of the authoring agency. If the name can be abbreviated and remain identifiable, you may spell out the name the first time only and put the abbreviation immediately after it, in brackets. For subsequent references to that source, you may use only the abbreviation (American Psychological Association [APA], 1993) . . . (APA, 1994).

5. Authors with the same last name

To avoid confusion in citing two or more authors with the same last name, include each author's initials in every citation (J. M. Clark, 1994) (C. L. Clark, 1995).

6. Quotation from an indirect source

Use the words *as cited in* to indicate when a quotation or any information in your source is originally from another source.

> Lester Brown of Worldwatch believes international
> agriculture production has reached its limit and that "we're
> going to be in trouble on the food front before this decade is
> out" (as cited in Mann, 1993, p 51).

7. More than one work in a citation

As a general guideline, list two or more sources within a single parenthetical reference in the same order in which they appear in your reference list. List more than one work by the same author in chronological order with the author's name mentioned once and the dates separated by commas (Thomas, 1974, 1979).

Works by different authors in the same parentheses are listed in alphabetical order by the author's last name, separated by semicolons: (Miller, 1990; Webster & Rose, 1988).

8. Long quotation set off from text

Introduce long quotations (40 or more words) with a signal phrase that names the author and ends in a colon. Indent this entire block quotation five spaces. If you quote more than one paragraph, indent the first sentence of each subsequent paragraph five spaces. At the end of the quotation, after the final punctuation mark, indicate in parentheses the location of the quotation in the source—page numbers for a print document, a section and part number for an online source.

> According to Langlacker:
>
> > Language is everywhere. It permeates our thoughts, mediates our relations with others, and even creeps into our dreams. The overwhelming bulk of human knowledge is stored and transmitted in language. Language is so ubiquitous that we take it for granted, but without it, society as we now know it would be impossible. Despite its prevalence in human affairs, language is poorly understood. (1968, p. 3)

2 Conventions for footnotes

Footnotes are used to provide additional information that cannot be worked into the main text, information highly likely to be of interest to some readers but also likely to slow down the pace of your text or obscure your point for other readers. Therefore, even the footnotes you do choose to provide should be as brief as possible; when the information you wish to add is extensive, it is better to present it in an appendix. Footnotes are indicated by an asterisk to avoid confusion with endnote notations. Endnotes should be numbered consecutively with superscript numbers, should follow the reference list on a page headed "Endnotes," should be double-spaced, and should have their first line indented five to seven spaces.

3 Conventions for the reference list

All works mentioned in a paper should be identified on a reference list according to the following general rules of the APA documentation system.

Format. After the final page of the paper, title a separate page "References," with no underline or quotation marks. Center the title an inch from the top of the page. Number the page in sequence with the last page of the paper.

Double-space between the title and the first entry. Set the first line flush with the left margin; the second and all subsequent lines of an entry should be indented five spaces from the left margin. This format is called a hanging indent.

Also double-space both between and within entries. If your reference list exceeds one page, continue listing your references in sequence on an additional page or pages, but do not repeat the title "References."

Order of entries. Alphabetize the list of references according to authors' last names, using the first author's last name for works with multiple authors. For entries by an unknown author, alphabetize by the first word of the title, excepting nonsignificant words (e.g., *A, An, The*).

Authors. List the author's last name first, followed by a comma and the author's initials (not first and middle names). When a work has more than one author, list all authors (up to six) in this way, separating the names with a comma. When listing multiple authors for a single work, place an ampersand (&) before the last author's name. A period follows the author name(s). If there are more than six authors, after the sixth name, put a comma and then *et al.*

Titles. List the complete titles and subtitles of books and articles, but capitalize only the first word of the title and any subtitle, as well as all proper nouns. Italicize book titles and journal or publication titles, but do not underline article titles or place quotation marks around them. Place a period after the title.

Publishers. List publishers' names in shortened form, omitting words such as *Company*. Spell out the names of university presses and organizations in full. For books, use a colon to separate the city of publication from the publisher.

Dates. For magazines and newspapers, use commas to separate the year from the month and day, and enclose the publication dates in parentheses: (*1954, May 25*). If no date is given in the document, write (*n.d.*) in parentheses.

Page numbers. Inclusive page numbers should be separated by an en dash with no spaces: *361–375*. Full sequences should be given for pages and dates (not *361–75*.) If pages do not follow consecutively (as in newspapers), include subsequent page numbers after a comma: *pp. 1, 16*. Note that *pp.* precedes the page numbers for newspaper articles but not for journal articles, unless there is no volume number.

Abbreviations. State and country names are abbreviated, but months are not. Use U.S. postal abbreviations for state abbreviations.

1. Book by one author

Benjamin, J. (1988). *The bonds of love: Psychoanalysis, feminism, and the problem of domination.* New York: Prometheus Books.

2. Book by two or more authors

Zweigenhaft, R. L., & Domhoff, G. W. (1991). *Blacks in the white establishment.* New Haven, CT: Yale University Press.

Include all authors' names in the reference list, up to six. If there are more than six authors, after the sixth name, put a comma and then put *et al.*

3. More than one book by the same author

List two or more works by the same author (or the same author team listed in the same order) chronologically by year in your reference list, with the earliest first. Arrange any such works published in the same year alphabetically by title, placing lowercase letters after the dates. In either case, give full identification of author(s) for each reference listing.

Bandura, A. (1969). *Principles of behavior modification.* New York: Holt, Rinehart, and Winston.

Bandura, A. (1977a). Self-efficacy: Toward a unifying theory of behavioral change. *Psychological Review, 84,* 191–215.

Bandura, A. (1977b). *Social learning theory.* Englewood Cliffs, NJ: Prentice Hall.

If the same author is named first but has different coauthors, subalphabetize by the last name of the second author. Works by the first author alone are listed before works with coauthors.

4. Book by a corporation, association, or organization

American Psychological Association. (1994). *Publication manual of the American Psychological Association* (4th ed.). Washington, DC: Author.

GENERAL FORMAT FOR BOOK, APA

Author/editor(s). (Year of publication). *Book title.* City of publication: Publisher.

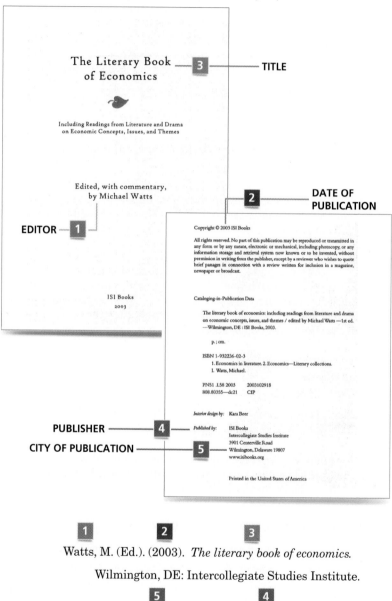

TITLE

EDITOR — **1**

DATE OF PUBLICATION

PUBLISHER — **4**

CITY OF PUBLICATION — **5**

The Literary Book of Economics — **3**

Including Readings from Literature and Drama on Economic Concepts, Issues, and Themes

Edited, with commentary, by Michael Watts

ISI Books
2003

Cataloging-in-Publication Data

The literary book of economics: including readings from literature and drama on economic concepts, issues, and themes / edited by Michael Watts —1st ed. —Wilmington, DE : ISI Books, 2003.

p. ; cm.

ISBN 1-932236-02-3
    1. Economics in literature. 2. Economics—Literary collections.
    I. Watts, Michael.

PN51 .L58 2003   2003102918
808.80355—dc21   CIP

Interior design by: Kara Beer

Published by: ISI Books
                Intercollegiate Studies Institute
                3901 Centerville Road
                Wilmington, Delaware 19807
                www.isibooks.org

Printed in the United States of America

1   **2**   **3**

Watts, M. (Ed.). (2003). *The literary book of economics.*

Wilmington, DE: Intercollegiate Studies Institute.

5   **4**

1 AUTHOR.

List the author's last name first, followed by a comma and the author's initials (not first name). When a work has more than one author, list all authors in this way, separating the names with a comma, placing an ampersand (&) before the last author's name, and ending with a period (*Smith, A. C., Jones, B., & Watts, M.*). If more than one work by the same author, list the earliest first.

> Watts. M. (1987). Student gender and school district differences affecting the stock and flow of economic knowledge. *Review of Economics and Statistics, 69,* 561–566.
>
> Watts. M. (Ed.). (2003). *The literary book of economics.* Wilmington, DE: Intercollegiate Studies Institute.

2 DATE.

Following author's name, give year of publication in parentheses.

3 TITLE.

List the complete titles and subtitles of books, but capitalize only the first word of the title and subtitle, as well as all proper nouns (*The literary book of African economics*). Italicize book titles and place a period after the title.

4 PUBLISHER.

List publishers' names in shortened form, omitting words such as *Publishers, Inc.,* or *Company.* Spell out the names of university presses and organizations in full (*New England University Press*). Use a colon to separate the place of publication from the publisher (*Wilmington, DE: Intercollegiate Studies Institute*).

5 CITY OF PUBLICATION.

Use U.S. postal abbreviations for state and country (*VT for Vermont, etc.*).

Alphabetize corporate authors by the corporate name, excluding the articles *A, An,* and *The.* When the corporate author is also the publisher, designate the publisher as *Author.*

5. Revised edition of a book

Peek, S. (1993). *The game inventor's handbook* (Rev. ed.). Cincinnati, OH: Betterway.

6. Edited book

Schaefer, Charles E., & Reid, S. E. (Eds.). (1986). *Game play: Therapeutic use of childhood games.* New York: Wiley.

Place *(Ed.)* or *(Eds.)* capitalized, and in parentheses, after the singular or plural name of the editor(s) of an edited book.

7. Book in more than one volume

Waldrep, T. (Ed.). (1985–1988). *Writers on writing* (Vols. 1–2). New York: Random House.

For a work with volumes published in different years, indicate the range of dates of publication. In citing only one volume of a multivolume work, indicate only the volume cited.

Waldrep, T. (Ed.). (1988). *Writers on writing* (Vol. 2). New York: Random House.

8. Translated or reprinted book

Freud, S. (1950). *The interpretation of dreams* (A. A. Brill, Trans.). New York: Modern Library-Random House. (Original work published 1900)

The date of the translation or reprint is in parentheses after the author's name. Indicate the original publication date parenthetically at the end of the citation, with no period. In the text, parenthetically cite the information with both dates: *(Freud 1900/1950).*

9. Chapter or article in an edited book

Telander, R. (1996). Senseless crimes. In C. I. Schuster & W. V. Van Pelt (Eds.), *Speculations: Readings in culture, identity, and values* (2nd ed., pp. 264-272). Upper Saddle River, NJ: Prentice Hall.

The chapter or article title is not underlined or in quotation marks. Editors' names are listed in normal reading order (surname last). Inclusive page numbers, in parentheses, follow the title of the larger work.

10. Anonymous book

Stereotypes, distortions and omissions in U.S. history textbooks. (1977). New York: Council on Interracial Books for Children.

11. Government document

U.S. House of Representatives, Committee on Energy and Commerce. (1986). *Ensuring access to programming for the backyard satellite dish owner* (Serial No. 99-127). Washington, DC: U.S. Government Printing Office.

For government documents, provide the higher department or governing agency only when the office or agency that created the document is not readily recognizable. If a document number is available, list it after the document title in parentheses. Write out the name of the printing agency in full, as the publisher, rather than using the abbreviation *GPO*.

12. Religious and classical texts

References are not required for well-known classical or religious works. However, the first in-text citation should identify the edition used. For example, referencing *The Quran: The Final Testament (Authorized English Version)* would require, in parentheses, following the naming of the text (Authorized English Version).

DOCUMENTING PERIODICALS

13. Article in a journal paginated by volume

Hartley, J. (1991). Psychology, writing, and computers: A review of research. *Visible Language, 25,* 339-375.

If page numbers are continuous throughout volumes in a year, use only the volume number, underlined, following the title of the periodical.

14. Article in a journal paginated by issue

Lowther, M. A. (1977). Career change in mid-life: Its impact on education. *Innovator, 8*(7), 1, 9-11.

GENERAL FORMAT FOR JOURNAL ARTICLES, APA

Author(s). (Year of publication). Article title. *Journal Title, volume number* (issue number), inclusive page numbers.

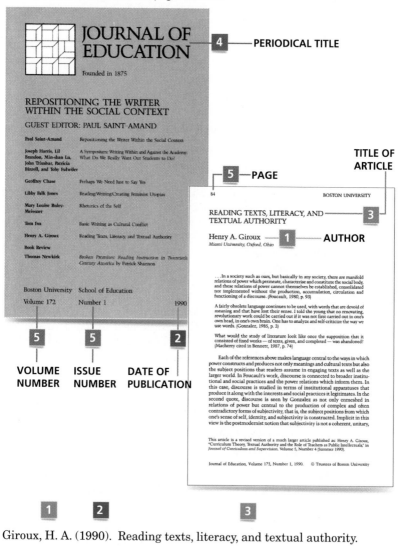

4 ——— PERIODICAL TITLE

5 — PAGE

TITLE OF ARTICLE

3

1 ——— AUTHOR

5 VOLUME NUMBER

5 ISSUE NUMBER

2 DATE OF PUBLICATION

1 **2** **3**

Giroux, H. A. (1990). Reading texts, literacy, and textual authority. *Journal of Education, 172*(1), 84–103.

4 **5**

1 AUTHOR.
List the author's last name first, followed by a comma and the author's initials (*Giroux, H. A.*). When a work has more than one author, list all authors in this way, separating the names with a comma and place an ampersand (*&*) before the last author's name (*Giroux, H. A., Smith, D., & Jones, M.*).

2 DATE OF PUBLICATION.
Following author's name, give year of publication in parentheses (*1990*). For magazines and newspapers, use a comma to separate the year from the month or month and day, and enclose in parentheses (*1954, May 25*). If no date is given in the document, write *n.d.* in parentheses followed by a period (*n.d.*).

3 TITLE OF ARTICLE.
List the complete titles and subtitles of articles, but capitalize only the first word of the title and subtitle, as well as all proper nouns. Period. Do not underline article titles or place quotation marks around them (*Reading texts, literacy, and textual authority: A study of American culture*).

4 TITLE OF PERIODICAL.
Italicize jounal or publication titles. Capitalize the first letter of all words in the title, except articles, prepositions, and conjunctions less than four letters long.

5 VOLUME, ISSUE, AND PAGE NUMBERS.
In an article in a journal paginated by volume (continuous pagination), include only the volume number (*in italics*), not the issue. In an article in a journal paginated by issue, list the volume number (*in italics*) followed by the issue number in parentheses but not in italics: *172*(1). Comma. Inclusive page numbers for pages and dates should be written out in full, separated by an en-dash with no spaces (*361–375 not 361–75; 204–205, not 204–05*). If pages do not follow consecutively (as in newspapers), include subsequent page numbers after a comma (*pp. 1, 16*). Note that *pp.* precedes the page numbers for newspaper articles but not for journal articles.

Include the issue number in parentheses if each issue of a journal is paginated separately.

15. Magazine article

Garreau, J. (1995, December). Edgier cities. *Wired,* 158-163, 232-234.

For nonprofessional periodicals, include the year and month (not abbreviated) after the author's name.

16. Newspaper article

Finn, P. (1995, September 27). Death of a U-Va. student raises scrutiny of off-

campus drinking. *The Washington Post,* pp. D1, D4.

If an author is listed for the article, begin with the author's name, then list the date (spell out the month); follow with the title of the newspaper. If there is a section, combine it with the page or pages, including continued page numbers as well.

17. Review

Ross, A. (2005, March 28). [Review of the play *Kafka's trial*]. *New Yorker,* 80.

Entries for reviews should begin with the reviewer's name, if known, followed by the complete date, then the words "Review of [genre, *title*]." If a review is unsigned, list it as *Rev. of* [genre, title] and alphabetize it by the name of the work reviewed.

18. Article by an unknown author

Conventionalwisdomwatch. (2005, June 13). *Newsweek,* 5.

DOCUMENTING FIXED ELECTRONIC SOURCES

APA conventions for documenting fixed electronic sources such as CD-ROMs, diskettes, and magnetic tapes list author, date, and title followed by the type of electronic source—for example, *[CD-ROM]*—in brackets and the complete information for the corresponding print source if available.

19. CD-ROM

Krauthammer, C. (1991). Why is America in a blue funk? [CD-ROM]. *Time, 138,*

83. Abstract from UMIACH file: Periodical Abstracts Item: 1126.00

20. Computer software

HyperCard (Version 2.2) [Computer software]. (1993). Cupertino, CA: Apple

Computer.

Provide the version number, if available, in parentheses following the software name. Add the descriptive term [*Computer software*] in brackets, followed with a period. Do not underline the names of computer programs.

DOCUMENTING ONLINE SOURCES

An APA Internet citation should provide essentially the same information as any textual source: author (when identified), date of site creation, title (or description of document), date of retrieval, and a working address (URL).

Try to reference specific documents or links, whenever possible, rather than general home or menu pages since such pages commonly contain many links, only one of which you are citing.

To transcribe a URL correctly, keep your word-processing file open and copy the URL directly from the Internet site to your paper. (Make sure your word processor's automatic hyphenation feature is turned off since an automatically inserted hyphen will change the URL; if you need to break a URL, do so after a slash or before a period.) APA does not recommend using angle brackets to indicate an Internet address.

If electronic sources don't provide page numbers, use paragraph numbers only if numbered in the document: (*para 4*). If the source is divided into chapters, use chapter and paragraph numbers: (*chap 2, 12*). If the source is divided into sections, use section and paragraph numbers to identify the source location: (*section 6, 8*).

For more details than the following examples can provide, consult the APA's Web page at http://www.apa.org/journals/webref.html.

21. Online periodical article

Kapadia, S. (1995, November). A tribute to Mahatma Gandhi: His views on

women and social exchange [12]. *Journal of South Asia Women's Studies*

[on-line serial], *1*(1). Retrieved December 2, 1995, from http://www.shore

.net/~india/jsaws

Indicate the number of paragraphs in brackets after the title, and add the term [*On-line serial*] in brackets between the journal name and the volume number.

GENERAL FORMAT FOR ONLINE SOURCES, APA

Author(s). (Date of electronic publication). Title of site. Date of access, electronic address

AUTHOR(S)   **URL**   **DATE**

`1`   `3`   `3`

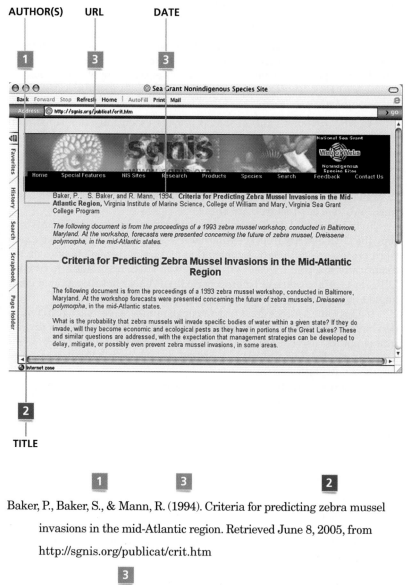

`2`

TITLE

`1`   `3`   `2`

Baker, P., Baker, S., & Mann, R. (1994). Criteria for predicting zebra mussel invasions in the mid-Atlantic region. Retrieved June 8, 2005, from http://sgnis.org/publicat/crit.htm

`3`

1 **AUTHOR OF MATERIAL ON WEB SITE.**
Follow rules for citing books and periodicals. Last name, followed by initials for first and middle names (*Baker, P., Baker, S., & Mann, R.*). If no author is listed, begin with page title.

2 **TITLE OF MATERIAL ON WEB SITE.**
Capitalize first word in site title and subtitle and any proper names only. Period. Do not enclose in quotation marks (*Criteria for predicting zebra mussel invasions in the Mid-Atlantic region*). If no title is obvious, use home page name as title (found in URL).

3 **PUBLICATION INFORMATION.**
List two dates for each Internet site: first, the date the site was created or last revised (*1994*). Second, list the date you accessed the site with the words *Retrieved from* followed by the date and electronic address, no concluding period (*Retrieved June 8, 2005, from http://sgnis.org/publicat/papers/crit.htm*).

If you have viewed the article only in its electronic form, you should add *Electronic version* in brackets after the article title as in the following example:

Smithsonian Institution's Ocean Planet: A special report. (1995). [Electronic
    version]. *Outdoor Life, 3,* 13-22. Retrieved November 1, 1999, from
    http://www.epinions.com/mags-Outdoor Life

22. World Wide Web site

To document a specific file, list the author, the date of publication, the titles of the document, and the complete work (if any). Add relevant information such as volume or page numbers of a print source. Conclude with a retrieval statement.

Williams, Scott. (1996, June 14). Back to school with the quilt. *AIDS Memorial*
    Quilt Website. Retrieved June 14, 1996, from http://www.aidsquilt.org/
    newsletter/stories/backto.html

Start with the title if no author is identified.

GVU's 8th WWW user survey. (n.d.). Retrieved August 8, 2000, from
    http://www.cc.gatech.edu/gvu/usersurveys/survey1997-10/

23. Work from an online database.

Conniff, R. (May 1993). Approaching *Walden. Yankee, 57*(5), 84. Retrieved June 2,
    2005, from ArticleFirst database.

Give the print publication information and when it was retrieved from which database. No URL is required.

24. Weblog entry

Rickey, A. (8 June 2005). Three years of hell to become the devil. Retrieved June
    10, 2005, from http://www.threeyearsofhell.com/

25. File transfer protocol (FTP), telnet, or gopher site

After the retrieval date, supply the FTP, telnet, or gopher search path.

Altar, T. W. (1993). *Vitamin B12 and vegans.* Retrieved May 28, 1996, from
ftp://ftp.cs.yale.edu

Clinton, W. (1994, July 17). Remarks by the President at the tribute dinner for
Senator Byrd. Washington, DC: Office of the White House Press Secretary.
Retrieved February 12, 1996, from gopher://info.tamu.edu.70/00/.data/
politics/1994/byrd.0717

King, Jr., M. L. (1963 August 28). I have a dream [Speech]. Retrieved January 2,
1996, from telnet://ukanaix.cc.ukans.edu

26. Synchronous communications (MOO, MUD, IRC)

To document a *real-time communication,* such as those posted in
MOOs, MUDs, and IRCs, describe the type of communication (e.g., *Group
discussion, Personal interview*) if it is not indicated elsewhere in the
entry.

Harnack, A. (1996, April 4). Words [Group discussion]. Retrieved April 5, 1996,
from telnet://moo.du.org/port=8888

27. Web discussion forum

Holden, J. B. (2001, January 2). The failure of higher education [Formal
discussion initiation]. Message posted to http://ifets.mtu.edu/archives

28. Listserv (electronic mailing list)

Weston, H. (2002, June 12). Re: Registration schedule now available. Message
posted to the Chamberlain Kronsage dormitory electronic mailing list,
archived at http://listserv.registrar.uwsp.edu/archives/62.html

Note that APA prefers the term *electronic mailing list* to *listserv.*

29. Newsgroup

Hotgirl. (2002, January 12). Dowsing effort fails. Message posted to
news://alt.science.esp3/html

30. Electronic newspaper article

Kolata, G. (2002, February 12). Why some people won't be fit despite exercise. *New York Times*. Retrieved February 12, 2002, from http://www.nytimes.com

31. Document available on university program or department Web site

McClintock, R., & Taipale, K.A. (1994). *Educating America for the 21st century: A strategic plan for educational leadership 1993–2001*. Retrieved February 12, 2002, from Columbia University, Institute for Learning Technologies Web site: http://www.ilt.columbia.edu/ilt/ docs/ILTplan.html

32. E-mail messages

Under current APA guidelines, electronic conversations are not listed on the References page. Cite e-mail messages in the text as you would personal letters or interviews (R. W. Williams, personal communication, January 4, 1999).

Following is an in-text parenthetical reference to a personal e-mail message:

James Tolley (personal communication, November 2, 2002) told me that the practice of dowsing has a scientific basis.

DOCUMENTING OTHER SOURCES

33. Film, recording, and other nonprint media

Curtiz, M. (Director). (1942). *Casablanca* [Film]. Hollywood, CA: Warner Bros.

Alphabetize a film listing by the name of the person or persons with primary responsibility for the product. Identify the medium in brackets following the title, and indicate both location and name of the distributor (as publisher). Other identifying information should appear in parentheses.

34. Audio recording

Springsteen, B. (2005). Devils & dust. On *Devils & dust* [CD]. New York: Sony BMG Music Entertainment.

Depending on the focus of your essay, begin with the artist, composer, or conductor. Continue with the date and the title of the whole work. Specify medium. End with the company label.

35. Television or radio broadcast, single episode

Carson, D. (Director).(1993). Emissary [Television series episode]. In *Star Trek: Deep Space Nine.* West Palm Beach: Fox.

For a single episode, begin with the director's name. If the broadcast is not an episode of a series or the episode is untitled, begin with the program title. Include date of broadcast, series title, city, and network. Leading off with other information—such as narrator, writer, or performers—depends on the purpose of your citation.

31 e Sample APA research paper

The research essay "Green Is Only Skin Deep: False Environmental Marketing," by Elizabeth Bone, was written to identify and explain one problem in contemporary American culture. Elizabeth's essay is documented according to the conventions of the American Psychological Association (APA). This sample includes title page and abstract; check with your instructor to find out whether these are required for course papers. The References page shows hanging indent style, with each first line full measure and subsequent lines in an entry indented five to seven spaces. In APA style, student papers may use a first-line indent instead. Check to see which style your instructor prefers.

APA APA APA

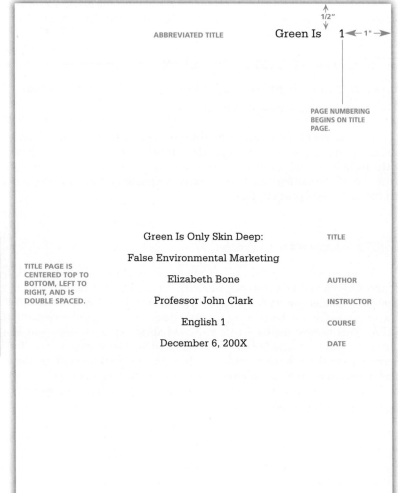

ABBREVIATED TITLE   Green Is   1

1/2"

1"

PAGE NUMBERING
BEGINS ON TITLE
PAGE.

Green Is Only Skin Deep: TITLE

False Environmental Marketing

TITLE PAGE IS
CENTERED TOP TO
BOTTOM, LEFT TO
RIGHT, AND IS
DOUBLE SPACED.

Elizabeth Bone   AUTHOR

Professor John Clark   INSTRUCTOR

English 1   COURSE

December 6, 200X   DATE

Title page for a student essay in APA format

ABSTRACT SHOULD BE PRINTED
ON A SEPARATE PAGE
FOLLOWING THE TITLE PAGE.

1"

1/2"

Green Is 2 ← 1" →

Abstract HEADING CENTERED

NO
PARAGRAPH
INDENT

DOUBLE
SPACE

Most Americans consider themselves environmentalists and favor supporting environmentally friendly or "green" companies. However, companies use a number of false advertising practices to mislead the public about their green practices and products by (1) exaggerating claims, (2) masking false practices behind technical terminology, (3) mis-sponsoring green events, (4) not admitting responsibility for real problems, (5) advertising green by association, and (6) solving one problem while creating others. Consumers must be skeptical of all advertisements and take the time to find out the truth behind advertising.

THE
ABSTRACT
SUMMARIZES
THE MAIN
POINT OF
THE PAPER.

Abstract for a student essay in APA format

TITLE IS REPEATED FROM
TITLE PAGE.

1"

1/2"

Green Is   3   ← 1" →

Green Is Only Skin Deep:

False Environmental Marketing

DOUBLE
SPACE

A recent Gallup poll reported that 75%

of Americans consider themselves to be

environmentally (Smith & Ouelch, 1993, p. 86). In

AUTHOR'S
NAME,
DATE,
AND PAGE
NUMBERS
ARE IN
PARENTHESES.

the same study, nearly half of the respondents said

they would be more likely to purchase a product if

they perceived it to be environmentally friendly or

"green." According to Smith and Ouelch (1993),

since green sells, many companies have begun to

promote themselves as marketing products that are

INFORMATIONAL
THESIS IS
AT END OF
FIRST
PARAGRAPH.

either environmentally friendly or manufactured

from recycled material. Unfortunately, many of these

companies care more about appearance than reality.

The most common way for a company to

FIRST EXAMPLE
OF FALSE
ADVERTISING IS
INTRODUCED.

market itself as pro-environment is to stretch the

definitions of terms such as "biodegradable" so that

consumers believe one thing while the product

delivers something else. For example, so-called

← 1" →

biodegradable plastic, made with cornstarch, was

introduced to ease consumers' fears that plastic lasts   ← 1" →

forever in the environment. However, the cornstarch

plastic broke down only in specific controlled

1"

First text page of a student essay in APA format

Green Is   4

laboratory conditions, not outdoors and not in
compost bins. The Federal Trade Commission
has updated its regulations to prevent such
misrepresentations so that now Glad and Hefty trash
bags are no longer advertised as biodegradable
(Carlson, Grove, & Kangun, 1993, p. 30.).

> PARAGRAPH INDENT IS 5-7 SPACES.

The use of technical terms can also mislead
average consumers. For example, carbon fluoride
compounds, called CFCs, are known to be
hazardous to the protective layer of ozone that
surrounds the earth, so their widespread use in air
conditioners is considered an environmental hazard
(Decker & Stammer, 1989). Chrysler Corporation
advertises that it uses CFC-free refrigerant in
its automobile air conditioners to appeal to
environmentally concerned consumers ("Ozone
Layer," 1994). However, Weisskopf (1992) points
out that the chemical compounds that replace CFCs
in their air conditioners pose other environmental
hazards that are not mentioned.

> SECOND EXAMPLE IS GIVEN.

> APA APA APA

> PAGE NUMBER IS NOT REQUIRED FOR PARAPHRASE OR SUMMARY.

> AUTHOR QUOTED BY NAME IN THE TEXT IS FOLLOWED BY PUBLICATION YEAR IN PARENTHESES.

Another deceptive greening tactic is the
sponsoring of highly publicized environmental
events such as animal shows, concerts, cleanup

> TRANSITIONS KEEP THE READER ON TRACK.

Green Is   5

programs, and educational exhibits. For example,
Ocean Planet was a well-publicized exhibit put
together by the Smithsonian Institution to educate
people about ocean conservation. Ford Motor
Company helped sponsor the event, which it then
used in its car advertisements: "At Ford, we feel
strongly that understanding, preserving, and
properly managing natural resources like our oceans
should be an essential commitment of individuals
and corporate citizens alike" (Smithsonian
Institution's Ocean Planet, 1995, para 8).

INCLUDE
PARAGRAPH
NUMBER FOR
INTERNET
SOURCE.

While sponsoring the exhibit may be a
worthwhile public service, such sponsorship has
nothing to do with how the manufacture and
operation of Ford automobiles affect the environment.
In fact, Ford was ranked as among the worst polluters
in the state of Michigan in 1995 (Parker, 1995).

Some companies court the public by
mentioning environmental problems and pointing
out that they do not contribute to those problems.
For example, the natural gas industry describes
natural gas as an alternative to the use of ozone-

SHORTENED
TITLE IS USED
WHEN NO
AUTHOR IS
CREDITED ON
REFERENCES
PAGE.

depleting CFCs ("Don't You Wish," 1994). However,
according to Fogel (1985), the production of natural

Green Is   6

gas creates a host of other environmental problems
from land reclamation to carbon dioxide pollution, a
major cause of global warming. By mentioning
problems they don't cause while ignoring ones they
do, companies present a favorable environmental
image that is at best a half-truth, at worst an
outright lie.

Other companies use a more subtle approach
to misleading green advertising. Rather than make
statements about environmental compatibility,
these companies depict the product in unspoiled
natural settings or use green quotations that have
nothing to do with the product itself. For example,
one Chevrolet advertisement shows a lake
shrouded in mist and quotes an environmentalist:
"From this day onward, I will restore the earth
where I am and listen to what it is telling me"
("From This Day," 1994, p. 19). Below the quotation
is the Chevy logo with the words "Genuine
Chevrolet." Despite this touching appeal to its love
of nature, Chevrolet has a history of dumping toxic
waste into the Grest Lakes (Allen, 1991). Has this
company seriously been listening to what the earth
has been telling it?

QUOTATION
OF FEWER
THAN 40
WORDS IS
INTEGRATED
INTO THE
TEXT.

Green Is   7

The most common manner in which companies attempt to prove they have a strong environmental commitment is to give a single example of a policy or action that is considered environmentally sound. Chevron has had an environmental advertising campaign since the mid-1970s. Most recently the company's ads feature Chevron employees doing environmental good deeds (Smith & Quelch, 1993, p. 94). For example, a recent ad features "a saltwater wetland in Mississippi at the edge of a pine forest . . . the kind of place nature might have made" and goes on to explain that this wetland was built by Chevron employees ("Shorebirds Who Found," 1998, para 1). However, LaGanga (1993, p. A1) points out that during the time this advertisement was running in magazines such as *Audubon,* Chevron was dumping millions of gallons of nasty chemicals (carcinogens and heavy metals) into California's Santa Monica Bay, posing a health risk to swimmers. The building of the wetland in one part of the country does not absolve the company of polluting water somewhere else.

ELLIPSIS POINTS INDICATE MISSING WORDS IN QUOTATION.

Green Is   8

It should be clear that the environmental image a company projects does not necessarily match the realities of the company's practice. The products produced by companies such as Chrysler, Ford, General Motors, and Chevron are among the major causes of air and water pollution: automobiles and gasoline. No amount of advertising can conceal the ultimately negative effect these products have on the environment (Kennedy & Grumbly, 1988). According to Shirley Lefevre, president of the New York Truth in Advertising League:

> It probably doesn't help to single out one automobile manufacturer or oil company as significantly worse than the others. Despite small efforts here and there, all of these giant corporations, as well as other large manufacturers of metal and plastic material goods, put profit before environment and cause more harm than good to the environment. (Personal communication, May 1995)

Consumers who are genuinely interested in buying environmentally safe products and

Green Is   9

supporting environmentally responsible companies need to look beyond the images projected by commercial advertising in magazines, on billboards, and on television. Organizations such as Earth First! attempt to educate consumers to the realities by writing about false advertising and exposing the hypocrisy of such ads ("Do People Allow," 1994), while the Ecology Channel is committed to sharing "impartial, unbiased, multiperspective environmental information" with consumers on the Internet (Ecology, n.d.). Meanwhile the Federal Trade Commission is in the process of continually upgrading truth-in-advertising regulations (Carlson et al., 1993). Americans who are truly environmentally conscious must remain skeptical of simplistic and misleading advertisements while continuing to educate themselves about the genuine needs of the environment.

WHEN NO DATE IS FOUND ON A SOURCE, WRITE *N.D.*

SECOND CITATION OF MORE THAN THREE AUTHORS IS SHORTENED TO FIRST AUTHOR'S NAME AND *ET AL.*

THESIS IS REPEATED IN MORE DETAIL AT END.

APA APA APA

Green Is 10 ← 1" →

References HEADING CENTERED

AUTHORS ARE LISTED ALPHABETICALLY.

Allen, F. E. (1991, March 10). Great Lakes cleanup enlists big volunteers. *The Wall Street Journal,* p. B1.

DOUBLE SPACE

INITIALS ARE USED FOR FIRST AND MIDDLE NAMES.

Carlson, L., Grove, S. J., & Kangun, N. (1993). A content analysis of environmental advertising claims: A matrix methods approach. *Journal of Advertising, 22*(9), 27-39.

ONLY FIRST WORD AND PROPER NAMES ARE CAPITALIZED IN ARTICLE TITLE.

P, OR PP. IS NOT USED TO INDICATE PAGES IN A PROFESSIONAL JOURNAL.

Decker, C., and Stammer, L. (1989, March 4). Bush asks ban on CFC to save ozone. *Los Angeles Times*, p. A1.

Do people allow themselves to be gullible? (1994, September). *Earth First!, 9,* 6.

DATE FOLLOWS AUTHOR (OR TITLE IF NO AUTHOR IS IDENTIFIED).

Don't you wish we could just do this to CFC's? (1994, December 7). [Natural gas advertisement]. *Audubon, 12,* 7.

USE N.D. WHEN NO DATE IS GIVEN IN ONLINE SOURCE.

The ecology channel (n.d.). Retrieved November 12, 1999, from http://www.ecology.com

NOTE ORDER OF MONTH, DAY, YEAR.

Fogel, B. (1985). *Energy: Choices for the future.* New York: Franklin Watts.

BOOK AND PERIODICAL TITLES ARE ITALICIZED.

From this day onward I will restore the earth where

INDENT 5-7 SPACES.

I am. (1994, November-December). [Chevrolet advertisement]. *Audubon, 11-12,* 18-19.

References list from a student essay in APA format

Green Is   11

Kennedy, D., & Grumbly, T. P. (1968). Automotive

emissions research. In A. Watson, R. R. Bates,

& D. Kennedy (Eds.), *Air pollution, the*

automobile, and public health (pp. 3-9).

Cambridge, MA: National Academy Press.

LaGanga, M. (1993, February 4). Chevron to stop

dumping waste near shoreline. *Los Angeles*

Times, pp. A1, A10.

The ozone layer has protected us for 1.5 billion

years: It's time we returned the favor. (1994,

November-December). [Chrysler

advertisement]. *Audubon, 11-12,* 40-41.

Parker, L. (1995, March 28). GM, Ford among top

polluters in state. *Detroit News,* p. A2.

The shorebirds who found a new wetland. (1998).

Retrieved November 12, 1999, from

http://www.audubon.com/water

Smith, N. C., & Quelch, J. A. (1993). *Ethics in*

marketing. Boston, MA: Richard D. Irwin.

Smithsonian Institution's Ocean Planet: A special

report. (1995). [electronic version]. *Outdoor Life,*

3, 13–22. Retrieved November 1, 1999, from

http://www.epinions.com/mags-Outdoor_Life

Weisskopf, M. (1992, February 23). Study finds CFC

alternatives more damaging than believed.

The Washington Post, p. A3.

P. OR PP. IS
USED FOR PAGE
NUMBERS IN
BOOKS OR
POPULAR
PERIODICALS.

ONLY THE
FIRST WORD
AND PROPER
NAMES ARE
CAPITALIZED
IN BOOK TITLE.

TITLES OF
PERIODICALS
ARE
CAPITALIZED
NORMALLY.

TITLE IS USED
WHEN NO
AUTHOR IS
IDENTIFIED IN
THE SOURCE.

INCLUDE
THIS NOTE
WHEN ONLY
THE ONLINE
SOURCE OF
A PUBLISHED
SOURCE HAS
BEEN
CONSULTED.

APA APA APA

chapter 32

CMS: Writing in the Humanities

This chapter describes the aims, style, forms, and documentation conventions associated with the humanities disciplines other than languages and literature: history, philosophy, religion, and the fine arts.

The purpose of studies in the humanities is to understand the human experience as it is expressed and interpreted in a variety of media. History examines the many documents that a civilization produces that provide clues to how its people thought and lived. Philosophy and religion examine the nature of humanity by scrutinizing texts produced by past thinkers and prophets. Studies in art and communications examine texts that are often nonverbal, including paintings, sculptures, and films.

In the humanities, the study and practice of writing is a primary means of making meaning. Students of history and philosophy, for example, spend a lot of time reading texts, reading about texts, listening to lectures based on texts, and writing texts that demonstrate an understanding of historical or philosophical knowledge. However, unlike literary texts, those in history, philosophy, and religion, as well as art and musical history, are often stepping-stones toward defining broader contexts, larger issues, or fuller understanding of human thought and expression. And unlike texts in the sciences and social sciences, those in the humanities involve matters of interpretation and debate rather than proofs and statistics. To be credible, interpretive papers need to be carefully reasoned, well supported, and clearly written.

32 b Style

In the humanities, thoughtfulness, variety, and vitality of expression are especially important. Though writing in the humanities is often explicitly argumentative, it is also fair and objective, presenting issues or positions reasonably and completely, and with a minimum of bias and subjectivity. The more neutral and analytical your tone, the more likely readers will take your ideas seriously. When you treat a text fairly, even one with which you disagree, readers are more likely to hear you out, which lays the foundation for strong and believable criticism. At the same time, the stylistic rules in the humanities are more variable than in most social science and science writing since individuality and uniqueness of expression are highly prized.

32 c Writing about texts

Two common forms of writing in the humanities are critical reviews and research papers.

1 Critical reviews

Writing critically requires many interwoven skills including careful description and explanation of the work under review as well as analysis, synthesis, and judgment of its ideas and arguments. For example, a writer might review a dramatized version of a historic event, a biographical analysis of an artist's work, a museum exhibit or concert performance—each of which, for the reviewer's purpose, would be considered a text. An effective critical review would point out both strengths and limitations of the "text," whatever its form, and also celebrate or question its connection to current culture and comparable texts.

2 Research papers

Research papers in the humanities may be descriptive (for example, tracing the effect of a particular invention on a society's economic or cultural life) or argumentative (for example, positing a radically different interpretation of a philosopher's beliefs). Whatever the aim, the best research papers demonstrate a mastery of a variety of informational sources as well as originality of thought and insight. In addition to locating sources previously unknown to the writer, most research papers in the humanities require *analysis* and *synthesis* of both **primary sources** (such as original documents, historical accounts, and statements of ideas) and **secondary sources** (what other writers have said about those primary sources)—all of which need to be documented in a clear, reasonable, and efficient manner.

32 d   CMS style: Documenting sources

The most widely used documentation system in history, philosophy, religion, and the fine arts is found in *The Chicago Manual of Style* (15th ed., University of Chicago Press, 2003). This manual actually includes two documentation systems, one using notes and bibliographies, the other using in-text citations with reference lists similar to those of the MLA and APA styles, but with subtle differences. Since Chicago style, or CMS, as this set of guidelines is commonly called, is the only major system that still uses the note/bibliography format, that is the form described briefly. The full note appears in close proximity to the reference—at the bottom of the page or at the end of the chapter—so it is the easiest system for readers who want to know quickly the full source of a citation. Sample pages in Chicago style are provided at the end of this chapter. If you are required to write a major project using Chicago style, we recommend consulting the latest edition of *The Chicago Manual of Style* or checking their Web site at www.press.uchicago.edu.

1 Conventions for marking in-text citations

Each time you quote, paraphrase, or summarize source material in your text, you need to mark it by inserting a raised (superscript) Arabic number immediately after the sentence or clause containing the information. The superscript number must follow all punctuation except dashes. Each new reference to source material requires a new number, and numbers are arranged consecutively throughout the text as follows:

> Frank Lloyd Wright's "prairie style" was characterized
>
> initially by the houses he built around Chicago "with low
>
> horizontal lines echoing the landscape."[1] Vincent Scully sees
>
> the suburban building lots for which Wright was designing as
>
> one of the architect's most important influences.[2]

Each superscript number corresponds to a note at the end of the paper or bottom (foot) of the page on which the number appears as seen below:

1. *Concise Columbia Encyclopedia,* s.v. "Wright, Frank Lloyd."

2. Vincent Scully, *Architecture: The Natural and the Manmade* (New York: St. Martin's, 1991), 340.

The first note does not require a page reference because it cites an alphabetized reference book. (See item 8 in 32d.)

2 Conventions for positioning notes and bibliography

Endnotes are typed as a single list at the end of a text. Endnotes are easy to format since they can be typed separately on a sheet of paper without calculating the space needed on each page. Footnotes can be difficult to place because the space taken up by the notes sometimes moves a footnote marker-number to the next page, requiring you to refigure the placement of your text. Many word-processing programs have a built-in footnote-formatting function, but it can also be done manually as well. Endnotes are more convenient for the writer as they allow you to use the full page for text rather than taking up space with footnotes and can be added to or deleted without affecting the body of the text.

The *endnote page* follows the last page of text and is numbered in sequence with the rest of the paper. Title the first page of the endnote section "Notes"—centered, without quotation marks, and one inch from the top of the page. Double-space throughout—between this title and the first entry, within the notes or entries themselves, and between entries. Order entries consecutively according to the note numbers in your paper. Indent the first line of each entry five spaces from the left margin, and place each subsequent entry line flush with the margin.

Footnotes are convenient because instead of turning to the back of a text to check a numbered source, readers can find the information simply by glancing at the bottom of the page they are reading. Footnotes must always be placed at the bottom of the same page on which the marker-number appears, four lines below the last line of text, indented and single-spaced.

A **bibliography** page is optional. Because notes include all necessary reference information, instructors may or may not require a final "bibliography" page listing sources alphabetically by author. If such a page is required, it may be called "bibliography," "works cited," or "references consulted." In form, it follows the conventions of MLA's "Works Cited" page.

3 Conventions for endnote and footnote format

The following guidelines are based on *The Chicago Manual of Style,* fifteenth edition (Chicago: University of Chicago Press, 2003), which follows the endnote and footnote format similar to that found in the *MLA Handbook for Writers of Research Papers.*

Numbers and spacing. Each entry is preceded by an Arabic number with a period that is indented five spaces and followed by a space. Any subsequent lines for an entry begin at the left margin. Double-space endnotes throughout. Single-space individual footnotes and double-space between footnotes.

Authors. Authors' names are listed first name first, spelled as they appear in the book. You may spell out the first name or use initials.

Punctuation. Separate authors' names and all titles with commas, and enclose all book publication information and periodical dates in parentheses. Underline or italicize the book title. Set in quotation marks the titles of articles in a periodical or anthology. Use colons to separate the place of publication from the publisher and commas to separate the publisher from the date. Colons should also be used to separate journal dates from page numbers. End all entries with a period.

Page numbers. Each entry for a book or periodical should end with the page number(s) on which the cited information can be found. (Note: Do not add *p.* or *pp.* unless from journals or newspapers *that do not use volume numbers.*)

The following are examples of the most common endnote citations required in undergraduate humanities papers.

DOCUMENTING BOOKS: FIRST REFERENCE

1. Book by one author

1. Jessica Benjamin, *The Bonds of Love: Psychoanalysis, Feminism, and the Problem of Domination* (New York: Prometheus Books, 1988), 76.

2. Book by two or more authors

2. Richard L. Zweigenhaft and G. William Domhoff, *Blacks in the White Establishment* (New Haven: Yale University Press, 1991), 113.

For three or more authors, follow each name with a comma.

3. Revised edition of a book

3. S. I. Hayakawa, *Language in Thought and Action,* 4th ed. (New York: Harcourt Brace Jovanovich, 1978), 77.

4. Edited book and one volume of a multivolume book

4. Tom Waldrep, ed., *Writers on Writing,* vol. 2 (New York: Random House, 1988), 123.

5. Translated book

5. Albert Camus, *The Stranger,* trans. Stuart Gilbert (New York: Random House, 1946), 12.

6. Reprinted book

6. Elizabeth E. G. Evans, *The Abuse of Maternity* (1875; reprint, New York: Arno Press, 1974), 74-78.

7. Work in an anthology or chapter in an edited collection

7. Mona Charen, "Much More Nasty Than They Should Be," in *Popular Writing in America: The Interaction of Style and Audience,* 5th ed., eds. Donald McQuade and Robert Atwan (New York: Oxford University Press, 1993), 207-8.

8. Article in a reference book

8. *The Film Encyclopedia,* 2nd ed. "Beaty, Ned" (HarperCollins Publishers, 1994).

No page number is needed for an alphabetically arranged book. Begin the entry with the author's name, if available.

9. Anonymous book

9. *The World Almanac and Book of Facts* (New York: World Almanac-Funk & Wagnalls, 1995).

DOCUMENTING PERIODICALS: FIRST REFERENCE

10. Article, story, or poem in a popular or general-circulation magazine

10. Matthew Hawn, "Stay on the Web: Make Your Internet Site Pay Off," *Macworld,* April 1996, 94-98.

11. John Updike, "His Mother Inside Him," *New Yorker,* 20 April 1992, 34.

11. Article in a daily newspaper

12. Peter Finn, "Death of a U-Va. Student Raises Scrutiny of Off-Campus Drinking," *Washington Post,* 27 September 1995, sec. D, p. 1.

GENERAL FORMAT FOR BOOKS, CMS

Author(s) or Editor(s), *Book title.* City of publication: Publisher, Date of publication.

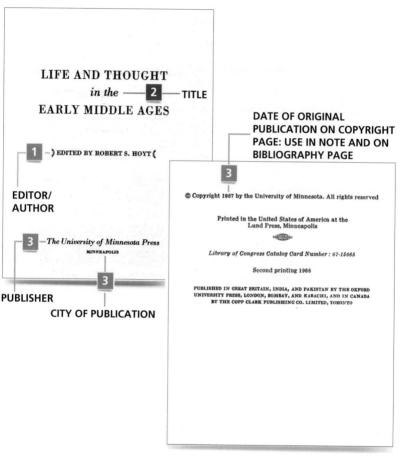

TITLE

DATE OF ORIGINAL PUBLICATION ON COPYRIGHT PAGE: USE IN NOTE AND ON BIBLIOGRAPHY PAGE

EDITOR/ AUTHOR

PUBLISHER

CITY OF PUBLICATION

LIFE AND THOUGHT
in the — **2**
EARLY MIDDLE AGES

1 —) EDITED BY ROBERT S. HOYT (

3 —*The University of Minnesota Press*
MINNEAPOLIS

3

3

© Copyright 1967 by the University of Minnesota. All rights reserved

Printed in the United States of America at the
Lund Press, Minneapolis

Library of Congress Catalog Card Number: 67-15065

Second printing 1968

PUBLISHED IN GREAT BRITAIN, INDIA, AND PAKISTAN BY THE OXFORD
UNIVERSITY PRESS, LONDON, BOMBAY, AND KARACHI, AND IN CANADA
BY THE COPP CLARK PUBLISHING CO. LIMITED, TORONTO

1   **2**

Hoyt, Robert S., ed. *Life and Thought in the Early Middle Ages.*

    Minneapolis: University of Minnesota Press, 1967.

3

1 AUTHOR OR EDITOR NAME.

Note: Name in normal order for individual or multiple authors or editors (*John Smith and Jim Jones*). Period. In subsequent notes to same author, include last name only, shortened title, and page number (*Smith and Jones, Life and Thought, 78*). Add *ed.*, after name for editor.

Bibliography page (may also be called Works Cited or References): Follow MLA format for assembling this page, alphabetically, with last name first, and so on.

2 BOOK TITLE.

List titles and subtitles fully, capitalized and italicized (*Life and Thought in the Early Middle Ages.*). Period. In subsequent notes, use shortened title. (*Life and Thought*).

In a bibliography entry, follow MLA style.

3 CITY, PUBLISHER, AND DATE OF PUBLICATION.

In the first note to a work, include all publication information as it appears on copyright page, in parentheses before the page number (*(Minneapolis: University of Minnesota Press, 1967), 103*). Period. In subsequent notes, omit publication information.

In a bibliography entry, follow MLA style.

GENERAL FORMAT FOR JOURNAL ARTICLES, CMS

Author(s). "Article Title." *Journal Title volume number, issue number* (Year of publication): inclusive page numbers.

2 — PERIODICAL TITLE

PAGE **TITLE OF ARTICLE**

3 **2**

1 — AUTHOR

3 **3** **4**

VOLUME ISSUE DATE OF
NUMBER NUMBER PUBLICATION

1 **2**

Giroux, Henry A. "Reading Texts, Literacy, and Textual Authority."

Journal of Education 172, no. 1 (1990): 84–103.

2 **3** **4** **3**

1 AUTHOR NAME.

In a note, list name in normal order for one, two, or three authors, each separated by a comma, with *and* before last author (*Alan Charles Smith, Brian Jones, and Michelle Watts*). Period. If four or more authors, list only first author followed by *and others*. In subsequent notes, cite author's last name, shortened title, and page number (*Giroux, "Reading Texts," 85*).

2 TITLE.

List titles and subtitles fully, capitalizing and put quotation marks around the titles of articles, poems, and short works within the periodical. Period. Italicize book titles within **article titles** ("A Reassessment of Faulkner's *As I Lay Dying*"). Use single quotation marks around the titles of short works within article titles ("T.S. Eliot's 'Ash Wednesday' Revisited"). *Italicize* or underline **periodical titles** (*ADE Bulletin*).

3 VOLUME, ISSUE, AND PAGE NUMBERS.

For journals paginated separately by issue (as in this example), list volume number, a comma, word "no.," and then issue number followed by date (in parentheses) and a colon: then page numbers: *(1990): 84–103*. Period. For journals paginated continuously, include volume number before the year and issue if available. Separate inclusive page numbers with an en dash (*42–54*). Only give the page numbers of pages referred to, or the first and last pages if referring to the article as a whole.

4 DATE OF PUBLICATION.

In magazines and newspapers, date of publication is placed within parentheses, followed by a colon and a space. For weekly or bi-weekly magazines give both day and month of publication in normal word order (Feb. 12, 2001). If no date of publication is given, put *n.d.* in parentheses (*n.d.*). Period.

12. Article in a journal paginated by volume

13. Jennie Nelson, "This Was an Easy Assignment: Examining How Students Interpret Academic Writing Tasks," *Research in the Teaching of English* 34 (1990): 362-96.

13. Article in a journal paginated by issue

14. Helen Tiffin, "Post-Colonialism, Post-Modernism, and the Rehabilitation of Post Colonial History," *Journal of Commonwealth Literature* 23, no. 1 (1988): 169-81.

14. Review

15. Review of Bone, by Faye Myenne Ng, *New Yorker,* 8 February 1992, 113.

16. Steven Rosen, "Dissing 'HIStory,'" review of *HIStory: Past, Present, and Future—Book I,* by Michael Jackson, *Denver Post,* 3 July 1995, sec. F, p. 8.

DOCUMENTING ONLINE SOURCES: FIRST REFERENCE

15. Material on CD-ROM database, periodically updated

17. Oregon Trail II, Ver. 1.0 Mac. (Minneapolis: Educational Computing Corp., 1995), ERIC, CD-ROM, SilverPlatter, March 1996.

Software titles are not italicized (underlined) in CMS style.

16. Work from an online database

18. Richard Conniff, "Approaching Walden." *Yankee,* 5, no. 5, May 1993, 84, <http://firstsearch.oclc.org>.

Give the print publication information same as for periodicals and add the URL.

17. World Wide Web (WWW) site

19. *Victorian Women Writers Project.* Ed. Perry Willett. April 1997. Indiana U. [cited 5 March 1998]; available at http://www.indiana.edu/~letrs/vwwp.

List the author's full name in normal order (if available), site title, date of publication (if available), date of access, and electronic address.

18. Home page—personal

20. Anna Fulwiler. Home page, <http://www.uvm.edu/~afulwile>.

19. Home page—college course or academic department

21. Jeffrey Hughes. Fundamentals of Field Science, course home page, Sep.-Dec. 2005, Botany department, University of Vermont, May 6, 2005, <http://www.uvm.edu/~plantbio/grad/fn>.

Include date accessed only for time-sensitive material such as a catalogue listing.

20. E-mail, listserv, or newsgroup (Usenet) message

22. Robert Jones. "Writing Guidelines." University of Vermont, 1998 [cited 29 March 1998]; available from jones213@rocket.pu.edu.

If you quote a personal message sent by somebody else, be sure to get permission before including his or her address on the reference page.

21. Synchronous communications (MUD, MOO, IRC)

23. Andrew Harnack. "Words." [Group discussion.] 1996 [visited 12 June 1996]; available from telnet.moo.du.org/port=8888.

Before the posting date, include the type of discussion (e.g., personal interview, group discussion), date visited, and electronic address.

GENERAL NOTE FORMAT FOR ONLINE SOURCES, CMS

Number. Period. Author(s). "Title," Name of site or sponsoring body, Date of electronic publication, electronic address.

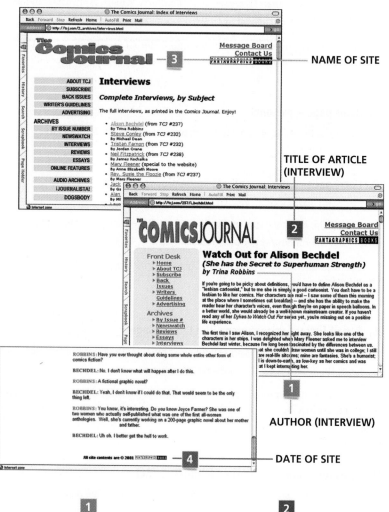

NAME OF SITE

TITLE OF ARTICLE (INTERVIEW)

AUTHOR (INTERVIEW)

DATE OF SITE

3. Trina Robbins, "Watch Out for Alison Bechdel (She has the Secret to Superhuman Strength)," *The Comics Journal*, 2001, http://tcj.com/237/i_bechdel.html.

1 **AUTHOR OF MATERIAL ON WEB SITE.**
Note: Name in normal order for individual or multiple authors (*John Smith and Jim Jones*). Period. In subsequent notes to same author, include last name only, shortened title, and page or paragraph number (*Smith and Jones, para. 12*). Add *ed.,* after name for editor.

Bibliography page (may also be called Works Cited or References): Follow MLA format for assembling this page, alphabetically, with last name first, and so on.

2 **TITLE OF MATERIAL ON WEB SITE.**
Enclose title and subtitle in quotation marks (*"Watch Out for Alison Bechdel (She Has the Secret to Superhuman Strength)"*). Period. If no title is obvious, use the home page name as the title (found in URL). Use same guidelines as for periodicals.

3 **NAME OF SITE OR SPONSORING ORGANIZATION.**
Usually found at top or bottom of home page followed by date (*The Comics Journal, 2001*).

4 **PUBLICATION INFORMATION.**
List only the date the site was created or last revised (usually at bottom of page) followed by the electronic address without angle brackets (*http://tcj.com/237/i_bechdel.html*). Period. CMS does not request date of access unless material is time-sensitive.

CMS CMS CMS

DOCUMENTING OTHER SOURCES: FIRST REFERENCE

22. Material on diskette

24. Diane Greco, *Cyborg: Engineering the Body Electric* [diskette] (Watertown: Eastgate, 1996).

23. Personal interview

25. John Morser, interview by author, Chicago, 15 December 1993.

24. Personal or unpublished letter

26. Paul Friedman, letter to author, 18 March 1992.

25. Work of art

27. Hans Holbein, Portrait of Erasmus, Musée du Louvre, Paris, in The Louvre Museum, by Germain Bazin (New York: Abrams, n.d.), p. 148.

DOCUMENTING SUBSEQUENT REFERENCES TO THE SAME WORK

26. Subsequent references to a work

The second and any subsequent times you refer to a source, the Chicago style calls for you to include the author's last name, a comma, a shortened version of the title, another comma, and the page number(s).

28. Benjamin, Bonds, 76.

29. Evans, The Abuse, 74-78.

The traditional Latin abbreviations *ibid.* ("in the same place") and *op. cit.* ("in the work cited") are seldom used in contemporary scholarly writing, though it is not incorrect to do so.

30. Ibid, 79.

32 e   Sample page with endnotes

The illustration that follows shows how citations are documented by endnotes.

Owsley 2

recorded "in exultant tones the universal neglect that had overtaken pagan learning."[2] It would be some time, however, before Christian education would replace classical training, and by the fourth century, a lack of interest in learning and culture among the elite of Roman society was apparent. Attempting to check the demise of education, the later emperors established municipal schools, and universities of rhetoric and law were also established in major cities throughout the Empire.[3]

The beginning of a page from the middle of a paper in CMS format. The superscript numbers 2 and 3 indicate that citations are documented in endnotes.

Owsley 12

Notes

1. Rosamond McKitterick, <u>The Carolingians and the Written Word</u> (Cambridge: Cambridge University Press, 1983), 61.

2. J. Bass Mullinger, <u>The Schools of Charles the Great</u> (New York: Stechert, 1911), 10.

3. James W. Thompson, <u>The Literacy of the Laity in the Middle Ages</u> (New York: Franklin, 1963), 17.

Endnote page with references in numerical order in CMS format

32 f   Sample page with footnotes

Footnotes appear on the same page with the citations, as the illustration on page 472 shows.

Kelly 5

The Teatro Olimpico was completed in 1584, the statues, inscriptions, and bas-reliefs for the <u>frons-scena</u> being the last details completed. Meanwhile, careful plans were made for an inaugural, which was to be a production of <u>Oedipus</u> in a new translation.[10] Final decisions were made by the Academy in February of 1585 for the seating of city officials, their wives, and others, with the ruling that "no masked men or women would be allowed in the theatre for the performance."[11]

The organization of the audience space was "unique among Renaissance theaters, suggesting . . . its function as the theater of a 'club of equals' rather than of a princely court."[12] The Academy is celebrated and related to Roman grandeur by the decorating over the monumental central opening, where its motto, "Hoc Opus," appears.[13] It is difficult to make out the entrances.

10. J. Thomas Oosting, <u>Andrea Palladio's Teatro Olimpico</u> (Ann Arbor, MI: UMI Research Press, 1981), 118-19.

11. Oosting, <u>Palladio's Teatro</u>, 120.

12. Marvin Carlson, <u>Places of Performance: The Semiotics of Theater Architecture</u> (Ithaca, NY: Cornell University Press, 1989), 135.

13. Simon Tidworth, <u>Theaters: An Architectural and Cultural History</u> (London: Praeger, 1973), 52.

A sample page from a paper using footnotes in CMS format

chapter 33

Writing in the Physical Sciences

This chapter describes the general aims and style of scientific writing and provides an overview of common forms and specialized documentation systems shared by the scientific community. If you write extensively in the sciences, consult one of the more detailed style manuals listed in 33d2.

33 a Aims

Scientific study examines the fundamental structures and processes of the natural world. In analyzing particular phenomena and organisms, scientists ask questions such as the following:

- What is it? Can it be isolated and observed? How can it be described?

- How does it function? What forces are in operation? How can these forces be explained?

- Why does it function the way it does? Can governing principles be identified, explained, and understood? Can predictions be made?

- What can be learned about other phenomena or organisms based on the evidence of particular studies?

Scientists approach and attempt to answer such questions using the *scientific method* of observation, prediction, experimentation, and analysis.

Observation. A chemist notices, for example, that when liquid A is mixed with liquid B, the solution of the two (C) has a higher temperature than A or B alone.

Prediction. On the basis of this observation, the chemist predicts that whenever these amounts of A and B are mixed together, C will always have a higher temperature. This prediction is called a *hypothesis*—a preliminary generalization or explanation based on the observed phenomena.

Experimentation. To test the hypothesis, the chemist devises an experiment (in this example, the mixing of the two liquids under controlled conditions), watches the results, and carefully notes what happens.

Analysis and conclusions. The results of the experiment may lead the scientist to conclude, "Yes, when specific amounts of A and B are mixed, reaction C occurs." This finding can be shared with other scientists and could provide the basis for further hypotheses. If the results are different from the hypothesis, new questions must be asked and new hypotheses formulated to explain why the results differed from the initial observations.

Writing plays a central role throughout the investigative and experimental process. To develop a hypothesis, scientists record observations, questions, and possible explanations. In conducting an experiment, scientists take full and accurate notes to keep a running account of methods, procedures, and results. To understand the significance of the results, scientists report or publish the results so other scientists can read about them and respond.

Scientific writing does not report the writer's opinions, values, or feelings; it aims for objectivity and accuracy when reporting observations and findings. When you write in the sciences, try to separate your observations from your expectations or biases. Record only what you see and hear and what the instruments tell you, not what you hope to discover. Keep in mind that your primary purpose is to present information accurately—not to persuade, argue, or entertain.

33 b   Style

Most science writing seeks to convey information specifically, directly, economically, and accurately. But this common goal does not mean that the style of all science writing is uniform. For example, the form and style of a laboratory report is quite different from the laboratory notebook on which it is based. An article in *Scientific American* (written for a general readership) is quite different from one in *The Journal of Chemical Education* (written for college chemistry instructors).

Stylistic Guidelines for Writing in the Sciences

In writing in the sciences, keep the goals of clarity and directness in mind.

- Choose **simple words** rather than complex words when the meaning is the same, and use disciplinary terminology carefully and accurately.
- Prefer **simple sentences** to complex.
- Maintain a **third-person point of view,** to avoid the pronoun *I.* Use the **passive voice** when necessary to describe procedures: *The liquids were brought to a temperature of 35℃.*
- Use the **present tense** to refer to established knowledge or to discuss conclusions. Use the **past tense** to describe methods and results.
- Insert **subheadings** to help readers predict what is coming.
- Include **tables** and **figures** when they can help explain your methods or results. Label each of these clearly, and mention them at appropriate points in the text.

33 c Writing about texts

Scientific reports have set forms that allow readers to locate information in predictable places. Two common forms of writing in college science courses are laboratory notebooks and laboratory reports.

1 Laboratory notebooks

Laboratory notebooks are journals that scientists keep to monitor day-to-day laboratory work and experimentation. They are used to record data—dates, times, temperatures, quantities, measurements—as well as to aid memory and provide records. These notebooks are also used to speculate about the meaning of the data. The privately kept notes serve as the basis for the information made public in formal laboratory reports.

SCI SCI SCI

∎ Laboratory notebook pages are usually numbered and bound rather than loose-leaf. This unalterable order guarantees an accurate record of exactly what happened in the laboratory, when it happened, and in what order.

∎ Double-entry notebooks, with a vertical line down the center of each page, are especially useful. Record data on the left; on the right make notes and speculations about the data.

∎ Laboratory notebooks must be complete and detailed. It is crucial to record all information about an experiment or observation.

2 Laboratory reports

Laboratory reports are formal reports that describe exactly what happened in any given experiment. The reader of a laboratory report should be able to replicate (or duplicate) the experiment by following the information in the report. While *labs* (as they are commonly called) vary slightly in format conventions from discipline to discipline, they all follow the same basic structure.

Introduction. The first section of the report defines the reasons for conducting the particular study, summarizes the findings of previous studies (a literature review), and states the researcher's hypothesis.

Methods and materials. Sometimes called "Procedure," this section details how the experiment was conducted and identifies all the equipment used. The experimental design is explained, and the methods of observation and measurement are described.

Results. Next, the researcher reports the specific factual findings of the study, describing the data and patterns that emerged but refraining from any judgment or interpretation.

Discussion. The final section of a laboratory report examines whether or not the results support the hypothesis. It can be somewhat speculative, focusing on the possible implications and limitations of the experiment and its results. It may also point out the relationship of the current study to other researchers' results, suggest further hypotheses that could be tested, and draw theoretical conclusions.

References cited. If you have mentioned published sources in your report, you need to include a list of *references cited*. (See 33d2.)

33 d   Number systems: Documenting sources

The life sciences (biology, botany, zoology), the applied sciences (chemistry, computer science, mathematics, physics), and the medical sciences (medicine, nursing, general health) all use a number system of documentation.

1 Conventions for number citation

In the number system of citation, writers alert readers to the use of other sources by citing a number, either in parentheses or with a *superscript,* a character raised a small space above the baseline of the surrounding text: [2] (as you can see, superscript numbers are also typically reduced in size for a neater appearance). This citation number corresponds to a numbered list of sources at the end of the paper. Math and life science disciplines generally prefer parenthetical numbers; chemistry, physics, the medical fields, and computer science disciplines generally prefer superscript numbers.

If, in using the number system, you use an author's name in a sentence, place the number immediately after the name, if possible.

> Linhoffer (3) reported similar results.

> Linhoffer[3] reported similar results.

If no author's name is used in the sentence, place the number immediately after the use of the source material. Science writers using parenthetical numbers have the option of including the author's last name before the number: (*Smith 3*).

According to the conventions of scientific writing, the numbers cited in the text can be organized either sequentially or alphabetically. In *sequential arrangement,* the first source cited in the text is numbered *1,* the second cited source is numbered *2,* and so on. Any subsequent reference to an already cited source is given the same number. Sequential reference is preferred by writers in chemistry, computer science, physics, the life sciences, and medicine.

In *alphabetic arrangement,* writers assign numbers according to the alphabetical order of the authors' last names as they appear on the reference page(s). For example, a reference to an author named Smith, even if the first source cited in the text, should be accompanied by the number *12* if Smith is the twelfth name on the alphabetical list of references. Alphabetical arrangement is preferred in mathematical writing.

SCI SCI SCI SCI

When using the sequential system, number the bibliography sequentially as you write, and continue to use the same number each time you cite that authority. When using the alphabetical system, arrange your bibliography alphabetically and number accordingly.

2 Conventions for the list of references

The "Literature Cited" or "References" section provides publication information for all sources cited in the text.

Each scientific discipline has its own format for documenting sources; select the style appropriate to your discipline or consult your instructor. The following brief examples are illustrative only; they suggest that minor differences occur from discipline to discipline within scientific fields. Should you need to write a substantial paper in any of these disciplines, consult the appropriate reference source listed below.

Life sciences

Biology, botany, zoology, anatomy, and physiology follow the documentation system recommended in the *CBE Style Manual,* 6th ed. (New York: Cambridge University Press, 1994), published by the Council of Science Editors. CBE bases its standards for documentation on those presented in *National Library of Medicine Recommended Formats for Bibliographic Citation* (NLM 1991), available full text online at <http://www.nlm.nih.gov/pubs/formats/internet.pdf>.

In-text number citations are given sequentially in parentheses. Title the list of references "Literature Cited," "References Cited," or "References," and use the following general styles.

BOOK ENTRIES

1. Quammen, D. Natural acts: a sidelong view of science and nature. New York: Schocken Books; 1985. 221 p.

Book with more than one author

2. Martini FH, Timmons MJ, McKinley MP. Human anatomy, third edition. Upper Saddle River, NJ: Prentice Hall; 1999. 886 p.

Book with an editor

3. Roberts GG, editor. The Prentice Hall anthology of science fiction and fantasy. Upper Saddle River, NJ: Prentice Hall; 2001. 1184 p.

Do not underline titles, and capitalize only the first word. Place a semicolon after the name of the publisher, and place a colon after the date if page range numbers are given. Leave no space(s) on either side of the colon that follows the date.

PERIODICAL ENTRIES

4. Brown, SG; Wagsten, MV. Socialization processes in a female lowland gorilla. Zoo Biol 1986;5(12):269-80.

Newspaper article

5. Garfinkel P. Medical students get taste of real-life doctoring. New York Times 2001 Oct 23;Sect F:7(col 2).

Magazine article

6. Kinsley M. In defense of denial. Time 2001 Dec 17:72-3.

Do not place in quotation marks or underline article or journal titles. Use no space(s) between year, volume and page numbers, and place an issue number, if required, immediately after the volume number, in parentheses.

ELECTRONIC SOURCES

An online journal article

7. Alfred J. Fast fly maps at SNP. Nature reviews genetics [serial online] 2001 Dec. Available from: http://www.nature.com/cgitaf/DynaPage.taf?file=/nrg/journal/v2/n12/full/nrg1201-912b_fs.html. Accessed 2001 Dec 7.

An online book

8. Olson S. Shaping the future: biology and human values [book online].
Washington DC: National Academy Press; 1989. Available from:
http://www.nap.edu/books/0309039479/html. Accessed 2001 Dec 7.

Web site

9. Plant Conservation Unit. Smithsonian Institute. [Internet]. c1997 [revised
2005, Jan.]. Available from: http://www.nmnh.si.edu/botany/projects/pcu
.htm. Accessed 2005, June 12.

Include three dates, if available, in a Web site reference: (1) the date of publication or copyright; (2) the most recent revision (immediately after publication date [revised 2003, Jan.]); and (3) date of access at end of citation.

Email message

10. Weaver, G.T. Notice of meeting [electronic mail on the Internet]. Message to:
Mark Smith, 2005, June 1, 7:00 AM [cited 2005, June 2]. [two para].

Include author, subject line of message, the
words [electronic mail on the Internet],
Message to: addressee's name, date of message, length of message.

Chemistry

Documentation style in chemistry is
based on the American Chemical Society's
*The ACS Style Guide: A Manual for Authors
and Editors,* 2nd edition. Edited by Janet
S. Dodd (Washington, DC: American Chemical Society, 1997); online see http://pubs
.acs.org/books/references.shtml. In-text citations should be superscript numbers and
arranged either sequentially or by author
name and date. For entries on the reference
list, which should be titled "Literature
Cited," use the following general styles.

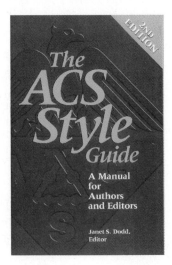

The ACS Style Guide

A Manual for Authors and Editors

Janet S. Dodd, Editor

BOOK ENTRIES

1. Siggia, S.; Hanna, J. G. Quantitative Organic Analysis via Functional Groups, 4th ed.; R. E. Krieger: Malabar, FL, 1988; pp. 55-60.

PERIODICAL ENTRIES

2. Scott, J. M. W. J. Chem. Ed. 1992(69)600-602.

For papers in the chemistry style, do not include article titles. If an issue number is required, place it immediately after the volume number (*69* in this example), in parentheses. Leave no spaces between date, volume, and page numbers for periodicals, and use all digits for page sequences.

Physics

Physics writing follows the style of the *AIP Style Manual,* 4th ed. (New York: American Institute of Physics, 1990–1997). The full text of the fourth edition can be downloaded free at http://www.aip.org/pubservs/style/4thed/toc.html.

Following this citation style, number in-text citations in sequence and in superscript. In the reference page, which is titled "References," use the following styles.

BOOK ENTRIES

[1] Pagels, H. R. Perfect Symmetry: The Search for the Beginning of Time (Bantam, New York, 1986), pp. 78-86.

PERIODICAL ENTRIES

[2] Crawford, F. S. Am. J. Phys. (60)751-752(1992).

In the physics system of citation, article titles are not included in the entries. If issue numbers are required, place them immediately after the volume number, in parentheses, and follow them with a comma. Place the date last, with single spaces between volume, page number(s), and date.

SCI SCI SCI

This chapter describes the aims, style, and common forms of writing in the business and professional world. Like writing in the social and physical sciences, business writing puts a premium on information; like writing in the humanities, it is highly influenced by the relation between writer and reader.

34 a Aims

The guiding objectives of successful companies are efficiency, accuracy, and responsibility. Procedures are designed for minimal waste of time and energy, care is taken to avoid errors, and transactions are conducted fairly.

Communication in business mirrors these precepts. Business writing is primarily practical and instrumental, because its goal is to get things done. For efficiency, it should be simple, direct, and brief; for accuracy, it should convey correct information and conform to standard conventions; and for responsibility, it should be honest and courteous.

Business writers must be aware of their audience. They must ask: To whom is the communication being written? What information do they already have? What else do they need to know? What does this communication need to include in order to have its intended effect? What, if any, secondary audience is likely to read this communication? Business writers must also be concerned about presentation. To make a good impression, any piece of writing must be neat, clean, and correct.

34 b   Style

Because clear communication is highly valued, writing for business purposes should be simple, direct, economical, and conventional. In general, the preferred tone is objective and fairly formal (although when addressing someone you know well, a more personal, informal tone may be appropriate).

Stylistic Guidelines for Business Writing

For most business writing, the following guidelines should be considered:

- **Start fast.** State the main point immediately, and avoid digression or repetition. In business, your reader's time—as well as your own—is valuable.
- **Write in a simple, direct style.** Keep your sentences as straightforward and readable as possible.
- **Choose the active voice** (*start fast*) rather than the passive voice (*fast starting is a principle to be followed*).
- **Use technical terminology or jargon sparingly.** Write out complete names of companies, products, and titles. Explain any terms that could be misunderstood.
- **Avoid emotional or biased language** (sexist, racist) as well as stereotypes and clichés. Try to maintain a level of courtesy even when lodging a complaint.
- **Use numbers, bullets, or descriptive headings** to help readers locate information quickly.
- **Use graphs, charts, and other illustrations** when they convey information more clearly than verbal language.

34 c   Common forms of writing in business

1 Memos

Memo is short for *memorandum,* meaning literally "a thing to be remembered." A memo is a note written to make a request, pass along information, or help either the sender or recipient remember something. Memos are less formal than business letters, partly because they are often sent between people who know one another and work together, usually in the same company. If you're writing to a stranger, a letter is more appropriate.

Format for Memos

June 8, 2005

1" margins ———————

Subject: or Re:
(regarding) ———————
no salutation ———————

block paragraph
style ———————

very direct ———————

no closing———————

From: Isabel Barahona
To: Design team
cc: Management group
Subject: Commendation

Everyone on the design staff made a terrific effort last week to put the finishing touches on the Rialto project. Janet, Kazuo, Sandy, and Jack, it's always a pleasure to make a presentation based on your work and to see its impact on customers. Thanks for going the extra mile under such a tight deadline.

E-mail within an organization often follows memo style in its directness and informality. (See 18b.)

2 Business letters

Tone is crucial. Thinking about what you're trying to say (purpose) and to whom (audience), helps you set an appropriate tone. Notice how tone changes as your *purpose* changes:

- *Inquiring*—seeking information about a job opportunity or a product. "Can you tell me whether your company makes a mower that meets these specifications?"

- *Promoting*—providing information about a product or service and encouraging the reader to purchase it. "The Neighbor Kids lawn service will have your yard looking neat and trim on the very first visit. To schedule, call 555-5555."

- *Communicating*—transmitting the results of a decision or an information-gathering process. "I'm pleased to inform you that your company is the apparent low bidder. Please call my office so we can complete a contract."

- *Confirming*—documenting terms agreed to elsewhere. "As we discussed over lunch, I will work with you to identify suitable investment properties. My consulting rate is $120 per hour plus travel expenses. I look forward to being of assistance."

- *Complaining*—specifying a problem, documenting it, and requesting a solution. "Although you billed me for twelve ink cartridges, I received only six. I enclose copies of my order and your packing slip. Please forward the remaining items immediately or refund the balance."

- *Relating*—maintaining lines of communication. "I enjoyed visiting with you at the convention and look forward to doing business with you."

Your tone will also change depending if you're writing to a stranger, a business acquaintance, or someone with whom you have an established working relationship. Your relationship to your *audience* and how you want to present yourself and your company help determine your writing approach.

New contact: When making an initial contact by letter, identify yourself right away, then state your purpose. If you can identify yourself by referring to a mutual acquaintance or shared experience, so much the better.

Dear Mr. Zenkov,

My name is Rob Cirul. My partner Chris Adams and I operate the Neighbor Kids Lawn Care service. I live at 234 Hollow Hills Lane, and your neighbor Ellen Jones is one of our regular customers.

Format for Business Letter

Heading with business address and contact information. Can also appear below signature line. ———

Neighbor Kids Lawn Care
234 Hollow Hills Lane
Hamilton, OH 45014
(513) 555-5555
OhioYardboys@aol.com

1" margins, block paragraphs ———

March 18, 2005

inside address ———

Yvelisse da Silva
2352 Sixteenth Street
Hamilton, OH 45014

Salutation. Note colon. ———

Dear Ms. da Silva:

Identify yourself, relationship to addressee, and purpose of letter.

I am Rob Cirul, one of the partners in Neighbor Kids lawn care service.

You and I met at the Highland Garden Center last week and talked about

yard work.

In body of letter, inquire, confirm, inform, or persuade.

My partners, Cal Ortiz and Jillian Wong, and I have been mowing lawns

and doing yard cleanup for three seasons, and we would be happy to

have you as a customer. Our rates are reasonable, and we have more than

a dozen repeat customers in the neighborhood who have been happy

with our work.

Summarize, and ask for the action you seek.

We will be working on your block this weekend. I'll stop by to talk with

you, or you can reach me at 555-5555. We hope to be able to work for

you.

Signature ———

Sincerely yours,

Rob Cirul

Rob Cirul

Established relationship: A letter to an established customer can be more familiar, but keep the tone appropriate to business communication.

> Dear Mr. Clark,
>
> It's hard to imagine spring is just around the corner, but I see your daffodils budding and know that I'll soon be mowing lawns again. I'm writing to confirm that you'll want your regular Friday afternoon lawn spot in the schedule.

Form

Think of a business letter as a brief essay, with an opening, supporting detail, and a conclusion. First, identify yourself and your relationship to the recipient, and state your business purpose. Next, detail your proposal or request. Then summarize your case and request or specify the next action to be taken.

3 Resumés

A *resumé* is a brief summary of an applicant's qualifications for employment. It outlines education, work experience, and other activities and interests so a prospective employer can decide quickly whether or not an applicant is a good prospect for a particular job. Try to tailor your resumé for the position you are seeking by emphasizing experience that is most relevant to the position. Preparing a resumé on a computer lets you revise it easily and quickly.

Generally, a resumé is sent out with a *cover letter* that introduces the applicant, indicates the position applied for, and offers additional information that cannot be accommodated on the resumé itself. Print out your resumé and cover letter on good-quality $8\frac{1}{2}'' \times 11''$ stationery. Even if you fax these documents to prospective employers, you should have attractive copies to take with you on interviews. Examples of a resumé and cover letter appear in 59c1.

Resumés should be brief and to the point, preferably no more than a page long (if relevant experience is extensive, more than one page is acceptable). Resumé formats vary in minor ways, but most include the following information:

Personal information. Resumés begin with the applicant's name, address, and phone number, usually centered at the top.

Objective. Many resumés include a line summarizing the applicant's objective, either naming the specific job sought or describing a larger career goal.

Education. Most first-time job applicants list their educational background first, since their employment history is likely to be fairly limited. Name the last two or three schools attended (including dates of attendance and degrees), starting with the most recent. Indicate major areas of study, and highlight any relevant courses. Also consider including grade point average, awards, and anything else that shows you in a good light. When employment history is more detailed, educational background is often placed at the end of the resumé.

Work experience. Starting with the most recent, list all relevant jobs, including company name, dates of employment, and a brief job description. If you are applying for your first full-time job, listing summer jobs, work-study programs, and similar employment, even in a different industry, will show prospective employers that you have some work experience. Unpaid volunteer work may also be relevant. Use your judgment about listing jobs where you had difficulties with your employer.

Special skills or interests. It is often useful to mention special skills, interests, or activities that provide additional clues about your abilities and personality.

References. The line *References available on request* indicates that you have obtained permission from two or three people—teachers, supervisors, employers—for prospective employers to contact them for a recommendation. To avoid embarrassment, select people who are likely to speak well of you, and secure their permission well in advance of your job search. Listing references on your resumé is acceptable but is not recommended. Most employers include a place to list references on their application form, and some have specific requirements such as listing only people who know you through previous work experience or not using relatives as references.

Following are two sample resumés that contain essentially the same information. However, the **traditional resumé** emphasizes employment history, listing information in approximately the order outlined above, and would be appropriate for applying to any position. The **skills-based resumé** emphasizes capabilities more than past experience and would be advantageous for a candidate with wide, varied, or extensive skills that might be of special interest to a particular employer.

Chris Aleandro
405 Martin Street
Lexington, Kentucky 40508
(606) 555-4033

Objective: Internship in arts administration.

Education

University of Kentucky: 1998 to present.

> Currently a sophomore majoring in business administration with a minor in art history. Degree expected May 2003.

Henry Clay High School (Lexington, KY.): 1995 to 1998.

> College preparatory curriculum, with emphasis in art and music.

Related Work Experience

Community Concerts, Inc.: 1998 to present.

> Part-time promotion assistant, reporting to local director. Responsibilities include assisting with scheduling, publicity, subscription/ticketing procedures, and fund-raising. Position involves general office duties as well as heavy contact with subscribers and artists.

Habitat for Humanity: September to November 1998.

> Co-chaired campus fund-raising drive that included a benefit concert, raising $55,000.

Art in the Schools Program: 1998–1999.

> Volunteer, through the Education Division of the Lexington Center for the Arts. Trained to conduct hands-on art appreciation presentations in grade school classrooms, visiting one school a month.

Other Work Experience

Record City: 1995 to 1998 (part-time and summers).

> Salesclerk and assistant manager in a music store.

Special skills: WordPerfect 5.1: desktop design of brochures, programs, and other materials.

References: available on request.

Traditional Resumé

Susan Anderson

CURRENT ADDRESS   222 Summit Street, Burlington, VT 05401
TELEPHONE AND E-MAIL   (802) 864-XXXX;
susan.anderson@XXX.XXX

OBJECTIVE: Researcher/writer for nonprofit environmental organization.

EDUCATION

> **University of Vermont.** School of Natural Resources, Geology
> and English double major. GPA: 3.6. Expected graduation,
> May 2004.

> **Fairfield High School.** Fairfield, OH. 1996–2000. Activities
> included debate team, Spanish club, student newspaper,
> field hockey, swimming.

SKILLS

> **Field research.** Extensive experience analyzing natural plant
> communities, quantifying data, surveying field sites, and
> drawing topographical site maps.

> **Newsletter publication.** Familiar with all aspects of editorial and
> feature writing, layout, production, and fund raising for
> nonprofit newsletters.

> **Computer literacy.** Fluent in *MS Word, Excel, PowerPoint, Adobe
> Premier, Sigmaplot, INFORM, Quark Xpress.*

> **Oral communication.** Confident public speaker to large and small
> audiences after three years on the university debate team.

> **Spanish.** Fluent after four years of secondary and college study,
> including AFS summer abroad in Quito, Ecuador.

RELEVANT ENVIROMENTAL COURSEWORK

> Field Ecology Methods
> Landscape and Ecosystem Ecology
> Fundamentals of Field Science
> Landscape Inventory and Assessment

RESEARCH EXPERIENCE

Southwest Earth Studies, June–August 2003. Internship to research public policy of acid mine drainage in the San Juan mountains, National Science Foundation.

Field Research of the Newark Rift Basin, June 2002. Internship to study water flow in the Newark rift basin, Newark Environmental Foundation program.

COMMUNICATION EXPERIENCE

Teaching Fellow, School of Natural Resources, University of Vermont, January 2003–present. Teach lab for a course, Environmental Problem Solving.

Editorial Assistant, *Wild Gulf Journal,* The Chewonki Foundation, January 2002–December 2003. Edited a quarterly journal of environmental education.

Tutor, Writing Center, University of Vermont, September 2001–December 2002. Counseled students in writing undergraduate papers in introductory and intermediate geology courses.

LEADERSHIP EXPERIENCE

English Majors' Student Representative, University of Vermont, September 2001–May 2002. Elected to represent 200 English majors and participate as a voting member at faculty meetings and curriculum revision committee.

Local Foods Coordinator, Onion River Coop. Burlington, VT. January 1999–May 2000. Ordered and coordinated pick-ups from local farms.

REFERENCES: Available upon request.

Skills-Based Resumé

34 d Documentation and format conventions

The format and style of documentation for business reports usually follow the guidelines of the American Psychological Association (APA). (See 31e.)

PART eight

Editing

Editing Section

Editing for Effectiveness

chapter 35

The Editing Process

As you plan, draft, and revise, you focus primarily on your **purpose**—on what you are trying to say. As you begin to edit, your focus shifts subtly to anticipating how your **audience**—your readers—will understand you.

Imagine reading your work for the first time. Think about your intended readers: What do they already know about your subject? Which new ideas will you need to explain? If you are presenting an argument, will readers be sympathetic or skeptical?

Such anticipation—call it seeing with the eyes of the reader—can help you identify places where you haven't made your ideas clear, where readers may misunderstand, or where they are likely to raise the toughest questions.

There are three crucial steps in the process of editing:

1. **Identify potential problems.** Do this by asking yourself repeatedly, "Will readers understand this as I intend?"

2. **Generate alternatives.** Rewrite the passage in question, perhaps more than one way, to improve understanding.

3. **Choose.** In light of your purpose and what you know about your audience, which alternative is best?

To edit well, you need a working knowledge of the conventions or standards of written English and the skill to apply those conventions according to your purpose, audience, and situation. Beyond following convention comes *polishing*—refining your writing to make paragraphs, sentences, and individual words communicate with clarity, style, and grace.

For your writing to be effective, your ideas need to come across with power and persuasiveness—and few wasted words. Strive for *clarity,* to make your purpose readily apparent. Set a *tone* appropriate for the subject, the audience, and your relation to that audience. Finally, edit for *grace*—a sense that the text is not only clear but enjoyable, moving, even memorable.

Seeing with the "Eyes of the Reader"

Anticipating readers' reactions is a primary editing skill. Here's how to develop it.

- **Budget time for editing.** Leave as much time for editing as you planned for drafting or revising.
- **Step back.** Take a break before beginning to edit.
- **Print a draft copy.** Moving from the computer screen to paper freshens your vision.
- **Work from large scale to small.** Read quickly from start to finish to see whether the paper achieves the goals you set out at its beginning. Are the opening and conclusion effective? Does the argument flow clearly? Does any element seem unexpected or jarring? Does the evidence support your claims? Make notes, but don't stop to make changes. Try to get a clear overview.
- **Act on your findings.** Return to the computer. For each problem, generate alternative solutions, and choose among them.
- **Print a copy and read again.** This time, look for points to emphasize, word choices to improve, and transitions to smooth. Again, make notes, then implement your changes in the computer file.
- **Repeat, reading aloud.** Print another copy of your paper and read it aloud, listening and looking for errors of grammar, punctuation, and spelling. Read all the way through, making notes; then make corrections on the screen.

If you practice editing in this pattern, you'll become more skillful at recognizing problems and at solving them. As your skills grow, you'll be able to work more easily on large-scale and small-scale questions at the same time, but the ability to focus on different areas will remain valuable.

Here's one more tip:

- **Exchange drafts with a trusted partner or with a writing group.** Notice how easy it is to get a large-scale overview, how sharply strong and weak passages stand out when you're reading something for the first time. When you edit your own work, try to place yourself in that first-reading frame of mind.

Most writers edit by attacking paragraph structure, grammar, and punctuation all at once, but to simplify discussion, we focus on one issue at a time. We have divided editing into four broad areas: effectiveness, grammar, punctuation, and mechanics.

35 a   Editing techniques

This section outlines some major editing techniques to sharpen your writing. Each technique is cross-referenced to a subsequent chapter or section for more information.

1 Editing for unity

Edit paragraphs so that each advances and amplifies one idea. Make sure each sentence illustrates the main idea in some logical way. For example, Issa discovered when writing his essay "On the Trail" (see Chapter 10) that the following paragraph would be better unified if he edited out the third sentence, which diverges into a different topic:

> **When mountain bikes first came on the scene, hikers and environmentalists convinced state and local officials to ban the bikes from wilderness trails (Buchanan 81; Kelly 104). . . . These trail closings have separated the outdoor community into the hikers and the bikers.** *Each group is well organized, and each group believes it is right.* **Is any resolution in sight?**

To test this choice, the writer read the paragraph through with and without the sentence in question and decided which was more effective. (See Chapter 36.)

2 Editing to grab readers' attention

Your opening paragraph needs to make readers want to continue. There is no one way to structure a good opening. Sometimes a colorful quotation or a surprising statistic works well. At other times a clear thesis or a provocative question is needed. In the narrative example below, an internal monologue reveals the author's vulnerability in the middle of a championship tennis match:

> Bounce. Bounce. Bounce. The sound is driving me insane, but I just can't get the nerve to toss up the ball and serve. Am I scared? Yes. Of what, this girl or this match? This girl—this girl scares me. She's a natural talent. How many times is that crosscourt forehand shot going to rip past me? Well, if I'm going to lose, let's get on with it.

(See Chapter 37.)

3 Editing for rhythm

Readers notice sentences that please the ear. For example, parallel constructions create rhythms that reinforce a comparison or contrast. Note the several kinds of parallel constructions used in these sentences from "On the Trail":

Educated mountain biking, like ~~other environmental pursuits,~~ *hiking and horseback riding,* *respects the environment* **and** *promotes peace and conservation,* **not** *noise and destruction.* **Making this case has begun to pay off, and the battle over** *who walks* **and** *who rides* **the trails should now shift in favor of peaceful coexistence.**

Other environmental pursuits was accurate, but altering the phrase to make it parallel to the first idea made the passage more rhythmic. (See Chapter 38.)

4 Editing for emphasis

In an essay, a paragraph, or a sentence, the most emphatic place is usually at the end. To end-weight a sentence, place less-essential information early; then end with the idea you want your reader to remember. For example, if we wrote the second sentence of this paragraph with the most important information first, it would read this way: "*The most emphatic place is usually at the end of a whole essay, a paragraph, or a sentence, for example.*" Our point has nearly vanished. (See Chapter 39.)

5 Editing for variety

Varying sentence structures often makes paragraphs clearer and more enjoyable. In the following example from her essay in 8g, Judith uses a variety of sentence lengths. She also varies sentence types.

> It is already afternoon. I fiddle with the key to lock the apartment door after me. I am not accustomed to locking doors. Except for the six months I spent in Boston, I have never lived in a place where I did not trust my neighbors. When I was little, we couldn't lock our farmhouse door; the wood had swollen and the bolt no longer lined up properly with the hole, and nobody ever bothered to fix it.

(See Chapter 39.)

6 Editing for specific details

In the following paragraph, Betsy describes members of a ballet rehearsal. By using a variety of specific nouns and adjectives, she helps us see her subjects:

> Dancers are scattered around the room, *stretching, chatting, adjusting shoes and tights.* Company members, the professionals who are joining us for this performance, wear *tattered gray legwarmers, sweatpants that have lost their elastic, and old faded T-shirts* over mismatched *tights and baggy* leotards. Their hair is *knotted into buns* or, in the case of male dancers, *held tight with sweatbands.* You can tell the students by the *runless pink tights, dress-code leotards, and immaculate hair.*

Specific nouns and adjectives create vivid and lively images—*"tattered gray legwarmers," "baggy leotards,"* and *"runless pink tights"*—that would be lost with a more general description: *"Dancers are scattered around the room, adults and students, each group dressed differently."* (See Chapter 40.)

7 Editing for dynamic verbs

Dynamic verbs show the subject of a sentence doing something: *walk, stride, jump, fly, sing, sail, stop, hear, believe, doubt, stumble,* or *fumble.* In contrast, **state-of-being** verbs show the subject of a sentence in a state of being, existing rather than acting: *be, appear, become, seem,* or *exist.* Look for dynamic verbs to make writing more vital and hold readers' attention.

                swirls turbulently
The water is turbulent between the rocks.
                        ^

The concluding paragraph of Judith's essay "Writing in Safety" (see 8g) uses dynamic verbs effectively (italics added):

> Hours later—my paper *started,* my exam *studied* for, my eyes *tired*—I *retrace* the path to my apartment. It is dark now, and I *listen* closely when I *hear* footsteps behind, *stepping* to the sidewalk's edge to let a man *walk* briskly past. At my door, I again *fumble* for the now familiar key, *insert* it in the lock, *open* the door, *turn* on the hall light, and *step* inside. Here, too, I am safe, ready to *eat, read* a bit, and *finish* my reflective essay.

Judith's two state-of-being verbs—*is* and *am*—provide a quiet contrast to the otherwise active paragraph. (See Chapter 40.)

8 Editing for conciseness

Delete words that do not add meaning, rhythm, or emphasis. Look at these sentences, each of which says essentially the same thing:

> In almost every situation that I can think of, with few exceptions, it will make good sense for you to look for as many places as possible to cut out needless, redundant, and repetitive words from the papers and reports, paragraphs and sentences you write for college assignments. [48 words]

> In most situations it makes sense to cut unneeded words from your college papers. [14 words]

> Whenever possible, omit unneeded words from your writing. [8 words]

> Omit unneeded words. [3 words]

(See Chapter 41.)

9   Editing for tone

Your **tone** reveals your attitude toward your subject and audience: whether you are distant or closely involved, neutral or partisan, dispassionate or emotional. To choose an appropriate tone, think of your purpose and imagine your audience: For whom are you writing? What effect do you want to create? For example, look again at the four sentences listed in 35a8 and notice how the tone increases in confidence and authority as you move from the tentative first version (*"In almost every situation that I can think of"*), through the gentle suggestion of the second (*"In most situations"*), to the stronger direction of the third (*"Whenever possible"*), to the command of the fourth (*"Omit"*). (See Chapter 42.)

10   Editing to control bias

Using ethnic, racial, national, gender, or sex-preference stereotypes in your writing will make you appear **biased.** For example, using the word *man* or *men* to stand for *human beings* or *people* is considered sexist because such terms ignore half of the population. Reliance on a stereotype to describe an individual also invites accusations of bias. (See Chapter 44.)

11   Editing for grammar

Your audience for academic writing—instructors and fellow students—places a high value on **grammatical correctness** and the conventional use of language. Errors in sentence structure, verb agreement, or modifier placement will undermine your credibility and distract readers from your ideas. Sharpening your working knowledge of grammar will help you write better and keep you from writing nonsensical sentences such as this one:

In a study of
~~Studying~~ the effects of cigarette smoking, monkeys smoked the
equivalent of dozens of cigarettes a day.

The monkeys were not conducting the study. This first part of the sentence is a dangling modifier.

(See "Grammar," Chapters 45–50.)

ESL *The Language of Gender Bias*

Languages vary in their conventions for indicating gender, so recognizing gender bias in English can be a challenge for speakers of other languages. For example, the expression *man and wife* is considered biased because the term *wife* identifies the woman by her relationship to the man, but the word *man* does not refer to the relationship. Using parallel words, either *man and woman or husband and wife,* eliminates the gender bias.

When you are revising a paper, ask a native English speaker in your writing group or another trusted advisor to help you identify possible examples of gender-biased language in your writing.

12 Editing for punctuation

Correct **punctuation** also marks you as a skilled writer. Using commas, periods, quotation marks, and other punctuation carefully will give you a familiarity with the rules so you will spot errors like this one:

The Justice Department has expanded its investigation of Medicare fraud, and has launched several grand jury inquiries.

No comma is needed between parts of a compound predicate; the basic elements of the predicate in this sentence are expanded . . . and . . . launched.

(See "Punctuation," Chapters 51–57.)

13 Editing mechanics

The term **mechanics** refers to questions that arise in presenting your finished writing, on paper or in electronic form. You must choose an appropriate and readable format. You must spell correctly, capitalize, abbreviate, and italicize according to standard practice. The last editing act is **proofreading**—reading to make sure your manuscript is correct in every way. Good proofreading requires reading line by line, word by word, and letter by letter. (See "Mechanics," Chapters 58–62.)

35 b   The meaning of "error"

Getting facts wrong—identifying the North Star as Sirius rather than Polaris, for example—can destroy a reader's confidence in you. Readers also judge your reliability by your command of written language: mastery of the language implies mastery of the subject.

More importantly, writing problems can make it hard for a reader to understand you. The reader's only way of interpreting the words on a page is a knowledge of how those words have been used in the past. Every departure from **convention**—the way words are customarily used—presents a challenge to the reader. If that challenge proves too formidable, all but the most dedicated reader will turn away from reading in favor of, say, taking a nap.

Some conventions are so widely accepted that they are regarded as **rules,** and departures from them are considered **errors.** These rules do not result from any one person or committee deciding what ought to be right and issuing edicts accordingly. On the contrary, the rules are based on many writers' and grammarians' descriptions of how English has been written and spoken in the past. Other conventions are more flexible. However, if you stretch the boundaries of what readers expect, you risk being misunderstood or losing their attention.

EDITING 1: EXPLORATION ....

Look at the comments and corrections on a paper handed back to you by your instructor. Which comments concern rules, and which concern conventions? How could the changes suggested improve communication? For what other reasons might your instructor have made the comments? If you cannot understand the proposed changes, discuss them with your instructor.

....

35 c   Working with others

1 Editing someone else's work

When you edit someone else's writing, make constructive suggestions that the writer can act on, not judgments that will leave the writer feeling attacked. The most effective editing relationship relies not on one person's authority but on cooperative efforts between writer and editor.

Read critically, trying to understand what the writer is attempting to do. Be alert to places where you as a reader have difficulty. Comment on the ways in which he or she has succeeded. Identifying strengths helps the writer build on them. Then discuss the things you think the writer needs to clarify or correct. (See Chapter 16.)

2 Accepting editorial advice

Everyone has had the painful experience of having a paper returned with curt corrections in red ink. But being edited by others is a fact of life. In college, other students as well as teachers may comment on your writing. If you write for publication or at a job, staff editors or supervisors will edit your work. As a writer, you should accept comments with an open mind. Focus on how other people's reactions and verbal or written responses show what is working and not working in your writing. Adopt the suggestions you agree with and discuss the ones you don't. No matter how tactlessly or brusquely an editor communicates with you, remember that the comments are about a particular draft—not about all the writing you've ever done and certainly not about you yourself. Respond objectively and not defensively. Adopting a professional attitude will facilitate your interactions with those editing your work.

EDITING 2: EXPLORATION

Think of the teacher who has helped you most with your writing. How did he or she express comments and suggestions about your work? How did you respond? Can you also recall comments or corrections that hurt your feelings? What was the impact on your writing? Were you able to distinguish between the meaning of the comments and their effect on you? How?

35 d   Editing on a computer

If you're not already in the habit of drafting on a computer, your next paper is a good time to start. Many of the techniques for inventing and discovering discussed in Chapter 7 can be used in a word-processing program. Freewriting and looping particularly lend themselves to a computer because, for most people, a keyboard is faster than a pencil and paper. A list of concepts or a cluster diagram can easily be turned into an outline using a word processor.

The editing step of generating alternatives (see 35a) also is easier on a computer. You can make several copies of a troublesome paragraph, try out various editing moves, and choose the one that works best.

For example, that last paragraph went through several versions:

DRAFT 1   Generating alternatives for editing also becomes easier on a computer. You can copy a passage several times, change each one in different ways, and choose the best one.

FIRST REVISION   Generating alternatives while editing (see 35a) becomes easier on a computer. You can make several copies of a paragraph, change each one in different ways, and choose the one that works best.

If you create a new file for each major revision and editing step, you'll have a record of your own writing process. After you finish a project, tracing your steps can provide insight into how you work and what works best for you.

Using Computer Editing Tools

Many word-processing programs include a spell-checker, a dictionary, a thesaurus, and sometimes a grammar-checking program. Take advantage of these features, but use them with care.

▪ Some writers don't like to be bothered while they're drafting, so they turn off spell checking. If you're one of these, be sure to run a spell-check when you're editing.

▪ Beware of relying entirely on spell-checkers. *Two, to,* and *too* are spelled correctly, as are *there, their,* and *they're*. A spell-checker won't notice if you've used the wrong one of these or any of the troublesome pairs listed in 58a or in Chapter 64, "Glossary of Usage."

▪ Rely even more cautiously on grammar-checkers. Few of them can correctly anticipate all possible sentence structures. A warning from a grammar-checker is reason to make sure you know what is right. If you don't know why a computer program is suggesting a change, figure out its reasoning before accepting the suggestion.

EDITING 3: APPLICATION ....

Explore the use of computers as writing tools. Ask about the word-processing habits of your classmates. Do any of their methods have advantages over yours? What are their favorite editing strategies and techniques?

35   e   Proofreading

When you **proofread,** you check for errors. The key to proofreading is to see what is *actually* on the page rather than what you *intended* to put there. Somehow you must look with fresh eyes at words you have already read several times. Plan to proofread twice: once on the final, edited draft from which you prepare your final manuscript, and once on the final manuscript itself.

Proofread to correct punctuation and typographical errors, but of course fix any others you find as well. Listing errors in your journal can help you avoid them in the future. Here are some useful techniques to help you proofread:

▪ **Proofread on hard copy.** If you have been composing on a computer, proofread on a printout. You will be surprised how many errors or awkward passages leap out at you from the printed page.

▪ **Read your paper aloud.** One test of good writing is whether it sounds clear and natural when read aloud. Reading aloud is also an effective way to find dropped words, misspellings, and punctuation errors.

▪ **Ask someone else to read your paper.** You can get a pair of fresh eyes by borrowing someone else's. Ask a friend to proofread for errors, omissions, or passages that seem unclear. Have your friend read your work aloud, and listen for awkward wordings and usage problems.

▪ **Read backward.** In proofreading for spelling, read the manuscript one word at a time. In practice, this is hard to do, since most people read at the level of phrases and sentences. Try reading backward, starting at the last word and proceeding to the first. Some writers use a ruler to focus on one line at a time: other writers use a pencil to point out each word.

▪ **Use your computer's spell-checker.** A computer's spell-checking function will never make the mistake of seeing what it expects to see instead of what is there. However, be aware that it can tell you only when you have misspelled a word, not when you have used the wrong word (such as *their* for *there*) or left one out. Most spell-checkers point out repeated words, but you must reread the sentence to determine whether the repetition is an error. (See Chapter 58 for more on spelling and using a spell-checker.)

▪ **Make corrections.** To indicate corrections on a manuscript, use standard proofreading and editing marks. (See the inside back cover.) These standard notations will be easy to understand if someone else is entering them in a computer file. It is acceptable to make a minor correction on a final typescript, but reprinting a page is easy and looks better. Be sure the replacement page begins and ends with the same words as the original.

ESL Strategies for Proofreading

In addition to the suggestions given in this section for effective proofreading, you may need to read your paper very carefully to check for common grammatical errors and incorrect word forms.

- Plan to read your paper several times to look for grammatical errors.

- Make a list of any frequent errors you are aware of. For example, you may consistently leave the final -s off plural nouns. Or you may use a verb tense that is not appropriate for the context. If you are not sure of your frequent errors, ask your instructor or tutor to help you create a list of them.

- Read your paper through once for each of these error types. In other words, concentrate on only one error type at a time. At first this process will be slow, but gradually your proofreading skills will improve; you will be able to proofread faster and to check more items at one time.

- You could also make a list of words that you frequently misspell. When you proofread for spelling, refer to your list and pay special attention to such words.

EDITING 4: PRACTICE ....

Proofread the following passage, correcting all errors in spelling, grammar, punctuation, and mechanics. Use standard proofreading marks.

Marian Anderson, who died in 1993 was the first black opera singer to preform at the Metropoliton Opera 1955 and became an inspiracion to generations of black performers throughout the U.S. Yet she was not able to make a name for herself in her own county until late in her life because of raical discrimmination. Althrough her grate talent was recognised early in her life (she won a voice contest in New York in 1925,) she could not get any rolls in opera, and her carrer was going nowhere. In the 1930s, Anderson decided to go to Europe to perform, and she quicky became an international singing star. When she returned to the U.S. and was invited to sing in Washington, DC, the D.A.R. (Daughters of the American Revolution) denied her acess to Constitution Hall, it's national headquarters. Eleanor Roosvelt (along with several other women) resined from the D.A.R. over this disgracefull incident, and she aranged for Anderson to perform outside at the Lincoln Memorial. 75,000 people came to hear Anderson sing, and her peformence in front of Lincolns statute became a powerful cymbal of the civil right's movement.

35 f   Editing when English is your second language

Editing in English can be challenging for people who grew up speaking another language because they have had less time to develop an ear for what "sounds right"—something native speakers often rely on. Certain aspects of English are often confusing to nonnative speakers and writers, such as the sequence of verb tenses used to illustrate the time at which events occurred:

By the time the sun *sets* tomorrow, I *will have been walking* for fifteen days.

The first part of the sentence uses the present tense to describe an action in the future; the second part describes an action that began in the past and will continue into the future but will be finished by the time indicated in the first part (sunset tomorrow).

In seemingly arbitrary ways, adjectives and articles (*the, a, an*)—or their absence—convey significant information about the nouns they precede:

ONE BOOK	*A book* is missing from the library.
AN INDEFINITE NUMBER	*Books* are missing.
ALL OF THE IDENTIFIED BOOKS	*The books* are missing.
NOT ALL OF THE BOOKS	*Some books* are missing.
ONE OF SEVERAL	*A biology book* is missing.
THE ONLY ONE OF ITS KIND	*The biology book* is missing.

To edit for issues of this kind, read your work aloud, and have someone else read it to you. You will hear things you didn't catch on the page. More generally, work to improve your English-language skills in general. The best way to gain command of the language is by reading widely, listening and observing how language is used, and examining your own English to see how it resembles or differs from standard usage. Of course, this advice applies to all of us, native and nonnative speakers alike.

ESL   *Editing Other Students' Writing*

As a nonnative speaker of English, you might question your ability to edit your classmates' writing. Keep in mind, however, that you probably know a lot about what makes a piece of writing readable and effective. You are a part of the audience a classmate wants to reach. If something is unfamiliar or unclear to you, that information may be valuable to the writer. You can offer helpful feedback about clarity of purpose, variety of sentence structure, words or phrases that seem unnecessary, and many other elements of an essay that are discussed in this chapter.

35 g   Using Part Eight

Many college instructors use a handbook like this one to show students how to make their writing stronger. Teachers reading dozens of student papers weekly will usually focus their written comments on large-scale issues, such as organization, logic, and the development of ideas. Rather than correct grammatical errors in detail, many instructors simply mark passages and refer students to the appropriate sections of the handbook for help.

What I liked most was⁄ the opportunity to explore different kinds

of writing.   No comma between verb and complement.
       See commas, 52j.

This instructor suggests that the student refer to 52j to review the use of commas, in particular the rule that a single comma should not separate a verb from a complement. Your instructor may also simply use a proofreading mark or correction symbol:

Every doctor has <u>their</u> own way of working.   agr

Proofreading marks and correction symbols are widely used and largely standardized. The symbol *agr* here stands for agreement between a pronoun (*their*) and its antecedent (*doctor*). To see what a symbol means, look it up in the chart on the inside back cover of this book; the chart will refer you to a relevant section of the book. Standard proofreading marks are listed on the inside back cover.

EDITING 5: APPLICATION ....

Select two or three comments that were marked on the last draft of a paper handed back to you by your instructor. Use the index or table of contents of *The Blair Handbook* to find out where the handbook addresses these issues, and then read those sections. Were the issues matters of effectiveness, of grammar, of punctuation, or of mechanics? What have you learned that you didn't know before? Use the editing advice in *The Blair Handbook* to edit the relevant sentences and correct any problems.

....

Paragraphs are the organizing units of writing, showing which ideas go together and how they relate to each other. Good paragraphing gives readers clues. When a new paragraph begins, readers expect a new step in the development of your ideas.

Readers expect each sentence within a paragraph to develop a single main idea—that the paragraph will be **unified.** They expect the paragraph to present its ideas in a clearly perceptible order—that it will be well **organized.** And they expect each succeeding sentence to relate to what came before, advancing the central point—that the paragraph will be **coherent.**

36 a Unity

In most college writing, each paragraph directly states a central idea, or topic, which is usually made explicit in a topic sentence. Sometimes a paragraph's topic can be communicated more subtly: readers may be able to infer a topic from a series of related sentences that do not include an explicit topic sentence.

In either case, a paragraph should contain only one main idea. Elements that do not support or clarify this idea should be eliminated. You can simply delete stray words or sentences; you can move them to another paragraph, or you can create a new paragraph where they will be more effective.

In a passage about minimizing the effect of divorce on children, Amy identified the first sentence as the topic sentence: *For various reasons, some unhappy couples remain married.* When she read each of the other sentences carefully to see whether they described reasons for staying married, she realized that the fourth sentence was out of place. She decided to move this sentence to the next paragraph, which dealt with a new topic.

> **For various reasons, some unhappy couples remain married. Some are forbidden to divorce by religion, others by social custom. Still others stay together "for the sake of the children." In recent years, psychologists and sociologists have studied families to determine whether more harm is done to children by divorce or by parents who stay together despite conflict.** ~~But by staying together, such parents feel~~ *believing* **they are sparing their children the pain of divorce.**
>
> **In his study of family conflict, Robert S. Weiss found that children in such families were often happiest "when Daddy is at work" . . .**

EDITING 1: PRACTICE

A.   The following paragraph, part of an information manual for new employees at a college radio station, discusses gifts and promotions. With this audience in mind, edit the paragraph to improve unity.

> College radio stations do not receive lavish gifts, but they are not neglected in the grand sweep of promotions that back college-targeted records. This station has received everything from posters to gold records to bottles of liquor. Whether the promotions actually get the records played is hard to document at college radio stations, and ours is no exception. The most common gifts are passes to performances and free copies of records.

B.   This paragraph is from an editorial that explains to local citizens the workings of the city planning board. With this audience in mind, edit the paragraph to improve unity.

> The idea of planning seems simple enough. Communities are asked to designate areas for specific purposes, such as commercial, residential, or industrial use. The state's new requirement that every city and township formulate a plan may create a shortage of planners. People take city planning very seriously. Sometimes such an innocuous topic as zoning leads to turmoil—for instance, when one group wants to open

a restaurant in what others consider a residential zone. Trying to pin-point exactly what a planner does is a little more complicated.

Select a paragraph from a paper you are working on. As you reread the paragraph, ask yourself these questions: (1) What is my topic sentence? and (2) How does this paragraph fit into my paper? If any sentences do not contribute to the main idea of the paragraph, try omitting or moving them. Eliminate any other elements that detract from the main point. If you find that some of your ideas need elaboration, write additional sentences with the above questions in mind.

How does your edited paragraph compare with the original? Does it advance your purpose more effectively?

36 b Organization

Ideas that are presented in no apparent order can confuse your readers, so clear organization within a paragraph is important. When editing, you must decide whether you have organized each paragraph in the way that most effectively accomplishes your purpose. You may decide to move your topic sentence or to reorganize the whole paragraph.

1 Placement of the topic sentence

Often the topic sentence or main idea is most effective at the beginning of a paragraph. If you find a topic sentence buried in the middle of a paragraph, consider moving it to the beginning.

In 1987, a man lost his job for taking a few puffs of a cigarette during his lunch break because smoking on or off the job violated his department's policy. He took his employers to court to get his job back, but the judge ruled that smoking was not comparable to the privacy rights protected by the Constitution. Court decisions have limited smokers' rights to pursue their habit. Other cases have established nonsmokers' right to protection from secondhand smoke.

A topic sentence can also be placed at the end of a paragraph, which is another way of emphasizing it.

> In 1987, a man lost his job for taking a few puffs of a cigarette during his lunch break because smoking on or off the job violated his department's policy. He took his employers to court to get his job back, but the judge ruled that smoking was not comparable to the privacy rights protected by the Constitution. Court decisions ^like these have limited smokers' rights to pursue their habit. Other cases have established nonsmokers' right to protection from secondhand smoke.

2 Common patterns of organization

The sentences and ideas within a paragraph should be arranged to convey the point of the paragraph.

General to specific

One common pattern for organizing paragraphs is *general to specific*. Begin the paragraph by stating the principal idea; edit subsequent sentences to support, explain, or expand on that idea.

GENERAL STATEMENT

Many athletes have improved their performance by using steroids. One such athlete is track star Ben Johnson, who won the Olympic gold medal in 1988 in the hundred-meter dash. After a couple of days, Johnson's medal was taken away because he had tested positive for the use of steroids. His steroid use had increased his leg strength and therefore made him a faster runner. Another example is Benji Ramirez, a former student at Central State University. He played on the JV team for two years and wanted to be good enough for the varsity squad. He decided to do this by increasing his physical strength, and the method he chose was using steroids. By his senior year, he was a starter on the varsity team.

SPECIFIC EXAMPLE

Specific to general

A specific-to-general pattern of organization begins with a series of details or examples and ends with a general statement, the topic sentence. In this personal narrative, Anita saved the topic sentence for last to give it impact:

SPECIFIC
EXAMPLE

I began by oversleeping—somehow I had forgotten to set my alarm clock. Then I had to drink my morning coffee black and eat my cereal dry becuse my roommate hadn't replaced the quart of milk she finished yesterday. After missing my bus and arriving late for my first class, I discovered that the paper I thought was due next week was actually due today. And because my lab partner was still mad at me about the mess I made of things last week, we accomplished almost nothing in two hours. All in all, it was a terrible day.

GENERAL
STATEMENT

Chronological order

Related events can be organized in **chronological order,** the order in which they happened. The topic sentence, a general statement summarizing the events and perhaps interpreting them, can appear at the beginning or, as in the paragraph above, at the end.

Sometimes paragraphs relating a series of events are better arranged in *reverse chronological order,* which looks back from the most recent to the most distant past, as in the example below. Here the topic sentence can appear at the end or at the beginning:

GENERAL
STATEMENT

At first a little hesitant to talk about painful memories, Leo started by describing his background. He ended the war as a refugee, he said, having escaped with only what he could carry. He then told me that on September 1, 1939, the Germans attacked Poland. They left his town alone for three days. On the third, they collected all the males from fifteen to sixty years of age and put them in a yard. The men were given trash and told to bury it with their hands. A friend of Leo's resisted and they shot him. He was buried along with the refuse.

EVENT 1

EVENT 2

EVENT 3

EVENT 4

In this vignette from a personal profile, Mark shows his interview subject opening up as he reaches farther into the past. Mark has structured the narrative to build up to its chilling conclusion.

Climactic order

An appeal to logic might be arranged in **climactic order,** beginning with a general statement, presenting specific details in order of increasing importance, and ending with a dramatic statement, a climax. Here Patrick is using scientific predictions to arouse and alarm a general, nonscientific audience:

GENERAL
STATEMENT

Consider the potential effect of just a small increase in the earth's atmospheric temperature. A rise of only a few degrees could melt the polar ice caps. Rainfall patterns would change.

SPECIFICS IN
INCREASING
IMPORTANCE

Some deserts might bloom, but lands now fertile might turn to desert, and many hot climates could become uninhabitable. If the sea level rose only a few feet, dozens of coastal cities would

CLIMAX

be destroyed, and life as we know it would be changed utterly.

Spatial order

A physical description can be organized in **spatial order,** moving from one detail to another as the eye would move. As in the chronological paragraph, a topic sentence summarizing and interpreting the details can appear at the beginning or end. Janelle intended this description to give the reader the feeling of sitting in one place, observing carefully:

SPECIFICS
ARRANGED
SPATIALLY

Above the mantelpiece hung an ancient flintlock musket that gave every indication of being in working order. A small collection of pewter, most of it dating from the colonial period, was arrayed across the mantel. To the left of the hearth stood a collection of wrought-iron fireplace tools and a bellows of wood and leather with brass fittings. At the right, a brass hopper held several cut limbs of what might have been an apple tree. On an iron hook above the coals hung a copper kettle, blackened with age and smoke. The fireplace looked as though it had changed

GENERAL
STATEMENT

little since the Revolution.

EDITING 3: PRACTICE ....

The following paragraph is from a news release that was sent to local newspapers in the townships near White Glen Park. Strengthen the paragraph by improving its organization.

One Saturday each month, Mike Perkins, a local golf pro, gives a free golf clinic at White Glen Park. Enthusiasts gather round while Mike discusses the finer points of the game. He addresses one aspect of the golf swing each session. He demonstrates the relevant concept, using someone from the crowd as a model. The public course donates six bushel baskets of golf balls and the use of its driving range for the event. Usually about sixty to eighty people show up. Saturday afternoons with Mike are always fun and informative. Last month he discussed proper hip movement in the iron swing. Then, after the lesson, Mike's monthly students hit practice shots until they used up the balls. The event is quite popular.

EDITING 4: APPLICATION ···

Make a copy of three paragraphs from a paper you are working on, and experiment to find the best possible organization for them. First, disassemble the paragraphs so that each sentence stands alone, starting each sentence on a new line on the computer screen. Next, find the topic sentences and set them aside. Decide which sentences belong in which paragraph. Then play with the order of the sentences until you find one that seems particularly effective; you might try some of the patterns of organization discussed in 36b. Decide whether the topic sentence belongs at the beginning or the end of each paragraph. Finally, rewrite the paragraphs using the new organization, making any necessary changes in wording. How does this edited version compare with the original?

···

36 c Coherence

In a *coherent* paragraph, each sentence connects with the next in a way that readers can easily recognize. Shortening long paragraphs, using transitional expressions, and sparingly repeating key words all can help achieve coherence.

1 Shortening long paragraphs

Long paragraphs can lack coherence simply because readers may lose track of what you are saying. Breaking a long paragraph into several smaller ones can give the reader a chance to rest, and it often results in greater coherence within each of the new paragraphs.

During a divorce, parents have the ability to shield a child from most of the potential harm. Most couples who stay together believe that the two-parent structure is important to the child's well-being and that changing this pattern upsets a child. ¶ A child's security is based on his or her relationship with each parent individually, according to studies by Judith Wallerstein, who found that stable, caring relationships between a child and each parent are the most significant ingredient in raising a child. If these relationships are

maintained, the effect of divorce on a child's emotions is much reduced. Indeed, maintaining even one stable relationship would appear to be better than a weak connection with both parents. In the
early stages of a breakup, both parents are often distracted by
other issues. The child may suffer as a result. A child's performance
in school and interactions with others may deteriorate, so everything should be done to aid the child in transition.

Breaking up the paragraph clarifies important points.

2 Making clear transitions

Whenever your flow of ideas shifts, let the reader know which way you
are headed. Otherwise readers may be confronted with a seemingly unrelated string of facts. Words or sentences that signal a change are called
transitions.

Transitional Expressions

Within a paragraph, a few words are often enough to signal a contrast, a connection,
or a change of direction. These **transitional expressions** connect distinct ideas, indicating how one idea expands, exemplifies, summarizes, or relates to another:

- **Expanding:** also, and, besides, finally, further, in addition, moreover, then
- **Exemplifying:** as an illustration, for example, for instance, in fact, specifically, thus
- **Qualifying:** but, certainly, however, to be sure, only
- **Summarizing:** and so, finally, in conclusion, in short, in sum, this experiment shows,
  thus we see
- **Relating logically:** as a result, because, by implication, for this reason, from this we can
  see, if, since, so therefore
- **Comparing:** also, as well, likewise, similarly
- **Contrasting:** but, even though, nevertheless, still, yet, despite
- **Relating in time:** after, before, between, earlier, later, longer than, meanwhile, since
- **Relating in space:** above, adjacent to, behind, below, beyond, in front of, next to, north
  of, over, through, within

Transitional Sentences and Paragraphs

To signal an important relationship between paragraphs, to change the subject, or to introduce an entirely new avenue of discussion, a transitional phrase might be inadequate. Consider using a transitional sentence or even a transitional paragraph to explain what kind of material is coming next and how it relates to what went before.

It is clear from these connections that many elements of the blues can be found in early rock 'n' roll. But before making any claims about the exclusive origins of rock 'n' roll in the blues, we need to look at the interwoven threads from other musical genres, including country music, gospel, and even the English music hall. Considering all these sources should make it clear that many races and cultures can claim some parentage of America's famous youth music.

After summarizing prior discussion, the writer says, "Hold that thought while I introduce some other information you might want to consider as well. And here's where this new information will lead."

As you edit, examine each change of subject, time, point of view, or setting to see whether you have adequately marked the transition. Changes you make while restructuring paragraphs may make new transitions necessary. Look again at the edited example from the paper about divorce, in which one long paragraph was broken into three. To clarify how the three new paragraphs related to one another, Amy added two transitional sentences, the first to highlight a logical contrast and the second to introduce a change of subject.

During a divorce, parents have the ability to shield a child from most of the potential harm. Most couples who stay together believe that the two-parent structure is important to the child's well-being and that changing this pattern upsets a child.
This, however, appears not to be the case.
A child's security is based on his or her relationship with each parent individually, according to studies by Judith Wallerstein, who found that stable, caring relationships between a child and

each parent are the most significant ingredient in raising a child. If these relationships are maintained, the effect of divorce on a child's emotions is much reduced. Indeed, maintaining even one stable relationship would appear to be better than a weak connection with both parents.

The issue during divorce, then, is how well a child can maintain at

In the early stages of a breakup, both parents are often distracted by other issues. The child may suffer as a result. A child's performance in school and interactions with others may deteriorate, so everything should be done to aid the child in transition.

least one secure relationship.

3 Using deliberate repetition

Selective repetition of key words or concepts creates a path for readers, connecting one sentence to the next. In the following example, *controversy* and *dispute* as well as *opposes, opponents,* and *proponents* are key words that help readers follow the argument:

Strategies for Editing Paragraphs

Most writers paragraph intuitively when they draft. When you edit, make conscious decisions about paragraphs:

- **Look at length.** Does each paragraph begin and end in the appropriate place? Should it be shorter? Should it include part of the following paragraph? Are there too many long paragraphs or too many short paragraphs in a row?
- **Check for unity.** Does each paragraph express and develop a single idea? Eliminate or move distracting elements.
- **Consider organization.** Is the pattern of each paragraph appropriate for your purpose?
- **Assess coherence.** Check the flow from each sentence to the next to ensure that the paragraph is clear and logical.
- **Provide transitions.** Within and between paragraphs, be sure relationships and changes of direction are clearly identified.

The *controversy* over Northgate Mall has continued for five years. The *dispute* has divided the city into two camps. A small group *opposes* the mall, but its members are vocal and energetic. The *opponents* maintain that it would rob trade from existing businesses downtown and contribute to traffic congestion. *Proponents* say that the growth it would bring would be easily manageable.

EDITING 5: PRACTICE ....

The following paragraph is from an oral report for a debate class. Strengthen the paragraph by editing to improve coherence. Consider the use of transitional expressions, the order of sentences, and the use of repetition. More than one edited version is possible. Be ready to explain your editing choices.

Accidents involving bicyclists usually increase when the college students—and their bicycles—return to classes. Many drivers in the city resent the high number of cyclists. They claim that the streets are too busy and too narrow for bike travel. Cyclists often will ignore traffic signals and stop signs and cut in and out of traffic without warning. If opposing traffic is slow in starting after a light changes, cyclists frequently will turn in front of it to move ahead. Usually few cyclists attempt to keep up with traffic, which creates a long line of cars unable to pass. These tendencies can be dangerous. At the corner of Tenth Street and Indiana the other day, a cyclist was struck by a car turning right when he tried to pass on the inside. He suffered no injuries, but some victims have to be hospitalized.

....

EDITING 6: PRACTICE ....

The following passage is from a newspaper account summarizing the history of a zoning proposal for a new mall and its impact on a mayoral election. Revise (1) to improve its unity, organization, and coherence and (2) to make it more interesting. You may have fun with your revision, so long as you do not alter the facts. You may begin new paragraphs as you see fit.

The zoning board rejected the proposal. The plan was the subject of three evenings of raucous debate. Then the city council took it up on appeal. The disagreement continued there for months. Some members said their first responsibility was to promote economic development in any form. The debate on the council reflected the divisions in the community. Growth should be regulated so that it does not harm existing businesses or the city as a whole, others believed. The project was approved two weeks after the new mayor took office. Amanda Robbins campaigned for mayor by rallying downtown businesspeople, historic preservationists, and neighborhood activists against the mall. Council member Steven McMillan ran on a prodevelopment, pro-mall platform. Both candidates said they wanted voters to end the deadlock on the proposal. The election was won by McMillan.

chapter 37

Improving Openings and Conclusions

Y ou never get a second chance to make a first impression. The **opening** of an essay must entice readers to continue. Your opening should give readers a reliable guide to what will follow: it should introduce your topic and your thesis or main idea and give readers an idea of what you intend to say.

An essay's **conclusion** merits equal attention because your parting words will linger in the reader's mind. The conclusion provides your last opportunity to tie together everything you have covered in clear, simple terms.

There are no formulas for openings or conclusions; each must suit your purpose and audience. On rare occasions, the first words of an essay may spring to mind as you begin to write, or the last words may flow effortlessly from the preceding paragraphs, and you may never need to change them. More often, however, you will find it distracting, while drafting, to worry about an opening or conclusion. First, draft the main portion of the paper, and worry later about the opening and conclusion. After drafting and revising, go back to your openings and conclusions. The editing stage is the best time to sharpen your focus, check directness, and polish wording.

37 a Engaging openings

In a short essay, you start like a sprinter and run flat-out for the full fifty meters. An opening of one paragraph is standard in much college writing. In a longer paper, you can set a more leisurely pace, engaging readers' attention, then guiding it and focusing it by the time you state the main argument.

In either case, readers should quickly be able to recognize both your **subject,** the general area you are writing about, and your **topic,** that particular aspect of the subject on which you are focusing. They should also understand your *main idea,* the central point you will make about that topic in your paper. In argument and research writing, this main point is presented in a **thesis,** an explicit statement usually placed in the opening paragraph. In personal experience and reflective writing, the thesis can take an unstated form as an implicit **theme** that is referred to throughout.

> Nikorn Phasuk, a Bangkok policeman who is also known as Plastic Man, steps onto a stage of asphalt under the glare of a blazing sun. He crouches, then retreats with mincing footwork as he coaxes vehicles toward him with fluid arm gestures, part of an artful ballet he uses to keep traffic rolling, no small feat in the city that may have the most congested streets in the world.
>
> As the last motorist accelerates by, the officer stabs a white gloved hand toward the heart of the city in a gesture that ends in a pirouette. Below dark sunglasses his teeth flash in a full grin, one that commuters irked by delays cannot help but emulate.
>
> "It relieves the tension, makes everybody less serious, and it's fun," Nikorn said. "And traffic seems to move faster."
>
> As he walked me back to my car, he held hands with a Bangkok journalist who had stopped by. Such intimacy, while common among Asian men, might be hard to imagine in New York City. But this was Thailand, where most actions seem choreographed for gentleness, and smiles are the expressions of choice.
>
> NOEL GROVE, "THE MANY FACES OF THAILAND"

Taking a few paragraphs to introduce a lengthy essay, Grove gives his readers a verbal film clip of downtown Bangkok that signals to his audience that they will be visiting an unfamiliar but delightful culture.

Your opening should be appropriate to your topic and main idea. Here are some techniques for matching your openings to specific purposes.

1 General-to-specific pattern

Many opening paragraphs for college papers start with a general statement of the main idea in a topic sentence. Subsequent sentences contain specific examples that support or expand on that statement, and the paragraph ends with a thesis statement.

> Language is the road map of a culture. It tells you where its people come from and where they are going. A study of the English language reveals a dramatic history and astonishing versatility. It is the language of survivors, of conquerors, of laughter.
>
> RITA MAE BROWN, "TO THE VICTOR BELONGS THE LANGUAGE"

2 Striking assertion

This opening features a statement so improbable or far-reaching that the reader will want to see proof.

> John Milton was a failure. In writing "Paradise Lost," his stated aim was to "justify the ways of God to men." Inevitably, he fell short of accomplishing that and only wrote a monumental poem. Beethoven, whose music was conceived to transcend Fate, was a failure, as was Socrates, whose ambition was to make people happy by making them reasonable and just. The inescapable conclusion seems to be that the surest, noblest way to fail is to set one's own standards titanically high.
>
> LAWRENCE SHANIES,
> "THE SWEET SMELL OF SUCCESS ISN'T ALL THAT SWEET"

3 Anecdote

Try telling an **anecdote,** or brief story, about people or incidents to introduce your topic and illustrate your thesis.

> Once I met a woman who grew up in the small North Carolina town to which Chang and Eng, the original Siamese twins, retired after their circus careers. When I asked her how the town reacted to the twins marrying local girls and setting up adjacent households, she laughed and said: "Honey, that was nothing compared to what happened before the twins got there." Get the good gossip on any little mountain town, scratch the surface and you'll find a snake pit!
>
> FRANCINE PROSE, "GOSSIP"

Near the end of this paragraph, you can see Prose's thesis coming and are ready to agree with it.

Strategies for Openings

To engage readers' interest, try one of the following strategies:

- Move from **general to specific** in your opening paragraph.
- Make a **striking assertion** in your opening.
- Add an **anecdote** that arouses your readers' curiosity.
- Grab their attention with an **interesting detail or quotation.**
- Ask a **provocative question** that leads to your topic.

4 Interesting detail, statistic, or quotation

An interesting detail, statistic, or quotation can place readers in an unfamiliar situation, making them eager for the explanation you are about to provide.

> People are often surprised, even alarmed, to learn that many of their cells crawl around inside them. Yet cell crawling is essential to our survival. Without it, our wounds would not heal; blood would not clot to seal off cuts; the immune system could not fight infections. Unfortunately, crawling contributes to some disease processes, too, such as destructive inflammation and the formation of atherosclerotic plaques in blood vessels. Cancer cells crawl to spread themselves throughout the body: were cancer just a matter of uncontrolled cell growth, all tumors would be amenable to surgical removal.
>
> THOMAS P. STOSSEL, "THE MACHINERY OF CELL CRAWLING"

Was your reaction the same as ours, "Yuck"? Then Stossel had you right where he wanted you!

5 Provocative question

An opening can ask a provocative question, which the essay attempts to answer.

> Look around you in most locations in the United States and Australia, and most of the people you'll see will be of European ancestry. At the same sites 500 years ago everyone without exception would have been an American Indian or an aboriginal Australian. This is an obvious feature of our daily life, and yet it poses a difficult question, one with a far from obvious

answer: Why is it that Europeans came to replace most of the native population of North America and Australia, instead of Indians or native Australians replacing the original population of Europe?

JARED DIAMOND, THE ACCIDENTAL CONQUEROR

EDITING 1: PRACTICE

Edit the following opening paragraph to make it more engaging. First assume you are writing a paper on economics for an economics class. Then edit the paragraph again, assuming you are writing about economics for an audience of noneconomists. What should your opening achieve in each case? What goals are the same, and which ones differ?

> Dr. Ravi Batra, an economist at Southern Methodist University, has described a long-term cycle of economic indicators. Those indicators, he believes, forecast a depression in the next few years. The World Futurist Society also predicts a global economic collapse rivaling the Great Depression of the 1930s. Both predictions cite a rash of bank failures in recent years, implying that the first indication of wider economic troubles will be the downfall of financial institutions.

37   b   Strong openings

Wanting to sound well informed and self-assured, writers sometimes lapse into misdirection, wordiness, overgeneralization, and cliché, which can be catastrophic in openings. Readers are more likely to keep reading when each sentence, each word, is important. To that end, edit any elements that may distract your readers.

1 Being direct

Ernie's draft starts on one topic and moves to another. Can you tell where his paper is headed?

> Isaac Asimov is among the first to have written about robotics. *I, Robot* is a collection of short stories on the subject, the earliest of which is from 1940. Even when going to the moon was science fiction, Asimov predicted that people would come to fear their own creation, a concept that dates back at least as far as Mary Shelly's *Frankenstein*.
> A movie that demonstrates the paranoia Asimov wrote about is *Terminator,* in which a computer takes control of machines, then attempts to

eradicate the human race. This is the paranoia Asimov predicted: humanity the slave master has an innate fear of rebellion among its slaves.

A robot is defined as "any mechanical device operated automatically, especially by remote control." The subject I will be addressing is the argument that robots are stealing jobs from humans, that painters, spot welders, machinists, skilled laborers of all kinds are being replaced by machines.

Does Ernie mean to focus on the workplace or the psyche? Keeping his literary examples as context, Ernie edited a new opening to make his position clear.

The claim that robots are stealing jobs from humans is nothing new; it is an old fear in a new form. Many writers and filmmakers have explored the underlying anxiety.

Isaac Asimov was among the first to write about robotics. . . .

Beware of *telling* the reader "My paper will be about. . . ." Delete such phrases and jump right in to *show* the reader what you mean.

2 Sharpening focus

Too broad an opening can dull readers' interest. Limit opening generalizations so that readers understand your main idea right away, as Julie did in a reflective essay on the relations between men and women:

Communication has become very important in our everyday lives. Without this ability to relate, friendships and marriages would fail. Furthermore, the different ways men and women communicate can result in serious problems at home and in the workplace.

Her first sentences were too obvious, so Julie sharpened her focus. Her edited sentences outline the territory she plans to cover.

Men and women have different ways of communicating that can create problems in marriages and work relationships. Overcoming these differences is essential to friendships and marriages alike.

3 Emphasizing the main idea

An opening should quickly establish your topic and tell readers what your point will be. Anything that slows their progress toward your main idea should be eliminated. In this draft, Dwayne intended to explore the morality of capital punishment, but he started with a dry definition likely to bore his readers:

What exactly is capital punishment? According to the *Academic Encyclopedia,* capital punishment is the lawful imposition of the death penalty. In biblical times, the death penalty was prescribed for murder, kidnapping, and witchcraft. In England in the 1500s, major crimes such as treason, murder, larceny, burglary, rape, and arson carried the death penalty.

Between 1977 and 1991 in the United States alone, 2,350 persons faced the death penalty, and at least 150 were executed. Although use of the death penalty has strict legal limitations, Americans have differing views on its value in protecting society. Is capital punishment right or wrong?

By asking the definition of a common term, Dwayne wasted his opening words. When editing, he sharpened the question he planned to explore, summarized a major disagreement, and tightened everywhere.

Can capital punishment be morally justified?

Americans disagree about whether the death penalty protects society. Its supporters argue that the fear of death deters some criminals and that execution stops others from striking again. Opponents believe that even noble ends cannot justify such terrible means.

Lawful execution has been around since biblical times, when it was prescribed for murder, kidnapping, and witchcraft. . . .

EDITING 2: EXPLORATION

Read the following two paragraphs, which begin Ambrose Bierce's essay "Disintroductions." Consider the strategies Bierce has used to engage the reader's interest, and evaluate the effectiveness of this opening. Be prepared to discuss your views with other members of your class.

The devil is a citizen of every country, but only in our own are we in constant peril of an introduction to him. All men are equal; the devil is a man; therefore, the devil is equal. If that is not a good and sufficient syllogism I should be pleased to know what is the matter with it.

To write in riddles when one is not prophesying is too much trouble; what I am affirming is the horror of the characteristic American custom of promiscuous, unsought, and unauthorized introductions.

EDITING 3: PRACTICE

Read the following opening paragraph. What do you think are the writer's audience, purpose, and thesis? Generate at least two alternative versions of the paragraph. Evaluate your alternatives according to your understanding of audience, purpose, and thesis.

My research paper is on the clunker law and why people are in favor
of it or opposed to it. The controversy exists between large corporations
and individuals who own old cars. The law proposes that cars dated
1981 or older that do not pass emission standards be destroyed or limited in their annual mileage. The law will affect the automobile industry and the economic welfare of the lower class. The clunker law is a
short-term solution to the problem of pollution. I will state my own
opinion about the clunker law. It's a fight between David and Goliath.

EDITING 4: EXPLORATION

Read several opening paragraphs by an author whose writing you admire,
and select one that seems particularly effective to you. Jot down what you
think were the writer's purpose, the intended audience, and the thesis or
main idea. What techniques has the author used to engage your attention?
How has the author focused your thoughts on the main idea? Which of these
techniques can you use in your own writing?

EDITING 5: APPLICATION

Read the opening paragraph of a paper you are working on, and evaluate
its effectiveness. Are you addressing your audience appropriately? Will it
grab readers' attention? Have you focused on your central idea? Generate
an alternative version with those questions in mind, and compare it to the
original. What are the strengths and weaknesses of each?

37 c   Satisfying conclusions

Imagine that, after reading all your evidence and arguments, readers
will remember only one paragraph. What would you want that paragraph
to say? That's your conclusion: the strongest statement of your case that
you can make based on the information you've assembled.

Here are some strategies for driving home your point:

1 Rhetorical question

One way to close an argument is to end with a **rhetorical question,**
one not meant to be answered but that creates a situation in which the
readers cannot help but agree with you.

Drug violence will continue as long as citizens tolerate the easy availability of guns on the streets; as long as the public shells out money for violence glorified in television and film; as long as drug customers, deprived of effective treatment, pour money into disadvantaged neighborhoods. How can society sit by and do nothing?

The reader isn't really expected to answer this question but rather to respond by saying, "We must do something!"

Valid Conclusions

Here are some pitfalls to avoid in conclusions:

■ A conclusion that simply asserts your own belief—unsupported by evidence—is unlikely to persuade anyone not already disposed to agree with you.

■ Last-minute appeals to beliefs or authority will not sway anyone who holds other beliefs or does not share your respect for your chosen authority.

■ A conclusion that goes far beyond what your evidence will support also is unlikely to be persuasive.

■ If you have not yet given readers an explicit statement of your main idea, you must do so in your conclusion.

2 Summary

Another strategy is a concise **summary** of your main points, followed by a *reflective* point about their meaning. This works well when your exploration has raised questions rather than provided firm answers, as in Teresa's exploration of the nature of death:

Death is a reality we confront every day. Morticians package death and sell it as interminable slumber. The military suggests that to be killed for a cause is an elevating experience that guarantees heroic stature. The medical profession struggles to preserve life beyond any reasonable hope for a significant future. One way or another, everyone has beliefs about an afterlife, but what happens beyond the grave, the world will never know. What happens lies beyond a door that one day each of us must unlock.

Teresa didn't want to say death was one thing and not another; she wanted her readers to ponder what death means to each of them.

3 Call to action

What better purpose in marshaling your powers of persuasion if not to mobilize readers on behalf of change? In so doing, you have to presume that your readers accept your argument and are ready to help you change the world.

> Media violence may not be the only cause of aggressive behavior, but it clearly has an adverse effect on viewers. Children are most affected because they readily learn new behavior by imitation. Their lessons are reenacted on playgrounds and on the streets. As citizens and as parents, it's time we demanded better.

4 Speculation

You can also conclude with *speculation* about the future, showing your readers a better world—if they act as you have urged in your argument. Anthropologist Margaret Mead ends her discussion of capital punishment by presenting a vision of a better future:

> The tasks are urgent and difficult. Realistically we know we cannot abolish crime. But we can abolish crude and vengeful treatment of crime. We can abolish—as a nation, not just state by state—capital punishment. We can accept the fact that prisoners, convicted criminals, are hostages to our own human failures to develop and support a decent way of living. And we can accept the fact that we are responsible to them, as to all living beings, for the protection of society, and especially responsible for those among us who need protection for the sake of society.

> MARGARET MEAD, "A LIFE FOR A LIFE"

Strategies for Conclusions

- Ask a **rhetorical question,** one that does not need answering but will ring in the readers' ears.

- **Summarize** the important points of your paper, driving home any connections you want to make or any final overarching point that needs to be made.

- Sound a **call to action** when writing papers that argue for change; it's a good way to engage your readers in further thought.

- **Speculate** about the future, leaving your readers to weigh the outcome of the issues you have presented.

EDITING 6: PRACTICE ....

Edit the following conclusion to make it more satisfying. More than one edited version is possible. Be ready to explain your editing choices.

Computers have already radically altered our society and will undoubtedly continue to do so. But how far will computers take us? Will we like our destination? From the banking and finance industries to recreation and art, every aspect of our lives has been affected by the ramifications of RAM and ROM. Much as the industrial revolution and the agricultural revolution did in past centuries, the computer revolution will fundamentally transform our culture in ways we cannot yet imagine. The three distinctive characteristics of computer transactions—speed of computation, ease of replication, and access through networking—are unremarkable in themselves, but when combined they change the very nature of information, the currency of our culture. No longer is knowledge accumulated over the centuries, unalterably fixed on pieces of paper and painstakingly consulted when needed. Today's information resembles a rushing torrent, always changing, impossible to contain or chart, and ready to sweep aside all limits or restrictions.

....

37 d Strong conclusions

Here are some common ways to improve conclusions.

1 Broaden

Take care not to limit your conclusion unnecessarily or to end on a secondary point. Mara originally drafted this conclusion arguing against religion's playing a formal role in public schools. When editing, she realized that she had made her conclusion seem narrower than the rest of her paper.

> **Praying, reading from the Bible, and presenting the teachings of any one religion tend to exclude people who are not believers in that religion. In the public school system, the prayers and beliefs of Christians would predominate and make non-Christians feel "different" and excluded. This is why religion should be kept out of the public schools and kept in the place of worship and the home. ~~However, I do think that holiday concerts and "Season's Greetings" decorations around Christmas and Hanukkah will continue.~~**

2 Focus

Raise questions or make generalizations that follow from your discussion. Kyle's essay discussed his college's requirement that students acquire computers, explored the educational applications of computers, and touched on the problems students encountered using them. Yet his conclusion wandered far off into speculation. He eliminated that distraction and created a smooth transition.

With computers as prevalent in college as they are in business, people are beginning to wonder where the computer age is taking us. Will computers become an integral part of everyday life? ~~Exactly how they will change people's lives remains to be seen, but~~ ~~**Will programmable machines make human minds obsolete?**~~ predicts changes more gradual than sweeping: **One university official** ~~seems to think not.~~ **"When it comes to just plain living and thinking, the computer is not really much help."**

3 Be direct

Wordiness saps the vitality of any conclusion. Transitional phrases such as *in conclusion, all in all,* or *to sum up* normally need not be used to signal that a conclusion is approaching. The structure and language of your concluding paragraphs should show readers that you're winding up. Furthermore, unnecessary words make you sound unsure of yourself.

A **qualifying phrase** such as *I think* or *I believe* also can weaken your conclusion. Such a construction is appropriate when you need to distinguish your conclusion from someone else's: *While Robinson concludes that the data clearly link low-frequency radiation to these illnesses, I would argue that the evidence is far from conclusive.* Usually, however, readers will understand that the ideas expressed in the conclusion are your own.

In drafting her paper on sharks, Aliah concluded with a repetition of other people's opinions or facts, ones that she had carefully documented earlier. By qualifying them in the first person, her conclusion seemed to be merely her own opinion, not a carefully formulated result based on research and analysis. When editing, Aliah removed the first-person references, and rather than telling what her conclusions would be, she simply stated them.

~~I can only hope that I have given some information to help you~~

Sharks
~~see that~~ sharks are not the fearsome creatures humans seem to
^   Millions of years old,
think they are. They have their place in the scheme of things like
                              ^
every other animal. The sooner we accept that the oceans are

their domain, the sooner we can learn to share the oceans with

them. ~~Sharks are millions of years old; I don't want to be part of~~

~~their destruction. I hope you too will consider helping to save~~

~~humankind's ancient enemy, the shark.~~/

EDITING 7: PRACTICE

Edit the following conclusion to make it more satisfying. More than one
edited version is possible. Be ready to explain your editing choices.

Everyone acknowledges that history is important, but there is a lot
of debate over just what kind of history should be studied and
taught. History matters. Some people mean different things when
they say this, though. A form of social history that focuses on the
lives and experiences of ordinary people has come into prominence
in recent years. Traditionally, history was the study of "great men"
and their wars. Economic conditions are also considered by some to
be at the center of what we mean by "history." Issues of race and
gender are now more prominent than they were before. There is no
agreement. So where does that leave those of us who want to study
history now? What model are we supposed to follow? There are so
many facts and ideas to learn in studying history. When you don't
know what facts and ideas you are supposed to be learning, it makes
the whole process overwhelming. You can't learn everything, can
you? If historians rethink what their discipline is all about, maybe
things will work themselves out. History is too important for this
issue to be ignored.

EDITING 8: EXPLORATION

Select an essay that looks interesting to you because of its title but that
you have not read before. First read only the opening paragraph. What can
you tell about the essay from this paragraph alone? What is the topic of the
essay? What will the author's position on this topic be? Think about the

author's relation to the subject matter (expert, tourist, researcher, story-teller?). Who is the intended audience, and how does the author relate to that audience? What is the tone or mood of the essay?

Next read the conclusion. Compare your understanding of the audience, purpose, topic, position, and tone with your impressions of the opening. How are they different? Judging only from the opening and the conclusion, try to determine what were the important points made in the essay.

Last, read the entire essay and see how accurate your predictions were. How good were your guesses?

··

EDITING 9: APPLICATION ··

Find two essays that you have enjoyed recently and compare their conclusions. Then try rewriting the conclusions of the first essay in the style of the second (and vice versa). Compare the effectiveness of the new conclusions with that of the old. Does one seem better than the other? Why? You might try this exercise using essays representing different genres (an expository essay and a proposal, a reflective essay and an essay that seeks to explain a concept, etc.). Do some types of conclusions work well in different kinds of writing while others do not? Think about why this might be the case.

··

38

Strengthening Sentences

blood-black

wn breaks open

Thus their head

ful falseness of

hus their hands

I f each of your ideas stands alone in a separate sentence, readers may see them as isolated facts. By combining ideas within sentences, you can show how they relate to one another. Of course, how you combine them depends on what connections you want to show.

38 a Coordinating ideas

Some ideas can be linked, compared, or contrasted.

The rock formations on the ceilings of caves are called *stalactites.* , and the

The ones rising from the floor are *stalagmites.*

This connection of ideas that are comparable or roughly equal is called **co-ordination.**

1 Coordinating conjunctions

The words *and, but, yet, or, nor, for,* and *so* are called **coordinating conjunctions** because they connect (or *conjoin*) similar elements. The resulting two-part sentence, called a **compound** sentence, presents ideas as equally important and the reader must pay attention to both (or all).

Sentence Types

The most basic sentences consist of a subject and a verb.

subject	verb
John	ran.

More common is a sentence consisting of a subject, a verb, and an object.

subject	verb	object
John	hit	the ball.

A sentence like this, with one subject, one verb, and possibly an object or modifiers, is called a **simple sentence.** It also can be called an **independent clause,** meaning it is grammatically complete and can stand alone.

A **compound sentence** contains two or more simple sentences (or independent clauses).

independent clause	independent clause
John ran far,	but he didn't run very fast.

A **complex sentence** contains an independent clause and another clause that cannot stand alone as a complete sentence.

independent clause	dependent clause
John runs	whenever he has time.

Whenever he has time is a clause (it has a subject and a verb), but by itself it doesn't make sense. It needs to be linked to an independent clause, so it is called a **dependent clause.**

A **compound complex sentence** includes at least two independent clauses and one dependent clause.

independent clause	dependent clause	independent clause
John ran	*as though he were lost in thought,*	but actually he was counting the cracks in the sidewalk.

Using a coordinating conjunction and a comma is the most common way of connecting sentences. (For more on punctuating compound sentences, see 52a and 53a.) Each of the words *and, or, nor, for, but, yet,* and *so* expresses a different relationship.

> **Incoming students must pass a placement examination to meet the**
>   , or they
> **foreign language requirement.** ~~Those who fail~~ **must take an intro-**
>   ^
> **ductory language course.**

Or specifies an alternative way to meet the requirement.

2 Semicolons

A semicolon can also join two sentences into one. It implies a close re-lationship between two ideas.

> The formations on the cave floor are *stalagmites*. Those that "stick
>
> tight" to the ceiling are *stalactites*.

(inserted edit: ; those)

3 Correlative conjunctions

Another way to coordinate two sentences is by using a pair of **correlative conjunctions** such as *both . . . and, either . . . or,* or *not only . . . but also.*

> Lavar won honors in mathematics and physics. He also was rec-
>
> ognized for achievement in biology.

(inserted edits: not only ; , but he)

4 Conjunctive adverbs

A conjunctive adverb such as *however, moreover,* or *nevertheless* used with a semicolon can also join two independent clauses.

> An Advanced Placement Test score will be accepted. The test must
>
> have been taken within the last year.

(inserted edit: ; however, the)

5 Improving coordination

Look for places where the right kind of coordination can help readers.

> The project was a huge undertaking, yet I was exhausted at the end.

(inserted edit: so)

The conjunction yet *implies contrast, but that is not what the sentence means. The conjunction* so *states the proper cause-and-effect relationship.*

Too much coordination begins to sound like baby talk. If a sentence with several coordinate structures seems weak, decide which elements belong together and which should stand alone. The following paragraph, for example, could be edited like this.

. When
Coordination can be overdone,/and when it is used too much, it can
. Readers ^
begin to sound repetitive,/and readers may begin to imagine the voice
^

Coordinating Conjunctions, Correlative Conjunctions, Conjunctive Adverbs

Relationship	Coordinating Conjunctions	Correlative Conjunctions	Conjunctive Adverbs
addition	and	both ... and	also, besides, moreover
contrast	but, yet	either ... or	instead, however
choice	or	not only ... but also	otherwise
causation	so, for		therefore, accordingly, consequently
negation	nor	not ... but neither ... nor	otherwise
substitution		either ... or	alternatively

ESL Not Only ... But Also

If you join two sentences with *not only ... but also,* you will need to change word order in the first clause.

■ If the first clause has an auxiliary verb—*has, could, would, might*—or if the main verb is *be,* reverse the order of the subject and the auxiliary verb or *be.*

Not only *has the computer science department* added several new courses this year, but the faculty has also updated the curriculum.

Not only *is California* a large state geographically, but it also has many cities with large populations.

■ If the first clause has no auxiliary, add an appropriate form of *do* before the subject. The verb must be in its base form. (See 47a.)

Not only *did the voters express* a lack of confidence in their governor, but they also showed concern about the effectiveness of the Congress.

of a child speaking in sentences that go on and on, strung together
with *and*, ~~and soon they~~ will get confused or bored, ~~and as~~ a writer
you should try to prevent that.

. They (insertion above "and")

_. As_ (insertion above "bored")

EDITING 1: PRACTICE

Edit the following passage, using coordination to relate ideas of equal importance. More than one edited version is possible. Be ready to explain your editing choices.

The workers were instructed to seal the oily rags in cans. They forgot to do it. At night the rags caught fire. The fire spread rapidly through the storage area. A smoke detector went off. No one noticed. The alarm was relayed to the fire station. Firefighters raced to the warehouse. Flames were already darting through the windows. Smoke poured through the ceiling. Glass cracked in the heat. It shattered. The fire commander turned in a second alarm. Another company sped toward the scene.

EDITING 2: EXPLORATION

Read the following passage from a personal narrative by N. Scott Momaday. How has Momaday used coordination? How many examples can you find of ideas joined by coordinating conjunctions? by semicolons? Could any of these ideas have been joined in other ways? If they had been, how would the effect of the passage have been different?

Once there was a lot of sound in my grandmother's house, a lot of coming and going, feasting and talk. The summers there were full of excitement and reunion. The Kiowas are a summer people; they abide the cold and keep to themselves, but when the season turns and the land becomes warm and vital they cannot hold still; an old love of going returns upon them. The aged visitors who came to my grandmother's house when I was a child were made of lean and leather and they bore themselves upright. They wore great black hats and bright ample shirts that shook in the wind. They rubbed fat upon their hair and wound their braids with strips of colored cloth. Some of them painted their faces and carried the scars of old and cherished enmities.

N. SCOTT MOMADAY, *THE WAY TO RAINY MOUNTAIN*

38 b Using subordination

To emphasize one idea over another within a sentence, try **subordination.** (The word means "making less important.") Here are two ideas presented as separate sentences, with neither given more weight than the other.

John Playford collected seventeenth-century music. He was an English musician.

To emphasize one element, put the other in a dependent clause.

John Playford, *who was an English musician,* collected seventeenth-century music.

John Playford, *who collected seventeenth-century music,* was an English musician.

A subordinate element may appear as a clause, a phrase, or a single word. The less important the element is grammatically, the less attention it demands from the reader.

NO
SUBORDINATION
The director wrote a plan. She intended to cover every major contingency.

CLAUSE
The plan *that the director wrote* was intended to cover every major contingency.

PHRASE
The plan *written by the director* was intended to cover every major contingency.

WORD
The *director's* plan was intended to cover every major contingency.

Subordinating Conjunctions

Relationship	Subordinating conjunctions
cause, effect	as, because, since, so, so that, in order that
condition	if, even if, if only, unless
contrast	although, even though, despite
comparison	as if, as though, than, whereas, while
choice	rather than, than, whether
sequence	after, as, as long as, before, once, since, until, when, whenever, while
space	where, wherever

Choose the subordination strategy that best expresses the relationship you intend. Subordinating the wrong element can change the meaning.

INDEPENDENT
SENTENCES
Scientists have carefully examined this theory. Some have criticized it.

INCORRECT
SUBORDINATION
Some scientists who have criticized this theory have carefully examined it.

This sentence inadvertently implies that some opponents have not been so careful.

CORRECT
SUBORDINATION
Some of the scientists who have carefully examined this theory have criticized it.

Be careful not to suggest an inaccurate cause-and-effect relationship.

that began shortly after

The nation was plunged into a deep recession ~~when~~ Ronald Reagan took office in 1981.

The writer did not mean to imply that Reagan's election caused the recession.

Also beware of excessive subordination.

Sometimes you may create passages that use too much subordination~~,~~ . That ~~which~~ can make them sound insipid ~~because every~~ . Every point seems to be qualified, while nothing is said directly.

EDITING 4: PRACTICE

Edit the following passage to improve coordination and subordination. More than one edited version is possible. Be prepared to explain your choices.

Last term I ended up with a low grade-point average, and my academic advisor thought that it was because I was taking too many difficult courses at the same time, so he recommended that I try to make a more sensible schedule this semester. I took his advice, yet I found myself with a much more manageable workload. I am taking calculus, which is difficult for me, and a photography course, which offers me different challenges, but I am finding the variety to be helpful.

ESL *Using Subordinating Conjunctions*

- When you use *whereas, while, although, though,* or *even though* in a dependent clause, do not use *but* before the independent clause.

  Although a smile shows happiness in most cultures, ~~but~~ in some it may be a sign of embarassment.

  Alternatively, you could delete although *and keep* but.

- When you use *because* or *since* in a dependent clause, do not use *so* in the independent clause.

  Because Rudolf Nureyev defected from Russia, ~~so~~ for many years he could not return to dance in his native country.

  You could also delete because *and keep* so.

- *Because* and *because of* are not interchangeable. *Because* is a conjunction—a word that introduces a clause containing both a subject and a verb.

  Because snow peas die in hot weather, you should plant them early in the spring.

- *Because of* is a two-word preposition, followed by a noun or pronoun.

  Because of the hot weather, the peas did not grow well.

When I am tired of doing problem sets, I can go out and take pictures, so when the weather is bad, I can stay in and do math. I don't waste time the way I did last term. Because of this new sense of balance, right now I am doing much better in all my classes, so I hope the pattern will continue.

EDITING 5: EXPLORATION

The following passage from an essay argues that politics has influenced the decisions of art galleries such as the Corcoran Gallery of Art in Washington, D.C. How many examples of subordination can you find in the passage? Why has the author used subordination rather than coordination to join ideas?

Whatever grave reservations regarding Congress may have motivated the directors of the Corcoran, they weakened the entire social fabric by yielding their freedom. Their decision should have been to show the work, whose merit they must have believed in to have scheduled the exhibition. Since then individual members of Congress have revealed themselves as enemies of freedom by letting their aesthetic attitudes corrupt their political integrity as custodians of the deepest values of a democratic society.

ARTHUR C. DANTO, "ART AND TAXPAYERS"

38 c Using parallelism

When you deliberately repeat a pattern within a sentence or paragraph, you've created a **parallelism.** This technique can highlight a comparison or emphasize a point: *The better the parallel, the more memorable the message.* In the following examples, the parallelisms create pleasing rhythms.

I came, I saw, I conquered.

JULIUS CAESAR

Of the people, by the people, for the people . . .

ABRAHAM LINCOLN

It was the best of times, it was the worst of times.

CHARLES DICKENS, *A TALE OF TWO CITIES*

To die, to sleep. To sleep, perchance to dream.

WILLIAM SHAKESPEARE, *HAMLET*

Although parallelism is sometimes thought of as a special technique, it appears in many common writing situations, so getting it right is important.

1 Compound elements

Compound elements are pairs joined by a coordinating conjunction (*and, or, nor, for, but, yet,* or *so*). For clarity, such elements should be grammatically similar.

working
They spend their time praying, reading, and ~~work~~ with the poor.
                                                   ^

2 Comparisons

Items being compared also must be in matching grammatical forms.

Laura likes painting as much as she likes ~~to read.~~

reading.

He believes communication is more a matter of thinking clearly
than ~~to write~~ well.

writing

3 Lists

Elements of a series or list joined with *and* or *or* also must be parallel in grammatical form.

Her favorite activities are painting, walking, and she liked ~~to visit~~

visiting
museums.

4 Completing parallels

Watch for words unintentionally omitted from parallel structures: prepositions (*to, for, at*), subordinating conjunctions (*although, since, because*), and relative pronouns (*who, which, what*).

The researchers tried to ensure that interviewees were representative of the campus population and their opinions reflected those

that
of the student body.

Without the second that, *it is unclear whether* their *refers to researchers or interviewees.*

5 Effective parallelism

Few devices achieve greater power, gravity, and impact than the force-ful, rhythmic, and formal words of a careful parallel construction.

With local leaders afraid of the "no growth" label, the quality of local decision making has declined. The question facing communities like Alta Mira is ~~whether they will do enough planning to avoid uncontrolled development.~~ not whether they will plan to have no growth but whether they will face growth with no plan.

The parallelism of not whether . . . but whether *and* no growth . . . no plan *helps the conclusion resonate.*

Strategies for Strengthening Sentences

When editing, consider the following ways to clarify the relationships between your ideas:

- Use **coordination** for alternatives, comparisons, contrasts, and extensions.
- Use **subordination** to clarify logical relationships between ideas.
- **Combine** choppy sentences.
- Use **parallelism** for emphasis.

EDITING 6: EXPLORATION

Find each instance of coordinate or parallel construction in the following sentence from Thomas Jefferson's draft of the Declaration of Independence. Identify the individual elements of each use of coordination or parallelism. What is the effect of parallelism?

> We therefore, the representatives of the United States of America in General Congress assembled, in the name of and by the authority of the good people of these states reject and renounce all allegiance to the kings of Great Britain and all others who may hereafter claim by, through or under them; we utterly dissolve all political connection which may heretofore have subsisted between us and the people or parliament of Great Britain; and finally we do assert and declare these colonies to be free and independent states and that as free and independent states, they have full power to levy war, conclude peace, contract alliances, establish commerce, and do all other acts and things which independent states may of right do.

EDITING 7: EXPLORATION ....

The following passage by Alice Walker discusses the position of African American women. Where has she used parallelism? What ideas are emphasized through this use of parallelism? How is the passage as a whole strengthened?

> When we have pleaded for understanding, our character has been distorted; when we have asked for simple caring, we have been handed empty inspirational appellations, then stuck in the farthest corner. When we have asked for love, we have been given children. In short, even our plainer gifts, our labors of fidelity and love, have been knocked down our throats. To be an artist and a black woman, even today, lowers our status in many respects, rather than raises it: and yet, artists we will be.
>
> ALICE WALKER, "IN SEARCH OF OUR MOTHERS' GARDENS"

EDITING 8: PRACTICE ....

If you employ complex forms of parallelism, match the elements of each structure carefully, and make sure the passage as a whole warrants the emphasis. Some writers use parallel structures inside other parallel structures, like sets of concentric circles. The effect is not only clarity but also the power, grace, and rhythm of a chant, useful on the most solemn of occasions.

> We can never be satisfied as long as our bodies, heavy with fatigue of travel, cannot gain lodging in the motels of the highways and the hotels of the cities. We cannot be satisfied as long as the Negro's basic mobility is from a smaller ghetto to a larger one.
>
> MARTIN LUTHER KING, JR., "I HAVE A DREAM"

EDITING 9: APPLICATION ....

Select a page from a draft you are working on, and evaluate the sentence structures. First identify examples of coordination by circling coordinating conjunctions and semicolons. Next draw a line under subordinate elements. Are coordination and subordination used where they are most effective? Are there any places where ideas would be better joined through another method? Is either coordination or subordination overused? Look for parallel structures. Are the words and ideas similar enough? Find places where you might consider using parallel structures. Edit the page to improve any weak sentence structure. How does the edited passage compare with the original?

chapter 39

Creating Emphasis and Variety

To focus the reader's attention, emphasize important ideas. You can establish *emphasis* by varying sentence structures and rhythms. *Variety* also ensures that you don't lose readers' attention.

When editing, decide what ideas you want to emphasize and where in your paper you might change rhythm or pattern to focus readers' attention.

Strategies for Achieving Emphasis and Variety

When editing to achieve emphasis and variety, try several of the following strategies; then choose ones that best suit your goals.

- Use the emphatic first and final positions.
- Edit sentence length.
- Vary sentence types.
- Vary sentence openings.
- Use deliberate repetition.
- Create elliptical constructions.

39 a   First and final positions

If you want something to be noticed, place it at a beginning.

I think that we're all mentally ill; those of us outside the asylums only hide it a little better—and maybe not all that much better, after all. We've all known people who talk to themselves, people who sometimes squinch their faces into horrible grimaces when they believe no one is watching, people who have some hysterical fear—of snakes, the dark, the tight place, the long drop . . . and of course, those final worms and grubs that are waiting so patiently underground.

STEPHEN KING, "WHY WE CRAVE HORROR MOVIES"

While first words grab attention, those that come last can have an enduring impact. The last words of a sentence, a paragraph, or an entire essay resonate in the reader's mind, lingering to provoke further thought.

Early civil rights bills nebulously state that other people shall have the same rights as "white people," indicating that there were "other people." But civil rights bills passed during and after the Civil War systematically excluded Indian people. . . . *Indians were America's captive people without any defined rights whatsoever.*

VINE DELORIA, JR., "CUSTER DIED FOR YOUR SINS"

Look for ways to use the emphatic first and final positions of each sentence, each paragraph, and each essay, especially in your opening and conclusion. (See Chapter 37.)

The costs
~~Whatever the rewards~~ of prohibition, ~~its costs~~ will always exceed ~~them.~~ *its rewards.* Users, who will always exist, are harmed not only by drugs but also by the law. The more effective the law, the more nonusers are victimized by crimes committed for drug cash. The higher drug prices go, the more desperate and sophisticated drug gangs become. ~~With~~ *with* a stroke of a pen, ~~society~~ *Society* could eliminate drug profits and drug crime.

Editing the concluding paragraph of her argument, Darla phrased her first sentence more boldly. She then moved the phrase with the stroke of a pen *to the emphatic final position.*

EDITING 1: APPLICATION

Select two pages from a paper you are working on. Underline the first and last sentence in each paragraph. Reading only these sentences, would a

From Old to New

As you edit for emphasis, consider what information you have already given your readers. Presenting information that readers already know—"old" information—before introducing "new" information helps readers see the connection to earlier ideas. This mental linking helps readers recognize the continuing thread of the discussion.

If the old-to-new pattern is not observed, the ideas are hard to follow, and the reader can't identify the main point.

Most artificial food colorings are synthetic chemicals.

new?

Hyperactivity in children was once thought to be increased by

old?

these colorings.

What is the main point that the writer will go on to explore? food colorings? hyperactivity? As it is written, we can't know.

See how much clearer the old-to-new pattern can be:

Most artificial food colorings are synthetic chemicals.

old   **new**

These colorings were once suspected of increasing hyperactivity in children.

Watch the flow of information from old to new from this masterful writer. The reader has already met Big João, so the passage starts with a familiar reference. The words in blue are familiar information (at that point in the reader's progress). Those in red are new at that point.

Big João **was born** near the sea, **on a** sugarcane plantation in Recôncavo, **the** owner of which **was a great** lover of horses. He boasted of possessing **the most** spirited sorrels **and of having** produced these specimens **of** first-rate horseflesh without any need of English studs, **thanks to the** astute matings **which** he **himself supervised.**

MARIO VARGAS LLOSA, *THE WAR OF THE END OF THE WORLD*

reader see the most important ideas in each paragraph? Edit each paragraph so that the most important idea is in either the first sentence or the last.

Next, on one of the edited pages, underline the most important element in each sentence, whether a thing, an action, or a description. How often does the most important element fall at the beginning or at the end of the sentence? How often is it buried somewhere in the middle? Edit each sentence, moving important elements to the first or final position wherever possible. Now, look for places where the flow of old information to new is reversed or interrupted. Edit to improve that flow.

Compare the edited version with the original to determine which you prefer. Does strengthening emphasis help achieve your goals?

39 b   Sentence length

Some writers write short sentences. They seldom use dependent clauses. They use few modifiers. Other writers never use simple sentences when elaborate ones, decorated with ribbons of dependent clauses, can be substituted, and thus they sometimes keep the reader waiting, hoping—perhaps even praying—eventually to find a period and, with it, a chance to pause for breath. (Whew!) Short sentences and longer ones both have their uses. When you edit, vary sentence length to direct and focus readers' attention.

1 Short sentences

Short sentences pack power. They command attention. They can show intense feelings, impressions, and events. In the following scene, Richard Rodriguez describes distributing bread in a poor neighborhood in Tijuana. Notice how his brief sentences make his confrontation with hunger and need all the more chilling:

> Five or six children come forward. All goes well for less than a minute. The crowd has slowly turned away from the altar; the crowd advances zombie-like against the truck. I fear children will be crushed. Silent faces regard me with incomprehension. *Cuidado* [careful], damn it!
>
> RICHARD RODRIGUEZ, "ACROSS THE BORDERS OF HISTORY"

To achieve such a dramatic effect—a critical scene in a personal narrative or in the summation of an argument—condense your ideas into as few words as possible and break up long sentences into shorter ones.

As soon as I hit the ball and took my first step, my knee collapsed,
and I was on the ground in blinding pain. I heard my teammates
yelling, "Get up! Run!" but I could no more run than I could fly.

(editing marks: "a" above first; "My" inserted; "The pain was" inserted; corrections deleting "As soon as", "my first", "my", "in blinding pain", "but", "I could")

2 Longer sentences

Most academic writing requires that you elaborate on your ideas and
show the connections between them. Longer sentences give you the room
to develop more complex thoughts and the structure to show the relationships between them. (See also Chapter 38.) If you find a patch of short sentences that say little and don't emphasize an important point, consider
combining some sentences to emphasize the main ideas.

Recent snows have renewed a problem in the town of Palmyra.
The problem is sinkholes. Water eroding underground limestone
deposits causes them. They are like huge potholes. They appear
quickly and grow rapidly. A few years ago a sinkhole opened in a
car dealer's lot, swallowing a few cars. Last February a fuel truck
making a delivery ended up in a sinkhole. Another sinkhole
swallowed a yard and threatened a house. Heavy snows are
melting rapidly. We face the problem of a sinking town.

(editing marks: ":" after Palmyra; ", which are caused by water" inserted; "that" inserted; ", while another" inserted; "With heavy" inserted; ", we" inserted; deletions of "The problem is", "Water", "causes them", "They", "Another", "Heavy snows are", "We")

You can create emphasis by mixing short and longer sentences. Try
changing abruptly from long sentences to a sparsely worded, simple sentence that stresses one of your key points. The break in rhythm can stop
readers in their tracks. Try it. It works.

EDITING 2: PRACTICE

Edit the following passage, which appears just before the end of a personal
narrative, mixing the length of the sentences to improve emphasis and variety. More than one edited version is possible. Be ready to explain your choices.

When I heard the mail drop through the slot in the door, my heart
leapt. After I practically flew downstairs, I pounced on the mail that lay
scattered on the floor. There, finally, was a letter for me from Iowa State
University. "Today's the day," I said to myself, "the day that will seal my

fate." At last I would have the answer to the all-important question of whether I had been accepted at the school of my choice. I wondered where I would spend the next four years. I wondered if I would be in Ames, Iowa, or at home in Deerfield, Illinois. After I took a deep breath and counted to three, I ripped open the envelope.

39 c   Sentence types

Sentences can vary by *rhetorical type* or by *functional type*. Because readers' attention will be drawn to an atypical sentence—a question or command, for instance—varying sentence types provides another way to create emphasis.

1   Rhetorical types and word order

Within a sentence, should you put the main point first and the less important information later? Or should you first establish the context and then deliver the main message? Such decisions refer to rhetorical sentence types. The first strategy—placing the main idea first—results in a **cumulative sentence.**

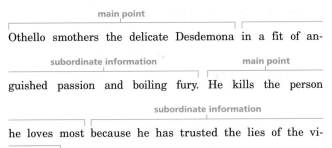

main point

Othello smothers the delicate Desdemona in a fit of an-

subordinate information   main point

guished passion and boiling fury. He kills the person

subordinate information

he loves most because he has trusted the lies of the vi-

cious Iago.

The second strategy—which saves its punch for the end—results in a **periodic sentence.**

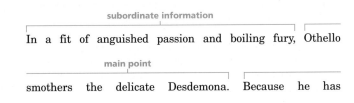

subordinate information

In a fit of anguished passion and boiling fury, Othello

main point

smothers the delicate Desdemona. Because he has

subordinate information   main point

trusted the lies of the vicious Iago, he kills the person he loves most.

Notice how the effects differ despite the very slight variation in wording.

Cumulative sentences allow a writer to make a major point, then support it. Yet writing composed solely of cumulative sentences can be monotonous, so consider using a periodic sentence to emphasize a point.

A *Small Place* is an unsettling book. In it, Jamaica Kincaid discloses shocking details about the tourist paradise Antigua, where she grew up. We see the poor condition of the school, the library, the hospital, and even the government, all problems she links to English and American imperialism. An American feels defensive and ashamed *when* confronted by the consequences of unthinking exploitation.

Alternatively, you can put important information first by using **inverted word order,** in which the verb precedes the subject: *Heavy hangs the head that wears the crown.* Although such inversion is uncommon, it can be used to strong effect in a special situation such as an opening or an ending.

2 Functional types

Most writing relies primarily on **declarative sentences**—sentences that make statements. However, an occasional *question, exclamation,* or *command* can grab the reader's attention.

Yes, I love the church. *How could I do otherwise?* I am in the rather unique position of being the son, the grandson, and the great-grandson of preachers. Yes, I see the church as the body of Christ. *But, oh! How we have blem-*

ished and scarred that body through social neglect and through fear of being nonconformists. [Italics added.]

MARTIN LUTHER KING, JR., "LETTER FROM BIRMINGHAM JAIL"

Notice how the emotional color of the paragraph changes as King changes sentence types using questions and exclamations.

The church was a hub of Black children's social existence, and caring Black adults were buffers against the segregated and hostile world that told us we weren't important. But our parents said it wasn't so, our teachers said it wasn't so, and our preachers said it wasn't so. The message of my racially segregated childhood was clear: *let no man or woman look down on you, and look down on no man or woman.* [Italics added.]

MARIAN WRIGHT EDELMAN, "A FAMILY LEGACY"

Edelman stresses the message by putting it in a command, which the reader can hear as Edelman heard it herself.

EDITING 3: EXPLORATION

Extreme examples of periodic and cumulative sentences were much more common in the past than now. Here are two excerpts from an essay by the eighteenth-century writer Samuel Johnson in which he relates the demise of an "adventurer in lotteries"—a gambler. What can you infer of Johnson's audience and purpose? Which sentence is periodic, and which is cumulative? What effect does each one have on you, the reader? Try to write sentences modeled on these examples, following their general patterns and rhythms but using different topics.

As I have passed much of life in disquiet and suspense, and lost many opportunities of advantage by a passion which I have reason to believe prevalent in different degrees over a great part of mankind, I cannot but think myself well qualified to warn those, who are yet uncaptivated of the danger which they incur by placing themselves within its influence. . . . My heart leaped at the thoughts of such an approach of sudden riches, which I considered myself, however contrarily to the laws of computation, as having missed by a single chance; and I could not forbear to revolve the consequences which such a bounteous allotment would have produced, if it had happened to me.

SAMUEL JOHNSON, "THE HISTORY OF AN ADVENTURER IN LOTTERIES"

ESL Reversing Subjects and Verbs for Emphasis

In English, placing certain elements at the beginning of a sentence requires unusual word order. This unusual word order—reversing the position of the subject and the verb or part of the verb—creates emphasis.

These *introductory elements* create word order much like that of a question, with the verb or an auxiliary verb coming before the subject.

```
                                auxiliary   base verb
          introductory element   | subject |
        ┌─────────────────────┐ ┌─┐┌─┐┌───┐
```
Under no circumstances did we wish to cut funding for this program.

These introductory elements require changing subject-verb order:

NEGATIVE ADVERBS	*Seldom* has a verdict created such an outrage among citizens.
OR ADVERB PHRASES	*In no way* should funding for this program be cut.
	(Others: *rarely, scarcely, hardly ever, only once, in no case, not until* [+ *time*], *not since* [+ *time*])
ADVERB OF EXTENT OR DEGREE	*So* intense was the hurricane that it destroyed much of the small town.
CONDITIONAL CLAUSES	*Only if we take measures now* will we rescue our city from urban blight.
	Only when there is justice will there be peace.

Certain other introductory elements require you to place the subject after both the auxiliary (if there is one) and the main verb.

ADVERB OF POSITION	*Beyond the hedge* stood a small shed.
COMPARATIVES	*More intriguing than the main plot of the novel* are several of the subplots.
PARTICIPLES WITH MODIFIERS	*Lying on my desk* should be a large sealed envelope.

39 d   Sentence openings

Consider repositioning elements so that some sentences begin with elements other than the subject. Doing so will slightly emphasize that sentence.

> Increasingly, doctors
> ~~Doctors~~ rely ~~increasingly~~ on advanced diagnostic equipment.

> Overworked and often underpaid, single
> ~~Single~~ parents, ~~who are overworked and often underpaid,~~ are among the most marginalized members of society.

> Until researchers learned to translate its hieroglyphs, much ⊙
> ~~Much~~ of ancient Mayan culture remained a mystery ~~until researchers learned to translate its hieroglyphs.~~

39 e   Deliberate repetition

Deliberately repeating words, phrases, or sentence structures links the repeated elements and emphasizes them. (See 36c on repetition and paragraph coherence.) Repetition also can create powerful rhythms. A succession of similar phrases, falling on the reader's ear like waves striking the shore, can soothe or build to a climax. Getting just the right amount of repetition is difficult, however. When in doubt, err on the side of too little rather than too much. You can also use synonyms, rather than repeat the same word.

To use repetition effectively, look for words, phrases, or structures that are important to your meaning. Make sure that the element you have repeated deserves the emphasis and that the rhythmic effect you create is appropriate for your subject and audience. In this passage, Mark was trying to recreate the magic spell his mother cast by reading to him regularly:

> She   and saw
> ~~When she~~ read to me, I ~~could see~~ faraway islands fringed with
> She read to me, and with
> coconut palms. ~~With~~ Jim Hawkins, I shivered in the apple barrel
> She read to me, and
> while the pirates plotted. I ran with Maori warriors to raid the
> She read to me, and
> villages of neighboring tribes. I saw Captain Cook slain on a

beach of the Sandwich Isles. I saw the Tahitians welcome British sailors. I watched Fletcher Christian mutiny against Captain Bligh, and I marveled that Bligh reached safety in an open boat. As she read to me, I heard Ahab's peg leg thump on the deck overhead, and I marveled at the whiteness of the whale.

Also notice the repetition of I saw, I shivered, I ran, I watched.

EDITING 5: EXPLORATION

In the following passage, identify repetition. How does it contribute to the passage's effectiveness? What ideas are emphasized?

His need for food stamps, quite obviously, is minimal now. But his need is not minimal for a reminder of those days when his father worked as a shipping clerk in a refrigerator plant and his mother stayed home to raise three children before she died so prematurely that her youngest son's heart still aches to think of it.

To reach the goal he has set for himself, to reach the level Sugar Ray Leonard once occupied at the top of boxing's craggy Mount Olympus, he must not lose a fight, but just as important, he must not lose his way.

He must avoid the normal pitfalls a fighter faces like the jabs to the nose and hooks to the liver, but this fighter must avoid more than that. He must avoid the eroding powers of money and fame, two things that build a man up and bring him crashing back to earth with the same swiftness.

RON BORGES, "A GOLDEN BOY WITH A PLATINUM PLAN"

39 f   Elliptical constructions

Sometimes, for the sake of brevity or to create a special rhythm, you can deliberately omit words that your reader will be able to supply mentally. Such an omission is called an **elliptical construction.**

Fire when ~~you are~~ ready.

I like the second one better ~~than the first.~~

The omitted words are often dropped from the second part of a parallel construction, after the idea has been introduced.

Our souls belong to our bodies, not our bodies to our souls.

HERMAN MELVILLE

His words suggested one thing, his actions ~~suggested~~ another.

Sometimes a comma is needed to show where words were dropped.

The architect receives high praise; the carpenter, none.

Elliptical constructions work only when all the words you omit are identical to words that remain.

Of Shakespeare's female characters, Lady Macbeth is the most ruthless, Desdemona and Juliet are **the most loving, and Portia** is **the most resourceful.**

The omitted verbs must match exactly the verb that remains: is. *But the plural subject* Desdemona and Juliet *requires the verb* are, *so the omitted verbs must be reinstated.*

For tips on pronouns in elliptical constructions, see 49p.

EDITING 6: EXPLORATION

The ways a writer achieves emphasis and variety are central to his or her writing style. Select a few pages of writing by one of your favorite authors and study the sentences for the techniques mentioned in this chapter. Does the author favor one technique? Which technique(s) are most effective? Why? What does the author's use of variety and emphasis say about his or her style? Answers to these questions could tell you a great deal about why you like your favorite author's work.

EDITING 7: PRACTICE

Edit the following passage from a personal narrative for emphasis and variety. You will, of course, have to choose what to emphasize and which elements to preserve as you create variety. Think of at least two alternatives for each choice, and note the reasons for your decisions. If you have to make assumptions about audience or purpose, note them as well.

Sunday dinner at Grandma's house was about as appealing to me as a day without recess for me, an energetic nine-year-old. It meant leaving the other kids at the playing field at the bottom of the eighth inning. I had to take a bath in the middle of the day and wash behind my ears. The worst thing was that I had to put on my best clothes and try to keep them clean. For me to keep my clothes clean seemed beyond the realm of possibility in those days. My parents would look absolutely delighted as I emerged from the bath every week. I looked, frankly, nothing like myself. My father would exclaim, "She's as clean as a hound's tooth!" Yet I would arrive at Grandma's week after week looking like Raggedy Ann, despite my parents' best efforts. My shirt would inevitably be stained; my stockings would inevitably be split; my shoes would inevitably be scuffed. My mother would look at me in disbelief as I climbed out of the car. She was amazed, no doubt, that such a metamorphosis could have occurred in a twenty-minute ride. My disheveled appearance, to be honest, never seemed to bother Grandma. She always exclaimed, "Don't you look nice!" I don't know to this day whether she was losing her eyesight or just being kind.

EDITING 8: APPLICATION

Select a passage from a paper you are working on and look for places that need emphasis or variety. Generate alternative versions using the various techniques discussed in this chapter—position, sentence length, sentence type, sentence openings, repetition, and ellipsis. Pick the version—alternative or original—that best suits your audience and purpose, and explain your choices.

chapter 40

Building Vital Sentences

What brings writing to life? Why does one writer's prose dull the senses while another's, on the same subject, rivets readers' attention? Sentence *vitality*—liveliness—helps create compelling writing. By delighting the imagination, a vital sentence encourages readers to think and interact with your words. Clarity, descriptiveness, action, and specific examples all contribute to vitality.

For example, many readers would find this description dull.

The sky and the sunrise are reflected by the snow. There is a road in front of me that goes down the slope toward the stone formations.

But this is what Edward Abbey actually wrote in *Desert Solitaire*.

The snow-covered ground glimmers with a dull blue light, reflecting the sky and the approaching sunrise. Leading away from me the narrow dirt road, an alluring and primitive path into nowhere meanders down the slope and toward the heart of the labyrinth of naked stone.

Why is the second passage so much more vital? The first uses **general** nouns with few modifiers: *sunrise, road, stone formations.* The second uses **specific** nouns and modifiers to create tangible images: *alluring and primitive path, labyrinth of naked stone.* The first uses weak, **state-of-being verbs:** *is, goes.* The second uses **dynamic verbs** that evoke actions readers can visualize: *glimmers, meanders.* Finally, while the verb in the first passage is in the **passive voice** (*are reflected*), the second passage uses verbs in the **active voice.**

Think of Each Sentence as a Story

Like any story, a sentence has actors (nouns and pronouns) and actions (verbs). Help readers imagine the story unfolding before their eyes. Let the person or thing the sentence is about and the grammatical subject be one and the same. Express the principal action of the sentence in its main verb.

Not

Festivities were held by Derry Street residents and their children to celebrate the opening of a new community playground.

but

Children and residents of Derry Street *celebrated* the opening of a new community playground.

or perhaps

Dozens of toddlers christened a new *playground* on Derry Street today, *clambering* on the climbing structures and *teetering* on the teeter-totters.

Can you envision much from festivities, children, residents, *or even* celebrated? *But* toddlers, christened, clambering, teetered—*such words can awaken the imagination.*

A sentence shouldn't be a who-done-it mystery. If you know who did it, say so.

WEAK   At a hearing before the selection committee, three sites were taken out of consideration, and a fourth was placed under further study.

STRONGER   At a hearing, *the selection committee took* three sites out of consideration and said it would study a fourth.

STILL STRONGER *The selection committee eliminated* three sites *and agreed to study* a fourth.

*Using the principal character (*the committee*) as the grammatical subject and putting the key actions in the main verbs (*eliminated, agreed*) brings the sentence to life—and shortens it!*

40 a   Concrete, specific nouns

If a sentence is to tell a story, your first task is to identify the actors in it so that readers can recognize them fully. Whether a character is a person, an object, or an idea, try to make that element come alive in readers' minds. Compare the mental pictures you get from the phrases *an old blue car* and *a rusted blue VW Beetle.* The first evokes images of a number of cars, the second a specific car.

As you edit, examine your choice of language. Is your language abstract or concrete? **Abstract** words refer to ideas and concepts that cannot be perceived by the senses: *transportation, wealth, childhood, nutrition.* **Concrete** words name things that can be seen, touched, heard, tasted, or smelled: *cars, dime, child, broccoli.*

Next, is your language general or specific? **General** words refer to categories and groups: *pets, stores, doctors.* **Specific** words identify individual objects or people: *Rover, the Reading Terminal Market, pediatrician Andrea McCoy.*

The terms *abstract* and *concrete* are not absolute, nor are *general* and *specific.* Think of them as representing the ends of a continuum, with varying degrees of abstraction in between.

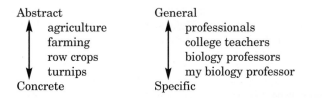

These two ways of characterizing words can overlap. *Music,* for example, is concrete in that you can hear it, but the word is also a general term embracing everything from Bartok to bagpipes to Busta Rhymes.

Human thought depends on the ability to make connections between the general and the specific. Some kinds of thought require abstract terms: we could not think, speak, or write about *truth, insurance, constitutionality, political risk,* or *angular velocity* without using words developed for such concepts. Yet writing composed exclusively of abstractions can seem like nothing but "hot air." On the other hand, it may be hard to glean general truths from writing consisting only of details. Writers often err on the side of too many generalizations, so look for ways to enliven abstract terms with specifics.

We stand for a brighter future, a renewed hope, a better America.

Who doesn't want those things? How can you tell what this writer stands for?

We stand for a brighter future, a renewed hope, a better America, in which the unemployed find work, the sick receive health care, the old and the young are nurtured, and all of us are treated with respect.

What this writer means by a better America is clearer now, and the reader is free to agree or disagree with the specifics provided.

When writing about an abstract concept, provide a definition or example definition shortly after introducing it. Then make sure you ground the abstraction with clear, tangible examples so that it has meaning for your readers.

—money the government has borrowed in order to operate—
Concern about the national debt inspired efforts to balance the
˄
federal budget.

, like those that created the welfare system,
Liberal policies are bringing this country to ruin.
˄

, by slashing environmental protections, show they
Conservatives don't care about people, only business.
˄

When writing academic papers, you may want to use general statements in openings and conclusions. Make sure that elsewhere in the paper you have developed the specific and concrete details needed to support them. (See Chapter 38.)

40 b   Strong verbs

After you have identified the actors in each sentence, describe their actions in equally vivid language by using strong verbs.

1 Replacing state-of-being verbs

Verbs drive sentences the way an engine powers a car. *Dynamic verbs*—those that express motion or create vivid images—add horsepower to your writing. Verbs that simply show a state of being, such as *be, appear, become, seem, exist*—can leave your sentences underpowered. As you edit, look for weak verbs and consider replacing them with dynamic verbs.

threatens   *more*
Nothing is more dangerous to future economic stability than
˄   ˄
inflation.

oppose
Even some forest-product corporations have taken a stand against
˄
deforestation, which is spreading rapidly.

Sometimes a form of *be* obscures a stronger verb that can become the main verb of the sentence.

The most effective writers ~~are those who~~ write as though they were simply talking.

Expletive constructions, those that begin with *there is / are* and *it is,* often can be replaced with stronger verbs.

~~There are~~ several moons ~~orbiting~~ *orbit* Jupiter, Galileo found.
<small>Several</small> <small>orbit</small>

~~There are~~ several techniques ~~that researchers~~ *Researchers* employ to prevent self-selection in opinion surveys.

~~There are many~~ people ~~who~~ still believe that Elvis Presley is alive, even though ~~it is~~ only tabloids ~~that~~ report such "news" seriously.
<small>Many</small>

2 Replacing weak dynamic verbs

Not all verbs that describe action spark clear images. Overuse has exhausted the image-making power of such verbs as *do, get, go, have, make,* and *think.* As you edit, watch for weak dynamic verbs and substitute stronger verbs when you can.

He ~~has~~ several antique cars.
<small>owns</small>

She ~~does her carvings~~ with great skill.
<small>carves</small>

Beavers ~~make~~ dams that slow erosion.
<small>build</small>

Often a verb that relies on a modifier or other words for its descriptive power can be replaced. Choose the verb that best describes what you intend to convey.

He ~~walked rapidly~~ out of the room.
<small>rushed</small>

He ~~walked rapidly~~ out of the room.
<small>ran</small>

He ~~walked rapidly~~ out of the room.
<small>scurried</small>

Using Expletive Constructions

Expletive constructions such as *it is* and *there are* often serve useful functions. They can create emphasis by slightly delaying the subject of the sentence and by allowing opportunities for parallelism. (See 39e and 39f.)

> *It is* a far, far better thing that I do, than I have ever done; it is a far, far better rest that I go to, than I have ever known.
>
> CHARLES DICKENS, A TALE OF TWO CITIES

Expletives are also necessary in certain expressions about time and the weather.

> *There* were showers this morning, but right now *it's* sunny outside.

> *It's* five o'clock, sir; *it's* time to go.

---

3 Turning nouns into verbs

The ease with which English words can be changed from one part of speech to another gives the language a marvelous flexibility. With the help of a suffix such as *-ance*, *-ment*, or *-ation*, verbs such as *deliver, announce,* or *tempt* can become useful nouns: *deliverance, announcement, temptation.*

Nouns thus made from verbs are called **nominalizations.** A nominalization can sometimes conceal the real action of a sentence by requiring the use of a verb such as *do, have, make,* or *be.* If you have entombed the action of your sentence in a nominalization, dig up the buried verb to give your prose new life.

Pickett's Charge ~~has a continuing fascination for~~ *still fascinates* historians of the Battle of Gettysburg.

Some nouns and verbs have the same form: *cause, dance, march, tie, love, hate.* If you use them as nouns, then you have to find new verbs, which are usually weaker. There is no reason to *perform a dance* when you can simply *dance,* no sense in *holding a march* when you can simply *march.*

The signs told us to ~~make a~~ detour around the construction.

We plan to ~~hold a meeting~~ *meet* in two weeks.

Not every noun can be turned into a verb. Some grammarians object to using *host* as a verb; instead of *Jay Leno hosts the Tonight Show,* they prefer *Jay Leno is the* host *of the Tonight Show.*

Changing Nouns to Verbs

To enliven your writing, replace these common expressions with the dynamic verbs that are buried within them.

Expression	Buried Verb
put forth a proposal	propose
hold a discussion	discuss
formulate a plan	plan
reach a decision	decide
arrive at a conclusion	conclude
hammer out an agreement	agree
hold a meeting	meet
call a strike	strike
make a choice	choose

EDITING 1: EXPLORATION

These two passages show what magic can be wrought when you make the topic of each sentence its grammatical subject and put its principal action in the main verb. Read each one, and pick out the actors and the actions in each sentence. How often are they represented by the subject and the verb?

The war has naught to do with slaves, cried Congress, the President, and the Nation; and yet no sooner had the armies, East and West, penetrated Virginia and Tennessee than fugitive slaves appeared within their lines. They came at night, when the flickering camp-fires shone like vast unsteady stars along the black horizon: old men and thin, with gray and tufted hair; women, with frightened eyes, dragging whimpering hungry children . . .

W. E. B. DUBOIS, *THE SOULS OF BLACK FOLK*

Through the port comes the moon-shine astray!
It tips the guard's cutlass and silvers this nook;

But 'twill die in the dawning of Billy's last day.
A jewel-block they'll make of me to-morrow,
Pendant pearl from the yard-arm-end
Like the ear-drop I gave to Bristol Molly—
O, 'tis me, not the sentence they'll suspend.

HERMAN MELVILLE, BILLY BUDD, FORETOPMAN

40 c Active or passive voice

When a verb is in the **active voice,** the person or thing performing the action is the subject.

Donald *spent* the money.

Donald, the actor performing the action, is the subject of the sentence. *Money,* the recipient of the action, is the direct object.

When a verb is in the **passive voice,** things get turned around. The recipient of the action—*money*—becomes the grammatical subject, and *Donald* becomes the **agent** of the action in the prepositional phrase *by Donald.*

The money *was spent* by Donald.

Donald can appear as above or disappear entirely, depending on how important it is that the reader know who the agent of the action was: *The money was spent, and the club folded.* Perhaps there is no agent at all:

Mistakes *were made.*

1 Using the active voice to emphasize actors and actions

By making the actor the subject of the sentence, the active voice helps readers visualize the action of a sentence. Active-voice sentences usually use fewer words and proceed more directly than passive-voice sentences. Edit to favor the active voice.

Manson and his followers planned the
~~The~~ Tate and LaBianca murders ~~were planned by Manson and his~~
~~followers~~ to incite a race war. ~~Whites were expected~~ They expected whites to rise up in
alarm at the killings.

2 Using the passive voice for special purposes

The passive voice deemphasizes the actor and highlights the recipient of the action. At times, this may be exactly what you want to do. Use the passive voice to accomplish the following special purposes:

■ To stress the topic

A constitutional amendment outlawing flag burning *was rejected* by the Senate.

■ To leave the agent unstated

According to investigators, the fire *was* deliberately *set.*

By whom? No one knows at this point.

■ To assert objectivity in research writing

In the experiment, samples of food *were* first *contaminated* with bacteria. The samples *were* then *irradiated.* The samples *were tested* to see whether the bacteria survived.

The passive voice deemphasizes the role of an individual and suggests other researchers could produce similar results.

■ To strengthen flow between sentences

ACTIVE   Two crises threaten the economic security of the nation. Economists, business leaders, and politicians *have documented* the first crisis, the decay of manufacturing industries. They have all but ignored the second, however.

PASSIVE   Two crises threaten the economic security of the nation. The first crisis, the decay of manufacturing industries, *has been documented* by economists, business leaders, and politicians. They have all but ignored the second, however.

Notice how the change helps the sequence of topics flow from one sentence to the next.

■ To take advantage of an emphatic position

Two crises threaten the economic security of the nation. The first crisis, the decay of manufacturing industries, has been documented by economists, business leaders, and politicians. *The second,* however, *has* all but *been ignored.*

Using the passive moves the key word ignored *to the emphatic final position.*

Verbs That Can't Be Passive,
ESL *Verbs That Can't Be Active*

Most verbs in English can be either active or passive:

Charles Darwin *wrote* the famous book *The Origin of Species*. It *was written* after his expedition to the Galapagos Islands.

But not all English verbs have both active and passive forms. **Intransitive verbs,** verbs that do not take a direct object, can't be passive.

The improvement ~~was~~ resulted from his work with a tutor.

The baby ~~was~~ weighed seven pounds.

But weigh *used as a transitive verb can be used in the passive voice: The baby* was weighed *by the doctor.*

Certain other verbs, even though they may have objects, also cannot be used in the passive voice.

five   *has*
~~Five~~ boroughs ~~are had by~~ New York City.

Do not use these verbs in the passive voice:

arrive	exist	occur	stay
come	fall	rain	vanish
cry	go	result	walk
consist	happen	rise	weigh + amount
die	have	seem	
disappear	live	sleep	

Do not use these verb phrases in the active voice:

be born	be killed	be made	
be given	be located	+	preposition

is located
The capital of the United States ~~locates~~ in Washington, D.C.

But locate *can be in the active voice when not followed immediately by a preposition: Can you* locate *Washington on the map?*

EDITING 3: EXPLORATION ....

The following passage by James Baldwin makes extensive use of expletive constructions and the passive voice. Read it carefully, and try to decide why the author has used these techniques. Do they influence the meaning of the passage? its effect? Where do they focus your attention? Do they create a particular mood or atmosphere?

There is a custom in the village—I am told it is repeated in many villages—of "buying" African natives for the purpose of converting them to Christianity. There stands in the church all year round a small box with a slot for money, decorated with a black figurine, and into this box the villagers drop their francs. During the *carnival* which precedes Lent, two village children have their faces blackened—out of which bloodless darkness their blue eyes shine like ice—and fantastic horsehair wigs are placed on their blond heads; thus disguised, they solicit among the villagers for money for the missionaries in Africa. Between the box in the church and the blackened children, the village "bought" last year six or eight African natives.

JAMES BALDWIN, "STRANGER IN THE VILLAGE"

EDITING 4: PRACTICE ....

Edit the following paragraph from a paper arguing against pesticide use by substituting the active voice whenever you think it is effective. Make any changes in wording to make the passage flow better or have greater impact. More than one edited version is possible. Be ready to explain your editing choices.

We are all affected by pesticides. Hundreds of synthetic chemicals have been developed by scientists to destroy the insects and rodents that are called "pests" by farmers and Sunday gardeners. Once these deadly toxins are used, however, they are retained in the land for years sometimes. They are maintained in the environment, where our crops and water supply are contaminated and desirable species of birds and fish are killed off. Ironically, pesticides are even known not to work very well in the first place, since usually a pest population that is resistant to the chemicals is created. And within a few years, the problem is as large as ever. The effect of pesticides on the environment and on our lives should be questioned. Perhaps even the right to use them at all should be questioned.

40 d   Vital modifiers

1 Using concrete, specific modifiers

Use the same considerations when selecting modifiers as you do for nouns: choose specific and concrete modifiers over abstract and vague terms. Some descriptive modifiers, such as *pretty, dull, dumb, nice, beautiful, good, bad, young,* and *old,* have become almost meaningless through overuse. They paint a very general picture. Rather than ask readers to accept your impression, give them the specific details so they can see things for themselves.

VAGUE   A row of old brick houses stands along the street.

SPECIFIC   Dilapidated brick houses line the street, their shutters sagging and their windows boarded.

VAGUE   She played poorly.

SPECIFIC   She played hesitantly, making several jarring mistakes.

2 Untangling noun clusters

A remarkable quality of English is its use of nouns as modifiers. Instead of saying *a cabinet for files,* we can say *a file cabinet.* We can also string noun modifiers together. *A metal file cabinet* is far easier to say than *a cabinet of metal for files.*

Like any good thing, using nouns as modifiers can be done to excess. A long string of nouns used as modifiers is called a **noun cluster:** *do-it-yourself home improvement instruction videotape recordings.* Readers, upon finding a large noun cluster, must decide which nouns serve as modifiers and which is the "real" noun. Untangle noun clusters by moving some of the modifiers elsewhere.

Michael Graves's architecture attempts to revitalize a ~~building~~
of building forms
~~form~~ language that was lost during the heyday of International
Style modernism.

Sometimes writers are tempted to introduce a person with a long string of identifying modifiers in a special kind of noun cluster called a *false title.* Pick the elements about the person that you want to emphasize and move the other descriptive modifiers elsewhere.

ESL *Order of Adjectives*

Some types of adjectives typically occur before others. For example, an adjective describing size typically occurs before one describing color; *the large white house,* not *the white large house.* Shown below is the typical order of adjectives before nouns.

1.	Article	a, an, the
	Or possession	my, our, your, his, her, its, our, their
	Or demonstration	this, these, that, those
2.	Number	one, second, eleven, next, last, few, some, many
3.	Evaluation	good, pretty, ugly
4.	Size	big, small, tiny
5.	Shape	round, oblong, rectangular
6.	Condition	broken, shiny, rickety
7.	Age	old, young, new
8.	Color	blue, red, magenta
9.	Material	wooden, cotton, iron
10.	Noun as adjective	sports, flower, city

        1 2   6   7   10
He never forgot his first shiny new sports car.

1 2   4   5   9
A few large round wooden containers were stacked on the floor.

Not all types of adjectives can be used together. For example, if you use an article, you shouldn't use a possessive: *the next project* or *my next project* but not *the my next project.* And generally, you should avoid long strings of adjectives.

We met Texas-style chili cook-off champion ~~Minnie Peppers~~. [*Minnie Peppers, the* inserted before "Texas-style"]

The team signed 170-pound Big Ten Conference rushing and ~~kick-return leader Carter McIlroy~~. [*Carter McIlroy, who led the* ... *in kick returns.*]

EDITING 6: EXPLORATION

Read the following paragraph from Nancy Gibbs's description of modern American zoos. What choices has Gibbs made to give vitality to the passage?

At some 150 American zoos . . . , the troubles are not very different. The sharks eat the angelfish. The Australian hairy-nosed wombat stays in its cave, and the South American smoky jungle frog hunkers down beneath a leaf, all tantalizingly hidden from the prying eyes of the roughly 110 million Americans who go to zoos every year. Visitors often complain that as a result of all the elaborate landscaping, they cannot find the animals. But this, like almost everything else that goes wrong these days, is a signal that America's zoos are doing something right.

NANCY GIBBS, "THE NEW ZOO: A MODERN ARK"

EDITING 7: PRACTICE

Edit the following paragraph to create vital sentences. You may invent and add any details you think are necessary. More than one edited version is possible. Be ready to explain your editing choices.

Most dog owners don't realize in advance how much time, money, and energy must be spent on a puppy. First, there is housebreaking the puppy and teaching it basic puppy obedience skills: how to accompany its owner while on a leash, how to respond to its name, how to stay near its owner. There are also other things—fetching, standing, and so on. And even when owners have the time for training, they probably don't have the necessary expertise. This means enrollment in expensive obedience school classes is required. Puppies create other expenses as well. Veterinarian visits, food and bedding, leashes and playthings, and grooming—a must for any well-bred dog—are all costly. And at least one nice rug or one pair of shoes must be replaced because a bad dog has chewed through them. Still, as any devoted dog owner will tell you, the expense is justified by the rewards; there's nothing like coming home from a hard day and being greeted by someone who loves you unconditionally and absolutely.

EDITING 8: APPLICATION

Read through a paper you are working on and pay close attention to the vitality of your sentences. Do your sentences "tell stories"? Have you chosen specific, concrete nouns and modifiers wherever possible? Are your verbs precise? Do they convey aciton? If you have used the passive voice, do you have a good reason for doing so? Can you find noun clusters? Keep the elements that you like and improve those that you don't like.

chapter 41

Being Concise

I n most writing situations, the goal is to convey information clearly and efficiently. Vagueness, wordiness, and needless complexity can tire or annoy readers. Therefore, make your writing direct: express your ideas plainly. Be **concise:** use no more words than you need to achieve your purpose.

It is natural—indeed a good idea—to throw lots of ideas into your first draft just to get them all down; but when editing, make your writing concise. Some writers call this process *boiling down,* referring to the cooking process that turns large quantities of thin broth into hearty, full-flavored soup. The drafts of this book required a lot of boiling down. The following is our original draft of a paragraph that appears later in this chapter:

> In a famous piece of advice, public speakers are urged, "Tell them what you're going to say, say it, then tell them what you said." In other words, say the message at least three times so that the audience will understand it clearly. This advice reflects the patterns of spoken language.

The second sentence seemed to do little more than rephrase the first, so we combined it with the third sentence.

In ~~other words, say~~ the message ~~at least three times so that~~ the

> spoken language, repeating   will help

audience ~~will~~ understand it clearly. ~~This advice reflects the~~

~~patterns of spoken language.~~

We edited further to eliminate other unnecessary words:

In spoken language, ~~repeating the message will help the audience~~ *repetition helps listeners*

understand ⟲ ~~it clearly.~~

At every step, we tested our results: we compared the new edited version both with the previous one and with our understanding of what we were trying to say. We guarded against losing meaning, but we were willing to lose subtle shadings if we could state our point more clearly. If you polish relentlessly, your prose will shine.

41 a   Vague generalities

As we think and reason, we absorb specific information and experiences and then make associations to generalize about these data: *That radiator burned my hand when I touched it. Radiators can be dangerous.*

Writing that consists only of specific details may fail to convey broader ideas. On the other hand, writing with too many generalizations may omit useful details. Overly broad generalizations are called **generalities,** and they need editing.

It is our duty today to take responsibility for our actions.

When was it not everyone's duty to be responsible?

Some generalities attempt to make a point but result in circular reasoning: *During the harsh winters of the 1870s, the weather was very cold.* (A harsh winter is cold by definition.) Some don't really say anything at all: *Many factors played a part.* (What factors?)

Generalities don't advance discussion. Eliminating them will usually improve your writing.

Fetal alcohol syndrome affects one of every 750 newborn babies.

~~**It is clearly not good for them,**~~ **causing coordination problems,**

malformed organs, small brains, short attention spans, and

behavioral problems.

When you delete a generality, you may have to move some information from it to another sentence.

Is college worthwhile? ~~Whether or not to go to college is a decision~~

~~that many eighteen-year-olds must face after graduating from high~~
                          high school
~~school,~~ Each graduate must decide according to his or her

finances, career opportunities, and, most important, personal

interests and goals.

Although generalities can occur anywhere in a paper, carefully check
your openings and conclusions, where you may be pushing for sweeping
statements or impressive summaries. (See Chapter 37.)

41 b   Idle words

Eliminate idle words. To determine whether a word is working or idle,
remove it: if no meaning is lost, leave it out.

1 Condensing automatic and wordy phrases

The speech habit of embellishing sentences with unnecessary words
can become a writing habit. It is a fact that most writers do it all the time.
For example, in the previous sentence, *it is a fact that* adds no meaning.
Phrases such as *it appears that* or *it has come to my attention that* merely
preface what the writer is about to say, a sort of authorial "throat-clearing."
Most sentences are better off without them.

Think of such phrases as **automatic phrases.** They often seem to
write themselves, but when examined, they add little if any meaning. When
you find an automatic phrase, test it for meaning: if something seems missing without it, try inserting a condensed version of the phrase.

          To
~~In order to~~ understand the effects of the law, consider the following

example.

          Today   often
~~In this day and age,~~ children ~~in many instances~~ know more about

dinosaurs than they know about American history.

Wordy phrases can be condensed. Look for unnecesssary uses of the
preposition *of* and for phrases containing *of* that can be reduced to a single

word. Abstract nouns such as *area, aspect, factor, kind manner, nature, tendency, thing,* and *type* should be suspect. Often you can delete them, condense them, or find more concrete substitutes. (See 40a.)

The author spent little time outside ~~of~~ his small circle of friends.

The architect had a specific ~~type of~~ construction method in mind.

2 Deleting useless modifiers

Modifiers such as *clearly, obviously, interestingly, undoubtedly, absolutely, fortunately, hopefully, really,* and *totally* are often used to intensify a whole sentence, making it sound more forceful or authoritative. Sometimes they add a nuance, but more often they can be deleted. Always test for altered meaning.

The strike against General Motors ~~clearly~~ disrupted production on the Buick assembly line. It was undoubtedly intended to do so.

Anna considered, but decided against, deleting undoubtedly, *which tells the reader that the assessment is her own conclusion.*

41 c   Simplifying grammatical constructions

Consider simplifying grammatical constructions. Changing a **passive-voice** sentence to the **active voice** usually shortens it slightly. (See 40c.) Eliminating **expletive constructions** such as *there were* and *it is* allows the use of strong verbs. (See 40b.)

Also consider shortening dependent clauses to phrases and phrases to single words. Look especially at **modifier clauses**—those that begin with *which, that, who, whom, because, before, when, where, while, if,* or *although.* To shorten a modifier clause to a phrase, try using just the past participle of the clause's main verb.

CLAUSE   The research project *that we were assigned to complete* involves a complex experiment.

PHRASE   The research project *assigned to us* involves a complex experiment.

WORD   *Our* research project involves a complex experiment.

Finding Unneeded Words

Automatic phrases that "write themselves" and wordy phrases from informal speech can introduce unneeded words. Edit with a critical eye for words that do no work.

Delete	**Or Substitute**
it is a fact that	in fact
it is clear that	clearly
there is no question that	unquestionably, certainly
the reason is that	because
without a doubt	undoubtedly
beyond the shadow of a doubt	surely, certainly
it is my opinion that	I think

Wordy	**Concise**
most of the people	most people
all of the work	all the work
due to the fact that	since, because
despite the fact that	although
at that point in time	then
communicate to	tell
voice concern	say
in this day and age	today
in those days	then
in any case	anyway
in most instances	usually
in some instances	sometimes
subsequent to	after
in the event of	if
in the final analysis	finally

In some situations, using the fewest words may not be the best solution. Take care that you do not create an awkward cluster by simplifying too many constructions. (See 40d.)

AWKWARD   The committee report listed sixteen alleged international illegal military-weapons dealers.

BETTER   The committee report listed sixteen alleged international dealers of illegal military weapons.

BETTER   The committee report alleged that sixteen international dealers illegally sold military weapons.

41 d   Redundancy

In a famous piece of advice, public speakers are urged, "Tell them what you're going to say, say it, then tell them what you said." In spoken language, repetition helps listeners understand.

In writing, some repetition is important, even necessary, to provide continuity. (See 36c and 39c.) But there is such a thing as too much repetition; it's called **redundancy.**

Exactly what constitutes redundancy remains for you to determine. Test each instance by omitting the repetition. Reread the passage, comparing it to the earlier version and to what you want to say. Does the repetition help link ideas, sustain rhythm, create emphasis, or prevent confusion? If not, leave it out. Have someone else read the passage for excessive repetition. Explain whom you are writing for and what you are trying to accomplish.

The most obvious redundancies arise from thoughtlessly using words that mean the same thing.

The ~~general~~ consensus ~~of opinion~~ among students was that the chancellor had exceeded her authority.

Consensus means a general agreement.

The raccoon warily circled ~~around~~ the tree.

An unnecessary definition is also usually easy to spot:

Foresters ~~who study trees~~ report that acid rain is damaging the state's population of hemlocks.

If you find yourself repeating a word or a similar one, try to eliminate one.

About ninety percent

~~A very high percentage~~ of the prison's inmates take advantage of the education program, ~~about ninety percent.~~

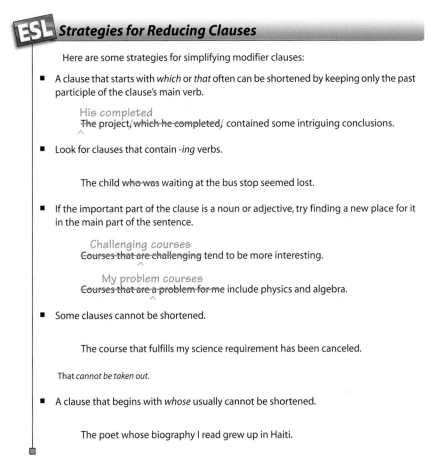

ESL *Strategies for Reducing Clauses*

Here are some strategies for simplifying modifier clauses:

■ A clause that starts with *which* or *that* often can be shortened by keeping only the past participle of the clause's main verb.

> His completed
> ~~The~~ project, ~~which he completed,~~ contained some intriguing conclusions.

■ Look for clauses that contain *-ing* verbs.

> The child ~~who was~~ waiting at the bus stop seemed lost.

■ If the important part of the clause is a noun or adjective, try finding a new place for it in the main part of the sentence.

> Challenging courses
> ~~Courses that are challenging~~ tend to be more interesting.

> My problem courses
> ~~Courses that are a problem for me~~ include physics and algebra.

■ Some clauses cannot be shortened.

> The course that fulfills my science requirement has been canceled.

That *cannot be taken out.*

■ A clause that begins with *whose* usually cannot be shortened.

> The poet whose biography I read grew up in Haiti.

EDITING 1: EXPLORATION

Look for generalities, idle words, and redundancies. Magazine articles and mass-market nonfiction books are often good sources. Collect two or three examples, and edit them to make them more concise. Bring your examples and edited versions to class to share with your classmates. Be ready to explain what you found in the originals and how your editing improves them.

Redundant Phrases

first and foremost	basic fundamentals
full and complete	initial preparation
past history	terrible tragedy
round in shape	final result, end result
red in color	free gift
the general consensus of opinion	true facts
a faulty miscalculation	completely destroyed
old and outdated	circle around
first ever	irregardless
cross over	misunderestimate
refer back	

EDITING 2: PRACTICE ....

Make the following passage more concise by eliminating generalities, idle words, and redundancies and by simplifying grammatical constructions. More than one edited version is possible. Be ready to explain your editing choices.

Many languages have influenced the development of English. The first instance of important influence came from the north in the form of Viking invaders who spoke a Scandinavian language. It appears that when these Vikings settled down and became farmers and traders who were peaceful, they wanted to be able to communicate with and speak to their Anglo-Saxon neighbors. There were several factors involved. Both groups spoke Germanic languages with similar vocabularies but with systems of grammar and inflection that were somewhat different. Clearly the easiest of the ways to smooth communication was for each group to drop the elements of their language that gave the other group difficulty. This explains why it is the case that modern English lacks the elaborate systems of verb endings and gender that characterize and distinguish other Indo-European languages.

....

41 e   Pretentious language

Sometimes writers believe that to impress their readers, they need to use technical or obscure language. They write *institutionalized populations* instead of *people in prisons*. Other writers overdecorate sentences: *In this sacrosanct institution of higher learning, we continually rededicate ourselves to the elevated principle that knowledge is empowering.* In other words, *In this university, we believe that knowledge gives power.*

While professors do expect students to demonstrate familiarity with the technical terms of their discipline (see 43g), needlessly complex language is termed **pretentious.** A special class of pretentious language is called **bureaucratese** after the government functionaries who so often use it. Another kind of pretentious language uses **jargon**—the specialized vocabulary of a profession or a social group—when addressing people who are unfamilar with that vocabulary.

Pretentious language often avoids names and personal pronouns by using the third person and the passive voice. Editing it into plain English often forces you to choose subjects for verbs and find direct ways of addressing readers.

PRETENTIOUS   The range of services provided includes examinations to determine visual or auditory impairment and the specification, provision, and instruction in the use of prosthetic devices including corrective lenses and auditory amplification devices.

EDITED   We can examine your eyes and ears, prescribe and sell glasses and hearing aids, and teach you to use them.

Pretentious Language

Pretentious	Direct
client populations	people served
voiced a concern	said, worried
range of selections	choice
minimizes expenditures	saves money
of crucial importance	important
institution of higher learning	college or university
have apprehension	fear
impacted	affected

41 f Euphemism

A **euphemism** is a word chosen for its inoffensiveness to substitute for one considered harsh or indelicate. Social conventions make it difficult for us to speak of certain subjects, especially money, death, and the human body. For example, many people would consider it more delicate to say *I lost my grandmother last week* than *My grandmother died last week.*

Euphemisms are also used by writers or speakers who fear negative reaction to plain talk about bad news. This use is called **doublespeak,** a term coined by George Orwell in his novel about totalitarianism, *1984.* Someone reading of *unemployment compensation reductions* may not understand immediately that it means *Workers without jobs will get less money from the government.*

~~As a result of the reordering of budget priorities,~~ the library ~~was~~
Short of money,
~~forced to defer acquisitions and suspend maintenance activities.~~
stopped buying books and maintaining its building.
^

EDITING 3: EXPLORATION

In the following passage, humorist Russell Baker lampoons contemporary rhetoric. How many examples of pretentious and euphemistic language can you find? Try editing the passage by replacing each example of pretentious language or euphemism with a more direct expression. Have you rescued "Little Red Riding Hood"?

> Once upon a point in time, a small person named Little Red Riding Hood initiated plans for the preparation, delivery and transportation of foodstuffs to her grandmother, a senior citizen residing at a place of residence in a forest of indeterminate dimension.
>
> In the process of implementing this program, her incursion into the forest was in mid-transportation process when it attained interface with an alleged perpetrator. This individual, a wolf, made inquiry as to the whereabouts of Little Red Riding Hood's goal as well as inferring that he was desirous of ascertaining the contents of Little Red Riding Hood's foodstuffs basket, and all that.
>
> RUSSELL BAKER, "LITTLE RED RIDING HOOD REVISITED"

EDITING 4: PRACTICE

Eliminate pretentious language and euphemisms from the following passage. More than one edited version is possible. Be ready to explain your editing choices.

> We conducted employee reviews and maintained a high standard of objectivity. Despite high performance reviews for your department,

however, we have decided to downsize the entire production staff by 40 percent. While we regret that this downsizing may inconvenience you in your relations with your subordinates, we know you, too, will understand our need to remain competitive in our market. Your continued loyalty—and that of your staff—will ensure that our company continues to set the standard of excellence for others to follow.

Testing Euphemisms

In academic writing, your purpose is to inform, not to obscure or mislead, so if you push too far for a delicate phrase, you will obscure meaning. When editing euphemisms from your writing, select a more direct alternative. Then test—consider how comfortable you feel with the more direct wording and whether your audience will be offended by your directness. If in doubt, check with a peer or an instructor.

DRAFT
Some Republicans in Congress *held* the Speaker of the House *responsible* for their party's *difficulties* in the election.

FIRST ALTERNATIVE
Some Republicans in Congress *blamed* the Speaker of the House for their party's *poor showing* in the election.

SECOND ALTERNATIVE
Some Republicans in Congress *blamed* the Speaker of the House for their party's *defeat* in the election.

Which is the best choice? Unless you have reason to soften your language, the second alternative is the most direct and therefore preferable.

Editing for Conciseness and Directness

When editing for conciseness and directness, keep the following guidelines in mind:

- Eliminate generalities.
- Remove automatic or idle words.
- Simplify grammatical constructions.
- Eliminate redundancy.
- Avoid pretentious language.
- Minimize euphemism.

EDITING 5: PRACTICE

Edit the following passage from a paper for a history class. More than one edited version is possible. Be ready to explain your editing choices.

My great-grandfather emigrated from Poland when he was a young man. Several of his cousins already lived in small Pennsylvania mining towns. When my great-grandfather arrived in America, he joined his cousins and began working in the mines.

There were several things he found discouraging. The dirty work, which was also dangerous, was far different from the life of agricultural splendor he had expected to lead, but he refused to let these types of circumstances ruin his happiness. It eventually was the case that he brought two of his brothers over to this country, and together the three of them saved money that was sufficient to buy a good-sized farm. By the age of thirty-four my great-grandfather had once again started a new life: he moved into his farmhouse, married a local woman, and began raising a family that would eventually be blessed by the arrival of fourteen bundles of joy.

EDITING 6: APPLICATION

Select a page from a paper you are working on. Examine each sentence carefully, looking for instances of wordy or indirect language. Using the checklists in this chapter, find euphemisms, pretentiousness, redundancy or any other problems, and draft alternatives. Working with a friend or a fellow student, compare versions and decide which most effectively suits your purpose.

speaker's tone of voice can express warmth, anger, confidence, hesitance, friendship, hostility, enthusiasm, regret. The **tone** of a piece of writing expresses the writer's attitude toward the subject and the audience. Do you sound hesitant or authoritative about your subject? enthusiastic? concerned? How do you address your audience? as friends? authority figures? Are you attempting to inform, persuade, or inspire them?

Tone isn't something you add to writing; it's already there as an important element of **voice,** which communicates a sense of the person who is writing. (See 5d.) The tone of your writing should represent you accurately and appropriately. Just as you wouldn't lecture in a small, hesitant voice to an auditorium full of people, you won't want to use street slang or an overly casual tone in formal academic writing.

42 a Appropriate tone

In academic writing, your audience includes the instructor who assigned the paper and perhaps other students as well. Try to imagine them reading your paper, and adjust your tone if you think your readers might not get the right impression.

When you are describing personal experiences, your tone can be *informal,* as if you were capturing a conversation with a friend or addressing your audience—even the instructor—directly in a friendly manner. A reflective essay may strike a thoughtful, questioning, or contemplative tone as you explore the possible meanings of an experience or an event. (See Chapter 8.) You might use informal language when you want the audience to get to know something about yourself and your attitudes. However, some kinds of language interfere with an informal tone, so edit anything, such as colloquialisms, jargon, or excessive formality that muddies the writing.

My brother and I ~~grew acquainted with~~ met the other kids who ~~attended~~ went to our elementary school; Tommy even ~~went so far as to exchange~~ swapped his favorite slingshot ~~in return~~ for a pet frog.

To explain how something works or to interpret a work of literature, adopt a tone that assures readers of your confidence and expertise. (See Chapters 9 and 11.) Avoid unnecessary qualifications that make you sound hesitant, and edit out any informalities that weaken your authority.

The marooned students in Golding's *Lord of the Flies* are ~~probably~~ typical schoolboys, but they ~~somehow~~ degenerate into barbarism.

What is Title IX? ~~The original name of Beethoven's last symphony? No. Title IX~~ It is part of the Educational Amendments of 1972 that gave women the same rights as men in all aspects of education, including athletics.

Use *formal* language when you want to downplay your personal involvement and emphasize facts, reports, or descriptions that can be verified or experienced by other observers. Research papers benefit from more formal language. (See Chapter 22.)

~~In a search of the library, I found three 19th~~ Three nineteenth- century authors ~~who~~ discuss this aspect of Mill's theory of liberty.

When arguing a position, use a dispassionate tone to marshal evidence and appeal to readers' reason. Sometimes you can select language that appeals primarily to emotion to convince your readers, but make sure that any emotional appeals are not too strident. (See Chapter 10.)

EDITING 1: EXPLORATION

Read a few paragraphs aloud from your last three papers. First try to describe your tone in each paper. For whom were you writing, and what was your purpose? Does your tone vary greatly, or do you hear a similar tone throughout? Next try to picture the sort of person your readers would imagine as the writer of your papers, if they could judge only from the tone of the papers. Is that image accurate? Is it the one you want them to have? Finally, decide whether you would do anything to change your tone in these papers. Are there aspects of one paper's tone that you would like to use elsewhere?

Developing an Appropriate Tone for Academic Writing

The tone of academic writing differs from that of other kinds of writing. For example, popular magazines tend to be informal and conversational, and advertising copy often relies more on emotional impact than on appeals to reason. Writing on the Internet often tries to portray the writer (and by extension, the reader) as well informed or "hip." To present yourself to an academic audience as an open-minded, careful researcher and thinker, avoid unnecessary slang and informal language. Guard against inflammatory language that might make you seem biased. (See Chapter 44.) Here are some strategies you can use:

- Pay attention to tone as you read texts of all kinds. Analyze how authors achieve different tones for different purposes.

- Collect a list of questions about tone to discuss with peers or your instructor. Discuss differences in tone you have observed between academic English and other kinds of writing.

- Read your writing aloud, or have a friend read it to you. Ask yourself what kind of tone you hear, and decide whether it is appropriate.

- Ask a friend to read your drafts and to comment on the tone.

- Flag any terms that are considered informal (*guy, kid*) or slang (*awesome, cool, rad*). Keep a list of such terms that crop up in your writing. When you edit for formal tone, use the list to remind you to evaluate them as you edit. Substitute alternatives and test for improvement in tone.

42 b   Point of view

A writer's **point of view** signals the writer's relation to the subject and the audience. One principal way in which a writer articulates a point of view is by selecting a **governing pronoun:** the first-person *I* or *we*, the second-person *you*, or the third-person *he, she, it,* or *they*.

Use the **first person** to relate personal reflection and personal experience. The first person is also appropriate in argument and research writing to describe your own observations or conclusions.

Everyone seemed a lot more upset than necessary about my Saturdays with Miss Dawson, which then made me really want to do it. I told my mother I was going to help the poor. She was disgusted, afraid of disease, toilet seats. I even knew that the poor in Chile had no toilet seats. My friends were shocked that I was going with Miss Dawson at all. They said she was a loony, a fanatic, and a lesbian, was I crazy or what?

LUCIA BERLIN, "GOOD AND BAD"

For about a month I spent most of each day either on the Peak or overlooking Melinda Valley. . . . Piece by piece, I began to form my first somewhat crude picture of chimpanzee life.

JANE GOODALL, *IN THE SHADOW OF MAN*

Using the **second person** can thrust your readers into the center of the scene or imply a close relationship between the writer and the reader. Address them directly using *you.*

Madrid—The window of the hotel is open and, as *you* lie in bed, *you* hear the firing in the front line seventeen blocks away. [Italics added.]

ERNEST HEMINGWAY, *BY-LINE: ERNEST HEMINGWAY*

The second person is appropriate for instructions such as formulas or recipes, which are often written as commands with the pronoun *you* omitted. (See 47f.)

To calculate the area of a rectangle, multiply its length by its width.

The subject of the verb multiply *is understood to be* you.

You in the sense of "people in general" is not acceptable in formal writing. Try replacing it with an impersonal construction or a more suitable noun or pronoun. (Also see 49c.)

Water can be separated
~~You can separate water~~ into its constituent elements by running an electric current through it and collecting the gases at the electrodes.

The **third-person** point of view focuses the writing directly on the subject rather than on the audience. It is the most widely used approach in formal academic writing.

One of the most important signs in the text is the color of Diane Chambers's hair. *She's* a blond, and blondness is a sign of considerable richness and meaning. America is a country where "gentlemen prefer blonds," and blond coloring is the most popular color sold. But what does blondness signify? [Italics added.]

ARTHUR ASA BERGER, "'HE'S EVERYTHING YOU'RE NOT....';
A SEMIOLOGICAL ANALYSIS OF *CHEERS*"

Consider which point of view seems appropriate for your essay. In most cases, research papers and position or interpretive papers do not describe your personal experience but record what you as an investigator find and think. For these, the third-person point of view is best; it keeps the attention on the subject and supports your scholarly objectivity. (See Chapters 9–11.) If your essay is reflective or drawn from personal experience, the first person can convey a sense of immediacy and authenticity. (See Chapter 8.)

42 c Level of formality

The **level of formality** of writing, sometimes called the **register**, depends on word choice, sentence structure, and rhythm. Do you refer to your *home* or your *crib*? Are your sentences conversational in pattern or built of elaborate structures? As you edit, check that your level of formality is appropriate.

A *familiar tone* is common in everyday speech or in your personal journal but rare in academic writing. Familiar language includes slang, sentence fragments, and even vulgarity without regard to rules or conventions.

Really got into it with Jones today. The turkey can't see the value in anything. Thinks team sports make kids "aggressors" or some bull like that.

Familiar language also assumes that the audience already understands the context—who Jones is, for example.

An *informal tone* is appropriate in a letter to a friend or in a personal essay. Writing informally, you give readers a little more context than a purely familiar tone would allow. Complete your sentences and use language that omits slang but still allows your personal feelings to show through.

I had a real argument with Professor Jones in my behavioral psychology class. He was trying to tell us that team sports teach people to be "aggressive" and "insensitive." He can't see the value in them at all.

Understanding Formality

In academic writing, slang and inappropriate informality are likely to make your ideas appear less serious and committed than the work of others. An appropriate tone amounts to speaking responsibly to your fellow scholars.

Anyone who watches contemporary cartoons, such as
~~Just check out any of the cartoons today~~—*Beavis and Butthead, Ren & Stimpy*, or

Mighty Morphin Power Rangers~~If you watch a whole show, you can best believe you~~
      great deal   ^
will witness a ~~whole lot~~ of violence.
              ^

Use a *formal tone* for a research paper, in which you focus not on emotion or conflict but on evidence and argument. Choose precise language that minimizes the personal aspects of the dispute. To establish a formal tone, write well-developed sentences, eliminate contractions, identify sources, and use language appropriate to academic readers.

Citing similarities between sports teams and primitive hunting bands, some scholars, including Professor Wilkin Jones in his writings on Aztec ball games, have suggested that competitive sports breed aggression. Other researchers, however, have found that team sports also foster self-discipline and cooperation.

EDITING 2: EXPLORATION

Read the following passage taken from Oliver Goldsmith's 1765 essay "On National Prejudice" and evaluate his tone. Then rewrite the passage, adopting a more colloquial tone, one that you consider more appropriate for a modern audience. Think about what changes you would make and why. Then compare the two passages. Has anything been lost in the translation?

As I am one of the sauntering tribe of mortals, who spend the greatest part of their time in taverns, coffee houses, and other places of public resort, I have thereby an opportunity of observing an infinite variety of characters, which, to a person of a contemplative turn, is a much higher entertainment than a view of all the curiosities of art or nature. In one of these my late rambles, I accidentally fell into the company of half a dozen gentlemen, who were engaged in a warm dispute about some political affair; the decision of which, as they were equally divided in their sentiments, they thought proper to refer to me, which naturally drew me in for a share of the conversation.

Amongst a multiplicity of other topics, we took occasion to talk of the different characters of the several nations of Europe; when one of the gentlemen, cocking his hat, and assuming such an air of importance as if he had possessed all the merit of the English nation in his own person, declared that the Dutch were a parcel of avaricious wretches; the French a set of flattering sycophants; that the Germans were drunken sots, and beastly gluttons; and the Spaniards proud, haughty and surly tyrants: but that in bravery, generosity, clemency, and in every other virtue, the English excelled all the world.

This very learned and judicious remark was received with a general smile of approbation by all the company—all, I mean, but your humble servant.

EDITING 3: PRACTICE

Edit the following two paragraphs, adjusting the tone to the appropriate level of formality. The first paragraph is from a paper relating a personal experience; the second is from a formal research paper. More than one edited version of each paragraph is possible. Be ready to explain your editing choices.

PERSONAL EXPERIENCE ESSAY

Who would find it credible that two adults would have trouble convincing one eight-pound feline that the time had come for his annual physical examination? Upon spotting his cage, the cat exits the room as quickly as he can. Under the bed, over the bed, up the staircase, down the staircase, he rushes with extreme celerity from one room to the next, ever eluding our grasp. When his outrageous behavior ceases and we have him cornered, I stealthily approach him and apprehend him. I loudly proclaim myself triumphant as I deposit him in his place of confinement and secure the top.

FORMAL RESEARCH PAPER

At the Dryden Correctional Center, the guys who run the education department try to prepare the inmates for living on the outside. That way criminals won't (they hope!) turn back to a life of crime. OK. Sounds like a good idea. But how do they do it? Well, they make sure that as soon as the criminals get tossed in the slammer they hit the books. This is so that they will have a better chance of getting jobs when they get out. The way they figure it is if the punks get jobs, they won't have to cross the line to make money. The educational programs are completely voluntary. Lots of the inmates take them, though.

42 d   Consistent tone

An unnecessary shift in tone or point of view will throw your readers off balance.

> **The assassinations of President Kennedy and Martin Luther King,**
>
> **Jr., the Vietnam War, the September 11 tragedy—each of these**
>
> **events shook public confidence in the nation and made it seem that**
> ~~had gone mad.~~
> **the world** ~~was out of whack.~~

Some shifts are necessitated by content. A deliberate shift in tone can be appropriately humorous, moving, or even compelling. In the following passage, Stephen Jay Gould shifts from an amusing story, told in casual language, to an argument based on logic and hard evidence, written in a more formal tone:

> When Muhammad Ali flunked his army intelligence test, he quipped (with a wit that belied his performance on the exam): "I only said I was the greatest; I never said I was the smartest." In our metaphors and fairy tales, size and power are almost always balanced by a want of intelligence. Cunning is the refuge of the little guy. Think of Br'er Rabbit and Br'er Bear; David smiting Goliath with a slingshot; Jack chopping down the beanstalk. Slow wit is the tragic flaw of a giant.
>
> The discovery of dinosaurs in the nineteenth century provided, or so it appeared, a quintessential case for the negative correlation of size and smarts. With their pea brains and giant bodies, dinosaurs became a symbol of lumbering stupidity. Their extinction seemed only to confirm their flawed design.
>
> STEPHEN JAY GOULD, "WERE DINOSAURS DUMB?"

Using a deliberate shift is like telling a joke in front of a group of strangers: you have to be sure it's a good joke, and you have to deliver it smoothly and with expert timing.

EDITING 4: APPLICATION

Read through a paper you are working on, paying close attention to its tone. How would you describe the tone? How do your choices of point of view, level of formality, and wording contribute to this tone? Given your subject

Refining Your Tone

When editing for tone, ask yourself the following questions:

- Is the tone **appropriate to the audience** I am writing for **and for the goal** I want to accomplish? If not, you may need to adjust your point of view or level of formality.

- Have I chosen the **point of view** that best illustrates my relationship to my subject? Test other points of view and then choose the one that helps you succeed in your goals for the paper.

- Is the **level of formality** right for my intended audience? If not, go back and consider your presentation of ideas and choice of words throughout.

- Have I maintained a **consistent tone?** If not, you need to edit your writing to eliminate elements that are incompatible with the tone you want.

and your purpose, is the tone appropriate? Have you maintained this tone throughout? If not, do your shifts in tone help the effectiveness of your paper or harm it? As you edit your paper pay full attention to its tone, keeping the aspects that you like and improving the aspects that you don't like.

chapter 43

Choosing the Right Word

Writers in English can choose among many words with similar meanings. For example, the place you live could be called, in a formal manner, your *residence, domicile,* or *habitation;* less formally, it could be called your *home, house, quarters,* or *lodging.* Informally, it could be called your *shack, digs, spot,* or *pad.* Not every word is effective in every context. At every turn, you have to choose which word can best—given your purpose and audience—convey the shade of meaning you intend. Enlarge your vocabulary by reading widely and listening actively to the words others use. Make word lists to study; **paraphrase** new words right away and use them in sentences, and try to learn the meaning of unfamiliar words from context.

43 a   The history of English

The special richness of the English vocabulary results from the merging of many languages. As waves of invasion and migration swept over the British Isles during the past three thousand years, each group of new arrivals brought a language that blended with existing speech.

After the Romans arrived in the British Isles in 43 B.C., they conquered the Celtic-speaking inhabitants and ruled much of what is now England for nearly five hundred years. When the Romans retreated, the Celts kept a few Latin words, such as *plant, candle,* and *wine.*

In the fifth century A.D., Germanic peoples from northern Europe—the Jutes, Saxons, Frisians, and Angles (for whom England is named)—invaded Britain, bringing with them their Germanic language, the basis of modern English. In what is now England, the Celtic language was largely replaced by that of the newcomers as Celtic speakers were displaced to Cornwall, Wales, and Scotland. Celtic words surviving in English include *clan, bin, gull,* and *crag.*

The invaders' early form of English, which became the dominant language for much of England, is called Old English. Many words in our modern vocabulary can be traced to this period: *work, bite, god, gold, hand, land, under, winter, word.*

Another wave of Latin began at the end of the sixth century with the arrival of missionaries sent from Rome to convert the Anglo-Saxons to Christianity. A flood of Latin religious and secular words gradually became part of English: *abbot, altar, Mass, acolyte, lily.*

In the eighth century, new invaders, known as Danes or Vikings, brought their Scandinavian language, Old Norse. Although they came as conquerors, many Danes settled alongside the Angles and Saxons. Words adopted from the Danes' conquest include *fellow, hit, law, rag, take, want,* and many words that begin with an *sk* sound (*scorch, scrape, scrub, skill, skirt, sky*).

In 1066 the Normans, from what is now western France, conquered England and brought with them their own language, Old French. Following the Norman Conquest, French became the language of the noble classes, the law, the monetary system, and learning. French words such as *parliament, justice, crime, marriage, money,* and *rent* seeped into common usage, as did *art, ornament, mansion, pleasure, joy,* and thousands more. English retains two sets of words for many things, an indication of the social divisions of Norman England. For example, farmers used the English words *pig, deer, sheep, cow,* and *calf,* but the ruling class, whose primary contact with these animals was consumption, used French names for their meat: *pork, venison, mutton, beef,* and *veal.* Eventually English became the predominant language among all classes, but by then French words had thoroughly infiltrated its vocabulary.

In the sixteenth century, a renewed interest in classical Greek and Latin learning—history, mythology, and science—brought into English a torrent of new words. From Greek came *democracy, hexagon, monogamy, physics, rhythm,* and *theory.* From Latin came *client, conviction, index, library, medicine, orbit,* and *recipe.* Since the nineteenth century, Greek and Latin roots have continued to provide a wealth of scientific and technical terms, many of which are invented words made up of ancient roots, prefixes, and suffixes: *cholesterol, cyanide, radioactive, telegraph, telephone, television.*

English also has absorbed words from other languages as its speakers have spread across the globe and as speakers of other languages have settled in English-speaking lands. Modern American English includes words from dozens of languages, including Spanish (*canyon, mustang, poncho, rodeo*), Italian (*balcony, balloon, carnival, ghetto*), Arabic (*alcohol, algebra, candy, lemon*), Hindustani (*bungalow, cot, jungle, loot, shampoo*), Japanese (*kimono, samurai, zen, karate*), and various African languages (*banana, yam, voodoo, banjo*).

These linguistic riches place at your disposal an array of words with similar meanings. Is a particular man *male, manly, macho, virile,* or *masculine?* Does a particular woman have a *job,* a *profession,* a *vocation,* or a *calling?* The choice depends on the shade of meaning you desire and the effect you want your words to have on your readers.

EDITING 1: PRACTICE

For each of the words below, think of as many synonyms and near synonyms as you can. Try to guess what language each word came from. Use a dictionary to check your guesses. You may want to compare your word lists with those of your classmates.

assist	chutney	hope	scream
calendar	good	name	truth
calculate	handle	number	vampire
cash	health	potlatch	verse
church	home	safari	warmth

43 b   Using the dictionary and thesaurus

Writers commonly rely on reference books to guide them in their use of language. The most widely used are a dictionary, a thesaurus, and a guide to usage.

1 The dictionary

An *unabridged* dictionary offers information on word origins as well as definitions and usage samples. *Webster's Third New International Dictionary* (Springfield, MA: Merriam-Webster, 2002), which contains 472,800 words, is among the most widely used. The most comprehensive is the 616,500-word *Oxford English Dictionary,* 2nd edition, 20 vols. (Oxford: Oxford University Press, 1989), which since 1928 has attempted to chronicle the first appearance and usage history of every word in the language. It is available in a searchable edition on CD-ROM, as are many recently published dictionaries.

An *abridged* dictionary omits some less common words, so it may be easier to use than a huge unabridged volume. *Merriam-Webster's Collegiate Dictionary,* 11th edition (Springfield, MA: Merriam-Webster, 2003) offers 225,000 entries focused on contemporary usage. The Internet edition at http://www. m-w.com/ includes the main A–Z listings of the print edition. Another widely used abridged dictionary, *The American Heritage Dictionary of the English Language,* 4th edition (Boston: Houghton Mifflin, 2000), is available in print, on CD-ROM, and on the Internet at http://www.bartleby.com/61/. It offers tips on usage and includes new

Browser window showing: "language. The American Heritage® Dictionary o..."

Address: http://www.bartleby.com/61/14/L0041400.html

CONTENTS · INDEX · ILLUSTRATIONS · BIBLIOGRAPHIC RECORD

The American Heritage® Dictionary of the English Language: Fourth Edition. 2000.

language

SYLLABICATION: lan·guage

PRONUNCIATION: lăng′gwĭj

NOUN: **1a.** Communication of thoughts and feelings through a system of arbitrary signals, such as voice sounds, gestures, or written symbols. **b.** Such a system including its rules for combining its components, such as words. **c.** Such a system as used by a nation, people, or other distinct community; often contrasted with *dialect.* **2a.** A system of signs, symbols, gestures, or rules used in communicating: *the language of algebra.* **b.** *Computer Science* A system of symbols and rules used for communication with or between computers. **3.** Body language; kinesics. **4.** The special vocabulary and usages of a scientific, professional, or other group: *"his total mastery of screen language— camera placement, editing—and his handling of actors"* (Jack Kroll). **5.** A characteristic style of speech or writing: *Shakespearean language.* **6.** A particular manner of expression: *profane language; persuasive language.* **7.** The manner or means of communication between living creatures other than humans: *the language of dolphins.* **8.** Verbal communication as a subject of study. **9.** The wording of a legal document or statute as distinct from the spirit.

ETYMOLOGY: Middle English, from Old French *langage,* from *langue,* tongue, language, from Latin *lingua.* See **dn̥ghū-** in Appendix I.

coinages such as *dot-com* and *soccer mom*. The annually updated *Random House Webster's College Dictionary* (New York: Random, 2003) lists more than 315,000 words, giving the most common definition first.

What's in a Dictionary Entry?

Most dictionaries follow the format found in the tenth edition of *Merriam-Webster's Collegiate Dictionary* (Springfield, MA: Merriam-Webster, 1996).

① entry word   ② pronunciation   ③ part of speech label   ④ inflected forms

com·mu·ni·cate \ kə- ' myü-nə-kāt \ *vb* **-cat·ed; -cat·ing** [L *communications*, pp. of *communicare* to impart, participate, fr. *communis* common—more at MEAN] *vt* (1526) **1** *archaic* : SHARE **2 a** : to convey knowledge of or information about : make known <~ a story> **b** : to reveal by clear signs <his fear *communicated* itself to his friends> **3** : to cause to pass from one to another <some diseases are easily *communicated*> ~ *vi* **1** : to receive Communion **2** : to transmit information, thought, or feeling so that it is satisfactorily received or understood **3** : to open into each other : CONNECT <the rooms ~ > — **com·mu·ni·ca·tee** \ -ₗ myü-ni-kə- ' tē \ *n* — **com·mu·ni·ca·tor** \ -' myü-nə-ₗkā-tər \ *n*

⑤ derivation

⑥ definitions

1. The **entry word** appears in bold type. Bars, spaces, or dots between syllables show where the word may be hyphenated. If two spellings are shown, the first is more common, although both are acceptable. If two spellings are dissimilar, entries are cross-referenced: **gaol** (jal) *n. Brit. sp.* of JAIL. A superscript numeral before an entry indicates that two or more words have identical spellings.

2. **Pronunciation** is spelled phonetically, set in parentheses or between slashes. (The phonetic key is usually at the bottom of the page.) If two pronunciations are given, the first is more common, although both are acceptable.

3. **Parts-of-speech labels** are set in italic type. The abbreviations are *n* for noun, *vb* for verb, *vt* for transitive verb, and so forth.

4. **Inflected forms** are shown, including plurals for nouns and pronouns, comparatives and superlatives for adjectives and adverbs, and principal parts for verbs. Irregular spellings also appear here.

5. The **derivation** of the word from its roots in other languages is set between brackets or slashes. *OE* and *ME* = Old English and Middle English; *L* = Latin; *Gr* = Greek; *OFr* = Old French; *Fr* = French; *G* = German; and so on.

6. **Definitions** appear with major meanings numbered and arranged from the oldest to the most recent or from the most common to the least common. An example of the word's use may be enclosed in brackets.

▪ **Synonyms** or **antonyms** may be listed, often with comments on how the words are similar or different.

▪ **Usage labels** are used for nonstandard words or meanings.

archaic: from a historic period; now used rarely if at all

colloquial [coll.]: used informally in speech or writing

dialect [dial.]: used only in some geographical areas

obsolete [obs.]: no longer used, but may appear in old writings

slang: highly informal, or an unusual usage

substandard [substand.]: widely used but not accepted in formal usage

British [Brit.], Irish, Scottish [Scot.] and so on: a word used primarily in an area other than the United States. Some dictionaries use an asterisk to mark Americanisms.

▪ **Usage notes** may follow definitions. They may also comment on acceptability or unacceptability.

2 The thesaurus

A **thesaurus** lists **synonyms**—words with similar meanings—for each entry. Many thesauruses list **antonyms**—words with opposite meanings—as well. *Roget's Thesaurus of English Words and Phrases* lists words in six major classifications and many related concepts. By contrast, *Roget's 21st Century Thesaurus* lists words in alphabetical order and contains a concept index.

A thesaurus can suggest words you can use to fit a particular context or level of formality. But be sure to check any unfamiliar words in a dictionary before using them. Some may be entirely inappropriate to your situation or may have unwanted connotations. For example, if you are eagerly gathering information on a particular subject, you may be said to *assimilate* it, *absorb* it, *ingest* it, or perhaps *digest* it, but not *imbibe* it, since the last of these terms means "to drink."

Online thesauruses include *Merriam-Webster's Collegiate Thesaurus* at http://www.m-w.com/, *Lexico* at http://www.thesaurus.com/, and *Roget's Thesauri* at http://www.bartleby.com/thesauri/.

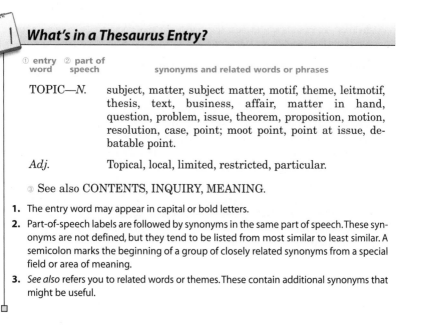

What's in a Thesaurus Entry?

① entry   ② part of
word   speech   synonyms and related words or phrases

TOPIC—*N.*   subject, matter, subject matter, motif, theme, leitmotif,
               thesis, text, business, affair, matter in hand,
               question, problem, issue, theorem, proposition, motion,
               resolution, case, point; moot point, point at issue, de-
               batable point.

Adj.   Topical, local, limited, restricted, particular.

③ See also CONTENTS, INQUIRY, MEANING.

1. The entry word may appear in capital or bold letters.

2. Part-of-speech labels are followed by synonyms in the same part of speech. These synonyms are not defined, but they tend to be listed from most similar to least similar. A
   semicolon marks the beginning of a group of closely related synonyms from a special
   field or area of meaning.

3. *See also* refers you to related words or themes. These contain additional synonyms that
   might be useful.

3 Guides to usage

Should you use *appraise* or *apprise? Compose* or *comprise? Affect* or
effect? Much or *many?* These are questions of **usage,** the choice of the
appropriate word. A guide to usage offers what a thesaurus does not:
advice on which word is appropriate or customary in which context. Some
choices include *A Dictionary of Modern American Usage* (Oxford: Oxford
University Press, 2003); *Choose the Right Word,* 2nd edition (New York:
HarperCollins, 1994); and *The American Heritage Book of English Usage*
(Boston: Houghton Mifflin, 1996). For a quick reference, consult Chapter
64, Glossary of Usage.

4 Specialized dictionaries

Specialized dictionaries list the vocabularies of various disciplines.
For example, if you need terms for the architectural features of medieval
cathedrals, consult the *Dictionary of Architecture and Construction.*
Specialized dictionaries also cover the regional and cultural varieties of
English, such as the *Dictionary of American Regional English.* The *New*

Dictionary of American Slang lists words used in conversational (or colloquial) English. Some dictionaries focus on word origins, or **etymology.** Others cover branches of the language, from Canadian to Jamaican and Bahamian English.

ESL *Bilingual Dictionaries*

If English is not your first language, a **bilingual dictionary**—sometimes called a **translating dictionary**—can be a great help. The most useful kind is one that translates both from English into your native language and vice versa, such as the *Oxford Spanish Dictionary: Spanish-English/English-Spanish* (Oxford: Oxford University Press, 1994). A collection of basic bilingual dictionaries is available online at http://dictionaries .travlang.com/. You can look up the English equivalent of a word in your first language, or you can look up the meaning of an English word you're not certain about. For academic writing, it's a good idea to consult a more comprehensive dictionary because abridged or pocket versions often offer several translations but provide no clue which one to choose.

EDITING 2: PRACTICE

Use a dictionary and a thesaurus to look up any words in the following passage that seem unfamiliar or that might be misused. Substitute more familiar words and correct any misuses but preserve the intended meaning. Be ready to explain your editing choices.

The role of Emma Woodhouse in Jane Austen's novel *Emma* often receives censure for her supercilious behavior. Many readers consider her attitude toward her neighbors to be unconscionable: she avoids calling on them whenever possible and suffers their visits with scarcely concealed ennui. And it's certainly true that Emma regards all social functions as opportunities to display her better charms and talents. Yet Emma may be understood as Austen's portrayal of an exceptional individual constrained by a mediocre society.

43 c Expanding your vocabulary

You can enlarge your tool kit of words, your **vocabulary,** in several ways. If you pay attention to the words others use, you will learn new words and usages. When you encounter a passage containing a new word, paraphrase it in familiar words; it helps fix the new word in your mind. Here are other ways to improve your vocabulary.

1 Learning from context

You often can infer the meaning of words from the words around them, the **context.** Suppose you read the following:

> The integration deal means that customers will be able to plug Pipes' *middleware* directly into Sybases's message server, which provides wireless communications and transaction security. Combining both vendors' message systems gives users flexible *middleware* to bridge heterogeneous systems.

Even without knowing much about computers, you can guess that *middleware* is a computer device or program (*ware,* as in *software* and *hardware*) that connects different (*heterogeneous*) systems so users can send messages to each other.

2 Learning from roots, prefixes, and suffixes

You can find clues to a word's meaning by looking at roots, prefixes, and suffixes.

Roots

A **root** is a base word, the part of a word from which other words are formed. Sometimes words are formed with two roots, as in many scientific and technical terms. For example, the word *photograph* is composed of the roots *photo,* from the Greek word meaning "light," and *graph,* meaning "writing." Other root words combined with *graph* make *telegraph,* meaning "distant writing"; *phonograph,* an instrument for recording sound; and *chronograph,* an instrument for recording time. This process works also in words like *software, shareware,* and *middleware,* all created by analogy with *hardware.*

One root may be spelled in several different ways, especially in words formed long ago. Thus *justice* and *jury* are both related to the Latin word *jus,* for "law." *Transcribe* and *manuscript,* as well as *inscription, conscript,* and *scripture,* not to mention *scribble,* share the Indo-European root *skeribh,* "to cut or incise," and hence, "to write."

Prefixes

A **prefix** is a group of letters attached to the beginning of a root to change its meaning. For example, the word *prefix* itself consists of a root, *fix,* meaning "attach," and a prefix, *pre-,* meaning "before." Changing a prefix can dramatically alter the meaning of a word. For example, *democracy* means "rule" (*-cracy*) "by the people" (*demos*); *autocracy* means "rule by one person"; *theocracy* means "rule by God or divine authority."

Suffixes

A **suffix** is a group of letters attached to the end of a root. Adding a suffix changes the meaning of the word and often changes the part of speech. For example, the verb *educate* means "to teach"; the noun *education* means "the process of teaching"; the adjective *educational* means "having to do with education or teaching."

Knowing some prefixes, suffixes, and roots can help you guess the meanings of words. Be careful to check your guesses; sometimes words similarly spelled have quite different meanings. *Disinterested* means "impartial or unbiased" while *uninterested* means "not interested or not concerned."

3 Keeping a word list

Reserve a page or two in your journal for a word list, and every time you encounter an unfamiliar word—whether in school or in a book—write it down. Write down your best guess of the word's meaning. Review the list regularly. Look up the words, and jot down the exact definitions. Immediately try out your new words in sentences in your journal and then in conversation.

43 d Connotations

The direct and literal meaning of a word is its **denotation.** For example, *fragrance, odor,* and *smell* all denote something detected by the sense of smell. But their associations differ: saying "You have a distinctive fragrance" is quite different from saying "You have a distinctive odor." The indirect meaning, based on such associations, is a word's **connotation.** As you edit, pay attention to the connotations of your words because they will affect the meaning you convey.

Common Prefixes

Prefix	Meaning	Example
a-, an-	without	atheist, anhydrous
ante-	before	antecedent
anti-	against	antiwar
auto-	self	autopilot
co-	with	cohabit
com-, con-, cor-	with	compatriot
contra-	against	contradiction
de-	away from, off	deplane
	reverse, undo	defrost, decode
dis-	not	dislike
en-	put into	encode
ex-	out, outside	exoskeleton
	former	ex-president
extra-	beyond, more than	extraterrestrial
hetero-	different	heterogeneous
homo-	same	homogeneous
hyper-	more	hyperactive
hypo-	less than	hypobaric
il-, im-, in-, ir-	not, without	illogical, immoral, insensitive, irresponsible
in-	into	inject
inter-	between	intercollegiate
intra-	within	intravenous
macro-	very large	macroeconomics
micro-	very small	microscope
mono-	one	monomania
non-	not, without	nonsense
omni-	all, every	omnipotent
post-	after	postmodern, postmortem
pre-	before	preheat
pro-	forward	promote
sub-	under	submit
syn-	with, at the same time as	synchronize
trans-	across	transcontinental
tri-	three	triangle
un-	not	unloved
uni-	one	unicorn

Common Suffixes

NOUN SUFFIXES

Suffix	Meaning	Example
-ance, -ence,	act	adherence
-ation, -ion, -sion, -tion	act, state of being	abstention, pretension
-dom	place	kingdom
	state of being	wisdom
-er, -or	one who	pitcher, actor
-hood	state of being	childhood
-ism	act, practice	terrorism
-ist	one who	psychologist
-ment	act	containment
-ness	state of being	wildness
-ship	state of being	professorship
	quality	workmanship

VERB SUFFIXES

Suffix	Meaning	Example
-ate	to make	activate
-en	to make	broaden
-fy	to become	liquefy
-ize	to make into	crystallize

ADJECTIVE SUFFIXES

Suffix	Meaning	Example
-able, -ible	able to	acceptable
-al, -ial	pertaining to	musical
-ate	having, filled with	passionate
-ful	filled with	fanciful
-ish	resembling	devilish
-ive	having the nature of	votive, active
-less	without	shameless
-like	prone to, resembling	warlike
-ly	pertaining to	motherly
-ose, -ous	characterized by	morose

ADVERB SUFFIX

Suffix	Meaning	Example
-ly	in a manner characterized by	easily

Some words have such strong connotations that using them will make you sound **biased.** (See Chapter 44.) Calling someone's hobby a *fixation* or an *obsession* rather than just a *pastime* implies that the person is mentally unstable, a judgment that will seem unfair unless you can support the implication with evidence. When you find words that make your writing seem biased, replace them with more balanced alternatives.

Another way in which connotations differ is in **level of formality.** (See 42c.) Some words are appropriate for informal contexts such as writing about personal experience, while others are appropriate for formal academic writing. Deciding whether you refer to an instructor as a *prof,* a *teacher,* a *professor,* an *educator,* or a *pedagogue* is partly a choice among increasing levels of formality.

EDITING 3: PRACTICE

Here's a way to have some fun with connotations. Pick an adjective and "conjugate" it as follows: *I am firm, you are obstinate, she is stubborn* or *I am thrifty, you are tight, he's an old skinflint.* Try it with these modifiers or others of your own choosing.

aging gracefully	adventurous	thoughtful
prudent	charming	sophisticated
bold	delicate	mature

43 e Confusing words

Homonyms, words with the same sound but different spellings and meanings, frequently create confusion. Even experienced writers sometimes use *their* when they mean *there* or *they're,* or confuse *write, right,* and *rite; its* and *it's;* or *principle* and *principal.*

Sometimes the confusion arises from spelling errors. If you write *to* for *two* or *too,* your computer spell-checker won't notice. Be aware of potentially confusing words, and examine each word to be sure it is used correctly. A list of problem homonyms appears in 58a.

43 f Prepositions and particles

Idioms are expressions or speech patterns that cannot necessarily be understood or predicted by rules of logic or grammar. Why do we ride *in* a car but *on* a train? Why do we *take* a picture but *make* a recording? Why

Verbs That Are Often Confused

Several pairs of verbs are similar in form but very different in meaning. You'll want to memorize them and edit for them when checking word choice.

SIT AND SET

Sit means "to be seated."

Set means "to put or place."

Neighbors *sit* on their screened porches every night.
I *set* a bowl of milk on the porch for our cat.

LIE AND LAY

Lie means "to recline."
Lay means "to put or place."

She *lies* down every day and meditates.
He *lays* the paper on the table every morning.

AFFECT AND EFFECT

Affect is almost always a verb; *effect* is usually a noun, although it has some uses as a verb.

Affect means "to produce an effect."
Effect, as a noun, means "the result of a change or action."
Effect, as a verb, means "to make happen."

Raising prices could *affect* sales volume.
Higher prices could have a bad *effect* on sales.
She was able to *effect* a change in policy.

COMPOSE AND COMPRISE

Compose means "to form."
Comprise means "consist of" or "include."

Fifty states *compose* the United States.
The United States *comprises* fifty states.

Other problem pairs are listed in the Glossary of Usage.

do Americans stay *in school* but not *in hospital* as the British do? In each case the correct word is determined by what is conventional and customary, or idiomatic.

Idiomatic expressions can cause problems even for native speakers; prepositions, for example, are often used in unexpected ways. We know that a **preposition**—*at, by, for, out, to, with*—shows a relationship between a noun or a pronoun and other words in the sentence. The only guide to the correct use of prepositions with nouns and verbs is to learn the conventional idioms.

This novel shows a great similarity *to* that one. The similarity *between* the stories is remarkable.

I will meet *with* you *in* the morning *at* the office.

Phrasal verbs are **two-word verbs,** verbs that need a second word to complete their meanings. These extra words, called **particles,** look like prepositions (*up, down, out, in, off,* and so on) and function with the verb to convey the full meaning, which may be quite different from the meaning of the verb alone. The meanings of the phrasal verbs in the following sentences, for instance, have very little in common with the verb *to come.*

How did this *come about?* (happen)

Of course, I expected things to *come out* all right. (end)

I was unconscious for a moment, but I soon *came to.* (revived)

Check your writing for idiomatic expressions. Be aware of potential trouble spots; try to make note of how these words are used in standard English, and whenever you are in doubt, consult a dictionary or other reference work.

ESL Frequently Confused Words and Phrases

Here are some words or phrases that can be confused.

Word or Phrase	Meaning or Function	Example
another	an additional one	I lost my library card. May I get *another* one?
the other	the second of two items	We have two cars. One is a station wagon; *the other* is a convertible.
few	not many	Frankly, I wouldn't ask him. He usually has *few* good ideas. [He has almost no good ideas.]
a few	some	Why don't you ask him? He always has *a few* good ideas. [He does have some good ideas.]
been	past participle of *be*	She has *been* gone all day.
being	present participle of *be*	Why do you think she is *being* so difficult?

Some Idiomatic Expressions

agree	We agreed *on* a place to have lunch. We agreed *to* leave at 12:30. We agreed *that* the food was excellent. We seldom agree *about* anything.
amuse	My cousin was amused *by* the clown. I was amused *at* my cousin's delight. The clown amused us *with* her tricks.
arrive	They arrived *at* the airport. They arrived *in* Los Angeles. They arrived *on* the scene.
differ	Margot differs *with* Harriet on this subject. Each one's opinion differs *from* that of the other. They differ *over* whether to go skiing.
identify	You can identify her *by* her appearance. You must identify her *to* the authorities. Do you identify *with* that character?
insist	I insist *on* going along. She insisted *that* my help wasn't needed.
occupy	The room is occupied *by* another group. Mario is occupied *with* his book.
prejudice	The jury was prejudiced *against* the defendant. They were prejudiced *by* improper evidence.
reward	The dog was rewarded *for* its behavior. It was rewarded *by* praise. It was also rewarded *with* a steak.
trust	He trusts you. You may trust *in* him. You may trust *that* he will do the right thing. He trusts you *to* do the right thing. Do not trust him *with* your money.
vary	The colors vary *in* intensity. They vary *from* light to dark. People's tastes vary *with* time. Their position has varied *over* the years.

....

Edit the following paragraph to make sure that words and expressions are used according to convention. More than one edited version is possible. Be ready to explain your editing choices.

> One of the most difficult things about small classes is that you never know when the instructor might call at you. Its easier to go unnoticed in a large lecture class where your one of a hundred faces in a crowd. When I'm in a small class, I try to set in the back row and make it obvious to my teachers that I'm taking a lot of notes. My theory is that if there convinced that your trying to write down what others are saying, they are less likely to call you.

....

ESL *Using Two-Word Verbs*

Some verbs join with a **particle**—a word such as *on, by, up, over,* or *through*—to create a new meaning. Here are some examples of such two-word verbs:

Verb	Particle	Meaning
call	off	cancel
call	out	summon
find	out	discover, learn
get	through	finish
make	up	invent, create
put	off	postpone
see	through	finish; not be deceived by
see	off	bid farewell
see	to	pay attention to

Here are some guidelines for using two-word verbs:

■ If the verb has no direct object, put the particle directly after the verb.

The photocopy machine *breaks down* often.

or

The photocopy machine often *breaks down.*

Some other two-word verbs in this group are *come back, come over, play around, lie down, roll over,* and *turn back* (retreat).

■ Two-word verbs with direct objects follow one of these four patterns:

1. Those that cannot be separated

Please *go over* this report carefully.

Watch your step as you *step off* the platform.

     Other verbs that follow this pattern include *come across, get on, get off, get over, get through* (finish), *look into,* and *see through* (not be deceived by).

2. Those that must be separated by the direct object

I tried to *get* the idea *across* to him.

I had to insist that he *do* it *over.*

     Only a few two-part verbs follow this pattern, including *get across* (communicate) and *see through* (finish).

3. Those that can be separated by a noun but not by a pronoun

You can write

The governor *called out* the National Guard to help in the flood.

or

The governor *called* the National Guard *out* to help in the flood.

     However, if the direct object is a pronoun rather than a noun, the verb parts must be separated.

The light was shining in my eyes, so I asked her to *turn* it *off.*

     Many phrasal verbs follow this pattern. They include *fill out, find out, give up, look over, leave out, make up, put down, put on, put away, turn off, turn on,* and *turn back* (reverse).

4. Those that can be separated by a pronoun but not by a noun

You can write

I *picked up* the mail.

or

I *picked* it *up.* (but not I *picked up* it.)

     Verbs that follow this pattern include many that use *up, down, in,* or *out.*

    If you are not sure how to use a two-word verb, consult an ESL dictionary or a native speaker.

43 g Slang, regionalisms, and jargon

Everyday speech is peppered with **slang,** highly informal language usually originating in small social groups: police officers are *cops;* computer programs have *bugs.* Some slang consists of new words of unknown origin: baseball players *shag* fly balls in practice; fugitives are *on the lam.* Other slang consists of old words used in new ways: *main squeeze* for girlfriend or boyfriend, *boot* to start a computer (from "pull itself up by its bootstraps"), *dis* for "treat with disrespect." Some slang words eventually join the mainstream and become part of standard English. Three examples are *bluff,* to scare off with a false show of confidence; *jazz,* which was once a slang sexual term; and *jeep,* from the World War II general purpose or "g.p." vehicle.

Regionalisms are expressions used in one part of the country but not standard nationwide. The generic word for *carbonated beverage,* for example, varies by region from *pop* to *soda* to *soft drink* to *seltzer.* Some expressions from regional dialects are regarded as substandard, not acceptable in formal writing.

A **colloquialism** is an expression common in spoken language but not usually used in formal writing. For example, the noun *pot* can refer not only to a cooking vessel but also to an illegal drug, the amount of money bet on a hand of cards, and ruination (*go to pot*).

Use slang, regionalisms, and colloquialisms sparingly, if at all. Such words may not be understood by everyone, and for academic writing they are usually too informal.

Specialized language particular to a field or discipline is called **jargon.** Each discipline develops special terms to express its ideas. Studying biology would be impossible without terms such as *chromosomes* and *osmosis.* Literary criticism employs such words as *climax* and *dénouement.* Politics has generated such terms as *spin, sound bite,* and *PAC* (political action committee). Unlike slang, jargon is often highly formal. Of course, a group's jargon may be unintelligible outside that group.

Be sure the special terms you use are appropriate for your audience. For example, a general audience would understand *thigh bone,* but an instructor reading a paper on a medical subject would expect you to use the technical term *femur.* To a specialized audience, correct and conventional use of technical language helps demonstrate your mastery of a subject.

If you adopt jargon for its own sake, however, you may sound stilted or pretentious. (See 41e.) Decide which special terms are essential and which are merely for show.

JARGON   It is incumbent on us to challenge the prevailing proposition that critical-theoretical approaches are the most enlightened ways of introducing students to the literary experience.

EDITED   We should question the widely held idea that using theories of criticism provides the best way to introduce students to literature.

Sometimes simple language cannot communicate a complex concept—you need a technical term. Introduce it in a way that helps the reader grasp its meaning. An explicit definition can help too. The following passage was written for car enthusiasts but not for mechanical engineers, so the writer had to explain the terms *lean* and *stoichiometric:*

> Running an engine *lean* means that there is less fuel in the cylinders than is needed to completely burn all of the available air. With gasoline, 14.7 pounds of air are required to burn 1 pound of fuel. This air–fuel ratio is referred to as *stoichiometric.*
>
> FRANK MARKUS, "LEAN-BURN ENGINES"

EDITING 5: PRACTICE

Edit the following paragraph from a paper describing computer enthusiasts to a general readership. Try a couple of versions, one minimizing jargon as much as possible and the other making the jargon reader friendly. What do you have to assume about your audience in either case?

> Virtually all the members of the campus Internet users group regard their computers as indispensable. These people spend most of their time logged on, cruising the net, swapping MP3s by e-mail, chatting online, or waging virtual combat in a multiuser dungeon. Word processing? spreadsheets? Old hat in this crowd! We're talking major bandwidth, personal Web sites, and Java scripts. The more adventurous of these folks speak UNIX like natives and are hacking around in mainframes that are supposed to be safe behind firewalls.

43 h   Figurative language

Figurative language, which likens one thing to another in an imaginative or fanciful way, can enliven your writing. Too much literal language can shackle your prose. Figurative language can unchain your thoughts, allowing an occasional leap of the imagination.

Figurative language makes connections through metaphor or analogy. This process is so deeply embedded in our language that we often overlook it. For example, the verb *overlook* in the previous sentence suggests we can fail to "see" a process or an idea in the same way that we can fail to see a physical object. Figurative language should be fresh, not hackneyed. Use it not for ornament or embellishment but to help readers understand.

A **mixed metaphor** combines two or more unrelated images, occasionally with unintended effects. If you find a mixed metaphor, consider eliminating the weaker image and extending the stronger.

He was ~~sitting on the fence~~ ^{undecided} about the election; he liked the challenger but didn't want to change horses in midstream.

EDITING 6: PRACTICE

Edit the following paragraph from a paper defending a popular TV show to improve its use of figurative language. More than one edited version is possible. Be ready to explain your editing choices.

Many people object to the television cartoon *The Simpsons* because they say it is over the top, but millions of children watch it with bated breath every week. Critics say shows like this are causing the American family to disintegrate and are teaching children that it is OK not to hit the books. They think that young people want to be like Bart Simpson, who is as proud as a peacock of being a bad student, and that the show is a stumbling block for students who want to be above par. I think it's crystal clear that children can tell the difference between television and reality. When they laugh at Bart talking back to his parents, they are just letting off steam because adults are always laying down the law.

43 i Clichés

An overused expression or figure of speech is called a **cliché.** The word itself, interestingly, is a metaphor. Cliché is a French word for the sound a stamping press makes in a process of making multiple identical images. In other words, something has become a cliché if it is ordinary, run-of-the-mill, like the following:

the last straw	needle in a haystack
strong as an ox	handwriting on the wall
better late than never	tried and true
lay the cards on the table	hit the nail on the head

To edit a cliché, try improving upon it. Go back to the original image and describe it in new words, add fresh detail, or introduce a play on the too-familiar words.

Outside, the wind ~~howled~~.
(keened)

If you cannot revive the cliché, replace it, striving for directness.

It was dark ~~as night~~ inside the cave.
(so that we waited in vain for our eyes to adjust)

EDITING 7: PRACTICE

Edit the following passage for an academic audience, examining word choice. More than one edited version is possible. Be ready to explain your editing choices.

If this has been a golden era for home shopping channels, it has also been one for mail-order catalogs. In the past five years the number of catalogs delivered to American homes has tripled. Vendors compose not only old favorites such as L.L. Bean and discount electronics distributors but also newer outfits created merely to take advantage of this trend. According to one survey, the average mail-order catalog junkie receives ten garb catalogs, nine catalogs for housewares and garden equipment, five catalogs for his or her favorite hobby, and six gift catalogs each month. Mail-order companies sell each other their lists of suckers, so once a consumer receives one catalog, chances are that he or she will be receiving catalogs to life.

EDITING 8: APPLICATION

Select one page from a paper you are working on. Remembering the purpose of the paper and its intended audience, examine your choice of words. Use the dictionary and thesaurus to check any word about which you are not sure. Does each word convey the precise meaning you intended? Do any words have connotations that are inappropriate in context? Have you mis-used any frequently confused words? Are your expressions idiomatically worded? Have you used any slang, regionalisms, colloquialisms or jargon? If so, why? Edit the page to improve word choices as necessary, and pay attention to word choice throughout the paper.

44

Eliminating Biased Language

eneralization means summarizing experience or observations: *Canada geese fly south for the winter.* From individual facts, we can make broad conclusions. Generalizing offers a powerful tool to understand patterns or anticipate future events. But relying too greatly on generalization can lead to error. Indeed, many but not all Canada geese are migratory; an increasing number stay put all winter in temperate regions.

Using a generalization about a group of people to predict the behavior or characteristics of an individual is particularly risky. Careless or unexamined generalizations, such as those based on race, ethnicity, cultural background, age, or lifestyle, are called **stereotypes.**

Writing that relies on stereotypes—*sleepy Southern town, typical New York attitude*—instead of specific description, reflects mental laziness. Appealing to prejudice to invoke what an audience "knows" about a group—*liberal politicians, religious fundamendalists*—or to provoke an emotional reaction is no substitute for reasoned discourse. Such writing is called **biased.** From your own experience as a reader, you know your audience is likely to mistrust any writer who relies on stereotypes rather than on specifics, evidence, and reason.

44 a Stereotypes

The danger of using a negative stereotype is obvious. But a positive stereotype—such as assuming that someone's ethnic background implies skill at mathematics—can be demeaning too—it substitutes a simplistic formula for appreciation of an individual.

To edit out stereotypes, consider qualifying a broad generalization or replacing sweeping statements with specific, relevant details. Some stereotypes simply need to be deleted.

Editing Stereotypes and Generalizations

As you edit your writing, look for stereotypes and generalizations. Ask yourself these questions:

- **Am I relying on stereotypes to make my point?** A stereotype such as *soccer moms* or *computer nerds* is a shorthand way of saying to readers, "You know what I mean." But readers may not know, or they may disagree. Show them specifics instead.
- **Does this generalization follow logically from factual evidence?** Two facts together don't imply that either one caused the other. That one Scot likes finnan haddock does not mean that all Scots like finnan haddock any more than it means that if you like finnan haddock, you must be from Scotland.
- **Am I generalizing responsibly?** Generalizations about a group, even valid ones, cannot predict the knowledge, abilities, attitudes, beliefs, or behavior of an individual. For example, anthropologists have suggested that Japanese culture emphasizes group values over individuality, but that does not support an automatic characterization of any one individual.
- **Does a positive description mask a stereotype?** Even a positive stereotype can be a slur in disguise, as when someone praises a woman for being an asset to her husband as though being a wife were her defining role in life.

Frank Peters, stooped from years in the woods ~~but still alert,~~ re-members the hot, dry summer of the Tillamook Burn.

The assumption that a man of Peters' age would not be alert is a stereotype.

I need someone who can understand my questions, so I hope my next course adviser will be a woman.

Someone's gender does not guarantee empathy. Does the following alternative raise the same issue?

I would feel more comfortable discussing my questions with a woman.

EDITING 1: EXPLORATION

Read the terms on the following list. Write down your reactions to each, and note what images and ideas spring to mind.

BMW drivers	African Americans	Muslims
baby boomers	whites	Jews
lawyers	Asians	career politicians
Generation X	bureaucrats	atheists
conservatives	liberals	religious fundamentalists

Now ask yourself the questions from the "Editing Stereotypes and Generalizations" box on page 622. Do any of your responses rely on stereotypes? How many people do you know in each category? Are your reactions based on your own experience, or do they come from what you have heard or read of other people's attitudes? Do you have similar impressions of everyone you have met in the group, or have you noticed variations? If you find yourself harboring stereotypes, remember to try to counterbalance them when you write.

44 b Labels

Everyone who communicates uses labels to identify groups: *whites, females, Democrats, psychiatrists, Taiwanese.* But labels inevitably focus on a single feature and have the potential to offend those who do not want to be characterized in one particular way. Also, some labels are considered derogatory; that is, they go beyond simple identification and evoke stereotypes. Here are some ways to judge how to use labels in your writing.

1 Using a group's own labels

Whenever possible, refer to a group of people by the label its members themselves prefer. Sometimes this is easy: members of the Rotary Club call themselves *Rotarians;* members of the Ancient Free and Accepted Masons are *Masons.*

With ethnic, racial, national, cultural, sexual, or gender labels, your choices become more difficult. Sometimes even those who belong to a group do not agree on what they should be called.

Designations of race, ethnicity, and nationality

Today some Americans whose birthplace or ancestry is in Spanish-speaking countries of South or Central America or Mexico refer to themselves as *Hispanics* while others prefer *Latino* and *Latina.* Some Mexican Americans prefer *Chicano* and *Chicana.* The term *Spanish Americans,* however, properly refers only to Americans whose country of birth or ancestry is Spain. Many *Native Americans* prefer that term to *Indian* or *American Indian,* but using the name of the tribe or nation is often a better choice: *Navaho, Lakota Sioux,* or *Seneca.* Some *Inuit* prefer that term to *Eskimo.* Some people use a term that indicates both their ethnic or national heritage and their American identity: *Chinese American, German American.*

Naming the specific country of someone's origin is always correct and worth the trouble: *Japanese, Vietnamese, Dominican, Chilean, Bosnian, Palestinian, Iraqi,* and so on. In some cases, you may need to identify people by ethnic origin as well as nationality: *Bosnian Serbs, German-speaking Poles, Israeli Arabs.*

The terms *black* and *African American* and the more general *people of color,* usually used to include Native Americans and Asians, are generally accepted, while *Negro* and *colored* are no longer acceptable.

If the religion of a particular group has a specific relevance in your writing, use the preferred terms: for example, a follower of Islam is a *Muslim.*

ESL Using Labels Derived from Adjectives

Many labels that describe groups are derived from adjectives: *the rich, the poor, the homeless.* Take care to use such collective nouns correctly.

- Always use the definite article *the* before the labeling noun.

  The legislature passed a law to assist ^the^ homeless.

- Use a plural verb when the collective noun is the subject.

  The poor ~~is~~ ^are^ always with us.

- A collective noun cannot refer to an individual. If you refer to one person in a group, use an adjective-plus-noun construction.

  We spoke to a homeless ^woman^ about her search for a job.

Designations of gender and sexual orientation

Most adult females prefer to be called *women* rather than *girls* or *ladies.*

When writing about sexual orientation, keep in mind that people have widely different views about the role of sexuality in public and private life.

Not everyone may share your perspective. The terms *homosexual, hetero-sexual, gay, straight, lesbian, bisexual,* and *transgendered* are all generally acceptable.

2 Checking labels for negative connotations

Labels that seem neutral can hide negative connotations. For example, the term *AIDS victims* can imply that such people are blameless, which you may intend, but also that they are helpless, which you may not.

As you edit, watch for unnecessary or unintended negative connotations, and substitute more neutral alternatives. (See 43d.) Focus when possible on people's strengths, referring to people as *living with cancer* or as *cancer survivors* rather than *suffering from cancer.* Focus on individuals first and their characteristics second: *a woman with quadriplegia* rather than *a quadriplegic.*

People's preferences for certain labels change frequently as connotations change. People with physical limitations often, but not universally, prefer *disabled* to *handicapped,* and the latter term one time seemed more neutral than *crippled.* The continuing attempt to avoid negative connotations has resulted in the use of *visually impaired* or *hearing impaired* for *blind* and *deaf* and in such constructions as *differently abled* for *disabled.* Such terms are easily lampooned as an excess of "political correctness," but you must balance the need for directness against the need for sensitivity. Sometimes the solution is not to label at all.

He was a fascinating ~~old~~ man with a lifelong passion for rare books and fine cognac.

EDITING 2: PRACTICE ....

Identify stereotypes in the following passages and describe the ways in which they may be thoughtless or offensive. If there is any useful information in the particular passage, edit it to communicate the information in a way that is not offensive. Be ready to explain your editing choices.

1. In order to achieve more diversity on college campuses, admissions officers are eager to accept foreigners, especially from poor countries.
2. Because of policies like this, during my freshman year I found myself living with an Oriental guy as well as with a Jew from New York City.

3. Since I had trouble in math and science, I asked my Vietnamese room-mate to help me in calculus and physics; I also asked him to show me some karate.
4. My other roommate, not surprisingly, was majoring in business.
5. All in all, I enjoyed the chance to live with a couple of minorities; it taught me a lot about how different people view things differently.

---

44 c   Nonsexist language

Words that embody gender stereotypes—also called sexist language—risk alienating half your potential audience (or more). Several kinds of gender bias arise from unexamined habits of thought and language.

1 In generic pronouns

Until recently, writers and readers alike accepted use of the pronouns *he, him,* and *his* in a generic sense when gender was unspecified or irrel-evant: *Anyone who believes those promises should have* his *head examined.* The "generic *he*" was understood to refer to females as well as males.

As acceptance of this convention wanes, some speakers substitute plural pronouns: *Everyone had fun on their vacation.* This is grammati-cally incorrect, since *everyone* is singular and thus requires a singular pro-noun. However, English has no singular personal pronoun of indefinite gender, only *he* or *she, him* or *her, his* or *hers.* In formal writing, you have to find ways around this dilemma.

her
Every nun has ~~their~~ own room.
                 ^

Nuns are women, so you can substitute her.

All attorneys have their   specialties.
~~Every attorney has his~~ own legal ~~specialty.~~
                 ^   ^

If you switch to the plural, watch for other agreement problems.

(For a complete discussion of gender agreement and avoiding the generic *he,* see 49j.)

2 In universal terms

The use of *man* and *mankind* to refer to the whole of humanity has fallen into disfavor because those terms seem to exclude or diminish the female half of the species. Substitute *humanity, the human race, humankind,* or *people.*

3 In occupational terms

In terms for a person's occupation, focus on the occupation, not the person's gender. Otherwise you risk suggesting that gender is a person's most important attribute or that some jobs are "naturally" held by either men or women.

Many occupational terms have a feminine form, with a suffix that indicates the female gender: *actor/actress, author/authoress, poet/poetess.* Avoid these, and use gender-neutral alternatives: for *stewardess,* use *flight attendant;* for *waitress,* use *server;* for *actress, actor.*

Occupational terms that end in *-man* imply that everyone who engages in that profession is male. Use sex-neutral substitutes.

BIASED	NEUTRAL
statesman	diplomat, national leader
congressman	representative to Congress, congressional representative
mailman	letter carrier, mail carrier
policeman	police officer
fireman	firefighter
businessman	executive, businessperson
chairman	chair, head, chairperson

Similarly, do not use language that implicitly assumes that an occupation determines a person's gender—that all nurses, secretaries, or teachers are female or that all airline pilots, business executives, or bronco busters are male.

The physician was assisted by a ~~male~~ nurse.

4 In descriptions

Treat the sexes equally. As you edit, notice comments about a woman's appearance or family life. If you would not have made similar comments about a man, delete them.

Dr. Jones, ~~mother of three,~~ was named to the hospital's peer review board.

5 In comparisons

Whenever you use a pair of terms for male and female, use terms that are directly comparable. The phrase *man and wife,* for example, identifies one partner as independent (*man*) and the other in terms of her relation to him (*wife*). Edit it as *man and woman* or *husband and wife.*

Her essay contrasted the novelists Dickens and ~~Jane~~ Austen.

6 In addressing your audience

Do not address a general audience as if it were made up of people of a single gender.

When you buy a house, ~~your wife~~ ^{you} will have to get used to a new kitchen.

EDITING 3: EXPLORATION

The following are excerpts from three political statements from earlier centuries, when ideas about the roles of the sexes and sexism in language were very different. To whom do you think Jefferson is referring? How about Lincoln? Is either statement ambiguous or open to more than one interpretation? How do you think Stanton interpreted Jefferson's text? In what ways is her use of male and female terms different from Jefferson's? In what ways is it similar to Jefferson's?

When in the course of human events it becomes necessary for one people to dissolve the political bands which have connected them with another, . . . a decent respect to the opinions of mankind requires that they should declare the causes which impel them to the separation.

We hold these truths to be self-evident, that all men are created equal, that they are endowed by their Creator with certain unalienable Rights. . . . That to secure these rights, Governments are instituted among Men deriving their just powers from the consent of the governed.

THOMAS JEFFERSON, DECLARATION OF INDEPENDENCE (1776)

Four score and seven years ago, our fathers brought forth on this continent a new nation, conceived in liberty and dedicated to the proposition that all men are created equal.

ABRAHAM LINCOLN, GETTYSBURG ADDRESS (1863)

When in the course of human events it becomes necessary for one portion of the family of man to assume among the people of the earth a position different from that which they have hitherto occupied, . . . a decent respect to the opinions of mankind requires that they should declare the causes that impel them to such a course.

We hold these truths to be self-evident: that all men and women are created equal; that they are endowed by their Creator with certain inalienable rights; . . . that to secure these rights governments are instituted, deriving their just powers from the consent of the governed.

ELIZABETH CADY STANTON, DECLARATION OF SENTIMENTS (1848)

EDITING 4: PRACTICE

Edit the following passage, eliminating any language that might be offensive. More than one version is possible. Be ready to explain your choices.

All of the old people at White Pines Residence agree that there couldn't be a better place for them to live. The modern residence has been designed to meet their every need, and in some ways it resembles a spa more than an old-folks' home. For one thing, the food is terrific. Every meal offers at least one exotic dish, always cooked to perfection. This isn't surprising, considering that the chef was born in Paris. In the medical area, facilities and services are first rate. A doctor is on call around the clock to provide care to all of the residents, many of whom suffer from cancer. With the handicapped in mind, doorways have been built that are wide enough for a cripple's wheelchair to pass through, and ramps are familiar sights, both inside and outside. Staff members have been carefully chosen for both their experience with old people and their personalities. They are all extremely popular with the residents. One of the best loved is a male nurse who always makes time in his busy schedule to read to the blind residents. Another nurse is a former actress; she has arranged for a local theater group to perform regularly at the residence. In addition, volunteers from the local college visit with the residents, providing them with companionship and friendship. Like so many old people, the residents at White Pines enjoy spending time with young people and telling stories about their youth.

EDITING 5: APPLICATION

In a paper you are working on, look for examples of biased language. Are there any stereotypes? If so, can you supply specific details to support your use of the stereotypes? Or should they be eliminated? Have you used labels to describe groups of people? Would these labels be acceptable to the people themselves? Have you used male pronouns to refer to both genders? Can you find any other examples of sexist language? If you discover such stereotypes or biased language in your paper, consider carefully why you might have written that way in the first place and how you can avoid doing so in the future. Then edit the relevant passages to eliminate the biased language. How does the edited version compare with the original?

Editing Section

Grammar

631

chapter **45** *Eliminating Sentence Fragments*

Does every sentence "start with a capital letter and end with a period"? As a character in *Porgy and Bess* says, "It ain't necessarily so." A group of words punctuated as a sentence that is not grammatically complete is called a **fragment.**

There are several ways to select text with the mouse. *A few of which may be known to you.*

In academic writing, most instructors regard sentence fragments as errors. One kind of fragment is missing something—a subject, a verb, or both. Another type has a subject and a verb but begins with an element such as *because* or *when* that makes it impossible for it to stand alone. While skilled writers sometimes deliberately use fragments for effect, less experienced writers tend to use them inadvertently.

45 a Fragments lacking subjects or verbs

A complete sentence—an **independent clause**—has a subject and a verb, but if one or the other is missing, you have found a fragment. You need to edit these fragments to create complete sentences. First, decide which element is missing. Then find a way to provide it.

1 Adding missing elements

Fill in the missing sentence element.

                          rocked
A fleet of colorful fishing boats at anchor in the bay.
                                      ^

Recognizing Fragments

A group of words can fail to form a complete sentence if it lacks subject or a verb.

■ **Does it contain a subject?** If not, it is a fragment.

>   *and*
> The protesters rested/ ~~And~~ talked about tomorrow's plans.

■ **Does it contain a verb?** If not, it is a fragment.

>   *ran by*
> A middle-aged jogger in beat-up Nikes.

Commands—sentences in the imperative mood—do not require explicit subjects: *Be there at noon.* (See 47f.)

Even if it contains a subject and a verb, a clause beginning with a word such as *when, because, after,* or *although* cannot stand alone as a sentence. It's a **dependent clause** because it must be connected to a clause that can stand alone—an **independent clause.** (See 45b and Chapter 63.)

>   *because*
> None of the research was completed on time/ ~~Because~~ of the delay in
>
> preparing the samples.

>   *it*
> Out of control, the careening truck hit the guardrail. Then spilled chickens and feathers halfway across the landscape.

> Symbolism figures prominently in Alice Walker's "Everyday Use."
> *The*
> ~~A~~ story ~~that~~ shows cultural differences between generations.

2 Joining the fragment

Another solution is to incorporate the fragment into a nearby sentence.

> Symbolism figures prominently in Alice Walker's "Everyday Use,"
> *which*
> ~~A story that~~ shows cultural differences between generations.

> I was in the library when I saw him. The new student from Hong
> Kong/ ~~He~~ was looking up something in the catalog.

Few employees interviewed held the company president in
high regard, ~~Or~~ *or* believed he could bring the business back to
profitability.

Join a fragment that is a list or set of examples to an introductory
statement.

Taking the boat out alone for the first time, I tried to think of
everything my father had shown me, ~~Centerboard,~~ *: centerboard,* halyards, jib
sheets, main sheet, tiller, and telltales.

Note: Following a colon, the first word of a list that is not a complete
sentence is not capitalized. (See 54b.)

ESL Preposition Fragments: Multiple-Word Prepositions

Fragments introduced by multiple-word prepositions can be more difficult to spot
than those introduced by one-word prepositions. Here is a list of common multiple-word
prepositions:

according to	for the sake of
along with	in contrast with
as a result of	in favor of
as compared with	in spite of
as for	instead of
aside from	on account of
as well as	regardless of
because of	relative to
contrary to	up until
due to	with respect to
except for	with the exception of

Whenever you use one of these prepositions in your writing, make sure the phrase it introduces is attached to an independent clause.

Our debate team was not invited to participate, ~~In~~ *in* spite of our winning record.

Edit the following passage to eliminate any fragments, making any changes in wording or punctuation that are necessary for smooth reading. More than one edited version is possible. Be ready to explain your editing choices.

There he stood. In the middle of the public square. Speaking at the top of his lungs about the end of the world. After two or three hours in the hot sun, he rested. Sat down in the shade of the clock tower. He opened his satchel and took out his lunch. A banana. A small can of apple juice. Three cookies and a wedge of cheese. I walked over to talk to him. He looked me right in the eye. For a long moment. Then spoke: "Have a cookie."

45 b   Dependent clause fragments

A **dependent clause** is a clause introduced by a **subordinating conjunction** (such as *after, although, since, because, when, where, whether*) or a **relative pronoun** (such as *who, which, that*). Even though it has a subject and a verb, a dependent clause such as *that extended from before dawn until long past dark* cannot stand alone as a sentence.

If you find a dependent clause punctuated as a sentence, try attaching it to a nearby independent clause that completes the thought.

Contemporary accounts describe a battle. ~~That~~ ^{that} extended from before dawn until long past dark.

Tests isolated the virus. ^{, which} ~~Which~~ can be deadly.

You also can remove the subordinating element so that the clause can stand alone.

^{The} ~~After the~~ leaves had all fallen. The trees stood bare.

On occasion, a fragment can be attached to a nearby sentence. In such a case, you will have to choose which sentence to use.

, although

It sounds like an excellent opportunity. ~~Although~~ the starting pay
is barely minimum wage. It provides more training than many
entry-level jobs.

The value of the opportunity is qualified.

It sounds like an excellent opportunity. Although the starting pay

, it

is barely minimum wage. ~~It~~ provides more training than many

entry-level jobs.

The value of the training provided is stressed.

(See 52b and 52c for punctuation of dependent clauses.)

EDITING 2: PRACTICE

Edit the following paragraph to eliminate dependent clause fragments.
More than one edited version is possible. Be ready to explain your editing
choices.

Despite the fact that doctors take an oath to protect life. Many physicians believe they should be allowed to help patients who want to com-
mit suicide. They want to do whatever they can to ease the pain of
death for those who are suffering. Because they believe people should
be able to die with dignity. Although euthanasia is not legal in most of
Europe, it is becoming more accepted in some countries. Especially in
the Netherlands. Which has one of the most liberal policies in the world.
There, specific guidelines allow a doctor to assist in the suicide of a patient who is terminally ill. As long as the patient requests it.

45 c   Fragments for special efects

Man is the only animal that blushes. Or needs to.

MARK TWAIN

Writers occasionally use fragments on purpose. Because a fragment
provides a dramatic break in rhythm, it can create dramatic emphasis. For
this reason, fragments abound in advertising.

The sun's harsh rays can wrinkle your skin. Even cause cancer. Introducing the ultraviolet protection of new No-ray Oil. A fluid that blends smoothly with your skin, penetrating and softening. To soothe and protect.

Here essayist Joan Didion uses fragments to underscore a major point:

> I knew that I was no legitimate resident in any world of ideas. I knew I couldn't think. All I knew then was what I couldn't do. All I knew then was what I wasn't, and it took me some years to discover what I was. *Which was a writer.*
>
> *By which I mean not a "good" writer or a "bad" writer, but simply a writer, a person whose most absorbed and passionate hours are spent arranging words on pieces of paper.*
>
> JOAN DIDION, "WHY I WRITE" (ITALICS ADDED.)

Because fragments are used infrequently in academic writing, you should consider carefully before using one deliberately. Will it be seen as an effective stylistic device or as an error? When your point warrants disrupting readers' expectations, a fragment might be in order. If it works.

EDITING 3: EXPLORATION

Look through popular magazines, essay collections, and other publications written for a general audience and note the use of intentional fragments. In each case, what effect does the fragment have on you, the reader? Defend or criticize the effectiveness of each fragment you find.

EDITING 4: PRACTICE

Read the following passage, which includes a number of intentional fragments. Identify each fragment and consider its overall effect. What do you think the writer was trying to achieve? Do you think the fragments are effective? To determine the overall effectiveness of the passage, edit it to eliminate fragments and then compare your edited version with the original.

There never was any question whether we would finish. Just how soon. It seemed every time we got ready to close up, another busload would come in. Tired and hungry. And the boss would say, "Can't turn away money," so we'd pour more coffee. Burn more toast. Crack more eggs. Over and over again. Because we needed the money too.

....

Edit the following passage to eliminate sentence fragments. Make any changes in wording that are needed for smooth reading. More than one edited version is possible. Be ready to explain your editing choices.

Ferdinand le Menthe Morton was born in New Orleans to a Creole family. Although he took classical piano lessons, he fell in love with another kind of music. Jazz and blues. Which he heard in the part of town called Storyville. In Chicago in the 1920s, he got a recording contract with RCA. He made some records and began calling himself "Jelly Roll." He claimed to have invented jazz. By himself. George G. Wolfe wrote a musical about his life. Called *Jelly's Last Jam* and written as though looking back from the moment of his death. At the end of his life, Morton had to acknowledge the contributions of other blacks to jazz. Which he had denied all his life. He came to recognize the heritage he shared with other black musicians. To accept and understand them. Although he had always thought of himself, a Creole, as different from blacks.

....

....

Examine your recent writings for sentence fragments. Do you write one kind of fragment frequently? If so, can you explain why? Practice editing any fragments you find by correcting each one in two or three different ways. Then decide which edited version of each sentence works best in your paper.

....

46

Fixing Fused Sentences and Comma Splices

An **independent clause,** one that includes a subject and a predicate and constitutes one complete idea, can stand alone as a complete sentence.

subject	predicate

Professional athletes can earn huge salaries.

Two or more independent clauses within a single sentence must be joined in one of four ways: with a comma and a coordinating conjunction, with a semicolon alone, with a semicolon and a conjunctive adverb or transitional phrase, or with a colon. These markers tell readers that a new idea is about to be presented and clarify the relationship between the ideas.

independent clause	independent

Professional athletes can earn huge salaries, yet some of them want

clause

still more.

In this example the comma and the conjunction *yet* mark the beginning of a new idea, a new independent clause. They help prevent misreading by limiting the number of possible ways the sentence can proceed from that point.

Two independent clauses joined without such a marker make a **fused sentence** (also called a *run-on sentence*). Readers get no warning when one thought ends and another begins.

independent clause

FUSED SENTENCE   Professional athletes can earn huge salaries some are

independent clause

paid millions of dollars per year.

Two independent clauses joined (or "spliced together") only by a comma make up a **comma splice.**

COMMA SPLICE   Professional athletes can earn huge salaries, millions of dollars a year isn't enough for some of them.

REVISED   Professional athletes can earn huge salaries; millions of dollars a year isn't enough for some of them.

Seeing the comma after salaries, *readers expect what follows to be part of the first clause rather than the beginning of a new one.*

Recognizing Common Causes of Sentence Errors

Comma splices and fused sentences, sometimes called *sentence errors,* often occur when two clauses express ideas closely linked in the writer's mind. Understanding why sentence errors occur can help you recognize them in your own writing. Here are some common situations that can lead to sentence errors:

- **Additional information.** The second clause explains, elaborates on, or illustrates the first.

  Every summer the tribes gathered along the banks of the river, ~~they~~ fished *to*

  and hunted and picked berries.

- **Contrast.** The meaning of the second clause contrasts with the meaning of the first.

  The Security Council supported the resolution, the United States vetoed it. *but*

- **Same or similar subjects.** The subject of the second clause renames the subject of the first clause.

. He
The professor asked us to write our thoughts down/~~he~~ said just to write

whatever came to mind as fast as we could.

■ **Incorrect use of conjunction or transition.** A conjunctive adverb or transitional phrase
is incorrectly used to join two sentences.

; however,
Forecasters predicted the storm would remain offshore/~~however~~ it made

landfall in North Carolina.

46 a   Comma and a coordinating conjunction

The **coordinating conjunctions** *and, but, yet, so, for, or,* and *nor* join
equal grammatical elements and specify a relationship between them, such
as addition (*and*), contrast (*but, yet*), causation (*so, for*), or choice (*or, nor*). (See
Chapter 38.) If the ideas in two independent clauses are equally important, you
can join them with a coordinating conjunction preceded by a comma. (See 52a.)

, and
The cyclone was especially savage it struck a particularly vul-

nerable area.

but
Maya Angelou has worked as an actress and director, her greatest

success has come as an autobiographer and poet.

46 b   Adding a semicolon

Another way to join two independent clauses is to add a **semicolon**
between the clauses to signify their equality.

1 Semicolon alone

Use a semicolon alone only when the clauses are closely and clearly related. (See 53a.) If they are not closely related, make them separate sentences. (See 46d.) If the relationship is unclear, use a conjunction to clarify it.

;
For years, free-market proponents have advocated legislation to

allow competitive auctions for broadcast licenses so far Congress

has refused.

Note: The second independent clause does not begin with a capital letter.

Semicolons are useful in sentences that contain more than two independent clauses, particularly when one or more items in a series have internal commas.

> **The sculpture, a poor imitation of the work of Dresner, was monstrous; its surface was rough and pitted; and its colors, ranging from fuschia to lime, were garish.**

When two or more independent clauses are short, closely related, and parallel in form, some writers use only a comma. However, the effect is somewhat informal.

> I washed the clothes, I dusted the furniture, I fed the children.

But a semicolon is necessary when the sentence becomes more complicated.

> **He dovetailed the joints of the drawers; he sanded, stained, and varnished.**

A semicolon is not needed before a **tag question.**

> A semicolon would look odd here, wouldn't it?

Conjunctive Adverbs

accordingly	incidentally	now
also	indeed	otherwise
anyway	instead	similarly
besides	likewise	still
certainly	meanwhile	subsequently
consequently	moreover	then
conversely	namely	therefore
finally	nevertheless	thus
furthermore	next	undoubtedly
hence	nonetheless	whereas
however		

2 Semicolon with a conjunctive adverb or transitional expression

Conjunctive adverbs, such as *finally, however,* and *therefore,* cannot be used with a comma to join two independent clauses. Neither can phrases such as *in fact* or *for example,* which are called **transitional expressions.** Use a semicolon instead. (See the list of conjunctive adverbs above; see 36c2 for a list of transitional expressions.)

The rebel forces were never completely defeated; moreover, they still control several strategic highland passes.

46 c Colon

When the second clause of two independent clauses explains, elaborates, or illustrates the first, you can use a **colon** to join the clauses.

This year's team is surprisingly inexperienced: seven of the players are juniors, and six are sophomores.

When the second independent clause conveys the main point of the sentence, some writers capitalize the first word after the colon.

My mother gave me one important piece of advice: Never wear plaids with stripes.

Such capitalization is optional; a lowercase letter after the colon is always correct. (See Chapter 54 and 59a.)

46 d Separate sentences

A comma-spliced or fused sentence may read better as two separate sentences, especially when one clause is much longer than the other or when the two clauses are dissimilar in structure or meaning.

The president outlined his new economic strategy on the same day that war broke out in the Middle East. Almost no one noticed his announcement.

Forming two sentences often increases emphasis on the second clause.

46 e   Subordinating one clause

To emphasize one of the two ideas in a fused or spliced sentence, put the less important idea in a **subordinate clause.** Subordinating one clause to the other will make it dependent—no longer able to stand on its own. (See 38b.) The effect is to bring important information into the foreground while leaving other information in the background.

Dependent clauses are introduced by a **subordinating conjunction** such as *after, although, as, because, if, than, whenever,* or *while* or by a **relative pronoun** such as *who, which,* or *that.* Choose the subordinating conjunction or relative pronoun that best describes the relationship you want to establish.

Because the
~~The~~ rain froze as it hit the ground , the streets were icy.
^   ^

that
The committee studied the issue ~~it~~ decided to recommend allowing
^
the group to participate.

46 f   Creating independent clauses

When two independent clauses are closely related, often you can collapse them into one clause.

and
This book held my attention, ~~it~~ gave a lot of information about the
^
colonial period.

Since book *and* it *are the same subject,* it *can be dropped.*

You can also turn one clause into a modifier phrase.

The huge chestnut oak cast a heavy blanket of shadow on the
dwarfing
ground beneath it, ~~it dwarfed~~ a few saplings.
^

, my favorite author,
Bobbie Ann Mason writes interesting stories about offbeat
^
characters. ~~She is my favorite author.~~

Edit each fused sentence or comma splice in the following passage by creating a single sentence or separate sentences. More than one edited version is possible. Be ready to explain your editing choices.

The weather report was over, we knew the storm was approaching rapidly. We were all very nervous hurricanes had struck our town many times before they did a lot of damage. My father came back from the hardware store with several rolls of masking tape, he gave each of us a roll and told us to tape the windows to keep the glass from shattering if hit by debris. Then mom sent me to check on our next-door neighbor he is extremely scared of storms. He still remembers the violent storms of his childhood, he was born in Texas. He returned with me to our house, we all waited in the basement we played cards and we listened to the radio. Fortunately, the storm dissipated when it hit the coast south of us, all the excitement was for nothing.

Edit the following passage to eliminate fused sentences and comma splices, using any strategy discussed in this chapter. Be ready to discuss your editing changes.

Expanding the airport will generate more flights, more flights will bring more travelers and money into the region. Each traveler spends an average of $7 in the airport on goods and services, when parking and ground transportation are added, the total approaches $25. The report said that developing the local economy would benefit the area, it said that air travel would make traffic problems worse on roads around the airport. According to the report, expanding the airport offers many advantages, including providing jobs, making travel more convenient, and boosting the economy.

However, the expansion plan faces some problems, it would cost $17 million and it would have to be built on land that might be valuable as wetlands. Opponents of the airport expansion appeared before the port commission, saying that new runways would endanger the nesting grounds of several rare migratory birds. The Department of Environmental Quality studied the bird migration patterns it said that the fifteen acres of wetlands in question were home to at least nineteen different species. The Southeast Region Chamber of Commerce has

Editing Comma Splices and Fused Sentences

There are several ways to correct fused sentences and comma splices:

- **Use a comma and coordinating conjunction** to specify the relationship between clauses.

    Columbus believed he would reach Asia, *but* his sailors had much less confidence.

- **Insert a semicolon** to signal a clear, close relationship of the clauses.

    He did not prove the world was round; he discovered the New World.

- **Precede a conjunctive adverb or transitional phrase with a semicolon.**

    Columbus continued to believe he had reached Asia; in fact, he did not realize he had discovered a "New World" until he found the mouth of the Orinoco River during his third voyage.

- **Use a colon when the second clause illustrates the first.**

    Columbus really did not know where he was; he insisted the islands he found were near Asia.

- **Divide the sentence into two sentences.**

    Columbus never set foot in North America. The closest he came to discovering "America" was landing in what is now Puerto Rico.

- **Subordinate one clause to the other.**

    Although Columbus believed he would reach Asia, his sailors had much less confidence.

- **Rewrite the sentence as one independent clause.**

    On Hispaniola, Columbus established a settlement called Isabella, ~~it was~~ the first European colony in the New World.

supported the airport expansion, claiming that the plan could create dozens of new jobs, the chamber president called those jobs more important than a few ducks.

EDITING 3: APPLICATION

Examine your own recent writing for fused sentences and comma splices. If you have used any, is there a pattern to your errors? Can you see why you made these mistakes? Edit any fused sentences and comma splices you found, and think about how best to correct or avoid these errors in the future.

Strong verbs convey a great deal of information. They help show *who* performed the action by changing form according to **person:** *I talk. He talks.* They show *how many* people performed the action by changing **number:** *She sings. They sing.* They show *when* it occurred by changing **tense:** *He thinks. He thought.* They show the speaker's *attitude* toward or *relation* to the action by changing **mood:** *You are an honors student. Be an honors student.* They also show whether the subject of the sentence acts or is acted upon by changing **voice:** *She took the picture. The picture was taken.*

Using verbs correctly in all these ways is not as difficult as it may seem. If you speak English fluently, you have been using the right person, number, tense, mood, and voice most of the time without thinking about it. In conversation, however, people often ignore the subtleties of correct usage. Additionally, what is "correct" varies from community to community. People who grew up speaking a dialect may find their use of verbs is considered nonstandard in formal academic writing.

This chapter gives an overview of verb forms, tense, and mood. The uses of the active and passive voice are discussed in Chapter 40. For questions of agreement between verbs and subjects, see 47h–47u.

VERB FORMS

47 a   Understanding forms

Except for the verb *be*, all English verbs have five forms.

Two forms express action occurring now: the **base form** and the **-s form.** The base form, also called the *plain form* or *simple form,* is used for present-tense action performed by *I, we, you,* or *they: I walk, you walk, they walk.* The -s form is used for *he, she,* or *it* (third-person singular): *he walks, she walks, it walks.*

Terms Used to Describe Verbs

The terms used to describe verbs are useful for discussing verb problems and their solutions.

■ **Person** indicates who or what performs an action. (See 47a–47b.)

first person	the one speaking	*I read.*
second person	the one spoken to	*You read.*
third person	the one spoken about	*He reads.*

■ **Number** indicates how many people or things perform the action. (See 47a–47b.)

singular	one	*I think.*
plural	more than one	*We think.*

■ **Tense** indicates the time of the action. (See 47d–47e.)

present	at this time	*I learn.*
past	before this time	*I learned.*
future	after this time	*I will learn.*

■ **Mood** indicates the speaker's attitude toward or relation to the action. (See 47f–47g.)

indicative	speaker states a fact or asks a question	*You* are *happy.* / Are *you happy?*
imperative	speaker gives a command or direction	Be *quiet!*
subjunctive	speaker expresses desire, wish, or requirement or states a condition contrary to fact	*I would be happier if you* were *quiet.*

■ **Voice** indicates whether the grammatical subject of the sentence performs the action or is acted upon. (See 40c.)

active	the subject acts	*She read the book.*
passive	the subject is acted upon	*The book was read by her.*

The Five Verb Forms

The five principal forms of English verbs are the base form, the *-s* form, the past tense, the past participle, and the present participle. Regular verbs add *-d* or *-ed* to form the past tense and past participle. Irregular verbs follow some other pattern. (The verb *be* has more than five forms. It is the most irregular verb in the English language. See 47b4.)

	Base Form	-s Form	Past Tense	Past Participle	Present Participle
REGULAR	act	acts	acted	acted	acting
	seem	seems	seemed	seemed	seeming
IRREGULAR	know	knows	knew	known	knowing
	eat	eats	ate	eaten	eating
	hit	hits	hit	hit	hitting

Two verb forms express action that occurred in the past: the **past tense** and **past participle.** For **regular verbs,** the past tense and past participle are formed by adding *-d* or *-ed* to the base form: *I walked. I have walked.* Verbs that form the past tense and past participle in other ways are called **irregular verbs.** Often the two past forms of an irregular verb differ from each other: *I knew. I have known.* The past tense and the past participle do not change to reflect who performed the action: *I tried. She tried. They tried.*

The fifth verb form, the **present participle,** is formed by adding *-ing* to the base form: *know, knowing.* It expresses continuing action in the present or the past. Like the past tense and past participle, it does not change according to person and number, and to serve as the main verb of a sentence it must be used with a form of *be: She is sleeping.* (See 47c.)

(For a discussion of the verb *be,* see 47b4; for more on other irregular verbs, see 47b2.)

47 b   Standard verb forms

1 Using *-s* and *-ed* forms correctly

Speakers of some dialects do not use the *-s* and *-ed* endings, but such usage is considered nonstandard in formal writing. As you edit your work, watch for missing *-s* and *-ed* endings.

wants
He ~~want~~ to go to the basketball game.
   ^

   asked   liked
The waiter ~~ask~~ me how I ~~like~~ the food.
       ^   ^

2 Using irregular forms correctly

Some patterns appear among irregular verbs. For example, some verbs, such as *bet, bid, burst, cast, cut, hit,* and *quit,* do not change form for the past tense or past participle. Certain vowel changes provide another pattern: *ring, rang, rung; sing, sang, sung; drink, drank, drunk.* But these patterns are not reliable enough to predict. The past tense of *think* is not *thank,* nor is its past participle *thunk;* both the past and past participle are *thought.*

Since irregular verbs cannot easily be predicted, you need to memorize them or consult a dictionary. Be sure to edit carefully for the correct verb forms. (See the examples on pp. 651–654.)

saw
She ~~seen~~ her mistake immediately.
   ^

known
I've ~~knowed~~ all along that she would.
   ^

Irregular Verbs

Base Form	Past Tense	Past Participle
arise	arose	arisen
awake	awoke, awaked	awaked, awoken
be	was, were	been
beat	beat	beaten, beat
become	became	become
begin	began	begun
bend	bent	bent
bet	bet	bet
bind	bound	bound
bite	bit	bitten, bit
blow	blew	blown
break	broke	broken
bring	brought	brought
broadcast	broadcast	broadcast
build	built	built
burst	burst	burst
buy	bought	bought

catch	caught	caught
choose	chose	chosen
cling	clung	clung
come	came	come
cost	cost	cost
creep	crept	crept
deal	dealt	dealt
dig	dug	dug
dive	dived, dove	dived
do	did	done
draw	drew	drawn
drink	drank	drunk
drive	drove	driven
eat	ate	eaten
fall	fell	fallen
feed	fed	fed
feel	felt	felt
fight	fought	fought
find	found	found
flee	fled	fled
fly	flew	flown
forbid	forbade	forbidden
forget	forgot	forgotten, forgot
forgive	forgave	forgiven
freeze	froze	frozen
get	got	gotten, got
give	gave	given
go	went	gone
grow	grew	grown
hang (suspend)	hung	hung
hang (execute)	hanged	hanged
have	had	had
hear	heard	heard
hide	hid	hidden
hold	held	held
hurt	hurt	hurt
keep	kept	kept
know	knew	known
lay (put)	laid	laid
lead	led	led
leap	leapt, leaped	leapt, leaped
leave	left	left
lend	lent	lent
let (allow)	let	let
lie (recline)	lay	lain
light	lit, lighted	lit, lighted

lose	lost	lost
make	made	made
mean	meant	meant
meet	met	met
mistake	mistook	mistaken
pay	paid	paid
prove	proved	proved, proven
quit	quit	quit
read	read	read
rid	rid	rid
ride	rode	ridden
ring	rang	rung
rise	rose	risen
run	ran	run
say	said	said
see	saw	seen
seek	sought	sought
sell	sold	sold
send	sent	sent
set	set	set
shake	shook	shaken
shoot	shot	shot
show	showed	shown, showed
shrink	shrank	shrunk
sing	sang	sung
sink	sank	sunk
sit	sat	sat
sleep	slept	slept
speak	spoke	spoken
spend	spent	spent
spin	spun	spun
spit	spit, spat	spit, spat
spring	sprang	sprung
stand	stood	stood
steal	stole	stolen
stick	stuck	stuck
sting	stung	stung
stink	stank, stunk	stunk
strike	struck	struck, stricken
swear	swore	sworn
swim	swam	swum
swing	swung	swung
take	took	taken
teach	taught	taught
tear	tore	torn
tell	told	told

think	thought	thought
throw	threw	thrown
wake	woke, waked	woken, waked
wear	wore	worn
win	won	won
write	wrote	written

3 Using *sit* and *set* and *lie* and *lay* correctly

Sit and *set* and *lie* and *lay* cause confusion because of their similar sounds and meanings. To distinguish them, remember that *sit* and *lie* never take direct objects (the ones with an *i* in them are **intransitive verbs**), while *set* and *lay* always take direct objects (they are **transitive verbs**). *Sit* means "to be seated"; *set* means "to put or place." *Lie* means "to recline"; *lay* means "to put or place."

INTRANSITIVE   People *sit* outside when it's warm.

I always *lie* down after lunch.

TRANSITIVE   We *set* the books on the table.

Every morning I *lay* the mail on her desk.

Sit/Set *and* Lie/Lay

Base Form	Past Tense	Past Participle	Present Participle
sit (to be seated)	sat	sat	sitting
set (to put or place)	set	set	setting
lie (to recline)	lay	lain	lying
lay (to put or place)	laid	laid	laying
lie (to tell a falsehood)	lied	lied	lying

4 Using *be* correctly

The verb *be* is an irregular verb that has many different forms. Every other English verb uses only two forms in the present tense: the base form and the -s (or -es) form: *I work, you work, we work, they work, she works.* The

Sure and, Try and, Got to, Have Got, Could of

The colloquial expressions *be sure and, try and,* and *got to* should be avoided in formal writing. The correct equivalents are *be sure to, try to,* and *must.*

Be sure ~~and~~ get there on time.
     ^ *to*

He promised to try ~~and not~~ be late.
         ^ *not to*

You ~~have got to~~ finish by Friday.
      ^ *must*

In formal writing, use a form of *have* in place of *has got* to indicate possession.

He's ~~got~~ a huge collection of fishing flies.
    ^ *has*

Do not use *could of, must of,* or *should of* in place of *could have, must have,* or *should have.*

She should ~~of~~ finished by now.
        ^ *have*

---

verb *be,* however, has three present-tense forms, all different from the base form: *I am, you (we, they) are, he is.*

These books ~~is~~ due back at the library next week.
           ^ *are*

Some speakers use the base form *be* instead of the correct present-tense form, and others drop the verb entirely. Such usage is regarded as nonstandard in formal writing.

He ~~be~~ happy watching television.
    ^ *is*

We on our way over.
  ^ *are*

Using *be* as an auxiliary (see 47c2) with the present participle is also nonstandard.

I ~~be~~ working harder this term than last term.
    ^ *am*

The Forms of Be

The most irregular verb in English is *be,* which has three forms in the present tense and two forms in the past tense.

	Singular	**Plural**
PRESENT	I am	we are
	you are	you are
	he, she, it is	they are
PAST	I was	we were
	you were	you were
	he, she, it was	they were

These are the principal parts of *be:*

Base Form	**-s Form**	**Past Tense**	**Past Participle**	**Present Participle**
be	is	was, were	been	being

Before the past participle *been,* always use a form of the auxiliary *have.*

have
I been practicing three hours every night.
^

ESL Gerunds and Infinitives as Nouns Following Verbs

Gerunds and infinitives are called **verbals** because although they are derived from verbs, but they do not function as verbs in sentences. A **gerund** is the *-ing* form of the verb used as a noun. An **infinitive** consists of *to* plus the base form of the verb.

Gerund   Infinitive
I stopped *eating* and started *to work.*

Gerunds and infinitives often follow verbs. By tradition, some verbs can be followed only by gerunds or gerund phrases: *I enjoy eating,* not *I enjoy to eat.* Other verbs can be followed only by infinitives: *I plan to swim* not *I plan swimming.* And a third category of verbs can be followed by either gerunds or infinitives (or gerund phrases or infinitive phrases): *I like reading. I like to read.*

It is sometimes difficult to remember whether to use a gerund or an infinitive with a particular verb. Here are some common verbs in each of the three categories.

■ **Some verbs can be followed directly only by a gerund,** not an infinitive.

visiting
He recommended ~~to visit~~ the botanical gardens.
^

admit	avoid	consider	delay
appreciate	complete	defend	deny

discuss	include	practice	resent
dislike	mention	quit	risk
enjoy	mind	recall	suggest
finish	miss	recommend	tolerate
imagine	postpone	regret	understand

■ **Some verbs can be directly followed only by an infinitive,** not a gerund.

> *to finish*
> I expect ~~finishing~~ my paper today.
>   ^

agree	deserve	learn	refuse
appear	desire	mean	seem
arrange	expect	need	tend
ask	fail	offer	threaten
choose	forget	plan	volunteer
claim	hesitate	prepare	wait
decide	hope	pretend	want
demand	intend	promise	wish

Some verbs followed by infinitives require a noun or pronoun between the verb and the infinitive.

> *my friends* ⊙
> She persuaded to stay ~~my friends.~~
>   ^   ^

Verbs that require a noun or pronoun before the infinitive include these:

advise	encourage	invite	reach
allow	expect	order	tell
cause	forbid	permit	urge
command	force	persuade	warn
convince	hire	remind	
dare	instruct	require	

■ **Some verbs can be followed by either a gerund or an infinitive.**

We began *watching/to watch* the documentary.

advise*	continue	prefer	stop
allow*	hate	regret	try
begin	like	remember	urge*
cause*	love	start	
cease	permit*		

The verbs marked with an asterisk (*) need to be followed directly by a noun or pronoun before an infinitive.

NO	The instructor *allows* to miss each student one class.
YES	The instructor *allows* each student *to miss* one class.
YES	The instructor *allows missing* one class.

Edit the following passage, using the correct -*s* and -*ed* forms and irregular forms of verbs.

The waiter sat down two hot chocolates topped with whipped cream at the table where we were setting. The bell over the door rung repeatedly as a steady stream of hungry diners enter. The winter sun shined brightly through the large glass panes next to us as we drunk our chocolate. I be resting comfortably in the corner of the booth when suddenly I seen the woman at the next table as she sprung up and walk toward the door. I gave my companion a questioning look and asked, "What do you think she meaned by that?"

---

47 c   Auxiliary verbs

1 Understanding auxiliary verbs

In some circumstances, the main verb of a sentence requires the presence of one or more **auxiliary verbs** (also known as *helping verbs*). The auxiliary and the main verb together form a **verb phrase**.

Verb Phrase

Auxiliary Main Verb

Tyler has been working.

The most common auxiliary verbs include forms of *be, have,* and *do.* They help form certain tenses (see 47d–47e), add emphasis, ask questions, make negative statements, and form the passive voice.

PRESENT PROGRESSIVE	The solids *are precipitating* out of the suspension.
EMPHASIS	They *do seem* to be settling rapidly.
QUESTIONS	*Have* the committee members *received* the proposal?
NEGATIVE STATEMENT	They *do not intend* to act on it tonight.
PASSIVE VOICE	The plans *were approved* by the committee.

The auxiliary verbs *can, could, may, might, must, shall, should, will,* and *would* are used with a main verb to express condition, intent, permission, possibility, obligation, or desire. Known as **modal auxiliaries,** they do not change form for person, tense, number, or mood. A modal auxiliary cannot stand alone as a main verb; it must appear with the base form of a verb, unless the base form can be inferred from context.

Can she *dance?* Yes, she *can* (dance).

2 Using auxiliary verbs correctly

In standard English, neither a present participle (*running, believing*) nor a past participle (*gone, forgotten*) can function alone as the main verb of a sentence. It must be preceded by a form of *be* or *have*. (See 47d–47e.)

> is
> **Sheila running for the city council.**
> ^

> has
> **She spoken to our club about her campaign.**
> ^

In some dialects, *don't* (for *do not*) is used with a third-person singular subject: *She don't want to finish the assignment.* However, this usage is nonstandard. Be sure to use *doesn't* (for *does not*) with third-person singular subjects.

> doesn't
> **He ~~don't~~ have to work tonight.**
> ^

EDITING 2: PRACTICE

Complete the following sentences by supplying an appropriate auxiliary verb in each blank. Some sentences may have more than one possible answer. Be ready to discuss your editing choices.

1. Throughout central Missouri, no one _____ seen such severe flooding in the twentieth century.
2. The major rivers _____ broken through their levees, threatened homes, businesses, and farms, and people _____ only watch as their lives _____ uprooted.
3. But the Great Flood of '93 created dozens of human interest stories as scores of volunteers built new levees so that others _____ not lose their homes.

4. Even residents who _____ lost their homes already _____ stuffing sandbags alongside those of their neighbors.
5. As a result, several small towns that _____ flooded completely _____ saved.
6. As the floodwaters receded, Congress approved $5.7 billion in disaster relief so that flood victims _____ begin to rebuild their homes and businesses.

ESL *Phrasal Modals*

In addition to one-word modal auxiliary verbs (*can, should*), English has **phrasal modals,** consisting of more than one word.

Phrasal Modal	Meaning
be able to	possibility, ability
be allowed to	permission, possibility
be going to	future action, obligation, intent
be supposed to, be to	obligation
had better	obligation
have to	obligation
ought to	obligation
used to	habitual past action

Unlike one-word modals, most of these phrasal modals change form to show number, person, and tense. The main verbs following them do not change form.

She *has* to take the bus today.

They *have* to take the bus today.

The phrasal modals *had better, ought to,* and *used to* do not change form:

We *used to* spend time in the library every day.

You *ought to* spend time in the library every day.

VERB TENSE

47 d Understanding tense

The **tense** of a verb helps show when its action occurred and how the action relates in time to other actions.

Special Uses of the Present Tense

The present tense usually indicates action happening now, at this instant: *I feel tired.* But the present tense also has some other conventional uses.

HABITUAL OR REGULAR ACTIONS

Use the present tense to describe characteristic or regularly repeated actions.

I *run* three miles every weekday morning.

FUTURE ACTIONS

The present tense may be used to indicate future action when other words locate the action in the future.

He *speaks* tomorrow night.

UNIVERSAL TRUTHS

Use the present tense to state a universal truth—a scientific fact, a definition, or an accepted piece of wisdom. (See 47e1.)

Newton showed that the moon's orbit *is* an effect of gravity.

Jarosite *is* a hydrous sulfate of iron and potassium.

LITERARY PRESENT

Use the present tense to discuss literary or artistic works.

Flannery O'Connor's characters *are* often sinners, rarely saints.

If you use the literary present, use it consistently.

In *The Tempest,* the wizard Prospero seems to control the very heavens.

As Shakespeare ~~described~~ *describes* him, he ~~had~~ *has* extraordinary powers.

The three **simple tenses** place action in the present, past, or future. Notice that the future tense is expressed with the use of a modal auxiliary, *will.*

PRESENT   He *looks* happy today.

PAST   He *looked* a little depressed yesterday.

FUTURE   He *will look* different ten years from now.

The three **perfect tenses** indicate *action completed at a specific time.* They also are divided into present, past, and future.

The *present perfect tense* indicates action that was completed in the past or a completed action that has some relationship to the present.

PERFECT
PRESENT

She *has looked* for the file already.

She *has looked* for it every day this week.

The *past perfect tense* indicates action completed before another past action took place.

PAST PERFECT

She *had looked* for the file several times before she *found* it.

The *future perfect tense* indicates action that will be completed at some specific time in the future.

FUTURE PERFECT

After she checks the computer room, she *will have looked* everywhere.

The three *progressive tenses* describe *continuing action in the present, past, or future.*

The *present progressive tense* describes continuous, temporary, or ongoing action in the present.

PRESENT
PROGRESSIVE

She is *anticipating* the holidays.

The *past progressive tense* describes continuous or ongoing action in the past, although not always with a specified conclusion.

PAST
PROGRESSIVE

Before her father's illness, she *was anticipating* the holidays.

The *future progressive tense* describes continuous or ongoing action in the future, often dependent on some other action or condition.

FUTURE
PROGRESSIVE

Once her father is better, she *will be looking* forward to the holidays again.

The three **perfect progressive tenses** describe *action continuing up to a specific time of completion in the present, past or future.*

The *present perfect progressive tense* describes ongoing action that began in the past and continues in the present.

PRESENT PERFECT
PROGRESSIVE

He *has been looking* for a job since August.

The *past perfect progressive tense* describes continuing action that was completed before some other action.

PAST PERFECT
PROGRESSIVE

Before he found work, he *had been looking* for a job since August.

The *future perfect progressive tense* describes continuous action that will be completed at some future time.

FUTURE PERFECT
PROGRESSIVE

Come August, he *will have been looking* for a job for six months.

Verbs That Do Not Have a Progressive Form

Verbs that express actions, processes, or events can usually be used in a progressive *-ing* form to indicate that something is in progress: *She is writing lyrics for the new musical.* Most verbs fit into this category.

Other verbs express attitudes, conditions, or relationships. These verbs are seldom used in a progressive *-ing* form.

believe
I am believing your story.
  ^

Here are some verbs that are not often used with *-ing* forms:

admire	cost	like	prefer
agree	disagree	love	seem
appear	dislike	need	sound
believe	hate	own	understand
belong	know	possess	want
contain			

47 e Appropriate sequence

The *dominant* or **governing verb tense** in a piece of writing affects the choice of tense for nearly every verb. "If a melody in a major key is transposed into a minor key," Theodore M. Bernstein writes in *The Careful Writer*, "it is not just the first few notes that are modified; almost every phrase that follows undergoes change." In other words, all the verbs throughout a passage must relate logically to the governing tense. This logical relation is called the **sequence of tenses.**

Within a single sentence, the tense of the main clause limits what tenses make sense in a dependent clause. For example, the present-tense sentence *I think that I am lost* becomes *I thought that I was lost* in the past tense. It would make no sense to say *I thought that I am lost.* Still, many combinations of tenses are possible.

present   present

I think that you like foreign films.

present   past

I think that you misunderstood me.

present   future

I think that you will enjoy this movie.

Changing the tense of any verb in a sentence can change the meaning of the sentence. As you edit, check to make sure that all your choices make sense.

1 Sequence with habitual actions and universal truths

When a dependent clause expresses a habitual action or a universal truth, the verb in the dependent clause remains in the present tense regardless of the tense in the main clause.

He *told* me that he *works* for Teledyne.

Copernicus *showed* that the earth *revolves* around the sun.

Notice that this use of the present tense distinguishes between statements accepted as true and assertions that may or may not be true.

He *told* me he *worked* for IBM, but I *learned* later that he *works* for Teledyne.

Only the second dependent clause uses the present tense works *because only it is accepted as true.*

2 Sequence with direct and indirect quotation

Verbs in a direct quotation are not affected by the tense of other verbs in the sentence. The words within quotation marks should be precisely the words used by the speaker.

Nancy *said,* "My dog *is* chasing a squirrel!"

However, when you express someone else's words using indirect quotation, or indirect discourse, you should paraphrase, changing person and tense to make the quotation grammatically compatible with the rest of the sentence. (See 27e, 50a5.)

Nancy said that her dog ~~is~~ **was chasing a squirrel.**

3 Sequence with infinitives and participles

The tense of an infinitive or a participle is affected by the tense of a main verb. The base form of a verb preceded by *to* is the *present infinitive* (*to know*), sometimes called simply the infinitive. Use the present infinitive to show action occurring at the same time as or later than the action of the main verb.

PRESENT INFINITIVE   Many children like *to play* video games.

The liking *and the* playing *take place at the same time.*

The professor *plans to conduct* a seminar for poets.

The seminar is in the future.

The *perfect infinitive* consists of the past participle preceded by *to have:* *to have known.* Use the perfect infinitive to indicate action that occurred before the action of the main verb.

PERFECT INFINITIVE   The mayor *appears to have decided* not to seek reelection.

The deciding has already taken place.

EDITING 3: PRACTICE

Edit the following passage twice, changing the verbs first to the present tense and then to the future tense.

For one week at the beginning of each semester, sororities opened their houses to prospective members. The women wore their best dresses and carefully put on their makeup. Along with frozen hair went frozen smiles. Hundreds of young women moved from house to house, where they were looked over and judged. For some women this was an exciting time; for others it was humiliating and degrading.

EDITING 4: PRACTICE

Edit the following passage, using appropriate verb tenses and putting them in a logical sequence. More than one edited version is possible. Be ready to explain your editing choices.

Many people thought that it will never happen, but Los Angeles finally opened a subway system. Perhaps you imagine that the name L.A. will never be associated with public transit, because it was practically synonymous with the word *automobile*. When questioned, some people say that the new system, although it is modest so far, was a turning point for the city. If you have visited New York, which has more than 450 stations and hundreds of miles of tracks, you realize that the new system is quite small. On opening day, supporters of the new system had said that they hoped to have put the city's dollars toward building stations rather than freeways.

VERB MOOD

47 f   Understanding mood

The **mood** of a verb expresses the speaker's attitude toward or relation to the action described.

▪ The **indicative mood** makes statements and asks questions.

He *believes* that the theory *is* valid.

When *did* she *graduate?*

▪ The **imperative mood** gives commands, orders, or directions. It consists of the base form of the verb and usually omits the subject, which is understood to be *you.*

Open your exam book and *read* the instructions.

Mix the eggs, milk, and vanilla and *fold* them into the dry ingredients.

▪ The **subjunctive mood** expresses wishes, desires, requirements, or conditions that the speaker knows not to be factual.

The *present subjunctive* is simply the base form of the verb for all persons and numbers.

I asked that she *leave* early to avoid traffic.

The *past subjunctive* is the same form as the simple past tense for all verbs except *be,* which uses *were* for both singular and plural subjects. The time implied, however, is present or future.

Even if I *had* time, I would not take up golf.

If she *were* rich, would she be different?

The *perfect subjunctive* uses the past perfect tense form (*had* with the past participle) to show that the statement is not factual.

Had he *caught* the bear, he would have been very sorry.

For correct use of *could* and *would,* see 47g3.

47 g Subjunctive mood

1 In standard idiomatic expressions

The subjunctive appears in some idiomatic expressions such as *if I were you, as it were,* and *far be it from me.* As with other idioms, take care to word these phrases in the customary way.

Long *live* the Queen!

If he *were* on time, then all would go smoothly.

2 After *as if, as though,* or *if*

In clauses beginning with *as if* or *as though,* which always specify conditions that are not factual, use the past or perfect subjunctive.

He screamed as though the house ~~was~~ on fire.
were
^

When a dependent clause beginning with *if* describes a condition contrary to fact, use the past or perfect subjunctive.

were
If only it ~~was~~ sunny, he would be happy.
            ^

Note: When the *if* clause expresses an actual condition, the subjunctive is not needed.

If it was sunny, he was happy.

To suggest that the *if* clause expresses something uncertain rather than untrue, use the indicative rather than the subjunctive.

was
If she ~~were~~ awake, she should have heard the doorbell.
      ^

3 With *might, could, should,* and *would*

When one of the modal auxiliaries that express conditionality—*might, could, should, would*—is used in an independent clause, the verb in the dependent clause can be either a subjunctive verb (*I would go if they invited me*) or an indicative (*I would go if they invite me*). However, if the dependent clause verb is a form of *be,* use the subjunctive.

were
I would go if there ~~would be~~ a good reason.
                ^

With *might have, could have, should have,* or *would have* (the conditional perfect) in the independent clause, use the perfect subjunctive, not another modal auxiliary, in the dependent clause.

had
The president could have won if he ~~would have~~ fought harder.
                                ^

4 To express a wish, a requirement, or a request

Use the past or perfect subjunctive in dependent clauses expressing wishes, which are usually contrary to fact.

had been
I wished there ~~was~~ some way to help them.
              ^

Dependent clauses following verbs stating requirements—such as *demand, insist, recommend, request, specify,* and *ask*—should use the present subjunctive.

dress
Courtesy requires that he ~~dresses~~ formally.
^

go
Barbara insisted that she ~~goes~~ alone.
^

The subjunctive makes a request sound a little more formal, and therefore perhaps a little more polite, than the indicative or the imperative.

SUBJUNCTIVE   We ask that you *be* seated.

INDICATIVE   We ask you *to be* seated.

IMPERATIVE   *Be* seated.

EDITING 5: PRACTICE

Edit the following passage, using the correct form, tense, and mood of each verb. More than one edited version is possible. Be ready to explain your editing choices.

Until the early years of this century, the Constitution does not extend to women the right to vote. Suffragists wished that every woman citizen was able to vote and they strived to amend the Constitution so that no state can deny any citizen the right to vote on account of sex. For this to happen, the Constitution required that three-quarters of the states were in favor of the amendment. Many of the arguments against women's suffrage struck us as absurd now. Some people argued that women do not understand the business world; others said that the cost of elections will go up. If women would get the vote, some worried, next they would want to hold office. Some felt that a woman is represented by her husband and that when he voted it was as though she is voting. Some also fear that a vote for women will be a step toward feminism, which many people consider a radical and dangerous idea.

SUBJECT–VERB AGREEMENT

47 h   Agreement

Verbs and their subjects must **agree,** or correspond, in **person** and in **number.** A singular subject requires a singular verb; a plural subject requires a plural verb. The first-person pronoun *I* requires a different verb form from a third-person subject. Such **agreement,** especially in a long sentence like this one in which many words separate the subject from the main verb, helps readers see relations between parts of the sentence. After seeing a singular subject, such as *agreement* in the previous sentence, readers look for a singular verb, in this case *helps,* as the main verb of the sentence.

To solve agreement problems, first identify the subject. Next, determine whether the subject is singular or plural. Then use the appropriate verb form.

Matters of agreement often come down to a single letter: *s.* Most English nouns form plurals by adding *-s* or *-es.*

SINGULAR	PLURAL
house	houses
rock	rocks
box	boxes

Most present-tense, third-person singular verbs end in *-s* or *-es.*

I
you } think
we
they

he
she } thinks
it

A simple rule can guide you through many agreement problems: If the subject ends in *-s* or *-es* (is plural), the verb probably shouldn't; if the verb ends in *-s* or *-es* (is singular), the subject probably shouldn't.

The *road winds* through the mountains.

The *roads wind* through the mountains.

Plural nouns such as *children* and *men* also require a verb without an *-s* or *-es: The children walk home.* Another exception is nouns that end in *-s* but are singular: *Economics is called "the dismal science."*

47 i Intervening words

When a verb immediately follows its subject, it usually is easy to tell whether the verb should be singular or plural. When a word or words come between the subject and the verb, however, confusion can arise. Restating the sentence in its simplest form—just subject and verb—can help clarify your choice.

People interested in helping reelect an incumbent representative typically (*volunteer / volunteers*) time as well as money.

Reduced to subject and verb, the sentence reads People volunteer; *both subject and verb are clearly plural.*

Often, the intervening words are **prepositional phrases,** groups of words introduced by a preposition such as *of* or *with.*

The bowl of apples (*is / are*) very tempting.

Is the subject of the verb the singular bowl *or the plural* apples? *Here,* of apples *is a prepositional phrase.* Bowl *clearly is the subject, so the verb should be singular:* The *bowl* of apples *is* very tempting.

Intervening phrases that begin with such words as *including, as well as, along with, together with,* and *in addition to* are not part of a compound subject. (See 47l.) You should ignore them in making decisions about subject–verb agreement. Try to think of them as parenthetical asides.

The president, along with many members of his party, ~~support~~ supports

stringent reforms.

47 j Subject following verb

In some sentences, the subject follows the verb.

Underneath the freeway overpasses (*huddle / huddles*) a ramshackle collection of cardboard shelters.

Mentally restoring normal word order to the sentence can help you find the subject.

A ramshackle *collection* of cardboard shelters *huddles* underneath the freeway overpasses.

The subject is collection, *which is singular, so* huddles *is correct.*

In a question, part of the verb almost always precedes the subject. As you edit, look for the subject after the verb, and make sure the verb agrees with it.

Are those *seats* next to you empty?

With so many chores, *is Juan* able to finish on time?

Expletives are words such as *it, here,* and *there* that begin a sentence with inverted word order. *Here* and *there* are never subjects, so look for the subject elsewhere in the sentence.

There *are* a million *stories* in the Naked City.

There *was* a *chance* that Marlin would catch Gordon.

However, when *it* is used in an expletive construction, it is considered the grammatical subject of the sentence. Because *it* is singular, it is always followed by a singular verb.

It is administrators who want this change, not students.

The constructions *there is, there are,* and *it is* are usually considered weak; for alternatives, see 40b1.

47 k   Linking verbs

Linking verbs include *be, become,* and *seem* and the sensory verbs *appear, look, feel, taste, smell,* and *sound.* They link the subject of a sentence to an element, called a **subject complement,** that renames or identifies the subject. Think of a linking verb as an equal sign between two equivalent terms.

Angela is captain.   Angela = captain
That looks difficult.   that = difficult

The term to the left of the equal sign is the subject; the term on the right of the equal sign is the subject complement.

Subject   Subject Complement

My paper's title is Eliot's "Rite of Spring."

Subject   Subject Complement

Eliot's "Rite of Spring" is my paper's title.

The verb in such a sentence should always agree with the subject, not necessarily with the complement.

The thing that keeps him going <del>are</del> his hobbies.

^is^

Thing *is the subject;* hobbies *is the complement.*

EDITING 6: PRACTICE

Edit the following passage to make verbs agree with their subjects. Take special care in identifying the subject.

Throughout its history, the National Aeronautics and Space Administration (NASA) have been at the center of both controversy and praise. The exploration of the solar system, along with the research conducted by space shuttle crews, are hailed as significant human endeavors. The costs of these achievements, though, often becomes the subjects of newspaper headlines. Currently, there are many who think that federal government allocate too much money to NASA. Supporters, however, who credit the agency for spearheading developments in the aeronautics industry, points out that NASA's budget is the smallest of all major governmental agencies. Moreover, they say that the agency generate more revenue nationwide than it consume because of the new industries built upon space-exploration technology. Aeronautics, personal computers, telecommunications, and even weather forecasting depends on this technology, and these industries employ millions of Americans. Behind some of the most significant technological advances in American society are the team of researchers, engineers, and scientists working for NASA. Without them and the technology they have developed over the years, some entire industries today would not exist.

---

47   I   Making verbs agree with subjects joined by *and*

When the conjunction *and* links two or more parts of a subject, it creates a **compound subject.** (Also see 49g.) Such a subject is almost always considered plural and thus requires a plural verb.

Peter and Patrick *appear* in the first act.

This rule has several exceptions. When the two elements joined by *and* are regarded as a single entity, the subject is considered singular and requires a singular verb.

Hare and hounds ~~are~~ my favorite game.
  is
  ^

If all parts of a compound subject refer to the same person or thing, a singular verb is appropriate.

My friend, my partner, and my mentor ~~have~~ brought wisdom and
  has
  ^
courage to this firm.

The writer is referring to one person who is all three things.

When singular elements joined by *and* are preceded by *each* or *every,* use the singular.

Each river, brook, and stream in the county ~~have~~ suffered pollution.
  has
  ^

However, when *each* comes after a *compound subject* rather than before it, the subject is plural.

Government and industry each ~~deserves~~ credit for the success of
  deserve
  ^
cleanup efforts.

47 m   *Or, nor*

The conjunctions *or, nor, either . . . or, not only . . . but also,* and *neither . . . nor* also create compound subjects by linking two or more elements. When one element of the subject is singular and another is plural, convention dictates that the verb agree with the part of the subject closer to it.

Neither the witnesses nor the senator *is* ready for the hearing.

If a singular verb sounds awkward, try rearranging the subject to put the plural part closer to the verb.

Neither the senator nor the witnesses *are* ready for the hearing.

Edit the following sentences to make verbs agree with their compound subjects. Circle the number of any sentence that is correct.

1. Neither the police officers nor the detectives knows how the intruder entered or left the house.
2. Each window and door are locked securely.
3. In addition, the outside security system and inside motion sensors shows nothing unusual last night.
4. Nonetheless both the house and the safe was broken into and all the money taken.
5. On the living room sofa, the banker and his wife sits weeping, lamenting their loss.
6. Not only their savings bonds but also their expensive jewelry was gone forever.

47 n   Collective nouns

Collective nouns refer to groups of people or things: *couple, flock, crowd, herd, committee.* They can cause confusion because the words themselves have a singular form even though they refer to several individuals. Whether a collective noun takes a singular or plural verb depends on whether the members of the group are acting as individuals or as one unit. If the members of a group act individually, use a plural verb.

The jury *have* returned to their homes.

If such a construction sounds awkward to you, try replacing the subject with one that is clearly plural.

The members of the jury *have* returned to their homes.

If an action is taken by an entire group together as a unit, use a singular verb.

The jury *has* reached a verdict.

The collective noun *the number* takes a singular verb.

The number of tourists *has* declined in recent years.

ESL *Verb Agreement with Noncount Nouns*

Count nouns name persons, places, or things that can be counted: *one apple, two oranges.* **Noncount nouns** refer to things that can't be quantified, such as abstract concepts, emotions, and qualities.

Mass Nouns	Abstract Concepts	Emotions	Qualities	Food
equipment	behavior	anger	confidence	butter
furniture	education	happiness	honesty	rice
homework	health	love	integrity	oat meal
money	knowledge	surprise	sincerity	

Noncount nouns are usually used only with singular verbs. In English these words usually have no plural form.

equipment makes
Good ~~equipments makes~~ the job easier.

This information   is
~~These informations~~ about subject–verb agreement ~~are~~ intended to help you edit.

For information on using articles (*a, an, the*) with nouns, see the box in 48a.

However, the expression *a number of* means "several" or "more than one," so it needs a plural verb.

A number of visitors *have* complimented the park management on the new trail markers.

47 o Indefinite pronouns

Whether a pronoun is singular or plural usually depends on whether the word or words it refers to are singular or plural. In the sentence *My uncle enjoys fishing, and he often goes on fishing trips,* the pronoun *he* is singular (and takes a singular verb, *goes*) because it refers to a singular noun, *uncle.*

However, an **indefinite pronoun,** such as *someone, some, few, everyone, each,* or *one,* often does not refer to a specific person or thing. Most indefinite pronouns are either always singular or always plural.

SINGULAR   Everybody *has* heard that old joke already.

PLURAL   Luckily, few of the passengers *were* injured.

Although pronouns such as *everybody* and *someone* are singular, many people in everyday speech treat them as if they were plural in order to avoid sexist language: *Everybody has their mind made up.* In formal writing, this usage is considered incorrect. (See 44c for alternatives in formal writing.)

Some, any, all, more, most, what, and *none* can be either singular or plural depending on what they refer to.

Of the *time* that remained, more *was* spent in arguing than in making decisions.

Of the *hours* that remained, more *were* spent in arguing than in making decisions.

As you edit, try mentally recasting the sentence without the indefinite pronoun, using *it* or *they* if necessary to determine whether the pronoun is singular or plural.

Some of the children (*is / are*) eager to leave.

They are eager to leave.

Common Indefinite Pronouns

ALWAYS SINGULAR

someone	anyone	no one	every	either
somebody	anybody	nobody	everyone	neither
something	anything	none	everybody	each
		nothing	everything	one
			much	

EITHER SINGULAR OR PLURAL

some	any	all	most	more
				what

ALWAYS PLURAL

few	both	several	many

All is plural when it means the total number in a group; it is singular when it means "everything" or "the only thing."

All of us *are* preparing for the examination.

All I have *is* twenty dollars.

None, which means "not one," is always singular: *None of the workers was injured.*

None of the information *was* missing.

ESL Verb Agreement with Quantifiers

- *Few and a few*

  Few means "not many." *A few* means "some," "several," or "a small number." *Few* and *a few* take plural verbs.

Many law students are taking the bar exam today. *A few* have taken it in other states.

Few have failed it more than once.

- *Little* and *a little*

  Little means "not much." *A little* means "some" or "a small amount." *Little* and *a little* take singular verbs.

Doctors have done considerable research on heart disease. However, *little has been done* with women as subjects.

Be careful pouring that hot sesame oil. *A little goes* a long way.

- *Most of the* and *most*

  Most of the (or *most of*) means "the majority of"; it takes a plural verb when it is followed by a plural noun or pronoun and a singular verb when it is followed by a noncount noun or a singular pronoun.

PLURAL   *Most of the dogs* in the neighborhood *bark* in the morning.

PLURAL   *Most dogs are* tied while their owners are at work. [adjective *most* modifying plural *dogs*]

SINGULAR   *Most of the violence* on TV *is* unnecessary.

SINGULAR   *Most is* treated as harmless by TV producers. [pronoun *most* referring to *most of the violence*]

47 p **Who, which, that**

To decide whether a verb following the **relative pronouns** *who, which,* or *that* should be singular or plural, find the word for which the pronoun stands (its **antecedent**). (See 49a and 49f–49j.)

> are
> **The dean and the provost, who ̶i̶s̶ on the search committee, will**
>   ^
> **meet with the candidates.**

If the dean and the provost are both on the committee, the verb should be plural. If only the provost is, the verb should be singular.

> slips
> **A bale of shingles that ̶s̶l̶i̶p̶ off the roof could hurt someone.**
>   ^

That *refers to bale, so* slips *is singular.*

Relative pronouns can be troublesome when they follow the construction *one of the* or *the only one of the.* If the relative pronoun refers to *one,* it is singular.

> The only *one* of the experiments that *works* is mine.

If the relative pronoun refers to whatever comes after *one of the* or *the only one of the,* it is plural.

> *One* of the areas that *were* cut most heavily *is* social spending.

EDITING 8: PRACTICE ....

Edit the following sentences to make verbs agree with collective noun subjects, indefinite pronoun subjects, and relative pronoun subjects. Circle the number of any sentence that is correct.

1. The pictures in the exhibit, which are open every night, feature children from Third World countries.
2. Many of the children photographed in Mexico was casualties of the earthquake.
3. Most people think that the look of sadness on their faces are most moving.

4. The best of the photographers, who spend three months every year in Southeast Asia, has won numerous awards.

5. Adding photography exhibits to the museum was one of many good ideas of the curator, who is herself a photographer.

47 q   Amounts

Words that describe amounts of time, money, distance, measurement, or percentage can take singular or plural verbs. As with collective nouns, the number depends on whether the subject is considered as a group of individuals (plural) or as a single unit or sum (singular).

Four *hours have* passed since we saw each other last.

The hours pass one at a time, individually.

Fifteen *minutes is* too long to keep the boss waiting.

The minutes here are a block of time, a unit.

47 r   Noun phrases and clauses

Noun phrases and **noun clauses** are groups of related words that function as a subject, object, or complement in a sentence. A *noun phrase* often lacks a subject or a predicate or both; a *noun clause* has both a subject and a predicate. All noun phrases and noun clauses are singular.

NOUN PHRASE   *Planning to write* is easy; actually writing is harder.

NOUN CLAUSE   *That he would not listen to us* was surprising.

47 s   Titles, words used as words

Titles of books, plays, and movies are treated as singular even if they are plural in form. The name of a company is also singular.

Friends was a popular TV series.

In discussing a word itself, use a singular verb even if the word is plural.

"Hyenas" *was* what my father lovingly called us children.

47 t   Subjects ending in -s

Although words such as *statistics, politics, economics,* and *aesthetics* seem to be plural because they end in -s, they take singular verbs when used in a general sense to mean a field of study, a body of ideas, or a profession. However, some of these words can be plural when referring to specific instances, activities, or characteristics.

Economics *is* a field that relies on statistics.

The economics of the project *make* no sense.

Words that refer to an ailment such as AIDS or measles are usually singular. So is the word *news*.

47 u   Troublesome plurals

Words such as *media* and *data* look like singular words in English, but they are Latin plurals and should take plural verbs. The corresponding singular forms are *medium* and *datum*. Look out, too, for *curriculum* and *curricula, criterion* and *criteria, phenomenon* and *phenomena*. The use of *data* as singular is gaining ground, especially in reference to computers, but you should avoid it in writing.

          love
The media ~~loves~~ a political scandal.

               support
The experimental data ~~supports~~ the theory you advanced.

Dictionaries list the preferred plural and singular forms of these and other words of foreign origin; some, like *stadium,* have lost their original plural forms completely.

Some nouns, such as *pants, sunglasses, binoculars,* and *scissors,* refer to single objects but take plural verbs.

The scissors *are* no longer sharp.

When the construction *pair of* is used, the verb is singular.

This pair of scissors *is* sharper.

ESL Some Collective Nouns That Require Plural Verbs

Some collective nouns are derived from adjectives and refer to a group of people: *the wealthy, the homeless, the elderly.* These nouns are considered plural and take plural verbs.

The *young* often *ignore* the advice of their elders.

The collective nouns *people* and *police* are always plural. The singular forms are *person* and *police officer.* The article *a* or the adjective *one* may be used before *people* to refer to a national or ethnic group, but the word is still plural. *A* is not used before *police.*

One people who *are* proud of their language *are* the French.

People are wondering who will be the next governor.

That *person is* wondering when to register to vote.

Police have been stationed in front of the house all afternoon.

A *police officer is* always on duty inside the courthouse.

EDITING 9: PRACTICE

Edit the following sentences by making verbs agree with their noun phrase or noun clause subjects, subjects that are titles or words used as words, or troublesome singular or plural subjects. Circle the number of any sentence that is correct.

1. Although a course in statistics often baffle college students, studying aesthetics is also challenging, particularly in courses that compares the arts.
2. Sometimes one artistic medium, like painting and sculpture, tell us something new about a novel, for instance.
3. This semester we read *Pride and Prejudice,* which were written by Jane Austen, but we also examined paintings of country houses.
4. Comparing the novel with the paintings provide a clearer picture of Austen's descriptions.
5. Preparing for exams for my interarts classes sometimes seem difficult because we cover a lot of material.

Editing for Subject–Verb Agreement

To solve problems of agreement, first identify the subject. Next determine whether it is singular or plural. Then use the corresponding verb form. Remember the following tips as you edit.

- Ignore words between the subject and the verb.
- Identify the subject even when it follows the verb.
- Identify the subject of a linking verb.
- Determine whether subjects joined by *and* are singular or plural.
- Determine whether subjects joined by *or* or *nor* are singular or plural.
- Determine whether collective nouns are singular or plural.
- Determine whether indefinite pronouns such as *everything* and *some* are singular or plural.
- Determine whether relative pronouns such as *who, which,* and *that* are singular or plural.
- Determine whether subjects that refer to amounts are singular or plural.
- Use singular verbs with noun phrases and noun clauses.
- Use singular verbs with titles and with words used as words.
- Identify singular subjects that end in *-s.*
- Use plural verbs with troublesome plurals.

EDITING 10: PRACTICE ....

Edit the following passage to make verbs agree with their subjects. More than one edited version is possible. Be ready to explain your editing choices.

The county employees and volunteers who run the prison education program focuses on illiteracy. Statistics shows that among prison inmates nationwide, some 60 percent is illiterate, and neither substance abuse programs nor vocational training seem as effective as literacy education in limiting the return of repeat offenders. The core of the program, therefore, are reading and writing skills. Each employee and volunteer go through a three-week training program in literacy education. If they can demonstrate sufficiently high reading levels, inmates may also train to become tutors.

EDITING 11: APPLICATION ....

Examine a paper you are working on to find any verbs that do not agree with their subjects. What kinds of mistakes did you make? Do you make one kind more than others? If so, why do you think you do?

....

chapter 48 | *Using Modifiers Correctly*

A djectives and adverbs *modify* other words—that is, they describe, specify, or limit the meanings of other words. **Modifiers** can enrich description, changing a simple sentence like *The explorers were lost* into an expressive one like *The polar explorers were thoroughly, hopelessly, horribly lost.* To be effective, modifiers must be used carefully and according to convention.

48 a Adjectives or adverbs

Adjectives modify nouns and pronouns.

             noun   noun

Many *deciduous* trees in the *mid-Atlantic* states are subject to attack

       noun

by *voracious* insects.

pronoun

They are especially *vulnerable* during a drought.

Adverbs modify verbs, adjectives, or other adverbs.

685

verb

Drought *rapidly* weakens the trees' natural defenses, sometimes with

adjective

truly devasting consequences.

ESL Using Articles with Nouns

An **article** (*a, an, the*) is a special kind of adjective. Which one you select depends on the context and on the type of noun it precedes.

■ Use the **indefinite article** *a* or *an* when you first mention a noun. At that point, its meaning is indefinite, not yet specified.

There is *a problem* with his approach. [an unspecified problem]

■ Before unspecified singular nouns, you may also use *one* or a personal pronoun.

one person   our child

■ Don't use an article before an unspecified plural noun.

Geese can be aggressive.

■ Don't use an article before a noncount noun. (For a definition of noncount nouns, see 47n and Chapter 63.)

The refugees demand *justice.*

■ Before a plural or noncount noun, you may use *some* (or, in a negative sentence, *any*).

They want *some answers.* [plural]

They have not been given *any information.* [noncount, negative]

■ Once the noun has been mentioned, use the **definite article,** *the.*

The problem begins in his assumptions. [the problem just mentioned]

■ Use the definite article if the noun is made specific by context.

The premises that support his argument should not be accepted without question. [The premises are immediately specified.]

■ Use the definite article when referring to a unique person, place, or thing.

The moon was setting as we awoke.

ARTICLES WITH PROPER NOUNS

Most proper nouns have no articles, but there are some exceptions. Ignore *The* as part of the formal name of an organization unless that organization is an important part of your audience, as in a job application to *The New York Times* or an admission letter to *The Ohio State University.*

Britain	(*but* the United Kingdom)
America	(*but* the United States—singular)
Lake Michigan	(*but* the Mississippi River)
Hawaii	(*but* the Hawaiian Islands)
Roger Smith	(*but* the Smiths—plural)
Second Street	(*but* the second street from here—common noun)

Many adjectives and adverbs are formed by adding **suffixes,** or endings to other words. (See 43c.) Adjectives are often formed by adding *-able, -ful, -ish,* and other endings to nouns or verbs: *acceptable, beautiful, foolish.* Many adverbs are formed by adding *-ly* to an adjective: *nearly, amazingly, brilliantly.*

In speaking, some people substitute adjectives for adverbs: *It worked real well* rather than *It worked really well.* If this is a speech habit of yours, be careful to use only adverbs to modify verbs, adjectives, or other adverbs. Use adjectives only to modify nouns and pronouns.

badly
We played bad in the first inning.

An *-ly* suffix does not always mean that a word is an adverb: *brotherly, friendly,* and *lovely,* for example, are adjectives. Also, many adverbs do not end in *-ly: often, always, later.* Still other words can be used as either adjectives or adverbs, such as *hard* or *fast.* To be sure of the correct form, consult a dictionary. (Also see 48c.)

EDITING 1: PRACTICE

Edit the following sentences, using adjectives and adverbs in the proper places.

1. When I first started running competitive, I had all kinds of problems.
2. My track coach said that breathing too heavy was causing my cramps.
3. He suggested I take short, even breaths to help me run smooth.
4. But once I perfected my breathing, my feet began to hurt real bad.
5. I found out that I was pigeon-toed and that my shoes did not fit correct.
6. After a lot of looking, I found special track shoe.

48 b   After linking verbs

Confusion about whether to use an adjective or an adverb arises occasionally with **linking verbs,** such as *be, become, feel, seem, appear, look, smell, taste,* and *sound.* A modifier after a linking verb usually modifies the subject of the verb, not the verb itself, so the modifier should be an adjective, not an adverb.

bad
I felt ~~badly~~ about not being able to help.

Some of these verbs can also express action, in which case they do not function as linking verbs.

LINKING VERB   The ghost of Hamlet's father *appears* anxious.

Anxious is an adjective modifying the noun ghost.

ACTION VERB   The ghost of Hamlet's father *appears* suddenly.

Suddenly is an adverb modifying the verb appears.

EDITING 2: PRACTICE

Edit the following sentences, using adjectives and adverbs correctly after linking verbs. Circle the number of any sentence that is correct.

1. One day, when Shelly first woke up, she seemed deliriously.
2. She started talking, but her voice sounded harshly and raspy.
3. I walked across the room and saw that she was pale and that her forehead was splotchy.
4. I put my hand on it and, sure enough, her brow felt coldly and clammy.
5. Fortunately one of our neighbors was a doctor, and she came over to see us.
6. After she gave her some antibiotics, Shelly was able to sleep, and a few days later, she felt strongly and healthy again.

48 c   Confusing modifiers

Several pairs of modifiers are commonly confused in everyday speech.

Bad and *badly*

In standard English, *bad* is always an adjective, *badly* always an adverb. Be sure to use them correctly, especially after linking verbs.

           bad   *badly*
She felt ~~badly~~ about doing ~~bad~~ on the test.

Good and *well*

Good and *well* share the same comparative and superlative forms: *good, better, best; well, better, best.* (See 48e.) *Good* is always an adjective. *Well* can be either an adjective or an adverb. As an adjective, *well* means "healthy," the opposite of *ill.* As an adverb, *well* means, among other things, "satisfactorily" or "skillfully." Do not use *good* as an adverb or *well* as an adjective meaning "satisfactory."

         well
She read ~~good~~ enough to get the part.

              good
My hat looked ~~well~~ on my mother.

Real and *really*

Real is properly used as an adjective meaning "genuine, true, not illusory": *They wondered whether the ghost was real. Really* is an adverb meaning "truly" or "very."

        really
He talks ~~real~~ fast.

Less and *fewer*

Use *less* to describe something considered as a whole unit: *less hope, less misery, less money.* Use *fewer* for quantities that can be counted: *fewer dreams, fewer problems, fewer dollars.*

                                fewer
The house would lose less heat if ~~less~~ windows were open.

Few is always an adjective, but *less* can be used as an adverb.

Ventilation makes the heating system *less* efficient.

48 d Double negatives

In English, one negative modifier (*no, not, never, none*) is sufficient to change the meaning of a sentence. Although double negatives are common in some dialects, particularly when one of the negatives is a contraction, be sure in editing to make negative statements with only one negative modifier.

He didn't want ~~no~~ dinner. *(any)*

He ~~didn't have~~ no money. *(had)*

Using *no* or *not* with an adverb such as *hardly, barely,* or *scarcely* creates a double negative.

She ~~didn't~~ hardly ~~have~~ time to catch her breath. *(had)*

Sometimes you need a double negative to make a *positive* statement.

The issue was *not* that he had *no* money; he simply did not want to spend it.

He had money.

One acceptable double negative is *not without*.

The Curies's research on radium was *not without* risk.

There was some risk.

EDITING 3: PRACTICE

Edit the following passage, using the correct form of any commonly confused modifiers and correcting any double negatives. More than one editing choice is possible.

Alan whispered to me one day in class that he was real hungry. I told him that I didn't have no food with me. He started mumbling something about how he couldn't be expected to do good on a chemistry exam when his stomach felt so badly. I couldn't see hardly no reason for him to complain so much. Everybody knew that he always brought lunches to school with him. In fact, the more I thought about it, the more I realized that nobody had less reasons to complain about being hungry than Alan. What made me even angrier, though, was that now he had made me want a snack.

ESL *Using Negatives:* **Not** *vs.* **No**

■ Use *not* in a negative verb phrase.

I *do not* agree with the author's opinion.

The professor *did not assign any* homework.

> *Use* any *with the object of a negative verb. (See 48d.)*

■ Use *no* or *not one* with nouns.

The professor assigned *no homework.*

There are *no places* to sit in the theater.

There is *not one* empty seat.

> *Use* not one *only with a count noun. (See 47n and Chapter 63.)*

■ These negative adverbs can be used in verb phrases:

never	almost never
rarely	hardly ever
seldom	scarcely

We *seldom* agree.

Rarely do I cook for myself.

> *Starting a sentence with one of these negative adverbs calls for inverted word order.*

■ Note the difference in the meanings of these negated pronouns:

No one can solve that problem.

> *It cannot be solved.*

Not everyone can solve that problem.

> *Some people can solve the problem, but others cannot.*

■ Note the difference in the meanings of the negated pronoun and the negated verb in the following examples:

Not everyone is here yet.

> *Some are here, but not all.*

Everyone is *not* here yet.

> *No one is here yet.*

▪ To emphasize negation, negate a noun with *no* instead of negating the verb with *not*. Note the change from *do not see* to *see no*.

NEGATIVE   *I do not see any* reason to assume he is lying.

EMPHATIC   *I see no reason* to assume he is lying.

48 e   Comparatives and superlatives

The basic or **positive form** of an adjective or adverb describes a quality or property: *large, delicious, late, graciously.* The **comparative form,** which usually ends in *-er* or is preceded by *more,* compares two people or things.

She arrived *later* than I did but was greeted *more graciously.*

The **superlative form,** usually ending in *-est* or preceded by *most,* makes a comparison among three or more people or things.

Of all their guests, she always arrived *latest* and was greeted *most graciously.*

Your choice of a comparative or a superlative modifier gives readers an important clue about the nature of the comparison.

Of the brothers, Joe was the *stronger* athlete.

Of the brothers, Joe was the *strongest* athlete.

The first sentence says that there are only two brothers, while the second indicates that there are at least three brothers.

1 Forming regular comparatives and superlatives

Most one-syllable adjectives and adverbs add *-er* and *-est* to form comparatives and superlatives: *smarter, closest.* There are exceptions such as *wrong, more wrong,* not *wronger.* Adjectives of three or more syllables, adjectives ending in *-ful,* adverbs of two or more syllables, and most adverbs ending in *-ly* generally use *more* and *most: more impressive, most hopeful, most often, most sharply.* With many two-syllable adjectives, the choice is yours (*happiest, most happy; luckiest, most lucky*), although the *-er* and *-est* endings are more common.

ESL **Articles with Comparatives and Superlatives**

When a comparative adjective (*warmer, easier*) is used by itself, do not use an article (*a, an,* or *the*).

This house is ~~the~~ *larger* than the other one.

DEFINITE ARTICLE *THE*

Use *the* when a comparative or superlative adjective is followed by a specific noun or by a pronoun renaming a specific noun.

This house is *the larger* one.

This is *the largest.*

The use of *the* is optional when the comparative or superlative adjective is used without a noun but the noun is implied.

Of the two houses, which one is *the larger?* [implied; *the larger* house]

Of the two houses, which is *larger?*

INDEFINITE ARTICLES *A/AN*

Use *a* or *an* with comparative adjectives modfying a noun that is not specific.

I've never seen *a larger* grapefruit.

Compare

Juanita ate the larger grapefruit. [a specific one]

Use *a* or *an* with superlative adjectives only if the superlative has the meaning "very."

That was *a most refreshing* glass of grapefruit juice.

Compare

That was the most refreshing glass of juice I've ever had.

For more about article usage, see the box in 48a.

Negative comparisons are formed using *less* for comparatives and *least* for superlatives: *less often, least hopeful.*

2 Avoiding double comparatives and superlatives

Use either *-er* or *more,* not both. Use either *-est* or *most,* not both.

Eating made him feel ~~more~~ better.

3 Forming irregular comparatives and superlatives

A few adjectives and adverbs form comparatives and superlatives in irregular ways. Take care to memorize them, especially if English is not your first language.

> Paul did ~~gooder~~ ^{better} on the test than I did.

> She said she felt ~~weller~~ ^{better} today.

4 Using only the positive form of absolute modifiers

Some modifiers, called **absolutes,** do not logically form comparatives or superlatives because their meaning suggests comparison is inappropriate. Words such as *perfect, unique, equal, essential, final, total,* and *absolute* should not be intensified. As you edit, make sure that you have not used *more* or *most* with such words.

> The turbo engine makes this car ~~even more~~ unique.

Irregular Adjectives and Adverbs

Positive	Comparative	Superlative
good	better	best
well	better	best
bad	worse	worst
badly	worse	worst
ill	worse	worst
many	more	most
much	more	most
some	more	most
little*	less	least

*Little in the sense of "not much" is irregular. *Little* in the sense of "small" is regular: *She wanted a little dog, but mine is littler than hers, and my cousin's is littlest of all.*

Choosing the Right Modifier

As you edit, examine your adjectives and adverbs carefully and make sure to do the following:

- Choose an adjective or adverb according to the part of speech that it modifies.
- Use adjectives after linking verbs.
- Choose correctly between commonly confused modifiers.
- Avoid double negatives.
- Use comparatives and superlatives correctly.

EDITING 4: PRACTICE

Edit the following passage, using the correct comparative and superlative forms of adjectives and adverbs. More than one edited version is possible. Be ready to explain your editing choices.

Do students from other countries perform better or worser than American students? Over the past decade, American scores on standardized tests have been declining steadilier in the United States than in other countries. Scores in Japan and Germany are often much more strong. Of those two countries, Japan's scores are usually highest. U.S. educators need to take a more closer look at preparing students for the challenges of an international labor market. Traditional methods of teaching may not be the most perfect. The most new methods may help students learn gooder.

EDITING 5: PRACTICE

Edit the following passage, using adjectives and adverbs correctly. More than one edited version is possible. Be ready to explain your editing choices.

The "guru of alternative medicine," Andrew Weil, M.D., has harshly criticism for mainstream doctors and their methods. He draws his ideas various from traditional Asian methods, Native American traditions, and more new disciplines such as hypnosis, magnetism therapy, and feedback control. He argues that mainstream medicine relies too heavy on scientific methods, ignoring the important role of the mind in controlling disease, which he believes is real important. To Weil, much diseases can be best understood in terms of the mind's relationship to the body. To his critics, Weil's work shows few evidence of the kind of careful collected data that mainstream medicine relies on to evaluate its methods. Those critics, including Arnold S. Relman, editor-in-chief emeritus of the *New England Journal of Medicine,* claim Weil's ideas need to be tested thorougher in the same ways that new surgical techniques or pharmaceutical products receive routinely evaluation.

48 **f**   **Placing modifiers**

In English, word order affects meaning: *The man ate the fish* does not mean the same thing as *The fish ate the man.* If a modifier's placement does not make clear what it modifies, readers may misinterpret the sentence. *They want only her to sing this song* means something different from *They want her to sing only this song.*

Because readers assume that a modifier modifies the nearest grammatically acceptable element, a **misplaced modifier** can seem to modify the wrong element, not the one the writer intended. When editing, move the modifier close to the word modified.

We wanted our ordeal to end desperately.

Unless the writer intended things to turn out badly, the adverb desperately *is misplaced.*

in a glass jar
He took a frog to biology class ~~in a glass jar.~~

It seems unlikely that the biology class was held in a glass jar.

Modifiers such as *almost, even, hardly, just, merely, nearly, only, scarcely,* and *simply* are called **limiting modifiers.** They create an implicit contrast: to say that *only A is true* implies that *B* and *C* are not true. Readers understand a limiting modifier to modify the sentence element that directly follows it. Consider the difference in meaning created in the following sentences by moving the limiting modifier *just:*

Just the children applauded the conductor.

Only the children, not the adults, applauded.

The children *just* applauded the conductor.

They applauded but did nothing else.

The children applauded *just* the conductor.

The children applauded the conductor and no one else.

A **squinting modifier,** one that seems to modify two things at once, appears between two sentence elements that it might modify—and seems to look in both directions at once.

Students who follow directions *consistently* score well on standardized tests.

What occurs consistently, the following of directions or the scoring well on tests?

To edit a squinting modifier, reposition it so that no misinterpretation is possible.

Students who follow directions ~~consistently~~ **score well on** *consistently* **standardized tests.**

Students who follow directions ~~consistently~~ **score well on** *consistently* **standardized tests.**

EDITING 7: PRACTICE

Edit the following passage, moving any misplaced modifiers. More than one edited version is possible. Be ready to explain your editing choices.

Most people assume that black bears hibernate incorrectly all winter. During the winter, although sleeping deeply, a true state of hibernation is not achieved by black bears. Their body temperature only drops a little, and one can wake up a black bear with just a little effort. Preparing to sleep for several months, a very large amount of food is eaten by the bears. This way, they can store fat and feed off it all winter while they are sleeping. The female surprisingly gives birth to her young at this time.

48 g   Dangling modifiers

A **dangling modifier** cannot be attached logically to anything in the sentence. Either the element that the modifier is intended to modify does not appear in the sentence, or it does not appear in a grammatically appropriate form. Readers interpret a dangling modifier as modifying the nearest grammatically acceptable element, which may not be what the writer had in mind. Often a dangling modifier consists of a prepositional phrase or verbal phrase at the beginning of a sentence.

Running through the rain, our clothes got soaked.

Clearly, it was we *who were running through the rain, not* our *clothes. But* we *does not appear in the sentence, only* our, *which cannot be modified by the phrase* Running through the rain.

In a sense, it is the reader who is left dangling, wondering what the writer meant. When editing a dangling modifier, introduce an element that logically can be modified, or change the form of an existing element. Then place it directly after the modifier.

she earned an A on

Having done well on her research, the paper ~~earned her an A.~~ ⊙

When her *becomes* she *and is inserted after the modifying phrase, the sentence makes sense.*

When the main clause is in the passive voice, an introductory phrase often has no subject to modify. One solution is to place the sentence in the active voice. (See 40c.)

we fixed

Preparing for the experiment, several slides ~~were fixed~~ **with dye.**

Who was preparing? The sentence doesn't say, so insert a subject.

researchers have forced

To study the effects of cigarette smoking, monkeys ~~have been forced~~ **to inhale the equivalent of a hundred cigarettes a day.**

Clearly, the monkeys are not conducting the research.

Edit the following passage, clarifying squinting modifiers and eliminating dangling modifiers. More than one edited version is possible. Be ready to discuss your editing choices.

Examining the patient death rates of more than fifty doctors, the results were compared by a panel to a statistical average. Having a better than average rate, a minus score was entered for those doctors. A positive score was entered for those who had worse than average rates. Consisting of only the doctors with positive scores, the panel released a list of names to a local newspaper. After reading the article, a protest was lodged by the county medical society. Doctors who criticized the study strongly argued that the scoring was biased.

48 h   Disruptive modifiers

A modifier that disrupts the flow of a sentence can confuse readers or distract, inadvertently, their attention from your meaning. In the previous sentence, for example, there are several better places for *inadvertently*. **Disruptive modifiers** include those that split an infinitive, those that divide verb phrase, and those that needlessly separate major sentence elements.

1 Modifiers that split infinitives

An infinitive consists of the base form of a verb preceded by *to: to fly, to grow, to achieve.* Whenever possible, avoid placing modifiers between *to* and the verb, which is called **splitting an infinitive.** Many instructors and readers regard this construction as a mark of careless writing.

He attempted to ~~smoothly~~ mix the ingredients. smoothly.

Many instructors will not object to a split infinitive if it is difficult to find a natural-sounding alternative.

The snow was just enough *to lightly dust* the city, which twinkled in the evening light.

The alternatives lightly to dust the city *or* to dust the city lightly, which twinkled *both sound forced.*

ESL   *Placing Frequency Adverbs within Verb Phrases*

When an adverb is used between elements of a verb phrase—such as *has been happening* or *will remember*—it usually appears after the first auxiliary verb.

Our baseball stadium has *rarely* been filled to capacity this season.

In questions, the adverb appears after the first auxiliary verb and the subject and before the other parts of the verb.

In the past, have you *usually* found yourself writing a paper the day before it's due?

When *not* is used to negate another adverb, it should appear directly after the first auxiliary verb and before the other adverb.

This newspaper does *not usually* put sports news on the front page.

    Not *negates* usually; not usually *means "seldom."*

However, do not split an infinitive with a lengthy modifier.

as soon as possible.

She wanted to ~~as soon as possible~~ try rock climbing.

You can also edit the sentence to eliminate the infinitive altogether.

wanted a vivid re-creation of

The director ~~wanted to vividly re-create~~ a bullfight.

2 Modifiers that split verb phrases

A **verb phrase** consists of one or more auxiliary verbs, such as a form of *be* or *have,* and a participle or base form: *had been formed, does happen.* Most instructors will accept a single adverb (or *not* plus another adverb) placed between the elements of a verb phrase.

Some early settlements in the New World have *inexplicably* vanished without a trace.

However, an intervening phrase or clause will be considered disruptive, so rewrite the sentence.

By

~~The Roanoke colony had,~~ by the time a supply ship arrived four
the Roanoke colony had
years later, disappeared without a trace.

3 Modifiers that separate major sentence elements

When deciding where to put a modifier clause or phrase, try to mini-mize disruption and yet place the modifier so that what it modifies is clear.

Because of her great popularity with audiences,
Mary Pickford, ~~because of her great popularity with audiences,~~
^
became the first silent film actor to be publicized by name.

never a stronghold of slavery,
Kentucky was, even though it had residents who fought for the
^
Confederacy during the Civil War, ~~never a stronghold of slavery.~~
^

Positioning Modifiers Appropriately

When editing to position modifiers appropriately, do the following, consulting this chapter as necessary:

- Reposition misplaced modifiers close to the word modified.
- Clarify which element is modified by a squinting modifier and move it.
- Eliminate dangling modifiers by adding the elements they should modify.
- Find a better position for any modifier that disrupts the sentence flow.

EDITING 9: PRACTICE

Edit the following passage for correct use of modifiers. More than one edited version is possible. Be ready to explain your editing choices.

Striking millions of Americans, some people only are afflicted by in-somnia occasionally, while other people live with it for several years. Having experienced mild, occasional sleeplessness, your insomnia shouldn't be considered a major concern. The causes from which it stems most often are quite simple. Having something troubling or ex-citing on your mind, exerting too much physical or mental activity be-fore bedtime, having a mild fever, drinking too much caffeine, or eating a heavy meal, sleeplessness might occur. Changing your schedule or surroundings, insomnia can also result. The way to best ensure a good night's sleep is to consistently follow a few simple steps. Try to go to bed at the same time every night. Sleep on a comfortable bed in a dark room. Realizing that it is still, after twenty minutes, hard to fall asleep, it is helpful for you to get up and do something, such as read, until you feel drowsy. And remember to always avoid caffeine and heavy foods as well as strenuous activity before bedtime.

chapter 49

Using Pronouns Correctly

Pronouns serve as stand-ins for nouns or other pronouns. Unless readers can tell what word a pronoun such as *she* refers to, they will ask, "She who?" Readers should know whether you are talking about Maya Angelou or Joan of Arc.

The word for which a pronoun substitutes is called its **antecedent** (from Latin roots meaning "to go before"). Although pronouns usually follow their antecedents, sometimes a pronoun appears before its antecedent. In either case, you must try to avoid confusing readers. This chapter focuses on clarifying pronoun reference, on ensuring that pronouns agree with their antecedents, and on choosing the correct pronoun case.

PRONOUN REFERENCE

49 a Clear antecedents

A pronoun with more than one possible antecedent can create confusion.

Vice President Cheney met with President Bush after *he* returned to Washington.

Who was returning, Bush or Cheney? Because *he* could refer to either, the meaning is unclear. Edit such a sentence so that the pronoun has only one possible antecedent. You can eliminate the pronoun if the result does not seem awkward.

Vice President Cheney met with President Bush after ~~he~~ returned to Washington.
Cheney

You can also place the pronoun so that confusion is less likely.

After
~~Vice President Cheney~~ met with President Bush ~~after~~ he returned
to Washington~~.~~ *, he*

You can use *the former* or *the latter* instead of a pronoun.

the former
Vice President Cheney met with President Bush after ~~he~~ returned
to Washington.

Paraphrasing a direct quotation can sometimes create confusion about antecedents. Using the direct quotation can sometimes avoid the problem.

, "You *"*
Peter told Patrick ~~that he had~~ passed the test.

The closer a pronoun and its antecedent appear to each other, the more easily readers can spot the relationship between them. If many words intervene, the reader may lose the connection. In the following passage, by the time readers get to *he* in the fourth sentence, they may have forgotten *Galileo* is the antecedent. Find a place to introduce the pronoun earlier, or use the antecedent again.

> **In the seventeeth century, the Italian scientist Galileo Galilei up-**
> **set the Catholic church by publishing a scientific paper asserting**
> **that the Earth revolved around the sun. That assertion contra-**
> **dicted contemporary church belief, which held that the Earth was**
> **the center of the universe. The paper also violated a papal order**
> *that Galileo had accepted*
> **~~of~~ sixteen years earlier not to "hold, teach, or defend" such a**
> *Galileo*
> **doctrine. Under pressure from the church, ~~he~~ recanted his theory**
> *Galileo*
> **of the Earth's motion, but even as he recanted, ~~he~~ is said to have**
> **whispered, "Eppur si muove" ("Nonetheless it moves").**

EDITING 1: PRACTICE ....

Edit the following passage by making each pronoun refer clearly to a single antecedent. More than one edited version is possible. Be ready to explain your editing choices.

Diane spotted Laura as she was beginning her regimen of stretching exercises. It was twenty minutes before the race was due to begin. Diane told Laura that she thought she would win the race. She was just plain faster. Laura responded that she had a good chance but that she was going to be tough to beat. Nodding in agreement, Diane shook hands with Laura. "Good luck," she said. "Have a good race."

Pronouns

PERSONAL

I, me, my, mine	it, its
you, your, yours	we, us, our, ours
he, him, his	they, them, their, theirs
she, her, hers	

INDEFINITE

all	each	many	none	some
any	either	more	no one	somebody
anybody	everybody	most	nothing	someone
anyone	everyone	much	one	something
anything	everything	neither	several	what
both	few	nobody		

DEMONSTRATIVE

this	that	these	those

RELATIVE

that	whatever	whichever	whoever	whomever
what	which	who	whom	whose

INTERROGATIVE

what	which	who	whom	whose
whatever	whichever	whoever	whomever	

REFLEXIVE AND INTENSIVE

myself	yourself	himself	herself	itself
ourselves	yourselves	themselves	oneself	

RECIPROCAL

each other	one another

49 b   Explicit antecedents

Most pronouns need explicit antecedents. (Indefinite pronouns, such as *somebody, everybody,* and *no one,* are exceptions. See 49j.) A pronoun whose antecedent is merely implied may confuse readers.

> Interviews with several computer programmers made *it* seem like a fascinating career.

What does *it* stand for? A reader might guess that *it* stands for *computer programming,* since this is a possible career, but *computer programming* does not appear in the sentence. To edit such a sentence, substitute a noun for the pronoun, use another pronoun that can refer to something already explicit in the sentence, or provide a clear antecedent for the pronoun.

> programming
> **Interviews with several computer programmers made ~~it~~ seem like a fascinating career.**

> theirs
> **Interviews with several computer programmers made ~~it~~ seem like a fascinating career.**

> people in programming
> **Interviews with several ~~computer programmers~~ made it seem like a fascinating career.**

1 Providing grammatically acceptable antecedents

An antecedent must be a noun, a noun phrase, or another pronoun. Usually, it cannot be the possessive form of a noun, an adjective, or other modifier. As you edit, make sure that any pronoun refers to a grammatically acceptable antecedent.

> among the committee members
> **The ~~committee's~~ bitter argument reflected badly on all of *them*.**

> Committee's *cannot be an antecedent for* them.

A possessive form of a noun or pronoun can be an antecedent, however, if the pronoun that refers to it is also possessive.

> The *committee's* argument reflected badly on all of *its* members.

2 Supplying explicit antecedents for *this, that,* and *which*

Confusion can arise when *this, that,* or *which* has two possible antecedents.

No one has suggested taxing health care. *This* is unlikely.

What is unlikely, the taxing of health care or the chance that anyone would sug-
gest it? You can usually clarify the reference by restating the antecedent that
you intend.

                                           tax
No one has suggested taxing health care. This is unlikely.
                                                 ^

When *which* and *that* (and *who* and *whom*) introduce clauses, they are
called **relative pronouns.** Usually, a relative pronoun introduces a clause
that immediately follows the pronoun's antecedent.

This book, *which I heartily recommend,* is out of print.

If other elements intervene or if the relative pronoun has more than one
possible antecedent, confusion can result. To clarify, you can provide an
unambiguous antecedent, or you can replace *which* or *that* with another
construction.

                          a response that
She took the situation seriously, ~~which~~ I found laughable.
                           ^
                          though   it
She took the situation seriously, ~~which~~ I found laughable.
                           ^   ^

ESL *Using* This *and* That

The demonstrative adjectives *this* and *that* mean "near" and "far," respectively. This
concept of distance can apply to space or time.

This vase right here is a better choice than *that* one in the back of the store.

That article I showed you last week was very technical.

This book I just found is more readable.

She has been very happy from *that* day to *this.*

EDITING 2: PRACTICE ....

Edit the following passage by making all pronouns refer to explicit antecedents. More than one version is possible. Be ready to explain your choices.

Thank you for giving me the chance to tour your videotape recycling facility. It gave me an excellent glimpse of what it is all about. I especially enjoyed the knowledge and wit of Bob Jones, our tour guide, which kept everyone in our group interested in the process. Bob showed us examples of tapes before and after they are refurbished, and that was incredible. Before processing, the tapes are scuffed and covered with labels, and after the workers finish their efforts, they look brand new. I know some people are skeptical about recycled videotapes, which I find somewhat understandable. But your recycling lines help the environment, even if in a small way. He made this clear to us before we left it.

....

49 c *It, they, you*

In casual speech, people often use *it, they,* and *you* with no definite antecedent. In academic writing, however, indefinite uses of *it, they,* and *you* should be avoided in favor of more specific constructions.

> ~~It said on the~~ news this morning that the game was canceled.
> *(The report said)*

> ~~They~~ tow away any car that is illegally parked.
> *(The police)*

> If the weather doesn't clear, ~~you~~ could see flooding.
> *(local residents)*

You may be used to address the reader directly (as in *You should use specific nouns whenever possible*), but in academic writing, do not use *you* to mean "people in general." One way to avoid reliance on *you* is to use indefinite pronouns such as *one* or *someone* that refer to an unspecified third person.

The pronoun *it* has three common uses. First, *it* can function as a personal pronoun: *I want to read the book, but Shana won't let me borrow* it. Second, *it* can be used to introduce a sentence in which the subject and verb are inverted: It *is necessary to apologize.* (See 47j.) Third, *it* appears in idiomatic constructions about time, weather, and distance: It *is ten past twelve.* In speech, few people notice if these senses of *it* are mixed. In writing, however, you should avoid using the same word in different senses in the same sentence.

Remember
~~It is important to remember~~ that once the exam begins, it will be

two hours before ~~it breaks for~~ intermission.

EDITING 3: PRACTICE

Edit the following passage by clarifying all uses of the pronouns *it, they,*
and *you.* Make any changes in wording needed for smooth reading. More
than one edited version is possible. Be ready to explain your editing
choices.

They say that you shouldn't believe everything you read in the newspaper. It is foolish to assume that it is possible for it to report the news
accurately all of the time. You can't expect that reporters and editors
will never make mistakes. Sometimes they receive late-breaking stories and have to rush to edit them before it goes to press. Occasionally
you even can see contradictions between two articles on the same topic.
It will say one thing in one article and then it will say something different in the other. It is when this happens that it is hard for you to
know which article you should believe.

49 d   *Who, which, that*

In general, *who* refers to people or to animals with names; *which* and
that refer to objects, ideas, unnamed animals, and anonymous people or
groups of people.

Black Beauty is a fictional horse *who* lives in a world that has now
disappeared.

Jake tried to rope the last steer, *which* twisted to avoid him.

This is the policy *that* the administration wants to enforce.

The tribes *that* built these cities have long since vanished.

(The difference between *who, whom,* and *whose* is one of case. See 49q.)
Most writers avoid using *which* to refer to people.

whom
I have met many actors, of ~~which~~ Jim Carrey is the funniest.

If using *of which* to refer to an inanimate object results in an awkward construction, substitute *whose*.

                whose

This is an idea ~~the~~ time ~~of which~~ has come.
             ^

Choosing Between Which *and* That

How can you tell whether to use *which or that?* The choice often depends on whether the modifier to be introduced is restrictive or nonrestrictive.

- A **restrictive modifier** is one that is necessary to identify what it modifies. It restricts, or limits, what it modifies in such a way that it is essential to the meaning of the sentence. It can be introduced by either *which* or *that* and is never set off by commas.

  All the courses *that are offered free of charge* are held in the evenings.

  The modifier that are offered free of charge *restricts (limits) the larger entity. All the courses* to those held in the evening. *The implication is that there may be other courses that are not free.*

- By contrast, a **nonrestrictive modifier** merely adds more information, not affecting the meaning of the sentence. It is introduced only by *which* (not by *that*) and is set off by commas.

  All the courses, which are offered free of charge, are listed in the catalog.

  All the courses are listed. The commas indicate that which are offered free of charge *doesn't limit or help identify the subject.*

- Although some people prefer *that* for all restrictive modifiers, *which* is acceptable as well.

  When in the course of human events it becomes necessary for one people to dissolve the political bands *which* have connected them with another ... a decent respect for the opinions of mankind requires that they should declare the reasons *which* impel them to the separation. [Italics added]

                                                       DECLARATION OF INDEPENDENCE

- *Who* may introduce either restrictive or nonrestrictive modifiers.

  NONRESTRICTIVE   Americans, *who* tend to eat a richer diet than Europeans, have rising rates of heart disease.

  The nonrestrictive who *clause adds information about Americans in general.*

  RESTRICTIVE   Americans *who* curb their appetites for rich foods may live longer than those *who* don't.

  The restrictive who *clause is necessary to identify the subject fully—in this case, just certain Americans.*

For more on restrictive and nonrestrictive clauses, see 52c.

Strategies for Clarifying Pronoun Reference

To clarify pronoun reference, edit your sentence using the following strategies.

■ Make sure a pronoun clearly refers to a single antecedent.
■ Place a pronoun close to its antecedent.
■ Provide an explicit antecedent.
■ Use *it, they,* and *you* appropriately.
■ Avoid overusing *it.*
■ Choose *who, which,* or *that* according to the antecedent.
■ Eliminate unneeded pronouns.

EDITING 4: PRACTICE

Complete the following passage, filling in the blanks with the correct pronoun: *who, whom, which,* or *that.*

None of the carpenters _____ works here has any use for imported nails. They swear that American-made nails are the only ones _____ are worth using. A nail _____ bends when it is driven in was probably made in Canada, they say. One box of nails, _____ they got from Japan, had heads _____ broke off if they tried to pull them out. There are problems every time the contractor brings them boxes _____ are imported. These men, every one of _____ works with nails every day, believe that they can tell where a nail comes from as soon as they hit it with a hammer. One thing is certain: a nail never bends because a carpenter hit it crooked.

49 e   Unneeded pronouns

Speakers of some dialects use a pronoun immediately following its antecedent.

After the shot, the deer i̶t̶ just took off.

EDITING 5: PRACTICE

Edit the following passage by making sure that all pronoun references are clear and that all pronouns are used appropriately. More than one edited version is possible. Be ready to explain your editing choices.

Studies have shown that alcoholism is a major problem in this city, that has a high percentage of unemployed and homeless people. This is true in other metropolitan areas as well. However, it affects not only the down-and-out but also working people, the elderly, and teenagers which have begun to experiment with drinking. We interviewed some social workers, which said that being homeless caused some people to drink.

We learned from interviewing homeless people, though, that many of those which are homeless now say they were drinking before they were on the street. Excessive drinking may force you to lose your home, if you're not careful, it seems from their experience.

- -

EDITING 6: APPLICATION -

Read through a paper you are working on. Are pronoun references unclear? Can you see any pattern to the problems? Edit any sentences in which you found pronoun reference problems, and think about how best to identify and correct these mistakes in your future editing.

- -

PRONOUN–ANTECEDENT AGREEMENT

49　f　Agreement

To be clear and correct, personal pronouns should **agree** with, or correspond to, their antecedents in number, person, and gender.

- Personal pronouns should agree with their antecedents in **number**—singular or plural. Most agreement problems involve confusion about number.

A *pronoun* is singular if *it* has a singular antecedent.

Pronouns are plural if *they* have plural antecedents.

- Personal pronouns should agree with their antecedents in **person**—first (*I, we, my, our*), second (*you, your*), or third (*he, she, it, they, his, her, its, their*).

I write in *my* journal at least once a week.

Robert writes in *his* journal every day.

ESL *Gender of Possessive Pronouns*

In many languages, the gender of a noun determines the gender of any element that modifies it. In French, for example, the word *mère* (mother) is feminine, so any word modifying it must be feminine as well, including possessive pronouns.

his mother	*sa mère*
her mother	*sa mère*

In English, however, the gender of a possessive personal pronoun must match the gender of its antecedent, not that of the word it modifies.

her mother	her father
his mother	his father

■ Singular personal pronouns should agree with their antecedents in **gender**—feminine, masculine, or neuter.

Rosanna finds that writing in *her* journal helps *her* clarify *her* thoughts.

Jimmy says *it* helps *him* analyze *his* research.

49 g Joined by *and*

A **compound antecedent** is one in which two or more parts are joined by a conjunction such as *and, or,* or, *nor: you* and *I, ducks or geese, neither rain nor snow.* When *and* links elements, the resulting grouping is usually considered plural, so a pronoun that refers to a compound antecedent joined by *and* should be plural as well.

Wind energy and solar power should soon take *their* place as major energy sources.

There are a few exceptions. A compound antecedent preceded by *each* or *every* takes a singular pronoun. (Also see 47o.)

Each leaf and twig was put in *its* own envelope.

When the parts of a compound antecedent refer to the same person or thing, the pronoun should be singular.

As *the systems manager and my immediate supervisor, she* oversees my work.

Also when the elements linked by *and* constitute a single entity, use a singular pronoun.

Hansel and Gretel is a chilling fairy tale. Like *Cinderella, it* offers an archetype of conflict between children and stepparents.

49 h   Joined by *or, nor*

The conjunctions *or* and *nor* can also be used to form a compound antecedent. When both elements are singular, a pronoun that refers to the compound antecedent is singular.

Either *hunger* or bad *weather* will take *its* toll on the soldiers.

When one element of a compound antecedent is singular and the other is plural, a pronoun clearly cannot agree with both of them. The convention is that the pronoun should agree with the antecedent closer to it.

Either the supply problems or the *weather* will take *its* toll.

If following this convention seems awkward, put the plural part of the antecedent nearer to the pronoun

Either the weather or the supply *problems* will take *their* toll.

49 i   Collective nouns

Collective nouns, such as *couple, flock, crowd, herd,* and *committee,* often cause agreement problems because they are singular in form yet they refer to groups or collections that can be regarded as plural. Take your cue from the intended meaning of the sentence. Use a plural pronoun if members of the group are acting separately.

The *crew* gather *their* belongings and prepare to leave the ship.

Use a singular pronoun if the group acts as a unit.

The *flock* arose in flight and made *its* way to the shelter of the trees.

EDITING 7: PRACTICE ....

Edit the following passage by making pronouns and antecedents agree. Be especially careful about compound and collective antecedents.

Often conflict at the workplace is inevitable, especially when an employee cannot agree with their supervisor's decisions. Sam experienced this conflict firsthand. Both he and his supervisor are unhappy with his relationship with each other. The supervisor makes Sam write memos about his many overtime hours to justify it. Sam believes his boss works him too hard because she doesn't like them. Neither the personnel director nor Alicia, Sam's closest friend at work, can use their influence to help Sam transfer because the staff unanimously gives their support to the supervisor.

49 j   Indefinite antecedents

An **indefinite pronoun**—such as *anyone, everyone, someone, nothing, everything*—does not require an explicit antecedent. You can write *Everyone likes ice cream* without further identifying your subject.

When another pronoun has an indefinite pronoun as its antecedent, it can be difficult to determine whether a pronoun that refers to an indefinite pronoun should be singular or plural.

Most indefinite pronouns are always singular: *anyone, everyone, someone, anybody, everybody, somebody, anything, everything, something, either, neither, each, nothing, much, one, no one.*

Each of the samples was placed in *its* own petri dish.

Neither of the Boy Scouts had brought *his* compass.

These singular indefinite pronouns also raise problems of gender agreement.

Someone has lost *his or her* briefcase.

In conversation, many people would say *Someone has lost* their *briefcase.* But this is incorrect in formal writing, since *someone* is singular. Using *his or her* avoids the implication that you're ignoring females, but that construction quickly becomes awkward. (For alternatives to the generic *he,* see the box below. For other tips on avoiding sexist language, see 44c.)

Because the word *none* is derived from *no one,* it is singular. (See also 47c.)

         has   its
None of the puppies ~~have~~ had ~~their~~ shots.

Avoiding the Generic He

Here are four ways to avoid the generic *he:*

■ If there is no doubt about the gender of the antecedent, you can use the pronoun of the same gender.

                                         her
    Anyone who wants to be an operatic soprano must train ~~their~~ voice carefully.

■ You can make the antecedent plural and edit any other agreement problems.

    All attorneys have their   specialties
    ~~Every attorney has his~~ own legal ~~specialty~~.

■ Use *his or her.* Use this strategy sparingly because *his or her* becomes monotonous with repetition.

                    or her
    A lawyer is only as good as his preparation.

■ Restructure the sentence to eliminate the pronoun. This strategy can be the most effective because it avoids the problem.

    All writers wrestle
    ~~Everyone wrestles~~ with this problem ~~in his own writing~~.

Some indefinite pronouns are always plural: *few, many, both, several.*

Hundreds of baby turtles climb out of the sand and crawl toward the

sea. *Few* survive *their* first week.

Still other indefinite pronouns can be singular or plural depending on context: *any, all, more, most, some.*

Most of the work *was* tedious because *it* was so repetitious.

Most *refers to* work, *which is singular, so* it *is singular.*

Most of the fans *have* left *their* seats and headed for *their* cars.

Most *refers to* fans, *which is plural, so* their *is plural.*

EDITING 8: PRACTICE

Edit the following passage by making pronouns and antecedents agree. More than one edited version is possible. Be ready to explain your editing choices.

Most people make many pronoun agreement mistakes in his or her speech because spoken English is much more informal than written English. Almost everyone knows that they shouldn't say "they" when they're talking about one person, but often they do so anyway when speaking. In conversation, even a professor, a freelance writer, or anyone else who works with words professionally won't always make a pronoun agree with the noun they refer to. But when someone writes, they should make sure that "something" is an "it" and not a "they." Otherwise, the reader will think the writer doesn't know what they are doing.

EDITING 9: PRACTICE

Edit the following passage for agreement. (You might have to change some verbs and nouns as well.) More than one edited version is possible. Be ready to explain your editing choices.

Changes in facial hair, a higher or a lower voice, and a decreased sex drive: this is some of the side effects of taking steroids. Yet many continue using this dangerous drug to improve their performance. Athletics is ever more competitive, and athletes are always striving to be the best he or she can be. In a race, mere seconds are a long time to an athlete when they mean the difference between a gold and a silver medal. Perhaps the athlete does not know what harm they are doing to their bodies. Someone cannot be physically addicted to steroids; any addiction to it is psychological and based on the fact that athletes like what they see. Unfortunately, the athlete cannot always see what lies ahead for them. Ben Johnson and some others should count himself lucky. All Johnson lost was a gold medal and the chance to compete again. Benjamin Ramirez was not so lucky. Nor were the many like him who lost his Iife.

EDITING 10: APPLICATION

Read through a paper you are working on to find pronouns that do not agree with their antecedents. Can you see why you made mistakes? Edit any sentences with agreement problems, and think about how best to avoid them. Write a brief set of guidelines to help yourself in the future.

PRONOUN CASE

49 k Choosing case

In speaking, we automatically choose among the pronouns *I* or *me* or *my, he* or *him* or *his.* We say *I saw him* rather than *me saw he,* or *my car* rather than *I car.* These changes of form, the grammatical property of nouns and pronouns called **case,** help indicate a word's role in a sentence. The **subjective case** (*I, he, she,* or *they,* for example) serves grammatically as a subject—the person or thing that performs the action of a sentence or a clause. The **objective case** (*me, him, her, them*) is used for an object—the person or thing that receives the action. The **possessive case** (*my, mine, your, yours, his, hers*) shows possession or ownership.

Most problems with case arise from the choice between subjective and objective pronouns: *I* or *me, we* or *us, she* or *her, who* or *whom.* Often the difficulty arises because nonstandard usages that are acceptable in everyday speech (*It's me!*) are inappropriate in formal writing (in which you would write

Determining Pronoun Case

PERSONAL PRONOUNS

SINGULAR	Subjective	Objective	Possessive
First person	I	me	my/mine
Second person	you	you	your/yours
Third person			
Masculine	he	him	his
Feminine	she	her	her/hers
Neuter	it	it	its
PLURAL			
First person	we	us	our/ours
Second person	you	you	your/yours
Third person	they	them	their/theirs

INTERROGATIVE OR RELATIVE PRONOUNS*

	Subjective	Objective	Possessive
	who	whom	whose
	whoever	whomever	—

*These pronouns are called **interrogative pronouns** when used to ask questions: Whose *book is that?* They are called **relative pronouns** when used to introduce dependent clauses: *The writer* whose *book we read visited the university.*

It is I). The key to choosing correct case is to analyze whether the pronoun in question is serving as a subject or as an object or is indicating possession.

49 I *And, or, nor*

Joining two or more words by *and, or,* or *nor,* and thus creating a compound element, does not affect their case. One test for correctness is to take out one word and the *and* or *or* and see how the sentence reads.

Joe and ~~me~~ talked to him.

If you mentally remove *Joe and,* you are left with *me talked to him.* Some people, trying to avoid this mistake, assume that *and me* is always wrong and thus make errors such as *He talked to Joe and I.* But we say *He talked to me,* not *He talked to I,* so we should also say *He talked to Joe and me.*

1 Subjective case for subjects

A subject that has two or more parts joined by *and, or,* or *nor* is a **compound subject.** Use the subjective case for each part of a compound subject. When one part of a compound subject is in the first person (*I, me*), put that part last.

> and I
> ~~Me and~~ Sandy found five lost lottery tickets.
>   ^

2 Objective case for objects

With **compound objects,** as with compound subjects, case is not affected by *and, or,* or *nor.* Use the objective case for each part of a compound object, whether it is the object of a verb or of a preposition.

>   him   me.
> The judges chose neither ~~he~~ nor ~~I.~~
>   ^   ^
>   them
> I spoke to Olga and ~~they~~ about the competition.
>   ^

To clarify the correct choice, mentally drop all but one pronoun from the compound object: *The judges chose him. The judges chose me. I spoke to them.*

The preposition *between* is used with two things, *among* with three or more. As with any preposition, the objects should be in the objective case.

>   me
> Between Jack and ~~I,~~ we sold more than four dozen souvenir
>   ^   among   me.
> T-shirts. We divided the money ~~between~~ him, Janet, and ~~I.~~
>   ^   ^

3 Subjective case following linking verbs

A **linking verb**—such as *be, become, seem, appear*—links its subject to a **complement** that follows the verb and renames the subject. In writing, both the subject and the complement should be in the subjective case.

>   I
> The first contestants were Laura and ~~me.~~
>   ^

If you have trouble choosing case following a linking verb, try turning the sentence around and simplifying the compound structure to a single pronoun: *I was the first contestant.*

Using the Pronoun Cases

SUBJECTIVE CASE

Use the subjective case (*I, you, he, she, it, we, they, who, whoever*) for the subject of a sentence or of a dependent clause.

She researched the origins of the tune.

James knew *who* would answer.

Also use the subjective case for a subject complement, which follows a linking verb (*be, seem, become, appear*) and renames the subject.

It is *they* who will benefit most.

OBJECTIVE CASE

Use the objective case (*me, you, him, her, it, us, them, whom, whomever*) for the object of a verb or of a preposition.

The judges chose *her* first.

They awarded the prize to *us*.

USING THE OBJECTIVE CASE WITH *MAKE, LET,* AND *HAVE*

Use objective case pronouns when infinitives follow *make, let,* and *have* even though these infinitives do not have the form *to* in front of them.

He let *us* retake the exam.

We made *him* tell us the secret recipe.

She had *me* turn the computer on.

POSSESSIVE CASE

Use the possessive case to show ownership, possession, or connection. The adjective form (*my, your, his, her, its, our, their, whose*) is used before a noun.

I wrote in *my* journal.

We met the singer *whose* songs we liked.

The noun form (*mine, yours, his, hers, ours, theirs*) can stand alone, without a noun.

The black coat is *hers*.

His is the plaid one.

EDITING 11: PRACTICE ....

Edit the following sentences, using the appropriate pronoun case for compound subjects and objects.

1. To him and I they provide hours of entertainment and neither he nor me ever seems to tire of them.
2. I don't remember whether it was him or me who first started watching them.
3. Others may not appreciate our passion for these shows, but they never seem boring to either he or I.
4. The best ones make me and him laugh every time we see them, and, thanks to the invention of the DVD, him and I can see them over and over.
5. Me and him have seen some shows so often that we have practically memorized them.

....

| 49 m | **Appositive pronouns** |

An **appositive** is a noun or pronoun that renames a preceding noun. (See 52c.) Pronouns used as appositives must be in the same case as the nouns they rename.

> **The losers—Tomoko, Rodney, and ~~me~~—all wanted a rematch.**
> _I

The appositive renames the subject, losers, *so the pronoun is in the subjective case.*

> **It was her sons, Paul and ~~him~~, who missed their mother most.**
> ^{he}

The appositive renames the subject complement, sons, *so it is in the subjective case.*

> **They asked the medalists, Katya and ~~I~~, to pose for a picture.**
> ^{me}

The appositive renames medalists, *the object of the verb* asked, *so it is in the objective case.*

To decide between the subjective and objective case in such sentences, simplify the construction: *They asked me to pose for a picture.*

49 n   *Us, we*

Pronouns immediately followed by nouns can cause confusion, but the correct case again depends on whether the pronoun is a subject or an object. (The noun following the pronoun is an appositive renaming the pronoun. See 52c.)

> We
> U̶s̶ bikers were worried about the weather.
>   ^

>   us
> They told w̶e̶ bikers not to worry about the weather.
>   ^

Mentally dropping the noun following *us* or *we* can make the choice clearer: *We were worried about the weather. They told us not to worry about the weather.*

EDITING 12: PRACTICE

Edit the following paragraph for pronoun case.

> Fishing with our dad, Charley and me hadn't caught any fish all week. We decided it was up to the two of us, him and I, to find some way to catch something. Us two kids borrowed a rowboat and, with him and me rowing, went way out in the middle of the pond. We dropped anchor and began fishing, him out of one side of the boat and I out of the other side. Charley asked me if I was sleepy and I said, "Not me," but then a splash of water woke me, and the boat was rocking. Charley was pulling madly on his rod, and it seemed as if his catch would tip the boat over and he and I with it. It took ten minutes for us, Charley and I, to get that catfish on board. Dad said it was turning out that the real fishers in the family were Charley and me. Dad made both Charley and I feel really proud.

49 o   Verbals

Participles, gerunds, and infinitives are called **verbals** because they are derived from verbs. However, they cannot function by themselves as verbs in sentences. A **past participle** (*worked, eaten, brought*) or **present participle** (*working, eating, bringing*) without an auxiliary verb can be used as a modifier. A **gerund** is the *-ing* form of the verb used as a noun. An **infinitive** is the base form of the verb, usually preceded by *to*.

PRESENT PARTICIPLE	A person *waking* at that hour is often groggy.
PAST PARTICIPLE	He seemed *tired*.
GERUND	*Waking* at that hour can ruin my day.
INFINITIVE	I hate to *wake* so early.

1 Objective case for objects of verbals

Verbals can have objects. In the sentence *I like to read books,* for example, the object of the infinitive *to read* is *books.* Choose the objective case for a pronoun that is the object of a verbal.

Watching *her* was fascinating.

He hadn't intended to lose *them*.

2 Objective or possessive case before *-ing* verbals

The choice of pronoun case before an *-ing* verbal depends on whether the verbal is used as a noun or as a modifier. Which of these pairs is correct? Either, depending on the meaning.

He heard their shouting.

What did he hear? He heard shouting.

He heard them shouting.

What did he hear? He heard them.

My
~~Me~~ leaving made them all sad.

me
He heard ~~my~~ leaving just before midnight.

49 p *Than, as*

The subordinating conjunctions *than* and *as* often appear in **elliptical constructions**—clauses that have one or more words intentionally omitted. Understanding exactly what is omitted is the key to choosing the correct case for a pronoun that follows *than* or *as*.

> Alex is as strong as (*I* / *me*).

Restore the omitted word *am* at the end of the sentence, and it is easy to choose the correct pronoun: *Alex is as strong as I am.*
Sometimes the omitted words will call for the possessive case.

> Jen's luggage weighs as much as *mine* [my luggage].

The subjective case could also be meaningful in this sentence:

> Jen's luggage weighs as much as *I* [weigh].
>
> *The objective case,* me, *would not be correct in any sense here.*

By using the correct case, you can help the reader understand sentences that offer more than one possibility for omitted words.

> My sister has more respect for her friends than *I* [have].

> My sister has more respect for her friends than [she has for] *me.*

EDITING 13: PRACTICE ....

Edit the following sentences, using the correct pronoun case after *than* or *as*. Circle the number of any sentence that is correct.

1. We're both columnists, but I think my columns are consistently better than her.
2. Our fellow writers consider I as funny as she.
3. But apparently our readers find she funnier.
4. Maybe I just have different taste than them.
5. Someday I know my writing will become more popular than her.

----

49 q *Who, whom*

The distinction between *who* and *whom* and between *whoever* and *whomever* has all but disappeared from everyday speech, so your "ear" for the correct form may be of little help. Yet in formal writing, the wrong choice is considered an error. When you encounter one of these pronouns, remember to use *who* and *whoever* only for subjects, *whom* and *whomever* for objects.

As a test, answer a question posed by *who* or *whom* with a sentence using *he* or *him.*

> (*Who / Whom*) got here first? *He* got here first.

> Who *and* he *are both subjective, so use* who.

> (*Who / Whom*) do you trust? I trust *him.*

> Whom *and* him *are both objective, so use* whom.

Use *who* when the answer uses *he;* use *whom* when it uses *him.*

1 To introduce questions

Who, whom, whoever, and *whomever* can introduce questions; when they do, they are **interrogative pronouns.** If the pronoun is the subject of the question, use *who* or *whoever: Who is going? Whoever could be calling at this hour?*

When the pronoun is the object of the verb, use *whom* or *whomever: Whom did you see? Whomever did he want?*

Also use *whom* or *whomever* when the pronoun is the object of a preposition: *To whom are you speaking?*

> Who
> ~~Whom~~ had the authority to enter the building at night?
>   ^

Test: He *had the authority. Use* who.

> Whom
> ~~Who~~ did you admit to the building?
>   ^

Test: You did admit him. *Use* whom.

> whom
> To ~~who~~ did you give authority to enter the building?
>   ^

Test: You did give authority to him. *Use* whom.

Don't be fooled by other clauses inserted nearby.

> Who
> ~~Whom~~, may I ask, is calling?
>   ^

Drop out may I ask *and the correct choice is clear.*

He was a student ~~whom~~ people thought would succeed.

who

Test: People thought he *would succeed, so use* who.

Be careful when a preposition is left at the end of a question. Pronouns that are objects of such prepositions still need to be in the objective case.

Whom did you give it to?

Moving the preposition can make the choice clear.

To whom did you give it?

2 In dependent clauses

Who, whom, whoever, and *whomever* are *relative pronouns* when they introduce dependent clauses, but the same rules about case apply. Use *who* and *whoever* when the pronoun is the subject of its clause, *whom* and *whomever* when it is the object of its clause. The case of a relative pronoun is determined by its role in the dependent clause, not by anything in the surrounding sentence.

The man *who* lives next door is a rock climber.

Who *is the subject of the clause* who lives next door.

The fellow *whom* I met last week is also a rock climber.

Whom *is the object of* met.

As with interrogative pronouns, the question test can help you choose the right case. Turn the dependent clause into a question introduced by the pronoun, and then answer that question with *he* or *him.* If the answer uses *he* (subjective case), then *who* is correct. If the answer uses *him* (objective case), then *whom* is correct.

I want a list of everyone ~~whom~~ visited the plant today.

who

Test: Who/Whom *visited the plant?* He *did, so use* who.

The police will interrogate ~~whoever~~ the foreman accuses.

whomever

Test: Who/Whom *does the foreman accuse? The foreman accuses* him, *so use* whomever.

EDITING 14: PRACTICE ···

Edit the following passage, using *who, whom, whoever,* and *whomever* correctly.

> Whomever took the last piece of German chocolate cake has caused an uproar in our household. Dad had vowed vengeance on whomever touched it. But this afternoon it was gone. Only a crumb-filled plate remained. Mom said she would not defend whoever Dad suspected. Dad fumed and fussed and brooded and interrogated whoever looked guilty. None of my brothers and sisters confessed to the crime, even when he threatened whoever the guilty party was helped by. In the end, though, we learned that the culprit was Mom, whom had made the cake for his birthday and said she just wanted a midafternoon snack. What could Dad say? If he complained too much, she wouldn't bake for him anymore.

···

49 r Reflexive pronouns

The pronouns *myself, yourself, himself, herself, itself, ourselves, yourselves,* and *themselves* are called **reflexive pronouns.** A reflexive pronoun reflects the action of the verb back toward its subject, making it clear that the object and the subject of the verb are one and the same: *I looked at myself in the mirror.* These pronouns are called **intensive** when they are used to rename and emphasize an element appearing earlier in the sentence: *He did it* himself.

Never use a reflexive pronoun as a subject. This error is most common when the subject should be *I* or *me.*

My friend and ~~myself~~ plan to attend.

When the subject and the object of a verb refer to the same person or persons, use a reflexive pronoun for the object.

himself
John cut ~~him~~ with the scissors.

Himself makes it clear that the person who has been cut is the same as the person who did the cutting.

me
John cut ~~myself~~ with the scissors when he handed them to me.
     ^

The words myself *and* John *do not name the same person, so* myself *is incorrect.*

A reflexive pronoun should be used as the object of a preposition only when it and an earlier noun or pronoun in the sentence name the same person or persons.

               myself,
I speak only for ~~me,~~ not for my roommate.
                  ^

Myself *is correct because* I *precedes it in the sentence.*

                   me,
As for Carlos and ~~myself,~~ we want to work in software design.
                     ^

Myself *is incorrect because* I *does not precede it.*

Editing for Correct Pronoun Case

To edit for pronoun case, do the following:

- Check pronoun case in elements joined by *and, or,* or *nor.*
- Check the case of pronouns used as appositives.
- Determine whether you need *us* or *we* before a noun.
- Check the case of pronouns used with verbals.
- Check the case of pronouns after *than* or *as.*
- Choose between *who* or *whom, whoever* or *whomever.*
- Use reflexive pronouns only as objects, only when necessary.

EDITING 15: PRACTICE ....

Edit the following passage, using the appropriate pronoun case throughout.

In the memories of my siblings and myself, our house used to be surrounded by a forest on three sides. Us children—my three brothers and me—used to hunt for snakes and salamanders in the woods by overturning the rocks that they lived under. One of the best hunting grounds for ourselves was the land to the south of our yard. When I was eight years old, I saw a garter snake catch a frog and devour it whole. It eating the frog upset my brothers and I terribly. Us, with our childish minds, thought that snakes were nasty, cruel creatures and that frogs were clearly nicer than them. Now that I am grown up, I realize that the snake eating the frog was not an act of cruelty. Each creature on earth lives and dies according to the natural order of things.

EDITING 16: APPLICATION

Examine a paper you are working on to see if you have used inappropriate pronoun case. Do you make one kind of error more than others? Think of ways to avoid such errors. Edit your work.

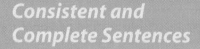

chapter 50

*Consistent and
Complete Sentences*

ike bus riders, readers like to know where
they are being taken. A good writer respects
readers' expectations the same way that a
good driver keeps passengers comfortable: by
avoiding needless detours and sudden changes in
destination.

50 a Unnecessary shifts

Readers generally expect continuity in point of view and in references
to time. Within sentences, readers expect a logical consistency in the person and number of subjects (see 47h–47u), in the forms of verbs (see
47a–47c), and in the way quotations are reproduced. A change in any of
these elements is called a **shift.** Often a writer's meaning does require a
shift, such as a change of subject from third person to first person or from
singular to plural.

As Ichiro rounded the bases, *we* in the stands erupted in a frenzy of
cheers and applause.

However, a shift in verb tense in the same sentence would be unnecessary
and confusing: *As Ichiro rounded the bases, we in the stands erupt in a frenzy
of cheers and applause.* Unnecessary shifts disrupt communication.

731

1 Shifts in person and number

We refer to ourselves in the **first person** (*I, we*), to our audience in the **second person** (*you*), and to other subjects in the **third person** (*he, she, it, one, they*). Unnecessary shifts in **person** often arise in sentences about groups or about unidentified people. Some writers shift unnecessarily to the second person, particularly when trying to make a comprehensive statement. To avoid unnecessary shifts to the second person, use *you* in formal writing only when referring to the reader. (See 49c.)

The chemistry students learned that ~~you~~ they had to be careful.

As one enters the building, ~~you see~~ one sees little evidence of fire.

Unnecessary shifts in **number**—from singular to plural and vice versa—generally occur when a writer has used a singular noun or pronoun of indeterminate gender (*student, one*) and then uses a plural pronoun to refer to it, perhaps to avoid the appearance of sexism. (See 44c and 49c.) You can avoid such shifts by making the antecedent plural or by substituting a singular pronoun.

~~Every student~~ Students makes their own schedule.

Each student is responsible for ~~their~~ his or her own work.

The first-person plural—*we*—has many uses. Some writers use *we* to speak inclusively of themselves and their audience: *We all use informal constructions in everyday speech.* Other writers use *we* to refer to themselves (the **editorial *we***) even when only one person is writing: *We have shown that most colloids are stable only within a limited range of temperatures.* Be careful not to mix different senses of *we*.

We asked a dozen people to share their opinions about ~~our~~ Americans' apparent national obsession with politicians' personal lives.

2 Shifts in tense

Tense places the action of the verb in time: *Today I go. Yesterday I went. Tomorrow I will go.* Different verbs in a sentence or paragraph may logically use different tenses to reflect actions occurring at different times. (See 47d–47e.)

We *will play* tennis before we *eat* breakfast but after we *have had* our coffee.

The tense you select to describe most of the actions in your paper is called the **governing tense.** Once you establish it, do not use another tense without a good reason.

> **When the contract was finished, it ~~sets~~ a firm deadline.**
> _set_

The **literary present tense** is used to describe literature or art. (See 47d.) If you use it, do so consistently.

> **In _The Glass Menagerie,_ Tom realizes how trapped he is after the Gentleman Caller ~~departed.~~**
> _departs_

Shifting Tense within a Paragraph

Sometimes verb tense shifting within a paragraph is necessary when you support or comment on an idea. Following are some acceptable reasons for shifting tense.

SHIFTING FROM PRESENT TENSE TO PAST TENSE

- To provide background information
- To support a claim with an example from the past
- To compare a present situation with a past one

Truly dedicated writers _find_ time to write regardless of the circumstances. Austen _wrote_ most of her novels in short bursts of activity between receiving visitors and taking care of household duties.

SHIFTING FROM PAST TENSE TO PRESENT TENSE

- To express a comment, opinion, or evaluation

On May 6, the town council _voted_ against the school bond. Their decision _is_ unfortunate.

3   Shifts in mood

English verbs are used in one of three **moods.** The **indicative mood** is used for statements and questions: _Rain fell, Did you hear it?_ The **imperative mood** expresses commands, orders, or directions: _Close the door._ Unnecessary shifts from the imperative to the indicative mood commonly occur in instructions.

> **First cover your work surface with newspapers, and then ~~you~~ make sure your materials are within easy reach.**

By contrast, the **subjunctive mood** expresses wishes or statements that are known to be not factual: *He wishes chocolate* were not *fattening. If he were a millionaire, he'd be happy without it.* (See 47f–47g.) Often, you will find that using the subjunctive mood and the indicative mood in the same sentence is appropriate. In the next two examples, the verbs in the independent clauses (*wishes* and *would be*) are in the indicative, while the verbs in the dependent clauses (*were* in both cases) are in the subjunctive.

My professor *wishes* that I *were* more diligent.

The world *would be* nicer if everyone *were* as kind as you.

Avoid unnecessary shifts from the subjunctive to the indicative or to the imperative.

The contract requires that you be in Denver on July 1 and that you ~~will~~ **be in Houston on August 1.**

4 Shifts in voice and subject

The subject of an **active-voice** verb performs the verb's action: *He hit the ball.* The subject of a **passive-voice** verb is acted upon: *The ball was hit by him.* (See 40c.) If a sentence has two verbs with the same subject, a shift of voice can be acceptable.

The students *completed* the project and *were given* first prize.

*The verbs shift from active (*completed*) to passive (*were given*) but have the same subject,* students. *The shift is acceptable because it keeps the focus on the subject.*

A shift from the active to the passive voice (or vice versa) can be distracting and unnecessary, however, when it requires a shift in subject as well.

As we peered out of the tent, the waning moon ~~was seen~~ we saw **through the trees.**

5 Shifts between direct and indirect quotation

Direct quotation, sometimes called *direct discourse,* reproduces someone's exact words, which are enclosed in quotation marks.

"I love my work," he insisted.

Indirect quotation, or *indirect discourse,* is a paraphrase of some-one else's words; it is not placed in quotation marks. (See Chapter 27.)

He insisted that he loved his work.

As you edit, watch for shifts from indirect to direct quotation that are not clearly needed. Either use indirect quotation consistently, or rewrite the sentence so that the direct quotation is introduced by a new verb and is enclosed in quotation marks.

He loved his work and why ~~was~~ *(wondered)* the job being *(was)* eliminated *(?)*

He loved his work and ~~why~~ *(asked, "Why)* is the job being eliminated *(")*?

Avoid using one verb (such as *said*) to introduce both an indirect quo-tation and a complete sentence of direct quotation. You have three editing choices: use indirect quotation in both instances, quote less than the full sen-tence directly, or start a new sentence.

Dr. Ryan claims that the play was composed before 1600 and ~~"It~~ *(that it was certainly written by)* ~~shows the clear hand of~~ **Shakespeare.**~~"~~

Dr. Ryan claims that the play was composed before 1600 and *(that it ")* **"It shows the clear hand of Shakespeare."**

Dr. Ryan claims that the play was composed before 1600 ~~and "It~~ *(He says, "It)* **shows the clear hand of Shakespeare."**

EDITING 1: EXPLORATION

Throughout the following excerpt from his essay "Computers," Lewis Thomas uses the pronouns *you* and *we* inconsistently. Consider what effect Thomas hoped to achieve with this unconventional use of pronouns. Do you think he was effective?

It would be nice to have better ways of monitoring what we're up to so that we could recognize change while it is occurring, instead of waking up as we do now to the astonished realization that the whole century just past wasn't what we thought it was, at all. Maybe computers can be used to help in this, although I rather doubt it. You can make sim-ulation models of cities, but what you learn is that they seem to be be-yond the reach of intelligent analysis; if you try to use common sense

Transforming Direct Quotations to Indirect Quotations

You must make certain changes when you transform a direct quotation into an indirect quotation.

VERBS

You often must change the tense of verbs in a direct quotation to be consistent with the rest of the sentence and avoid confusing shifts.

Direct Quotation	**Indirect Quotation**
Present tense	**Past tense**
He said, "They *are* tired."	He said that they *were* tired.
Past tense	**Past perfect tense**
She said, "They *lost* their keys."	She said that they *had lost* their keys.
Present perfect tense	**Past perfect tense**
He said, "She *has written* a great short story."	He said that she *had written* a great short story.

Some auxilliary verbs change from present to past tense.

Direct Quotation	**Indirect Quotation**
can	could
may	might
must, have to	had to
will	would

He said, "They *can* travel quickly."   He said that they *could* travel quickly.

PRONOUNS

In some cases, you may have to change pronouns when you transform a direct quotation into an indirect quotation. Pay attention to meaning when considering these changes.

Direct Quotation	**Indirect Quotation**
She said, "*I* was wrong."	She said that *she* was wrong.
She said to me, "*You* can sing."	She said that *I* could sing.
She said to them, "*You* can sing."	She said that *they* could sing.

FOR QUESTIONS

When a direct quotation is a question, you may need to change the word order or add a word such as *if* or *whether* when transforming it into an indirect quotation.

Direct Quotation	**Indirect Quotation**
She asked, "*What is the answer?*"	She asked *what the answer was.*
He asked, "*Is this correct?*"	He asked *whether that was correct.*

FOR COMMANDS AND REQUESTS

When a direct quotation that is a command or a request is transformed into an indirect quotation, it should be introduced with a verb such as *tell, order,* or *ask* and should contain an infinitive. It may also need to specify who was given the command or request.

Direct Quotation	**Indirect Quotation**
I said,"*Don't* get up."	I *told him not to* get up.
She said,"*Please* leave."	She asked *him* to leave.

to make predictions, things get more botched up than ever. This is interesting, since a city is the most concentrated aggregation of humans, all exerting whatever influence they can bring to bear. The city seems to have a life of its own. If we cannot understand how this works, we are not likely to get very far with human society at large.

EDITING 2: PRACTICE

Edit the following sentences to avoid distracting or awkward shifts. Some sentences have more than one possible answer. Be ready to explain your editing choices. Circle the number of any sentence that is correct.

1. Last night, Karen reminded me about the time of the exam and says, "You had better not be late this time."
2. Fortunately, this morning she also gave me a wake-up call; she says she knew that I would oversleep.
3. I arrived at the examination room about five minutes early and was given an answer booklet and a seating assignment by the proctor.
4. We were allowed one hour for the examination, and do not use any books.
5. When it was time to begin, we were told first to review, and then you can begin to answer the questions.
6. As I turn to the first section, though, I saw a truly horrible sight.
7. My test dealt with second-year organic chemistry, but I was enrolled in American history.
8. I start sweating, and then, when I looked next to me, I saw another student busily scribbling in their answer book.
9. Suddenly, it dawns on me that I don't recognize anyone in the room, and I began to panic.
10. Just then the phone rang, and I hear Karen saying "Get up!" and telling me that she knew I would oversleep.

50 b Mixed constructions

The term **mixed construction** applies to a sentence that begins one way and then takes a sudden, unexpected turn, so that readers are unsure what it means. One kind of mixed construction uses a grammatically unacceptable element as a subject or predicate. Another kind of mixed construction links subject and verb in an illogical way.

1 Making subjects and predicates grammatically compatible

In English, a prepositional phrase cannot be the subject of a sentence.

Listening
~~By listening~~ closely and paying attention to nonverbal signals
    ^

helps a doctor make a better diagnosis.

A doctor can make a better diagnosis by   ⊙
~~By~~ listening closely and paying attention to nonverbal signals
^   ^
~~helps a doctor make a better diagnosis.~~

A modifier clause also cannot be the subject of a sentence. A modifier clause begins with a subordinating conjunction such as *after, before, while, because, if, although,* and *unless.* To edit such a sentence, provide a new subject for the sentence.

The doctor's status as
~~Because the doctor is~~ an expert does not mean a patient should
    ^

never question a diagnosis.

Another kind of grammatically mixed sentence uses an inappropriate element as a predicate. A dependent clause cannot contain the main verb of a sentence.

The fact that most patients are afraid to ask questions,~~which~~ gives

doctors complete control.

Removing which *turns* gives *into the main verb.*

2 Making subjects and predicates logically compatible

Sometimes a sentence combines elements that logically do not fit. Although the intent might be understood, something is wrong at the level of literal meaning. If you sense that some elements do not work together, reduce your sentence to its most basic elements—subject and verb—to see where the problem lies.

> ~~The opinion of most~~ **people believe that dogs make better pets than cats.**
>
> Most

Reduce the sentence to subject and verb: The opinion *cannot* believe; people *can. So* people *makes a more logical subject.*

> ~~The increase in the~~ **number of cat owners in the United States has doubled since 1960.**
>
> The

The increase *hasn't doubled;* the number of cat owners *has doubled.*

> **Repeat offenders whose licenses have already been suspended for drunk driving will ~~be~~ revoked.**
>
> have their licenses

It is not offenders *who will be revoked but rather their licenses.*

A subject complement must rename the subject in a logical way.

> **My father's favorite kitchen appliance is ~~using~~ our microwave.**

Using *is not an appliance. When* oven *functions as the subject complement renaming* appliance, *the sentence makes sense.*

3 Eliminating faulty predication

A type of mixed construction called **faulty predication** is both ungrammatical and illogical. Sentences with faulty predication use a modifier clause starting with *when, where,* or *because* to rename the subject. Some contain the phrase *The reason is because.*

> **A stalemate is ~~where neither player can~~ win.**
>
> the inability of either player to

> ~~Pop art is where~~ **an artist reproduces images from commercial products and the popular media.**
>
> In pop art,

Such constructions are ungrammatical because a modifier cannot rename a subject. They are illogical because a person or thing (the subject) cannot be a *when, where,* or *because.*

Reserve *when* and *where* clauses to modifiers specifying time and place. Whenever you see *the reason is because,* substitute *the reason is that* or restate the subject.

> The reason little has been done is ~~because~~ ^{that} the committee is deadlocked.

> ^{Little} ~~The reason little~~ has been done ~~is~~ because the committee is deadlocked.

EDITING 3: PRACTICE

Edit the following passage by eliminating mixed constructions. More than one edited version is possible. Be ready to explain your editing choices.

> The reason some readers feel that Ernest Hemingway's fiction is overrated is because his style seems so simple and repetitive. By focusing on the subtleties of his language, though, can tell us a great deal about the psychology of his characters. In "The Big Two-Hearted River," for example, the intention of Hemingway tries to give the reader a sense of Nick Adams's struggle to maintain some degree of emotional stability by focusing on the minute details of a trout-fishing excursion. By repeatedly reminding himself that he had made a "good camp" shows that Nick feels a sense of anxiety on some other, subconscious level. In an example like this, then, we can see that Hemingway's unique style is using small details to offer deeper insights into his characters' minds.

50 c   Missing words

Sentences can be incomplete because of inadvertently omitted words, faulty elliptical constructions, or ambiguous comparisons.

1 Checking for omitted words

Little words like *the, a, an, is, was, in, at, to,* and *that* are easy to omit, either in haste or in the interest of brevity. As you edit, check that you have not omitted necessary words.

>   *to*   *was*
> **When she told me ^ meet her at the office, I ^ sure she meant her office.**

When you read silently, your eye has a tendency to "fill in" what it expects to see; therefore, a good way to check for missing words is to read your writing aloud.

2 Completing elliptical constructions

In **elliptical constructions,** words are intentionally omitted that readers can be expected to understand. Elliptical structures are often used in parallel constructions. (See 38c, 39f.)

In an elliptical construction, make sure that the words omitted are identical to the words already used in the other part of the parallel.

>   *were*
> **The sun shone brilliantly and the clouds ^ radiant.**

The second clause requires a different verb from the verb in the first clause, shone, *so the second verb cannot be omitted.*

Consider repeating conjunctions and prepositions, especially in long parallel structures.

>   *in*
> **Little words are easy to omit, either in haste or ^ the interest of brevity.**

3 Making comparisons complete

Comparisons may be incomplete or illogical if a writer leaves out words that are necessary for reader understanding. Comparisons must be complete and explicit. Beware of inadvertently equating a person with a thing.

>   *Cooper's*
> **Many of Melville's novels are superior to ~~Cooper.~~ ^**

Do not leave readers in doubt about what you are comparing.

she likes
It seems that Goodall likes apes more than other people.
                                                        ^

Does she like apes more than she likes other people, *or* more than other people
do? *Rather than make readers choose, make the comparison clear and complete.*

(For more on comparisons, see 48e, 49p.)

Composing Consistent and Complete Sentences

Check to make sure that your sentences are consistent and complete:

- Make sure sentences include no unnecessary or distracting shifts.
- Make subjects and predicates relate to one another grammatically and logically.
- Make sure not to omit words necessary to express ideas clearly.

EDITING 4: PRACTICE

Edit the following passage, making all of the sentences consistent and complete. More than one edited version is possible. Be ready to explain your editing choices.

I'll bet that most people sit down to their dinner between six and seven o'clock each night. You can tell because that's when the infuriating salespeople from the local paper call. He pretends that I already have a subscription, and then he'll ask you, "Was your paper delivered on time today?" or whether it was late. It is especially annoying is where they ask the same question every time. And they think that if you say, "No, I'm not a subscriber," somehow I will agree to listen to their sales pitch. What makes it even worse is a terrible newspaper. If they were trying to sell me *The New York Times* would be a different story.

EDITING 5: APPLICATION

Examine a paper you are working on, and see whether you have written any sentences that are inconsistent or incomplete. Is there one kind of mistake that you make frequently? Can you see why you might have made this mistake? Edit those sentences, and think about how best to avoid these problems in the future.

Editing Section

Punctuation

743

The full stop at the end of every written sentence requires one of three marks of **end punctuation:** a *period,* a *question mark,* or an *exclamation point.* Sometimes the only clue to the meaning of a sentence is the end punctuation: *They won. They won? They won!* Periods are also used with abbreviations, and question marks are sometimes used in parentheses to indicate uncertainty.

As you edit, be aware of the conventional uses of end punctuation.

51 a Periods

Use a period at the end of a statement, a mild command, or a polite request.

The administration has canceled classes.

Do not attempt to drive to school this morning.

Please forward an application to the address above.

Also use a period after an indirect question (one that is reported, not asked directly). (See 50a5 and 51b.)

I wonder who made the decision?.

Use a period in abbreviations that end in lowercase letters.

Mr., Mrs., Ms.	a.m., p.m.	in., ft., yd., mi.
Dr., Rev., Jr., Sr.	sec., min., hr.	etc., eg., i.e., vs., ca.
Gov., Sen.	wk., mo., yr.	p., para., fig., vol.
exceptions: mph, rpm		

Do not use periods in other abbreviations unless they stand for personal names.

US   UK   BC   AD   BA   PhD   MD
W. E. B. Du Bois

Do not use periods in acronyms, which are abbreviations formed from the first letters of a series of words to simplify the names of government agencies, corporations, and other entities.

| NASA | NATO | AIDS | CNN | SAT | FBI | CIA | EPA |
| IRS | IRA | NCAA | IBM | RSVP | mph | rpm | |

When an abbreviation containing a period falls at the end of a sentence, use a single period to end the sentence.

The flight leaves at 6:00 a.m.

EDITING 1: PRACTICE ....

Edit the following sentences by using periods correctly.

1. Sandra Booker, M.D., is a role model for our community.
2. Dr Booker focuses her practice on pediatric care for homeless children, beginning her day as early as 5:00 a.m..
3. She volunteers two days a week at an A.I.D.S. clinic.
4. She has worked with the US. Department of Housing and Urban Development (H.U.D.) to develop programs for at-risk families.
5. She even conducts a learning lab. for high school students who are considering becoming doctors.
6. I wonder who else in the community does so much?

....

51 b   Question marks

Use a question mark at the end of a **direct question.** Direct questions are usually signaled either by *who, when, what, where,* or *why,* or by inverted word order, with part of the verb before the subject.

Where is Times Square?	*How* can I get there?
Can I take the subway?	*Do you* know the fare?

A sentence that ends with a **tag question** also takes a question mark. (See 52e for the use of commas with tag questions.)

This train goes to Times Square, doesn't it. ?

Direct questions in a series may each be followed by a question mark, even if they are not all complete sentences (See 59a for advice on capitalizing fragmentary questions.)

Where did Mario go? To the library? To the cafeteria?

When a quotation is itself a question, put the question mark inside the quotation marks. No additional comma or period is needed.

I asked, "Should I go".?

Gertrude Stein was reportedly asked on her deathbed, "What is the answer?" "What is the question?," she replied.

When a quotation that is not a question appears in a sentence that is a question, put the question mark outside the quotation marks.

Did you say, "I should go?"

When both the sentence and the quotation it contains are questions, use a question mark inside the quotation marks.

Did you say, "May I go too?"?

The same rules apply to exclamation points (see 51c).

Writers sometimes phrase questions in normal word order, as if they were statements; a question mark indicates that they should be read as questions.

Sylvester Stallone will play Hamlet next year? Don't count on it.

Unlike direct questions, **indirect questions**—ones that are reported rather than asked directly—are not followed by question marks. In other words, if the independent clause in a sentence is a question, then use a question mark. If the independent clause is not a question, don't use a question mark.

Are you asking me which subway you should take?

He wants to know how he can get to Times Square.

(For more on indirect questions, see 50a5.)

Use a question mark in parentheses to indicate uncertainty about a specific fact such as a date or the correct spelling of a word.

The plays of Francis Beaumont, 1584(?)–1616, ~~1584–1616,~~ were as popular in their

day as Shakespeare's.

Do not use question marks in parentheses to suggest sarcasm or irony.

Some people think it is funny ~~(?)~~ to humiliate others.

EDITING 2: PRACTICE ....

Edit the following sentences by using question marks correctly.

1. "You say that by learning another language a person can learn a lot about another culture," I asked.
2. I wonder how long it takes to be able to think in a different language?
3. What is the best way for me to learn to speak French, converse with my friends, go to the language lab, go to France?
4. The best way to learn to speak another language is to speak it as often as possible, isn't it.
5. Some students think it's entertaining (?) when classmates make mistakes.
6. Don't you know that we learn by making mistakes.

....

51 c Exclamation points

Use an exclamation point to convey emphasis or strong emotion in exclamations, forceful commands, interjections, and statements or questions that require special intensity.

What a mess!   Wow! It's getting late!
Stop the train!   Was that train fast!

When the words in a direct quotation are an exclamation, put an exclamation point before the closing quotation marks.

    "Ouch" ! my brother cried. "That hurts!"

If a sentence that requires an exclamation point ends with a quotation that does not, put the exclamation point outside the quotation marks.

    Don't call it "Frisco!"

If both the sentence and the quotation within it are exclamations, put an exclamation point inside the quotation marks.

    Quick, yell "Fire!"

Do not use an exclamation point, even in parentheses, to indicate amazement or sarcasm. Do not use more than one exclamation point or a combination of exclamation points and question marks to indicate amazement.

    The judges selected Carl (!) to represent us in the regional competition.

    Can you believe that the baby slept through the night!!?!

Because exclamation points signal emphasis, they make demands on readers' attention and energy. Use only one or two in a passage; pick the most important exclamation point and replace the others with periods.

EDITING 3: EXPLORATION

Find four or five examples of popular writing that overuse exclamation points. A good place to start your search is in advertising and comic strips in newspapers or magazines. What effect do the exclamation points have?

EDITING 4: PRACTICE

Edit the following sentences by using exclamation points correctly. Some sentences have more than one possible answer. Be ready to discuss your editing choices.

1. Our mother told us to be careful! not to slip on the ice when we were running for the bus.
2. "Be careful," she called out as we hurried down the icy driveway.
3. "Oh! No! Here comes the bus now. Hurry up."
4. "Too late. Now we'll have to walk to school."
5. "Are you crazy!? It's a four-mile walk to school."
6. "Don't tell me you can't walk four miles?" I exclaimed.

EDITING 5: PRACTICE

Edit the following by using all end punctuation correctly. More than one edited version is possible. Be ready to explain your editing choices.

Have you always assumed eating sugar will make you gain weight. This fact (?) is increasingly subject to debate. According to recent research, the main problem with sugar is that it usually accompanies fat in a diet Dr Adam Berg, a nutritionist, wondered what makes some people gain weight more than others? His research has led him to believe that excess fat is actually more likely than sugar to cause problems with weight and health! A study by the US Food and Drug Administration shows that the average American eats about two ounces of sugar a day. According to Berg, the level of sugar consumption found by the F.D.A. applies to both moderately overweight and obese people. Does the difference lie in amount of exercise? genetic makeup. calorie intake. Berg believes it is a combination of these, but he notes specifically that the eating patterns of obese people reflect a particularly high consumption of fatty foods. He suggests cutting out the doughnuts (!) and eating low-fat sweets instead. If only it could be so easy.

Commas shape the phrasing of written sentences in the same way that brief pauses shape the phrasing of spoken sentences. Commas can indicate how a sentence is divided. By showing which words go together and which should be separated, commas help readers understand a sentence's meaning.

Consider, for example, how difficult it is to understand the meaning of the following sentence, from which all commas have been deleted:

A quarter of a century after the introduction of television into American society a period that has seen the medium become so deeply ingrained in American life that in at least one state the television set has attained the rank of a legal necessity safe from repossession in case of debt along with clothes cooking utensils and the like television viewing has become an inevitable and ordinary part of daily life.

With its commas restored, however, this complex sentence is actually quite clear:

A quarter of a century after the introduction of television into American society, a period that has seen the medium become so deeply ingrained in American life that in at least one state the television set has attained the rank of a legal necessity, safe from repossession in case of debt along with clothes, cooking utensils, and the like, television viewing has become an inevitable and ordinary part of daily life.

MARIE WINN, "THE PLUG-IN DRUG"

Guidelines for Using Commas

As you edit use the following guidelines for placing commas in your paper:

■ Before a coordinating conjunction that joins independent clauses. (See 52a.)

[Independent Clause],   [Independent Clause]

I had studied for hours, but I still found the exam difficult.

■ To set off an introductory element (See 52b.)

[Introductory Element],   [Main Clause]

Concentrating intensely, I completed the exam in twenty minutes.

■ To set off any nonrestrictive element. (See 52c.)

[Main Clause],   [Nonrestrictive Element]

They toured the *Balclutha,* which was moored near Fisherman's Wharf.

[Nonrestrictive Element]

Dr. Parke-Cookson, our chemistry professor, gives exams weekly.

■ To set off parenthetical expressions and elements of contrast, (See 52d.)
■ To set off interjections, tag sentences, and direct address. (See 52e.)
■ Between items in a series. (See 52f.)

[Item], [Item],   [Item]

English, history, and philosophy are my favorite subjects.

■ Between coordinate adjectives. (See 52g.)

[Coordinate Adjective], [Coordinate Adjective], [Noun]

Well-written, well-researched papers receive the best grades.

■ Between quotations and attributory phrases. (See 52h.)
■ With numbers, dates, names, and addresses. (See 52i.)
■ To prevent misreading. (See 52j.)

52 a   Coordinating conjunctions

An **independent clause** is a group of words that contains a subject and a predicate and that can stand alone as a complete sentence. A **compound sentence** contains two or more independent clauses. If those clauses are joined with a **coordinating conjunction** (*and, or, but, for, nor, yet, so*), use a comma before the coordinating conjunction.

Campaign workers distributed leaflets, and posters lauding the candidates were hung throughout the hall.

When two short independent clauses are related, the comma may be omitted.

The sun rose and the fog lifted.

To prevent misreading of a compound sentence when the independent clauses contain internal commas, you may use a semicolon rather than a comma before the coordinating conjunction that joins the independent clauses.

Cruise passengers may disembark to shop, tour the island, or snorkel, or, if they wish, they may swim, view a movie, or just relax on the ship.

Do not use a comma without a coordinating conjunction to join independent clauses. If you do, the result is an error known as a **comma splice.** (See Chapter 46.)

His hobby is raising geese, he proudly displays the blue ribbons he has won at the state fair.

Do not use a comma before a coordinating conjunction joining two dependent clauses.

When the board meets, and when the vote is officially recorded, the decision will be final.

Also do not use commas between other compound elements, such as compound subjects and compound verbs. (See 52j2.)

EDITING 1: PRACTICE ....

Edit the following sentences, using commas correctly with coordinating conjunctions joining independent clauses. Circle the number of any sentence that is correct.

1.   The highway department sets speed limits on state roads and highways and it determines standards for intersecting roads.

2. Every new business or residence along a highway needs an access road but first the highway department must approve its design and location.

3. The developer of a new housing development or commercial center must complete an application, and must submit it for the highway department's review.

4. The regulations set standards for sight distances and markings so a developer can tell whether a driveway is acceptable.

5. The minimum sight distances vary with the speed limit and the grade of the road and the standards for driveway construction vary with the expected volume of traffic.

6. The highway department does not have to permit a driveway that does not meet its standards or that would require modifications to the roadway.

---

52 b Introductory elements

When a sentence begins with an element other than the subject (and its modifiers), put a comma after that introductory element.

DEPENDENT CLAUSE   *When Elizabeth I assumed the throne of England in 1558,* the country was in turmoil.

PREPOSITIONAL PHRASE   *In every taste test,* the subjects chose the new flavor over the old.

INFINITIVE PHRASE   *To do the job properly,* they need more time.

PARTICIPIAL PHRASES   *Praised by all the critics,* the movie was still not a hit.

Barking furiously, the little dog lunged at me.

ABSOLUTE PHRASE   *His dream of glory destroyed,* the boxer died an embittered man.

A comma is optional when an introductory phrase is brief and there is no possibility of confusion: *In 1963 an assasin's bullet shocked the world.*

Do not use a comma after an introductory phrase when the word order of the sentence is inverted so that the verb precedes its subject.

In the back of the closet,̷ was an old box.

In this sentence, box *is the subject and* was *is the verb.*

Do not use a comma after a phrase that functions as the subject of the sentence rather than as a modifier.

Hearing that song,̷ evokes warm memories.

In this sentence, hearing that song *is the subject.*

EDITING 2: PRACTICE ....

Edit the following passage, using commas after introductory elements.

> Despite his own admission that he had lived a life full of failings Mickey Mantle died a hero to many Americans. During the 1950s and 1960s Mantle was the most popular player on the New York Yankees. Because of that team's unsurpassed success on the baseball diamond Mantle's personal achievements took on an even greater luster than they otherwise might have. However it was not just his skills as a player that made him beloved. In fact Mantle's warmth as a human being endeared him to fans and sportswriters more than did any other trait. When Mantle died in 1995 his passing was felt deeply by many who had seen him play. Although years separated them from their childhood days at the ballpark many older Americans took time to cherish their memories of watching "the Mick" play. To many he was the symbol of a less cynical and materialistic era.

52 c   Nonrestrictive elements

A modifier is **restrictive** if it provides information that readers must have in order to understand the meaning of the word or words modified. It "restricts" or limits the meaning from a general group to a more specific one.

Students *who are late* will be prohibited from taking the exam.

The modifier who are late *is restrictive because it limits the meaning to a specific group of students—those who are late.*

A modifier is **nonrestrictive** if it provides additional information but is not essential to the meaning of the word or words it modifies.

Qualified doctors, *who must be licensed,* are in short supply.

The modifier who must be licensed *tells the reader more about doctors but does not restrict the meaning to a specific group of doctors.*

When something or someone is identified by name, it has been adequately specified; therefore, any modifier is nonrestrictive.

Ernesto Seguerra, *who used to run a hardware business,* is now running for mayor.

Use commas to set off nonrestrictive modifiers but not restrictive ones. Often, the only clue to whether a modifier is restrictive or nonrestrictive—and to the writer's meaning—is how the sentence is punctuated.

Company employees *who receive generous benefits* should not complain.

Company employees, *who receive generous benefits,* should not complain.

The restrictive modifier in the first sentence limits the meaning to a specific group of employees, implying that not all employees *of the company receive generous benefits. The nonrestrictive modifier in the second sentence says something different: by not specifying a specific group, it implies that all employees receive generous benefits.*

To determine whether a modifier is restrictive or nonrestrictive, try omitting it. Omitting a nonrestrictive modifier usually will not change the basic meaning of a sentence, but omitting a restrictive one will.

RESTRICTIVE   Athletes who take steroids want a shortcut.

Athletes want a shortcut.

These two sentences have very different meanings; the modifier is restrictive.

NONRESTRICTIVE   Olympic athletes, who all have trained intensely, are usually in top physical shape.

Olympic athletes are usually in top physical shape.

These two sentences mean about the same thing; the modifier is nonrestrictive.

Another way to see whether a modifier is restrictive or nonrestrictive is to ask a question about the identity of the subject. If the answer requires the information contained in the modifier, the modifier is restrictive.

RESTRICTIVE   A cat that neglects to groom itself will have matted fur.

What will have matted fur? A cat that neglects to groom itself. Restrictive.

NONRESTRICTIVE   A cat, a nocturnal mammal, hunts small rodents.

What hunts small rodents? A cat. Nonrestrictive.

1 Modifier clauses

Adjective clauses—clauses that begin with *that, where, which, who, whom,* and *whose*—can be either restrictive or non-restrictive. *That* is used only in restrictive clauses. *Which* is used for nonrestrictive clauses, but it can be used for restrictive as well. (For more information on *that* and *which,* see 49d.)

RESTRICTIVE   Anyone *who visits the National Air and Space Museum* can touch a piece of the moon.

A clause modifying an indefinite pronoun, such as anyone, *is usually restrictive.*

NONRESTRICTIVE   The festival will honor Spike Lee, *who directed* Malcolm X.

A clause modifying a proper noun is almost always nonrestrictive.

Adverb clauses—those that begin with subordinating conjunctions such as *because, when,* and *before*—are usually restrictive, needing no commas.

I usually do well on tests *when I am prepared.*

When an adverb clause introduces a sentence, however, a comma is required. (See 52b.)

When I am prepared, I do well on tests.

2 Appositives

An **appositive** is a noun or noun phrase that immediately follows another noun and renames it. An appositive is restrictive only when it is more specific than the noun it renames. (See 49m.)

RESTRICTIVE   Poet *Gary Soto* has written several novels for young adults.

His poem *"Oranges"* is about having a crush on someone.

Gary Soto *is more specific than* poet. "Oranges" *specifies which of many poems.*

NONRESTRICTIVE   Gary Soto, *a popular poet,* writes novels for young adults.

"Oranges," *my favorite of his poems,* seems autobiographical.

A popular poet *is less specific than* Gary Soto. My favorite of his poems *is not more specific than* "Oranges."

EDITING 3: PRACTICE

Edit the following passage, using commas correctly.

Anger an emotion all of us experience at one time or another generally arises, when we feel we can't control a situation or we don't get what we want. Anger may be natural but researchers say that people, who get angry often, may be giving in to a learned response. Such uncontrolled fits of anger which can actually kill a person may be controlled if people, can learn to deal with their anger, in a positive way. C. Mack Amick a counselor from North Carolina advises people to ask themselves three questions when they get angry. The first question, recommended by Amick, is "Is this really important to me?" The answer well may be "no" which means it's time to cool off. The second question that he recommends is "Is this the right time to get angry?" The final question designed specifically to help one gain control is "Do I have an effective response?" Finding a response, that is assertive but not aggressive, is the key to controlling one's anger.

52 d   Parenthetical expressions and elements of contrast

Parenthetical expressions are words and phrases that interrupt the flow of a sentence to offer a comment, a supplemental explanation, or a transition. In many cases, **transitional expressions** and **conjunctive adverbs** (such as *furthermore, for example, as a result, therefore, however,* and *meanwhile*) serve as parenthetical expressions and are set off with commas. Other conventional parenthetical expressions include *in fact, of course, without a doubt, by the way,* and *to be honest.* Phrases that begin with *according to, such as,* and so forth are also parenthetical expressions.

One Saturday, *for example,* we had marshmallows for breakfast.

Parenthetical expressions can often be moved within a sentence without affecting its meaning. No matter where they appear in a sentence, they are set off with commas.

The commissioner was not amused by the report, *however.*

The commissioner, *however,* was not amused by the report.

However, the commissioner was not amused by the report.

Commas may also be used to set off **elements of contrast**—words, phrases, or clauses that emphasize a point by describing what it is not or by citing an opposite condition.

The experience was illuminating, but unnerving, for everyone.

The article mentioned where he obtained his degree, not when he received it.

EDITING 4: PRACTICE ....

Edit the following sentences, using commas correctly. Circle the number of any sentence that is correct.

1. Soothing music it seems is effective for reducing stress.
2. Many physicians in fact are recommending relaxing music not tranquilizers to patients with high levels of stress.
3. One Boston doctor surprisingly enough has produced a recording of music that according to him uses the rhythms of a healthy heartbeat.
4. He believes exposure to such rhythms can promote a slower and more regular heartbeat in patients.
5. Other physicians however suggest that patients should select their own favored music not a doctor's prescription.
6. A Phoenix psychologist for example advises patients to start with music that is the same as not calmer than their energy level; they can later switch to music of a lower intensity.

....

52 e   Tag sentences, direct address, and interjections

Use commas to set off nonessential elements such as tag sentences, direct address, and some interjections.

1 Tag sentences

Use a comma before **tag sentences**—short statements or questions at the ends of sentences that express or elicit an opinion.

You received my application in time, *I hope.*

We are not so trusting of strangers these days, *are we?*

2 Direct address

Use a comma or commas to set off words of **direct address**—words that name the person or group to whom a sentence is directed.

That, *my friends,* is not the end of the story.

We appreciate your generous contribution, *Dr. Collins.*

3 Interjections

Use a comma or commas to set off mild **interjections,** expressions of emotion. (Set off a stronger interjection by treating it like a separate sentence: *Hooray! I got an A on my exam!*)

Oh, what good times we had together.

The replacement players, *alas,* were doomed from the start.

Yes and *no* are treated similarly.

Yes, I enjoyed the party, but *no,* my date didn't.

EDITING 5: PRACTICE ....

Edit the following sentences, using commas correctly. Circle the number of any sentence that is correct.

1. Oh the promises politicians make.
2. They always begin with something like, "My fellow citizens it is my goal to follow the will of the people."
3. Then they tell us, "You realize that my first concern is my constituents I hope."

4. They can't really expect us to believe their promises can they?

5. Ah we're just disillusioned with politicians these days my friends, so no wonder turnout on election day gets lower every year don't you think?

---

52 f Items in a series

A **series** consists of three or more words, phrases, or clauses that are equal in grammatical form. A coordinating conjunction—*and, or, but, nor, so, for, yet*—usually precedes the final item in the series. Use a comma after each item in the series except the last.

He studied all of the notes, memos, letters, and reports.

To accelerate smoothly, to stop without jerking, and to make complete turns/ can require many hours of driving practice.

Unless a comma is required by another rule, do not use one before the first item or after the last item of a series.

The primary colors are/ red, yellow, and blue.

They visited Nevada, Utah, and Arizona/ on their trip west.

When individual items of a series include commas, you can help readers avoid confusion by separating the items with semicolons instead of commas. (See 53b.)

---

52 g Coordinate adjectives

Coordinate adjectives are two or more adjectives that modify the same noun: *warm, sunny day.* Coordinate adjectives are independent of each other in meaning and in their relationship to the noun. Use commas to separate coordinate adjectives.

To see whether adjectives are coordinate, try inserting *and* between them or reversing their order. If the resulting sentence still makes sense, the adjectives are coordinate and require commas. If the adjectives are not coordinate, do not separate them with a comma. Such adjective combinations, called **cumulative adjectives,** build on one another and together modify a noun.

COORDINATE ADJECTIVES

YES   He put on a *clean, pressed* shirt.

YES   He put on a clean and pressed shirt.

YES   He put on a pressed, clean shirt.

CUMULATIVE ADJECTIVES

YES   I found *five copper* coins.

NO   I found five and copper coins.

NO   I found copper five coins.

Do not use a comma between the last adjective and the noun it modifies, whether the adjectives are coordinate or not.

They walked with delicate, deliberate/ steps across the ice.

(See the ESL box in 40d2.)

EDITING 6: PRACTICE ....

Edit the following sentences, using commas correctly. Circle the number of any sentence that is correct.

1. Burlington International Airport, like any other airport, has a tower, a radar room and many safety devices.
2. Inside the airport are a comfortable spacious lounge, three departure gates, and a restaurant.
3. The airport leases the space to a number of companies, including airlines car rental agencies food concessions and gift shops.
4. The airport's representative explained that the airport is run like larger airports that it leases out its buildings and that it takes a percentage of the profits made by the independent businesses.
5. The majority of air travel at the airport is between Boston Newark and Chicago although travel is by no means limited to these three, major cities.
6. Over the next ten years, the airport hopes to replace the few, remaining pre-1950s buildings with large modern facilities.

52 h   **Quotations**

Direct quotations are often accompanied by **signal phrases,** which identify the source of the quotation. In general, use commas to set off a signal phrase, whether it appears before, after, or in the middle of the quotation.

> In 1948, Jack Kerouac first declared, "We're a beat generation."

A comma before a signal phrase goes *inside* the quotation marks.

> "Scratch a lover," said Dorothy Parker, "and find a foe."

When a signal phrase appears between two complete quoted sentences, it is followed by a period. If the quotation ends with a question mark or exclamation point, do not add a comma.

> **"Dead, did I say?,̸" Chief Seattle concludes. "There is no death, only a change of worlds."**

Do not use a comma before a partial quotation preceded by *that* or when there is no true signal phrase.

> **He closed by saying that,̸ "time will prove us right."**

> **According to one critic, the program is,̸ "a sinkhole for public dollars."**

> **The slogan,̸ "You deserve a break today,̸" was particularly successful.**

In general, do not use a comma before indirect quotations.

> **Jones claimed,̸ he had not yet begun to fight.**

A comma may, however, follow an introductory phrase before indirect quotation.

> According to Jones, he has not yet begun to fight.

(See Chapter 56 for more on punctuating quotations.)

Edit the following sentences, using commas correctly.

1. "Love looks not with the eyes" according to Shakespeare "but with the mind."

2. In her novel *Jacques,* George Sand writes "No human creature can give orders to love."

3. "How do I love Thee?," asked Elizabeth Barrett Browning. "Let me count the ways."

4. "Man must evolve for all human conflict a method which rejects revenge, aggression, and retaliation" said Martin Luther King, "The foundation of such a method is love."

5. Dr. King also said "I believe that unarmed truth and unconditional love will have the final word in reality."

6. "Love is heaven" wrote Walter Scott "and heaven is love."

---

52 i Numbers, dates, names, and places

1 Numbers

For numbers of five digits or more, use a comma before every three digits, counting from the right.

2700 (*or* 2,700)   79,087   1,654,220

Do not use a comma in years, page numbers of four digits, or numbers in addresses.

That example is found on page 1269.

In 1990, our address was 21001 South Street, Lodi, Ohio 43042.

2 Dates

Use a comma between the words for the day and month and between the numbers for the date and year.

Friday, March 22   June 10, 1999

Also use a comma after the year when a date giving month, day, and year is part of a sentence.

Our family reunion was held on July 22, 2005, in Chicago.

Don't use commas when only the month and year are given in a date or when the month separates the date and year. (The day, month, year order is more common in British English than in American English.)

The war broke out in *August 1914* and ended on *11 November 1918*.

3 Names

Use commas to set off an abbreviation or title following a name.

Joyce B. *Wong, MD,* supervised the CPR training session.

Renee *Dafoe, vice president,* welcomed the new members.

Edwin M. *Green, Jr.,* was the first speaker.

Do not use commas to set off roman numerals following a name.

Frank T. Winters III

4 Places and addresses

Use a comma before and after the state when naming a city and state in a sentence.

She was born in *Lexington, Kentucky,* and raised in New York.

When a full address is given in a sentence, use a comma to separate each element except the postal code, which should have no comma before or after it.

My address is *169 Elm Street, Apartment 4, Boston, Massachusetts 02116* through the end of June.

For an address in block form, as on the front of an envelope, do not use a comma at the end of each line.

EDITING 8: PRACTICE ....

Edit the following sentences, using commas correctly.

1. In the week before Christmas, the mail order company where I worked filled 84567 orders.

2. I started my job in February, 1998 and the last day I worked was January 15 1999.
3. During that time, I answered 3456 calls and sold merchandise worth more than $200000.
4. The worst customers are the ones with names like Jane Jones Ph.D. or John Johnson, III, who insist on having their titles appear on all their mail.
5. You may write to my former employer at this address: National Mail Order Products, 19123 Fifth Avenue New York New York 10001.
6. With $1500 in my savings account, I did not need to worry about getting another job until March 1999.

---

52 j To prevent misreading

Commas may occasionally be used, even when they are not required by any specific rule, to prevent misreading.

We will all pitch in, in the event of a problem.

I believed, once I had seen the evidence.

Those of us who can, preserve the memories fondly.

They found that in 1990, 256 people were affected.

If a clause that begins with *because* follows the main clause but could modify more than one element in the sentence, a comma can help clarify the meaning.

We knew that she called her brother because her mother asked her to do so.

We knew that she called her brother, because we saw the phone bill.

Usually a modifier modifies the closest suitable element. If that's not the case, the comma helps alert the reader.

....

Make up sentences that are awkward, confusing, or humorous without commas. Read them to your classmates to see if they are able to understand them. Examples:

> In the winter time seems to stand still.

> I dressed and fed my cats.

....

52 k Misuse

Failing to include commas where they are conventionally expected can confuse readers. It can be equally distracting, however, to use commas where they are not required.

Misuses of commas already discussed in this chapter are summarized in the box on page 770. This section covers several other common misuses.

1 Avoid putting single commas between subjects and verbs, verbs and objects or complements, or objects and complements

Subject and verb

A *season* of drought, *worried* the farmers.

Verb and object

The agreement *entails*, *training* for part-time staff.

Verb and complement

The laid-off workers *seem*, surprisingly *understanding*.

Object and complement

The extra pay made *him*, quite *happy*.

However, a pair of commas, such as those used to set off nonessential elements, may separate subjects from verbs.

David *Hill, the chief researcher,* developed the method.

Comma Troubleshooting

Pay special attention to the commas that help readers understand your ideas. (From a reader's point of view, some commas are more important than others.)

- As an editing strategy, put brackets around structures that need commas so that you can easily identify where phrases or clauses begin and end.

    My English teacher [who is new this year] just graduated from Stanford.

    [If we consider the source of humor for this joke] we see that it depends on something that is contrary to our expectations.

- Check for commas following all adverb clauses (*because, although, when,* etc.) that begin sentences. Find the end of the clause and add a comma if necessary.

    Because the library was closed I studied at home.

- When using *that* to introduce a clause, make sure that you have not set it off by commas. (See 52k3.)

    In the library, we found the materials/ that we needed to complete the project.

- If you have listed three or more items in a series, make sure that you have put a comma and the word *and* or another coordinating conjunction before the last item. (See 52f.)

    , and
    We studied similies, metaphors analogies.

2 Avoid putting commas between two compound elements

Compound subject

The *members* of the senior class/ and their *parents* were invited.

Compound verb

Maria quickly *turned off* the lights/ and *locked* the door.

> ## Checking for Commas That Occur in Pairs
>
> ▪ Always make sure to use a pair of commas to set off the following when they appear in the middle of a sentence: **nonrestrictive modifiers** and **appositives** (52c); **parenthetical elements** and **elements of contrast** (52d); **interjections** and **words of direct address** (52e); and **years in full dates, titles, abbreviations after names,** and **state names preceded by city names** (52i).
>
> > This book, which he had read three times, was quite tattered.
> > $_\wedge$
> >
> > The instructors, rather than the students, are being tested.
> > $_\wedge$
> >
> > I bought it from a Joplin, Missouri, publisher.
> > $_\wedge$
> >
> > It will be January 3, 2004, before I receive my degree.
> > $_\wedge$
>
> ▪ Delete single commas that separate the subject from the verb, no matter how many words make up the subject (unless it has phrases or clauses after it that need commas). (See 52b and 52k.)
>
> > The city in the southern United States that I like the most / is New Orleans.

Compound object

> Sean put the *books* on the shelf / and the *pens* in the drawer.

Compound complement

> He found the work *easy to learn,* / but *hard to continue.*

Commas are used to separate the independent clauses of a compound sentence. (See 52a.)

> The rain finally stopped , and then the sun came out.
> $_\wedge$

3 Avoid putting commas following a relative pronoun or subordinating conjunction

> The map *that,* / we requested turned out to be incorrect.

Our legislators have no idea how to proceed *because¦ we have not*
come to a consensus.

A pair of commas, such as those used to set off parenthetical elements, may
separate these elements.

We found that, according to the latest data, the population had doubled.

(See 52h for uses of commas with quotations.)

EDITING 10: PRACTICE ....

Edit the following passage for correct comma use.

> More kids than ever before are playing video games, to fill up their
> leisure time. Some popular, video games have inspired movies that be-
> came a huge, financial success. Playing such a game, is thought by some
> to have a negative influence on behavior, though. Some, recent studies
> suggest that children, witnessing simulations of extreme violence, are
> more likely, than others, to behave violently, themselves. On the other
> hand, many others argue that video games are a harmless way for peo-
> ple, to relieve stress, and aggression. In their view, human beings are
> naturally prone to violence, and to claim that the elimination of a sin-
> gle, video game would make a difference, is sheer fantasy.

EDITING 11: PRACTICE ....

Edit the following passage for correct comma use.

> In two, recent scientific studies researchers have found what might be
> called, an "excitability gene." This genetic variation as it is called is
> found in people who crave, excitement, thrills and new experiences.
> They are also themselves excitable, and prone to temper flare-ups. If the
> discovery holds up after further research it will represent the first link
> ever discovered between a gene and normal nonpathological behavior.
> "Success in mapping genes for a normal personality trait may signal a
> fruitful way to map genes for psychopathology" according to one of the
> researchers C. Robert Cloninger M.D. Cloninger who is on the staff of
> Washington University, proposed the hypothesis that, people's need for
> excitement is related to how dopamine a neural chemical is processed
> by the brain. This process is governed by a specific gene that in fact
> occurs in two variant forms, as a series of seven sequences or a series

Editing Unneeded Commas

Do not use a comma for the following:

■ To join independent clauses without a coordinating conjunction. (See 52a and Chapter 53.)

> We won the game͵ it was the first of many victories.

■ After an introductory phrase when the verb precedes the subject in a sentence. (See 52b.)

> Along with every challenge͵ comes an opportunity for success.

■ After a phrase that is the subject of the sentences (See 52b.)

> Eating sensibly and exercising regularly͵ improved my health.

■ To set off restrictive elements. (See 52c.)

> The materials͵ that you requested͵ have arrived.

> A bird͵ with only one wing͵ has little chance of survival.

> Singer and guitarist͵ John Hall͵ will appear at the benefit.

■ Before the first element or after the last element of a series, unless required by another rule. (See 52f.)

> We contributed to͵ United Way, World Watch, and the Red Cross͵ last year.

> Rice, beans, and peppers͵ provide the basis for many local dishes.

■ Between adjectives that are not coordinate. (See 52g.)

> There are three͵ different patterns of male baldness.

of four. What researchers discovered was that people, who could be called "novelty-seekers," generally had the longer seven-sequence version of the gene. This does not mean however, that the behavioral trait is governed solely by this single gene and researchers caution that other factors such as personal experience come into play.

EDITING 12: APPLICATION

Take a few moments to reflect on the difficulties you most commonly have in using commas. Make a brief list that ranks your problems in order from greatest to least amount of difficulty. Now examine a paper you are working on and look for any examples of misused or omitted commas. Do you notice consistent patterns? How accurate was your initial prediction of where your difficulties would lie? Edit any sentences in which you have misused or omitted commas.

chapter 53 — *Semicolons*

While a comma marks a pause within a sentence, a *semicolon* marks a stop within a sentence, telling readers that what precedes it is complete and that what follows is also complete but related. The semicolon always comes between sentence elements of equal rank; it is not used to introduce, enclose, or end a statement.

Although using a period or a comma is often mandatory, using a semicolon is usually a choice; in certain situations it may be an alternative to a period, and in other circumstances, it may replace a comma.

53 a Between independent clauses

An **independent clause** is a group of words that contains a subject and a predicate and that can stand alone as a complete sentence. Two or more such clauses may be joined with a semicolon to indicate that the clauses are related.

The storm raged all night; most of us slept fitfully, if at all.

A semicolon can emphasize contrast or contradiction.

Most dogs aim to please their owners; cats are more independent.

A semicolon must be used between independent clauses joined with a **conjunctive adverb** (*however, furthermore, therefore*) or a **transitional expression** (*for example, on the other hand*). (See 38a3, 46b2.)

Many in the community were angry; however, they lacked an articulate leader.

The contract was approved; indeed, no one questioned the restrictions.

Do not use both a coordinating conjunction and a semicolon to join simple independent clauses. Either delete the conjunction, or replace the semicolon with a comma.

Hundreds of volunteers assisted in the cleanup effort; ~~and~~ many worked from dawn to dusk.

To feel compassion is natural¸ but to help someone is truly virtuous.

You may use a semicolon with a coordinating conjunction to join complex or lengthy independent clauses, particularly if they contain commas.

If the weather clears, we plan to leave for our climb at dawn; and if it doesn't, given the dangerous trail conditions, we'll pack up and go home.

(For more on joining independent clauses, see Chapter 38.)

Eliminate any semicolon between an independent clause and a dependent clause. If the dependent clause precedes the independent clause, use a comma. (See 52b.) No punctuation is needed if the independent clause is first unless punctuation is required by another rule or convention.

Torrential rains fell every day¸ when we visited Florida last summer.

As soon as the rain stopped¸ the mosquitos came out.

EDITING 1: PRACTICE ....

Edit the following sentences, using semicolons as necessary to join independent clauses.

1. The amount of crime shown on television has been criticized for inciting aggression in viewers, in fact, it may be equally criticized for unreasonably raising viewers' fears.
2. Some experts estimate that 55 percent of prime-time characters experience a violent confrontation in the course of a week, the actual figure in life is less than 1 percent.

Using Semicolons Sparingly

As a stylistic device, the semicolon can be overused, creating a monotony of rhythm and sentence structure. Save the semicolon for the sentences in which it is most effective.

Tax incentives can distort the economy ⊙ For
; for example, real estate tax shelters

helped create the glut of empty office buildings that forced developers into

bankruptcy and caused a banking crisis due to defaults on loans. More tax

breaks are not the answer ⊙ They
; they would only create more distortion.

Politicians, however, compete to think up special tax cuts; it must be an

election year.

The editing reserves the semicolon to set up the statement that requires the most emphasis.

3. Studies have found that frequent viewers of television are likely to overestimate the statistical chance of violence in their lives, no matter what their gender, educational level, or neighborhood, and, moreover, fear, mistrust, and even paranoia can be the result.

4. For example, among city dwellers almost half of those identified as frequent viewers see crime as a very serious problem, only a quarter of infrequent viewers do.

5. Many Americans today rate crime as the country's number one problem, in fact, only a small segment of the population is likely to experience a violent crime.

6. Television-related misconceptions about crime may lead citizens to clamor for more protection, local governments to request additional funding, and politicians to raise taxes, and, worse, they may also contribute to increasing social mistrust.

53 b   In a series

Items in a series are generally separated by commas. (See 52f.) In some situations, however, you can use semicolons instead.

Use a semicolon between elements in a series if any element of the series includes a comma.

The candidates for the award are Maria, the winner of the essay competition; Elanie, the top debater; and Shelby, the director of the senior play.

Some writers use a semicolon to separate a series of long phrases or clauses, even when they contain no internal commas.

As a nation, we need to understand why these regional conflicts occur; how they are rooted in the power vacuum that followed the fall of the Soviet Union; and what kinds of responses we can offer in settling them.

As with commas, a series should not be preceded or followed by a semicolon unless another rule requires it.

Use a colon, not a semicolon, when an independent clause introduces a list. (See 54a.)

It was a fine old house, but it needed work; plastering, repainting,

rewiring, and a thorough cleaning.

When Is a Semicolon Needed?

- To separate two independent clauses
- In a series to separate items containing commas

EDITING 2: PRACTICE ....

Edit the following sentences, using semicolons as necessary. Circle the number of any sentence that does not need semicolons.

1. Our vacation to New England included trips to Mystic, Connecticut, Ogunquit, Maine, Boston, Massachusetts, and Keene, New Hampshire.
2. Several different craft can be seen on the Charles River; including sculls rowed by students from the universities in the area, canoes, rowboats that can be rented for a small fee, and motorboats.
3. To learn about a new place quickly, obtain a detailed map of the area you plan to visit, walk to as many places as possible, always wearing shoes with good soles, and talk to the residents, provided they look friendly.

4. If you go to Boston's Museum of Fine Arts, don't miss the Paul Revere silver, the Egyptian mummies, the Athenian vases, and the terrific collection of paintings, including works by Gauguin, Degas, Monet, van Gogh, and Whistler.

5. In addition to its art collection, New England has been home to some of the greatest writers in America: Henry David Thoreau, who wrote *Walden,* Henry Wadsworth Longfellow, whose house on Brattle Street in Cambridge is a historic landmark, and Nathaniel Hawthorne, a resident of Salem, Massachusetts, and author of *The Scarlet Letter.*

EDITING 3: PRACTICE

Edit the following sentences by replacing any incorrectly used semicolons with the correct mark of punctuation or by rewording the sentence. Some sentences can be edited in more than one way. Circle the number of any sentence that is correct. Be ready to explain your editing choices.

1. Farley Mowat's books are not depressing though, they make one think about the role of humans in the universe.

2. His writing abounds with examples of the greedy nature of human beings; however, it does not convey a sense of helplessness.

3. Mowat clings to a spark of hope that it is not too late for humans to develop a respectful attitude toward our planet and the animals that inhabit it; although he regards humans as covetous.

4. A self-designated advocate for nonhuman animals, Mowat reveals the precariousness of the relationship between humans and animals; with unforgiving honesty for the most part.

5. He can be delightfully witty when he describes a positive, healthy relationship but also merciless when he condemns one; especially when it is destructive and exploitative.

6. After describing the harsh conditions in the village of Burgeo in the north of Newfoundland, he reveals the paradoxical lure of the place; abundant fish, seals, dolphins, and whales.

EDITING 4: PRACTICE

Edit the following passage, using semicolons correctly. More than one edited version is possible. Be ready to explain your editing choices.

Often students will not use the semicolon because they are unsure how to use it. They find the rules confusing; or hard to follow, or they have trouble applying the examples from textbooks to their own writing. Consequently, they avoid using semicolons whenever possible. A person does not have to be a professional writer, however, to use semicolons correctly. The following three rules might help; use semicolons between independent clauses when they are closely related, use semicolons to separate items in a complex series, and finally, do not use semicolons too often or your reader will think you don't know what you're doing—an important consideration; especially if you are writing for an instructor.

54

Colons

L ike the semicolon, the *colon* indicates a stop within a sentence. As a mark of introduction, the colon alerts the reader that the information preceding it is illustrated by what follows. The colon is also required as a mark of separation in certain other situations, such as in writing the time of day in numerals.

The colon is a strong and rather formal mark of punctuation. Be careful not to overuse it.

54 a Marks of introduction

Use a colon to introduce an example, explanation, list, or quotation. The colon must be preceded by an **independent clause,** one that contains a subject and a verb and can stand alone as a complete sentence.

An example or explanation can be a single word, a phrase, or a clause.

He has but one objective: success.

Much remains to be done: updating our computers, for example.

The budget agreement erected a wall between health care and education: no money was to be transferred between the two.

Capitalizing the first word of an independent clause following a colon is optional, but be consistent throughout a paper.

Use a colon to introduce a list that follows an independent clause. Frequently, an independent clause before a list will contain an expression such as *the following* or *as follows*.

Almost everything you buy travels to you by truck: paper products, food, medicine, even pickup trucks.

To complete the dish, proceed as follows: transfer the meat to a warm platter; arrange the cooked vegetables around it; ladle on some of the sauce, and sprinkle with chopped parsley.

A colon is used to introduce a quotation that is preceded by an independent clause.

As he left, he quoted Puck's final lines from *A Midsummer Night's Dream:* "Give me your hands, if we be friends, / And Robin shall restore amends."

Editing Misused Colons

In most sentences, a colon should follow only an independent clause. Otherwise, use other punctuation conventions.

- Eliminate a colon that comes between a verb and its object or complement.

   For lunch, he usually eats: fruit, salad, or yogurt.

   My favorite fruits are: peaches, grapes, and bananas.

- Delete any colon between a preposition and its object.

   She has traveled to: New Orleans, San Francisco, and Boston.

- Eliminate any colon that follows an introductory expression (*including, such as, like, for example,* etc.).

   The show displayed several unusual pets, including: iguanas, raccoons, a civet, and a black widow spider.

- Do not use more than one colon in a sentence.

   Wesley's visits always meant gifts: records, magazines, and books: ᵒᶠ pirate tales, mystery stories, and epic sagas.

However, use a comma, not a colon, before a quotation if the words preceding it do not constitute an independent clause.

As the song from *South Pacific* puts it, "You've got to be carefully taught."

(See Chapter 56 for more on punctuating quotations.)

A long quotation set off from the main text in block format may also be preceded by a colon. (See 56a2.)

54 b   Marks of separation

Between numerals expressing hours, minutes, and seconds

The winning car's official elapsed time was 2:45:56.

Between a main title and a subtitle

Blue Highways: A Journey into America

"A Deep Darkness: A Review of *Out of Africa*"

Between chapter and verse numbers in biblical citations

Isaiah 14:10–11

After business letter salutations and in memo headings

Dear Mr. Nader:

To:	Alex DiGiovanni
From:	Paul Gallerelli
Subject:	2007 budget

Colons are also used to separate elements in bibliographies and reference lists in research papers. (See Part Seven.)

EDITING 1: PRACTICE ....

Edit the following sentences, using colons correctly.

1. One thing is certain, the new crewmate on a whale watch always has to do the worst chores.

2. Given the terrible weather of the last few days, I was relieved by what I saw out in the distance, a nice, calm ocean.

3. I stepped on the deck and spoke these words from Melville's *Moby-Dick,* "Call me Ishmael."

4. The sight of my first whale made me think of Jonah 1.17–2.10.

5. Finally, I began the job I had been hired to do, preparing snacks and beverages in the galley.

6. We spotted various kinds of whales on the excursion, right whales, humpback whales, finback whales, and minke whales.

7. There is one thing whale watch enthusiasts should always remember to do, wear rubber-soled shoes.

8. The people on the deck wore clothes to keep them dry ponchos and garbage bags.

9. When we returned to land at 6.00, I wanted nothing more than to go home and sleep.

10. One more chore awaited me, however, scrubbing the slime off the sides of the boat.

chapter 55 | *Apostrophes*

T he *apostrophe,* used primarily to form the possessive of a noun or an indefinite pronoun, also indicates certain unusual plural forms and shows where a letter has been dropped in a contraction. (For this symbol's use as a single quotation mark, see Chapter 56.)

55 a Possessive nouns and indefinite pronouns

The **possessive case** of a noun or pronoun shows ownership or an association between that noun or pronoun and another word: *Sarah's book.*

Singular nouns

To form the possessive of any singular noun that does not end in *-s,* use an apostrophe and *-s.*

Denzel Washington's new movie is one of his best.

The *camera's* shutter speed is fixed.

For singular nouns ending in *-s,* it is always correct to form the possessive by adding both an apostrophe and *-s.* However, if pronouncing the

782

additional syllable is awkward—as with last names that sound like plurals—some writers add only an apostrophe.

Don't waste the *class's* time.

John Adams' [or *Adams's*] presidency was marked by crisis and conflict.

Plural nouns

For plural nouns ending in -*s,* add only an apostrophe to form the possessive.

They examined the structure of several *moths'* wings.

The *Mertzes'* apartment was beneath the *Ricardos'.*

For irregular plural nouns not ending in -*s,* form the possessive by adding an apostrophe and -*s.*

We studied the *media's* coverage of *children's* issues.

Compound nouns

Use an apostrophe and -*s* on only the last word to form the possessive of a hyphenated or unhyphenated compound noun.

He borrowed his *mother-in-law's* car.

The *secretary of state's* office certified the election results.

Two or more nouns

When nouns joined by *and* are considered a unit and are jointly in possession, add an apostrophe and -*s* to only the last noun.

My *aunt and uncle's* anniversary party was a disaster.

When nouns joined by *and* are considered individuals in separate possession, add an apostrophe and -*s* to each noun.

The documentary compared *Aretha Franklin's* and *Diana Ross's* early careers.

Using Apostrophes with Proper Nouns

Sometimes writers use apostrophes incorrectly with proper nouns. One common problem is the use of 's to form the plural of family names. Edit your papers to eliminate any apostrophes used to form nonpossessive plural nouns.

For more than forty years, the Kennedy/s have fascinated the American public.

    Thomases
The ~~Thomas's~~ live on Maple Street.

An apostrophe may seem to be called for in the names of certain companies, organizations, and publications that appear to include the possessive form of a noun. Check these names in a directory or in a copy of the publication in question to find out whether to use an apostrophe and, if one is required, whether the possessive noun is singular or plural. The following are a few examples of different treatments of the issue of possessive forms in proper names:

    Bloomingdale's
    Publishers Weekly
    Reader's Digest
    Saks Fifth Avenue
    Service Employees International Union

Indefinite pronouns

An **indefinite pronoun** is a pronoun that does not refer to any specific person or thing, *someone, anybody, no one, one, another.* Use an apostrophe and *-s* to form the possessive case of some indefinite pronouns.

Someone's umbrella was left in the assembly hall.

It is *no one's* business but mine.

Do not use an apostrophe and *-s* to form the possessive of the indefinite pronouns *all, any, both, each, few, many, most, much, several, some,* and *such.* Indicate the possessive by using a preposition such as *of,* or use a pronoun that has a possessive form.

                                     the
For the Dickinson and Crane seminar, we must read ~~both's~~
      of both.
complete works.

everyone's
Unfortunately, we cannot respond to ~~each's~~ questions.
                                                              ^

EDITING 1: PRACTICE ....

Edit the following sentences, using apostrophes correctly to form the possessive forms of nouns and indefinite pronouns. Circle the number of any sentence that is correct.

1. Some people believe that students' test scores have fallen in recent years.
2. In fact, high school juniors and seniors scores on many commercial achievement tests are higher than they have ever been.
3. It seems that the medias need to report negative news is a large factor in leading people to believe that young peoples' knowledge today is not as great as it was in the past.
4. What older people do not always realize is that no ones knowledge of the world at eighteen is as comprehensive as it will be after another ten or twenty or thirty year's worth of learning.
5. Many also do not consider that student's work today is generally more advanced than in the past, particularly in the sciences.
6. Todays' high school biology textbooks, for example, include lessons on DNA, RNA, gene splicing, and biochemical engineering.
7. During my mother and father's high school years, such subjects were reserved for college or even graduate school.
8. Even in terms of history and geography, areas in which the current generations knowledge has been shown to be weak, critic's reports of declining standards seem to be exaggerated.
9. A 1943 survey of college freshmen found that even elite students knew nothing at all about Thomas Jefferson and Abraham Lincoln's presidencies and could not identify the Mississippi River's location on a map!

....

55 b   Plurals of words used as words, letters, numbers, and symbols

Use an apostrophe and -*s* to form the plural of a word used as a word.

Analysis reveals more *the*'s than *and*'s in most writing.

Also use an apostrophe and an -*s* to form the plural of letters, numerals, and symbols.

Tic-tac-toe is played on a grid with *x*'s and *o*'s.

We have no size *8*'s in that style but five size *10*'s.

Today most telephone dial pads include #'s and ✳'s.

A word, number, or letter used this way is usually set off by italics or underlining. (See 61d.) However, note that the apostrophe and the -*s* in the plural form are not italicized or underlined.

To form the plural of centuries and decades, you may use an apostrophe and -*s* or an -*s* alone, as long as you are consistent. (The Modern Language Association prefers an -*s* alone.) Do not use an apostrophe when the century or decade is expressed in words.

the 1800s (*or* the 1800's)

the '60s (*or* the '60's) *but* the sixties

(See 55c2 for the use of the apostrophe to indicate omitted digits in a year.)

For plurals of abbreviations ending with periods, use an apostrophe and -*s*. Use -*s* alone for abbreviations without periods.

My science professor has earned two Ph.D.'s.

Like all politicians, she has some IOUs.

(See Chapter 62 for more on abbreviations.)

55 c Omission of letters

1 Contractions

Apostrophes can indicate that letters have been omitted from a word. A **contraction** shortens two words into one by replacing one or more letters with an apostrophe. The following list shows the correct use of the apostrophe in some common contractions:

cannot	can't	will not	won't
do not	don't	would not	wouldn't
does not	doesn't	was not	wasn't
she would	she'd	it is	it's
who is	who's	you are	you're
I am	I'm	they are	they're
let us	let's	we have	we've
there is	there's	he has, he is	he's

Contractions help to create a friendly conversational tone (which is why we've used them in this book). But because of their informality, contractions are not appropriate for most academic writing.

2 Omitted letters in colloquial expressions and digits in a year

Apostrophes also can indicate omitted letters in certain colloquial expressions and omitted digits in a year.

spic 'n' span   rock 'n' roll   the class of '99

An apostrophe is not used, however, when digits are omitted from the second year in a range of years: *Rembrandt van Rijn (1606–69)*.

Pronouns and Apostrophes

Pronouns do not use apostrophes—as nouns do—in the possessive form. For example, the possessive of *she* is *hers* (not *her's*), and the possessive of *they* is *theirs* (not *their's*).

When pronouns appear with apostrophes, they form contractions, such as *it's* for *it is* and *I'll* for *I will*. If you want to use a contraction, remember to include the apostrophe, or you may produce a totally different word from the one you intend. For example, *I'll* becomes *Ill* without the apostrophe.

The possessive pronouns *its, whose, your,* and *their* sound like the contractions *it's, who's, you're,* and *they're,* so be especially careful to choose the form that expresses your intended meaning.

A good test is to substitute the spelled-out form of the word whenever you see a pronoun with an apostrophe in your writing. (Consider using the search function on your computer to locate apostrophes.) If the result makes no sense, then you have incorrectly used a contraction.

The storm was brief, but it's [it is] *its* effects were devastating.

She is the candidate who's [who is] *whose* views most reflect my own.

3 Letters omitted to show pronunciation

Writers sometimes use apostrophes in dialogue to indicate letters omitted from certain words, suggesting the speaker's pronunciation.

"Courtin' was diff'rent in my day," the old man said.

Plural and Possessive Forms

Singular	Singular Possessive	Plural	Plural Possessive
school	school's	schools	schools'
box	box's	boxes	boxes'
class	class's	classes	classes'
Duvalier	Duvalier's	Duvaliers	Duvaliers'
Jones	Jones's	Joneses	Joneses'

When spoken, the plural, the singular possessive, and the plural possessive sound the same for most words. In writing, the spelling and the placement of the apostrophe help readers distinguish among the three forms.

Apostrophe or No Apostrophe?

WHAT NEEDS AN APOSTROPHE?

- Possessive cases of nouns or indefinite pronouns: *Janey's* book, *somebody's* dog.
- Plurals of words used as words, numbers, letters, symbols: *if's, Ph.D.'s, A's, $'s.*
- Contractions: *Who's* coming? *We're* late. *It's* raining.

WHAT CAN'T HAVE AN APOSTROPHE?

- Personal pronouns: *you, yours; she, hers; he, his; it, its; we, ours; they, theirs.*
- Relative pronouns: *that, which, who, whose.*
- Interrogative pronouns: *Whose* are these?
- Demonstrative pronouns: *this, these, that, those.*
- Reflexive pronouns: The hunters found *themselves* lost in the fog. I consider *myself* honest.

EDITING 2: PRACTICE

Edit the following sentences, using apostrophes correctly to form contractions.

1. If your a fan of the outdoors, youll enjoy exploring the Hudson River Valley, which isnt far from New York City.
2. In the summer, a boat will take passengers from the city to Bear Mountain, where hiking enthusiasts wont be disappointed.

3. The views from the mountain's 1300-foot summit cant be surpassed; youll see wilderness stretching out before your eyes in every direction.
4. A trip to the country wouldnt be complete without a stop at Buddy's Café n Deli.
5. Similarly, you shouldnt visit Hyde Park without stopping by FDR's country home, which has been preserved as it was when he died in 45.
6. Both the Hudson River Valley and New York City offer plenty to do for the outdoor buff whos interested in stunning scenery, fine hiking, and rich history.

EDITING 3: PRACTICE

Edit the following sentences, being careful to distinguish plurals, contractions, and possessives.

1. Charles Dicken's brief experience of a debtor's prison with it's deplorable conditions had a profound effect on him.
2. Its perhaps surprising to learn that Dickens didn't start out as a novelist; instead, he trained as a lawyer's clerk.
3. The author, who's literary career began during the 1830s, started out writing for magazines' under the pseudonym "Boz."
4. Society's evil, corruption, and crime were concerns to Dickens, and their frequently found as themes throughout his novel's.
5. They're style and structure were affected by the fact that Dickens wrote his novel's for publication in monthly installments.
6. Dickens's first novel, *Pickwick Papers,* was illustrated by a popular artist, who's plates contributed to the success of the work.

EDITING 4: EXPLORATION

During the next week, keep your eye out for what you consider mistakes in the use of apostrophes, and write down any that you find. Look in newspapers, in magazines, on billboards, on the sides of commercial vehicles, on storefronts, and in television advertising. Do these mistakes make any difference in how the words are read and understood? What would be the advantages or disadvantages of leaving out apostrophes?

Edit the following passage, using apostrophes correctly.

The computer industrys' most important "enhancement" these days may be many software companies expansion of they're call-in help desks. With the enormous growth in the number of computer owners' over the past five years has come a corresponding growth in those owners need for truly helpful technical support, particularly considering that the average first-time buyer of a computer today has very little understanding of it's operation or functions. Just a few years ago, most companies technical support staff's consisted only of technicians and computer experts, who's attitude often suggested that a customers' questions were too stupid to be taken seriously, implying that "the problem is yours' not our's." Worse, their advice could be so technical that it's usefulness to customers was almost nonexistent. Today, however, companies are beginning to realize that ones success in an increasingly competitive market will depend on good customer service. Now when all those *Es* for "Error" appear on a users' screen, real help will be only a telephone call away.

chapter 56

Quotation Marks

Using another person's exact words is called **direct quotation.** When you quote directly, you must tell readers you are doing so by indicating the source and by enclosing the person's exact words in quotation marks (or by setting off long quotations). Restating someone else's idea in your own words is called **paraphrasing** or **indirect quotation.** When quoting indirectly, you still must identify the source, but do not use quotation marks.

Quotation marks are also used to distinguish certain words, such as titles, from the main body of the text. Italics are used for this purpose as well. (See 61a.)

The guidelines for presenting quotations vary somewhat from discipline to discipline. This chapter follows the conventions of the Modern Language Association, the style for papers written in the languages and literature. (For information on this and other disciplinary styles, see Chapters 29–34.)

Using Quotation Marks

Quotation marks are like shoes: use them in pairs. In written American English, there are two types of quotation marks: **double quotation marks** (" ") which identify quotations, titles, and so on, and **single quotation marks** (' ') which identify quotations within quotations (or titles within titles). In print and in handwriting, a distinction is made in the direction of the curve between an opening quotation mark (") and a closing quotation mark ("). Many word processing programs automatically set opening and closing quotation marks using the same key. However, most typewriters use the same straight quotation mark or marks at both ends of a quotation.

56   a   Direct quotations

The conventions are different for using quotation marks when quoting short passages and long ones. (See examples in Chapter 27.)

1 Short passages

Use quotation marks to enclose brief quotations, those from one word up to four typed lines of prose or three lines of poetry. If a parenthetical citation of the source is provided, place it after the closing quotation marks but before the period or other punctuation. (See 56e for advice about using other punctuation marks with quotation marks.)

> Boswell calls this relationship a "collateral adoption," a term
>
> other experts do not use (97).

> In *Lives Under Siege,* Ratzenburger argues that "most
>
> adolescents are far too worried about the next six months and
>
> far too unconcerned about the next sixty years" (84).

When quoting poetry, use a slash preceded and followed by a single space to indicate line breaks. (See 57e.)

> Shakespeare concludes Sonnet 18 with this couplet: "So long as
>
> men can breathe or eyes can see, / So long lives this, and this
>
> gives life to thee."

Forgetting the quotation marks at the end of a quotation is a common typographical error, so check for these carefully as you edit.

2 Long passages

Longer direct quotations are set off from the main text in **block format.** Start a new line for the quotation; indent all lines of the quotation one inch or ten spaces, and do not use quotation marks. If the signal phrase introducing a block quotation form a complete sentence, they are usually followed by a colon, although a period is also acceptable. (See 54a.) If the signal phrase does not constitute a complete sentence, a comma or no punctuation at all is used, depending on context. If a parenthetical citation of the source is provided, place it two spaces after the final punctuation.

A recent editorial describes the problem:

> In countries like the United States, breastfeeding, though
> always desirable, doesn't mean the difference between
> good and poor nutrition—or life and death. But it does in
> developing countries, where for decades infant food
> manufacturers have been distributing free samples of infant
> formulas to hospitals and birthing centers. (<u>Daily Times</u> 17)

The editorial goes on to argue that the samples last only long
enough for the mothers' own milk to dry up; then the
mothers find they cannot afford to buy the formula.

A single paragraph or part of a paragraph in block format does not use a
paragraph indent. For two or more quoted paragraphs, the first line of each
new paragraph after the first is indented three additional spaces.

When quoting poetry, reproduce as precisely as possible the line breaks,
indents, spacing, and capitalization of the original.

> Lawrence Ferlinghetti's poem opens with a striking image of
> the poet's work:
>
> > Constantly risking absurdity
> >   and death
> >   whenever he performs
> >   above the heads
> >   of his audience
> >   the poet like an acrobat
> >   climbs on rime
> >   to a high wire of his own making

If a quotation appears within a quotation, use single quotation marks
for the inner quotation.

> After the election, the incumbent said, "My opponent will soon
> learn, as someone once said, 'You can't fool all of the people all
> of the time.' "

If a quotation appears within a quotation that is displayed in block format, and that therefore is not within quotation marks, use double quotation marks for the inner quotation.

56 b   Dialogue

Use quotation marks when reproducing dialogue, whether real or fictional. Start a new paragraph to show every change of speaker. Once the pattern is established, readers can tell who is speaking even if not every quotation has attributory words.

> "Early parole is not the solution to overcrowding," the prosecutor said. "We need a new jail."
>
> The chairman of the county commission asked, "How do you propose we pay for it?"
>
> "Increase taxes if you must, but whatever you do, act quickly."

If one speaker's words continue for more than a single paragraph, use quotation marks at the beginning of each new paragraph but at the end of only the last paragraph.

(See 52h for advice about using commas to set off attributions.)

EDITING 1: PRACTICE

Edit the following sentences, using quotation marks correctly with brief direct quotations.

1. Remembering a trip with her parents in 1947, black American poet Audre Lorde writes in her memoir, *Zami,* The first time I went to Washington, D.C., was on the edge of the summer when I was supposed to stop being a child.
2. "Preparations were in the air around our house before school was even over, she recalls. We packed for a week."
3. Once in Washington, Lorde remembers, I spent the whole next day after Mass squinting up at the Lincoln Memorial where Marian Anderson had sung after the D.A.R. refused to allow her to sing in their auditorium because she was Black. Or because she was "Colored," my father said as he told me the story. Except that what he probably said was "Negro," because for his times, my father was quite progressive.
4. Lorde goes on to observe that later in the evening, "The family stopped for a dish of vanilla ice cream at a Breyer's ice cream and soda fountain.

5. When the waitress first spoke, they didn't understand her, so then, writes Lorde, "The waitress moved along the line of us closer to my father and spoke again. 'I said I kin give you to take out, but you can't eat here. Sorry.'"

6. The young Lorde's feelings about this casual racism in the nation's capital seems to be summarized by the first lines of a poem she wrote many years later: There are so many roots to the tree of anger / that sometimes the branches shatter / before they bear.

EDITING 2: APPLICATION

Look through some of your recent papers and locate a passage that could have been written in dialogue. Edit the passage to turn it into dialogue, following the guidelines described in this section.

---

56 c Titles

Use quotation marks for titles of brief poems, short stories, essays, book chapters and parts, magazine and journal articles, episodes of television series, and songs. (Italics are used to indicate titles of longer works such as books, magazines, journals, television series, recordings, films and plays. See 61a.)

> "Araby" is the third story in James Joyce's book *Dubliners*.

> This chart appeared with the article "Will Your Telephone Last?" in November's *Consumer Reports*.

> In my favorite episode of *I Love Lucy*, "Job Switching," Lucy and Ethel work in a chocolate factory.

If the title of a part of a work or series is generic rather than specific—for example, Chapter 8—do not use either quotation marks or italics.

Use single quotation marks to indicate quoted material that is part of a title enclosed in double quotation marks.

> We read "'This Is the End of the World': The Black Death" by historian Barbara Tuchman.

Titles are indicated by quotation marks only in text, so do not put quotation marks around the title at the beginning of your own essay, poem, or story. However, use quotation marks wherever your title includes a quotation or title.

An Analysis of the "My Turn" Column in *Newsweek*

Titles Within Titles

Use the following models when presenting titles within other titles. These same guidelines apply to other words that normally are indicated by quotation marks or italics (such as foreign words or quotations) when they appear in titles.

■ A title enclosed in quotation marks within an italicized title

"A Curtain of Green" and Other Stories

■ An italicized title within a title enclosed in quotation marks

"Morality in *Death of a Salesman*"

■ A title enclosed in quotation marks within another title enclosed in quotation marks

"Symbolism in 'Everyday Use' "

■ An italicized title within another italicized title

Modern Critics on Hamlet *and Other Plays*

(For more on using italics, see Chapter 61.)

EDITING 3: PRACTICE

Edit the following sentences, using quotation marks correctly with titles. Circle the number of any sentence that is correct.

1. Jeff read a review of *Sunset Boulevard* in The Theater, a column in *The New Yorker* magazine, and he wants to see the play tonight.

2. Jan prefers to stay at home and finish reading *A View from the Woods,* one of the stories in Flannery O'Connor's *Everything That Rises Must Converge.*

3. As usual, Kim will be watching *Star Trek* reruns on television. Her favorite episode is Who Mourns for Adonis?

4. Erik will spend the evening reading "Why I Write," an essay that Orwell wrote the year after he published his novel *Animal Farm.*

5. Alan wants to stay home and study Thomas Hardy's poem *At the Word "Farewell."*

6. Jeff decides to stay at home and listen to his jazz records. He always turns up the volume when the song *Basin Street Blues* comes on.

---

56 d   Translations, special terms, irony, and nicknames

1 Translations

When a word or phrase from another language is translated into English, the translation may be enclosed in quotation marks. The original word or phrase is italicized. (See 61d.)

> I've always called Antonio *fratellino,* or "little brother," because he is twelve years younger than I.

2 Specialized terms

A specialized term or new coinage is often introduced in quotation marks when it is first defined.

> The ecology of this "chryocore"—a region of perpetual ice and snow—has been studied very little.

3 Irony

You may indicate that you are using a word in an **ironic** sense—that is, with a meaning opposed to its literal one—by putting the word in quotation marks; but use this technique sparingly in academic writing.

> Jonathan Swift's essay "A Modest Proposal" offers a quick "solution" to Ireland's poverty and overpopulation: eat the children.

4 Nicknames

An unusual nickname may be enclosed in quotation marks at first mention, particularly when it is introduced as part of the full name.

> When I joined the firm, the president was a man named Garnett E. "Ding" Cannon.

56   e   With other punctuation

1 Periods and commas

Periods and commas go inside quotation marks.

Juliet Schor refers to "the rise of what some have called 'postmaterialist values.'"

Note that the period or comma goes inside both single and double quotation marks.

2 Colons and semicolons

Colons and semicolons go outside quotation marks.

The sign read "Closed": there would be no sodas for us.

Willie Nelson wrote "Crazy"; Patsy Cline made the most famous recording of it.

3 Question marks, exclamation points, and dashes

Question marks, exclamation points, and dashes go inside the quotation marks if they are part of the quotation or title.

Dr. King asked, "How does one determine whether a law is just or unjust?"

Robert Frost's famous poem "Out, Out—" was published in 1916.

When they are not part of the quotation or title but rather apply to the whole sentence, these marks go outside the quotation marks.

Who invented the expression "Have a nice day"?

To make matters worse, from the altar the bride sang "I Got You, Babe"!

When both the quoted material and the sentence as a whole require one of these marks, use only the question mark or exclamation point inside the quotation marks. (See 51b, 51c.)

Was it Rodney King who asked, "Why can't we all just get along?"

If the logic of a sentence dictates that a quotation end with a question mark or an exclamation point but sentence grammar calls for a period or comma as well, use the stronger mark (the question mark or exclamation point) and delete the weaker one (the period or comma).

As soon as we heard someone shout "Fire!"ʲ we began to run for the exit.

4 Parentheses and brackets

Parentheses and brackets can be used to indicate comments on or alterations to a quotation. Words that are not part of the quotation are set off in parentheses when they are *outside* the quotation marks and in brackets when they are *within* the quotation marks.

For example, you may add italics for emphasis in a quotation, but always indicate that you have done so by enclosing the phrase "italics added" in brackets at the end of the passage, after the closing quotation mark but before the period.

According to this study, in 1992 "the *average* major league baseball player earned more than $1 million a year" [italics added].

(For examples of bracketed material within quotations, see 57d.)

EDITING 4: PRACTICE ....

Edit the following sentences, adding quotation marks as needed and making sure that they, as well as other punctuation marks, are used correctly.

1. No matter how many times you say it, Christie, Malcolm said, I still can't accept the idea that international law should have no bearing on how nations act.
2. "Wait a minute"! she retorted. That's not what I said at all.
3. Well, what did you say, then? Malcolm asked.
4. "My point, Christie said, is that a government can't allow itself to be constrained from acting to preserve its interests without some kind of guarantee that other countries won't take advantage of the opportunity".

5. But that's what international law is designed to do, isn't it? Clearly, there's an element of self-interest in any collective security arrangement, he argued, but that doesn't mean that there are no restraints on that interest.

6. "That's true", she replied, wearily. "But sometimes"—wait, let me finish"—governments use international law as a smokescreen. Besides, she continued, you have to admit that powerful countries are more likely to get what they want in the United Nations or the World Court."

7. I'm not so sure, Malcolm mused, grinning. I guess I'm just not as cynical as you are.

8. "Spare me, she replied, and will you stop jabbering and help me fix this flat"?

....

EDITING 5: PRACTICE ....

Edit the following passage to make sure that quotation marks and related punctuation are used correctly.

Tennessee Williams's play "The Glass Menagerie" opens with the character Tom speaking directly to the audience: "Yes, I have tricks in my pocket, I have things up my sleeve." "But I am the opposite of a stage magician." This opening monologue serves to set the stage for the story to come. "I am the narrator of the play, continues Tom, "and also a character in it. The other characters are my mother, Amanda, my sister, Laura, and a gentleman caller who appears in the final scenes." Amanda is an aging "Southern belle" living with her two adult children in a dingy St. Louis apartment and desperate to find a match for her daughter. Crippled and painfully shy, Laura often retreats to a fantasy world of glass animal figurines and old songs like Dardanella and La Golondrina played on a scratchy Victrola. When asked by Amanda how many gentleman callers are expected one afternoon, Laura replies "I don't believe we're going to receive any, Mother. "Not one gentleman caller?, Amanda exclaims. "It can't be true! There must be a flood, there must have been a tornado"! When Amanda enlists Tom to bring home a potential "beau" for Laura, the gentleman caller turns out to be a former high school classmate, Jim, whose nickname for Laura was Blue Roses. "Whenever he saw me, Laura recalls at one point, he'd holler, "Hello, Blue Roses!" Jim is already engaged, however, a situation that leads to a climactic confrontation between Amanda and Tom.

....

chapter **57** | *Other Punctuation*

Parentheses, dashes, ellipsis points, brackets, and slashes each have specific functions in sentences, and using them appropriately can bring extra polish to your writing. Use them sparingly, however, and for specific purposes. (For the correct use of hyphens, see Chapter 60.)

57 a Parentheses

Parentheses can enclose **parenthetical expressions,** elements that would otherwise interrupt a sentence: explanations, examples, asides, and supplementary information. They are also used to set off cross-references, citations, and numbers in a list.

1 Enclosing explanations, examples, and asides

In setting off explanations, examples, and asides, writers often have the choice using commas, parentheses, or dashes. (For a comparison, see the box in 57b.) Because parentheses tend to de-emphasize what they enclose, use them for material that is not essential to the meaning of the sentence or to the point being made.

> Current Hollywood stars whose parents were stars include Anjelica Houston (daughter of John) and Michael Douglas (son of Kirk).

801

Speaking little English (he had immigrated to the United States only a few months earlier), my grandfather found his first job in a tuna-packing factory.

Parentheses may also be used to enclose dates, a brief translation, abbreviations, or initials.

The Oxford English Dictionary was first published under the editorship of James A. H. Murray (1888–1933).

English also borrowed the Dutch word *koekje* ("cookie").

The North American Free Trade Agreement (NAFTA) continues to spark controversy.

2 Enclosing cross-references and citations

Use parentheses to enclose cross-references to other parts of your paper and to identify references and sources for quotations.

The map (p. 4) shows the areas of heaviest rainfall.

Nick Carraway felt unsettled to see Gatsby at the end of his dock beckoning in the direction of a "single green light" (21).

(See 56a and Chapters 30–34 for more about citing sources for quotations.)

3 Enclosing numbers or letters in a list

Use parentheses to enclose numbers or letters that introduce items in a list within a sentence.

The dictionary provides (1) pronunciation, (2) etymology, (3) past meanings, and (4) usage citations for almost 300,000 words.

4 Using other punctuation with parentheses

When information within parentheses is not a complete sentence, end punctuation appears outside the final parenthesis, thereby punctuating the sentence as a whole.

The strikers protested the company's practice of buying parts from other companies (outsourcing).

When one complete sentence is enclosed in parentheses but stands alone, the end punctuation is placed inside the final parenthesis, and the first word is capitalized.

> The damage caused by the storm is estimated at $1.5 million. (This figure does not include the costs of emergency medical aid.)

When a complete sentence enclosed by parentheses falls within another sentence, the first word is not capitalized, and no period is used. A question mark or exclamation mark may be used for effect.

> The damage caused by the storm (estimates run as high as $1.5 million) was the worst in more than three decades.

> After a visit to Buffalo (how can people there stand the cold weather?), it was a relief to return to the South.

A comma never comes directly before a set of parentheses. If a comma is required by the sentence structure, place it directly after the parentheses.

> **Working for the minimum wage, ($2.30 an hour at the time) I had very little money to spare.**

(For the use of brackets with direct quotations, see 56e4.)

EDITING 1: PRACTICE ....

Edit the following sentences, inserting parentheses where appropriate, deleting unnecessary parentheses, and correcting any nonstandard use of other punctuation with parentheses. (You may need to make other changes in punctuation.) Some sentences can be edited in more than one way. Be ready to explain the changes you made.

1. Buddhism is a religion and philosophy that was founded in India around 535 B.C.E. by Siddhartha Gautama, who is called Buddha "the Enlightened One".
2. Other names for Buddha are the Tathagata, "he who has come thus," Bhagavat, "the Lord," and Sugata, "well-gone."
3. Tradition has it that Gautama, also spelled Gotama, was born a prince but renounced the world at age twenty-nine to seek to understand the inevitability of human suffering.
4. Eventual spiritual enlightenment led him to the "four noble truths" of Buddhism: 1 existence is suffering; 2 suffering is caused by attachment

to the physical world; 3 the suffering humans experience can cease; 4 the path to release from suffering involves eight stages of thinking and behavior.

5. For the next forty-five years, (He was thirty-five when he reached enlightenment.) Buddha traveled and taught his doctrine to a growing number of disciples.

6. Central to the practice of Buddhism are meditation (and adherence to a set of clearly defined moral precepts).

7. These moral precepts, for example, injunctions against taking life, stealing, and dishonesty, continue to provide a primary basis of Buddhist practice.

---

57 b   Dashes

Dashes serve many of the same purposes as parentheses—that is, they set off explanations, examples, asides, and supplementary information that would otherwise interrupt the meaning of the sentence. However, dashes tend to emphasize the material they set off rather than subordinate it, as parentheses do. Dashes can also be used to highlight contrast and to indicate interruptions and changes in tone. Because dashes break the flow of a sentence, use them sparingly.

In word processing, use two hyphens with no space on either side to create a dash.

> A dash--when you use one--should look like this.

Note that unlike a single parenthesis, a dash can be used singly to set off material at the end of a sentence.

1 Dashes for explanations, examples, and asides

She donates a considerable sum to Georgetown University—her alma mater—every year.

At first we did not notice the rain—it began so softly—but soon we were soaked through.

Of all the oddities in Richard's apartment, the contents of the bathtub—transistors, resistors, circuit boards, and odd bits of wire—were the strangest of all.

2 Dashes to emphasize contrast

The restaurant is known for its excellent food—and its astronomical prices.

3 Dashes to indicate a pause, interruption, or change of tone

"Well, I guess I was a little late—OK, an hour late," I admitted.

"Hold on," she shouted, "while I grab this—"

4 Dashes with other marks of punctuation

If the words enclosed by dashes within a sentence form a sentence, do not capitalize the first word of the inner sentence or use a period. If the enclosed sentence is a question or an exclamation, you may use a question mark or an exclamation point, but do not capitalize the first word.

Ward and June Cleaver—who can forget their orderly world?—never once question their roles in life.

Choosing Commas, Parentheses, or Dashes

Commas, parentheses, and dashes can all be used to set off nonessential material within a sentence.

■ Use **commas** when the material being set off is closely related to the rest of the sentence. (See Chapter 52.)

A dusty plow, the kind the early Amish settlers used, hung on the wall of the old barn.

■ Use **parentheses** when the material being set off is not closely related to the main sentence and when you want to de-emphasize it. (See 57a.)

Two young boys found an old plow (perhaps as old as the first Amish settlement) hidden in an unused corner of the barn.

■ Use **dashes** when material being set off is not closely related to the main sentence but you want to emphasize it. (See 57b.)

The old plow—one his great-grandfather had used—was still in good working order.

Do not use a comma or a period immediately before or after a dash.

My cousin Eileen—she is from Ireland,—brought a strange flute with her when she came to visit.

With so many things happening at once—graduation, a new job—, Marcelle felt she had become a different person.

Avoid using more than two dashes in a sentence.

He never told his father about his dreams—he couldn't explain them—but silently began to make plans—plans that would one day lead him away from this small town.

EDITING 2: PRACTICE

Edit the following passage, deleting dashes where they are not effective. More than one edited version is possible. Be ready to explain your editing choices.

Jamaica Kincaid's most openly opinionated—and, to my mind, best—book—*A Small Place*—is a social critique of her home island—Antigua. In this book, her voice—humble yet strong, and sometimes filled with anger—speaks for her people. Her feelings—stemming from years of living in Antigua in the aftermath of British imperialism—are expressed in a simple—yet beautiful—manner.

57 c Ellipsis points

Ellipsis points are three periods, each preceded and followed by a space. They are used to mark an **ellipsis,** any deliberate omission of words from a direct quotation. Quotations are often shortened either to make a passage more emphatic or to achieve a usable length, but writers must be careful, when deleting portions of quotations, not to change the original passage's meaning. (See 27e.)

Consider the following paragraph from Betty Edwards's *Drawing on the Right Side of the Brain:*

Drawing is not really very difficult. *Seeing* is the problem, or, to be more specific, *shifting to a particular way of seeing.* You may not believe me at this moment. You may feel that you are seeing things just fine and that it's the drawing that is hard. But the opposite is true, and the exercises in this book are designed to help you make the mental shift and gain a twofold advantage: first, to open access by *conscious volition* to the right side of your brain in order to experience a slightly altered mode of awareness; second, to see things in a different way. Both will enable you to draw well.

Use ellipsis points to indicate an omission within a sentence.

Edwards tells the reader, "You may feel . . . that it's the drawing that is hard."

If an omission comes at the end of a complete sentence, include the period or other end punctuation before the ellipsis points.

Edwards addresses the reader directly with a provocative assertion: "Drawing is not really very difficult. . . . You may not believe me at this moment."

Likewise, if you end the quotation before the end of the original sentence, include a period before the ellipsis. (Note that in such cases, there is no space between the last quoted word and the period or between the final ellipsis point and the closing quotation mark.)

In Edwards's view, "Drawing is not really very difficult. *Seeing* is the problem. . . ."

However, when parenthetical documentation is included after a quote ending with an ellipsis, the period follows the parentheses.

Betty Edwards writes, "Drawing is not really very difficult. *Seeing* is the problem . . ." (2).

Ellipsis points are not necessary when what you quote is obviously not a complete sentence.

Edwards offers the reader paths to "a slightly altered mode of awareness."

If you omit a whole line or more when quoting poetry, indicate the omission by using ellipsis points for the length of a line.

She walks in beauty, like the night
. . . .
And all that's best of dark and bright
Meet in her aspect and her eyes.

In dialogue, ellipsis points can indicate a hesitation or a trailing off of speech, and in informal writing they may be used to create a pause for dramatic effect.

> I could only stammer, "What I mean is . . . well. . . ."

> For a moment there was silence . . . followed by a rush as the cat bolted from the underbrush.

EDITING 3: PRACTICE

Using ellipsis points, edit the following paragraph to shorten it for a paper on racism. More than one edited version is possible. Be ready to explain your editing choices.

> Until we label an out-group it does not clearly exist in our minds. Take the curiously vague situation that we often meet when a person wishes to locate responsibility on the shoulders of some out-group whose nature he cannot specify. In such a case he usually employs the pronoun "they" without an antecedent. "Why don't they make these sidewalks wider?" "I hear they are going to build a factory in this town and hire a lot of foreigners." "I won't pay this tax bill; they can just whistle for their money." If asked "who?" the speaker is likely to grow confused and embarrassed. The common use of the orphaned pronoun they teaches us that people often want and need to designate out-groups (usually for the purpose of venting hostility) even when they have no clear conception of the out-group in question. And so long as the target of wrath remains vague and ill-defined specific prejudice cannot crystallize around it. To have enemies we need labels.
>
> GORDON ALLPORT, "THE LANGUAGE OF PREJUDICE"

57 d   Brackets

Brackets are used to enclose words that are added to or changed within direct quotations. (See 27e.) They can also enclose comments about quotations and about material that is already inside parentheses. (If your typewriter or word processor does not have brackets, you can write them in by hand.)

Consider this passage from an article titled "Interview with a Sparrow" by E. B. White:

> As yet the onset of Spring is largely gossip among the sparrows. Any noon, in Madison Square, you may see one pick up a straw in his beak, put on an air of great business, twisting his head and glancing at the sky. Nothing comes of it. He hops three or four times and drops both the straw and the incident.

In quoting from this passage, it would be permissible to make small changes in order to clarify a pronoun reference, to add an explanatory phrase, or to make the quoted words read correctly within the context of the new sentence.

> E. B. White describes just such a spring day: "Any noon, in Madison Square, you may see [a sparrow] pick up a straw in his beak, [and] put on an air of great business, twisting his head and glancing at the sky."

> E. B. White describes a sparrow on a spring day: "Any noon, in Madison Square [in New York City], you may see one pick up a straw in his beak, [and] put on an air of great business, twisting his head and glancing at the sky."

> White concludes by noting that the bird "[hopped] three or four times and [dropped] both the straw and the incident."

ESL *Placement of Punctuation*

Only a few kinds of punctuation can begin a line of text in English.

Ellipsis points: ...

Opening quotation mark: "

Opening parenthesis: (

Opening bracket: [

All other types of punctuation should be placed within or at the end of a line. However, an opening quotation mark, an opening parenthesis, or an opening bracket may not be placed at the end of a line.

If you are using a word processing program, it will avoid most problems for you automatically, as long as you have not incorrectly inserted a space before or after a mark of punctuation.

Brackets are also used to change capitalization in the original quotation to make it correct in the new sentence.

> The fact that "[n]othing comes of it" is, for White, what makes the sparrow's activity worth noting.

Brackets can be used to indicate a spelling or punctuation error in quoted material that was present in the original. By enclosing the word *sic* (Latin for "such") in brackets directly after the error, you inform the reader that you see the error but are not responsible for it.

> In its statement, the commission said that its new health insurance program "will not effect [sic] the quality of medical care for county employees."

Within parentheses, use brackets to avoid double parentheses.

> (These findings are summarized in Table C [p. 12].)

EDITING 4: PRACTICE ....

Edit the following passage, using brackets correctly.

> According to the findings of a new study, people who smoke may be hurting not only themselves. "It (tobacco smoke) can be just as detrimental to nonsmokers as to smokers," a spokesperson for the study told reporters. "In fact, secondhand smoke may be even more dangerous," she added, "since they (nonsmokers) are inhaling it without a filter." This latest finding adds to the growing list of the dangers of cigarette smoking. (See related article on the effects of smoking on fetal development (p. 14).)

....

57 e   Slashes

A *slash* (/) is a slanted line, also known as a *solidus* or *virgule*. Use a slash, preceded and followed by a space, to mark the end of a line of poetry incorporated in text.

> Shakespeare opens *The Passionate Pilgrim* with a seeming paradox: "When my love swears that she is made of truth, / I do believe her, though I know she lies."

(See 56a for more on quoting poetry.)

Use a slash with no space before or after it in some common expressions indicating alternatives.

either/or proposition   pass/fail system   true/false test

When possible, however, in most formal writing use a conjunction and hyphens between the alternatives rather than a slash.

                      win-or-lose
A small business can be a ~~win/lose~~ investment.
                                    ^

In particular, the slashed alternatives *and / or, he / she,* and *s / he* are considered inappropriate for writing in the humanities.

    Also use a slash without spaces to separate numerals when they represent the parts of a date (*1 / 3 / 02*) and the numerator and denominator in a fraction (*1 / 2*). (In typescript, use a hyphen to separate a whole number from its fraction: *2-1 / 2*) Some word processing programs recognize 1/2 as a fraction and set a special character: $\frac{1}{2}$.

EDITING 5: PRACTICE

Edit the following paragraph, using parentheses, dashes, and brackets correctly. (You may have to alter some other punctuation.) More than one edited version is possible. Be ready to discuss your editing choices.

    One of my biggest pleasures when I am out driving is reading other drivers' bumper stickers. These little messages, often provocative, always revealing of the people who stick them so proudly on the backs of their cars, serve a number of functions. They allow people to express their views on politicians, "Impeach whoever happens to be in office," for example, or "Vote for Nobody," as well as their views on political issues more generally, "Visualize World Peace" and "Who Needs the Whales?" They work as advertisements, "Ask me about Avon," and as personal statements, "I live to fish." They even give parents a chance to show their pride in their children, "My child is an honor student at Pineview School," or to display their ignorance, "My child can beat up you're (sic) honor student." I don't have a bumper sticker myself, but I definitely will once an "I Love Bumper Stickers" version appears on the market!

Editing Section

Mechanics

chapter 58

Spelling

The spelling of English words seems sometimes to defy reason. One reason is that English spelling reflects the language's many etymological sources. As English has absorbed words from other languages, it has assumed or adapted their spellings; thus the spelling of a word in English often cannot be determined simply by its pronunciation. (See 43a for more on the history of the English language.)

Misspellings can undermine your credibility and, in some cases, lead readers to misunderstand. Always edit carefully for spelling, keeping in mind the guidelines that follow.

58 a Confusing words

1 Distinguishing between homonyms

Homonyms are words with the same sound but different meanings: *great, grate; fair, fare.* When you are drafting and revising, it is easy to confuse homonyms, writing *their* instead of *there,* for example, or *rite* instead of *write.* As you edit, check carefully to make sure you've chosen the correct word in every case.

Memory aids can help you distinguish between some homonyms. For example, *piece,* what you slice a pie into, has a *pie* in it, whereas *peace* does not. Knowing word origins or related words can also help. *Rite* is related to *ritual,* in the sense of ceremony. *Write* is descended from an Old English word, *writan,* meaning "to scratch, draw, or engrave." Sometimes examining roots, prefixes, and suffixes is helpful. For example, *migrate* ("to move from one place to another") serves as the root for both *emigrate* and *immigrate.* The prefix *e-* means "out of" or "away from," so to *emigrate* is to leave one place for another: *Many Soviet Jews* emigrated *to Israel in search of a better life.* The prefix *im-,* on the other hand, means "into" or "toward," so to *immigrate* is to come into one place from another: *Many nineteenth-century* immigrants *came to this country seeking economic opportunity or fleeing political upheaval.*

Homonyms and Similar-Sounding Words

accept (receive)
except (leave out)

access (approach)
excess (too much)

adapt (change)
adopt (choose)

advice (suggestion)
advise (suggest)

affect (influence)
effect (result)

allude (refer)
elude (escape)

allusion (reference)
illusion (deception)

altar (church table)
alter (change)

antidote (poison remedy)
anecdote (brief story)

ascent (climb)
assent (agree)

bare (uncovered)
bear (carry; the animal)

bazaar (market)
bizarre (weird)

birth (childbearing)
berth (place of rest)

board (plank; food)
bored (drilled; uninterested)

born (given birth to)
borne (carried)

break (smash, split)
brake (stopping device)

canvas (fabric)
canvass (examine)

capital (city; wealth)
capitol (building)

censor (prohibit)
sensor (measuring device)

cent (money)
scent (fragrance)
sent (past of send)

cite (mention)
site (place)
sight (vision)

coarse (rough)
course (way, path)

complement (make complete)
compliment (praise)

conscience (moral sense)
conscious (aware)

cursor (computer marker)
curser (swearer)

council (committee)
counsel (advise; adviser)

dairy (milk-producing farm)
diary (daily book)

dessert (sweet food)
desert (abandon)

dissent (disagreement)
descent (movement downward)
decent (proper)

dual (having two parts)
duel (fight between two people)

dye (color)
die (perish)

elicit (draw forth)
illicit (improper)

eminent (noteworthy)
imminent (impending)

ensure (make certain)
insure (indemnify)

exercise (activity)
exorcise (drive out)

fair (just)
fare (food; fee)

faze (disturb)
phase (stage)

formerly (at an earlier time)
formally (according to a pattern)

forth (forward)
fourth (follows *third*)

forward (to the front)
foreword (preface)

gorilla (ape)
guerrilla (fighter)

hear (perceive)
hear (in this place)

heard (perceived)
herd (group of animals)

heroin (drug)
heroine (principal female character)

hole (opening)
whole (entire)

holy (sacred)
wholly (entirely)

immigrate (come in)
emigrate (leave)

incidents (events).
incidence (frequency of occurrence)
instance (example)

its (possessive of *it*)
it's (contraction of *it is*)

know (be aware)
no (negative, not yes)

lead (to guide; metal)
led (guided)

lesson (instruction)
lessen (reduce)

lightning (electric flash)
lightening (making less heavy)

loose (opposite of *tight*)
lose (opposite of *find* or *win*)

meat (food)
meet (encounter)

miner (excavator)
minor (person under a given age)

pair (two)
pear (fruit)
pare (peel; reduce)

passed (went by)
past (an earlier time)

peace (absence of war)
piece (part; portion)

peer (look; equal)
pier (pillar)

plain (simple; flat land)
plane (flat surface; smooth off;
  aircraft)

pray (ask, implore)
prey (hunt down; what is hunted)

principle (rule)
principal (chief person; sum
  of money)

quiet (silent)
quite (really, positively, very much)

rain (precipitation)
reign (rule)

right (correct)
rite (ritual)
write (inscribe)

road (path)
rode (past of *ride*)

scene (setting, stage setting)
seen (perceived)

sense (perception)
since (from that time)

shone (past of *shine*)
shown (past of *show*)

stationary (not moving)
stationery (writing paper)

straight (not curved)
strait (narrow place)

tack (angle of approach)
tact (sensitivity; diplomacy)

taut (tight)
taught (past of *teach*)

than (word of comparison)
then (at that time)

their (possessive of *them*)
there (in that place)
they're (contraction of *they are*)

threw (past of *throw*)
through (by way of)

to (in the direction of)
too (also)
two (the number)

waist (middle of the torso)
waste (squander)

weak (feeble)
week (seven days)

wear (carry on the body)
where (in what place)

weather (atmospheric conditions)
whether (if, in case)

which (what one)
witch (sorceress)

whose (possessive of *who*)
who's (contraction of *who is*)

yore (past time)
your (possessive of *you*)
you're (contraction of *you are*)

See also Chapter 64, Glossary of Usage.

2 Distinguishing between expressions written as one or two words

Some words can be written either as one word or two: *We'll go there
sometime. We spent some time there.* In almost all cases, the two spellings
have two different meanings.

all ready (completely prepared)	already (previously)
all together (all in one place)	altogether (thoroughly)
all ways (all methods)	always (at all times)
a lot (a large amount)	allot (distribute, assign)
every day (each day)	everyday (ordinary)
may be (could be)	maybe (perhaps)
some time (an amount of time)	sometime (at some unspecified time)

Remember that *cannot* is always one word and that most dictionaries suggest spelling *all right* as two words.

A computer spell checker won't help you find **errors in meaning**—that is, when you want *affect* instead of *effect;* or *you're,* not *your;* or *dinner,* not *diner.* It's up to you as a writer and careful proofreader to catch these problems.

3 Distinguishing between words with similar spellings and meanings

Misspellings often occur with words that are closely related in meaning and spelled and pronounced similarly. The following pairs of words can be confusing because their meanings are related and the spelling in each case differs by only a single letter. (See also Chapter 64.)

advice (noun)	advise (verb)
breath (noun)	breathe (verb)
chose (past tense)	choose (present tense)
cloths (fabrics)	clothes (garments)
device (noun)	devise (verb)
envelope (noun)	envelop (verb)
later (after more time)	latter (in the final position)
prophecy (noun)	prophesy (verb)

Similar problems can occur where the only spelling difference is in the prefix or suffix: *perspective, prospective; personal, personnel.* If you have trouble with words like these, remembering differences in pronunciation can help you distinguish the correct spelling of the word you intend.

Watch out for confusion between contractions that include pronouns and the possessive forms of the same pronouns. Remember: a pronoun with an apostrophe is a contraction; a pronoun without an apostrophe is possessive. (See the box in 55c.)

CONTRACTIONS	POSSESSIVE PRONOUNS
it's (it is, it has)	its (belonging to it)
they're (they are)	their (belonging to them)
who's (who is, who has)	whose (belonging to whom)
you're (you are)	your (belonging to you)

EDITING 1: PRACTICE

Edit the following passage, looking for commonly confused words and for words misspelled because of how they may be pronounced.

"Were just about to have our desert. Would you care to join us?"

"Thanks allot, but no. I've all ready eaten—a fore-coarse meal."

"Oh, just have one small peace of pie. You can have it plane, without any topping."

"It looks extrordinary, but to tell you the truth, I'm a little afraid of the affect it'll have on my waste. I've been trying to loose wait; my cloths are getting so tight that I can hardly breath."

"Are you getting any exorcise? Their is probly no better way to lose weight."

"Well, I never was much of an athalete, as you know. I have a stationery bike, but I just can not seem to motivate myself to workout. I always seem to find an excuse to put it off until latter."

ESL Recognizing British Spellings

For some words, British spelling—also used widely in other countries, including Australia, Canada, and India—differs from the preferred American spelling: *centre* rather than *center, labour* rather than *labor.* In general, writers in the United States are expected to conform to American spellings, so if you've learned British spellings, you'll need to take note of such differences and edit your work accordingly. Also check the spelling of proper nouns that include these words: *New York State Theater* at Lincoln Center but *Helen Hayes Theatre.*

58 b Spelling rules

1 Remembering the *ie/ei* rule and its exceptions

You may already be familiar with this rule: Put *i* before *e* except after *c*, or when it sounds like "ay" as in *neighbor* and *weigh.* In most cases the rule holds true:

Pronunciation and Spelling

Careless pronunciation can throw off your spelling. If you spell the following words the way you often hear them, you will probably misspell some of them. Pronounce each of these words, paying careful attention to the italicized letters that many people drop or mispronounce. As you edit, check each of these words carefully.

accident*al*ly	math*e*matics	reco*g*nize
ar*c*tic	m*e*me*n*to	re*l*evant
ari*th*metic	mischie*vous*	roo*mm*ate
at*hl*ete	nu*clear*	san*dw*ich
can*d*idate	pos*si*bly	sim*i*lar
enviro*n*ment	prejud*ice*	su*r*prise
extr*a*ordinary	(noun)	temp*e*rature
Feb*r*uary	prejud*iced*	ten*t*ative
gover*n*ment	(adjective)	use*d* to
in*t*erference	prob*ab*ly	usu*al*ly
lab*o*ratory	pron*u*nciation	vet*e*ran
lib*r*ary	quan*t*ity	We*dn*esday
lit*e*rature	rea*l*tor	win*try*

i before e: belief, field, friend, mischief, niece, patience, piece, priest, review, shield, view

ei after c: ceiling, conceit, conceive, deceit, deceive, receipt

ei sounding like "ay": eight, feign, freight, sleigh

There are, however, several common exceptions to remember.

ie after c: ancient, conscience, financier, science, species

ei not after c or sounding like "ay": caffeine, codeine, counterfeit, either, feisty, foreign, forfeit, height, leisure, neither, seize, weird

2 Adding suffixes according to spelling rules

A **suffix** is a syllable or group of letters attached to the end of a word to change its meaning and, sometimes, its part of speech: *tap* + *ed* = *tapped*, *reverse* (verb) + *-ible* = *reversible* (adjective). (See 43c2.) Adding a suffix can sometimes change the spelling of the base word. In addition, remember to watch for similar-sounding suffixes that are commonly confused with one another. Adding a **prefix,** a syllable attached to the beginning of a word, almost never causes a spelling change in the base word. However, some prefixes require hyphens. (See 60b.)

Suffixes after words ending in *y*

If the letter before the final *y* is a consonant, the *y* changes to *i* when a suffix is added, *unless* the suffix itself begins with *i*.

CONSONANT BEFORE *Y*	friendly + -er	= friendlier
	happy + -ly	= happily
	apply + -ing	= applying
	baby + -ish	= babyish

If the letter before the *y* is a vowel, the *y* doesn't change to *i*.

VOWEL BEFORE *Y*	convey + -ed	= conveyed
	annoy + -ance	= annoyance
	pay + -ment	= payment

The few exceptions to these rules include (1) some short words ending in *-y* when the suffix begins with a consonant (*dryness, shyly*): (2) the adverb form of very short words ending in *-ay* (*daily, gaily*); and (3) the past tense of three irregular verbs ending in *-ay* (*laid, paid, said*).

Proper nouns ending in *-y* generally do not change spellings when suffixes are added (for example, *McCarthyism, Kennedyesque*).

(See 58b3 for rules about plurals of words ending in *y*.)

Suffixes after words ending in *e*

If the suffix begins with a consonant, keep the final *e* of the base word.

SUFFIX STARTING WITH CONSONANT	hate + -ful	= hateful
	polite + -ness	= politeness
	state + -ment	= statement
	sure + -ly	= surely

Using *-cede, -ceed, and* -sede

Because they have identical sounds, the syllables *-cede, -ceed,* and *-sede* are often confused. The most common is *-cede,* as in *accede, concede, intercede, precede, recede,* and *secede. -Ceed* appears in the words *exceed, proceed,* and *succeed. -Sede* appears only in the word *supersede.*

There are a few exceptions to this rule, which you should memorize: *acknowledgment, argument, judgment, duly, truly, wholly, awful, ninth.*

If the suffix begins with a vowel, usually drop the final *e* of the base word.

SUFFIX STARTING
WITH VOWEL

admire + -able = admirable
dance + -er = dancer
insure + -ing = insuring
use + -able = usable (but *useable* is an acceptable alternative spelling)

But keep the *e* if it is necessary to prevent misreading: *dye + -ing = dyeing* (not *dying*); *canoe + -ing = canoeing* (not *canoing*). In addition, keep the *e* when it follows a soft *c* (one that sounds like *s,* not *k*) or a soft *g* (one that sounds like *j* or *jh*) and the suffix starts with *a* or *o;* dropping the *e* in such cases would give the *c* or *g* a hard pronunciation.

BASE WORD WITH
SOFT C OR G

enforce + -able = enforceable
outrage + -ous = outrageous

Suffixes after words ending in a consonant

If a suffix begins with a consonant and is added to a word that ends in a consonant, simply add the suffix, even if doing so results in a double consonant.

SUFFIX
STARTS WITH
CONSONANT

cup + -ful = cupful
defer + -ment = deferment
girl + -like = girllike
open + -ness = openness

If a suffix beginning with a vowel is added to a word ending in a consonant, you may be unsure whether to double the final consonant of the base word. The rules are simple. Double the final consonant only if (1) the base word is one syllable or the stress in the base word is on the last syllable *and* (2) the final consonant is preceded by a single vowel.

abet + -or = abettor
admit + -ing = admitting
hop + -ing = hopping
occur + -ence = occurrence

refer + -al = referral
slap + -ed = slapped
star + -ing = starring (not to be confused with stare + -ing = staring)

If the stress in the base word is not on the last syllable, or if the final consonant is preceded by a consonant or two vowels, do not double the final consonant.

STRESS NOT ON FINAL SYLLABLE	barter + -ing = bartering danger + -ous = dangerous envelop + -ed = enveloped
FINAL CONSONANT FOLLOWS CONSONANT	hurt + -ing = hurting doubt + -able = doubtable enact + -ed = enacted
FINAL CONSONANT FOLLOWS TWO VOWELS	fuel + -ing = fueling repeat + -ed = repeated sweep + -er = sweeper

Two exceptions to this rule are *format* (*formatted, formatting*) and program (*programmed, programming*). In addition, if the base word is stressed on the last syllable but adding the suffix changes the pronunciation so the stress of the base word is no longer on that syllable, do not double the final consonant: *refer* + *-ence* = reference.

-ly or -ally

The suffix *-ly* or *-ally* turns a noun into an adjective or an adjective into an adverb. Add *-ally* to words that end in *-ic.* (An exception is *publicly.*)

automatically	characteristically
basically	dynamically

Add *-ly* to words that do not end in *-ic.*

absolutely	instantly
differently	interestingly

Most other words that end in *-ally* are formed by adding *-ly* to the adjective suffix *-al: nation, national, nationally.* When adding *-ly* to a word that ends in *-l,* keep both *l*'s: *actual* + *-ly* = actually; *real* + *-ly* = really.

3 Forming plurals according to spelling rules

Most English nouns are made plural by adding *-s: book, books; page, pages.* There are, however, many exceptions. Fortunately, most of these follow the general rules described here.

General rules for plurals

Nouns ending in *ch, s, sh,* or *x* usually are made plural by adding *-es.*

church, churches   glass, glasses   wish, wishes   box, boxes

Nouns ending in *y* are made plural by adding *-s* if the letter before the *y* is a vowel. Otherwise, the plural is formed by changing the *y* to *i* and adding *-es*.

day, days   dairy, dairies
alloy, alloys   melody, melodies

Nouns ending in *o* are often made plural by adding *-s*.

video, videos   trio, trios   duo, duos
burro, burros   Latino, Latinos   inferno, infernos

However, several nouns ending in *o* preceded by a consonant form their plurals by adding *-es*.

embargo, embargoes   hero, heroes
veto, vetoes   potato, potatoes
tomato, tomatoes

Other nouns ending in *o* may take either *-s* or *-es* in forming the plural.

cargo, cargos, cargoes   tornado, tornados, tornadoes
volcano, volcanos, volcanoes   zero, zeros, zeroes

Many writers make it a habit to refer to a dictionary for the accepted plural form of words ending in *o*.

Nouns ending in *f* sometimes change the *f* to *v* and add *-es* to make the plural.

calf, calves   leaf, leaves   self, selves
half, halves   loaf, loaves   thief, thieves

Other nouns ending in *f* simply add *-s*.

belief, beliefs   chief, chiefs   proof, proofs
brief, briefs   oaf, oafs   reef, reefs

Still others form the plural either way: *hoof, hooves, hoofs*.

Nouns ending in *fe* may change the *f* to *v* before adding *-s: wife, wives; life, lives; knife, knives*. But not all nouns ending in *-fe* follow this pattern: *safe, safes; fife, fifes*.

Irregular and unusual plural nouns

A few nouns are made plural without adding an *-s* or *-es*.

child, children   goose, geese   mouse, mice
foot, feet   man, men   woman, women

A handful of words have the same form for singular and plural.

deer, deer   series, series
moose, moose   sheep, sheep

Many loan words are made plural according to the rules of their original language. Words borrowed from Latin keep the endings used in Latin when forming plurals: *alumnus, alumni; alumna, alumnae; alga, algae; datum, data; medium, media.* Words from the Greek also keep their original endings: *analysis, analyses; criterion, criteria; phenomenon, phenomena.*

However, some loan words have Anglicized plurals that are more widely accepted than their original Latin or Greek plurals: *stadiums* rather than *stadia.* Some foreign plurals are regarded as singular in English because the singular form is so rarely used: *The agenda is brief.*

Plurals of proper nouns

In general, proper nouns form plurals by adding *-s* or *-es.* Adding *-s* when forming the plural does not create an extra syllable in pronunciation: *the Simpsons, the Kims, several Lisas.* When the plural is pronounced with one more syllable than the singular, add *-es.* This usually occurs with proper nouns that end in *ch, s, sh, x,* or *z: the Bushes, the Joneses, the Koches, the Ruizes.* Do not use an apostrophe to indicate the plural of a proper name.

Plurals of compound nouns

A **compound noun** consists of two or more words regularly used together. If the compound is written as one word, make the last part plural: *newspapers, henhouses, notebooks.* An exception to this rule is the word *passersby.*

If a compound noun is written as separate words or if it is hyphenated, make plural the word that expresses the central idea. This is usually the noun in the compound: *attorneys general, presidents-elect, professors emeritus.* When both parts of the compound are nouns, make plural the word that is modified by another word or by a prepositional phrase: *bath towels, sisters-in-law, soldiers of fortune.*

Plurals of letters, numbers, and words

To form the plural of a letter, number, or symbol, use an apostrophe and *-s.*

There are two *m*'s in *programmer.*

No sentence should end with two *?*'s.

For the plural of numbers referring to decades or centuries expressed in numerals, an apostrophe and *s* may be used, but the letter *s* alone is preferred. Be consistent.

the 1700s   the 1700's
the nineties

Plurals of abbreviations

Form the plural of an abbreviation or an acronym by adding *s*.

Several of my classmates have become MDs.

She keeps her money in two IRAs.

Spelling Tips

- Always consult a dictionary when you are in doubt about how to spell a word.

- When checking the spelling of an unfamiliar word, note its *etymology*, or origin, and the history of its usage. This information will help you understand why a word is spelled the way it is.

- Keep a personal spelling list of difficult words you encounter. Check to see whether a word that you find troublesome shares a root, prefix, or suffix with a word you already know; the connection helps you learn the meaning, as well as the spelling, of the new word.

- Use the spell checker on your word processor to proofread your papers. It locates transposed or dropped letters as well as some misspellings.

- Proofread your work carefully, even when you use a spell checker. If your spelling is right but the word is wrong, even the computer can't help. For example, if you confuse *to, too,* and *two,* or *its* and *it's,* the spell checker won't catch the error because it can't recognize the context in which a word is used.

EDITING 2: PRACTICE ....

Edit the following passage, using basic spelling rules to eliminate misspelled words.

Of all the holidaies, one of my least favorite is Thanksgiving. I know that it is traditionnal to beleive in Thanksgiving as a time for shareing a hearty meal with family and freinds, but to me all that outragous food—the huge turkies with two different gravies, the spicey dressing, the rich potatos, along with the butterred vegetables, the breads and rolls, and the multiple peices of pumpkin pie—just excedes the boundarys of civilized dinning. Then after the guestes have all stuffed themselfs, one group—usualy the women, of course—spends the rest of the afternoon cleanning up while the others—mostly the man, naturally— head for the den, ploping down in front of the television for a truely stimulateing afternoon of armchair quarterbackking. I conceed that I am in the minority, but I just can't concieve what anyone possibaly enjoies about Thanksgiving.

··

EDITING 3: APPLICATION ··

Keep a word list for one week. Look up in a dictionary any unfamiliar words that you encounter in your reading or writing, noting the origin and spelling of each word. Record these words on your word list. At the end of the week, review your list. Have a friend give you a spelling test, and cross off the words you get right. Start a new list with any you miss.

··

chapter 59 · *Capitalization*

Capital letters are conventionally used to indicate the beginning of a sentence and to distinguish names, titles, and certain other words. (For information on the capitalization of abbreviations, see 62c–62g.)

59 a   First word of a sentence

Use a capital letter at the beginning of a sentence.

In a series of fragmentary questions, it is equally acceptable to begin each fragment with a capital or lowercase letter.

> What was the occasion? a holiday? someone's birthday?

Whichever style of capitalization you choose for such questions, be consistent throughout your paper.

Sentences following colons

When two independent clauses are joined by a colon, capitalizing the first word of the second clause is optional, but be consistent throughout a paper.

> The senators' courage failed them: the [*or* The] reform bill was dead for another decade.

827

Always capitalize a numbered list of sentences (but not phrases) following a colon.

His philosophy can be reduced to three basic rules: (1) Think for yourself. (2) Take care of your body. (3) Never hurt anyone.

Sentences between parentheses or dashes

Capitalize the first word of a complete sentence within parentheses if it is not inside another sentence.

Congress attacked sex discrimination in sports with a 1972 law called Title IX. (Changes added in 1974 are called the Bayh amendments.)

Do not capitalize the first word of a complete sentence set off by parentheses or dashes when it falls within another sentence.

Title IX (the name refers to a section of U.S. civil rights law) has changed collegiate sports a great deal over thirty years. On many campuses Title IX has increased the number of competitive sports offered to women—even opponents of the law agree this is true—but its effect on men's sports is more difficult to assess.

59 b   Quotations and lines of poetry

1 Quotations

Capitalize the first word of a quoted sentence wherever it falls in your own sentence.

"We'd like to talk to you about the budget for women's sports," Jeannine told the athletic director. "The first question is from Ryan."

Ryan asked, "How many sports are offered?"

Do not capitalize the first word of the continuation of a quotation interrupted by a signal phrase.

"Indeed," Mr. Kott responded, "we field men's and women's teams in track, swimming, tennis, and golf."

If the first word of a quotation does not begin a sentence of yours or a sentence in the original, do not capitalize it.

Recognizing details familiar from his childhood, E. B. White feels "the same damp moss covering the worms in the fishing can."

When quoting from published prose sources, you may have to change the capitalization of the original to fit into your sentence. If you use a capital letter where the original has a lowercase letter, or vice versa, use brackets to show the change. (See 57d.)

2 Capitalizing quotations from poetry

When quoting poetry, always follow the capitalization of the original.

The poem opens with Frost's usual directness and rhythmic formality: "Whose woods these are, I think I know. / His house is in the village, though." Compare this to Lucille Clifton's offhanded "boys / i don't promise you nothing. . . ."

(See Chapters 56 and 57 for more on punctuating quotations.)

59 c Proper nouns

Proper nouns name particular persons, places, or things: *Toni Cade Bambara, Gulf of Mexico, Mercedes Benz.* In general, proper nouns are capitalized. (Articles, coordinating conjunctions, and prepositions in proper nouns are not capitalized.) **Common nouns,** on the other hand, name general classes of persons, places, or things: *writer, gulf, automobile.* Common nouns are not capitalized unless they are part of a proper noun.

In general, the following should be capitalized.

Names of individual people and animals

Catherine the Great	Eleanor Roosevelt
Snoopy	Vincent van Gogh

Note that capitalization of *van, de, la,* and so on varies, so consult a reliable print source for the conventional spelling of a particular name.

Religions, religious terms, deities, and sacred works

Allah	the Bible
Christianity, Christians	God
Judaism, Jews	the Koran
Protestant	Roman Catholic

Family Members

Words describing family relationships are capitalized only when they are used as names, not when they are preceded by a possessive pronoun.

The family gave a party for Dad and Uncle Fritz.

My dad and my uncle are twins.

Nationalities, ethnic groups, and languages

African Americans	Chicano	Chinese
French	Hindustani	Seminole

Titles

Formal and courtesy titles and their abbreviations are capitalized when they are used before a name and not set off by commas.

Coach Bill Parcells	Dame Agatha Christie
Dr. Wu	Prof. Mitchell Cox
Judge Marilyn Harris	Senator Dianne Feinstein

They are lowercased when used alone or separated from the name by commas.

Dianne Feinstein, senator from California

my physics professor, Mitchell Cox

Titles indicating high station or office may be capitalized when they are not followed by a name: *the President of the United States, the Queen, the Pope.* Derivatives of such titles, however, are not capitalized: *presidential, papal.*

Months, days of the week, and holidays

August 12, 1914	the Fourth of July
Presidents' Day	Tuesday, the twentieth of April

Seasons are not capitalized: *summer, fall.*

Geographic names

the Colorado River	the Grand Canyon
Little Rock, Arkansas	Madison Avenue
the Midwest	Puerto Rico
the Western Hemisphere	the Windy City

Note that *the* is generally not capitalized in these names. Common nouns like *river, avenue,* and *street* are lowercase when they are preceded by two or more proper nouns: *Bleecker and MacDougal streets.*

Although direction words are capitalized when they name a region (*the South*), they are not when they indicate compass directions: *We headed south on U.S. 61.*

Institutions, organizations, businesses, and trade names

Aquafresh	Congress
Big Mac	Habitat for Humanity
the League of Women Voters	Microsoft Corporation
the United Nations	Wesleyan University

Be sure to capitalize only the proper name of an institution, not a generic term referring to it: *Kenyon is ranked among the best small colleges in the country.*

Words such as *company, incorporated,* and *limited* and their abbreviations are capitalized when they are used as part of a business's formal name: *Jones Brothers Limited.* They are not capitalized when they are not part of the formal name: *The company is on the verge of bankruptcy.*

Historical documents, legislation, events, periods, and movements

the Constitution	Public Law 100-13
the Norman Conquest	the Renaissance
the Rationalist movement	the Stamp Act
an Impressionist painter	World War II

Ships, aircraft, spacecraft, and trains

the *Challenger*	the *Orient Express*
the *Spirit of St. Louis*	the *U.S.S. Constitution*

(See 61b for guidelines on italicizing names of vehicles.)

Derivatives of proper nouns

Beatlemania	Marxist
Newtonian	Texan

Prefixes before derivatives of proper nouns are not capitalized: *neo-Marxist, anti-American.* (See 60b for information on hyphenating prefixes before proper adjectives.)

Words derived from proper nouns that have taken on independent meanings often are no longer capitalized: *french fries, herculean, quixotic, ohm, vulcanization.*

59 d Titles

For the title of a book, play, essay, story, poem, movie, television series, piece of music, or work of art, capitalize the first word, the last word, and all other words except articles (*the, a, an*), coordinating conjunctions (*and, or, for, but, nor, so, yet*), prepositions (*in, on, with,* and so on), and the *to* in infinitives. Some publishers capitalize prepositions of five or more letters (*within, among,* and so on). Check the title if possible.

Beauty and the Beast	"The East Is Red"
Home Improvement	*Nude Descending a Staircase*
"What I Did for Love"	*The Taming of the Shrew*

I *and* O

Always capitalize the personal pronoun *I*, no matter where it falls in a sentence.

Whatever I play, I play to win.

Also capitalize the interjection *O*, used in prayers and to express wonder and surprise.

Descend on us, O Spirit of Peace.

Note that the interjection *oh* is not capitalized unless it begins a sentence: *We didn't succeed, but oh, how we tried.*

Follow the same rule for subtitles, including capitalizing the first word: *Women Playwrights: The Best Plays of 2002.*

If a title contains words joined by a hyphen, both words usually are capitalized, with the exception of articles, conjunctions, and prepositions (*The One-Minute Grammarian; The Social History of the Jack-in-the-Box*).

(See 56c and 61a on the use of quotation marks and italics for titles.)

What Needs Capitalization?

As you edit, make sure you've capitalized the following words:

- The first word of every sentence
- The first word of a quoted sentence within a sentence
- Proper nouns and their derivatives
- Important words in titles.

EDITING 1: PRACTICE

Edit the following passage, capitalizing correctly.

The Library of congress, established in Washington in 1800, has been called the National Library of the United states. Primarily responsible for its creation was vice president Thomas Jefferson (He was himself an avid book collector), who also supported it strongly during the course of his Presidency. When a fire destroyed much of the Collection in 1814, Jefferson donated his own personal library as a replacement. Ruined by another fire in 1851—Some 35,000 volumes were lost—the library languished until congress passed the copyright act of 1870, which required that all material copyrighted in the Country be deposited there. Today the imposing building on Independence avenue—beloved by many washingtonians—contains some 75 million items, including maps, prints, photographs, and an extensive collection of asian art and artifacts. Of course, it also houses such diverse prose works as a rare edition of *The Federalist papers* and a copy of Gary Larsen's *It Came From The Far Side.*

EDITING 2: APPLICATION ....

Examine a paper you are working on for mistakes in capitalization. Is there one kind of mistake in using capitalization that you consistently make? If so, think about how best to identify words that should and should not be capitalized when you edit your work. Edit any sentences in which you have made capitalization mistakes.

....

60

Hyphenation

The hyphen helps readers understand how words are to be read. A hyphen can link parts of a word that might otherwise be seen as separate or separate parts of a word that might be misleading or hard to read if written together. The hyphen has conventional uses in numbers, fractions, and units of measure.

60 a Ends of lines

If a word is too long to fit at the end of a line, you can divide it, using a hyphen to signal that the word continues on the next line. It is better not to divide words, but if you must, be sure to do so at an acceptable point. When in doubt, consult a dictionary. The divisions in the entry word indicate where it may be hyphenated. Here are a few guidelines:

- **Follow pronunciation.** Divide between pronounced syllables: *ro-dent, jew-el.* Generally, divide between two consonants—*car-pen-ter, or-bit*—unless the two consonants produce a single sound: *broth-er, tro-phy.* Divide between double letters: *mas-sive, car-ry.* (See prefixes and suffixes below for an exception involving *-ing* endings.)

- **Do not leave just one letter on a line.** Such words as *amount (a-mount), ideal (i-deal),* and *opaque (o-paque)* should not be hyphenated; *abandon* can only be divided as *aban-don, idolize* only as *idol-ize.*

▪ **Divide compounds between words.** If a compound is hyphenated, divide at the hyphen: *self- / esteem, son- / in-law,* or *son-in- / law.* Divide a one-word compound between its parts: *mother-land,* not *mo-therland*

▪ **Divide at prefixes or suffixes.** Try to leave both parts of the word recognizable: not *an-tibody* but *anti-body,* not *hy-phenate* but *hyphen-ate.* Before *-ing* endings, generally hyphenate after double letters that end a root word: *roll-ing,* not *rol-ling.* But if a consonant is doubled in adding the *-ing* ending, keep the added consonant with the suffix; *hit-ting, cut-ting.* (See 58b for rules on doubling consonants.)

Most word-processing programs can automatically hyphenate a document. If you choose not to hyphenate any words, most programs allow you to turn off hyphenation. If you take advantage of your computer's ability to hyphenate, be sure to double-check its choices, which may be less than perfect.

EDITING 1: PRACTICE ....

Indicate all possible hyphenation points, if any, for the following words. If there is more than one point, indicate the preferable hyphenation. Then check against a dictionary.

1. coordinated	**5.** crossbones	**9.** commitment
2. acquitted	**6.** minibus	**10.** antidote
3. preparedness	**7.** ignite	**11.** damming
4. width	**8.** overcast	**12.** damning

60 b   Prefixes

Although most prefixes are attached to root words without hyphens, there are a few exceptions. When in doubt, consult your dictionary. The following guidelines cover most of the common uses of hyphens following prefixes.

Use a hyphen to attach a prefix to a capitalized word or to a date. (The prefix itself is usually not capitalized.)

anti-Washington sentiment   post-1994 guidelines

Use a hyphen to attach a prefix to a term of more than one word. (See 60c.)

pro-school-choice candidates   pre-space-age technology

Use a hyphen after *all-, ex-* (when used to mean "former"), *self-,* and *quasi-.*

all-inclusive   ex-convict   self-hypnosis   quasi-judicial

A hyphen may be used when a prefix ends with the same letter that begins the base word: *anti-intellectual, co-ownership.* However, the hyphen has been dropped from many such words (*cooperate, preexisting, unnatural*). Check a dictionary.

A hyphen is occasionally used to distinguish between two different words spelled with the same letters, especially when there is a strong chance of a misreading.

We asked them to *refund* [give back] our money.

Congress will *re-fund* [fund again] the program for another year.

When two prefixes separated in a sentence by a conjunction apply to the same base word, add a hyphen after both prefixes, with a space after the first prefix.

We compared the *pre-* and *post-election* analyses.

60 **c**   **Compound words**

Two or more words used as a single unit form a **compound word.** A compound rewritten as one word is called a *closed compound: workhorse, schoolteacher.* Other compounds are written as two words, or *open compounds: hope chest, lunch break, curtain rod.* Others are hyphenated: *great-grandson, mother-in-law,* and *stick-in-the-mud.*

In deciding whether to hyphenate **compound nouns,** check a dictionary. If the compound is not listed in the dictionary, write it as separate words. Note that most compound nouns consisting of three or more words are hyphenated: *will-o'-the-wisp, jack-in-the-box.*

Compound adjectives consist of two or more words that function together as a single adjective before a noun: *a well-written essay, a late-night party, a touch-and-go situation.* They are usually hyphenated to make it clear which words go together to form the adjective. It is often necessary to do this to prevent a misreading. For example, compare the meanings of the following sentences:

Mr. Donovan is an old car collector.

He is an old *person who* collects cars.

Mr. Donovan is an old-car collector.

He is a person who collects old cars.

Note, however, that where a well-established compound noun functions as an adjective, misreading is unlikely and no hyphen is needed.

high school student   post office box

Also, a hyphen is never used after an adverb ending in *-ly*.

highly motivated employees   a strongly worded statement

When two compound adjectives before a noun have the same base word and are linked by a conjunction, the base word can be dropped from the first and a space added after the hyphen.

full- and part-time employees

60 d   Numbers, fractions, and units of measure

Hyphenate two-word numbers from twenty-one to ninety-nine. Do not hyphenate before or after the words *hundred, thousand,* or *million*.

fifty-seven   twenty-two hundred
two hundred fifty-seven   six hundred twenty thousand

Remember that long numbers are often easier to read when expressed in figures. (See 62a.)

Use a hyphen between the numerator and denominator of a spelled-out fraction unless one of them is already hyphenated.

one-half   two-thirds   twenty-one fiftieths

When a number includes a unit of measure (feet, inches, miles, pounds), hyphenate modifiers but not nouns.

An ordinary dump truck has a *nine-cubic-yard* bed.

Only a gardener would delight in *nine cubic yards* of manure.

Use a hyphen in ages when the expression functions as a noun or as an adjective preceding a noun.

I threatened to trade in my *ten-year-old* twins for one *twenty-year-old*.

Do not hyphenate when the word indicating time—in this case *years*—is plural: *The boy is ten years old.*

A hyphen can be used to suggest a range between numbers: *1987–90, 120–140 times a year.* However, readers generally find it clearer if the range is described in words: *from 1987 to 1990; between 120 and 140 times a year.* Do not mix the two methods: *They attended the college from 1987 to 1990* (not *from 1987–1990*).

Guidelines for Hyphenation

As you edit, make sure you have used hyphens appropriately for the following:

- For dividing words at the ends of lines, if necessary
- After certain prefixes
- In certain compound words
- In some fractions, numbers, and units of measure

EDITING 2: PRACTICE ....

Edit the following passage, hyphenating all words where necessary and deleting unnecessary hyphens. You may have to consult a dictionary.

Widely-available desktop publishing systems have led to an explosion in the publication of *zines,* the low tech equivalent of magazines. Generally published out of the editor owner's home, the average zine has a small print run (from 250–350 copies) and very low production costs (around $500). Zines, which are similar to under-ground publications of the 1960s and 1970s, reflect the offbeat personalities of their owners. Most make very-little money but enjoy a devoted reader-ship, approximately two thirds of which is under thirty-years-old in most cases. One of the best known zines is *Ersatz,* published by Sam Pratt, twenty seven, out of his loft in Manhattan's Hells' Kitchen. Reflecting the irreverent sensibilities of the postReagan era, *Ersatz* has included such pieces as a quasiserious article on the deeper significance of the Trix rabbit. As zines become more-and-more popular, bigger publishers have begun to look for ways to coopt their ideas.

....

Examine a paper you are working on for hyphenation mistakes. Is there one kind of mistake in using hyphens that you consistently make? If so, think about how best to remember hyphenation rules when you edit your work. Edit any sentences in which you have mis-used or omitted hyphens.

....

A /A K K
B B L L
C C M M
D D N N
E E O O
F F P P
G G Q Q
H H R R
IJ IJ S S

Most publications use a **roman** typeface—like this one—for the main body of the text. **Italic** typeface—*which looks like this*—is used to distinguish certain words, usually to indicate that they must be interpreted somewhat differently.

The equivalent of italics in typed and handwritten work is underlining. Many word processing programs now allow writers to shift to italic type, but make sure this is acceptable to your instructor; he or she may still prefer underlining to italics in student work.

61 a Titles

Italicize the titles of books, long poems considered to be independent works, plays, operas and other long musical works, movies, CDs or long-playing recordings, newspapers, magazines and journals, television or radio series, and works of art. Use quotation marks rather than italics for titles that are subdivisions of a larger work. (See 56c for more on using quotation marks for titles and for marking titles within titles.)

The titles of sacred works, parts of sacred works, and ancient manuscripts are not italicized.

the Bible   the Koran   Genesis

The titles of public documents also are not in italics.

the Constitution   the Declaration of Independence

Most academic stylebooks recommend neither capitalizing nor italicizing the article (*a, an,* or *the*) in the name of a newspaper or magazine, even if the newspaper or magazine includes it in its own name, as does [*The*] *New York Times.* However, when writing to or for a publication, follow its particular style.

Italics and Quotation Marks for Titles

Italics	Quotation Marks
Holy the Firm (book)	"Newborn and Salted" (chapter)
Here Lies (story collection)	"Big Blonde" (short story)
North of Boston (poetry collection)	"Mending Wall" (poem)
Song of Roland (long poem, independent work)	
Waiting for Godot (play)	
Porgy and Bess (opera)	
Carmina Burana (long musical work)*	
Pulp Fiction (movie)	
Voodoo Lounge (CD recording)	"Mean Disposition" (song)
Los Angeles Times (newspaper)	"Icy Words on Global Warming" (article)
New Republic (magazine)	
The Simpsons (television series)	"Homer Meets Godzilla" (episode)
All Things Considered (radio series)	
The Boating Party (painting)	
Reclining Nude (sculpture)	

*Note that a musical work identified by form and key is neither italicized nor put in quotation marks: Beethoven's Symphony No. 5 in D Minor.

61 b   Individual trains, ships, airplanes, and spacecraft

Italicize the official names of individual trains, ships, airplanes, and spacecraft but not the names of classifications of such vehicles.

a Polaris rocket   the *Shasta Daylight* (train)
Spirit of St. Louis (airplane)   a Trident submarine
the U.S.S. *Arizona* (ship)   *Voyager* (spacecraft)

61 c   For emphasis

Italics can indicate that a word or words should receive special emphasis in a sentence.

Despite popular perception, the rate of violent crime is actually *lower* today than it was twenty years ago.

Such emphasis can also help clarify a point.

Then Ms. Dillon asked *me* to sing.

Of all people, me!

Then Ms. Dillon asked me to *sing*.

Of all things, sing!

61 d   Words, numerals, and letters used as words

Use italics when you refer to a word or numeral itself. Also italicize letters referred to as part of the alphabet or as mathematical symbols.

How would you define the terms *liberal* and *conservative?*

Because I read the *1* as a *7*, my calculations were incorrect.

When I type quickly, I often substitute *w* for *s.*

Let *x* stand for test scores and *y* for hours of study.

61 e   Foreign words

Words and phrases from other languages are usually italicized unless they have become a familiar part of English usage.

Many old castles in Spain have been turned into *paradores* where visitors can spend the night.

The *Mille Miglia* was an auto race of a thousand miles.

The menu offered spaghetti, lasagne, and *pasticcio di faglioni.*

In deciding whether to italicize words from other languages, check a recent English dictionary. Words that do not appear should be italicized. Words that do appear should be italicized only if they are seldom used by English speakers.

Always italicize a word or phrase from another language that you are defining for the first time.

The Hawaiian word for that smooth, ropelike lava is *pahoehoe.*

Latin names used to classify plants and animals by genus and species are also italicized.

The biologists named their discovery *Symbian pandora.*

Common Uses of Italics

As you edit, check for your use of italics with the following:

- Titles of long published works, musical works, and works of art
- Names of trains, ships, and other specific vehicles
- Specific words you wish to give special emphasis
- Words, numerals, and letters used as words
- Words from languages other than English

EDITING 1: PRACTICE

Edit the following passage, making sure words are italicized according to convention.

Before planting a garden, it is a good idea to consult a reputable source for tips on successful gardening. Many newspapers, such as the New York Times, have a weekly column devoted to gardening. There are also many useful books, such as "A Guide to Growing Gorgeous Greenery," with its especially helpful introductory chapter, *Plan Before You Plant.*
First a gardener should learn about the different types of plants. Annuals is the term given to plants that complete their lifetime in one year; the term perennials is used for plants that grow back every year. Many annuals are popular with gardeners, especially the Begonia semperflorens and the Petunia hybrida.

EDITING 2: APPLICATION

Examine a paper you are working on for mistakes in italicizing. Is there one kind of mistake in using italics that you consistently make? If so, think about how best to remember which words to italicize when you edit your work. Edit any sentences in which you have misused or omitted italics.

chapter 62

Numbers and Abbreviations

Analysis and persuasion often depend on numbers. The more numbers used in a piece of writing, the more likely readers are to become confused or intimidated.

62 a   Figures and words

Conventions for choosing between figures and words for numbers vary according to discipline. For more information, consult the style guide for your discipline (Chapters 29–33).

In most nontechnical academic writing (including writing in literature and the humanities), spell the numbers one to one hundred as well as all fractions. (See 60d about using hyphens in numbers.)

thirty universities   fifty-three graduates
three-fourths of the class

Also spell out round numbers over one hundred if they can be expressed in two words. Otherwise, use figures.

five hundred students   517 students
more than fifty thousand trees   52,317 trees

In some publications, figures are used for numbers over ten and for numbers used with measurements of time (*7 hours, 3 weeks*) and size, including weight (*20 pounds, 6 grams*), length (*5 feet*), area (*2 square meters*), and volume (*1 teaspoon, 2 liters*).

It is sometimes clearer to express very large round numbers using a combination of words and figures: *The Census Bureau says that the U.S. population exceeds 250 million.*

In technical writing (including writing in the social and natural sciences), most numbers are written in figures.

The pressure increased by 3 kilograms per square centimeter.

Fewer than 5 percent of the eggs failed to hatch.

In both nontechnical and technical writing, spell out any number that begins a sentence. If doing so is awkward, rewrite the sentence.

Five hundred forty-seven
~~547~~ students attended the concert.

Attending the concert were
547 students ~~attended the concert~~.

Express any numbers that readers must compare with each other in the same way. If convention requires using figures for one number, do the same for the other numbers.

87
In Midville last year, ~~eighty-seven~~ cats and 114 dogs were destroyed by the city pound.

Figures or Spelled-Out Numbers?

When trying to choose between spelling out numbers or using figures, ask yourself the following questions:

- Is it a round number that can be expressed in one or two words? For most writing situations, spell these out.

- Does the number begin a sentence? Spell it out or edit the sentence so that it appears elsewhere.

- Am I addressing a technical audience? Use the conventions for technical writing and those explained in the discipline's documentation guidelines. (See Chapters 31 and 33.)

Singular and Plural Forms of Numbers

When the word for a number is used as a plural noun without another number before it, use the plural form of the word. You may also need to use the word *of* after it.

The news report said there were only a few protesters at the nuclear power plant, but we saw *hundreds*.

Dozens of geese headed south today.

When the word for a number is preceded by another number, use the singular form of the word, and do not use *of* with it.

There were approximately *two hundred* protesters.

At least *three dozen* geese flew over the lake today.

In a hyphenated adjective that includes a number, use the singular for the unit of measure.

That movie lasted *three hours*.

It was a *three-hour* movie.

62 b   Conventional uses

The following cases, by convention, require the use of figures, even in nontechnical writing.

In dates

11 April 1999   July 16, 1896   the year 2001

In addresses

2551 Polk Street, Apt. 3

San Francisco, CA 94109

With abbreviations and symbols

3500 rpm	37°C
65 mph	$62.23
74%	53¢

In discussions that use numbers infrequently, you may use words to express percentages and amounts of money if you can do so in two or three words: *seventy-four percent* and *fifty cents,* but not *sixty-two dollars and twenty-three cents.* If you spell out numbers, also spell out *percent, dollars,* and *cents.*

For time

12:15 A.M.   2330 hours

Note that numbers used with *o'clock, past, to, till,* and *until* are generally written out as words.

at seven o'clock   twenty past one

For decimal fractions

2.7 seconds   35.4 miles

For cross-references and citations

Chapter 56   line 25
volume 3, pages 13–17   act 3, scene 2

(See Chapters 30–33 for specific documentation formats.)

ESL *Punctuating Numbers*

Numbering systems throughout the world differ in their punctuation. Some numbering systems use a period to mark divisions of thousands, so that *ten thousand* is written *10.000.* In the United States, commas are used to mark divisions of thousands.

In 1989, the population of Ecuador was 10,262,271.

In the United States, the period is used as a decimal point to separate whole numbers from decimal fractions.

Seven and a half can also be written *7.5.*

EDITING 1: PRACTICE

Edit the following passage, making sure all numbers are handled appropriately for nontechnical writing.

For the last 10 years, I have been running at least five miles a day, six days a week, fifty-two weeks a year. That adds up to eighteen hundred twenty miles yearly. I figure that by the year two thousand, I will have run well over 20,000 miles. My running schedule almost never varies. I hit the streets just after I awaken, at 6 o'clock, and run for 3/4 of an hour. Then I make a ten-minute stop at a nearby diner for a quick orange juice before circling back toward home. 1,750 footfalls later I arrive home to shower and get ready for the day.

EDITING 2: PRACTICE

Examine a paper you are working on for numbers that you have handled incorrectly. Is there one kind of mistake in using numbers that you consistently make? If so, think about how best to remember how to handle numbers when you edit your work. Edit any sentences in which you have handled numbers incorrectly.

62 c   In nontechnical texts

Abbreviations—shortened forms of words—are frequently used in tables, footnotes, endnotes, and bibliographies to help readers proceed through the material quickly and easily. (Documentation and its acceptable abbreviations are discussed in Chapters 30–33.) They are also used often in scientific and technical writing. With a few exceptions, however, you should avoid abbreviations in the body of a general, nontechnical essay, paper, or report. This chapter discusses abbreviations that are acceptable in nontechnical text.

62 d   Titles and degrees

Personal or courtesy titles such as *Mr., Mrs., Dr.,* and *St.* may be abbreviated when they precede a full name. For such titles, capitalize the first letter and end with a period.

Mr. Samuel Taylor Darling   Dr. Leslie Hunter
St. Francis of Assisi   Prof. Karen Greenberg
Gen. Tommy Franks   Rep. Tom DeLay
the Rev. Martin Luther King, Jr.   Sen. John McCain

Never abbreviate *president* or *mayor.* (Note that *Miss* is not an abbreviation, so it is written without a period. The courtesy title *Ms.* ends with a period even though it is not an abbreviation.)

Except for *Mr., Mrs.,* and *Dr.,* spell out titles used before a surname alone: *Professor Greenberg, Senator Boxer.*
Titles that do not precede a name are not abbreviated or capitalized.

professor
Raisha Goldblum has been named assistant ~~prof.~~ of chemistry.

Titles or degrees such as *Esq, MD, LLD, JD,* and *PhD* that follow a name are always abbreviated, as are generational titles such as *Jr.* and *Sr.* They are set off by commas in a sentence. MLA guidelines omit periods in degree titles.

A new book by Dana Clark, MD, criticizes animal testing.

Do not use both *Dr.* and a degree.

~~Dr.~~ Barry Qualls, PhD, will speak at commencement.

62 e   Time, dates, amounts, and symbols

The following abbreviations and symbols are used only preceding or following numbers.

Time

Use A.M. and P.M. (or *a.m.* and *p.m.*) for specific times of day.

12:15 P.M. (*or* p.m.)   9:00 A.M. (*or* a.m.)

Avoid using these abbreviations without a specific hour or with *o'clock.* (See 62b.)

night.
We studied late into the ~~P.M.~~

in the evening.
The ceremony will begin at seven o'clock ~~P.M.~~

Dates

Use BC (*before Christ*) and AD (*anno Domini,* Latin for "in the year of the Lord") when necessary to distinguish dates. To avoid a religious reference, some writers substitute the abbreviations BCE (*before Common Era*) and CE (*Common Era*). Note that AD precedes the date, except when *century* is used.

425 BC (or 425 BCE)

AD 376 (or 376 CE)

the first century AD

Amounts or numbers

Acceptable abbreviations with amounts or numbers in nontechnical writing include *F* for *degrees Fahrenheit* and *C* for *degrees Celsius* in temperatures; *mph* (or *m.p.h.*) for *miles per hour;* and *No.* or *no.* for *number.*

The speed limit has been raised from 55 mph to 75 mph.

The British prime minister's official address is No. 10 Downing Street.

In scientific and technical writing, units of measure are abbreviated when they follow amounts, usually without periods.

To 750 ml of this solution was added 200 mg of sodium cyanate.

In other situations, abbreviations are often acceptable if they are clearly defined at the first mention.

The engine develops maximum torque at 2900 revolutions per minute (rpm). Peak power is achieved at 6500 rpm.

Symbols can also be used as abbreviations with amounts. Symbols acceptable in nontechnical writing include those for degrees (°), percentage (%), and dollars ($), when they are used with figures denoting specific quantities.

By definition, 100°C equals 212°F, the boiling point of water.

The bill came to $35.99.

The percentage of positive responses was surprising.

62 f   Geographic names

It is acceptable to abbreviate geographic names (except cities) in addresses on mail. For state names, use abbreviations recommended by the U.S. Postal Service. (See the box in this section.)

Lila Martin
100 W. Glengarry Dr.
Birmingham, MI 48009

When presenting a full address in text, spell out everything but the state name. When presenting less than a full address, spell out everything.

His address was 1109 Green Street, Harrisburg, PA 17102.

She was born in Harrisburg, Pennsylvania.

State Abbreviations

Use these U.S. Postal Service abbreviations (capitalized, with no periods) for the names of the fifty states and the District of Columbia only on mail, in full addresses in text, or in documentation.

State	Abbreviation	State	Abbreviation
Alabama	AL	Montana	MT
Alaska	AK	Nebraska	NE
Arizona	AZ	Nevada	NV
Arkansas	AR	New Hampshire	NH
California	CA	New Jersey	NJ
Colorado	CO	New Mexico	NM
Connecticut	CT	New York	NY
Delaware	DE	North Carolina	NC
District of Columbia	DC	North Dakota	ND
Florida	FL	Ohio	OH
Georgia	GA	Oklahoma	OK
Hawaii	HI	Oregon	OR
Idaho	ID	Pennsylvania	PA
Illinois	IL	Rhode Island	RI
Indiana	IN	South Carolina	SC
Iowa	IA	South Dakota	SD
Kansas	KS	Tennessee	TN
Kentucky	KY	Texas	TX
Louisiana	LA	Utah	UT
Maine	ME	Vermont	VT
Maryland	MD	Virginia	VA
Massachusetts	MA	Washington	WA
Michigan	MI	West Virginia	WV
Minnesota	MN	Wisconsin	WI
Mississippi	MS	Wyoming	WY
Missouri	MO		

It is acceptable to abbreviate *District of Columbia* in text: *Washington, D.C.* Also, *United States* may be abbreviated to *U.S.* when used as an adjective, but it should be spelled out as a noun.

The U.S. government is divided into three branches.

Voter turnout in the United States is disturbingly low.

62 g Latin terms

The following abbreviations for common Latin terms are not generally used in text but may be used in documentation or notes. (See Chapters 30–33.)

ABBREVIATION	LATIN	MEANING
c. or ca.	*circa*	about
cf.	*confer*	compare
e.g.	*exempli gratia*	for example
et al.	*et alii*	and others
etc.	*et cetera*	and so forth
ibid.	*ibidem*	in the same place
i.e.	*id est*	that is
N.B.	*nota bene*	note well
vs. or v.	*versus*	against (used in legal case names)

62 h Initials and acronyms

Initials or *initial abbreviations* consist of the first letter of each word in a phrase or name, such as *IMF* for International Monetary Fund, *U.K.* for the United Kingdom, or *CD* for compact disc. An **acronym** is a word consisting of initials and pronounced as a word: *NATO* for North Atlantic Treaty Organization, *UNICEF* for United Nations International Children's Emergency Fund. Both initials and acronyms consist entirely of capital letters.

Most initial abbreviations and all acronyms are written without periods. Abbreviated names of some countries do use periods: *U.S., U.K.* Initials that stand for people's names also use periods, followed by a space: *B. B. King, George W. Bush.* (Note, however, that conventional references to American presidents by their three initials use neither periods nor spaces: *JFK, FDR.*) If you are not sure how to punctuate an abbreviation, consult a dictionary.

For unfamiliar initials or acronyms, provide the full name at the first mention followed by the abbreviation or acronym in parentheses.

> World commerce is governed in large part by a set of treaties called the General Agreement on Tariffs and Trade (GATT).

In later references, use just the abbreviation or acronym.

> GATT keeps countries from imposing unilateral import duties.

EDITING 3: PRACTICE

Look for examples of abbreviations in your textbooks as well as in popular writing in magazines, newspapers, and fiction. Does the use of abbreviations in both types of writing follow the rules outlined in this chapter? Why do you think words have been abbreviated as they have in each kind of writing?

EDITING 4: PRACTICE

Edit the following passage, using abbreviations correctly.

> Although the United States Constitution is supposed to guarantee equal rights to all people regardless of color, in the first half of this century most African Americans in the southern U.S. lived in deplorable conditions. E.g., African Americans had to use separate washrooms, and they could not attend schools with whites. Not until the 1940s did the United States Supreme Court finally begin to outlaw practices that deprived African Americans of their rights. One small step toward equality was made when representatives from the National Association for the Advancement of Colored People (N.A.A.C.P.) persuaded the Court that maintaining separate schools for African Americans and whites was not equal. In 1954, under Chief Justice Earl Warren of Calif., the Court ordered the desegregation of schools in the U.S. Despite the new legislation, however, the southern states still resisted integration, and only Senator Lyndon Johnson from TX and two sen. from Tenn. (Estes Kefauver and Albert Gore, Senior) were in favor of desegregating the schools. Racial conflict raged throughout the southern states over the issue of integration; one area of conflict was Little Rock, Ark., where resistance was so great that the National Guard had to be

Using Articles with Degree Abbreviations, Initials, and Acronyms

Before **degree abbreviations** in the singular, you need to use an article: *a, an,* or *the.* The choice of *a* or *an* depends on how the first letter in the abbreviation is pronounced.

▪ Use *an* if the first letter of the abbreviation is a vowel or is a consonant that is pronounced with a vowel sound at the beginning.

He just finished *an* AA degree.

An MS is a Master of Science degree. [*Pronounced "em"-"ess."*]

▪ Use *a* if the first letter of the abbreviation is a consonant that is pronounced with a consonant sound.

She has *a* PhD in physics.

For **initials** and **acronyms,** check a reference book to see whether an article is needed before them.

▪ Many of these words do not require an article when they are used as nouns.

I just read a new article about *NATO.* [not *the NATO*]

▪ Some initial abbreviations require the article *the* just as the spelled-out version would.

The FBI was called in to investigate the fire.

If you spelled it out, you would write The Federal Bureau of Investigation.

▪ If you use an abbreviation as an adjective, you may need to add the article *a* or *an* before it, depending on the meaning of the noun that follows. As with degrees, pronunciation of the abbreviation determines whether you should use *a* or *an.*

Both of my parents work in television, my mother at *an* NBC affiliate and my father at *a* CBS station.

The photograph on the front page showed *a* NATO session.

The acronym NATO *is pronounced as a word, not as individual letters.*

used to enforce integration. Even this drastic step did not solve the problem, however, and the struggle for equal education and other civil rights for African Americans went on for many years.

Examine a paper you are working on for misused or omitted abbreviations. Is there one kind of mistake in using abbreviations that you consistently make? If so, think about how, in editing your work, you might best remember to abbreviate words correctly. Edit any sentences in which you have made errors in abbreviating.

PART nine

www.prenhall.com/fulwiler

abbreviation A shortened form of a word: *U.S.* for "United States." See Chapter 62.

absolute A modifier indicating a quality that cannot be made larger or smaller (*entire, unique, superior*). An absolute does not have a comparative or superlative form. See 48e4.

absolute phrase A phrase that consists of a noun or pronoun and a participle and that modifies an entire sentence, not just one part of it. *The work done, the boss called for a celebration.*

abstract Referring to an intangible idea or a group without reference to individual characteristics: *baked goods, liberty, mountains.* Compare *concrete, general, specific.* See 40a.

abstract database A database of whose entries are summaries or *abstracts.* See *database.*

acronym An abbreviation that forms a word out of the initials of the name or title that it shortens: *NATO, LILCO, MoMA, MADD.* See 51a, 62h.

active voice See *voice.*

adjective A modifier that describes nouns and pronouns. There are three types of adjectives: **descriptive** (*green, tall*), **proper** (*Italian, Buddhist*), and **limiting** (*few, all, a, the*). See also *article* and *modifier.* See 40d, Chapter 48.

adjective clause A dependent clause introduced by a relative pronoun (*who, which, that*) and functioning as an adjective. See 38b.

adverb A modifier that describes a verb, adjective, another adverb, or a whole sentence. See also *modifier.* See Chapter 35, 62d.

adverb clause A dependent clause introduced by a subordinating conjunction (*when, where, because*) and functioning as an adverb. See 38b.

agent The person or thing that performs an action. In a sentence in which the verb is in the passive voice, the agent, if indicated, is usually the object of the preposition *by.* See also *voice;* see 40c, 47a.

agreement Grammatical correspondence in number, person, and gender between subjects and their verbs and between pronouns and their antecedents. See 47h–47u, 49f–49j.

analogy Description by pointing out a similarity in otherwise unrelated objects or processes. See *figurative language.*

analytical interpretation   See *interpretive essay.*

anecdote   A brief story that illustrates the theme or thesis of a piece of writing. See 37a.

annotating   Writing comments on a text to record one's responses during critical reading.

antecedent   The element that a pronoun replaces. Pronouns agree with their antecedents in person, number, and gender. See also *agreement, gender, number,* and *person.* See Chapter 49.

antithesis   A thesis presented in opposition to another thesis in a position paper. See *synthesis.*

antonyms   Words whose meanings are the opposite of each another. See 43b.

appositive   A word or phrase that follows a noun or pronoun and describes or renames it: *Cliff, an old family friend, always helps out at harvest time.* See 49m, 52c2.

argument paper   An essay whose purpose is to persuade readers to support one side of an issue or accept an answer to a question. See also *interpretive essay, position paper.* See Chapter 10.

argument research   Research undertaken to collect information to support an argument. See also *informational research;* see Chapter 10, 22c.

article   *A, an* (**indefinite articles**) or *the* (**definite article**) are considered adjectives. See 35a, 35e.

attribution or attributory words   Words that indicate the person who is quoted in a direct quotation: *I said, Jonathan wrote.* Also called **signal phrase.** See Chapter 16, 52g.

audience   The readers to whom a piece of writing is directed. See 5b, 15c2.

automatic phrase   A phrase that is used habitually but adds little to a sentence's meaning. See 41b.

auxiliary verb   A form of the verbs *be, do,* or *have* or the verbs *can, could, may, might, must, shall, should, will,* or *would.* An auxiliary verb together with a main verb or a participle constitutes a *verb phrase.* Also called *helping verb.* See 34c1, 61c.

base form   The first- and second-person, singular, and plural present-tense form of a verb: *go, stop, sit, stand.* Also called *plain form* or *simple form.* See 47a.

biased language   Writing in which meaning is expressed by connotation, sterotype, or prejudice rather than by direct statements of fact, inference, or evidence. See Chapter 44.

bibliographic database   See *database.*

bibliography   A list of works related to a topic or of sources consulted in research. See 23b2, 30je, 32e.

Boolean operators   Words such as *AND, OR,* and *NOT* that limit the combination of words used in an Internet search to those most likely to locate the
topic of interest. See 24b.

brainstorming   An invention and discovery technique in which the writer
makes a list of possible solutions to a problem or answers to a question. See 7a.

browser   A computer program used to access the World Wide Web. See also
World Wide Web. See 24a.

bureaucratese   Jargon or pretentious language that is typical of governmental or institutional writing. See also *doublespeak, euphemism.* See 41e.

case   The form of a pronoun that shows whether it functions as a subject **(subjective case)** or an object **(objective case)** or whether it indicates ownership
(possessive case). Nouns change form only to show ownership (possessive
case). See 49k–49r, 55a.

cause-and-effect analysis   A writing strategy in which the writer identifies the action or actions (cause) that bring about a certain condition (effect).
See 8e1, 9d5.

chronological order   See *sequence of events.*

claim   A statement or assertion made in support of an argument. The argument's central claim is its *thesis.* A **counterclaim** is a claim made against the
thesis. See 10a.

class book   An edited, bound collection of student writing, usually featuring
some work from each student in a class. See 20d.

classification and division   A writing strategy in which the writer puts
ideas, things, or people in a category or class with similar items (classification)
and identifies distinguishing features (division). See 9d4.

clause   A group of words that includes both a subject and a predicate. See
also *dependent clause, independent clause;* see 38a–38b, 52a.

cliché   An expression used so often and for so long that it is no longer striking, vivid, or meaningful. See 43i.

climactic order   Presentation of specific details in order of increasing importance, ending with a dramatic statement, a climax. See 36b.

clustering   An invention and discovery technique in which ideas are
grouped nonlinearly, with relationships among them indicated by lines and
circles. See 7f.

coherence   The connection between ideas established by clear, focused, logical development and careful transitions. See 36c.

coined compound   A compound word (generally hyphenated) made up by a
writer to express an idea in a particularly concise or vivid way. See 60c.

collaborating   Working as a group with other writers. See 21a, 22b.

collective noun   A singular noun that names a group of things or people:
fleet, team, family. See 47n, 59i.

colloquialism   A term or expression used in spoken language but not accepted in formal writing. See 43g.

command   A sentence that gives an order or instruction. Also called *imperative sentence.* See 39c, 51a, 51c.

comma splice   The joining of two independent clauses with only a comma. See Chapter 46.

common noun   A noun that names a general person, place, or thing. Also called *generic noun.* See also *proper noun.* See 59c.

communicative writing   Writing whose primary purpose is to communicate information and ideas. The most common communicative purposes are to recount an experience, to report information, to explain an idea, and to argue a position. See 5a2.

comparative form   See *modifier.*

comparison and contrast   A writing strategy in which the writer describes similarities between two or more things or people (comparison) and then the differences between them (contrast). See also *contrast.* See 9c3.

complement   A word or phrase that renames a subject or object. A **subject complement** is an adjective or noun that follows a linking verb and renames the subject: *Tom is patient.* An **object complement** is an adjective or noun that follows an object and renames it: *They named him captain.* See also *linking verb.* See 47k, 49l3, 52j1.

complete predicate   See *predicate.*

complete subject   See *subject.*

complex sentence   A sentence that includes one independent clause and one or more dependent clauses. *While you were out, your mother called.* See 39c.

compound adjective   See *compound word.*

compound antecedent   An antecedent made up of two or more nouns or pronouns joined by a coordinating conjunction. See 49g–49h.

compound-complex sentence   A sentence containing two or more independent clauses and at least one dependent clause: *While you were out, your mother called, and the sink overflowed.* See 49c.

compound noun   See *compound word.*

compound object   An object of a verb or preposition composed of two or more nouns or pronouns joined by a coordinating conjunction. See 49l2.

compound predicate   Two or more predicates (verbs) that share a subject and that are joined by a coordinating conjunction: *My uncle Ron shaved and dressed.* See also *predicate.* See 52j.

compound sentence   A sentence containing two or more independent clauses and no dependent clauses: *I went to John's house, but he wasn't home.* See 38a, 39c, 52a.

compound subject   Two or more subjects that share a predicate and that are joined by a coordinating conjunction: *Her dog and her cat got sick.* See also *subject.* See 474l–47m, 49l1, 52j.

compound word   A single unit formed by combining two or more words. A *closed compound* is written as one word: *keyhole.* An *open compound* is written as two or more separate words: *soccer player;* other compounds are hyphenated. See 47c, 58b3.

concise   Writing that uses few words to achieve its purpose. See Chapter 41.

conclusion   The final section of a paper, in which the writer summarizes what has gone before and makes general statements about the topic that are needed to complete the paper's purpose. See 37c–37d.

concrete   A word or term that refers to an individual object or person, something specific or tangible: *apple strudel, Pike's Peak.* Compare *abstract, general, specific.* See 40a.

conjunction   A word or pair of words that connects two sentence elements and expresses a relationship between them. A **coordinating conjunction** joins elements of equal grammatical weight: *and, but, or, nor, so, for, yet.* A **correlative conjunction** is a pair of words that joins two grammatically equivalent elements: *both . . . and, either . . . or, neither . . . nor, not only . . . but also, whether . . . or.* A **subordinating conjunction** introduces a dependent clause and indicates its relationship to an independent clause. Subordinating conjunctions include *although, because, when,* and *while.* See also *conjunctive adverb.* See Chapter 38, 46a, 47l–47m, 49h–49i, 49l.

conjunctive adverb   A conjunctive adverb, together with a semicolon, joins two independent clauses: *however, therefore, furthermore.* See 52d.

connotation   A word's associations in addition to its literal meaning. See also *denotation.* See 43d.

context   Background information or setting provided for readers to understand a whole work. See 5b, 10c1.

contraction   A word or phrase shortened by the omission of one or more letters, which are replaced with an apostrophe. See 42c, 55c1.

contrast   Words, phrases, or clauses that emphasize a point by describing what it is not or by citing an opposite condition. Usually set off by commas. See 52d. See also *comparison and contrast.*

convention   The accepted, standard, or customary way of doing something. *Academic conventions* call for an objective style and a clear thesis statement. See 20e. Conventions for writing are a language's set of customs for using words, grammar, and punctuation. See 35b.

coordinate adjectives   Two or more adjectives with distinct meanings modifying a noun or pronoun separately: *The tired, discouraged, disgusted ballplayer slumped on the bench.* Coordinate adjectives are separated by commas. See also *cumulative adjectives.* See 52f2.

coordinating conjunction   See *conjunction*.

coordination   The grammatical connection of two or more ideas to give them equal emphasis and importance. See 38a, 39c.

correlative conjunction   See *conjunction*.

counterclaim   See *claim*.

count noun   A noun that names something that can be counted by unit or instance: *fifty laps, thirty-nine flavors, two apples.* See also *noncount noun.* See 35a.

creative writing   Writing whose primary purpose is the creation of a text that is enjoyable and rewarding in and of itself, in addition to the information or ideas it conveys. Fiction, poetry, and drama are commonly identified as creative writing, but all writing can be creative. See 5a3.

critical essay   See *interpretive essay*.

critical reading   An analysis of an author's assumptions, ideas, arguments, and conclusions to understand them better, test them, and determine their meaning in an overall sense. See Chapter 2 and Chapter 3.

critical thinking   The process of gathering, evaluating, and synthesizing information to reach one's own conclusions.

cross-reference   In-text notes that indicate relationships among text passages.

cumulative adjectives   Two or more adjectives that build on one another and together modify a noun: *The unsightly green chair had been in the family for five generations.* See also *coordinate adjectives.* See 39f2.

cumulative sentence   A sentence in which the main idea is stated at the beginning. See also *periodic sentence.* See 39c.

dangling modifier   A modifier, often a participle or participial phrase, that does not modify a clearly stated noun or pronoun: *Driving down the highway, the radar detector went off.* See 48g.

database   A large, structured collection of related information in print or electronic form. A **bibliographic database** lists articles or books by subject, title, and author. An **abstract database** contains summaries of the articles listed in addition to the bibliographic information. A **full-text database** contains a complete or nearly complete text of the articles listed. See 23b3, 23c.

deductive reasoning   Reasoning in which general statements lead to a conclusion about a specific case: *All cats purr. Rex is a cat. Therefore Rex purrs.* See also *inductive reasoning*.

definite article   See *article*.

definition   A writing strategy in which the writer describes something so that it can be distinguished from similar things. See 9c1.

degree   See *modifier*.

demonstrative adjective   See *demonstrative pronoun*.

denotation   A word's literal meaning. See also *connotation.* See 43d.

dependent clause A clause containing a subject and a verb but introduced by a subordinating conjunction or a relative pronoun: *We went because we had to.* A dependent clause cannot constitute a complete sentence. Also called *subordinate clause.* See 51b, 52c, 54c, 58b, 59e.

description A writing strategy in which the writer creates an image of something, using words that appeal to the five senses. See 9c2.

descriptive modifier See *adjective.*

design Deciding how to present written material visually, including selection of paper, type fonts, spacing, and placement of headings and titles among the considerations. See Chapter 17.

desktop publishing The art of using computers and computer-based programs to design documents visually. See Chapter 17, 19b–19c.

direct address A word or phrase that indicates a person or persons who are spoken to: *Don't forget, Amy, to lock the door.* See 52e.

direct discourse See *quotation.*

direct object See *object.*

direct question A sentence that asks a question and ends with a question mark: *Which way is north?* See also *indirect question, tag sentence;* see 51b.

direct quotation See *quotation.*

discovery writing Writing whose primary purpose is to uncover ideas and information stored in the writer's memory. See also *invention;* see Chapter 7.

disruptive modifier A modifier placed in such a way as to make the phrase or clause it modifies difficult to follow. See also *split infinitive;* see 48h.

division See *classification and division.*

documentation The practice and procedures for crediting and identifying source materials used in research writing. Standard documentation styles are MLA style for writing in language and literature, Chicago (CMS) style for writing in other humanities, and APA style for writing in the social sciences. See 27g, 30d, 31d, 32d, 33d, 34f, 35d.

double negative The nonstandard use of two negative modifiers that, in effect, cancel each other out. *This is not hardly good English.* See 48d.

doublespeak An extreme form of euphemism that purposely describes things so they seem the opposite of what they actually are. See 41f.

drafting The stage of the writing process in which the writer begins to produce a text. The complete text is called a **draft;** each subsequent revision of the piece of writing is considered a new draft. See also *editing, revising;* see 4c.

dynamic verb See *verb.*

editing The stage of the writing process in which the writer improves a draft by making sentences and words clearer, more powerful, and more precise. See also *revising;* see 4f, Chapter 35.

effect See *cause-and-effect analysis.*

effectiveness The quality of writing that makes it clear, interesting, and readable. See 3f, Chapters 35–44.

editorial *we* Reference to the writer in the first-person plural, even when only one person is writing. Used to indicate that the writing represents the work or opinions of the writer and his or her colleagues. See 50a1.

ellipsis The deliberate omission of one or more words from a quoted phrase or clause. An ellipsis must be indicated by ellipsis points (. . .). See also *elliptical construction;* see 57c.

elliptical construction A phrase or clause from which one or more words are omitted and are assumed to be understood: *I ordered the shrimp; Angelo, the lobster.* See 38f, 39f.

endnotes Notes at the end of a chapter or paper that list sources cited according to superscript numbers in the text. A documentation system that follows CMS style. See 32d2.

end punctuation One of three marks of punctuation—a period, a question mark, or an exclamation point—used to indicate a full stop at the end of a sentence. See Chapter 51.

error Departure from a rule. See 35b.

etymology The source and development of a word. See 43b4.

euphemism A polite term substituted for one considered unpleasant or impolite. See 41f.

evaluation Comment that places a value or rating on a piece of work or judges it. See also *suggestion.*

evidence Information presented in support of an argument. The most important types of evidence are facts, examples, inferences, informed opinions, and personal testimony. See 10a4, 10e.

evocative detail A description of setting or character that relies on an appeal to the senses to make the subject vivid. See 37a1.

exclamatory sentence A sentence that expresses strong feeling and that usually ends with an exclamation point. See 51c.

explanatory writing A presentation of information and ideas that will help readers understand the subject. Explanatory essays are sometimes called *informative papers, expository papers,* or *reports.* See Chapter 9.

expletive construction A sentence beginning with *it* or *there* (called an *expletive* when used in this manner), followed by a form of the verb *be* and the subject of the sentence: *There is a delay on Route 24 this morning.* See 40b1, 41c, 47j.

expository paper See *explanatory writing.*

fact A verifiable piece of information that most readers will accept without further argument. See *opinion.*

fallacy   Incorrect logic or weak reasoning. See 10e.

faulty predication   A mixed construction in which the subject and verb do not make sense together. See 50b3.

field research   Research conducted outside of the library by **interviewing** people who have information about a topic or by **observing** people and activities related to the topic. See Chapter 25.

figurative language   The use of imagery or comparison. The main types of figurative language are *analogy, hyperbole, irony, metaphor, paradox, personification, simile,* and *understatement.* See 9d, 43h.

finite verb   A verb that changes form to indicate person, number, tense, and mood. See also *infinitive, verbal.*

first person   See *person, point of view.*

flashback   See *sequence of events.*

footnote   A note at the bottom of a page listing, in numerical sequence, sources cited by superscript number in the text on that page. A documentation system that follows CMS style. See 32d2.

formality   A quality of language created by word choice and sentence structure and ranging from the very formal (or ceremonial) to the familiar. See 29c.

fragment   A word group that is grammatically incomplete but is punctuated as a sentence. See Chapter 45.

freewriting   An invention and discovery technique in which the writer writes quickly without stopping. See 7b.

full-text database   See *database.*

fused sentence   Independent clauses joined without a conjunction or proper punctuation. Also called *run-on sentence.* See Chapter 46.

gender   (1) The categorization of a noun or pronoun as masculine, feminine, or neuter. See also *agreement.* See 49f. (2) The categorization of a person as male or female. See 44c. Pronouns must agree with their antecedents in gender.

general   Categorization of a word or statement that includes or refers to an entire group, type, or category. See also *specific;* see 35a, 40a.

generality   A generalization that is essentially meaningless or empty. See 41a.

generalization   A conclusion based on a number of specific facts or instances, the result of *inductive reasoning.* See *inductive reasoning, inference, generality.* See 10e, 41a, Chapter 44.

gerund   The *-ing* form of a verb functioning as a noun: *Acting is her life.* See also *participle, verbal.* See 47b, 49o.

governing pronoun   Predominance of first, second, or third person used to convey a point of view in a piece of writing. See 42b.

grammar   A system for describing how sentences are organized and structured. See 35a11, Chapters 45–50.

helping verb   See *auxiliary verb.*

homonym   A word that sounds like another word but has a different spelling and meaning. See 43e.

hyperbole   Deliberate exaggeration for emphasis or effect. See *figurative language.*

idiom   A customary phrase or usage that does not make literal sense or follow normal rules. See 43f.

imperative   See *command.*

imperative mood   See *mood.*

implied subject   A subject that is not stated but that can be inferred from context. In commands, the subject *you* is usually implied: *Shut the door.* See also *subject.*

imply   To suggest a conclusion without explicitly stating it. Said of a speaker. See *infer.* See Chapter 64.

indefinite article   See *article.*

indefinite pronoun   A pronoun that refers to a nonspecific person or thing and therefore does not have a clear antecedent: *anybody, no one, everything, some, none.* See 47o, 49j.

independent clause   A clause with a subject and a predicate that can stand alone as a complete sentence. Also called *main clause.* See also *dependent clause;* see Chapters 32–33, 52a.

indicative mood   See *mood.*

indirect discourse   See *quotation.*

indirect object   See *object.*

indirect question   A sentence that reports a question, usually in a dependent clause, and ends with a period: *She asked whether I would go along.* See also *direct question, tag sentence.* See 51b.

indirect quotation   See *quotation.*

inductive reasoning   Reasoning in which specific facts support a probable general conclusion: *The alarm has rung at 8:30 on the past five mornings. The alarm will probably ring at 8:30 this morning.* See also *deductive reasoning.*

infer   To draw a conclusion from evidence or premises. Said of the reader or listener. See also *imply.* See Chapter 64.

infinitive   The base form of a verb preceded by *to.* An infinitive functions as a noun, adverb, or adjective. See also *verbal;* see 47b, 49o.

informal   See *level of formality.*

informational research   Research undertaken to collect information needed to answer a research question. See also *argument research;* see 22b.

informational thesis   See *thesis.*

informative paper   See *explanatory writing.*

initials   The first letter of each word in a phrase or name. See 62g.

intensive pronoun   A pronoun ending in *-self* or *-selves* used for emphasis: *I prefer steak myself.* See also *reflexive pronoun;* see 49r.

interior monologue   A portrayal of unspoken thoughts, often expressed with sentence fragments and made-up words; described as talking to oneself.

interjection   A term inserted into a sentence or standing alone that expresses strong feeling or reaction: *wow, jeepers.* See 52e3.

Internet   The international network by which computers send and receive information, in the form of data, images, and sound. Called the Net for short. See also *online, World Wide Web;* see Chapter 18, Chapter 24, 23b.

interpretive community   Any group that shares a set of beliefs or approaches to analyzing, discussing, and interpreting ideas. See 11c.

interpretive essay   An essay whose purpose is to analyze a text and present a persuasive explanation of its meaning. Sometimes called *analytical essay, critical essay, critical analysis, literary interpretation,* or *review.* A **personal interpretation** uses the writer's beliefs, experiences, and viewpoint to give meaning to the text. An **analytical interpretation** deemphasizes the writer's personal relationship to the text and focuses on the work being interpreted. See Chapter 11.

interrogative pronoun   A pronoun used to introduce a question: *who, whose.* See 49q1.

interrogative sentence   A sentence that asks a question. See also *direct question, indirect question, tag sentence.* See 51b.

interview   See *field research.*

intransitive verb   A verb that expresses action or being with no object or recipient. See also *transitive verb.* See 47b3.

introductory element   A dependent clause, phrase, or word that precedes the subject and verb of a sentence. Usually followed by a comma. See 52b.

invention   Writing or other activities undertaken to help the writer develop solutions to questions and problems encountered in the writing process. See also *discovery writing.* See Chapter 7.

inverted word order   The placement of words in a sentence in an unexpected sequence to ask a question or create emphasis.

invisible writing   An invention and discovery technique in which the writer uses a word processor for freewriting but darkens the screen so that the words on it are invisible. See 7b.

irony   An inconsistency between expectations and experience or between intended and apparent meaning: *Even as their leaders rail against the cultural influence of Hollywood culture, people flock to the movies.* See also *figurative language.*

irregular verb   A verb that does not follow the usual *-d* or *-ed* pattern in spelling its past tense and past participle. See also *regular verb.* See 47b2.

I-search essay   A piece of writing that focuses on the process of the search instead of the result. See 18b, 22e4.

issue   A topic that can be argued about, often stated in the form of a question. It raises a real question that has at least two distinct answers, one of which the writer is interested in advocating. See 10a–10c.

italics   Type characterized by slanted letters. See also *roman;* see Chapter 61.

jargon   Terms and expressions that arise within a specialty or field, often essential language for people in that field but not understood by others. See 43g.

journal   A record of a person's thoughts and ideas on any aspect of life, work, or studies. See Chapter 6.

judgment   See *evaluation.*

keyword   An important word related to a research topic, used to search for references. See 23b.

level of formality   See *formality.*

limiting modifier   A modifier that distinguishes the word modified from other similar things. See also *adjective;* see 48f.

linking verb   A verb that connects a subject to a complement, which is a word that renames or describes the subject. See also *complement;* see 47k, 48b, 49l3.

listserv   An e-mail program that automatically sends copies of messages to every subscriber on a list. See also *newsgroup;* see 24d.

literary interpretation   See *interpretive essay.*

literary present   The present tense used to describe the events of a literary work. See 47d.

logic   Systematic thinking that bases conclusions on reasonable relationships between pieces of evidence.

looping   An invention and discovery technique in which the writer creates a series of freewritings, each building on the most important idea uncovered in the previous one. Sometimes called *loop writing.* See also *freewriting;* see 7c.

main clause   See *independent clause.*

main verb   The verb that expresses the action of the sentence. See also *verb phrase.*

mechanics   The standardized features of written language, other than punctuation, that are used to clarify meaning. Elements of mechanics are spelling, capitalization, hyphenation, and italics. See 35a13, Chapters 58–62.

metaphor   To describe one thing in terms of another, without explicitly making a comparison: *The tree of liberty must be refreshed from time to time with the blood of patriots and tyrants.* See *figurative language.*

misplaced modifier   A modifier that is placed in a sentence so as to be unclear what it describes or which word it modifies. See also *dangling modifier;* see 48f.

mixed construction   A sentence combining sentence structures that do not fit together grammatically. See 50b.

mixed metaphor   An implied comparison in which unrelated elements are introduced from a different implied comparison: *We're all in the same boat, so we mustn't fumble.* See also *figurative language;* see 43h.

modal auxiliary   An auxiliary verb that does not change form for person or number. The one-word modals are *can, could, may, might, must, shall, should, will,* and *would.* See 47c1.

modifier   A word or group of words that describes another word, phrase, or clause. The most common modifiers are adjectives and adverbs. Modifiers have three forms: **positive,** which simply states a quality (*He worked hard*); **comparative,** which compares the degree of that quality between two persons or things (*He worked harder than his sister*); and **superlative,** which compares the degree of the quality among three or more persons or things (*He worked hardest of all the company's employees*). See Chapter 48.

modifier clause   A dependent clause that functions as an adjective or adverb.

modifier phrase   A phrase that functions as an adjective or adverb.

mood   The property that indicates the speaker's relation to the action of a verb, stating fact **(indicative),** giving a command **(imperative mood),** or expressing a wish or condition contrary to fact **(subjunctive).** See 47f–47g.

multiple-word verb   See *phrasal verb.*

newsgroup   A collection of postings on the Internet about a single topic. Also called a *usenet group.* See also *listserv;* see 24d.

nominalization   A noun made from a verb: *estrange* plus *-ment* equals the noun *estrangement.* See 40b3.

noncount noun   A noun that names something concrete that cannot be counted and given a number: *silver, tobacco, information.* Also called *mass noun.* See 47a.

nonrestrictive clause   See *restrictive and nonrestrictive clauses.*

nonsexist language   See *sexist language.*

nonstandard English   Usage that reflects the speech patterns of a particular community but does not follow the conventions of the dominant American dialect. Nonstandard English is inappropriate for academic writing.

noun   A word that names a person, animal, place, object, or idea. See also *common noun, count noun, noncount noun, proper noun.*

noun clause   A dependent clause that functions as a noun: *I explained <u>how I built the model</u>.* See 47r.

noun cluster   A group of words consisting of a noun and several other nouns used as modifiers: *hardwood parquet ballroom dance floor.* See 40d.

noun phrase   A noun and its modifiers. See 47r.

number   The characteristic of a noun, pronoun, or verb that indicates whether it is *singular* (referring to one person or thing) or *plural* (referring to more than one). See also *agreement.* See 47h–47u, 49f–49j.

object   A noun, pronoun, or noun phrase or clause that receives the action of a verb or a preposition. A **direct object** receives the action of a verb or verbal: *She read the newspaper.* An **indirect object** indicates to or for whom or what the action of the verb is directed: *She gave him the newspaper.* The **object of a preposition** follows a preposition: *They wrote a story about the event.* See *prepositional phrase.*

object complement   See *complement.*

objective case   See *case.*

objective stance   See *stance.*

observation   See *field research.*

online   Connected to the Internet. See 23c, Chapter 24.

opening   The beginning of an essay, which establishes the subject, the tone, and sometimes the theme or thesis of the essay. See 15d7, 37a–37b.

opinion   An idea that reflects an author's personal beliefs and conclusions, as distinguished from verifiable fact. See also *fact.*

organize   Arrange in a clearly perceptible order. See *sequence of events;* see also *climactic order, spatial order;* see 36b.

outline   Organized list of points to be made in an essay. See 7e, 15d, 27c.

paradox   An apparently self-contradictory statement that is nevertheless true: *The proper task of parenthood is preparing your children to leave you.* See also *figurative language.*

paragraph   A group of sentences about a single topic. Good paragraphs are unified, coherent, and well organized. See Chapter 36.

parallelism   The use of similar grammatical elements or structures—words, phrases, clauses, sentences, or paragraphs—for emphasis. See 38e–38f.

paraphrase   A restatement of the ideas of a written or spoken source in the writer's own words. See also *quotation, summary;* see 23e3, 27d2.

parenthetical expression   A word or word group that comments on or adds information to a sentence but is not part of the sentence structure and does not alter its meaning. Parenthetical elements appear between parentheses, commas, or dashes. See 52d, 57a–57b.

participial phrase   A phrase built around a present or past participle that functions as a modifier.

participle   A verb form that expresses continuing or completed action. A **present participle** is created by adding -*ing* to the base form. Used with auxiliary verbs, it forms the progressive tenses. Without an auxiliary verb, a present participle is a modifier when functioning as an adjective or a *gerund* when functioning as a noun. See also *gerund, verbal.* See 47b, 47c, 49o. A **past participle** is created by adding -*d* or -*ed* to the base form in regular verbs. In irregular verbs the past participle is formed differently for each verb. Used with auxiliary verbs, it forms perfect tenses. Used without an auxiliary verb, it functions as a modifier. See also *verbal;* see 47a, 47e, 49o.

particle   See *phrasal verb.*

part of speech   Designation of a word as a noun, pronoun, verb, adjective, preposition, conjunction, or interjection.

passive voice   See *voice.*

past participle   See *participle.*

past tense   See *tense.*

perfect progressive tense   See *tense.*

perfect tense   See *tense.*

periodic sentence   A sentence in which the main idea is placed at the end. See also *cumulative sentence.* See 39c.

person   The characteristic of a noun, pronoun, or a verb that indicates whether the subject or actor is the one speaking (**first person:** *I, we*), spoken to (**second person:** *you*), or spoken about (**third person:** *he, she, it, they*). See also *agreement;* see 42b, 47a, 47h, Chapter 49.

personal experience paper   A common college writing assignment whose purpose is to recount events experienced by the writer in an interesting and enlightening manner. See Chapter 8.

personal interpretation   See *interpretive essay.*

personal pronoun   A pronoun that refers to a particular person, group, or thing. Chapter 49.

personification   Speaking of an inanimate force or object as though it were a person: *The wind keened as though it had lost a child.* See *figurative language.*

perspective   The vantage point from which a paper is written. Perspective is established through point of view, tense, emphasis, and level of formality. See also *point of view, stance, tone;* see 8c, 9e.

persuasion   See *argument paper.*

phrasal preposition   Words that work together as a single preposition: *except for, according to.*

phrasal verb   A verb with more than one word. Phrasal verbs are formed by combining a one-word verb with one or more **particles** such as *to* or *off.* Together, the verb and the particle(s) create a meaning that is distinct from that of the original verb: *come up, come off.* Also called *two-word verb* or *multiple-word verb.* See 43f.

phrase   A group of words that does not include both a subject and a verb but that work as a grammatical element, such as a noun, verb, or modifier. See also *absolute phrase, modifier phrase, noun phrase, object, prepositional phrase, verbal phrase, verb phrase.*

plagiarism   Any use of someone else's ideas or words without explicit and complete documentation or acknowledgment. See 23e3, Chapter 28.

plain form   See *base form.*

planning   The stage of the writing process that consists of creating, discovering, locating, developing, organizing, and trying out ideas. See 4b.

plural   See *number.*

point of view   An indication of the writer's relation to and attitude toward his or her material. See also *person;* see 8c, 30b, 42b.

position paper   A type of argument paper that sets forth a position on an issue of local or national concern. See Chapter 10.

positive form   See *modifier.*

possessive case   See *case.*

predicate   The **simple predicate** is the main verb of the sentence. The **complete predicate** is the simple predicate plus its modifiers, objects, and complements. See also *compound predicate.*

predicate adjective   An adjective complement. See also *complement.*

predicate noun   A noun as a complement. See also *complement.*

prefix   A word segment attached to the beginning of a word to change its meaning. See 43c.

preposition   A word *(in, with, about, on)* that connects a noun or noun phrase (the **object** of the preposition) to another word, phrase, or clause and conveys a relation between the elements connected. See also *object, prepositional phrase.*

prepositional phrase   A preposition, its object, and any associated modifiers: *The newspaper had a story <u>about the peace plan.</u>*

present participle   See *participle.*

pretentious language   Excessively formal, old-fashioned, or complicated words and expressions used not for their appropriateness but to impress the reader. See 41e.

primary source   Firsthand information and raw data on a topic. See also *secondary source.* See 22e, 30a, 31c2.

progressive tense   See *tense.*

pronoun   A word used in place of a noun or noun phrase. See also *agreement, antecedent, demonstrative pronoun, intensive pronoun, interrogative pronoun,* *personal pronoun, reciprocal pronoun, reflexive pronoun, relative pronoun.* See Chapter 49.

proofreading The final stage of a writing project, rereading to catch typographical errors, misspellings, and incorrect capitalization. See 35a13.

proper adjective See *adjective.*

proper noun The name of a particular person, place, animal, organization, or thing. Proper nouns are capitalized. See also *common noun.* See 59c.

punctuation A system of standardized marks to clarify meaning. See 35a12, Chapters 51–57.

purpose The reason for generating a piece of writing; the goal a writer wants to accomplish. Four general purposes for writing are to discover, to communicate, to persuade, and to create. See 5a.

qualifying phrase An expression such as *I think* or *in my opinion* that identifies a statement as the writer's idea rather than the thoughts or beliefs of others. See 37d3.

quotation The reproduction of a writer's or speaker's exact words. **Direct quotation** (or *direct discourse*) reproduces another person's words exactly, within quotation marks. In **indirect quotation** (or *indirect discourse*), a writer rephrases another person's words and integrates them grammatically and logically into his or her own sentence. See also *paraphrase, summary;* see 22e3, 27d1, Chapter 28, Chapter 56.

reciprocal pronoun A two-word pronoun that refers to one part of a plural antecedent: *each other, one another.* See 49a.

recounting experience See *personal experience paper.*

redundancy Unnecessary repetition. See 41d.

referent See *antecedent.*

reflective essay A common college writing assignment in which the writer reflects on a significant subject, raises questions about it, and speculates on possible meanings. Sometimes called simply an *essay.* See Chapter 8.

reflexive pronoun A pronoun ending in *-self* or *-selves* whose antecedent is the subject of the sentence it appears in: *I could kick myself.* See also *intensive pronoun;* see 49r.

regionalism A nonstandard expression common in one geographic area. See 43g.

register See *level of formality.*

regular verb A verb that forms its past tense and past participles by adding *-d* or *-ed* to the base form. See also *irregular verb.* See 47b.

relative clause A dependent clause that functions as an adjective. See *relative pronoun.*

relative pronoun A pronoun that introduces a noun clause or an adjective clause: *who, whose, which, what.* See 49a, 49b2.

report   See *explanatory writing.*

reporter's questions   Questions that reporters use in gathering information, also useful for invention and discovery: *Who? What? Where? When? Why? How?* Also called *journalist's questions.* See 7d, 23b.

research essay   A common college writing assignment in which students conduct research and write about their findings. Sometimes called *research paper* or *research report.* See Chapter 22.

research question   The question that research is designed to answer. See 22b3.

researching   The stage of the writing process in which the writer gathers information and ideas about which to write. Research is a part of all writing assignments except those written completely from personal experience. See also *argument research, field research, information research, research essay.* See 4d, Chapters 22–28.

responding   The act of offering comments on a writer's material, ideas, or drafts. See also *collaborating, writing group;* see Chapter 16.

restrictive and nonrestrictive clauses   *Restrictive clauses* limit or further identify the nouns they modify and are essential to the meaning of a sentence: *I bought the books that were assigned.* Restrictive clauses are not set off with commas from the words they modify. *Nonrestrictive clauses* do not limit the nouns they modify and are not essential to the meaning of a sentence: *The books, which were on a special shelf, cost sixty dollars.* Nonrestrictive clauses are set off with commas. See 52c.

review essay   See *interpretive essay.*

revising   The stage of the writing process in which the writer improves a draft by making changes to its direction, focus, argument, information, organization, or other important features. Revision generally occurs at the level of ideas. See also *editing;* see 4d, Chapters 14–16.

revision strategies   Plans and methods for revising. See Chapters 14–16.

rhetoric   The use of language to achieve the writer's (or speaker's) purpose in communicating with an audience. See 4f.

rhetorical question   A question not meant to be answered that sets up a response from the writer. See 37c1.

Roman   A typeface characterized by vertical characters. In most printed material, the body of the text is set in roman type. See also *italic;* see Chapter 61.

root   The part of a word that stays the same as the word changes form with the addition of prefixes and suffixes. *Route* is the root of *routing, routine, reroute.* Also called *base word.* See 31c, 50b.

rule   A convention so widely accepted that not to follow it is considered an error. See 35b.

run-on sentence   See *fused sentence.*

sarcasm   The deliberate use of words to say the opposite of what they mean, often with the intent of expressing contempt or displeasure: *Houseguests for the summer? Oh, joy!* See also *figurative language.*

search engine   A computer program that searches for information based on a word or phrase. Users indicate by *Boolean operators,* such as *and, or,* and *not,* a combination of words to limit a search to the topic of interest. See 24b.

second person   See *person, point of view.*

secondary source   Reports and interpretations of and arguments about firsthand information and raw data. Many of the sources consulted in library research are secondary sources. See also *primary source;* see 22e, 30a, 32c2.

sentence   A group of words containing a subject and a predicate and conveying a comprehensible, complete idea or thought.

sentence element   Designation of a word or group of words according to its function in a sentence. See *subject, predicate, object, complement, phrase, clause.*

sequence of events   The order in which events are related. The most straightforward sequence of events is **chronological order,** the order in which events occurred. See 36b2. Another sequence of events is the **flashback,** in which earlier events are related after later ones. See 8e.

sequence of tenses   The relationship between the main verb and all the other verbs in a sentence. See also *governing tense* in **tense.** See 47e.

series   A list of words, phrases, or clauses separated by commas or semicolons. See 38f, 52f1.

server   A host computer that stores files of information and distributes them on request. See 24a1.

sexist language   Any language in which assumptions about gender are embedded: *policeman, each must do his best.* Choose nonsexist alternatives. See 44c.

-s form   The third-person singular, present tense of a verb, created by adding *-s* or *-es* to the base form. See also *base form;* see 47a.

shift   Any change in verb tense, number, or person within a sentence or between sentences that results in confusion for the reader. See 50a.

signal phrase   Words such as *He said* or *according to* that identify the source of a quotation or an idea. Also called *attributory words.* See Chapter 16, 52g.

simile   To describe one thing explicitly in terms of another: *My love is like a red, red rose.* See *figurative language.*

simple form   See *base form.*

simple predicate   See *predicate.*

simple sentence   A sentence that contains only one independent clause. See 39c.

simple subject   See *subject.*

simple tense   See *tense.*

singular   See *number.*

slang   Colorful, irreverent, informal expressions usually coined by small groups. Slang is usually not appropriate in formal writing. See 43g.

spatial order   Organization of a physical description by moving from one detail to another. See 36b.

specific   Categorization of a word or statement that refers to a single, particular thing. Compare *general;* see also *abstract, concrete.* See 35a, 40a.

split infinitive   An often awkward construction in which words intervene between the infinitive marker *to* and the verb: *to quickly go.* See 48h1.

squinting modifier   An ambiguously placed modifier that does not clearly modify one sentence element but could modify more than one. See 48f.

stance   The perspective adopted for a particular paper. An **objective stance** focuses on the topic under discussion rather than on the writer's own thoughts and feelings. A **subjective stance** incorporates the writer's thoughts and feelings into the account or analysis. See Chapter 5.

standard English   Usage that follows the rules and conventions of written English. Standard English is appropriate for formal academic papers. See 35b, 43g.

state-of-being verb   See *verb.*

stereotype   Overgeneralization about a person or group based on gender, race, ethnicity, and so on. See 44a.

structure   The way in which the content of a paper is put together, including the order and grouping of ideas. See 5b.

style   (1) A writer's distinctive way of expression, established through the level of formality and the simplicity or complexity of words, sentences, and paragraphs. See also *level of formality;* see 5b2, 5c2. (2) In visual design, the overall effect of such features as type fonts, graphics, size of margins, and placement of headings, titles, page numbers, and notes. See Chapter 17.

subject   (1) The noun or pronoun that performs the action of the verb, is acted upon by the verb, or is described by the verb. The **simple subject** is the noun or pronoun alone. The **complete subject** is the noun or pronoun plus its modifiers. See also *compound subject, implied subject.* See 47h–47u. (2) The idea about which a paper is written. See also *topic.*

subject complement   See *complement.*

subjective case   See *case.*

subjective stance   See *stance.*

subjunctive mood   See *mood.*

subordinate clause   See *dependent clause.*

subordinating conjunction   See *conjunction.*

subordination   Connection of two or more ideas (usually clauses) to make one of them dominant and the other or others logically secondary or subordinate. See 38b–38c, 46e.

suffix   A word segment attached to the end of a word root to change its meaning or form. See 43c, 58b.

suggestion   A recommendation for revising a piece of work. See also *evaluation.*

summary   A distillation of a source's ideas into a brief statement phrased in the writer's own words. See also *conclusion, paraphrase, quotation;* see 23e3, 27d3, 37c2.

superlative   See *modifier.*

survey   A structured interview in which respondents, representative of a larger group, are all asked the same questions. Their answers are tabulated and interpreted in an effort to discover attitudes, beliefs, or habits of the larger population they represent. See 25c.

suspense   A writing strategy that sustains readers' interest by raising a question or posing a problem and delaying the answer or solution.

symbol   Something that stands for something else. In type, a character that represents a word or words. See 62e.

synonym   Word with the same meaning as another word or with a similar meaning. See 43b.

synthesis   An element of critical thinking in which a writer or reader applies the process of summary, analysis, and interpretation to conflicting beliefs to produce new ideas. See also *antithesis, thesis;* see 10a.

tag question   See *tag sentence.*

tag sentence   A brief sentence at the end of another sentence (after a comma) for emphasis or to elicit a response. A tag sentence may be either a statement or a question: *Mark cannot join us, I'm afraid. You're tired, aren't you?* See 33b1, 38b, 39e1.

telling detail   A fact or observation that advances the characterization of someone without the writer's having to render an obvious opinion. See 8a.

tense   The form a verb takes to show when its action occurs. **Simple tenses** show events that occur in the past, present, or future: *I walked, I am walking, I will walk.* **Perfect tenses** indicate action completed in the past (*had sat*), present (*have sat*), and future (*will have sat*). **Progressive tenses** indicate action happening continuously, and not necessarily ending, in the past (*was sitting*), present (*am sitting*), and future (*will be sitting*). **Perfect progressive tenses** express actions happening over a period of time and then ending in the past (*had been sitting*), the present (*have been sitting*), or in the future (*will have been sitting*). The **governing tense** is the tense used in verbs describing most of the actions in a paper or story. See 8c, 47d–47e.

text Any symbolic work constructed by humans that is open to interpretation. Originally written texts (essays, novels, plays, poems) but also images (photography, painting, film). See Chapter 11.

theme The central idea of a personal or reflective essay. It can be implied rather than stated directly. See 8f, 11d, 30b.

thesaurus A word reference that lists synonyms and antonyms.

thesis A statement of the point the writer hopes to make in the essay. A **working thesis** is a statement of the point a writer thinks a finished essay will make. An **argument thesis** expresses an opinion that the essay will support. An **information thesis** presents a factual statement to be supported with explanation and detail. See 5a, 9c, 10a, 11d, 22c.

third person See *person, point of view.*

tone The writer's attitude toward the subject and audience, conveyed through the piece of writing. Tone is established primarily through word choice, point of view, and level of formality. See also *level of formality, point of view;* see 5b2, Chapter 42.

topic The central issue, idea, or situation of a paper. Also called *main idea.* See also *subject.* See 2a, 36a, 37a.

topic sentence The sentence that states the main idea of a paragraph. See 36a.

transition A phrase, sentence, or paragraph that marks a change in focus or the introduction of a new idea.

transitional expression A word or phrase that connects separate ideas or statements and describes the relationship between them: *for example, as a result, later.* See 36c2, 52b, 52d.

transitive verb A verb that expresses an action with an object or recipient: *We counted the starfish.* See also *intransitive verb.* See 47b3.

two-word verb See *phrasal verb.*

understatement Deliberately excessive restraint in description: *Madonna achieved some fame as a singer.* See *figurative language.*

unified In reference to a paragraph, having all its sentences develop a single topic. See 36a.

URL (uniform resource locator) The address of a Web site, entered or displayed on the command line of a *browser.* See also *World Wide Web;* see 13a2.

verb A word that indicates action or existence, expressing what a subject does or is. See 62c. An *action verb* expresses motion or creates vivid images. See 27b, 34d. A *state-of-being verb* expresses a subject's existence rather than action: *be, seem, become.* See 22a7, 27b.

verb phrase A main verb plus any auxiliary verbs. See also *auxiliary verb;* see 47c1, 48h2.

verbal A verb form that does not function as the main verb of a sentence: *driving, to drive, driven.* See also *gerund, infinitive, participle;* see 47b, 49o.

verbal phrase   A verbal and its modifiers, objects, and complements.

voice   (1) The sense of the writer conveyed to the reader by a piece of writing. See 5d, 8a1. (2) In grammar, an attribute of a verb showing whether the action of the verb is performed by the sentence's subject **(active voice:** *Mary reads the book)* or is performed on the sentence's subject **(passive voice:** *The book is read by Mary).* See 40c, 47a.

vocabulary   The words commonly used by an individual or a group of people. See 43c.

wordiness   Unnecessary words. See 41b.

working thesis   See *thesis.*

World Wide Web   An Internet function that can display text, graphics, animation, photography, and sound. A **Web site** is a collection of Web pages, or files, from one source. See 18a, Chapter 24.

writing group   Writers who help one another by responding to one another's work or collaborating. See 16e.

writing portfolio   A collection of a writer's work contained within a single folder. See 20a, 20b.

writing process   The activities writers go through to produce a finished piece of writing. Writing processes vary from person to person and from situation to situation. However, the typical writing process can be described as having five distinct but overlapping stages: planning, drafting, researching, revising, and editing. See Chapter 4.

T his glossary provides information about words that are commonly confused with one another or used incorrectly. Others listed are considered inappropriate for formal academic writing. If you are unsure about how to use a word or are having trouble choosing between words, check here first.

Good usage consists of more than clear distinctions and unvarying rules. Some usages described here are considered incorrect—*discreet* for example means "prudent" but *discrete* means "separate"—no one who knows that these are two different words would argue that they are interchangeable. On the other hand, some usages are considered acceptable by some authorities but not by others. For example, some writers prefer to use *farther* only when referring to physical distances and *further* only when referring to the more abstract distances of time, quantity, or degree. However, respected writers have been using them interchangeably for hundreds of years. To decide what is appropriate for your writing, carefully consider the expectations of your audience. Instructors will appreciate your using words as carefully and precisely as possible. When in doubt, follow the recommendations here or in a more comprehensive reference such as *Choose the Right Word* by S.I. Hayakawa [New York: Collins, 1994] or *Merriam-Webster's Dictionary of English Usage* [Springfield, MA: Merriam-Webster, 1994].

Some of the usages described in this glossary occur frequently outside formal academic writing. For example, **nonstandard** usages (such as *anyways* instead of the standard *anyway*) reflect the speech patterns of particular communities but do not follow the conventions of the dominant American dialect. **Colloquial** usages (such as *flunk* meaning "to fail" or *awfully* meaning "very") are often heard in speech but are usually considered inappropriate for academic writing. **Informal** usages (such as using *can* and *may* interchangeably) may be acceptable in some papers but not in formal research or argument essays.

Except as noted, the usages recommended in this glossary are those of **standard** written English, that is, the usages that most closely follow the rules and conventions of the language. Standard written English is appropriate for formal academic papers.

a, an   Use *a* before words that begin with a consonant sound (*a boy, a hero, a shining star*), even if the first letter of the word is a vowel (*a useful lesson*). Use *an* before words that begin with a vowel sound (*an antelope, an umbrella*).

accept, except   *Accept* is a verb meaning "to receive" or "to approve" (*I accept your offer*). *Except* is a verb meaning "to leave out" or "to exclude" (*He excepted all vegetables from his list of favorite foods*) or a preposition meaning "excluding" (*He eats everything except vegetables*).

adapt, adopt   *Adapt* means "to adjust" or "to accommodate"; it is usually followed by *to* (*It is sometimes hard to adapt to college life*). *Adopt* means "to take into a relationship" (*They considered adopting a child*) or "to take and use as one's own" (*I have adopted my roommate's habits*).

adverse, averse   *Adverse* is an adjective meaning "unfavorable" or "unpleasant" (*Adverse weather forced us to cancel the game*). *Averse,* also an adjective, means "opposed to" or "feeling a distaste for"; it is usually followed by *to* (*We are averse to playing on a muddy field*).

advice, advise   *Advice* is a noun meaning "recommendation"; *advise* is a verb meaning "to give advice to" (*I advise you to take my advice*).

affect, effect   *Affect* as a verb means "to influence" or "to produce an effect" (*That movie affected me deeply*). In psychology, *affect* as a noun means "appearance" or "outward display of emotion." *Effect* is a noun meaning "result," "consequence," or "outcome" (*That movie had a profound effect on me*); it is also sometimes used as a verb meaning "to bring about" (*Dr. Johnson effected important changes as president*).

aggravate, aggrieve   *Aggravate* is a verb meaning "to make worse." *Aggravate* is sometimes used colloquially to mean "to irritate" or "to annoy," but in formal writing use *irritate* or *annoy* (*I was irritated by my neighbors' loud stereo; my irritation was aggravated when they refused to turn it down*). *Aggrieve* means "having a grievance or a complaint." (*They thought I was unreasonable, but I was clearly the aggrieved party.*)

ain't   *Ain't* is a nonstandard (colloquial) contraction for *am not, is not, are not, have not,* or *has not. Ain't* is not acceptable in formal writing except in reproducing dialogue.

all ready, already   *All ready* means "full prepared" (*They were all ready to leave*). *Already* means "previously" (*They had already left*).

all right, alright   The two-word spelling is preferred; the one-word spelling is considered incorrect by many.

all together, altogether   *All together* means "all gathered in one place" (*The animals were all together in the ark*). *Altogether* means "thoroughly" or "entirely" (*The ark was altogether too full of animals*).

allude, elude   *Allude* is a verb meaning "to refer (to something) indirectly"; it is followed by *to* (*Derek alluded to a rodent infestation*). *Elude* is a verb meaning "to escape" or "to avoid" (*The mice eluded Derek at every turn*).

allusion, illusion *Allusion* means "an indirect reference" or "the act of alluding to, or hinting at, something" (*The phrase "I have a dream" is often an allusion to Dr. Martin Luther King, Jr.*). *Illusion* is a noun meaning "misleading image" or "misapprehension" (*Mr. Hodges created an optical illusion with two lines*).

a lot *A lot* should be written as two words. Although *a lot* is used informally to mean "a large number," avoid using it in formal writing (*The students had many* [not *a lot of*] *opportunities*).

a.m., p.m. or A.M., P.M. Use these abbreviations only with numbers to indicate time (6:30 p.m.). Do not use them as substitutes for *morning, afternoon, evening,* or *night*. Do not use them with *o'clock*.

among, between Use *among* to signify three or more choices (*Competition among the oil companies is intense*). *Between* means only two choices (*He divided the cake between the twins*).

amount, number Use *amount* to refer to quantities that cannot be counted (*Fixing up the abandoned farmhouse took a great amount of work*). Use *number* for quantities that can be counted (*A large number of volunteers helped*).

an See *a, an.*

and/or *And/or* is used in technical and legal writing to connect two terms when either one or both apply (*Purchasers must select type and/or size*). When possible, avoid and/or by using the construction "A or B or both" (*Students may select chemistry or physics or both*).

anxious, eager *Anxious* is an adjective meaning "worried" or "uneasy" (*Lynn is anxious about her mother's surgery*). Do not confuse it with *eager,* which means "enthusiastic" or "impatient" (*I am eager* [not *anxious*] *to leave*).

anybody, anyone; any one *Anybody* and *anyone* refer to an unspecified person (*Anybody may apply for the new scholarship. Anyone on the hill could have seen our campfire*). *Any one* means "unspecified, but only one" (*Each child may select any one toy from the box*).

anyplace, anywhere In formal writing, use *anywhere,* not *anyplace* (*You may sit anywhere you choose*).

anyways Use the standard word *anyway.*

as *As* may be used to mean "because" (*We did not go ice skating as the lake was no longer frozen*), but only if no confusion will result. For example, *We canceled the meeting as only two people showed up* could mean that the meeting was canceled either at the moment when the two people showed up or because only two showed up.

as, as if, like To indicate comparisons, *like* should be used only as a preposition followed by a noun (*Ken, like his brother, prefers to sleep late*). In formal writing, *like* should not be used as a conjunction linking two clauses. Use *as* or *as if* instead (*Ken sleeps late just as* [not *like*] *Carl does. Anne talks as if* [not *like*] *she has read every book by Ernest Hemingway*).

as to   Do not use *as to* as a substitute for *about* (*We inquired about* [not *as to*] *the company's affirmative action policies*).

assure, ensure, insure   *Assure* is a verb whose meaning is similar to "reassure" (*The lawyer assured her client that the case was solid*). *Ensure* and *insure* both mean "to make sure, certain, or safe," but *insure* generally refers to finance (*John hoped his college degree would ensure his future. He knew he would need to insure his house.*)

at present, presently   *At present* means "now, at this time." *Presently* means "soon."

averse   See *adverse, averse.*

awful, awfully   *Awful* is an adjective meaning "inspiring awe." In formal writing, do not use it to mean "disagreeable" or "objectionable." Similarly, the adverb *awfully* means "in an awe-inspiring way"; in writing, do not use it in the colloquial sense of "very."

awhile, a while   The one-word form *awhile* is an adverb that can be used to modify a verb (*We rested awhile*). Only the two-word form *a while* can be the object of a preposition (*We rested for a while*).

bad, badly   *Bad* is an adjective, so it must modify a noun or follow a linking verb, such as *be, feel,* or *become* (*John felt bad about holding the picnic in bad weather*). *Badly* is an adverb, so it must modify a verb (*Pam played badly today*).

being as, being that   *Being as* and *being that* are nonstandard expressions for *because* (*Since* [not *being as*] *her shoulder was injured, Anna withdrew from the tournament*). See *since.*

beside, besides   *Beside* means "by the side of" or "next to" (*The book is beside the bed*). *Besides* means "other than" or "in addition to" (*No one besides Linda can solve this problem*). *Besides* can also mean "furthermore" or "in addition" (*The weather is bad for hiking; besides, I have a cold*).

better   The phrasal auxiliary verb *had better* denotes obligation (*You had better hurry*). Do not use *better* alone in this sense.

between   See *among, between.*

biannual, biennial   *Biannual* refers to something that happens twice a year (*The biannual adjustments for daylight saving time occur in April and October*). The term *biennial* refers to something that happens every two years (*The Whitney Museum opens its biennial exhibit of American art next month*).

bisect, dissect   *Bisect,* pronounced bi-sect with a long i, means to divide into two parts (*In geometry, we learned to bisect an angle.*) *Dissect,* pronounced dis-sect with a short I, means to cut apart (*In biology, we had to dissect a frog.*)

breath, breathe   *Breath* is a noun (*I had to stop to catch my breath*). *Breathe* is a verb (*It became difficult to breathe at higher elevations*).

bring, take   The verb *bring* describes movement from far to near; the verb *take* describes movement away from a place (*Dr. Gavin asked us to bring our rough sketches to class; she said we could take them home after class*).

busted   *Busted* is a nonstandard past tense for *burst* (*The state Senate chamber was flooded when a water line burst*). As a synonym for *arrested, busted* is also nonstandard.

but, however, yet   Use these words alone, not in combination (*We finished painting, but* [not *but however*] *there is still much work to do*).

cache, cachet   *Cache,* pronounced like "cash," is a French term meaning "a hidden supply or source." *Cachet,* which rhymes with "sashay," means "a hidden charm."

can, may, might   In informal usage, *can* and *may* are often used interchangeably to indicate permission, but in formal writing, only *may* and its past tense *might* should be used this way (*May I borrow your dictionary?*). *May* also denotes possibility (*It may snow tomorrow. He said it might snow*). *Can* is used only to indicate ability (*I can see much better with glasses*).

capital, capitol   *Capital* is an adjective meaning "punishable by death" (*capital punishment*) or referring to uppercase letters (*A, B*). As a noun it means "accumulated wealth" (*We will calculate our capital at the end of the fiscal year*) or "a city serving as a seat of government" (*Albany is the capital of New York*). *Capitol* is a noun for the building in which lawmakers meet (*The civics class toured the state capitol last week*). Capitalize it when referring to a specific building: *The House and Senate meet in the Capitol.*

caveat   *Caveat,* from the Latin phrase *caveat emptor,* or "buyer beware," means "warning" or "caution." Do not use it to mean "condition" (*He approved the purchase on the condition that* [not *with the caveat that*] *the house pass a structural inspection.*)

censor, censure   *Censor* means to remove material from a text or an image; *censure* means "to blame or condemn sternly" (*Plans to censor song lyrics have been censured by groups that support free speech*).

center, epicenter   The *epicenter* is the spot on the Earth's surface directly above the site of an earthquake. Do not use *epicenter* when *center* will suffice.

center around, center on   *Center around* is colloquial for *center on* (*The discussion centered on the meaning of Darwin's theory to his scientific contemporaries*).

cite, site, sight   *Cite* means "to quote for the purposes of example, authority, or proof" (*Tracy cites several landmark cases in her treatise on capital punishment*). *Site* is usually used as a noun meaning "place" or "scene" (*Signs of prehistoric habitation were found at the site*). *Site* can also be used as a verb meaning "to place on a site." *Sight* is a verb meaning "to see" or a noun meaning "vision" (*Bligh's party finally sighted an island. The mariners thought it a beautiful sight.*).

climactic, climatic   *Climactic* derives from *climax,* a moment of greatest intensity (*In the climactic scene of the play, the murderer's identity is revealed*). *Climatic* derives from *climate* (*Pollution might cause climatic changes*).

compare to, compare with   *Compare to* means "to liken" or "to represent as similar" (*Jim compared our new puppy to an unruly child*). *Compare with* means "to examine to discover similarities or differences" (*We compared this month's ads with last month's*).

complement, compliment   *Complement* as a verb means "to fill out or complete"; it is also a noun meaning "something that completes or fits with" (*The bouquet of spring flowers complemented the table setting*). *Compliment* means "to express praise or admiration" or "an expression of praise or admiration" (*Russ complimented Nancy on her choice of flowers*).

compose, comprise   *Compose* means "to constitute or make up"; *comprise* means "to include or contain" (*Last year's club comprised fifteen members; only eight members compose this year's club*). Do not use *comprised of,* which makes no sense. Use *composed of* (*The club is composed of eight members*).

conscience, conscious   *Conscience* refers to a sense of right and wrong (*His conscience would not allow him to lie*). *Conscious* means "alert, awake," "marked by thought or will," or "acting with critical awareness" (*He made a conscious decision to be punctual*).

continual, continuous   *Continual* means "recurring" or "occurring repeatedly" (*Liz saw a doctor about her continual headaches*). *Continuous* means "uninterrupted in space, time, or sequence" (*Light refracted by raindrops forms the continuous band we call a rainbow*).

could have, must have, should have, would have   Do not use the preposition *of* instead of the auxiliary verb *have* (*I could have danced* [not *I could of danced*] *all night*). Do not use these modal auxiliary verbs in both clauses of a complex sentence (*If I had* [not *could have*] *stayed longer, I would have earned more.*)

council, counsel   *Council* is a noun meaning "a group meeting for advice, discussion, or government" (*The tribal council voted in favor of the new land rights law*). As a noun, *counsel* means "advice" or "a plan of action or behavior" (*The bishop gave counsel to the young men considering the priesthood*). *Counsel* may also be used as a verb meaning "to advise or consult" (*The priest counseled the young man*).

credible, incredible; credulous, incredulous   *Credible* and *incredible* describe whether something is believable or trustworthy (*His descriptions of life at sea seem credible enough, but his tales of his own heroism in battle are incredible*). *Credulous* means "willing to believe" and carries the connotation of "too willing to believe" (*Such a charismatic leader depends on credulous followers*). *Incredulous* means "unwilling to believe" (*The claim of controlled, low-temperature fusion was challenged by incredulous physicists around the world*).

criteria, criterion   *Criteria* is the plural of *criterion,* which means "a standard on which a judgment is based" (*Many criteria are used in selecting a president, but a candidate's hair color is not an appropriate criterion*).

data, datum   *Data* is the plural of *datum,* which means "a fact" or "a result in research." Some writers now use *data* as both a singular and a plural noun;

in formal usage it is still better to treat it as plural (*The data indicate that a low-fat diet may increase life expectancy*).

decent, descent, dissent   *Decent* means "good, proper." *Descent* means "the act of going down, the opposite of climbing." *Dissent* means "disagreement, especially political disagreement."

defuse, diffuse   *Defuse* means literally "to remove a fuse" (*They were able to defuse the controversy.*) *Diffuse* means "to dilute" or "diluted, scattered" (*A diffuse sample revealed no particular pattern.*)

detract, distract   *Detract* means "to take away from" (*This discovery should not detract from Einstein's achievement*). *Distract* means "to divert attention from" (*We should not let the controversy distract us from our purpose*).

device, devise   *Device* is a noun meaning "mechanism" or "invention" (*McCormick's reaper was an ingenious device for harvesting grain*). The verb *devise* means "to invent or discover" (*Perhaps you can devise a way to make an omelet without breaking eggs*).

differ from, differ with   *Differ from* means "to be unlike" (*This year's parade differed from last year's in many ways*). *Differ with* means "to disagree with" (*Stephanie differed with Tom over which parade was better*).

different from, different than   *Different from* is preferred to *different than* (*Hal's taste in music is different from his wife's*). But *different than* may be used to avoid awkward constructions (*Hal's taste in music is different than* [instead of *different from what*] *it was five years ago*).

discreet, discrete   *Discreet* means "prudent" or "modest" (*Most private donors were discreet about their contributions*). *Discrete* means "separate" or "distinct" (*Professor Roberts divided the course into four discrete units*).

disinterested, uninterested   *Disinterested* means "unbiased" or "impartial" (*It will be difficult to find twelve disinterested jurors for such a highly publicized case*). *Uninterested* means "indifferent" or "unconcerned" (*Most people were uninterested in the case until the police discovered surprising new evidence*).

don't   *Don't* is a contraction for *do not*, not for *does not*. The contraction for *does not* is *doesn't* (*He doesn't* [not *don't*] *know what to do about it*).

each   *Each* is singular (*Each tool has its own place; each is to be put away properly*).

effect   See *affect, effect*.

e.g.   *E.g.* is the Latin abbreviation for *exempli gratia*, which means "for the sake of example." In formal writing, use *for example* or *for instance*.

elicit, illicit   *Elicit* is a verb meaning "to draw forth" or "to bring out" (*The investigators could not elicit any new information*). *Illicit* is an adjective meaning "unlawful" or "not permitted" (*The investigators were looking for evidence of illicit drug sales*).

elude   See *allude, elude*.

emigrate, immigrate *Emigrate* means "to leave one's country to live or reside elsewhere" (*His grandparents emigrated from Russia*). *Immigrate* means "to come into a new country to take up residence" (*His grandparents immigrated to the United States*).

eminent, imminent *Eminent* means "prominent" (*Her operation was performed by an eminent surgeon*). *Imminent* means "impending" (*The hurricane's arrival is imminent*).

ensure See *assure, ensure, insure.*

enthused, enthusiastic In formal writing, *enthused,* the past tense of the verb *enthuse,* should not be used as an adjective; use *enthusiastic* (*Barb is enthusiastic* [not *enthused*] *about her music lessons*).

epicenter See *center, epicenter*

especially, specially *Especially* is an adverb meaning "particularly" or "unusually" (*The weather was especially cold this winter*). *Specially* is an adverb meaning "for a special reason" or "in a unique way" (*The cake was specially prepared for Sandy's birthday*).

etc. An abbreviation for the Latin expression *et cetera, etc.* means "and so forth." In formal writing, avoid ending a list with *etc.;* indicate that you are leaving items out of a list with *and so on* or *and so forth*. Use *etc.* alone, not with *and,* which is redundant.

eventually, ultimately Although these words are often used interchangeably, *eventually* means "at an unspecified later time" while *ultimately* means "finally" or "in the end" (*He knew that he would have to stop running eventually, but he hoped that he would ultimately win a marathon*). See also *penultimate.*

everybody, everyone, every one *Everybody* and *everyone* refer to an unspecified person (*Everybody wins in this game*). *Every one* refers to each single member of a group (*Every one of these toys must be picked up*).

except See *accept, except.*

expect *Expect* means "to anticipate or look forward to." Avoid using it colloquially to mean "to think or suppose." (*I suppose* [not *expect*] *I should go study now*).

explicit, implicit *Explicit* means "perfectly clear, direct, and unambiguous" (*Darrell gave me explicit directions to his house*). *Implicit* means "implied" or "revealed or expressed indirectly" (*His eagerness was implicit in his tone of voice*).

farther, further Although these words are often used interchangeably, some writers prefer to use *farther* to refer to physical distances (*Boston is farther than I thought*) and *further* to refer to quantity, time, or degree (*We tried to progress further on our research project*).

fewer, less Use *fewer* for items that can be counted (*Because fewer people attended this year, we needed fewer programs*). Use *less* for items that cannot be counted (*We also required less space and less food*).

finalize Many writers avoid using *finalize* to mean "to make final." Use alternative phrasing (*We needed to complete* [not *finalize*] *our plans*).

firstly, secondly, thirdly Use *first, second, third* instead.

former, latter *Former* is used to refer to the first of two people, items, or ideas being discussed, *latter* to refer to the second (*Monet and Picasso were important painters; the former is associated with the Impressionist school, the latter with Cubism*).

further See *farther, further.*

get The verb *get* has many colloquial uses. In formal writing, avoid using *get* to mean "to provoke or annoy" (*He gets to me*), "to start" (*We should get going on this project*), or "to become" (*She got worried when he didn't call*). Have *got to* should not be used in place of *must* (*I must* [not *have got to*] *finish by five o'clock*) or in place of *have* (*Do you have* [not *Have you got*] *a dollar for the toll?*).

goes, says Avoid the colloquial use of *go* for *says* (*When the coach says* [not *goes*] *"Now," everybody runs*).

good and *Good and* should not be used for *very* in formal writing (*My shoes were very* [not *good and*] *wet after our walk*).

good, well *Good* is an adjective; it should not be used in place of the adverb *well* in formal writing (*Mario is a good tennis player; he played well* [not *good*] *in the tournament*). But in response to the question *How are you?* most formal academic writers would prefer *I am well* to *I am good.*

half a, half of, a half a For distance, use *a half* (*They had walked a half mile in pitch darkness*). For other quantities, use *half of, a half,* or *half of a* (*Half of the audience was not amused. Half an apple was plenty for Eve. A half ton of coal takes up a lot of room.*). Avoid *a half a.*

hanged, hung *Hanged* is the past tense and past participle of *hang* in the sense of "execute" (*Two prisoners were hanged at this spot*). *Hung* is the past tense and past participle of *hang* meaning "to suspend" or "to dangle" (*All her clothes were hung neatly in the closet*).

hardly, scarcely *Hardly* and *scarcely* are adverbs meaning "barely," "only just." Do not use double negatives, such as *can't scarcely* and *not hardly*. (*I can scarcely* [not *can't scarcely*] *keep my eyes open*).

has got, have got See *get.*

have, of Use *have* (not *of*) with *could, would, should,* and *might* (*We could have* [not *of*] *gone to the concert*).

he/she, s/he, his/her When you require both female and male personal pronouns in formal writing, use *he or she* (or *she or he*) and *his or her* (or *her or his*) instead of a slash.

healthful, healthy *Healthful* means "tending to promote good health" (*I try to eat a healthful diet*). *Healthy* means "having good health" (*By doing so, I hope to stay healthy*).

height   Use *height,* not *heighth* (*The temple was roughly six meters in height, ten in length, and twelve in width*).

herself, himself, itself, myself, ourselves, themselves, yourself, yourselves   Use these pronouns only to reflect the action of a sentence back toward the subject (*He locked himself out of the apartment*) or to emphasize the subject (*I myself have no regrets*). Do not use these pronouns in place of personal pronouns such as *I, me, you, her,* or *him* (*He left an extra key with Bev and me* [not *myself*]).

hisself   *Hisself* is nonstandard; use *himself.*

hopefully   *Hopefully* is an adverb meaning "in a hopeful manner" (*The child looked hopefully out the window for her mother*). In formal writing, do not use *hopefully* to mean "I or we hope that" or "It is hoped that" (*I hope that* [not *hopefully*] *Bob will remember his camera*).

however   See *but, however, yet.*

hung   See *hanged, hung.*

i.e.   *I.e.* is an abbreviation for the Latin phrase *id est,* meaning "that is." In formal writing, use *that is* instead of the abbreviation (*Hal is a Renaissance man; that is* [not *i.e.*], *he has many interests*).

if, whether   Use *if* to state a condition (*If it snows, I will wear my new boots*). Use *whether* (or *whether or not*) in a clause that expresses or implies an alternative (*In the morning, I will decide whether to wear my boots*).

illicit   See *elicit, illicit.*

illusion   See *allusion, illusion.*

immigrate   See *emigrate from, immigrate to.*

imminent   See *eminent, imminent.*

implicit   See *explicit, implicit.*

imply, infer   *Imply* means "to express indirectly" or "to suggest"; *infer* is a verb meaning "to conclude" or "to surmise" (*Helen implied that she had time to visit with us, but we inferred from all the work on her desk that she was really too busy*). Speakers *imply;* listeners *infer.*

in, into   Use *in* to indicate position (*The sun is low in the sky*). Use *into* to suggest motion or change of position (*The rats moved cautiously into the maze*). The use of *into* to mean "involved in" or "interested in" is slang (*She is interested in* [not *into*] *astrology*).

in regards to   *In regards to* is an incorrect combination of two phrases, *as regards* and *in regard to* (*In regard to* [or *As regards*] *the first question, refer to the guidelines you received*).

incidents, incidence, instance   *Incidents* are occurrences or events; *incidence* (usually singular) refers to the extent or frequency with which something occurs; an *instance* is an example (*The incidence of crime has decreased* *this year. For instance, our town had 30 percent fewer incidents involving armed robbery than we experienced last year.*).

incredible, incredulous   See *credible, incredible.*

infer   See *imply, infer.*

ingenious, ingenuous   *Ingenious* means "resourceful" or "clever" (*Elaine came up with an ingenious plan*). *Ingenuous* means "innocent" or "simple" (*It was a surprisingly deceptive plan for such an ingenuous person*).

inside, inside of; outside, outside of   The prepositions *inside* and *outside* should not be followed by *of* (*The suspect is inside* [not *inside of*] *that building*).

insure   See *assure, ensure, insure.*

irregardless, regardless   The nonstandard *irregardless* is often mistakenly used for *regardless* (*We will have the party regardless* [not *irregardless*] *of the weather*).

is when, is where   Avoid these awkward expressions in formal writing to define terms (*Sexual harassment refers to* [not *is when someone makes*] *inappropriate sexual advances or suggestions*).

its, it's   *Its* is the possessive form of the pronoun *it; it's* is a contraction for *it is* or *it has* (*It's hard to tear a baby animal away from its mother*).

itself   See *herself, himself.*

kind, sort, type   *Kind, sort,* and *type* should be used with *this* (not *these*) and a singular verb (*This kind of mushroom is* [not *These kind of mushrooms are*] *very expensive*). The plural forms—*kinds, sorts,* and *types*—should be used with *these* and with a plural verb (*These three types of envelopes are the only ones we need*).

kind of, sort of   In formal writing, avoid using the colloquial expressions *kind of* and *sort of* to mean "somewhat" or "rather" (*My paper is rather* [not *kind of*] *short; my research for it was somewhat* [not *sort of*] *rushed*).

later, latter   *Later* means "after some time"; *latter* refers to the second of two people, items, or ideas (*Later in the evening, Jim announced that the latter of the two speakers was running late*). See also *former, latter.*

lay, lie   The verb *lay* means "to put or set down" and is followed by an object; its principal forms are *lay* or *laid*. The verb *lie* meaning "to recline" or "to rest in a horizontal position" has the principal forms *lie, lay, lain*. Do not confuse them (*I will lay out the blanket and lie down. He laid the book on the table as he lay on the bed*).

lead, led   As a verb, *lead* (rhymes with *seed*) means "to go first" or "to direct"; as a noun, it means "front position" (*Hollis took the lead in organizing the files*). Its past tense and past participle are *led* (*The path led to the cave*). The metallic element *lead* is pronounced like *led*.

learn, teach   Students *learn;* teachers *teach.* (*Our parents taught* [not *learned*] *us right from wrong*).

leave, let   *Leave* means "to depart"; it should not be used in place of *let*, which means "to allow" (*When you are ready to leave, let* [not *leave*] *me give you a ride*). The expressions *leave alone* and *let alone*, however, may be used interchangeably (*I asked Ben to leave* [or *let*] *me alone while I worked on my paper*).

led   See *lead, led.*

less   See *fewer, less.*

let   See *leave, let.*

liable, likely   *Liable* means "inclined" or "tending," generally toward the negative (*If you do not shovel the sidewalk, you are liable to fall on the ice*). *Liable* is also a legal term meaning "responsible for" or "obligated under the law" (*The landlord is liable for the damage*). *Likely* is an adjective meaning "probable" or "promising" (*The school board is likely to cancel classes if the strike continues.*)

lie   See *lay, lie.*

like   See *as, as if, like.*

likely   See *liable, likely.*

loose, lose   *Loose* is an adjective meaning "not securely attached." The verb *lose* means "to misplace" or "to undergo defeat" (*Be careful not to lose that loose button on your jacket*).

lots, lots of   *Lots* and *lots of* are colloquial expressions meaning "many" or "much"; avoid them in formal writing (*The senator has much* [not *lots of*] *support; she is expected to win many* [not *lots of*] *votes*).

man, mankind   These terms were once used to refer to all human beings. Now such usage is considered sexist; use *people, humanity,* or *humankind* instead (*What has been the greatest invention in the history of humanity* [not *mankind*]*?*).

may   See *can, might.*

may be, maybe   *May be* is a verb phrase (*Charles may be interested in a new job*); *maybe* is an adverb meaning "possibly" or "perhaps" (*Maybe I will speak to him about it*).

media, medium   The term *media,* referring to various forms of communication—newspapers, magazines, television, radio—is the plural form of the noun *medium;* it takes a plural verb (*Some people feel that the media were responsible for the candidate's loss*).

might   See *can, may.*

mine, mines   *Mine* is a pronoun meaning "belonging to me." Avoid *mines,* a nonstandard form (*Did you find yours? I found mine*).

moral, morale   *Moral* is an ethical principle or the lesson of a story or an experience (*The moral is to treat others as you wish to be treated*). *Morale* is the mental condition or mood of a person or group (*The improvement in good weather lifted the crew's morale*).

most   Do not use *most* to mean "almost." (*Prizes were given to almost* [not *most*] *all the participants*).

must have   see *could have, must have, should have, would have*

myself   See *herself, himself.*

nausea, nauseated, nauseating, nauseous   The noun *nausea* refers to the feeling of being sick to one's stomach. Something that makes you sick to your stomach is *nauseous* or *nauseating*. If you are sick to your stomach, you are *nauseated,* not *nauseous.*

nor, or   Use *nor* with *neither* (*Neither Paul nor Sara guessed the right answer*); use *or* with *either* (*Either Paul or Sara will have to drive me home*).

nowhere near   *Nowhere near* is an informal usage. Use *not nearly* instead (*This year's class is not nearly as unruly as last year's*).

number   See *amount, number.*

of   See *have, of.*

off of   Use *off* alone; *of* is not necessary (*The child fell off* [not *off of*] *the playground slide*).

OK, O.K., okay   All three spellings are acceptable, but this colloquial term should be avoided in formal writing (*John's performance was all right* [or *adequate* or *tolerable;* not *okay*], *but it wasn't his best*).

on account of   Avoid using *on account of* to mean "because of" (*The course was canceled because of* [not *on account of*] *lack of interest*).

or   See *nor, or.*

outside, outside of   See *inside, inside of; outside, outside of.*

passed, past   *Passed* is the past tense of the verb *pass* (*She passed here several hours ago*). *Past* refers to a time before the present (*She has forgotten many details about her past life; the past is not important to her*).

penultimate   *Penultimate* means "next to the last." The one before that is the *antepenultimate.* Do not use *penultimate* as a more intense version of *ultimate.*

people, persons   A *person* is an individual human being. Groups are usually *people* (*Only one person came, although we had hoped many people would attend*) except when emphasizing the individuality of the members of a group of people (*Three persons were injured in a single-vehicle accident on Rohrer Road*).

per   The Latin term *per* should be reserved for commercial or technical use (*miles per gallon, price per pound*). Avoid it elsewhere in formal writing (*Kyle is exercising three times each* [not *per*] *week*).

percent, percentage   The term *percent* refers to a specific fraction of one hundred; it is always used with a number (*We raised nearly 80 percent of our budget in one night*). Do not use the symbol % in formal writing except in tables, formulas, or technical writing. The term *percentage* is not used with a specific number (*We raised a large percentage of our budget in one night*).

perspective, prospective   *Perspective* is a noun meaning "a view"; it should not be confused with the adjective *prospective,* meaning "potential" or "likely" (*Mr. Harris's perspective on the new school changed when he met his son's prospective teacher*).

phenomena   *Phenomena* is the plural of the noun *phenomenon,* meaning "an observed fact, occurrence, or circumstance" (*Last month's blizzard was an unusual phenomenon; there have been several such phenomena this year*).

plenty   *Plenty* means "full" or "abundant"; in formal writing, do not use it to mean "very" or "quite" (*The sun was quite* [not *plenty*] *hot*).

plus   *Plus* is a preposition meaning "increased by" or "with the addition of" (*With wool socks plus your heavy boots, your feet should be warm enough*). Do not use *plus* to link two independent clauses; use *besides* or *moreover* instead (*Brad is not prepared for the advanced class; moreover* [not *plus*], *he can't fit it in his schedule*).

p.m., a.m. or P.M., A.M.   See *a.m., p.m. or A.M., P.M.*

precede, proceed   *Precede* is a verb meaning "to go or come before"; *proceed* is a verb meaning "to move forward or go on" or "to continue" (*The attendants preceded the bride into the church; when the music started, they proceeded down the aisle*).

presently   See *at present, presently.*

pretty   In formal writing, avoid *pretty* to mean "quite" or "somewhat" (*Dave is quite* [not *pretty*] *tired this morning*).

principal, principle   *Principal* is an adjective meaning "first" or "most important"; it is also a noun meaning "head" or "director" or "an amount of money" (*My principal reason for visiting Gettysburg was my interest in the Civil War; my high school principal suggested the trip*). *Principle* is a noun meaning "a rule of action or conduct" or "a basic law" (*I also want to learn more about the principles underlying the U.S. Constitution*).

proceed   See *precede, proceed.*

quotation, quote   *Quotation* is a noun, and *quote* is a verb. Avoid using *quote* as a noun (*Sue quoted Jefferson in her speech, hoping the quotation* [not *quote*] *would impress her audience*).

raise, rise   *Raise* is a transitive verb meaning "to lift" or "to increase"; it takes a direct object (*The store owner was forced to raise prices*). *Rise* is an intransitive verb meaning "to go up"; it does not take a direct object (*Prices rise during periods of inflation*).

rarely ever   Do not use *rarely ever* to mean "seldom." Use "hardly ever" or *rarely* alone (*We rarely* [not *rarely ever*] *travel during the winter*).

real, really   *Real* means "true" or "actual" (*The diamonds in that necklace are real*). *Really* is informally to mean "very" or "quite"; do not use *real* as an adverb (*Tim was really* [not *real*] *interested in buying Lana's old car*).

reason is because   The phrase *the reason is because* is redundant; use *the reason is that* or *because* instead (*The reason I am late is that* [not *because*] *I got stuck in traffic. Yesterday I was late because* [not *The reason I was late yesterday was because*] *I overslept*).

reason why   *Reason why* is redundant; use *reason* alone (*The reason* [not *The reason why*] *we canceled the dance is that no one volunteered to chaperone*).

regardless   See *irregardless, regardless*.

respectably, respectfully, respectively   *Respectably* means "in a manner worthy of respect" (*Although we did not win, we performed respectably*). *Respectfully* means "in a manner characterized by respect" (*Even when you disagree, you should listen respectfully*). *Respectively* means "in the order given" (*The programs on the environment, woodcraft, and herpetology are at 10:00 A.M., noon, and 3:00 P.M., respectively*).

rise   See *raise, rise*.

says   See *goes, says*.

scarcely   See *hardly, scarcely*.

sensual, sensuous   *Sensual* means "arousing or exciting the senses or appetites"; it is often used in reference to sexual pleasure (*His scripts often featured titillating situations and sensual encounters*). *Sensuous* means "experienced through or affecting the senses," although it generally refers to esthetic enjoyment or pleasure (*Her sculpture was characterized by muted colors and sensuous curves*).

set, sit   *Set* is a transitive verb meaning "to put" or "to place"; it takes a direct object, and its principal forms are *set, set, set* (*Mary set her packages on the kitchen table*). *Sit* is an intransitive verb meaning "to be seated"; it does not take a direct object, and its principal forms are *sit, sat, sat* (*I sat in the only chair in the waiting room*).

shall, will   In the past, *shall* (instead of *will*) was used with the first-person subjects *I* and *we*. Now *will* is acceptable with all subjects (*We will invite several guests for dinner*). *Shall* is generally used in polite questions (*Shall we go inside now?*) or for requirements or obligations (*Jurors shall refrain from all contact with the press*).

should have   See *could have, must have, should have, would have*.

sight   See *cite, sight, site*.

since   Use *since* to mean "continuing from a past time until the present" (*Carl has not gone skiing since he injured his knee*). Do not use *since* to mean "because" if there is any possibility that readers will be confused about your meaning. For example, in the sentence *Since she sold her bicycle, Connie has not been getting much exercise, since* could mean either "because" or "from the time that." Use *because* to avoid confusion.

sit   See *set, sit*.

site   See *cite, site, sight*.

so, so that   The use of *so* to mean "very" can be vague (*Gayle was so depressed*). Use *so* with a *that* clause of explanation (*Gayle was so depressed that she could not get out of bed*). *So that* means "with the intention that" (*Gayle got out of bed early so that she would be in class on time*).

somebody, someone, something   These pronouns take singular verbs (*Somebody calls every night at midnight and hangs up; I hope something is done about this problem before someone in my family becomes frightened*).

someplace, somewhere   Do not use *someplace* in formal writing; use *somewhere* instead (*The answer must lie somewhere* [not *someplace*] *in the text*).

some time, sometime, sometimes   *Some time* means "a length of time" (*We have not visited our grandparents in some time*). *Sometime* is an adverb meaning "at an indefinite time in the future" (*Let's get together sometime*); *sometimes* means "on occasion" or "now and then" (*Sometimes we get together*).

sort   See *kind, sort, type.*

sort of   See *kind of, sort of.*

stationary, stationery   *Stationary* means "not moving" (*All stationary vehicles will be towed*). *Stationery* means "writing materials" (*Karen is out of stationery*).

supposed to, used to   These expressions consist of a past participle (*supposed, used*) followed by *to.* Do not use the base forms *suppose* or *use* (*Ben is supposed* [not *suppose*] *to take the garbage out; he used* [not *use*] *to remember regularly.*).

sure, surely   In formal writing, do not use the adjective *sure* to mean "certainly" or "undoubtedly"; use the adverb *surely* or *certainly* or *undoubtedly* instead (*It is certainly* [or *surely;* not *sure*] *cold today*).

sure to, try to   Avoid using *sure and* and *try and* for *sure to* and *try to* (*Be sure to* [not *and*] *come to the party; try to* [not *and*] *be on time*).

take   See *bring, take.*

than, then   *Than* is used in comparisons (*Dan is older than Eve*). *Then* indicates time (*First pick up the files, and then deliver them to the company office*).

that, which   A clause introduced by *that* is always a restrictive clause; it should not be set off by commas (*The historical event that interested him most was the Civil War*). Many writers use *which* only to introduce nonrestrictive clauses, which are set off by commas (*His textbook, which was written by an expert on the war, provided useful information*); however, *which* may also be used to introduce restrictive clauses (*The book which offered the most important information was an old reference book in the library*).

thataway, thisaway   Both these terms are colloquial. Use *that way* or *this way.*

that there, these here, them there, this here   By themselves, *that, these, them,* and *this* indicate position (*this* for something close by, *that* for something farther away), so the colloquial constructions *that there, this here,* and so forth are redundant.

their, there, they're   *Their* is the possessive form of the pronoun *they* (*Did they leave their books here?*). *There* is an adverb meaning "in or at that place" (*No, they left their books there*). *They're* is a contraction of *they are* (*They're looking all over for their books*).

theirselves, themselves   *Theirselves* is nonstandard; use *themselves.*

then   See *than, then.*

'til, till, until   *Till* and *until* are both acceptable spellings; *'til,* however, is a contraction and should be avoided in formal writing (*We will work until we are finished; you should not plan to leave till then*).

to, too, two   *To* often indicates movement or direction toward something (*Nancy is walking to the grocery store*). *Too* means "also" (*Sam is walking too*). *Two* is a number (*The two of them are walking together*).

toward, towards   *Toward* is preferred, but both forms are acceptable.

try and   See *sure to, try to.*

type   In colloquial speech, *type* is sometimes used alone to mean "type of," but avoid this usage in formal writing (*What type of* [not *type*] *medicine did the doctor prescribe?*). See also *kind, sort, type.*

ultimately   See *eventually, ultimately.*

uninterested   See *disinterested, uninterested.*

unique   *Unique* is an adjective meaning "being the only one" or "having no equal." Because it refers to an absolute, unvarying state, it need not be intensified (by words such as *most* or *very*) (*Her pale blue eyes gave her a unique* [not *very unique*] *look*). The same is true of other adjectives that indicate an absolute state: *perfect, complete, round, straight,* and so on. But modifiers that qualify are acceptable (*almost perfect, nearly straight*).

until   See *'til, till, until.*

usage, use   *Usage* means "an established and accepted practice or procedure" (*He consulted the glossary whenever he was unsure of the correct word choice or usage*). Do not substitute *usage* for *use* (*Park guidelines forbid the use* [not *usage*] *of gas grills*).

used to   See *supposed to, used to.*

utilize   The verb *utilize,* meaning "to put to use," borders on pretentiousness; *use* is generally better (*We were able to use* [not *utilize*] *the hotel kitchen to prepare our meals*).

wait for, wait on   *Wait for* means "to await" or "to be ready for." *Wait on* means "to serve"; in formal writing they are not interchangeable (*You are too old to wait for* [not *on*] *your mother to wait on you*).

way, ways   Do not use *ways* in place of *way* when referring to long distances (*Los Angeles is a long way* [not *ways*] *from San Francisco by car*).

well   See *good, well.*

where Do not use *where* in place of *that* (*I read that* [not *where*] *several of the company's plants will be closed in June*).

where . . . at, where . . . to *Where* should be used alone, not in combination with *at* or *to* (*Where did you leave your coat?* [not *Where did you leave your coat at?*] *Where are you going?* [not *Where are you going to?*]).

whether See *if, whether.*

which See *that, which.*

which, who, that Use *which* to refer to places, things, or events; use *who* to refer to people or to animals with given names; use *that* for places, things, events or groups of people (*The parade, which was rescheduled for Saturday, was a great success; one man who* [not *which*] *attended said it was the best parade that he could remember*). *That* is also occasionally used to refer to a single person (*Beth is like the sister that I never had*). See also *that, which.*

who See *which, who, that.*

who, whom; whoever, whomever Use *who* and *whoever* for subjects and subject complements; use *whom* and *whomever* for objects and object complements (*Who revealed the murderer's identity? You may invite whomever you wish*).

who's, whose *Who's* is a contraction of *who is* (*Who's coming for dinner tonight?*). *Whose* is the possessive form of *who* (*Whose hat is that?*).

will See *shall, will.*

-wise The suffix *-wise* indicates position or direction in words such as *clockwise* and *lengthwise*. In formal writing, do not add it to words to mean "with regard to" (*My personal life is confused, but with regard to my job* [not *jobwise*], *things are fine*).

would have See *could have, must have, should have, would have.*

yet See *but, however, yet.*

your, you're *Your* is the possessive form of *you* (*Your table is ready*). *You're* is a contraction of *you are* (*You're leaving before the best part of the show*).

yourself, yourselves See *herself, himself.*

CREDITS

Page 1, EyeWire Collection/Getty Images-Photodisc; **p. 2,** EyeWire Collection/Getty Images-Photodisc; **p. 11,** Getty Images/Digital Vision; **p. 25,** Courtesy of the Library of Congress; **p. 27,** Courtesy of the Library of Congress; **p. 28, top,** Courtesy of Universal Studios Licensing, LLP; **p. 29,** © Teri Stratford. All rights reserved; **p. 30, top,** Dorothea Lange/ Getty Images Inc.-Hulton Archive Photos; **p. 30, bottom,** Walker Evans/Library of Congress/Corbis; **p. 31,** Courtesy of the Library of Congress; **p. 32,** Courtesy of the Library of Congress; **p. 34,** Courtesy of the Library of Congress; **p. 35, top,** Courtesy of the Library of Congress; **p. 35, bottom,** Courtesy of the Library of Congress; **p. 36,** Reprinted by permission of Intellectual Properties Management on behalf of the Estate of Martin Luther King, Jr.; **p. 38,** © The New Yorker Collection 2005 Mike Twohy from cartoonbank.com. All Rights Reserved; **p. 40,** Thomas E. Franklin/Getty Images; **p. 42, top,** © Hermann/Starke/CORBIS. All Rights Reserved; **p. 42, bottom,** © Chase Swift/CORBIS. All Rights Reserved; **p. 43,** Reprinted by permission of the National Center for Family Literacy; **p. 44,** Reprinted by permission of the National Crime Prevention Council; **p. 45,** Reprinted by permission of the National Trust for Historic Preservation; p. 46, Reprinted with permission © 2005 American Lung Association. For more information about the American Lung Association or to support the work it does, call 1-800-LUNG-USA (1-800-586-4872) or log on to www.lungusa.org; **p. 49,** Photos.com; **p. 59,** Photodisc/Getty Images; **p. 60,** Photos.com; **p. 74,** Photos.com; **p. 75,** Toby Fulwiler; **p. 84,** Photos.com; **p. 93,** Photos.com; **p. 94,** Photos.com; **p. 112,** Getty Images/Digital Vision; **pp. 125, 126, 131,** © Peyo-2006-licensed through Lafig Belgium-www.smurf.com; **p. 133,** John Marshall Mantel/Corbis/Bettmann; **p. 136,** Photos.com; **p. 154,** Peter DeSantis/New England Mountain Bike Association; **p. 155,** Duncan McNicol/Stone/Getty Images; **p. 159,** Reprinted by permission of Western New York Mountain Biking Association and Todd Scott, Executive Director of the Michigan Mountain Biking Association; **p. 164,** Photos.com; **p. 165,** "We Real Cool" from *Blacks* by Gwendolyn Brooks. Copyright © 1991 by Gwendolyn Brooks. Reprinted by permission of the estate of Gwendolyn Brooks; **p. 182,** Rachel Epstein/PhotoEdit; **pp. 182-83, 637,** Excerpt from "Why I Write" by Joan Didion. Copyright © 1976 by Joan Didion. Originally published in *The New York Times Book Review.* Reprinted by permission of the author; **p. 184,** From *Good Bones and Simple Murders* by Margaret Atwood. Copyright Doubleday, a division of Random House, Inc. Reprinted with permission; **p. 192,** SW Productions/Getty Images, Inc.-Photodisc; **p. 199,** Photos.com; **p. 200,** EyeWire Collection/Getty Images-Photodisc; **p. 207,** Photos.com; **p. 220,** Photos.com; **p. 229,** Photos.com; **p. 230,** Cary Wolinsky/Aurora & Quanta Productions, Inc; **p. 233,** Inc., Martin Paul Ltd/Index Stock Imagery, Inc.; **p. 238,** Alan Hayakawa; **p. 239,** Patrick Hayakawa; **p. 241,** Photos.com; **p. 244,** San Francisco Chronicle; **p. 248,** Copyright 2005 Internet Scout Project, http://scout.wisc.edu; **p. 251,** Reprinted by permission of Anil Dash; **p. 253,** Andrew Olney/Getty Images/Digital Vision; **p. 256,** Reprinted by permission of the Mendocino Wine Alliance; **p. 257,** Reprinted by permission of

ESL INDEX

INDEX

Note: **Boldface type** indicates page numbers for main text discussion of that topic.

WAC BOXES

WRITING ACROSS THE CURRICULUM